THE WORKS OF
JOHN WEBSTER

VOLUME TWO

This is the second volume to appear in the Cambridge edition of the works of John Webster. Volume one contains *The White Devil* and *The Duchess of Malfi*, and this volume has *The Devil's Law-Case*, *A Cure for a Cuckold*, and *Appius and Virginia*. While *The Devil's Law-Case* and *A Cure for a Cuckold* are available in modernized versions, *Appius and Virginia* has not been edited since early in the twentieth century. Furthermore, this Cambridge critical edition preserves the original spelling of all the plays, and incorporates the most recent editorial scholarship, including valuable information on Webster's share in the collaborative plays, and new critical methods and textual theory. In particular, the edition integrates theatrical aspects of the plays with their bibliographical and literary features in a way not previously attempted in a scholarly edition of a Jacobean dramatist. The edition presents all Webster's plays (with the exception of those collaborative plays already published in the Cambridge editions of Dekker, and Beaumont and Fletcher under the editorship of Fredson Bowers), and provides a brief biography, an account of the Webster canon, illustrations, and a critical and theatrical history of each play. The edition will be of interest to scholars and students of drama and English literature, and to theatre practitioners and historians.

THE WORKS OF
JOHN WEBSTER

―――

An Old-Spelling Critical Edition

―――

Edited by

David Gunby

David Carnegie

MacDonald P. Jackson

―――

VOLUME TWO

THE DEVIL'S LAW-CASE
A CURE FOR A CUCKOLD
APPIUS AND VIRGINIA

―――

CAMBRIDGE
UNIVERSITY PRESS

PUBLISHED BY THE PRESS SYNDICATE OF THE UNIVERSITY OF CAMBRIDGE
The Pitt Building, Trumpington Street, Cambridge CB2 1RP, United Kingdom

CAMBRIDGE UNIVERSITY PRESS
The Edinburgh Building, Cambridge CB2 2RU, UK
40 West 20th Street, New York, NY 10011–4211, USA
477 Williamstown Road, Port Melbourne, VIC 3207, Australia
Ruiz de Alarcón 13, 28014 Madrid, Spain
Dock House, The Waterfront, Cape Town 8001, South Africa
http://www.cambridge.org

First published 2003

Printed in the United Kingdom at the University Press, Cambridge

Typeface Monotype Bembo 11/13pt   *System* QuarkXPress™ [SE]

A catalogue record for this book is available from the British Library

ISBN 0 521 26060 4

Contents

THE DEVIL'S LAW-CASE

A CURE FOR A CUCKOLD

APPIUS AND VIRGINIA

Illustrations

General preface to Volume two

This, the second volume of the Cambridge edition of *The Works of John Webster*, is devoted to three plays from the last decade of Webster's career: *The Devil's Law-Case*, *A Cure for a Cuckold*, and *Appius and Virginia*. Of these, two were written in collaboration—*A Cure for a Cuckold* with Thomas Heywood and William Rowley and *Appius and Virginia* with Heywood—while the third constitutes Webster's sole unaided essay in the tragicomic mode. All have considerable merits, and close acquaintance has convinced the editors that all three deserve not only the detailed scholarly attention given them, but also the opportunity to prove themselves on the stage in productions by professional companies. It is to be hoped that these will follow their appearance in this volume.

The editing of the plays in Volume two has proceeded along the lines laid down initially for the edition, with each editor taking primary responsibility for one aspect of the editing process, but all three jointly as well as severally responsible for the outcomes. The only parts of the volume for which editors take individual responsibility are those credited to them: the Critical, Theatrical, and Textual introductions. And even here there has been considerable consultation, with editors reading and commenting on each others' work.

The aim of the editors has been to work by consensus, and this has rarely been difficult. As in Volume one, however, there has been no attempt to disguise the rare instances where there is disagreement—as for instance over a textual crux in *The Devil's Law-Case*, where two of the editors have published notes arguing diametrically opposed solutions. Such rare differences the notes record.

Again, as in Volume one, there is no separation of textual, literary, and theatrical notes, since the rationale for the edition is the interdependence of these three aspects of play texts. The collation, however, is provided separately.

The General preface to Volume one referred to what was then a major difficulty arising from the publishing of this edition seriatim: how to refer to works by Webster not in that volume. With the appearance of this second volume that problem is much diminished, but where reference is made to works not yet published the same solution is adopted as in

Volume one: use of the lineation of the Lucas edition, as (e.g.) *AQL* (Lucas) I.i.150–1. To save space abbreviation has again been widely employed, both for works by Webster and for other works referred to more than twice. A List of abbreviations is found on pp. xx–xxi. Where, in the Commentary, reference is made to another editor (e.g., Lucas or Weis) or to Dent without further detail, such reference is to the appropriate passage in their volumes.

Finally, it is with sadness that we record the death, in late 1996, of Antony Hammond, co-editor of Volume one, colleague, and friend. Tony died soon after the publication of the volume to which he had contributed so much, but before cancer struck him down he had also done considerable work on Volume two, and particularly on *The Devil's Law-Case*. Tony's brusque manner masked gentleness and generosity, and these qualities we miss, along with his wit, his enthusiasm, and his expertise—in fine wine and opera as in matters bibliographic.

Tony's replacement in the editorial team—one Tony enthusiastically endorsed when he knew he would be unable to continue—is another New Zealander, Mac Jackson of the University of Auckland, a bibliographer of great experience and reputation whose most recent work has been on the Oxford edition of Thomas Middleton. The transition has been a smooth one, and the team's range of skills has been most fortunately enlarged—given the presence in Volume two of two collaborative works—by Mac's expertise in determining authorship. Thanks to his work, building on that, earlier, of others such as Gray, Lucas, and Lake, it seems possible to argue with confidence not only who share with Webster the credit for *A Cure for a Cuckold* and *Appius and Virginia*, but also, with some degree of precision, what their shares are.

General textual preface

MacDonald P. Jackson

Basic principles and procedures remain those set forth in Volume one, but some further discussion seems in order. The three plays included here present a few problems of their own, not encountered in the editing of *The White Devil* and *The Duchess of Malfi*, and, for certain details, our interpretations of the original guidelines need clarification.

A significant modification to the format of Volume one involves the collation of departures from the lineation of the quartos that serve as foundation texts. Both the 1623 Quarto of *The Devil's Law-Case* and the 1661 Quarto of *A Cure for a Cuckold* have so much prose printed as verse, misaligned verse, and verse printed as prose that we have preferred not to clutter the collation notes at the foot of each page with the record of our editorial changes to lineation, but to consign the relevant data to special sections. This in turn means that, whereas prose 'set erroneously as verse in the copy-text' was 'not collated in detail' in Volume one[1]—a quarto's use of verse being signalled in a general way, without any indications of its line divisions—in Volume two we have included specific information about line endings, dealing with one speech at a time. Although *Appius and Virginia* requires far less adjustment to its lineation than the other two plays, we have, for the sake of consistency, treated it in the same way.

To save space in collating lineation changes, we have attached 'a' or 'b' to certain line-numbers to denote the first or second part of a line shared between speakers: in the few cases where this practice might lead to ambiguity, the opening and closing words of the passage under consideration have been given in the lemma. The formula 'This ed.' has not been used: any change to the foundation text's lineation that is not attributed to a previous editor originates with us. Thus the entry for *A Cure for a Cuckold*, II.iv, that reads '**38–9**] *verse* . . . not | Q' signals that our decision to print as prose has not been anticipated by earlier editors and that the Quarto prints as verse and divides after 'not'. In such entries, punctuation after words ending lines and spelling and typography of these words (in respect of 'u' and 'v', for example) are those of our edition, not of the foundation text. Lineation in quartos and other editions is indicated by line endings only. Although the main object is to record our own deviations from the quartos and our indebtedness to our predecessors, we have also collated a few plausible arrangements that we have not adopted.

Some of our decisions on how to arrange the verse have been affected by our attributions of authorship in collaborative plays. *A Cure for a Cuckold* was published as by John Webster and William Rowley, but our own investigations have confirmed Lucas's findings that Thomas Heywood contributed both to this comedy and to *Appius and Virginia*, published under Webster's name alone. Heywood's blank verse is more regular than Webster's, and Rowley's habit of at times dealing out ten-syllable lines with scant regard for patterns of stress has influenced our lineation in *A Cure for a Cuckold*, at II.iv.114–18 and V.ii.62–7, for example.

In the Quarto of *Appius and Virginia* verse lines start with lower-case letters unless a capital is used for some other reason—to begin a new sentence or to highlight a noun or other significant word. We have capitalized all verse lines, both in *Appius and Virginia* and in the other two plays, making the alterations silently even when stray lines in *The Devil's Law-Case* or *A Cure for a Cuckold* have anomalously been set in the original quartos without capitals. Naturally our relineation of the foundation texts also leads to the silent alteration of lower case to upper case when our change is from quarto prose to verse, and from upper case to lower case when our change is from quarto verse to prose.

'Silent emendation is one of the icebergs that may wreck even the most titanic edition', declared Antony Hammond and Doreen DelVecchio in introducing the subject in Volume one.[2] A few words may be added to their account of this edition's 'silent' modifications to the original texts. The most important of these concern speech prefixes and stage directions. As explained in Volume one, speech prefixes have been regularized, abbreviated forms having been expanded. Where the speaker is not in doubt and no typographical error occurs in the quarto, these adjustments to speech prefixes have not been collated. We have settled upon one particular form of the name: '*Oppius*', for example, in *Appius and Virginia*, rather than the '*Opius*' which he becomes from B4^r to C1^r (our I.iii) and from H2^v to H3^r (our V.i) and, in a stage direction, on I1^v (our V.iii); and, in the same play, '*Marcus Clodius*', rather than the '*Marcus*' or '*Clodius*', which, in full or abbreviated forms, he is also called. Similarly, uncontentious spelling variants of names in stage directions (such as '*Anabel*' on B2^r in *A Cure for a Cuckold*), instead of the usual '*Annabel*') have been silently regularized. The punctuation of speech prefixes has also been silently standardized: sporadic anomalies in the quartos—a comma or colon or the absence of any punctuation mark—have not been collated. On the rare occasions when a stage direction lacks a closing full stop in the foundation quarto, one has been provided. The expansion of unambiguous abbreviations in stage directions has not been collated, except where changes to their punctuation or placing have also been made.

Akin to stage directions are the scene headings that we have added within square brackets: [I.ii], and the like. All three plays in Volume two are divided into acts but not into scenes. Scene headings are collated when there is nothing corresponding to them in the relevant quarto. Thus Dyce has been credited with each scene division that he introduced.

One addition should be made to Volume one's list of silent normalizations of punctuation, such as the replacement of black-letter and italic stops with roman.[3] The varying lengths of dashes in the quartos seem quite arbitrary, bearing no relation to function. Choices appear to have been made mainly according to compositorial preference and, more significantly, the numbers and lengths of dashes in a compositor's case of type at any given time and the amount of space available in a particular line. In this volume we have standardized the length of the dash, rather than attempting to imitate the quarto variations in this purely typographical feature.

In *A Cure for a Cuckold* and *Appius and Virginia* the first word of each act's dialogue begins with a very large capital followed by one of normal size. This edition prints a normal capital followed by a lower-case letter.

Worth repeating is Volume one's statement that while changes of punctuation to the text have been collated, consequent changes in case (such as capitalization after the replacement of a colon with a full stop) have not, and that throughout this edition 'lowercase after final ?/! is silently capitalized'.[4] One kind of regularization of the foundation texts—specified in the General textual introduction to Volume one—has given rise to much careful deliberation. 'The exclamatory question mark has been replaced with the modern exclamation mark where it seems clear that an exclamation with no interrogative content was intended, on the grounds that the distinction between the two marks was still in the process of being established at the time Webster's works were first printed.'[5] In distinguishing between quarto question marks that are genuinely interrogative and question marks that are essentially exclamatory, and are therefore silently replaced by exclamation marks in this edition, we have been guided by our sense of how the dialogue would most appropriately unfold in performance.

The scholar who scrutinizes our collation notes will observe that adjustments to punctuation are more frequent than in most other twentieth-century old-spelling editions. This is partly because we want *The Works of John Webster* to be used by directors and actors, and, while acknowledging the fluidity of seventeenth-century syntax, have tried to clarify the shape of some of the longer speeches, so that they are more readily comprehensible than they appear in the quartos. Like all old-spelling editors, we have corrected foundation-text punctuation when it is patently wrong or misleading—when a comma ends a speech or a compositor has misunderstood a sentence and supplied stops that he would not have set had he interpreted the meaning rightly. But we have also made punctuation heavier or lighter when such changes result in clear gains in intelligibility and would have done so even for a seventeenth-century reader. In making adjustments we have aimed not to obscure the nature of a quarto's early modern punctuation, but to bring it a little closer to its own best standards.

Our interest in the theatrical qualities of these plays has also motivated a much fuller supplementation of the foundation texts' stage directions than previous editors have attempted. This process has been carried further than in Volume one. Our intention has been to help readers recreate in the mind's eye and ear the plays in performance on the pre-Restoration stage. Editors, mulling over the text line by line, can often deduce details about who is being addressed, what actions are being performed, what properties are visible, when characters must enter or exit, and so on, that a spectator would experience directly and immediately in the theatre, but that may remain obscure to a reader unwilling to undertake the slow process of reconstruction. The spectator observes that in *The Devil's Law-Case*, II.i.197–201, Ariosto addresses first Julio and then Romelio. A reader *works out* that Ariosto switches his attention in this way, and can do so only after pondering the sentences. By adding, in square brackets, '*to Julio*' and '*to Romelio*' we try to make reading the plays more closely resemble hearing and viewing them staged. In the same play Crispiano's entry with Ariosto at the beginning of III.i is recorded in the Quarto, but a reader will not visualize him as '*disguised as a merchant*'— though the subsequent dialogue makes his costume clear—without the stimulus of the words we have appended. Directions have, however, been augmented or amended only when we are confident that the dialogue demands the staging indicated. We have been anxious to avoid anything unduly 'prescriptive'. When alternative ways of presenting the dialogue, or of realizing the text in performance, are feasible, we have canvassed the possibilities in the Commentary.

Also mentioned in Volume one was that tildes 'have been expanded, and collated' and ampersands expanded (and collated) 'when there is evidence that they have been used to save space, but not elsewhere'.[6] In Volume two we have expanded (and collated) all tildes and ampersands, finding a distinction between ampersands 'used to save space' and other ampersands too difficult to draw. Most ampersands and tildes occur in tight lines, but even when they occur in well-spaced lines or lines ending against the right-hand margin in white space rather than lettering there is usually reason to suspect that the compositor has set them as an aid to justifying the line of actual type.

Likewise, in almost always preserving the spacing of contractions (whether 'I'm' or 'I 'm', for example), we have been aware that the less usual forms may have been chosen by the compositor for purposes of justification, but have altered the spacing (and recorded the alteration in the collation notes) only when what the quarto prints is so anomalous as to seem plainly not authorial.

Indeed, among the most conspicuous differences between our texts and Lucas's is our much greater willingness to preserve orthography common in the seventeenth century but regularized, and in fact modernized, by Lucas, even though his also was an old-spelling edition: for example, 'a kin', 'some what', 'over hear't', 'yester day', 'president' (for 'precedent'), 'too' (for 'to'), and such contractions as 'e'm' and 'or'e' (for 'over'), in which the placing of the apostrophe is 'illogical' but not unusual in the period. *LION: Drama* has been invaluable in revealing the prevalence of certain forms that Lucas preferred to emend. Nor have we followed Lucas in supplying apostrophes to possessives from which they are absent in the foundation texts: the meaning is seldom in the least ambiguous, and any difficult locutions are glossed in the Commentary.

Finally, in the lists of Press variants, line references ignore headlines, but otherwise count all lines of type, including lines of quads that leave white space.

1. *Webster*, I, 43.
2. Ibid., I, 42.
3. Ibid., I, 42–6.
4. Ibid., I, 45.
5. Ibid., I, 44.
6. Ibid., I, 44 and 48.

Acknowledgements

As with Volume one of this edition, our debt to previous editors is great, especially to F. L. Lucas's edition of *The Complete Works of John Webster* (London, 1927).

Thanks for research grants, leave, fellowships, and equivalent support are due to the Universities of Auckland and Canterbury, and Victoria University of Wellington, and to the Marsden Fund, administered by the Royal Society of New Zealand, for a major supporting grant (and Paul Froggatt of Victoria Link for keeping tabs on the money). Visiting fellowships have generously been granted by the Centre for Reformation and Renaissance Studies at Victoria University, University of Toronto; Clare Hall, Cambridge; Massey College, University of Toronto; St Catherine's College, Oxford; Trinity College, University of Toronto; and Trevelyan College, University of Durham.

We are again grateful to the librarians and staff of our own universities mentioned above, and of all the libraries where we have consulted texts, theatre archives, and other material, to Oxford University Computing Services, and to the Folger Shakespeare Library for permission to reproduce title-pages of the three plays. We also reiterate the thanks made in Volume one to the professional theatres and practitioners who have assisted our research.

To our research assistants Cassandra Fusco, Nicole Jackson, David Lawrence, Pauline Neale, Anna Renton-Green, David Watkins and especially to Hester Lees-Jeffries, we owe a great debt. Many colleagues and friends have supported our work, among whom mention should be made of Herbert Berry, Elizabeth Brennan, Katherine Duncan-Jones, Colin Gibson, Konrad Eisenbichler, Claus Ejlertsen, Jim Fowler, Paul Froggatt, Andrew Gurr, Michael Hattaway, David Hoeniger, Trevor Howard-Hill, Paulina Kewes, Kim Kippen, Soon-Ai Low, Jean MacIntyre, Brian Parker, Richard Proudfoot, Jennifer Shennan, Tim Stretton, Hans Werner, and Claire Worley. In addition, of course, we have imposed on our own colleagues and students, and particular thanks must go the student casts and crews who have undertaken productions of these seldom-performed plays. To our families and friends, as always, our heartfelt gratitude.

Special mention must be made of the invaluable contribution as music consultant for the edition of Professor Peter Walls, who saved us from many egregious errors.

We acknowledge also the patience and support of the staff of Cambridge University Press, particularly Sarah Stanton and Margaret Berrill.

The sad death of Tony Hammond, our co-editor for Volume one, must not obscure his contribution to this volume, for which he did nearly all the textual collation, and particularly for his early work in addressing the lineation problems in *The Devil's Law-Case*. We also acknowledge the immense support we received since the inception of the edition from Don McKenzie, whose death was a heavy blow.

David Gunby, Department of English, University of Canterbury,
Christchurch, New Zealand

David Carnegie, School of English, Film and Theatre,
Victoria University of Wellington, New Zealand

MacDonald P. Jackson, Department of English,
University of Auckland, New Zealand

List of abbreviations

Volume I of this edition is cited as *Webster*, I. Unless otherwise noted, all citations from classical works are from Loeb Classical Library editions, and all biblical quotations from the Geneva Bible. Shakespeare references use abbreviated titles without authorship citation (see under 'Shakespeare' below). Works prior to the eighteenth century are published in London unless specified otherwise.

I. WORKS BY WEBSTER

a. ABBREVIATIONS

See Webster canon (*Webster*, I, xxxii–xxxiv) for full titles, chronology, and publication details. Webster is referred to in the Commentary as W. 'Stage direction' is abbreviated as SD. References to works by Webster not contained in vols. I and II of this edition are signalled as being to the Lucas edition lineation: e.g., *AQL* (Lucas) I.i.150–1.

AddM	W's Additions to *The Malcontent*
AQL	*Anything for a Quiet Life*
AV	*Appius and Virginia*
CC	*A Cure for a Cuckold*
Char.	*Characters*
DLC	*The Devil's Law-Case*
DM	*The Duchess of Malfi*
FMI	*The Fair Maid of the Inn*
IndM	Induction to *The Malcontent*
KWW	*Keep the Widow Waking*
MonC	*A Monumental Column*
MonH	*Monuments of Honour*
NHo	*Northward Ho*
Ode	*Ode*
Prog.	*Progeny of . . . Prince James*
QV	*Qualis Vita*
SP	*A Speedy Post*

STW	*Sir Thomas Wyatt*
ToAM	*To . . . Antony Munday*
ToTH	*To . . . Thomas Heywood*
WD	*The White Devil*
WHo	*Westward Ho*

b. PRINCIPAL EDITIONS OF WEBSTER

Editions are cited by editor and, where necessary, date.

Brennan 1975	Elizabeth M. Brennan, ed., *The Devil's Law-Case*, New Mermaids (London, 1975)
Dilke	Charles Wentworth Dilke, *Old English Plays*, 6 vols. (London, 1814–15)
Dollimore and Sinfield	Jonathan Dollimore and Alan Sinfield, eds., *The Selected Plays of John Webster* (Cambridge, 1983)
Dyce 1	Alexander Dyce, ed., *The Works of John Webster*, 4 vols. (London, 1830)
Dyce 2	Alexander Dyce, ed., *The Works of John Webster* (London, 1857)
Gunby 1972	D. C. Gunby, ed., *John Webster: Three Plays* (Harmondsworth, 1972)
Hazlitt	William Hazlitt, ed., *The Dramatic Works of John Webster*, 4 vols. (London, 1857)
Lucas	F. L. Lucas, ed., *The Complete Works of John Webster*, 4 vols. (London, 1927)
Shirley	Frances A. Shirley, ed., *The Devil's Law-Case*, Regents Renaissance Drama (Lincoln, Neb., 1971)
Thorndike	Ashley H. Thorndike, ed., *Webster and Tourneur* (New York, 1912)
Weis	René Weis, ed., *The Duchess of Malfi and Other Plays* (Oxford, 1996)

2. FREQUENTLY-QUOTED AUTHORS

With authors for whom reference is made to several plays or other works, the author's name only may appear in this list, followed by the edition(s) cited. Thus, e.g., a note in the Commentary to Jonson, *Sejanus* may be amplified by reference in this list to *Ben Jonson*, ed. C. H. Herford and Percy and Evelyn Simpson, 11 vols. (Oxford, 1925–52).

Alexander	Sir William Alexander, *The Monarchicke Tragedies* (1607). The individual plays are cited as follows: *The Alexandraean Tragedie* (*Alex. Trag.*) and *Julius Caesar* (*Jul. Caes.*). Act and scene numbers are followed by signature references
Bartholomaeus, *Batman*	Anglicus Bartholomaeus, *Batman uppon Bartholome, his Booke De Proprietatibus Rerum*, tr. Francis Batman (1582)
Beaumont	Francis Beaumont and John Fletcher, *The Dramatic Works in the Beaumont and Fletcher Canon*, gen. ed. Fredson Bowers, 10 vols. (Cambridge, 1966–96)
Browne, *Works*	*The Works of Sir Thomas Browne*, ed. Sir Geoffrey Keynes, 4 vols. (London, 1964)
Cal. S. P. Dom. (Charles I)	*Calendar of State Papers, Domestic Series: Charles I*, ed. John Bruce, William Douglas Hamilton, and S. C. Lomas, 23 vols. (London, 1858–97)
Cal. S. P. Dom. (James I)	*Calendar of State Papers, Domestic Series: James I*, ed. Mary Anne Everett Green, 6 vols. (London, 1856–72)
Campion, *Works*	*The Works of Thomas Campion*, ed. Walter R. Davis (London, 1969)
Chamberlain, *Letters*	*The Letters of John Chamberlain*, ed. N. E. McClure, 2 vols. (Philadelphia, 1939)
Chapman	*The Plays of George Chapman: The Comedies*, ed. Allan Holaday (Urbana, 1970) *The Plays of George Chapman: The Tragedies*, ed. Allan Holaday (Cambridge, 1987) *The Poems of George Chapman*, ed. Phyllis B. Bartlett (New York, 1962)
Dekker	*The Dramatic Works of Thomas Dekker*, ed. Fredson Bowers, 4 vols. (Cambridge, 1953–61). Nondramatic works of Dekker are cited from early printed editions
de Serres, *General Inventorie*	Jean de Serres, *A General Inventorie of the Historie of France unto 1598*, tr. E. Grimeston (1607)

Donne	John Donne, *The Epithalamions, Anniversaries and Epicedes*, ed. W. Milgate (Oxford, 1978)
	John Donne, *The Elegies and The Songs and Sonets*, ed. Helen Gardner (Oxford, 1966)
Drayton, *Works*	Michael Drayton, *Works*, ed. J. William Hebel et al., corrected ed., 5 vols. (Oxford, 1961)
Earle, *Microcosmographie*	John Earle, *Microcosmographie* (1628)
Fletcher	Francis Beaumont and John Fletcher, *The Dramatic Works in the Beaumont and Fletcher Canon*, gen. ed. Fredson Bowers, 10 vols. (Cambridge, 1966–96).
Ford	John Ford, *The Broken Heart*, ed. T. J. B. Spencer, Revels Plays (Manchester and Baltimore, 1980)
Gerard, *Herball*	John Gerard, *The Herball or Generall Historie of Plantes* (1597)
Guazzo, *Civile Conversation*	Stefano Guazzo, *The Civile Conversation of M. Steeven Guazzo*, tr. G. Pettie (1581)
Guevara, *Diall*	Antonio de Guevara, *The Diall of Princes . . . With the Famous Booke of Marcus Aurelius*, tr. T. North (1557)
Hall, *Characters*	Joseph Hall, *Characters of Vertues and Vices: In Two Bookes* (1608). Characters written after 1608 are quoted from *The Works of Joseph Hall* (1625)
Harrison, 'Description'	William Harrison, 'Description of England', in Raphael Holinshed, *Chronicles* (1587)
Henslowe, *Diary*	*Henslowe's Diary*, ed. R. A. Foakes and R. T. Rickert (Cambridge, 1961)
Herrick, *Works*	*The Poetical Works of Robert Herrick*, ed. L. C. Martin (Oxford, 1956)
Heywood	Individual plays and other works by Thomas Heywood are, unless otherwise noted, cited from the first published edition, with act and scene numbers of the plays followed by signature references. This is a departure from the practice in Vol. I of citing from Shepherd's 1874 *Works*.
Heywood and Rowley	*A Critical Edition of Fortune by Land and Sea by Thomas Heywood and William Rowley*, ed. Herman Doh (New York, 1980)

Jonson	*Ben Jonson*, ed. C. H. Herford and Percy and Evelyn Simpson, 11 vols. (Oxford, 1925–52)
Kyd	*The Works of Thomas Kyd*, ed. Frederick S. Boas (Oxford, 1901)
Livy, *Romane Historie*	Titus Livius, *The Romane Historie*, tr. Philemon Holland (1600)
Lodge, *Works*	*The Complete Works of Thomas Lodge*, ed. Edmund Gosse, 4 vols. (London, 1883; repr. New York, 1963)
Lyly	*The Complete Works of John Lyly*, ed. R. W. Bond, 3 vols. (Oxford, 1902)
Marlowe	*The Complete Works of Christopher Marlowe*, ed. Fredson Bowers, 2nd ed., 2 vols. (Cambridge, 1981)
Markham, *Cavelarice*	Gervase Markham, *Cavelarice; Or the English Horseman* (1607)
Marston	John Marston, *Antonio and Mellida*, ed. W. Reavley Gair, Revels Plays (Manchester and New York, 1991) John Marston, *The Malcontent*, ed. G. K. Hunter, Revels Plays (London, 1975) John Marston, *The Wonder of Women, or the Tragedy of Sophonisba*, ed. William Kemp (New York, 1970)
Marston, *Poems*	*The Poems of John Marston*, ed. Arnold Davenport (Liverpool, 1961)
Massinger	*The Plays and Poems of Philip Massinger*, ed. Philip Edwards and Colin Gibson, 5 vols. (Oxford, 1976)
Matthieu, 'Continuation'	Pierre Matthieu et al., 'Continuation' of Jean de Serres, *A General Inventorie of the Historie of France unto 1598 . . . Continued out* [*of*] *the Best Authors*, tr. E. Grimeston (1607). [See also de Serres]
Matthieu, *Henry IV*	Pierre Matthieu, *The Heroyke Life and Deplorable Death of Henry the Fourth*, tr. E. Grimeston (1612)
Middleton	Thomas Middleton, *A Chaste Maid in Cheapside*, ed. R. B. Parker, Revels Plays (London, 1969) [Thomas Middleton], *The Revenger's Tragedy*, ed. R. A. Foakes, Revels Plays (London, 1966). [Authorship in this edition ascribed to Cyril Tourneur] Thomas Middleton, *Women Beware Women*, ed. J. R. Mulryne, Revels Plays (London, 1975)

Middleton and Rowley	Thomas Middleton and William Rowley, *A Fair Quarrel*, ed. R. V. Holdsworth, New Mermaids (London, 1974) Thomas Middleton and William Rowley, *The Changeling*, ed. N. W. Bawcutt, Revels Plays (London, 1958)
Montaigne, *Essayes*	Michel de Montaigne, *The Essayes or Morall, Politicke and Militarie Discourses*, tr. J. Florio (1600)
Montreux, *Honours Academie*	Nicolas de Montreux, *Honours Academie. Or the Famous Pastorall of Julietta*, tr. R. Tofte (1610)
Moryson, *Itinerary*	Fynes Moryson, *An Itinerary Written by Fynes Moryson Gent.* (1617)
Nashe, *Works*	*The Works of Thomas Nashe*, ed. R. B. McKerrow, 4 vols. (London, 1910)
North's Plutarch	Sir Thomas North, tr., *The Lives of the Noble Grecians and Romanes . . . by Plutarch* [ed. specified in citation]
Overbury, *Characters*	Sir Thomas Overbury, *New and Choise Characters, of Severall Authors* (1618 ed. unless otherwise specified)
Pepys, *Diary*	*The Diary of Samuel Pepys*, ed. Robert Latham and William Matthews, 11 vols. (London, 1970–83)
Pliny, *Nat. Historie*	[Caius Plinius secundus] *The Historie of the World*, tr. Philemon Holland (1601)
Scot, *Disc. Witchcraft*	Reginald Scot, *The Discoverie of Witchcraft, Wherein the Lewde Dealing of Witches is Notablie Detected, the Knaverie of Conjurors* (1584)
Selden, *Duello*	John Selden, *The Duello, or Single Combat* (1610)
Shakespeare	William Shakespeare, *The Riverside Shakespeare*, ed. G. Blakemore Evans et al. (Boston, 1974). Play titles, without Shakespeare's name, are abbreviated as in *A Complete and Systematic Concordance to the Works of Shakespeare*, ed. Marvin Spevack, 9 vols. (Hildesheim, 1968–80)
Sidney, *Works*	*The Complete Works of Sir Philip Sidney*, ed. Albert Feuillerat, 4 vols. (Cambridge, 1912–26)
Stow, *Annales*	John Stow, *The Annales of England . . . Continued unto 1614*, by E. Howes (1615)

J. W., *Valiant Scot*	*The Valiant Scot by J. W.: A Critical Edition*, ed. George F. Byers (New York and London, 1980)
Topsell, *Historie*	Edward Topsell, *The Historie of Foure-footed Beastes* (1607)

3. FREQUENTLY-QUOTED CRITICAL WORKS

Works are normally cited throughout by author (and, where necessary, date).

Abbott	E. A. Abbott, *A Shakespearean Grammar* (London, 1870)
Bawcutt	N. W. Bawcutt, ed., *The Control and Censorship of Caroline Drama: The Records of Sir Henry Herbert, Master of the Revels 1623–73* (Oxford, 1996)
Bentley	Gerald Eades Bentley, *The Jacobean and Caroline Stage*, 7 vols. (Oxford, 1941–68)
Bliss	Lee Bliss, *The World's Perspective: John Webster and the Jacobean Drama* (Brighton, 1983)
Boklund 1970	Gunnar A. Boklund, '*The Devil's Law-Case*: An End or a Beginning?', in Brian Morris, ed., *John Webster* (London, 1970)
Bradley	David Bradley, *From Text to Performance in the Elizabethan Theatre: Preparing the Play for the Stage* (Cambridge, 1992)
Brooke	Rupert Brooke, *John Webster and the Elizabethan Drama* (London, 1916)
Brown 1954	John Russell Brown, 'The Printing of John Webster's Plays (I)', *Studies in Bibliography* [hereafter *SB*] VI (1954), pp. 117–40
Brown 1956	John Russell Brown, 'The Printing of John Webster's Plays (II)', *SB* VIII (1956), pp. 113–27
Brown 1962	John Russell Brown, 'The Printing of John Webster's Plays (III)', *SB* XV (1962), pp. 57–69
Cary	M. Cary, *A History of Rome Down to the Reign of Constantine*, 2nd ed. (London, 1960)
Carnegie	David Carnegie, 'Seldon's *Duello* as a Source for Webster's *The Devil's Law-Case*', *N&Q*, n.s. XLVI (1999), pp. 260–2

Carnegie and Gunby	David Carnegie and David Gunby, '*The Devil's Law-Case* 2.1.149–51', *Explicator* LVII (1998), pp. 17–20
Carnegie and Jackson	David Carnegie and MacD. P. Jackson, 'The Crux in *A Cure for a Cuckold*: a Cryptic Message, a Doubtful Intention, and Two Dearest Friends', *MLR* XCVI (2001), pp. 14–20
Chambers	E. K. Chambers, *The Elizabethan Stage*, 4 vols. (Oxford, 1923)
Courtade	Anthony E. Courtade, *The Structure of John Webster's Plays* (Salzburg, 1980)
Cunnington and Lucas	Phillis Cunnington and Catherine Lucas, *Occupational Costume in England* (London, 1967)
Dent	R. W. Dent, *John Webster's Borrowing* (Berkeley and Los Angeles, 1960)
Dent 1984	R. W. Dent, *Proverbial Language in English Drama Exclusive of Shakespeare, 1495–1616* (Berkeley, 1984)
Dessen	Alan C. Dessen, *Elizabethan Stage Conventions and Modern Interpreters* (Cambridge, 1984)
Dessen and Thomson	Alan C. Dessen and Leslie Thomson, *A Dictionary of Stage Directions in English Drama, 1580–1642* (Cambridge, 1999)
Foakes	R. A. Foakes, *Illustrations of the English Stage 1580–1642* (London, 1985)
Forker	Charles R. Forker, *Skull Beneath the Skin: The Achievement of John Webster* (Carbondale, Ill., 1986)
Gardiner	Samuel R. Gardiner, *History of England from the Accession of James I to the Outbreak of the Civil War 1603–1642*, 10 vols. (London, 1883–4)
Goldberg	Dena Goldberg, *Between Worlds: A Study of the Plays of John Webster* (Waterloo, 1987)
Gosse	Edmund Gosse, *Seventeenth-Century Studies* (London, 1885)
Greg, *Bibliography*	W. W. Greg, *A Bibliography of the English Printed Drama to the Restoration*, 4 vols. (London, 1939–59). References for plays are to numbered entries, not pages
Greg,	W. W. Greg, *Dramatic Documents from the Elizabethan*

Documents	*Playhouses*, 2 vols.: Facsimiles, Commentary (Oxford, 1931)
Griffin	Robert P. Griffin, *John Webster: Politics and Tragedy* (Salzburg, 1972)
Gurr 1992	Andrew Gurr, *The Shakespearean Stage, 1574–1642*, 3rd ed. (Cambridge, 1992)
Gurr 1996	Andrew Gurr, *The Shakespearian Playing Companies* (Oxford, 1996)
Henke 1975	James T. Henke, *Renaissance Dramatic Bawdy (exclusive of Shakespeare)*, 2 vols. (Salzburg, 1975)
Henke 1988	James T. Henke, *Gutter Life and Language in the Early 'Street' Literature of England* (West Cornwall, Conn., 1988)
Hoeniger	F. David Hoeniger, *Medicine and Shakespeare in the English Renaissance* (Newark, Del., 1992)
Hoy 1980	Cyrus Hoy, *Introductions, Notes and Commentaries to Texts in 'The Dramatic Works of Thomas Dekker'*, 4 vols. (Cambridge, 1980)
Jackson 1985	MacD. P. Jackson, 'John Webster and Thomas Heywood in *Appius and Virginia*: a Bibliographical Approach to the Problem of Authorship', *SB* XXXVIII (1985), pp. 217–35
Jackson 1998	MacD. P. Jackson, 'The Compositors of *Appius and Virginia* (1654)', *Publications of the Bibliographical Society of America* XCII (1998), pp. 535–40
Jackson 1999	MacD. P. Jackson, 'Latin Formulae for Act Endings in Early Modern English Plays', *N&Q*, n.s. XLVI (1999), pp. 262–5
Jowitt	*Jowitt's Dictionary of English Law*, 2nd ed., ed. John Burke (London, 1977)
Kiernan	V. G. Kiernan, *The Duel in European History* (Oxford, 1988)
King 1965	T. J. King, 'Staging of the Plays at the Phoenix in Drury Lane, 1617–42', *Theatre Notebook* XIX (1965), pp. 146–66

King 1992   T. J. King, *Casting Shakespeare's Plays: London Actors and Their Roles, 1590–1642* (Cambridge, 1992)

Kusunoki   Akiko Kusunoki, 'A Study of *The Devil's Law-Case*: With Special Reference to the Controversy over Women', *Shakespeare Studies* (Tokyo) XXI (1982–3), pp. 1–33

Linthicum   M. Channing Linthicum, *Costume in the Drama of Shakespeare and His Contemporaries* (Oxford, 1936)

LION: *Drama* *Literature Online: English Drama* [database online] (Bell and Howell; Ann Arbor, Mich., 2000 [version current October 2000])

LION: *Poetry* *Literature Online: English Poetry* [database online] (Bell and Howell; Ann Arbor, Mich., 2000 [version current October 2000])

Lockyer   Roger Lockyer, *The Life and Political Career of George Villiers, First Duke of Buckingham, 1592–1628* (London, 1981)

MacIntyre   Jean MacIntyre, *Costumes and Scripts in the Elizabethan Theatres* (Edmonton, 1992)

MSR   Malone Society Reprints

Murray   Peter B. Murray, *A Study of John Webster* (Philadelphia, 1964)

Nares, *Glossary* Robert Nares, *A Glossary; Or, Collection of Words, Phrases, Names and Allusions to Customs, Proverbs, etc. . . . in the Works of English Authors, particularly Shakespeare and his Contemporaries*, ed. James O. Halliwell and Thomas Wright (London, 1872)

OCD   M. Cary et al., eds., *The Oxford Classical Dictionary* (Oxford, 1949)

OED   *Oxford English Dictionary*

Parker, *Coriolanus* R. B. Parker, ed., Shakespeare, *The Tragedy of Coriolanus* (Oxford, 1994)

Partridge 1955 Eric Partridge, *Shakespeare's Bawdy* (London, 1955)

Partridge 1984 Eric Partridge, *A Dictionary of Slang and Unconventional English*, 8th ed., ed. Paul Beale (London, 1984)

Pearson	Jacqueline Pearson, *Tragedy and Tragicomedy in the Plays of John Webster* (Manchester, 1980)
Ranald	Margaret Loftus Ranald, *John Webster* (Boston, 1989)
Reynolds	George Fullmer Reynolds, *The Staging of Elizabethan Plays at the Red Bull Theater 1605–1625* (New York, 1940; repr. New York, 1966)
Ronan	Clifford Ronan, *'Antike Roman': Power, Symbology and the Roman Play in Early Modern England, 1585–1635* (Athens, Ga., 1995)
Rubinstein	Frankie Rubinstein, *A Dictionary of Shakespeare's Sexual Puns and Their Significance* (London, 1984)
Seiden	Melvin Seiden, *The Revenge Motive in Websterean Tragedy* (Salzburg, 1973)
Shakespeare's England	*Shakespeare's England*, 2 vols. (Oxford, 1916)
STC	Alfred W. Pollard and G. R. Redgrave et al., *A Short-Title Catalogue of Books Printed . . . 1475–1640*, 2 vols., 2nd ed. (London, 1976)
Stoll, *Periods*	Elmer Edgar Stoll, *John Webster: The Periods of His Work as Determined by his Relations to the Drama of his Day* (Boston, 1905)
Stone, *Crisis*	Lawrence Stone, *The Crisis of the Aristocracy 1558–1641* (Oxford, 1965)
Sugden	Edward H. Sugden, *A Topographical Dictionary to the Works of Shakespeare and His Fellow Dramatists* (Manchester, 1925)
Sykes	H. Dugdale Sykes, notes cited by Lucas
Taylor	Gary Taylor, 'The Structure of Performance: Act-Intervals in the London Theatres, 1576–1642', in Gary Taylor and John Jowett, *Shakespeare Reshaped, 1606–1623* (Oxford, 1993), pp. 3–50
Tilley	Morris Palmer Tilley, *A Dictionary of the Proverbs in England in the Sixteenth and Seventeenth Centuries* (Ann Arbor, Mich., 1950)
Wiggins	Martin Wiggins, 'Notes on Editing Webster', *N&Q*, n.s. XXXXII (1995), pp. 369–77

Wing	Donald Goddard Wing et al., *Short-Title Catalogue of Books Printed . . . 1641–1700*, 4 vols., 2nd ed. (New York, 1972–98)
Wymer	Rowland Wymer, *Webster and Ford* (New York, 1995)
Young	Alan Young, *Tudor and Jacobean Tournaments* (London, 1987)

THE DEVIL'S LAW-CASE

Date

A firm *terminus ad quem* of 1619 for the dating of *The Devil's Law-Case* is provided by the title-page of the 1623 Quarto, which states that the play was 'acted by her maiesties Seruants'. For as Bentley and Gurr demonstrate,[1] *pace* Lucas, Queen Anne's Men ceased to refer to themselves by their old title at her death on 2 March 1619, a provincial troupe continuing as 'Servants to the Late Queen Anne', while a remnant of the London company, including Richard Perkins, continued to play at the Red Bull as the 'Players of the Revels'.[2] It thus seems almost certain that *The Devil's Law-Case* must first have been performed by Queen Anne's Men no later than February 1619.

A sound *terminus a quo* is harder to establish. Bentley, for once supporting Fleay, argues that 'the unusual insistence on the dates'[3] in the trial scene argues first performance in 1610, but this mathematically-derived solution—e.g. Romelio, aged thirty-eight, was born in 1572—finds no favour elsewhere, and a more viable *terminus* is likely to be found in Webster's borrowings (at I.ii.173 ff. and II.i.155 ff.) from Jonson's *The Devil Is an Ass*. As Lucas notes,[4] these passages show no signs of being later interpolations, so it seems reasonable to assume that the writing of some, at least, of *The Devil's Law-Case* postdates the first performance of *The Devil Is an Ass* in (probably) November or December 1616.[5]

Dating Webster's tragicomedy more closely within these limits is difficult and involves the assessment of several possible topical references, none of them conclusive. One is that at IV.ii.11–13, where the Second Surgeon comments: 'How? Goe to the East Indies! And so many Hollanders gone to fetch sauce for their pickeld Herrings! Some have bene pepperd there too lately.' Stoll argued a reference to a notorious incident in August (but actually October) 1619, when four English ships loading pepper off Sumatra were captured by the Dutch,[6] but this is ruled out by the March 1619 disbanding of the Queen's Men. On the other hand, as Lucas points out, 'hostilities were incessant in the East Indies between English and Dutch from the beginning of 1617 to the end of 1620',[7] and the first news of fighting reached England in April 1618, so that the passage may indicate a date of composition subsequent to that.

A less particular allusion is that argued by Bourgeois, who links references in V.iv to courage in the face of death to the legendary firmness before execution of Sir Walter Raleigh on 29 October 1618.[8] Bourgeois argues also that in the handling of Leonora's law suit, and particularly in the character of Winifrid, are to be found allusions to the scandalous Lake–Roos trial of January 1618 to February 1619 (see p. 10). The case is weak, however, and no more capable of substantiation than attempts to find in *The Devil's Law-Case* allusions to the long-running warfare between Chief Justice Coke and his wife, which began in 1617 as a quarrel over their daughter's marriage, or to any other example of what John Chamberlain, writing to Dudley Carleton on 12 February 1620, called 'the insolence and impudence of women'.[9]

In sum, the most that can be said concerning the dating of *The Devil's Law-Case* is that it was probably completed after November or December 1616 and performed prior to March 1619. The East Indies reference suggests, however, that (unless the allusion is a late insertion) the play was still being written in April 1618, while the allusions to Raleigh, if indeed they are such, argue that composition was still under way in November of that year. Such particularity, however, is speculative, and a conservative dating can be no more precise than 1617–19, with an inclination towards 1618 as the most likely date.

1. Bentley, I, 165; Gurr 1996, pp. 326–7.
2. Gurr 1996, p. 326.
3. Bentley, V, 1250–1.
4. Lucas, II, 213.
5. Jonson, IX, 250–1.
6. Stoll, *Periods*, p. 31.
7. Lucas, II, 214. See for details Gardiner, III, 167–71.
8. Baron A. F. Bourgeois, 'John Webster: the Probable Date of *The Devil's Law-Case*', *N&Q*, eleventh series, x (July–December 1914), pp. 41–2. Chamberlain writes of Raleigh's courage in letters dated 31 October and 7 November (Chamberlain, *Letters*, II, 175–80).
9. Chamberlain, *Letters*, II, 289.

Critical introduction

DAVID GUNBY

'What is striking about discussion of the work of John Webster', writes Neil Carson, 'is the absence of that larger area of agreement within which meaningful arguments about detail can take place. There is not a universally acceptable definition of Webster's peculiar genius.'[1] Where *The Devil's Law-Case* is concerned that problem—'the absence of that larger area of agreement within which meaningful arguments about detail can take place'—is exacerbated by the relative paucity of critical debate about Webster's only unaided foray, so far as we know, into the genre of tragicomedy. In 1970 Gunnar Boklund expressed the problem thus: 'Any critical treatment of *The Devil's Law-Case* will inevitably be hampered by the lack of a critical tradition on which to fall back. Few scholars have found the play worth serious consideration, and nothing like a generally accepted interpretation has consequently been achieved.'[2] In fact the situation had begun to improve when Boklund presented his paper at the York Conference on John Webster, since the first article devoted entirely to *The Devil's Law-Case* appeared in 1968,[3] and the first major discussion of chapter length, in Peter B. Murray's *A Study of John Webster*, in 1969. Prior to these there had, of course, been Lucas's introduction (pp. 222–8) to the play in the second volume of his edition of *The Complete Works of John Webster* (1927), but Lucas was not, for the most part, impressed by *The Devil's Law-Case*, and his introduction tends to damn with faint praise where it does not damn outright. Since Boklund wrote, however, there have been major contributions to the debate over *The Devil's Law-Case* from Jacqueline Pearson, Lee Bliss, and Charles Forker, and briefer but useful ones from Akiko Kusunoki, Rowland Wymer, Anthony Courtade, and René Weis. Agreement on what Webster is trying to do, and how he goes about it, is still far from universal, but at least there is a modest corpus of critical material on which those discussing the play can draw.

In the first critical comment we have (*c.* 1640) on *The Devil's Law-Case*, the clergyman Abraham Wright describes it as 'But an indifferent play'. The plot, Wright continued, 'is intricate enough, but if rightly scanned will be found faulty, by reasons many passages doe either not hang together, or if they doe it is so sillily as noe man can perceive them likely to bee euer done'.[4] Whether because of dissatisfaction with the plot, as Wright would have it, or for other reasons, *The Devil's Law-Case* has, in fact, been very rarely 'done' since the seventeenth century: only twice indeed on the professional stage, at York in 1980 and Bristol in 1989 (see pp. 52–4). Cynics might be inclined to suggest that the absence of bizarre and idiosyncratic Websterian productions, particularly such as some *The White Devil* has received, advances rather than hinders a critical understanding of his plays, but it is nonetheless unfortunate that there is so little in the way of theatre experience to support and illuminate the critical study of a 'poem' where, Webster himself confessed, in his address 'To the Juditious Reader', 'A great part of the grace . . . lay in Action'.

In slating the structure of *The Devil's Law-Case* Wright institutes a critical tradition which continues to the present day. 'The disjunctive tendencies of Webster's dramaturgy seem to threaten cohesion in *The Devil's Law-Case* even more radically than in *The White Devil*', writes Forker, adding that 'the drama gives an impression of having been conceived as a group of separate episodes or emotionally entangling situations that were only later spliced into a play.'[5] Boklund, earlier, had come to much the same conclusion, though linking the problem of incoherence with the absence of a single source on which Webster could rely: 'He had neither the natural continuity of an exciting story nor the elemental problems of a familiar exemplum to fall back on, and was apparently not able to bring his disparate ingredients together to a convincing dramatic whole.'[6] And Wymer, in the course of a generally sympathetic account of a play which he finds 'lively, disconcerting, highly theatrical and much more interesting than many more "competent" plays of the period . . . in other words, a suitable candidate for further revivals',[7] nonetheless comments that, 'Even for admirers of Fletcher's style of melodrama, Webster has overloaded the narrative complications to the point of incoherence.'[8]

Not all those who write on *The Devil's Law-Case* agree. Murray, for instance, praises 'the nearly perfect order of its plot',[9] while Pearson sees it as one of 'four perfectly structured plays' which Webster wrote.[10] Nonetheless, the balance of critical opinion tends towards the view that *The Devil's Law-Case* is deficient structurally. It also tends to see its conclusion as one of the play's least satisfactory features. One of the earliest and most damning comments on this aspect of the play is Madeleine Doran's:

A complicated plot of rivalries in love, duels and disappearances leads up to a fine trial scene in which the conscienceless Leonora's revengeful intentions against her own son are exposed and thwarted. But Webster does not let the findings of the trial govern the outcome of the play. He winds it up with a solution of affairs directly athwart every sympathy he has created, all sense of justice, and what might be called the 'leading' of the plot.[11]

Forker is less scathing in declaring that 'Webster's concluding scene may be said both to resolve and to sidestep the many complexities of plot, character, and meaning so assiduously cultivated in all that precedes',[12] but he, too, feels dissatisfaction at the 'pairing off' of the couples at the end: it is, he writes, 'oddly joyless and so unadorned by poetry or romance as to seem imposed—more like a convenience of the playwright than a psychologically valid, much less inevitable, harmonizing of dissonance'. 'An arranged rather than a felt or emergent symmetry', Forker concludes, 'is what Webster offers us at the end.'[13] The same concern is expressed by Wymer, who writes: 'We hardly care what happens to the various characters and their expressions of joy seem perfunctory in the extreme (though arguably less so in performance, where their words may be less important than their gestures).'[14] 'Webster's unlikely ending', Wymer observes, 'is neither amusing enough to work as a parody of the desire for improbable happy endings nor emotional enough to seem deeply significant.'[15]

By contrast, Pearson argues that the 'increasingly incomplete explanations of the behaviour and feelings of the people in the play' constitute 'a deliberate tragicomic strategy' in which The Devil's Law-Case 'falls apart into spectacle, short scenes and sketchy explanations, detaching us from the fiction and confronting us unavoidably with its theatrical nature'.[16] 'The Devil's Law-Case', Pearson concludes, 'is not failed tragedy that goes to pieces in the last act, but a successful play in a different mode, a critical and analytic tragicomedy with a strong theatrical self-consciousness.'[17]

Like Pearson, Wymer sees The Devil's Law-Case as 'extremely self-conscious about its theatrical status'.[18] But unlike Pearson, he links two major strands of criticism concerning the play, the perfunctory nature of its ending and the debate over its 'significance', and specifically over whether Webster's tragicomedy should be read in Christian, and indeed theological, terms. Wymer himself briefly discusses aspects of seventeenth-century Church of England theology which may have a bearing on the improbability of the ending, and particularly emphasis on the inscrutability of God's purposes and the hidden workings of grace, before concluding that 'The decisive objection to taking The Devil's

Law-Case as seriously as some critics have done is . . . its lack of emotional engagement at the end.'[19]

Wymer's is a reaction to, though not entirely a rejection of, a reading of *The Devil's Law-Case* which has its origins in the arguments of Gunby and Murray that the play is essentially a work of theodicy. The counter-argument, which rests, *inter alia*, on Elton's documentation of the impact of scepticism on belief in providence,[20] sees the fideism of the Capuchin as misplaced, and undermined by the action of the play. 'The Capuchin believes Heaven has redirected man's disastrous private drama into one harmonious and encompassing comedy,' writes Bliss, 'but his happy certainty hardly quiets our suspicion that for Webster fundamental questions remain unanswered.'[21] 'Webster's own tragicomedy offers little support', he concludes, 'for the pat assumption of happy endings created by divine fiat.'[22] Forker straddles the gap between these critical positions in maintaining both that 'We can hardly exclude Christian values from Webster's play without doing it violence' and that 'Neither, on the more skeptical side of the debate, can we ignore the damaging glibness of tone, the shrugging off of moral responsibility and the quasi-cynical fillips of plot that push the ending of the drama dangerously close to parody.'[23] Yet one senses in Forker's account of the play an uncertainty, displayed in constantly tentative phrasing, which suggests the difficulty of maintaining that position. In *The Devil's Law-Case*, Dena Goldberg claims, Webster 'is allowing himself to have his cake and eat it'.[24] A question to be addressed is whether the position taken by Forker can be similarly described, or whether it represents an unsustainable maintenance of opposites.

In much of what has been written above concerning disagreements over Webster's dramaturgy, over the meaning of *The Devil's Law-Case*, and the significance which is to be drawn from its ending, there is a sense of *déjà vu*. With the two tragedies, after all, and with *The White Devil* in particular, there is disagreement of a similar kind. In another respect, however, there is no sense of earlier disagreements revisited, since the topicality of *The Devil's Law-Case* and its evident connection with London, despite its Neapolitan setting, mark a new development in Webster, or rather a return to the world of the *Ho* plays of 1604–5. Nor is there major disagreement as to what the dramatist's purposes are in respect of his two major targets, the insolence of ungovernable women, and duelling. Both issues were topical in London in 1618 and both are handled in a manner which makes the dramatist's position clear.

Of the two issues, that of duelling is handled entirely in Act II, where

8

Contarino and Ercole fight, and nearly kill each other, over Jolenta. Julio
sees the two duellists as 'perfect lovers' (II.ii.41), since

> It has been ever my opinion,
> That there are none love perfectly indeed,
> But those that hang or drowne themselves for love:
> Now these have chose a death next to Beheading,
> They have cut one anothers throats, brave valiant Lads.   (II.ii.42–6)

The terms in which Julio praises the rivals, however, as having 'cut one
anothers throats' undermine his praise, as does the behaviour of the duellists themselves, whose elaborate dedication to protocol, and a punctilio
taken to perhaps comic extremes, serve to underline the pointlessness of
what they are doing. But it is the curt response of Prospero, here as elsewhere in the play seeming to have a choric function, in which we find
the condemnation which echoes the vehemence with which King James
himself opposed, and proscribed, duelling:

> Come, you doe ill, to set the name of valour
> Upon a violent and mad despaire.
> Hence may all learne, that count such actions well,
> The roots of fury shoot themselves to hell.   (II.ii.47–50)

Duelling is examined—and condemned—in the first half of the play.
What Crispiano describes as 'the insolencies | Of . . . women' (III.i.28–9)
is likewise examined—and likewise condemned—in the second half.
Courtade considers III.i 'misplaced', since 'Crispiano's revelation of his
secret mission is clearly expository as is the presentation of Ariosto's
honesty.'[25] 'The discussion of the abuse of the law by women and the
meeting of the two guardians of society's fragile soundness', Courtade
continues, 'might have better occurred as part of their first meeting in
II.i. The importance of the law and the eventual transfer of the law's
championship from the trusty old judge to the scrupulously honest
lawyer need to be established earlier in the play for better dramatic
impact.'[26] But Courtade misses the structural point, which is that the
handling of the issues of duelling and ungovernable women is predicated
on a two-part structure to the play, manifest in so many other aspects of
The Devil's Law-Case.

That what Crispiano calls 'the insolencies | Of . . . women' was a
major concern in England in the years 1615–21 is well documented.
During this period major scandals saw three men holding high public
office brought down through what were widely perceived as unscrupulous and domineering wives and a fourth made a laughing-stock. The

first to fall was Robert Carr, Earl of Somerset, who with his wife, the former Countess of Essex, was in May 1616 found guilty of the murder in September 1613 of Sir Thomas Overbury, imprisoned in the Tower of London. Though King James commuted the death sentences passed on his former favourite and his wife, they were not released from prison until 1622, and Carr's career was over.

The second case involved the Lord Treasurer, Thomas Howard, Earl of Suffolk, who in 1618 was dismissed on grounds of corruption. After a Star Chamber hearing in October and November 1619, he and his wife, accused of extortion, were found guilty, fined, ordered to make reparation, and imprisoned. Howard's public career, too, was over, and rumour had it that he had acted under the influence of his wife.

The third case, also brought to the Star Chamber, involved Sir Thomas Lake, who in February 1619 was dismissed as Secretary of State, not because of any failure in office, but because of his involvement in the scandalous Lake–Roos case. After a quarrel about property, Lady Lake had accused her son-in-law, Lord Roos, of an incestuous relationship with his stepgrandmother, the Countess of Exeter, whom Lady Lake likewise accused of trying to poison her and her daughter. A crucial point in the allegations was that the Countess had read and signed a confession of guilt in her house in Wimbledon, and that Lady Lake's maid, one Sarah Swarton, had observed this from behind an arras. The Countess brought a charge of defamation against the Lakes and Lady Roos, and James himself, in what Lucas describes as 'one of his flashes of Sancho Panzan shrewdness',[27] insisted on inspecting the room, and found that there was a gap of some two feet between the bottom of the arras and the floor, so that there was no way Sarah Swarton could have been present without discovery. In February 1619 the Lakes and Lady Roos were fined and imprisoned, Lady Roos being released in June on admission of guilt, as was Lake in January 1620. His wife, however, obstinately refused to admit her guilt, and was not released until May 1621. Again, the general view was that a husband had been the victim of an unscrupulous and domineering wife.

Besides these three cases, there was another, much longer-running, involving a public feud between the Chief Justice, Sir Edward Coke, and his wife, the former Lady Hatton. Their first falling-out (over property) had occurred soon after their marriage in 1598, but things came to a head in 1617 over the marriage of their daughter, Frances. When the case was brought before the Privy Council Lady Hatton's denunciation of her husband was such that, John Chamberlain reported to Sir Dudley Carleton on 24 May 1617, 'Burbage could not have acted better.'[28]

That these and other incidents, including the publication of Joseph Swetnam's virulent *Araignment of Lewde, Idle, Froward and Unconstant Women* (1615), fuelled strong anti-feminist feelings seems clear. Moreover the King himself shared these feelings, as was evident from his instruction in January 1620 to the Bishop of London. John Chamberlain writes:

> Yesterday [24 January] the bishop of London called together all his Clergie about this towne, and told them he had expres commaundment from the King to will them inveigh vehemently and bitterly in theyre sermons against the insolencie of our women, and theyre wearing of brode brimd hats, pointed doublets, theyr heaire cut short or shorne, and some of the stilletaes or poniards, and such other trinckets of like moment, adding withall that yf pulpit admonitions will not reforme them he wold proceed by another course.[29]

Less than three weeks later, Chamberlain wrote to Carleton describing the results:

> Our pulpits ring continually of the insolence and impudence of women: and to help the matter forward the players have likewise taken them to taske, and so to the ballades and ballad-singers, so that they can come no where but theyre eares tingle.[30]

That *The Devil's Law-Case* was written in response to the royal initiative is ruled out by its date of composition (see pp. 3–4). Kusunoki, however, argues that Romelio's comments on the violence of female jealousy, which has often 'raisd the Devil up | In forme of a Law-case' (III.iii.201–2), 'having no relevance to the dramatic context here', 'may well have been intended to remind the audience of the Lake–Roos case, which was caused partly by Lady Roos' jealousy of the Countess of Exeter',[31] though the more immediate purpose of the statement is proleptic, as an ironic prefiguration of the trial which Leonora is to instigate, and of which we get our first inkling later in the same scene. But that in *The Devil's Law-Case* Webster does address seriously the moral and social implications raised for his contemporaries by the actions of women seen as malicious and ungovernable is signalled throughout the play—and indeed in its sub-title—by the references to the devil. Apropos the Bishop of London's instruction to his clergy John Chamberlain wrote: 'the truth is the world is very far out of order, but whether this will mend yt God knowes'.[32] In Leonora, and in Romelio, we observe individuals 'very far out of order', but part of a dramatic world which at the last does 'mend' through divine intervention in support of the law and the church.

In support of his argument for 'the nearly perfect order' of the plot of *The Devil's Law-Case*, Murray advances the following summary:

the structure of the action divides the play into three balanced sections. The plot as a whole is organized around three great futile, inconclusive, violent human conflicts. Acts I and II culminate in an effort to settle a dispute by lawless duelling. Acts III and IV culminate in an effort to settle a dispute by law, and Act V winds everything up with a trial by combat, in which the violence of duelling is joined with the force of law in a doubly desperate attempt to determine truth.[33]

Thematically, Murray's tripartite 'structure of the action' has its merits, but in dramatic terms it is more productive to see *The Devil's Law-Case* as built on a two-part structure resembling those in *The White Devil* and *The Duchess of Malfi*. In *The White Devil*, III.iii constitutes a replaying, with ironic variations, of the opening scene of the play.[34] In *The Duchess of Malfi*, likewise, Act I is revisited in the first two scenes of Act III.[35] In *The Devil's Law-Case* the third act yet again forms the point at which new actions begin, often paralleling those instituted in the first act of the play, and often forming ironic variants on their earlier counterparts. The recasting of the sub-plot takes place in III.i, where links are established with II.i, but the more significant new actions, and parallels, are to be found in III.ii and particularly III.iii, where much relating to Romelio, Leonora, Contarino, and Jolenta is picked up from the first act, and reformulated.

In this reformulation, III.ii plays an important, though in a sense preliminary, part. It is here that Romelio, 'The fortunate Youngman' (I.i.12) of the first half of the play, makes his crucial mistake, in attempting to ensure Contarino's death by hastening the inevitable, and sets himself up as the unfortunate young man of the second half. More than that, though, we see (quite literally) the merchant whose pride is of a piece with his wealth metamorphose into a parody of Marlowe's Barabas. His two soliloquies reveal not only his malevolence but also his pleasure in hamming up the part of the stage Machiavel, but Webster's larger purpose is served by the way in which Romelio's preposterous appearance— almost certainly including a red wig and oversize nose (see p. 38)—signals his moral decline just as, more seriously, does the appearance of Francisco as Mulinassar the Moor in *The White Devil*.

Restored though he may be, in III.iii, to his merchant's garb, Romelio is no longer the supremely confident and successful young man of Act I. And what happens in III.iii, in various ways paralleling the events of Act I and initiating the second phase in *The Devil's Law-Case*, underlines that fact. In Act I, for instance, we find Romelio (assisted by Leonora), pressuring Jolenta to marry Ercole, and asserting that she is now contracted to him (the term 'contract' is used four times by them). Jolenta and

Contarino believe, however, that in the eyes of heaven they are contracted to one another, and Winifrid, taking a more earthy and pragmatic
view of events, suggests that they 'get . . . instantly to bed together'
(I.ii.261). They do not, but III.iii imparts an ironic twist to the situation
when, reacting to Romelio's pressure on her to pretend that the child
Angiolella is carrying is hers by Ercole, Jolenta asserts that she is pregnant
by Contarino. Romelio had said that scandal could be avoided by
affirming that a precontract between Jolenta and Ercole had existed 'By
the same words usde in the forme of mariage' (III.iii.52). Jolenta counters
by asserting, falsely, that she is pregnant, and that a 'Precontract shall
justifie it' (66). In Act I Romelio is able, by virtue of his position as head
of the family, and supported by Leonora, to force through something
akin to a contract. Now he is forced to seek Jolenta's complicity in his
plans, and the greater strength of her position is underlined by the way
she turns Romelio's terminology against him.

There is another parallel which even more strongly demonstrates
Romelio's new and vulnerable status, one pointed up by the use of
'picture' in its metaphorical and actual senses. In Act I Leonora's failure to
recognize that by 'picture' Contarino means Jolenta—a misunderstanding no doubt arising from Leonora's attraction to him—intensifies, if it
does not generate, her strong support for Romelio's efforts to force
Jolenta to marry Ercole. In III.iii, however, an actual picture features cru-
cially as Leonora plans to disgrace and disinherit him because of his
'murder' of Contarino. Having called for 'the picture | Hangs in my
inner closet' (III.iii.359–60), which the donor bade her 'looke upon'
'when I was vext' (367–8), she finds 'It has furnisht me with mischiefe'
(370).

That Leonora is now initiating action rather than reacting to the initia-
tives of others is another indicator of a turning point in the play. 'Here
begines | My part i'th play', she comments (III.iii.371–2), and in a sense
this is true. The first half of *The Devil's Law-Case* is dominated by
Romelio: the second half will, until the end of the trial, be dominated by
Leonora. And Romelio, so dominant earlier, will now be the victim.

One more parallel, marking the beginning of the second phase of *The
Devil's Law-Case*, remains to be mentioned: the replacement of
Contarino by Ercole in Jolenta's affections. Where in Act I Contarino is
the object of Jolenta's love, and Ercole's suit is rebuffed, in III.iii the situ-
ation is abruptly reversed: 'Why, I protest, | I now affect the Lord *Ercoles*
memory, | Better then the others' (III.iii.154–6). That the basis for
rejecting Contarino, and indeed swearing never to marry him (158–61),

is false does not reduce the significance of this switch of affections, which is proleptic not only of the final pairing of Jolenta and Ercole, but also, ironically, of Leonora and Contarino.

Another indication of the two-part structure of *The Devil's Law-Case* is the fact that several major actions are concluded by Act III. Save in the play's final moments, for instance, Jolenta and Contarino do not meet again after I.ii, nor she and Ercole, while the duel in II.ii ends the conflict between Ercole and Contarino, and the stabbing in III.ii Romelio's vengeful pursuit of Contarino. On the other hand Webster also uses the first half of the play to prepare the ground for actions which are largely confined to the second, introducing Ariosto and Crispiano in II.i, the Capuchin in II.iii and the Surgeons in III.ii. He also echoes in the second half actions which have taken place in the first, as with the duels of II.ii and V.vi, where the erstwhile opponents, Contarino and Ercole, become allies, and as with Ariosto, urging Romelio to patience in II.iii and to anger in IV.ii. Likewise, we find Romelio in meditation in both II.iii and V.iv.

The sub-plot of *The Devil's Law-Case*, concerning Crispiano, 'one of the most eminent Civill Lawyers in Spaine' (II.i.4–5), and his scapegrace son, Julio, serves the customary Jacobean purpose of providing comparisons and parallels with the main action. The comparisons may be described in a phrase: folly as opposed to vice. Julio's sins are venial; he is a stereotypical young man, spendthrift and morally insouciant. He also turns out to be something of a coward. Romelio, with whom he is to be compared, is a sinner of a darker hue altogether, a maker rather than a spender of money, and no coward. The parallels, on the other hand, are more extensive and complex. Murray notes that 'just as in the main plot mother and brother spy upon and seek to dominate their daughter–sister', so in the sub-plot 'a father spies upon and seeks to dominate his son'.[36] He continues:

> Crispiano is to spy on Romelio as well as on Julio, and in the climactic episode of the play he is alleged to be the father of Romelio as well as of Julio. This parallel with Julio is further enforced at the end of the play when they fight as a team in a duel against the other parallel set, the nearly interchangeable lovers, Ercole and Contarino.[37]

As Murray notes, there is also parallelism in Ariosto's delivery of moral lectures first to Julio (II.i) and then to Romelio (II.iii).

How far, though, does the sub-plot fit the two-part structure so evident in the main action? If Julio be the focus, not strongly, since there is only the parallelism of Julio's first, unwitting, meeting with his father in II.i and his recognition of Crispiano in IV.ii. If Crispiano, however, is taken as the point of reference, there is a decided shift in Act III akin to that involving Leonora in the main action. For Courtade, 'The first scene of Act III seems misplaced.' 'The discussion of the abuse of the law by women and the meeting of the two guardians of society's fragile sound-ness', he claims, 'might have better occurred as part of their first meeting in II.i.'[38] To argue thus is to miss the fresh impetus, and change of direction, which involves Crispiano. In II.i he explains his merchant's disguise as a means of observing his son's profligacy and in III.i he initially justifies it to Ariosto as cover for surveillance of Romelio's illegal gold trading. The latter, however, is never developed, and Crispiano's real role in the second half of the play is revealed in his vow to 'curbe the insolencies | Of . . . women' (III.i.28–9), this presumably being the 'other businesse of greater consequence' (II.i.9–10) not enlarged upon in the first half of the play.

The Devil's Law-Case opens with emphasis on Romelio's wealth and good fortune, but it rapidly turns to Contarino, whose arrival a servant announces (I.i.29). Prior to his entry, Prospero and Romelio provide differing assessments of the young nobleman, Prospero considering that 'There lives not a compleater Gentleman | In Italy, nor of a more ancient house' (34–5) and that Contarino 'loves [Jolenta] intirely, and she deserves it' (44). Romelio is contemptuous on both counts, convinced that Contarino's motive in wooing Jolenta is mercenary: he is selling land to pay debts, 'And thinkes if he can gaine my sisters love, | To recover the treble value' (42–3). This problematizing of Contarino's character and motives prior to his first entry—without parallel in The Devil's Law-Case—should alert us to the need to scrutinize with special care the evidence provided by Webster. So should the fact that we do not see him with Jolenta until after he has sought Romelio's and (obliquely) Leonora's consent to his marriage to her. That Contarino is a spendthrift is clear from the comments of Leonora and Romelio concerning his previous evening's gambling (I.ii.67–74); that he loves Jolenta he never in fact says, coming no closer than telling Romelio that 'your sister and I | Are vowed each others' (I.i.94–5). Interestingly, too, when eventually we do see the lovers together, late in I.ii, most of the seventy lines or so that they share are taken up with the opposition they face. Indeed, the most intimate moments are mute, and accompanied by Winifrid's rather breathless aside:

Oh you pretty ones, I have seene this Lord many a time and oft set her in's lap, and talke to her of Love so feelingly, I doe protest it has made me run out of my selfe to thinke on't; oh sweet breath'd Monkey, how they grow together! Well, tis my opinion, he was no womans friend that did invent a punishment for kissing.   (I.ii.240–4)

The staging is much akin to that in *The White Devil*, where the first embrace of Vittoria and Brachiano is accompanied by a commentary from Zanche and Flamineo, and likewise interposes between us and the lovers.

Prefaced as it is by a questioning of Contarino's motives, this largely constrained representation of the relationship of Jolenta and her noble suitor, and particularly of his feelings, is made the more problematic because of the language he uses in telling Romelio of his intention to marry Jolenta. He had, he tells the merchant, 'concealed from you a businesse' (I.i.85) partly to avoid the possibility of proceeding against his will, but (he adds),

> another reason
> Was, that I would not publish to the world,
> Nor have it whispered scarce, what wealthy Voyage
> I went about, till I had got the Myne
> In mine owne possession. (I.i.89–93)

'To Contarino, love is wealth,' writes Murray, 'and the loved one herself is the "Myne" he seeks.'[39] But the manner in which Contarino and his suit is presented suggests rather that his motives are at least contaminated by financial considerations, and the doubt that his language generates is accentuated by the fact that, even before we have seen the two together, Contarino doubts Jolenta's constancy. Her note is brief, and the *'businesse | That concernes both our honors'* (I.i.213–14) unexplained, but her subscription—*'Yours in danger to be lost'*—is entirely clear, so that Contarino's reaction seems at once unworthy and obtuse:

> Tis a strange Injunction; what should be the businesse?
> She is not chang'd I hope. Ile thither straight:
> For womens Resolutions in such deeds,
> Like Bees, light oft on flowers, and oft on weeds. (I.i.216–19)

As so often in Webster's tragedies, so here we might well feel that this, the scene's concluding couplet, serves purposes beyond those recognized by the speaker.

If we compare the presentation of Contarino with that of Ercole, some interesting differences emerge. With the latter there is no prejudgement, for good or ill, though Ercole's image is not enhanced by Romelio's insensitive pressing of his case, and Jolenta's contemptuous dismissal of it. Ercole himself remains silent until line 27, when he addresses Jolenta in a formal manner, but thereafter until the entry of Leonora at 66 his only comments are protests at having been misled by Romelio and made to look ridiculous. Following Leonora's entry he is again silent, as she and Romelio apply pressure to get Jolenta to renounce Contarino, until her distress draws from him the magnanimity of

> Lady, I will doe a manly Office for you,
> I will leave you, to the freedome of your owne soule,
> May it move whither heaven and you please. (I.ii.94–6)

This in turn draws from Jolenta an acknowledgement that Ercole expresses himself 'most nobly' (97), just as his departing speech does an acknowledgement by Jolenta that she will pray for him:

> I will leave you excellent Lady, and withall
> Leave a heart with you so entirely yours,
> That I protest, had I the least of hope
> To enjoy you, tho I were to wayt the time
> That Schollers doe in taking their degree
> In the noble Arts, 'twere nothing, howsoere
> He parts from you, that will depart from life,
> To doe you any service. (I.ii.153–60)

Ercole's suit is, of course, advanced with unremitting pressure by Romelio and Leonora, and he is, in some measure, compromised when, at 127, Romelio seizes Jolenta's hand and places it in his. Whether, in response to Romelio's urging, he follows this up with a kiss (130) is unclear, but he certainly abstains from the insensitive joking in which Romelio and his mother then indulge.

All in all, then, despite the fact that Jolenta is in love with Contarino (which naturally predisposes us to prefer him), and that Romelio and Leonora are pressuring her to accept Ercole, the latter emerges much the better from the opening act of the play. And the superiority is reinforced markedly when, having given Jolenta his word that he will not quarrel with either Romelio or Ercole, Contarino challenges the latter to a duel. He also accuses Ercole of 'falsehood' and 'malice' in loving Jolenta, to which Ercole replies, reasonably enough, 'Compare her beauty, and my youth together, | And you will find the faire effects of love | No myracle at all' (II.i.242–4). Wymer comments that 'neither of these supposedly noble rivals ever comes properly into moral focus', and suggests Webster perhaps intentionally puzzles us as to why 'Ercole chooses to lie about Romelio's furtherance of his suit to Jolenta.'[40] But Ercole in fact supplies a plausible reason for denying Romelio's involvement in telling Contarino why the latter may not believe him:

> you may thinke,
> I count it basenesse to ingage another
> Into my quarrell; and for that take leave
> To dissemble the truth. (II.i.267–70)

In naming Leonora, Ercole is ensuring that he alone will face Contarino, who would undoubtedly have challenged Romelio had the latter been named.

Ercole's behaviour here confirms him as the worthier suitor, while Contarino, in breaking his vow to Jolenta, confirms his inferiority. And the way Webster handles the two as they make their Lazarus-like recoveries provides further moral distinctions. For Ercole is remorseful at having 'fought for one, in whom I have no more right, | Then false executors have in Orphans goods, | They cozen them of' (II.iv.7–9), and recognizes that he 'rather chose the hazard of my soule, | Then foregoe the complement of a chollerick man' (10–11), earning from the Capuchin, who accompanies him, the accolade of 'You are divinely informed sir' (6). Contarino, on the other hand, shows no sign of such self-recognition. His first appearance after Romelio's radical surgery is moments before the trial begins, when he appears in the company of the two Surgeons, and disguised as a Dane. Wymer, discussing the prevalence of disguise in the trial scene, notes Nashe's caricature in *Pierce Pennilesse* of the stereotypical Dane: 'a mixture of braggart soldier and overdressed gallant', and comments: 'If Contarino's disguise was anything like this, then it must be connected satirically with the aristocratic pride which led him to fight the duel and with all the other instances of "insolent vain-glory" with which the play abounds.'[41] But while his disguise may indeed bring him closer in appearance to the young fop, Julio, its primary purpose is surely further to differentiate Contarino from Ercole, who observes the trial 'muffled'.

The revived Contarino's silence as to his actions in Acts I and II is accompanied by an almost complete silence as to his actions in Acts IV and V, and there is general critical puzzlement as to why he does not reveal himself earlier. For Wymer, 'no amount of critical ingenuity will explain away Contarino's . . . decision not to reveal that he survived both the duel and Romelio's attempt to murder him, a decision which puts four lives pointlessly at risk (including his own)'. Wymer notes that 'Webster foregrounds the problem by having Contarino exclaim, "Wherefore should I with such an obstinacy, | Conceale myselfe any longer"' (V.ii.15–16), but concludes that he 'cannot provide a satisfactory answer'.[42] Yet the very act of foregrounding Contarino's silence suggests that Webster (unless he is to be held remarkably incompetent) intends

Contarino's unwillingness to be interpreted—and in the light of the representation of the young man earlier in the play, there seems to be no other way to read his refusal to reveal himself—as impercipience, selfishness and, perhaps, as a continued inclination to duelling.

'Contarino and Ercole—and their function in the play's structure—suffer not from complex but from inconsistent characterization': so writes Bliss.[43] The evidence suggests the contrary, particularly in the case of Ercole, who is, *pace* Bliss, differentiated quite precisely from his rival. What, then, of Jolenta, for whom the two men contend? She is, in some ways, the archetypal comic trophy-heroine: the spoils to go to the victor. She appears in only four scenes, and for most of the play is caught up in situations where she can only react. Not, indeed, until the final scene is she able to take the initiative in a way which ensures that she will get what she wants. Yet Jolenta does manage, nonetheless, to be more than Pearson's 'passive pawn in the game for most of the play'.[44] Our first impression of her is of a young woman strong-minded and sharp-witted, easily holding her own in verbal jousting with Romelio (I.ii.1–26). More soberly, she continues to resist when Romelio and Leonora combine to exert pressure on her to accept Ercole, and only when Leonora kneels to reinforce that pressure with what will, if Jolenta refuses to comply, be a mother's curse, does she reluctantly submit with 'Your Imprecation has undone me for ever' (104). Her response to Romelio's jocose 'Smile me a thanke for the paynes I have tane' (167) is bitter and to the point: 'I hate my selfe for being thus enforst, | You may soone judge then what I thinke of you | Which are the cause of it' (168–70).

In Contarino's company, Jolenta continues to show up strongly, for the most part more strongly than he, and both in her reproof of Winifrid for suggesting that they 'get you instantly to bed together' (261) and in her insistence that Contarino swear on his honour that he will not quarrel with Romelio or Ercole (267–70) we see a woman strong and morally stringent. It is presumably for her performance in III.iii, therefore, that Forker excoriates her as 'both ingenue and bitch, both virgin and pretended sexual partner outside formal marriage'.[45] Quite what marks Jolenta as a 'bitch' is unclear (her 'bitter flashes' perhaps?), and the appellation 'ingenue' seems equally ill-fitting. Her virginity we need not doubt, and 'pretended sexual partner outside formal marriage' seems remarkably heavy-handed and moralistic as a response to her behaviour in III.iii, where Jolenta moves from grief to what she describes, accurately, as 'phantasticall sorrow' (III.iii.192), and pretends to be 'with child already' (64)—presumably occasioning Forker's 'pretended sexual partner outside formal marriage'—to 'a fatall purpose', since if Romelio 'had lov'd or tendred [her] deare honour, | [He] would have lockt [his] ponyard in [her] heart' (88–9).

The Jolenta who seeks refuge in 'phantasticall sorrow' in III.iii is akin to the Jolenta who jokes with Angiolella in V.i and then with her flees 'the noyse' (V.i.40) of 'the intended combate' (33). The Jolenta who appears in the final scene, *her face colour'd like a Moore* (V.vi.33.1–.2), on the other hand, is close kin of the Jolenta who in III.iii reveals considerable shrewdness in seeking explanations for, or challenging, parts of Romelio's account of the plotting of Leonora and Contarino. For as Pearson points out, her disguise 'is a visual riddle which becomes a test for Ercole, now her "sweet heart" (V.i.34), and also for the audience, who must also not be deceived by her "blackened" appearance'.[46] 'Contarino', Pearson continues, 'has failed her tests: he has mistrusted her, misunderstood her, lied to her, and finally left her for her own mother.'[47] It might be more accurate to say that Contarino has failed Webster's tests. We know, for instance, that he mistrusted Jolenta; we do not know that she knows. We become aware, also, that he has transferred his affection to Leonora just prior to Jolenta's entrance; it is not clear, however, that she knows it. The more important point, in any case, is that Ercole passes Jolenta's test. Like Bassanio in *The Merchant of Venice*, as Pearson notes, 'Ercole is asked to choose between appearances and reality, and must bring about the happy ending by rejecting "vaine shew"' (V.vi.44) and looking beyond 'the outward skin' to 'the Jewell that's within' (46–7).[48]

Jolenta, then, finally asserts herself, within societal constraints, and is united with the man whom she was forced, in I.ii, to accept on pain of a mother's curse. What, then, of Leonora, who threatened what was the ultimate sanction, one so powerful as, in *The White Devil*, to reduce Vittoria to tears? For Forker she remains 'shadowy, mysterious, and psychologically ambiguous' until in III.iii 'The long soliloquy in which the idea of revenge against her son germinates in Leonora's mind brings the complicated widow into full definition for the first time in the play.'[49] If she is 'mysterious' in the first half of *The Devil's Law-Case*, it is certainly not because we see little of her, since Leonora appears in eight scenes, twice as many as her daughter, and is present, strongly, in both scenes in Act I. 'The sexually frustrated widow, the dignified matron, the jealous lover, the witch, the implacable revenger, the alienated parent, the religious convert, and the dedicated wife all represent aspects of Leonora's character', comments Forker.[50] In I.i the first, and strong, impression is surely that of 'the dignified matron', since it is as such that she is described by Contarino prior to her first entry, and as such that she greets him. Forker also labels her a 'sexually frustrated widow', presumably because of the readiness with which she misunderstands Contarino's oblique request for her 'picture' and the way in which she phrases her exit speech:

> I would not have you come hither sir, to sell,
> But to settle your Estate. I hope you understand
> Wherefore I make this proffer. (I.i.203–5)

Only, indeed, one as imperceptive as Contarino would fail to realize what Leonora is driving at here, since she has gone as far as convention allows—and perhaps a little further—in trying to make her feelings clear. Even so, to label her 'sexually frustrated' is to categorize her in terms of Webster's 'character' of 'An ordinarie Widdow', sexually rapacious and socially aspiring. Like the Duchess of Malfi she is neither that nor (though in I.ii she quotes almost verbatim from it) the epitome of widowhood, 'A vertuous Widdow' who never marries again and devotes herself to her children and to pious works. As Wymer notes:

> This elderly but still sexually active lady, who competes with her own daughter for Contarino's affections, could easily have been treated with a mixture of grotesquerie and pathos as a stock type whose most famous embodiment was to be Congreve's Lady Wishfort. Yet in her reaction to Contarino's apparent death, her great speech of grief and anger trembling on the brink of madness (III.iii.265–309), she rises far above any misogynist stereotype.[51]

It is not only in her great speech in III.iii, however, with its outpouring of grief, frustrated desire, anger, and vengefulness, that Leonora impresses. In I.i her comments about the alienation of land are sound advice, while in II.iii she reveals (but attempts to hide) a powerful devotion to Contarino. In III.iii, likewise, she reveals in her dialogue with Winifrid not only her plans for revenge but also insight and compassion:

> Thou hast lived with me
> These fortie yeares; we have growne old together,
> As many Ladies and their women doe,
> With talking nothing, and with doing lesse:
> We have spent our life in that which least concernes life,
> Only in putting on our clothes; and now I thinke on't,
> I have been a very courtly Mistris to thee,
> I have given thee good words, but no deeds. (III.iii.394–401)

Leonora surprises, then, in a way which Ercole, Contarino, and Jolenta do not. And because we become aware that she has hidden—or rather, intermittently and fleetingly revealed—depths, we are prepared for the shift, in the second half of the play, from acceptance to action, as she takes over from Romelio the role of chief plotter. Equally, by the powerful devotion to Contarino which she struggles to hide in II.iii, we are prepared for the play's denouement, in which she and the spendthrift young nobleman are united. Pearson expresses surprise at this aspect of the denouement, commenting: 'Leonora, the character who really complicates the comic planning, might have been married off to Crispiano . . . More in line with Jacobean ideals about widows, Leonora might have withdrawn altogether from the marriage-stakes.'[52] But *The Devil's Law-Case* is a play which from the first—in steadily demonstrating that the young lovers are not suited, or destined, for one another, for instance—defeats conventional expectations, and Leonora's depiction—and her union with Contarino—are of a piece with much else in the play.

So, too, is the depiction of Romelio, whom we must call the play's central figure, even if 'hero' seems an inappropriate appellation. Like his mother, and like Bosola, whom he in this much resembles, Romelio surprises. In the first scene he is quintessentially the successful young merchant, supremely confident, arrogant, and possessed of a strong bourgeois contempt for the aristocracy, whom, as in the person of Contarino, he regards as idle relics of a past age. Yet for all his less than likeable attributes, he is also endowed with positive qualities, including the energy and drive evident in his advice to Contarino:

> Oh my Lord, lye not idle;
> The chiefest action for a man of great spirit,
> Is never to be out of action: we should thinke
> The soule was never put into the body,
> Which has so many rare and curious pieces
> Of Mathematicall motion, to stand still.
> Vertue is ever sowing of her seedes:
> In the Trenches for the Souldier; in the wakefull study
> For the Scholler; in the furrowes of the sea
> For men of our Profession, of all which
> Arise and spring up Honor. (I.i.64–74)

Contarino comments, after Romelio departs, 'I doe observe how this *Romelio*, | Has very worthy parts, were they not blasted | By insolent vaine glory' (I.i.116–18). Imperceptive he may be, but Contarino is nonetheless right in this. In the remainder of Act I other negative traits of the 'fortunate Youngman' (I.i.12) are revealed. In I.i we see Romelio's cynicism concerning Contarino's motives in seeking to marry Jolenta, and in I.ii his callousness and materialism in forcing through her betrothal to Ercole. Her marriage is 'this maine businesse of life' (I.ii.38), her tears seen as a conventional gesture of reluctance, to be ignored or treated as embellishment. By the end of the act, thus, Webster has laid out the main negative features of Romelio's persona. In the four remaining acts of *The Devil's Law-Case* we see how Romelio is brought low by commercial and personal disasters, and how the positive characteristics which he reveals intermittently, and under pressure of circumstance, allow him, at the last, to be regenerate, his 'very worthy parts' intact, but his cynicism, callousness, and 'insolent vaine glory' purged.

We see Romelio's positive side at several points in the play. In II.iii, for instance, the anger and cynicism of his exchanges with Ariosto are followed by a meditation on life and death at once satiric and reminiscent of a medieval anchorite (II.iii.93–124), while shortly afterwards he reveals a capacity for sympathy which surprises, to say the least:

> Poore *Jolenta*, should she heare of this!
> Shee would not after the report keepe fresh,
> So long as flowers in graves. (II.iii.134–6)

Then at the end of the scene we find, cheek by jowl in his brief soliloquy, what he describes as 'strange' thoughts, 'but . . . no good ones' (167). On the one hand he is going to 'visit *Contarino*', since 'upon that | Depends an Engine shall weigh up my losses, | Were they sunke as low as hell' (168–70), while on the other he acknowledges that the reason he has suffered such losses is that he was 'Lost in securitie' in a 'wicked world' that 'bewitches, | Especially made insolent with riches' (172–3).

In *The Devil's Law-Case*, Margaret Loftus Ranald claims, 'Psychological motivation is nonexistent and verisimilitude is ignored.'[53] This is clearly an exaggeration, but as the representation of Romelio demonstrates, Webster does move freely and frequently from something approaching verisimilitude, and certainly includes elements of motivation, to an older, and much more symbolic, mode. That the man who can in part at least recognize that he has brought disaster upon himself can also seek to murder Contarino is compassable as verisimilitude, but that Romelio the merchant should dress up as a Jew, and carry out his crime in a parody of Marlowe's great Machiavel, Barabas, requires explanation in another way. Like Jolenta's blackened face, or Francisco's in *The White Devil*, Romelio's disguise as a stage Jew represents a symbolic truth: that he is debasing (and making a fool of) himself in carrying out what is patently an unnecessary crime.

Yet even in disguise Romelio is not completely the Machiavel. His opening soliloquy is entirely comic and parodic, a speech in which, as he says, 'I loose my selfe' (III.ii.17), but the longer soliloquy, in which he winds himself up to the stabbing, is more complex. It is hard to agree with Forker that in the soliloquy Romelio 'wrestles with the conscience of which, but minutes earlier, he had appeared to be disburdened, and can finally strengthen his resolve only by reassuring himself that a death by stabbing is preferable to the shameful execution for the murder of Ercole that might be Contarino's fate in the event of his recovery',[54] since much of the soliloquy seems to be more or less parodically conscienceful. But in the last lines, at least, parody is replaced by direct statement:

> Yet this shall proove most mercifull to thee,
> For it shall preserve thee
> From dying on a publique Scaffold, and withall
> Bring thee an absolute Cure, thus.   (III.ii.113–16)

These lines are proleptically ironic, of course, since a cure is exactly what Romelio is effecting, but even before we recognize this, late in the scene, they feel different from what has preceded them, and more of a piece with the statements of the reflective Romelio glimpsed earlier.

In III.iii, on the other hand, we are back to the Romelio of Act I, a cynical materialist manipulating his sister with a mixture of lies and half truths, and then callously summing up his achievement and informing us of his plans for dealing with her—'Shee must never marry' (III.iii.208)—and with the Surgeons, who are to be 'waged' to the dangerously unhealthy 'East Indies' (210). It is the last statement of confidence that we hear from Romelio. Within moments he has bragged to Leonora of killing Contarino, and shortly after we are in a new world, dramatically, in which she is hatching her plot to disinherit Romelio, and he, for the remainder of the play, becomes the victim rather than the victor. At bay throughout most of the trial scene, he re-establishes himself briefly when Leonora's falsehoods are exposed, but he is once more under threat when Ercole reveals what he knows of Contarino's supposed murder.

Thereafter we do not see Romelio again until V.iv, when, accompanied by the Capuchin Friar, he enters *very melancholly* (V.iv.38.1). The Friar's opening aside makes plain his intention; having learnt from Winifrid of Contarino's recovery, he intends 'To sound *Romelio's* penitence' (42) before resolving all 'these errours by discovering, | What shee related to me' (43–4). What follows—the unsuccessful attempt by the Capuchin to get Romelio to prepare himself spiritually for the dangers he faces, the ritual entry of Leonora with the coffins and winding sheets, the apparent change of heart by Romelio and then the shock of discovering that his spiritual awakening is a sham—forms part of the problematic ending of *The Devil's Law-Case*, so much discussed, and so often condemned as unsatisfactory. It also raises the issue of the role of the Capuchin, which, together with that of Ariosto, needs discussion before the ending can be further considered, and a judgement on the play's outcome made.

The Capuchin makes his first appearance in II.iii, in a ritual entry, accompanied by two Bellmen. His ostensible purpose is to solicit prayers for 'two unfortunate Nobles, whose sad fate | Leaves them both dead, and excommunicate' (II.iii.71–2) for what canon law considers the equivalent of suicide. But the Capuchin's assertion that both Contarino and Ercole have been 'slaine in single combat' (79) raises questions. Does he indeed believe that they have died? If so, on what evidence? To state that it is odd to have him soliciting prayers for those merely rumoured to be dead is to skirt close to a misguidedly naturalistic critique not infrequently found in discussions of *The Devil's Law-Case*. But asking the question in these terms serves to foreground the likelihood here of an explanation for the ritual entry as non-naturalistic as the entry itself. For the most likely purpose of the ritual entry is surely that which it achieves: a shock administered to Romelio, drawing his meditation on death (93–124). The positive effect is only partial, for it is followed by the fatalism of his response to the Capuchin's expression of regret at his losses:

> Um sir, the more spatious that the Tennis court is,
> The more large is the Hazard.
> I dare the spitefull Fortune doe her worst,
> I can now feare nothing. (II.iii.127–30)

The Capuchin's response encapsulates a theological truth and suggests something at least of the course which the play will take:

> Oh sir, yet consider,
> He that is without feare, is without hope,
> And sins from presumption; better thoughts attend you. (II.iii.131–3)

The Capuchin's second entry, accompanying an Ercole 'preserved', so the Friar tells him, 'beyond naturall reason' (II.iv.1), is less evidently symbolic. Nonetheless the pun in the same line, 'Looke up sir', reinforced by another in the Capuchin's comment that Ercole is 'divinely informed' (6) in acknowledging the error of duelling over Jolenta, points up the Friar's role in *The Devil's Law-Case*: to offer spiritual guidance and comfort.

With Ercole this is easy: he has, so near to death, seen the error of his ways. The last part of the scene reverts to the tougher candidate for divine assistance, however. Romelio, we are told, 'has got a Nun with child' (41); this, forcing Jolenta into a loveless marriage contract, and precipitating the duel, the Capuchin comments, 'are crimes that either must make worke | For speedy repentance, or for the Devill' (42–3).

The Capuchin does not appear again until III.iii, when, in its to-the-moment appropriateness, his entry once more presses its significance upon us. Leonora has collapsed in grief, and the Capuchin enters by 'a private way which I command, | As her Confessor' (III.iii.292–3). Here again, however, what appears to be a beneficial spiritual intervention turns out to be less than successful. With Romelio the problem is one of attitude. With Leonora it is that the man 'miraculously saved' is not Contarino but Ercole. Hence the woman who eulogizes the Capuchin with 'Oh, may you live | To winne many soules to heaven, worthy sir, | That your crowne may be the greater' (309–11), meditates after he leaves upon revenge, and then, as a preparative to employing Winifrid in her plot, states: 'let's to my ghostly Father, | Where first I will have thee make a promise | To keepe my counsell' (414–16).

Thus, by the end of Act III the Capuchin has failed in his efforts to bring spiritual succour to both Romelio and Leonora. Nor, until well into Act V, will he have an opportunity to redress the situation. In the interim, however, the focus shifts to the law, and back to Ariosto, who has been, since Act II, an alternative force for reformation and regeneration in Romelio.

Like the Capuchin, Ariosto is introduced in Act II, but initially he seems to have more to do with the sub-plot involving Crispiano and his foolish son, Julio, than with the main action involving Romelio. Described as 'the very myracle of a Lawyer, | One that perswades men to peace, and compounds quarrels | Among his neighbours, without going to law' (II.i.105–7), he also 'will give counsell | In honest causes gratis' (109–10), which he does to Julio in II.i and to Romelio in II.iii. With the latter, angry at his losses, relayed to him by Crispiano, he counsels patience:

Ariosto.   Your losses I confesse, are infinite, yet sir, you must have patience.
Romelio.   Sir, my losses I know, but you I doe not.
Ariosto.   Tis most true, I am but a stranger to you, but am wisht by some of your best friends, to visit you, and out of my experience in the world, to instruct you patience.

(II.iii.1–6)

The way in which Ariosto's counselling of Romelio is presented—baldly, without preface, and with vagueness as to its provenance—argues a parallelism between his role and that of the Capuchin, who himself counsels Romelio later in the scene. The little lawyer's decision to 'talke to [him] like a Divine' (II.iii.31) strengthens the parallel, as does his challenge to Romelio over the arrogant names he gave his lost ships. Even more interesting, however, is Ariosto's final statement, as he exits, having failed to bring the angry Romelio to see the need for the traditional Christian virtue of patience:

> give me thy hand, my intent of comming hither, was to perswade you to patience; as I live, if ever I doe visit you agen, it shall be to intreat you to be angry, sure I will, Ile be as good as my word, beleeve it. (II.iii.57–60)

In the trial scene Ariosto does just that, prophesying that 'within this halfe houre [I] shall intreat you to bee angry, very angry' (IV.ii.53–4). When, irritated, Romelio asks directly, 'What are you sir?' (75), Ariosto replies, 'An angry fellow that would doe thee good, | For goodnesse sake it selfe' (76–7). He stands alongside Romelio, at the bar, but in the legal sense he is not his counsel, and as he emphasizes, is receiving no fee. This, of course, clears the way for him to assume the role of judge when Crispiano steps down, but it also underlines his anomalous position, highlighted by his earlier statement that he has 'now occasion to be at your elbow' (52–3).

As the trial continues and Romelio, derided as a 'Cuckow hatcht ith nest | Of a Hedge-sparrow' (127–8), listens to his mother's claim that 'penitence' drives her to reveal the truth about his paternity, he finds it increasingly difficult to maintain his calm detachment, and finally breaks out angrily in denunciation of her and all women. Ariosto, who has been monitoring the gradual breaking down of Romelio's shell of indifference, and who greets Romelio's outburst with 'Take heed you doe not cracke your voice sir' (315), can now cease to monitor Romelio's emotional state, and prepare to take over from Crispiano the role of judge.

In Act V, therefore, Romelio's spiritual and emotional well-being is again the responsibility of the Capuchin, and in V.iv, when he enters to encounter 'ROMELIO *very melancholly*' (V.iv.38.1), the final stage in the battle for the merchant's soul begins. In II.iii Romelio had responded to the entry of the Capuchin and Bellmen with a meditation on death, but the Capuchin had seen his fatalism as dangerous, since 'He that is without feare, is without hope, | And sins from presumption' (II.iii.132–3). And though Romelio had acknowledged that he was 'Lost

in securitie' (II.iii.172), he was not, clearly, recognizing that the
overconfidence which success had brought is what theologians call
'carnal security': a complacency about one's spiritual state brought about
by worldly success. In V.iv (which in this respect echoes II.iii) the discussion between the Capuchin and Romelio takes up where II.iii left off.
The Capuchin tells us, in an aside, that he has 'come | To sound *Romelio's*
penitence' (V.iv.41–2) and tells Romelio, in response to an irritated 'Who
has hired you to make me Coward?' (68), 'I would make you a good
Christian' (69). And when Romelio maintains his attitude of indifference
towards death and its implications, comments:

> O, I tremble for you:
> For I doe know you have a storme within you,
> More terrible then a Sea-fight, and your soule
> Being heretofore drown'd in securitie,
> You know not how to live, nor how to dye:
> But I have an object that shall startle you,
> And make you know whither you are going. (V.iv.112–18)

The 'object' is the pageant-like entry of Leonora *'with two Coffins borne by
her servants, and two Winding-sheets stucke with flowers'* (119.1–.2), to which
Romelio responds with a second meditation, in which he acknowledges
the evanescence of life, and the vanity of ambition. It should be noted,
however, that beautifully expressed though it is, 'All the Flowers of the
Spring' does not necessarily indicate a full spiritual awakening. Indeed,
the only statement Romelio makes which suggests that is when he speaks
of forgiving Leonora, since it is 'the way | To be forgiven yonder'
(143–4). The rest, as in his acknowledgement of 'how rankly we doe smel
of earth, | When we are in all our glory' (145–6), is rather a recognition
of mortality, and the vanity of human wishes. That the Capuchin recognizes this only partial reclamation is clear from his response:

> Why this is well:
> And now that I have made you fit for death,
> And brought you even as low as is the grave,
> I will raise you up agen, speake comforts to you
> Beyond your hopes, turne this intended Duell
> To a triumph. (V.iv.152–7)

'More Divinitie yet?' is Romelio's response, which might alert us to the
fact that his regeneration is indeed incomplete, that he has been brought
low, but not yet raised up. If we are alerted by this, then his locking of
Leonora and the Capuchin in the turret will seem less startling, but a *coup
de théâtre* it still is, and one which shocks and offends many critics. Forker,

for instance, comments: 'Webster seems to present us with two Romelios in rapid and contradictory juxtaposition—the moral philosopher whose noble words spring from a "heart of adamant" suddenly "melt[ed]" by a fresh recognition of human transience (V.iv.138–9) and the icy scoffer-manipulator for whom the attitude of penitence is just another useful (if derisory) disguise.'[55]

Yet Romelio's final outburst of cynicism is short-lived. Faced with death itself, rather than symbolic reminders of it, he feels the need 'at the last gaspe, | To have some Church mans prayer' (V.vi.13–14). His acknowledgement that 'I doe not well know whither I am going' (12) is in direct descent from the spiritual disorientation we find earlier in Vittoria, Flamineo, and Bosola, dying in a mist. 'Some evill Angell | Makes him deafe to his owne safetie' the Capuchin tells Leonora (V.v.3–4). At the last, though, unlike his tragic forebears, Romelio is given the opportunity to draw back from the spiritual abyss.

Reading Romelio's change of heart in quasi-naturalistic terms, we may assume that the efforts of the Capuchin (and of Ariosto) have in the end had their effect. Looking at it theologically, we may (without abandoning the quasi-naturalistic explanation) note, with Wymer, that 'Protestant theology emphasised faith rather than reason as the path to God', and that 'Calvinists, in particular, promoted the view that God's workings were secret and inscrutable, incapable of being understood or challenged by human reason.'[56] Forker notes the 'symbolic' staging at this point, commenting: 'The spatial relationship obviously carries theological over-tones. The Capuchin and widow now possess a kind of heavenly knowl-edge in a stage location appropriately near "the heavens," but their confinement and distance from the arena of human activity make their higher truth maddeningly unavailable to those it might benefit.'[57] Certainly the Capuchin, thus confined, is acutely aware of the ironic outcome of his (as of Romelio's) efforts

> To see how heaven
> Can invert mans firmest purpose! His intent
> Of murthering *Contarino*, was a meane
> To worke his safety, and my comming hither
> To save him, is his ruine.   (V.v.14–18)

But the Friar also urges the despairing Leonora, prepared to jump to her death in an effort to save Contarino's life, to 'looke upwards rather', since 'Their deliverance must come thence' (13–14), and in a sense the ironic setback constitutes a test of faith, which the Friar thus passes.

The ironies which attach to the events of V.iv and V.v are, of course, merely the latest in a play suffused throughout with irony, beginning in action with Leonora's misunderstanding of Contarino's asking for her picture, but earlier in language, when Romelio first deceives Contarino with a bitterly ironic statement of support for his marriage to Jolenta, and then adds, 'no doubt, | My mother will be of your mind' (I.i.114–15). Irony, both verbal and dramatic, is indeed central to *The Devil's Law-Case*, and as Pearson notes: 'Although its plot is complex, at each turn it depends on a repeated motif—an action which ironically produces quite a different result from that intended.'[58] Typical of such ironies, and in a sense the greatest, because of its layered complexities, is Romelio's appearance as the murderous Jewish Machiavel. Forker comments: 'The Jew of course, pretends to be working against Romelio, so that the paramount irony (from the audience's point of view) consists in the villain–hero's having created for himself a villainous alter ego who will actually advance his real interests, but appear to be defeating them.'[59] In fact the 'paramount irony' is the further twist, whereby the 'villainous alter ego who will actually advance [Romelio's] real interests, but appear to be defeating them' is in fact defeating them, since without his intervention Contarino would have died.

Given the pervasive, and ultimately beneficent, operation of irony in *The Devil's Law-Case*, and the way in which Ariosto and the Capuchin work throughout to reclaim Romelio, Boklund seems wide of the mark when he writes of the conclusion:

> Even if we adopt a purely pragmatic attitude to [Romelio's] activities and emphasize that he really does not marry off his sister against her will but only tries to, that he really does not murder Contarino but only tries to, that he really does not acquire Ercole's and Contarino's property but only tries to—an attitude that may be essential for the proper understanding of tragicomedy—it is still somewhat hard to have the sun of forgiveness shine equally on him and on his intended victims.[60]

Setting aside this narrowly moral objection to the ending of *The Devil's Law-Case*, however, we are still left with objections which, while including a moral dimension, relate particularly to the perfunctory nature of the play's closure. Forker, for instance, speaks of the 'near-arbitrary couplings and the evasions of serious ethical judgment that attend them'[61] and also of the play's 'slapdash and psychologically unconvincing unions'.[62] Comparing the ending of Webster's tragicomedy to those of *All's Well That Ends Well*, *Measure for Measure*, and *The Tempest*, in all of which he notes 'feelings of psychological incompleteness and of moral dubiety', he adds: 'despite the religious implication of Leonora's and

Romelio's "conversions", Webster shows us almost nothing of the con-
trition that would make their forgiveness theologically appropriate or
their marriages symbolic of new spiritual enrichment or social awareness'.[63]

At moments like this one senses the existence of particular difficulties
attending critical discussion of this, as other, Webster plays, difficulties
which perhaps stem from the uniqueness of Webster's art, and in particular its unlikeness to Shakespeare's. The unions of Bertram and Helena at
the end of *All's Well That Ends Well*, for instance, or of the Duke and
Isabella, and Angelo and Mariana at the end of *Measure for Measure*, are as
briefly handled as those of Romelio and Angiolella, Leonora and
Contarino, and Jolenta and Ercole, yet occasion less complaint, while the
conclusion of *Measure for Measure* carries theological implications as
strong as those of the closing scenes of *The Devil's Law-Case*.[64] Part of the
explanation for the critical unease in these respects may lie in Webster's
tendency, throughout his career, to avoid much exploration of his characters' inner feelings. Soliloquies, in Webster, tend to be used rather to
explain what has or is about to happen than to explore the workings of
the speaker's psyche, and motivation tends to be revealed as much in the
use of imagery, or the comments of others, as in remarks by individuals
themselves.

Likewise, Webster tends to provide, whether through language or
action, pointers to judgement, pointers such as, in *The Devil's Law-Case*,
make it abundantly plain by the end of Act II that Contarino is not suitable for, or destined to win, Jolenta, and well before the close that Jolenta
has shifted her affections to Ercole. We are not made privy to the feelings
of the characters in this regard, so much as to the rightness of these outcomes. In short, we are dealing, as we do not in Shakespeare, with an art
with strong didactic tendencies, and in which we need to accommodate
to the didacticism or feel dissatisfied.

Another area of complaint about *The Devil's Law-Case* concerns its frequent and sometimes disconcerting tonal shifts. We find dissatisfaction
with this in Forker's reference to a 'damaging glibness of tone',[65] and presumably underlying Bliss's comment that 'Ariosto's moral effect is
perhaps blunted by his clowning in scenes 1 and 3 of act 2 and as
Romelio's unwanted "counsel" in the trial.'[66] Both in II.iii and during
the trial, however, Ariosto is engaged in a very serious business: trying to
bring Romelio to recognize his spiritual plight. The manner in which he
does this ranges from the jocular to the serious, but the significance of
what he is attempting does not vary. Likewise, during II.i Ariosto

attempts to 'read [Julio] good counsell' (II.i.132), and the fact that he is joined by Romelio in a comic assault on Julio's profligacy does not make what he is attempting any less serious.

The unease evident in Bliss's comments on Ariosto (unease found also in Kusunoki's comment that Ariosto is 'frequently made to look ridiculous')[67] is reflected also in responses to Romelio, who is capable of chameleon shifts of tone. But here as in so much else, Romelio is a lineal descendant of Flamineo and Bosola, and the greater difficulty which critics seem to have in accepting such shifts in the merchant seems to stem from the problematic status of tragicomedy, and of Websterian tragicomedy in particular. Where Flamineo's mordant satiric comment and bizarre jocularity are acceptable alongside deep seriousness in *The White Devil*, the same mix in Romelio is found problematic in *The Devil's Law-Case*.

What kind of tragicomedy is this of Webster's? Forker comments that 'Even for tragicomedy—a mixed genre by definition—Webster's drama aspires to an unusual degree of inclusiveness',[68] and goes on to list the comic modes he finds in *The Devil's Law-Case*: cynical city comedy, humour comedy, romantic comedy, problem or dark comedy, and Fletcherian tragicomedy. For his part, Wymer, restricting himself just to various tragicomic models, finds three in terms of which Webster's sole experiment in the genre might be read:

> If Marston is seen as the dominant influence, then the satiric and intellectually challenging aspects of Webster's play will be emphasized, and its close continuity with the tragedies, particularly *The White Devil*, will be emphasized. If Fletcher is taken as the reference point, then the complex plotting, with its fortunate final twists will be highlighted and Webster will be convicted of sacrificing the artistic integrity of the tragedies for the sake of a fashionable but empty melodramatic formula which, moreover, he is incapable of imitating successfully. If the relation to Shakespeare is stressed, then the temptation will be to invest the miraculous happy ending with a religious and philosophical profundity of the kind that many critics have found in *Measure for Measure* or *The Winter's Tale*.[69]

For Bliss, however, the options lie between romance tragicomedy, in which 'the plot's shifting oppositions finally resolve themselves organically to transform the initial confusion and malice into a harmonious resolution undreamt of in the opening acts, yet also dependent upon the very sufferings which had then seemed insurmountable',[70] and what he terms 'ironic tragicomedy', which 'refuses fully to resolve and transcend the human sufferings and contradictions it explores'.[71] 'What distinguishes these plays from later romance tragicomedy', he comments, 'is their deliberate exploration of difficulties they cannot fully resolve. They allow and exploit generic dissonance.'[72]

In certain respects Bliss's category of ironic tragedy seems to fit the Websterian bill. There is 'generic dissonance' in *The Devil's Law-Case*: tonal instability is one marker of that. And since Bliss places Marston's *The Malcontent* in this category, we can blend his judgement with that of Wymer, and agree that in *The Devil's Law-Case* 'the satiric and intellectually challenging elements' are powerful. On the other hand, the play's outcome is not what Bliss finds in ironic tragicomedy: a comic conclusion which 'is gained by wit but held together by no more than dramatic convention'.[73] Rather, we find a somewhat austere version of 'a harmonious resolution undreamt of in the opening acts, yet also dependent upon the very sufferings which had then seemed insurmountable'.[74] Throughout, Webster has pointed the way to an eventual union of Ercole and Jolenta. That Romelio should marry Angiolella is an act of symbolic restitution akin to the union of Angelo and Mariana in *Measure for Measure*. The surprise is the coupling of Leonora and Contarino, but in a play which from the first sets out to show that the archetypal young lovers are unsuited to one another, it need come as no surprise that rather than pairing off Leonora with the suitably elderly Crispiano, or confirming her in widowhood—options which as Pearson suggests would have met Jacobean audience expectations[75]—Webster unites the wealthy widow with the spendthrift young aristocrat. In doing so he confounds, as he has done earlier in his portrayal of Leonora, the stereotypical representation of an ageing widow. *The Devil's Law-Case* was written at a time when feelings against domineering women were strong, but in a play which demonstrates that '*When Women goe to Law, the Devill is full of Businesse*', Webster invests Leonora with a degree of sympathy which is remarkable. In this, as in so many other ways, *The Devil's Law-Case* defies both expectation and categorization. In doing so, it proves itself a worthy descendant of *The White Devil* and *The Duchess of Malfi*.

1. Neil Carson, 'John Webster: the Apprentice Years', in G. R. Hibbard, ed., *The Elizabethan Theatre VI* (Hamden, Conn., 1978), p. 76.
2. Boklund 1970, p. 123.
3. D. C. Gunby, '*The Devil's Law-Case*: an Interpretation', *MLR* LXIII, 3 (July 1968), pp. 545–58.
4. In G. K. and S. K. Hunter, eds., *John Webster: A Critical Anthology* (Harmondsworth, 1969), p. 35.
5. Forker, p. 380.
6. Boklund 1970, p. 118.

7. Wymer, p. 85.
8. Ibid., p. 75.
9. Murray, p. 187.
10. Pearson, p. 2.
11. Madeleine Doran, *Endeavors of Art: A Study of Form in Elizabethan Drama* (Madison, 1954), p. 354.
12. Forker, p. 416.
13. Ibid., p. 417.
14. Wymer, p. 84.
15. Ibid., p. 85.
16. Pearson, p. 109.
17. Ibid., p. 114.
18. Wymer, p. 79.
19. Ibid., p. 84.
20. William R. Elton, *King Lear and the Gods* (Lexington, 1966), pp. 3–33.
21. Bliss, p. 182.
22. Ibid., p. 183.
23. Forker, p. 446.
24. Goldberg, p. 127.
25. Courtade, p. 113.
26. Ibid.
27. Lucas, II, 215.
28. Chamberlain, *Letters*, II, 77.
29. Ibid., II, 286–7.
30. Ibid., II, 289.
31. Kusunoki, p. 10.
32. Chamberlain, *Letters*, II, 287.
33. Murray, pp. 204–5.
34. See *Webster*, I, 64–6.
35. Ibid. I, 383–4.
36. Murray, p. 187.
37 Ibid.
38. Courtade, p. 113.
39. Murray, p. 194.
40. Wymer, p. 75.
41. Ibid., p. 81. For discussion of disguise, see pp. 38–9.
42. Ibid., p. 75.
43. Bliss, p. 174.
44. Pearson, p. 111.
45. Forker, p. 424.
46. Pearson, p. 111.
47. Ibid.
48. Ibid., p. 112.
49. Forker, p. 395.
50. Ibid., p. 424.
51. Wymer, p. 78. Since there is no evidence that Leonora is literally 'sexually active', Wymer's phrase is presumably a shorthand for 'still prepared to be sexually active'.

52. Pearson, p. 105.
53. Ranald, p. 66.
54. Forker, p. 390.
55. Ibid., p. 413.
56. Wymer, p. 83.
57. Forker, p. 414.
58. Pearson, pp. 102–3.
59. Forker, p. 391.
60. Boklund, p. 126.
61. Forker, p. 448.
62. Ibid., p. 449.
63. Ibid., p. 448.
64. Brief but resonant final statements, such as Mariana's to the Duke concerning Angelo—'O my dear lord, | I crave no other, nor no better man' (V.i.425–6)—are not, of course, provided in *The Devil's Law-Case*.
65. Ibid., p. 445.
66. Bliss, p. 186.
67. Kusunoki, p. 23.
68. Forker, p. 420.
69. Wymer, p. 74.
70. Bliss, p. 18.
71. Ibid.
72. Ibid.
73. Ibid., p. 19.
74. Ibid., p. 17.
75. Pearson, p. 105.

Theatrical introduction

DAVID CARNEGIE

THE PATTERN OF THE PLAY

THE SCRIPT

At over 3,000 lines *The Devil's Law-Case* is a long play for the period, even longer than *The White Devil*, so it may, like that play, have been cut in its original production.[1] Nevertheless, a production at the Theatre Royal, York in 1980 (hereafter York 1980) demonstrated that a relatively full text is playable even in modern conditions in under two and a half hours.[2] It is notable that the York production also gave full attention to spectacular elements such as the two fights and the procession of coffins in V.iv. The danger of cutting, as was clear in a production in Bristol in 1989, is that to assume that an audience will fail to engage with religious or ethical issues in, e.g., Romelio's satiric 'Meditation' (II.iii.89), the Capuchin's more serious speeches in V.v, or Jolenta's highly symbolic 'black and white' speech at the end of the play, may result in the play's overall theme and purpose being blurred or lost.

Religious language, whether satiric, serious, stylized, or even providential, is only one important linguistic mode in the play. Other significant discursive areas include the mercantile (trading, smuggling, or seeking a rich bride), honour (from gambling debts to duelling, from women's subservience to allegations of bastardy), and the legal (not only the obvious comedy and satire of the trial scene, but also the reformative comments of Crispiano and Ariosto and the deadly formulae of judicial combat in V.vi).

PRODUCTION

As in the two Italian tragedies, Webster is again concerned with the dramaturgy of spectacle, mood, and the stage picture, including costume, makeup, properties, music, and lighting.

Costume and makeup are of especial importance for such a convoluted plot as that of *The Devil's Law-Case*, but thematic and symbolic purposes also matter. The religious themes of the play, for instance, are emphasized by the prominence of the Capuchin, wearing the grey robe and large cowl of the order, and girded with a cord from which hangs his rosary. By Act V Ercole and Contarino are also in '*Friers habits*' (V.ii.13.1), since the judicial combat to come is specifically religious in its medieval reliance on God to 'Determine the right' (V.vi.10), and the combatants have therefore been '*at the Bathanites*' (V.ii.13.2). Unfortunately we do not know who or what the Bathanites were, but there is little doubt that we are to understand that the two men have been at a religious ceremony to confess and be shriven.[3]

The nun's habit worn by Angiollela (a grey or brown gown with a black veil; see V.i.0.1n) is rendered satiric by her evident pregnancy beneath it, and then highly symbolic as the 'white Nun' is contrasted with Jolenta's 'blacke one' (V.vi.39). The symbolism of white and black is primarily related to skin colour, since Jolenta has '*her face colour'd like a Moore*' (V.vi.34.1–.2), but it is possible that Jolenta, still in a black gown of '*mourning*' (III.iii.0.2), and veiled like Angiollela, might initially look very like a black-habited nun.[4] The Bristol 1989 decision not to have Jolenta in blackface at the end, but to add only a black shawl to her usual costume, clearly reduced the emphatic visual iconography that accompanies the words. At York 1980, by contrast, Jolenta wore a black veil that reached to the floor on all sides just like that worn by Leonora at the trial, both women thereby being turned into objects of mystery waiting to be revealed. Jolenta at York also wore a cross at her neck, echoing the 'large Rosary' of the Capuchin.

Religious identification is the basis also for the '*habit of a Jew*' (III.ii.0.1) which Romelio adopts, but in this case as a disguise. Both the stage direction and the scene itself suggest an immediately recognizable stage costume, probably akin to Shylock's 'Jewish gaberdine' (*MV* I.iii.112). A gaberdine was a long loose gown with wide sleeves, and stage tradition suggests that Shylock's was the coarse outdoor version of the garment like Caliban's (cf. *Tmp.* II.ii.37–8). Thomas Jordan in 1664 recalls of Shylock that 'His habit was a Jewish Gown, | That would defend all weather.'[5] Historically, Jews in Europe were required to wear a distinguishing mark, either a circular or other badge on the outer garment, or more usually a special hat, often yellow. Bacon says 'usurers should have orange-tawny bonets, because they do judaise'.[6] The gaberdine was neither compulsory wear for Jews nor exclusive to them, and was in wide use in the sixteenth century by all classes. However, a strong stage convention seems likely to be operating here;[7] as James Shapiro says, 'Like Barabas [in *The Jew of Malta*], Romelio summons up the familiar images of the Jew as murderer, poisoner, military and political threat, and economic parasite.' Shapiro, however, believes that it is 'only his Jewish "habit" that sets Romelio apart—no exaggerated "Jewish" physical features and hence no easy way to tell Christian from counterfeiting Jew (in this case played by a counter-feiting Christian)'.[8] Why Shapiro has come to this conclusion is not clear; we might well think it probable that Romelio followed other stage Jews by providing himself not only with the stock clothing, but also the artificial 'bottle nose' (cf. Marlowe, *The Jew of Malta*, III.iii.10) and red beard and wig that became part of the standard portrayal (see III.ii.3n).[9] This is the more likely because, as Rowland Wymer suggests, 'it is the dis-guise itself which is the real object of interest', in part because it gives Romelio (probably acted by Richard Perkins, who may already have been playing Barabas as well) an opportunity to 'allude to and re-create Marlowe's villain–hero'.[10]

Romelio's disguise is adopted by 2 Surgeon at the end of the play (adding to the bizarre visual image of a pregnant nun accompanied by a Moorish lady), but the Surgeons' earlier disguise during the trial scene is not specified (and Ercole is merely '*muffled*' [IV.ii.0.2]). Contarino, however, adopts foreign dress as a disguise for his presence at the trial scene. While it is not until much later that he is described as 'the Dane' (V.iv.4), his supposed nationality must be easily identifiable, since Ercole can refer to his 'Nation' at IV.ii.614. Identification of foreigners by their style of clothing is common on the stage; MacIntyre cites, for instance, Haughton's *Englishmen for My Money* with its 'three foreign suitors as Dutch, French, and Italian, dressed differently from each other and from the three Englishmen'.[11] Danish clothing seems also to have been distinc-tive, to judge by Henslowe's wardrobe (see IV.ii.6.1n) and contemporary satire: Dekker refers to 'the Danish sleeve sagging down like a Welsh wallet',[12] and in descriptive rather than satiric vein Fynes Moryson reports of the King of Denmark that 'the Kings Guard wore huge breeches puffed, and of diuers colours like the *Sweitzers* hose'.[13] These may have been the vastly ostentatious 'pludderhoser', which Cay Dollerup suggests were probably one of the three distinctive elements of Danish costume on the English stage, the other two being a 'high, egg-formed fur hat virtually devoid of brim', and a long 'gold chain wound several times around the neck'.[14] Thomas Nashe, in *Pierce Penilesse*, describes a typical 'foole braggart' Dane who wears a cockes feather in a redde thrumd hat like a caualier . . . his apparel is so puft vp with bladders of Taffatie, and his back like biefe [beef] stuft with Parsly, so drawne out with Ribands and deuises, and blisterd with light sarcenet bastings, that you would thinke him nothing but a swarme of Butterflies if you saw him a farre off.[15]

Nashe's marginal notes also refer to '*half a dozen siluer rings*', and the entire section is noted as '*The pride of the dane*'. Wymer comments that 'if Contarino's disguise *was* anything like this, then it must be connected satirically with the aristocratic pride which led him to fight the duel and with all the other instances of "insolent vainglory" with which the play abounds'.[16] This seems possible; but, alternatively or in addition, such an extravagant appearance may be designed to make him appear foolish, and to associate him visually with the foppish Julio.

Julio's father Crispiano, a lawyer and judge, is yet another character to adopt a disguise, in his case the 'habit of a Marchant' (II.i.5; at York 1980, a brown cloak concealing his own rich purple and silver). In addition to this clothing, he probably has a false beard, since in the court in IV.ii he is already wearing his proper resplendent scarlet judge's robes (see IV.ii.46.1n), but must be able to reveal his true identity quickly.[17] While Contilupo is more likely than Crispiano to resemble the engraving of the gowned lawyer Ignoramus, with his pen box and inkhorn, from George Ruggle's play of that name (see Fig. 5), the Cambridge students who per-formed *Ignoramus* before King James in 1615 'dressed Sir Ignoramus like Chief Justice Coke and cutt his beard like him and feigned his voyce';[18] and Sir Edward Coke (see Fig. 1) has some similarities to Crispiano. Aubrey reported that

Sir John Danvers, who knew him, told me that he had heard one say to him [Coke], reflecting on his great scraping of wealth, that his sonnes would spend his Estate faster than he gott it; he replyed, They cannot take more delight in the spending of it then I did in the getting of it.[19]

Sanitonella and Crispiano exchange similar words at II.i.19–30, and one wonders if Webster intended topical performance reference to Coke or some other mighty lawyer.[20] Contilupo, however, and even more so the disreputable law clerk Sanitonella with his vast bundles of paper, will clearly be much less well off.

Within the merchant class, too, there is likely to be a clear hierarchy of wealth, with Romelio and Jolenta in particular likely to be more richly dressed than Prospero and Baptista. Leonora, too, may be dressed in costly fabric, though she is presumably in the black of a widow. At Bristol 1989, Leonora's plunging neckline implied her active interest in appearing

1. Sir Edward Coke in the robes of Lord Chief Justice, *c.* 1613–16
(attributed to Paul Van Somer).

attractive to Contarino (in distinct contrast to a high-buttoned Jolenta). In III.iii Jolenta, too, wears black, and may remain '*in mourning*' (III.iii.0.2) for the rest of the play. If so, the change in her appearance will visually reinforce a sense of how much has altered since she was wooed by Contarino in Act I.

The 'great Lord *Contarino*' (I.i.29) will presumably be dressed in aristo-cratic fashion, but determining the rank and dress of his rival Ercole is more difficult. Initially Ercole is referred to by Romelio as a 'Gentleman' (I.ii.40), but a few lines later is 'my Lord' (64), and at IV.ii.608 a 'Noble man'. Wymer assumes he is a Knight of St John; while this is likely (he is called in the Dramatis Personae 'a Knight of Malta'), it is not the only basis on which the King of Spain might send him via Malta on 'an Expedition 'gainst the Turke' (I.ii.86), so conclusions about the 'moral irony'[21] of Ercole wearing a Maltese cross need to be treated with caution. Dramaturgically, the two young men are linked (by a shared past as students at Padua, rivalry for Jolenta, shared conceptions of the code of honour, as co-accusers in the judicial combat, and eventually, bizarrely, by betrothal into the same family), so it seems most likely they are dressed in equivalent fashion (so York 1980).

Some characters are likely to be generically identifiable by costume: the additional judge and lawyer in IV.ii, the Herald and perhaps the Marshal, and probably the Surgeons in comically blood-spattered aprons (so York 1980; but cf. III.ii.18.1n). In other cases costume is a more subtle code identifying personality and character, and the II.i exchange between Ariosto and Julio is of particular interest.

That Julio is a fop in his clothing can be deduced both from Crispiano's knowledge of his son's 'course of ryot' (II.i.21) and from the satiric descrip-tion of Julio's 'numerous Wardrobe' at II.i.167 ff. Ariosto, by contrast, the 'dapper fellow | In the long stocking' (100–1), is dressed in the now old-fashioned style of over forty years earlier when he was 'chamber-fellow to [Julio's] father, when they studied the Law together' (127–8). 'Dapper' is a term applied 'to a little person who is trim or smart in his ways and move-ments' (*OED* 1b), and his small stature is confirmed by Crispiano describ-ing him as 'but a little piece of flesh' (104). The 'long stocking' is clearly 'the long stocking portion of the trunk-hose to which they were joined high up on the thigh',[22] and the 'round slop' mocked by the modish Julio at 143 the small trunk hose 'round like a pumpkin or onion'[23] that go with the long stocking. The fashion is familiar from Elizabethan illustrations, but was by this time long out of date, and would be in sharp contrast to Julio's fashionable Jacobean baggy slops. This contrast is more than merely visual, however; the thematic point is, presumably, that the visual and verbal mockery of the sprightly old gentleman will ironically strengthen the end of the play, when the young fop receives his comeuppance from the old-fashioned moralist.[24]

Props, both large and small, sometimes have thematic import as well, perhaps nowhere more obviously than in the emblematic '*two Coffins . . . and two Winding-sheets stucke with flowers*' (V.iv.119.1–.2). These *mementi mori* are designed by the Capuchin and Leonora to 'startle' (117) Romelio out of his 'securitie' (115), and the possibilities for stage business and spectacle are considerable (at York 1980, for instance, special lighting and extra friars added to the solemnity, and extra flowers were provided to be thrown into the coffins at some point; at Wellington 1995 (see p. 55) the winding sheets were reminiscent of John Donne's death engraving (see 119.2–20n). While Romelio, however, pretends to be deeply affected by the religious implications of the presentation, Julio seems to become comically entangled in one of the winding sheets, though precisely how is hard to say (see 150–1n).

Similar *mementi mori* are seen earlier in the play, when Jolenta's grief at Contarino's reported death is illustrated not just by a change into the black dress of mourning, but also by '*A Table set forth with two Tapers, a Deaths head, a Booke*' (III.iii.0.1–.2). York 1980 added a 'jewel relic' (possibly indicating a jewelled reliquary) and a rosary, while Bristol 1989 gave Jolenta a hand mirror, recalling the emblematic mirror of the Duchess (see *DM* III.ii.69 SD n). Leonora's picture of Crispiano seems also to serve a symbolic role; Leonora comments that she 'was enjoyned . . . ever when I was vext, | To looke upon that' (III.iii.367–8), and although her initial impulse is 'mischiefe' (370), the Capuchin's resolution of the play entirely resolves her vexation. At the Cockpit, with no stage posts, the picture would presumably have been hung on the tiring-house wall when Leonora calls for it in III.iii, and then again in the same place when it appears in the trial scene, thus both conveniently adjacent to Crispiano's seat as a judge, and with a visual echo back to Leonora's inception of the suit at law.

In addition to the coffins and Jolenta's table, other large props include the bed in which Contarino is discovered (or which is thrust out) in III.ii, '*seats for the Judges*' (IV.ii.0.1), which presumably implies substantial chairs, possibly on a raised dais like a 'state' (see *Webster*, I, 101, and below, *Staging the trial scenes*). The lists which are set up for the combat in V.vi are also, presumably, of some substance, even if no more than posts and rails.

Hand-held props, such as the rapiers of the Act II duel and the long military swords of the Act V judicial combat (see below, *Staging the trial scenes*) tend to be, in this tragicomedy, double in their implications. The rapiers, for instance, are the mortal instruments of the murderous aristocratic code of honour; but they lose their aura somewhat as the two apparently dying rivals squabble 'like small boys fighting over their favourite toy'.[25] Similarly, the medieval swords (and, at York 1980, armour) of the final judicial combat are heavy, deadly, and weighted with God's judgement; but involvement of the irrepressibly comic coward Julio offers potential for low comedy (so Wellington 1995). The little stiletto in III.ii implies the horror of Italianate treachery, but also invokes, in Romelio's mind, domestic images of executing 'Barmotho Pigs', or lancing a pustule with a 'Shoo-makers aule' (III.ii.99, 105). Romelio's 'bag of double Duckets' (136) to bribe the Surgeons is similarly transmuted to comic mode by his analogy of purchasing 'the silence of a terrible scolding wife' (134). The lawyer's brief to disinherit Romelio would be serious in its implications were it not for its ludicrous bulk, and associations with wrapping cheese and figs (IV.i.9–14). Even then, Sanitonella's vast 'Buckram bagg' has not lost its capacity for low comedy: there is a 'very lovely Pudding-pye' yet to emerge (IV.ii.35, 41). The letters, too, which are essential to the intrigue and misconceptions throughout the play—Jolenta's midnight summons to Contarino, Ercole's letter of introduction from the King of Spain, Contarino's supposed will, and especially Jolenta's riddling letter to Ercole saying 'that the shame she goes withall, | Was begot by her brother' (V.ii.38)—seem reduced as a category to overtly theatrical comic contrivances by Leonora's 'paper' at V.vi.62, which will avoid the need for a lengthy recapitulation of the plot.

These shifts between tragedy and comedy can be assisted by music and, especially in modern productions, lighting. The Bellmen's dirge-like handbells will seem tragically serious in announcing both the death and excommunication of Contarino and Ercole, but Romelio's 'Meditation' (II.iii.93; and see n) which immediately follows, and which may have been sung or chanted, possibly even accompanied by the Bellmen, is comically satiric in its tone. And although Romelio's verse (or song) at V.iv.122–37 is free from the satire of the earlier meditation, and is accompanied by '*Soft Musicke*', the apparent harmony and sincerity of effect are almost immediately reversed by Romelio's cynical imprisoning of his mother and the Capuchin. Even the trumpets supporting the formalities of the judicial combat in V.vi are undercut and forced to sound their final charge twice because of the interruption caused by Romelio's sudden change of heart ('Stay, I doe not well know whither I am going' [V.vi.12]).

In the original productions candles may or may not have been used to suggest that by the time of Contarino's visit to Jolenta at the end of I.ii the time is midnight, as specified in her I.i letter, but the 'two Tapers' (III.iii.o.1) specified on Jolenta's table are clearly intended to reinforce the sense of melancholy. The modern stage lighting at York 1980 ensured that the stage was enveloped in shadows for this scene, whereas for much of the play the lighting was much brighter, and drenched in warm Mediterranean colours (with interior scenes indicated by great shafts of light penetrating the tall louvres of the set). Even Bristol 1989, with much more limited lighting, could emphasize their melodramatic interpretation of Contarino's stabbing by spotlighting him alone, leaving Romelio in the shadowy half light behind.

ACTING

Of all the roles in the play, only that of Romelio can with any confidence be associated with a particular early performer. Richard Perkins, who probably played Flamineo in *The White Devil* (see *Webster*, I, 93, 98), and certainly played Barabas in *The Jew of Malta* later if not at this period, was probably the first Romelio. These three characters share a number of attributes—villainy, self-conscious humour, and a high degree of complicity with the audience—but we have no specific knowledge of how Perkins might have approached the role of Romelio.

At both York 1980 and Bristol 1989 the Romelios were energetic, cynical, and comic, demonstrating how good a rapport Romelio can build with an audience. Damien Thomas at York had 'a Machiavellian saturnine mockery of smiling about him, and delights in his scheming'.[26] He also caught 'a good measure of Romelio's cynicism'.[27] Cornelius Garrett at Bristol carried energetic interplay with the audience even further, being described as hamming it up as 'a crowd-pleasing pantomime villain'.[28] Clearly Romelio, like Flamineo and Barabas, must find ways to make the audience complicit with his theatrical delight in his villainy. There is more to the character than that, however; Jacqueline Pearson commented about the York production, 'this striving for comedy also blunted some things in the play, and especially the last moments',[29] and Michael Coveney found the actor did not 'solve the central problem of how avarice and deception lead, in his case, to moral and poetical insight'.[30] This is evidently the biggest challenge facing any actor of Romelio. The role of the Capuchin is crucial here, since if he is a figure of fun, as at Bristol, he cannot exert a strong and serious redemp-

44

tive influence on Romelio (as at Wellington 1995). In that case Romelio is left to find his own salvation.

As with Romelio, the portrayal of Leonora must have a double focus: what the *Yorkshire Post* called 'the vain coquetry of her age, and the unflinching insistence of her revenge'.[31] At York many critics found Annette Kerr's Leonora too discreet and realist in style, feeling that she needed more 'reckless carnality'[32] and grotesquerie in order to justify her desire for Contarino, but Ned Chaillet liked the alternative: a 'pleasantly perverse . . . matronly pose'.[33] At Bristol she was more obviously sexy, in both costume and performance, and this was in distinct contrast to the prim Jolenta, whose portrayal, according to *The Stage*, showed 'a touch too much post-feminist strength and aggression . . . her manner clashing with her words'.[34] Joanne Pearce's Jolenta at York seems to have played a wider range of emotion, being praised for her 'adorable'[35] qualities as well as her fire and 'hysteria'.[36]

Of the young men, Jolenta's rival lovers Contarino and Ercole were criticized at York for seeming interchangeable, a problem, as Jacqueline Pearson pointed out, if the ending is to be explicable.[37] This criticism was despite the director's intention that Contarino should be seen as more concerned with money and Ercole with honour.[38] At Bristol, however, the swashbuckling Contarino was distinctly in comic mode, as was the 'extravagant'[39] Julio, unlike the more serious Ercole.

Among the older men, Bristol's pompous Crispiano was an audience favourite, but Ariosto's important thematic role as a secular equivalent to the Capuchin received no notice. Among the various other comic roles, the Surgeons (comically inept at York, compared to Sweeney Todd at Bristol), Contilupo, and Winifrid are most frequently mentioned.

What is clear from both the professional productions is that local comic effects are relatively easy for actors; what is more difficult, particularly in productions such as these with no strong directorial conception of the overall thematic structure, is to find the balance of characterization and tone that will add up to a satisfying interpretation of the play as a whole.

STAGE HISTORY

THE ORIGINAL PRODUCTIONS

The title-page of the 1623 Quarto of *The Devil's Law-Case* announces it as 'A new Tragecomoedy . . . As it was approovedly well Acted | by her Majesties Servants'. Queen Anne's Men had also performed *The White*

Devil in 1612, and Webster's preface to that play records his disenchant-
ment with their habitual theatre, the Red Bull (see *Webster*, I, 97). The
likely date of *The Devil's Law-Case* about 1617–19 (see pp. 3–4), however,
coincides with the period when the Queen's Men had moved from the
rowdy Red Bull to Christopher Beeston's elite indoor playhouse in
Drury Lane, the Cockpit (or Phoenix). The dating of the play is not
certain enough absolutely to rule out performance at the Red Bull prior
to 1617 (or during 1617, while the Cockpit was being rebuilt as the
Phoenix after being wrecked on Shrove Tuesday),[40] and performance by
the same company (as 'Comedians to the late Queen Anne', or as the
Company of the Revels)[41] may have continued back at the Red Bull even
after Beeston moved the Prince's Men into the Cockpit in mid–1619,
unless Beeston was already retaining plays to himself.[42] Nevertheless,
initial performance at the Cockpit/Phoenix seems more likely than not;
and aspects of the play itself support a cautious supposition that it may
have been written with an indoor 'private' playhouse in mind.

Indoor playhouses were smaller than the outdoor amphitheatres; and if
the Inigo Jones drawings for a hall theatre really are for Beeston's Cockpit
conversion in 1616–17, as is now widely accepted, we can be precise
about its dimensions. The railed stage shown in the drawings (see Fig. 2)
is, according to John Orrell and Andrew Gurr, 23 foot 6 inches (7.2
metres) wide by 15 foot (4.6 metres) deep, much the same size as the
Blackfriars stage for which Webster wrote *The Duchess of Malfi*. The
tiring-house facade has three entry doors, the central one 4 foot (1.2
metres) wide and with a high arch, surmounted by another similar arch at
the upper level. Seating is close to the stage in such a small theatre (52
foot [15.8 metres] by 37 foot [11.3 metres] internally), especially in the
side galleries containing four degrees rising from stage level, and the
other galleries adjacent to and above these.[43]

The Devil's Law-Case, like *The Duchess of Malfi* (see *Webster*, I, 421–3),
is well suited to such a small indoor playhouse with its moneyed and fashionable audience. Tragicomedy, whether Fletcherian or Marstonian (cf.
pp. 32–3), is aimed at a knowing audience. The call for '*Soft Musicke*' at
V.iv.122 is more typical of private playhouses than of the much larger
outdoor amphitheatres.[44] And fighting is restricted to duels, with the
judicial combat in Act V under careful regulation within the drama, even
to the extent of '*Lists set up*' (V.vi.0.1), which would, in addition to establishing the chivalric jurisdiction, have protected any on-stage spectators.
Since the two flanking doors were narrower and lower than the central
door, and in Orrell's view 'could hardly have been used for impressive

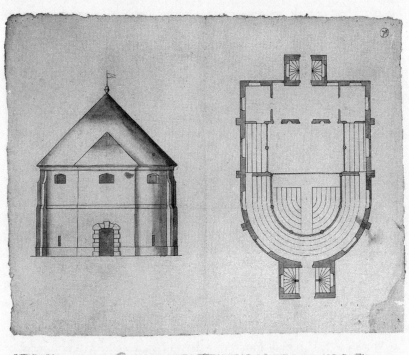

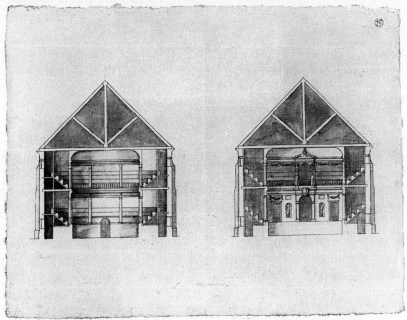

2. Inigo Jones's drawings, probably for the Cockpit in Drury Lane (the Phoenix).

3. A judicial combat, with lists and raised judges.

entries',[45] it is tempting to consider the imposing architecture of the Cockpit's central arched doorway when imagining the visual impact of Leonora's summoning the two Bellmen outside her 'gate' to enter 'into'th Court' (II.iii.67–8), or her processional entry at V.iv.119 with coffins, winding sheets, and flowers, or when thinking of the possible discovery of 'CONTARINO *in a bed*' (III.ii.71.1; but his bed could instead have been thrust out onto the stage). Crispiano and Ariosto as judges in V.vi may have been placed centrally, prior to the two side doors coming into use: '*Enter at one doore*, ERCOLE *and* CONTARINO, *at the other*, ROMELIO *and* JULIO' (V.vi.2.1–.2). Or, for this final scene, more space might have been made available on the small main stage by placing the judges at the equally imposing arched window at the upper level, a placing that would correspond with the actual position of judges in real tournaments (see Fig. 3). The upper level, although likely to have been the music room at most times, is certainly used when the Capuchin and Leonora appear '*above at a window*' (V.v.0.1). This complete short scene between two actors is unusual in being played entirely '*above*' without reference to actors present on the main stage, something that T. J. King, in his study of plays presented at the Phoenix, declares never to happen.[46] Nevertheless, it does happen in this play, and the window shown in the Cockpit drawing is ornate and wide enough to provide a very satisfactory frame.

Just as *The Duchess of Malfi*, however, was performed at both the

Blackfriars and the second Globe, so we must allow that *The Devil's Law-Case*, no matter how well suited to the Cockpit, could also have been performed in any known playhouse of the period. The repeated stage direction *'at one doore . . . at the other'* (IV.i.0.1–.2, V.vi.2.1–.2) could mean use of only two entry doors without creating problems for entries or exits. The Capuchin's 'private way' of III.iii.292, and the 'Closset' (IV.ii.3) from which Ercole watches the trial scene need be no more than a stage door or a gap in stage hangings. Reynolds, believing that both Contarino's bed in III.ii and Jolenta's table in III.i were discovered, had to postulate either 'an unmarked interval—hardly likely—or that two cur-' tained structures permitted these scenes to be discovered successively'.[47] But whether at the Phoenix or at the Red Bull, the bed may have been thrust forth rather than discovered, and the instruction for Jolenta's table that it be *'set forth'* tends not to support discovery.[48] Queen Anne's Men would have faced no difficulty in performing this play at the Red Bull.[49] Alexander Leggatt, indeed, includes the 'sight-gag of the pregnant nun' as typical of Red Bull fare: an 'older vein of comedy'.[50]

Queen Anne's Men would not have had their company resources stretched by *The Devil's Law-Case*. David Bradley concludes (based on assumptions about casting and doubling discussed in *Webster*, I, 98–100, 426–7) that the play could be performed by as few as fifteen men and four boys, but that sixteen men is more likely.[51] Of the major adult men's roles, Romelio, Contarino, Ercole, Crispiano, Sanitonella, Julio, Ariosto, and the two Surgeons cannot easily double. The Capuchin might be required to double; perhaps, since he cannot double Prospero, Baptista. Prospero might double Contilupo. On this basis, eleven actors could cover the main speaking roles, leaving five hired men to play the two Bellmen, the Register, the two Officers, the non-speaking Judge and Lawyer in IV.ii, the Marshal, the Herald, and the various servants, guards, and attendants. Bradley's assumption that four boys were needed for the four women's roles is almost certainly correct, though it would be just possible to double Winifrid and Angiollela.

Of the known members of Queen Anne's Men at this period,[52] Richard Perkins had been singled out for praise by Webster for his performance in *The White Devil*, probably as Flamineo (Epilogue, 7–9), and on this basis alone one might expect him to have played Romelio. There is the further possibility that Perkins was already playing Barabas in *The Jew of Malta* (a role he was certainly playing in another Beeston company in 1633). If so, Webster is putting in his mouth a doubly reflexive comment about being 'Excellently well habited' as 'a rare Italienated Jew'

(III.ii.1–3): not only Romelio comparing his disguise role to that of Marlowe's Barabas, but Perkins-as-Romelio drawing further attention to Perkins-as-Barabas. Other actors still in the company which performed *The White Devil* included Beeston himself (although he may have given up acting for management by this time),[53] Thomas Heywood, Robert Pallant, and the thin comic William Robbins (who, we may speculate, might have played Ariosto or Sanitonella).[54]

The audiences at the Cockpit who responded to these actors would have been more affluent than at the Red Bull (they had to be to afford the higher admission prices), and Andrew Gurr speculates about whether proximity to the Inns of Court led to Beeston commissioning plays aimed at a legal clientele.[55] If so, that may explain the dramatic focus on two very different trial scenes.

Staging the trial scenes (1)

Even more than in *The White Devil*, the IV.ii trial scene presents particular challenges to our understanding of possible staging. In *The White Devil*, it was argued, stage practice for III.ii would have followed the physical arrangements of Jacobean courts, with 'the judge or judges at one end, advisers and clerks at the sides, and the accused and lawyer standing outside the enclosure at the bar, facing the judge' (*Webster*, I, 101, and Fig. 4, I, 102). In both plays English legal terminology and procedure provide the underlying assumptions despite the Italian settings. In *The Devil's Law-Case*, however, the stage directions complicate matters by calling for two judges, two lawyers, and, remarkably, two bars: '*Enter* CRISPIANO *like a Judge, with another Judge*; CONTILUPO, *and another Lawyer at one Barre*; ROMELIO, ARIOSTO, *at another*; LEONORA *with a blacke vaile over her, and* JULIO' (IV.ii.46.1–.3). An earlier direction has '*Officers preparing seats for the Judges*' (IV.ii.0.1), presumably on a raised dais centrally and towards the back of the stage (see *Webster*, I, 101–3). The two bars are likely to be placed at this time, but the question is where.

A bar in an English court is in the first instance in front of the judge, although it can be at some distance from him, as in the Swetnam drawing (*Webster*, I, 102, Fig. 4); but English courts often had two bars, one close to the judge and one at a distance, with King's Counsel and serjeants allowed between the two bars while the accused and other counsel remained beyond the second bar. This arrangement on a Jacobean stage would mean that Contilupo and the mute lawyer with him are to be taken as King's Counsel (technically appointed by the court to manage the case, although there should be one for each party in a civil suit); but this not only sits uneasily with Leonora's hiring of Contilupo while Romelio has done nothing to 'provide [himself with] Counsell' (IV.ii.72), but it also sets up a stage dynamic that appears undramatic and probably unworkable. The actor of Contilupo would be trapped between the two bars, with Romelio, Ariosto, Leonora, and Sanitonella all behind the farther bar obscuring much of the audience's view of him.

A second and more likely option is that the two bars are set out so as to emphasize the adversarial nature of this trial, facing each other at opposite sides of the stage with the judges placed centrally and symmetrically between them at the back. The fact that the call for two bars is unique in the drama of the period suggests that it was a dramatic demand rather than a standard reflection of courtroom practice. In this staging, Leonora would join Contilupo behind one bar (with Sanitonella, Winifrid, and the other lawyer able to stay further back, possibly near one of the side entry doors), while Romelio and Ariosto would face them across the stage from the other bar. Julio and others not party to the case could easily stay well out of the way. Whether or not such adversarial arrangements were found in English courts, there is no question but that a physical opposition would serve the drama well.[56]

Staging the trial scenes (2)

Unlike the trial in IV.ii, the second trial is a judicial combat under the essentially feudal jurisdiction of the High Court of Chivalry in V.vi. Webster drew a number of verbal and other specifics for this scene from John Selden's antiquarian handbook *The Duello, or Single Combat* (1610).[57] Despite the title, Selden's information is for the highly regulated medieval trial by combat, and is quite apart from, presumably in dramatic opposition to, the irregular single duel fought between Contarino and Ercole earlier in the play. This contrast is likely to be reinforced in production by, for instance, the early duel being fought with fashionable rapiers while the final combat is fought with what Selden calls weapons '*Auncient, Vsuall, and Military*', i.e., on stage, bastard swords of four foot (1.2 metres) long or so.[58] The formality of the Marshal's control of the combat, through the Herald and trumpeters, is reinforced by the symmetrical entry of the four combatants, two at one door and two at the other (V.vi.2.1–.2). And, as discussed earlier, regular tournament practice would reinforce the possibility of the judges being placed in full view above the fighting, the more so as the small Cockpit stage would disadvantage on-stage spectators once the '*Lists*' were '*set up*' (V.vi.0.1). The dramaturgical importance of the scene to Webster is perhaps best illustrated by his desire to have '*The Combate continued to a good length*' (19.1).

For Webster to deliberately invoke a medieval juridical code based on divine justice asserting itself through an elaborate combat would not only be understood by Inns of Court men and others in an educated private theatre audience at the Cockpit; it also seems peculiarly appropriate as an ending to a play in which the devil's law-case is unable to be decided in any other way.

SUBSEQUENT PRODUCTIONS

After the original productions, no further professional presentations are known until 1980, when the Theatre Royal, York, presented the play as part of the York Festival. Michael Winter's textually full production was based on a belief 'that Webster had absorbed the vogue for tragi-comedies and was saying, somewhat cynically, "I want to give you a tragic ending, but the fashion is for a comic one and so here it is"'.[59] This was carried to the extent of all the characters on stage freezing at V.vi.11, and Romelio, under special lighting, making a theatrical choice to convert from tragedy to comedy.[60] This view of the play led to 'the spirit of the evening' being 'a literate and comic romp'.[61]

The actors, encouraged to guy the play, found a great deal of comedy. Romelio established a good rapport with the audience: 'a wry plotter . . . played with some wit by Damien Thomas. Perhaps his soul never seems truly at risk, but he captures the spirit of the evening.'[62] His winning over of Joanna Pearce's 'adorable Jolenta . . . a sweetmeat with a fiery centre'[63] in 'an ambiguously sexual candle-lit bedroom scene' (III.iii) was particularly praised, as was Jolenta's transition 'from virginal dismay to gleeful participant'.[64] Leonora, however, got mixed reviews, some critics appreciating her restrained clarity, but others finding her out of style with both the production and the play: 'Leonora should be a sexy old woman of 60 but Annette King hoses down the hot verse and turns the character into an up-market governess forced to handle soiled lines. She delivers them mildly with a cleansing smile which makes nonsense of the motivation.'[65] No such reservations were expressed about the incompetent Surgeons whose tongues were firmly in their cheeks at Romelio's miracle cure of Contarino, nor about the enthusiastic playing of the Contarino and Ercole. The duel at II.ii was based on the comic premise of mutual and honourable apology and unwillingness to fight, so that 'the participants embrace more frequently than they cross swords'.[66] Contarino was so concerned with fair play that when he injured Ercole's dagger hand ('You are hurt' [II.ii.16]) he stepped back, ready to regard honour as satisfied; but when Ercole insisted on continuing, Contarino put his own dagger aside so as not to have an advantage.[67] With its constant interruptions for friendship and protocol, the duel 'becomes a farcical "game" of honour which suddenly slips into tragedy and it is this directorial touch which makes the subsequent behaviour of the two men utterly convincing'.[68]

The production was played on a very bare set surrounded by high wooden louvred doors which lent themselves to highly atmospheric lighting: dark and melancholy for 'two Tapers, a Deaths head, a Booke, JOLENTA in mourning' (III.iii.0.1–.2), dappled green for the duel, and colour-saturated interiors suggesting Mediterranean warmth. Costumes were richly and colourfully Renaissance Italianate, and music also suggested the period. The presentation of coffins and winding sheets by the Capuchin and Leonora in V.iv was made a spectacular celebration of death by back-lighting the coffins as they came in simultaneously from doors back left and back right, and by the addition of two rows of monks in attendance.[69]

Although the more thoughtful of the critics sensed a lack of coherent purpose in the production, they all expressed their pleasure and approval at having the opportunity to see the play, and several suggested that more productions were likely to follow. In the event, there have been only two further professional productions, in Bristol in 1989 and in London in 2002.

A room upstairs at the Hen and Chicken pub in Bristol was the venue for the production by a small company called Show of Strength. Several characters were cut (notably Prospero and one of the two surgeons) to fit the play to the company's limited resources, and text was cut both to reduce running time and to excise symbolic and topical Jacobean references which, it was feared, audiences might find incomprehensible. As a result Jolenta and Julio lost sections of their repartee, Romelio lost his 'Meditation' (II.iii.89), Jolenta did not give her symbolic black and white speech at the end (V.vi.40–55), and Crispiano's scene of explanation to Ariosto of the reasons for his return (to investigate Romelio and 'to curbe the insolencies | Of these women' [III.i.28–9]) was cut altogether.

The director's aim was 'simply to create accessible and entertaining theatre',[70] and to this end Victorian setting and costumes 'served to high-light the melodramatic elements in the script'.[71] The Victorian setting suited the pub room with audience in close proximity, and costumes reinforced the typing of the characters: red military dress uniform for Ercole, a swirling velvet cloak for Contarino, Julio in white trousers with a white silk scarf, and a rather prim Jolenta's high-buttoned leg-of-mutton blouse contrasting with Leonora's plunging décolletage. Some performances tended also towards the easy laughs of melodrama: Cornelius Garrett's Romelio was 'a crowd-pleasing pantomime villain. Ric Jerrom brings long experience as a street entertainer to his character-isations of the hypocritical surgeon and the fake lawyer [i.e., Crispiano], and enjoys himself immensely—as does the audience.'[72] Contarino so embraced the comedy that he wore a Lone Ranger mask as his disguise.[73] Leonora and Jolenta, by contrast, played much more seriously, and *The Stage* felt that Jolenta showed 'too much post-feminist strength and aggression'.[74]

Despite 'an uneven series of performances'[75] the production success-fully mined the comedy of the play in a presentation that 'erred on the side of entertainment'.[76] The director's hopes that the Victorian setting would suggest a similar Jacobean preoccupation with commerce, greed, hypocrisy, Christian belief unsupported by practice, and male chauvin-ism,[77] seems to have been lost in the audience embrace of the conven-tions of simplified melodrama. The improbabilities of the plot were played as just that. The audience was delighted at the consequences of Romelio lancing Contarino's wound; and the instruction that he 'marry that Nun' (V.vi.83) brought the house down. The close confines of a pub room allowed a highly presentational style of performance which always sought and acknowledged the laughter of the audience. What was missing was any serious development of the iconic or providential aspects of the play.

The London production in early 2002 took place as this volume was at press. Michael Caines reported in the *Times Literary Supplement* that a company called Instant Classics presented the play, like the Bristol pro-duction, in a cramped space in a pub, the White Bear Theatre in Kennington. The text was abridged, with, for instance, Crispiano the sole judge in the trial scene. The setting, like that at Bristol, was Victorian, but apparently with a more serious purpose. David Cottis, the director, is quoted as choosing the period 'in keeping with [the play's] emphasis on litigation and moneymaking, and its resemblance in tone and incident to the London novels of Charles Dickens and the comic operas of Gilbert and Sullivan'.[78] While some parts of the production apparently slid into melodrama ('Romelio was reduced to a bulging and boorish villain'), others seem to have been more in keeping with

Fletcherian tragicomedy in triggering 'a transition from tragic mode to comic or vice versa'. On the comic side were, it seems, stage business with 'Tennis-court woolen slippers' (IV.ii.383), and 'a madcap double-act of two blackmailing surgeons'. In a deeper exploration of the themes, the Julio–Crispiano sub-plot became surprisingly important: 'in performance, their shifty relationship contrasts clearly with that of Leonora and [her] son'. This comment appears linked to the critic's reaction to the play as a whole and its Victorian setting, that 'there is something Dickensian in the play's distaste for legalistic fandango and its explicit didacticism (albeit from a "didacticist of genius"...)'.

In addition to these three modern professional stage productions, the play has been broadcast at least once on BBC radio (10 May 1968), and there have been a number of university student productions, including the University of York in 1964, Exeter in 1976, and Victoria University of Wellington, New Zealand, in 1995. This last performance was concerned to explore not only the comedy of the play, but also the redemptive role of the Capuchin in persuading Romelio towards an eventual change of heart.

Three professional productions and a handful of student performances do not constitute a performance tradition. Nevertheless, it is clear that the comedy of *The Devil's Law-Case* is rich, that audiences will follow the convolutions of the plot, and that the spectacle of duels, processions, trial, and chivalric combat is theatrically engaging. Serious attention to the theme of redemption has also demonstrated a theatrical viability. What is awaited is a professional production which will unite the comic and the serious, giving us Webster's tragicomedy with the same force as it must have had when originally staged.

1. See *Webster*, I, 84, and Andrew Gurr, 'Maximal and Minimal Texts of Shakespeare', *Shakespeare's Globe Research Bulletin* 4 (April 1998).
2. Stage management reports, Theatre Royal, York.
3. See V.ii.12.2n and Carnegie, p. 262.
4. See MacIntyre, pp. 113, 121, 275.
5. *Royall Arbor of Loyal Poesie* (1664), p. 37.
6. Quoted by M. Channing Linthicum, 'My Jewish Gaberdine', *PMLA* XLIII (1928), p. 765.
7. Reynolds, p. 175; MacIntyre, p. 114.
8. James Shapiro, *Shakespeare and the Jews* (New York, 1996), p. 93, and, citing Thomas Jordan on the red beard, p. 240 n. 96.
9. See MacIntyre, p. 114.
10. Wymer, pp. 80–1.
11. MacIntyre, p. 132.

12. Thomas Dekker, *The Gull's Hornbook*, in *The Wonderful Year and Selected Writings*, ed. E. D. Pendry (London, 1967), p. 77.

13. Moryson, *Itinerary*, pp. 169–70.

14. Cay Dollerup, 'Danish Costume on the Elizabethan Stage', *RES* n. s. xxv (1974), p. 58. He notes that with twelve Danish embassies to London between 1590 and 1615, often with upwards of a hundred members, Danish costume may have been well known.

15. Nashe, *Works*, I, 177–8.

16. Wymer, p. 81.

17. MacIntyre, pp. 243–4, notes that removing a false beard is likely to be the way Orlando Friscobaldo, in Dekker's *II The Honest Whore*, V.ii.178.1, '*discouers himselfe*'.

18. John Aubrey, *Brief Lives*, ed. Oliver Lawson Dick (1949; Harmondsworth, 1972), p. 77.

19. Ibid., pp. 226–7.

20. Aubrey was writing some sixty years after the play was first performed, and Danvers was already dead by then, so no weight can be placed on the verbal similarities.

21. Wymer, pp. 81–2.

22. C. Willett Cunnington, Phillis Cunnington, and Charles Beard, *A Dictionary of English Costume* (London, 1960), p. 128.

23. C. Willett and Phillis Cunnington, *Handbook of English Costume in the Sixteenth Century* (London, 1954), p. 114.

24. For a fuller discussion of this issue, see Carnegie and Gunby.

25. Private communication from Malcolm Ranson, the fights arranger at York 1980.

26. Desmond Pratt, *Yorkshire Post*, 6 June 1980.

27. Robert Cushman, *Observer*, 15 June 1980.

28. Shirley Brown, *Stage*, 18 January 1990.

29. *Research Opportunities in Renaissance Drama* XXIII (1980), p. 67.

30. *Financial Times*, 7 June 1980.

31. Pratt, *Yorkshire Post*, 6 June 1980.

32. Cushman, *Observer*, 15 June 1980.

33. *The Times*, 9 June 1980.

34. Brown, *Stage*, 18 January 1990.

35. Pratt, *Yorkshire Post*, 6 June 1980.

36. John Barber, *Daily Telegraph*, 10 June 1980.

37. *Research Opportunities in Renaissance Drama* XXIII (1980), p. 67.

38. Michael Winter, private communication. Critics, however, tended to find the characters interchangeable.

39. Judith Skorupski, *Bristol Observer*, 8 December 1989.

40. See Gurr 1996, pp. 123–7, for discussion of the troubled transition of the company from the Red Bull to the Cockpit/Phoenix.

41. Bentley, I, 165–70, Gurr 1996, pp. 326–8.

42. Gurr 1996, pp. 404–5, finds no evidence that the Prince's Men took over any of Queen Anne's Men's plays in 1619, though Beeston subsequently became 'a great acquirer of playing resources' (p. 419).

43. See Gurr 1992, pp. 160–4, and John Orrell, *The Theatres of Inigo Jones and John Webb* (Cambridge, 1985), pp. 39–77, Andrew Gurr with John Orrell, *Rebuilding Shakespeare's Globe* (London, 1989), pp. 125–48, Foakes, pp. 64–7, and, for isometric

drawings and model reconstructions, Richard Leacroft, *The Development of the English Playhouse* (London, 1973), p. 72, and Richard and Helen Leacroft, *Theatre and Playhouse* (London and New York, 1984), p. 65. Orrell, in *The Theatres of Inigo Jones*, pp. 53–4, suggests the probable colour scheme, and that the stage was probably 'covered in stretched green baize'.

44. Music was also played between the acts, and *The Devil's Law-Case* is clearly written in the expectation of act breaks, as the exit and re-entry of Leonora and Winifrid at the end of Act III and beginning of Act IV indicates. By this period, however, all theatres were using act breaks; see Taylor.

45. Orrell, *The Theatres of Inigo Jones*, p. 51.

46. King 1965, p. 157. King does not include *The Devil's Law-Case* in his study.

47. Reynolds, p. 150.

48. See King 1965, pp. 156, 158–9.

49. Cf. *Webster*, I, 100–1, for discussion of *The White Devil* at the Red Bull. A number of scholars, including Reynolds and Bentley, list the play in the Red Bull repertoire.

50. Alexander Leggatt, *Jacobean Public Theatre* (London and New York, 1992), p. 121.

51. Bradley, p. 240.

52. See Bentley, I, 171, Gurr 1996, p. 326.

53. Bentley, II, 365.

54. See *Webster*, I, 98, and, on Robbins, Bentley, II, 547–8.

55. Gurr 1996, p. 325.

56. Dena Goldberg, p. 126, argues correctly that 'Webster's portrait of Crispiano's court is not intended to be a realistic representation of a Jacobean courtroom'; but W. J. Jones refers to an instance of a judge becoming annoyed at the loud arguments of six Clerks of Chancery, and requiring them to stand three either side of the bar to give opposing views (*The Elizabethan Court of Chancery* [Oxford, 1967], p. 100). Although the trial is technically a civil case, Webster seems to be drawing on Common Pleas or King's Bench practice to some extent, and treating Leonora as if she were laying a criminal information against Romelio in a criminal case. I am grateful to Herbert Berry, Tim Stretton, and Clare Worley for private communication about the legal implications of this staging.

57. See Carnegie.

58. See Carnegie, p. 262.

59. Reported by Michael Chaddock, *Yorkshire Evening Post*, 3 June 1980.

60. Michael Winter, private communication. He also said he believed Webster was sending up Beaumont and Fletcher tragicomedy.

61. Ned Chaillet, *The Times*, 9 June 1980.

62. Ibid.

63. Pratt, *Yorkshire Post*, 6 June 1980.

64. Michael Coveney, *Financial Times*, 7 June 1980.

65. Nicholas de Jongh, *Guardian*, 7 June 1980.

66. Coveney, *Financial Times*, 7 June 1980.

67. Private communication from Malcolm Ranson, the fights arranger at York 1980.

68. de Jongh, *Guardian*, 7 June 1980.

69. Theatre Royal promptscript.

70. Nick Bamford, private communication.

71. S. M., *Gloucestershire Gazette*, 29 December 1989.

72. Brown, *Stage*, 18 January 1990.
73. Elizabeth Bowden (designer), private communication.
74. Brown, *Stage*, 18 January 1990.
75. A. C. H. Smith, *Guardian*, 4 December 1989.
76. Brown, *Stage*, 18 January 1990.
77. Nick Bamford, private communication.
78. Michael Caines, *Times Literary Supplement*, 12 April 2002. All quotations about this production are from this review.

Textual introduction

MACDONALD P. JACKSON

Like Webster's two Italian tragedies, *The Devil's Law-Case* was not entered on the Stationers' Register. The sole seventeenth-century edition is the quarto printed by Augustine Mathewes for John Grismand in 1623.[1] The title-page promised buyers '*The true and perfect Copie from the Originall. As it was approouedly well Acted by her Maiesties Seruants*'. The prefatory material—consisting of a list of characters (A1^v), Webster's dedication to Sir Thomas Finch, Knight Baronet (A2^r), and his address to the reader (A2^v)—is sufficient guarantee that the playwright facilitated publication.[2] Webster even mentions that he had declined the unsolicited offers of several friends to furnish him with commendatory verses, of the kind that graced *The Duchess of Malfi* in the same year.

Mathewes was involved with some two score of playtexts in the period 1622–35. In 1622 his shop had worked on reprints of Middleton and Rowley's *A Fair Quarrel* and the anonymous *The Troublesome Reign of King John*, both for Thomas Dew, and in the following year, besides printing Webster's tragicomedy, he reprinted Kyd's *The Spanish Tragedy*, some copies to be sold, like *The Devil's Law-Case*, by John Grismand and some to be sold by Thomas Langley. *The Devil's Law-Case* was evidently the first play to be set from manuscript in his printing-house. But of course his compositors may have had experience in setting type from manuscript playtexts in other establishments.

The Quarto collates A–L^4, with the text starting on A3^r and L4^v being blank. 'The identification of headlines is difficult in this quarto', as John Russell Brown noted,[3] but a few observations may be ventured. A two-skeleton method of printing was used for sheets B–E. Skeleton I evidently machined outer B, inner C, inner D, and inner E, and skeleton II machined inner B, outer C, outer D, and outer E. Thereafter, the distinction between the two sets of four headlines breaks down, with some interchange between skeletons, some headlines sustaining minor adjustments, and some new ones being created. Inner F uses at least two headlines from skeleton II, and inner G at least two from skeleton I. But formes in sheets F–L seem to draw on a pool of headlines. There are clear signs of continuity between outer H, inner I, inner K, and inner L, and between inner H, outer I, outer K, and outer L, but the formes of one group may also take an occasional headline from the other.[4]

This pattern, such as it is, gives us few clues as to how many compositors may have set the text or how, if there were two or more, they divided their labours, and the usual tests—of a wide range of spellings, variations in speech prefixes, punctuation marks and their spacing, precise width of measure, use of italics, and so on—reveal no clear signs of contrasting compositorial practices. The typographical combination 'ſsi' is invariable in the Quarto, rather than the much more common triple ligature 'ſſi' or the rare third alternative 'sſi'. Choices among these options can sometimes identify compositors, but the fount of type used for the Quarto may simply have lacked triple ligatures.[5]

Deviations from such predominant spellings as 'agen', 'been', 'businesse', 'doe', 'goe', 'here', 'keepe', 'Mistris', 'Oh', 'shee', '-cke', '-lesse', '-ly', and '-tie' fail to correlate in any significant fashion, while the proportions of spaces before and/or after the various punctuation marks remain tolerably consistent throughout, and such fluctuations as do occur seem unrelated to other variables. Often an anomalous spelling occurs within a few lines of the prevailing one, and several anomalies are obviously due to the exigencies of justification.[6] The contraction 'i'th' usually has the apostrophe (some thirty-five times); although eight of the ten cases in which it is omitted occur from F3^v onwards, four of them are on pages that also have an instance of the normal apostrophized form.[7] The variants are thus compatible with one man's increasing carelessness. The appellation 'sir' is used dozens of times in the play. It is capitalized on only eleven of the occasions on which it does not begin a sentence or a line: seven of these are in sheet A, three in B, and one on C1^r; in A the capitalized forms outnumber the uncapitalized (7:2), in B the reverse is the case (3:9), and after C1^r the capitals are dropped. The change is more likely to have taken place in the printing-house than to reflect the underlying manuscript, but it does not imply the work of two compositors.

Of possible significance, however, is a decisive shift in the spelling of the word 'though'. The modern spelling is used once on A3^v, to be followed by ten instances of 'tho' (A4^v, B3^r, B4^r twice, B4^v, E1^r, E1^v, E2^r, E4^r, F2^v); thereafter 'though' is invariable (H4^v, I1^r twice, K2^r, L3^r, L3^v). This hints at a change of compositors at a point corresponding to the reorganization of headlines within sheets F–G. But there is no very clear support from other orthographical and typographical variations.[8] The likelihood is that two or more compositors set type for the Quarto, but, if so, they must have either adhered closely to the spelling of their copy or had very similar personal preferences, so that their stints remain undetermined.

There are no obvious signs of setting by formes rather than seriatim: no evidence of type shortage creating meaningful patterns of substitution, no evidence of a compositor's attempt to waste space, and no certain evidence of his making any but the most minor adjustments to cramp the text to fit a page. On C3^v the word 'taking' (following 'paynes') is set on the same line as the catchword; on the last nine lines of F1^r a single word turnover, an ampersand, and the further shortening of speech prefixes for the two Surgeons ensure that the last speech need not carry over onto the next page; and on K1^r the spelling 'wil' and a tilde help get the last speech on that page into a single line, but this as much a matter of justifying the line as the page.[9] These are the kinds of small manoeuvres that save a line here and there.

The Quarto is not, however, generous with white space, and it becomes a little less so as it progresses. It is divided into acts but not into scenes, except in so far as entries beginning new scenes (as these were first determined by Dyce) are always centred, whereas most entry directions, along with exits, and directions for stage business, are placed towards the right of the page. The basic principle of differentiation between directions to be centred and directions to be placed right seems, however, to be length, since none of those that begin scenes could comfortably fit on the line above along with the preceding '*Exeunt*', and the only centred directions *within* scenes are also too long to go into the line above, with the sole exception of the first of ten, on B4^v. The placing of stage directions in *The White Devil* (1612), thought to have been set from Webster's holograph, has a similar rationale, though in that quarto there are also a few marginal directions. In *The Devil's Law-Case* the entries heading the acts are always preceded by a blank line, and the first two, that beginning the play on A3^r and that beginning Act II on C2^r, are also followed by a blank line. Three further scenes, all in the first half of the play, begin with entries preceded (but not followed) by a blank line: I.ii (B2^r), II.iv (E2^r), and III.iii (F1^v). The rest have no blank line before or after.

Brown drew attention to the fact that the catchword on A1^v, the page listing the dramatis personae, is a large 'The', which is appropriate to A3^r (which begins with the title of the play), but not to A2^r. He deduced that

'Webster probably brought (or sent) a dedication and preface to the printing-house' for late insertion, and found confirmation of this theory in some misalignment of the type of A2^r–A2^v with the surrounding pages.[10]

PRESS CORRECTION

Brown also thought that at least two press variants suggested Webster's own involvement in the process of stop-press correction, and most editors repeat this suggestion. Among the copies of the Quarto available for collation some thirty-three press variants have been found in seven formes; sixteen of these occur within G(i), and several could only have been made by the corrector's consulting the manuscript copy or through the direct intervention of the author. At IV.i.17 (G3^v) 'ith Margent sheet' is corrected to 'i'th Margent'. Brown judged that 'sheet' must have been in the copy, so that 'some other authority probably caused its excision'.[11] It is doubtful, though, whether the attributive or quasi-adjectival application of 'margent' (or 'margin') to a 'sheet' (of paper) is idiomatic or makes sense in the context. *OED* affords no parallel. So the presence of the word in the uncorrected forme may be due to a compositor's eyeskip from 'sheets of paper' five lines above, or to his being affected by a kind of memorial contamination from the phrase.[12] Likewise, the other change suspected to be authorial, from 'salt water' to 'rough water' at V.i.44 (K2^v), may simply represent the correction of a compositor's easy substitution of a familiar collocation for the less familiar one in his copy. Some press corrections go well beyond the kind of mechanical tidying up that can be done conjecturally, and must originate in an authoritative source, but there is insufficient reason to postulate proofreading by Webster rather than the corrector's recourse to the manuscript copy.[13]

Sheet G is the only one that is variant in both formes, and the number of press variants in G(i) is exceptional. It is tempting to see a connection with the breakdown of normal two-skeleton printing from sheet F onwards, but uncertainties over the identification of specific headlines leave no solid basis for speculation.

PRINTER'S COPY

In its corrected state, the Quarto requires very little substantive emendation. Brown carefully assessed the evidence for the nature of the printer's copy and hesitantly concluded that 'if the copy had any distinctive merits, they were those of a literary rather than a theatrical manuscript'.[14] The New Bibliographers, led by McKerrow and Greg, believed that a playwright's 'foul papers' would normally be turned over to a theatrical company, and that these would be transcribed to serve as a 'promptbook'. They conceded that if his working draft was especially 'foul' (or disorderly), a playwright might have been obliged to make his own fair copy, and that a sufficiently clean set of authorial papers might have been suitable to submit to the censor and, once it had received some annotation, to govern performances. Several scholars have recently doubted that any firm distinction between 'foul papers' texts and 'promptbook' texts can be maintained, and it has become clear that acting companies tolerated in their theatrical playscripts more muddle, variety, and authorial idiosyncrasy than was once thought possible.[15] It is nevertheless true that behind some printed plays we can gain clear glimpses of an author's habits of composition, while others show more obvious signs of having derived from manuscripts that had been prepared for use in the theatre.

Brown seems right in deciding that there are features of the Quarto pointing towards the author and none that point decisively towards adaptation of the underlying manuscript for use as the playhouse 'book'. Winifrid is simply '*A wayting Woman*' in the list of characters, and appears as such on her first entry and in the subsequent speech prefixes in I.ii (B4^v–C1^v), though she is addressed by Romelio as '*Winifrid*' thirty lines after her arrival. In III.iii (from G2^v onwards) and IV.i (from G3^v onwards) she is always given her name, whether in full or abbreviated, in directions and speech prefixes. Dramatists often think of their characters, especially minor ones, in generic terms before taking care to confer on them their specific names. Brown also noted that Baptista, who is mentioned in the play's third speech (A3^r) and is listed among characters entering at II.i.91.1 (C3^v) and II.ii.33.1 (D3^v), has nothing to say and is ignored in the dramatis personae. But as the Quarto text stands he is needed to stay in mimed conversation with Julio and be addressed by Ercole at II.i.212 and 224.

Some dozen exits are unmarked, including a few for more than one character, but there is widespread agreement that actors can be trusted to get themselves offstage at the right times, so the omissions would not be serious in a theatrical manuscript. Defective or absent entry directions are more telling, but there are only two: one for the Capuchin and Ercole in III.iii (G1^v) and one for Sanitonella at the beginning of V.vi (L3^r). The omissions could conceivably be due to a compositor's oversight.

The nature of the stage directions alters in an interesting fashion as the play develops. Act I provides only bare entrances and exits. Some descriptive directions appear in Act II: '*This is spoke aside*' (C4ʳ) and '*They sit downe*' (D1ʳ) in II.i, and '*They fight*', '*Fight*' and '*Contarino wounded, fals vpon Ercole*' in II.ii (D3ʳ). From Act III onwards there are several much more elaborate directions, such as '*A Table set forth with two Tapers, a Deaths head, a | Booke, Iolenta in mourning, Romelio sits by her*' at the head of III.iii (F1ᵛ). This evinces a Websterian fondness for emblems: there is nothing in the dialogue or subsequent directions to indicate that the specified items are actually *used* by the characters, so the catalogue must reflect Webster's own concern with the stage image and its emotional and moral suggestiveness, as betokening Jolenta's grief. The stools on which Jolenta and Romelio sit, properties demanded by the *action*, remain unmentioned, but Webster probably thought of these as already on stage.

Descriptions of business and spectacle continue to increase in number, and to become more varied, to the play's end. Contilupo enters in IV.i as '*a spruce Lawyer*' (G4ᵛ), Ercole enters '*muffled*' and the Surgeons '*disguised*' in IV.ii (H1ʳ); Leonora has '*a blacke vaile ouer her*' in the long and detailed entry a little later in the same scene (H2ʳ); Angiolella enters '*great bellied*' at the beginning of Act V (K2ʳ). The latter portion of the strange direction in V.ii, '*Enter Ercole with a letter, and Contarino comming | in Friers habits, as hauing bin at the Batha- | nites, a Ceremony vsed afore these | Combates*' (K3ʳ), is clearly authorial, being of no practical use in performance. Romelio enters '*very melancholly*' in V.iv (K4ᵛ), and the scene contains another Websterian death-emblem in Leonora's entry with two coffins '*and two Winding-sheets stucke with flowers*' (L1ᵛ), one of which she presents to Romelio and the other to Julio. The stipulation that the combat in V.vi be '*continued to a good length*' (L3ʳ) sounds authorial, as does the play's final entry: '*Enter Angiolella vail'd, and Iolenta, her face colour'd like a | Moore, the two Surgeons, one of them like a Iew*' (L3ᵛ). The two asides (besides that on C4ʳ there is '*Con. speaks aside*' on K3ʳ) have an author's wordiness, where the simple imperative would be normal.

What emerges is a strong impression of 'foul papers' directions, sparse at first but growing more elaborate as the playwright's imagination takes fire. In addressing the 'judicious reader' Webster calls *The Devil's Law-Case* 'this Poeme', and the Quarto seems to offer an essentially literary, pre-theatrical text.[16] Was it, however, set from autograph? The question raises the vexed subject of the Quarto's lineation.

LINEATION

The play begins with a short speech that is mislined because of the initial block ornamental capital. There are also many later passages where the Quarto's lineation is suspect, or where one cannot be confident that it correctly distinguishes between verse and prose. Editors have presented widely different arrangements, largely depending on how much of its irregular verse they regard as really prose, and on how far they are willing to go in creating an approximation to iambic pentameters out of the metrical fragments of consecutive speeches. Sometimes the beginning of one speech can be dovetailed onto the end of its immediate predecessor to form a perfect pentameter, and sometimes one or more very short speeches can be combined with one another or with adjacent speech endings or beginnings that are metrically incomplete in such a way as to maintain tolerably regular blank verse. But often the attempt to form such composite lines produces verse that is marred by extreme enjambments and seems excessively loose.

In this play, perhaps because of its tragicomic genre, Webster permitted himself a freer versification than ever before. Some lines are so crowded with unstressed syllables as to conform rather to an accentual than to an accentual–syllabic prosody. Speeches, and even whole exchanges, may seem to modulate from verse to prose or from prose to verse, and the distinction between rhythmic prose and relaxed iambics may be hard to sustain.

In the Quarto (1612) of *The White Devil*, judged to have been set from holograph, when a speech continues a line of verse the new prefix is set on that line. This, at least, is the ideal towards which the text aspires, and although there are a good many failures to attain it (often due to the difficulty of fitting the wording plus the speech prefixes within the 23-em measure), the Quarto practice affords a fair guide to the verse structure. In *The Devil's Law-Case* some speeches, along with their prefixes, are set or begin on the same line as the previous one, but the number increases after the first three sheets and again in the last three, and the nature of the running-on also changes. Per sheet (from A to L), the total number of speeches sharing a line with another is as follows: A: 2, B: 2, C: 1, D: 6, E: 3, F: 5, G: 7, H: 6, I: 16, K: 14, L: 13. Thus there are only five examples in the first three sheets, but forty-three in the last three sheets. Fifty of the complete total of seventy-five are very short speeches of only one to five words, and seven others *follow* similarly short speeches.[17] In only eighteen cases are the beginnings and endings of longer speeches involved, and all but one of these occur within sheets G–L, with sheets I–L providing fifteen. Moreover, an examination of *all* the Quarto's very short speeches reveals that whereas in sheets A–F there are twenty-two missed opportunities to make them share a line with the speech immediately before or after (plus five doubtful cases, where the line might have been unduly tight), there are only three in sheets G–L (plus four doubtful cases). This gives the following ratios of opportunities missed to opportunities taken: A–F 22:18, G–L 3:39.

Short speeches often enough share a line with the previous speech in tightly printed seventeenth-century play quartos, and in view of the other slight indications that Mathewes's printing-house was eager to fit *The Devil's Law-Case* and its preliminaries into eleven quarto sheets, the progressive saving of lines may have been a compositor's precautionary measure;[18] or the fact that the same-line placing of beginnings and endings of longer speeches is, with one exception, confined to $G2^r$–$L4^r$ and occurs even on the last two pages of the Quarto, when it must have been obvious that the play would finish on $L4^r$ with space to spare, might be connected with the slim evidence for a change of compositors at some point between $F2^v$ and $H4^v$. Alternatively, the pattern may, at least to some extent, reflect developments in the manuscript itself. What can be said with some assurance is that it cannot correspond to Webster's own sense of the structure of his verse. Even if, as seems unlikely, his autograph of the play exhibited a marked increase in same-line speeches towards the end, this could hardly have been for duly considered artistic reasons. The Quarto layout gives an editor little assistance in deciding whether to 'step' speeches in order to indicate their metrical attachment to a preceding part-line.

The situation is both like and unlike that in *The Duchess of Malfi*, probably printed from a transcript in the hand of the professional scribe Ralph Crane. In that Quarto (1623) same-line speeches are confined to $I1^v$–$M2^v$, a stretch of the play coinciding quite closely with IV.i–V.ii.[19] There too the majority of the fifty-eight speeches with prefixes set within the line are very short (totalling thirty-four) or are preceded by very short speeches (four examples). Brown refers the shift in practice to a printing-house decision: both compositors who set *The Duchess of Malfi* contributed substantially to $I1^v$–$M2^v$, as to the earlier and later sections of the text.[20] However, since same-line speeches are a regular feature of the putatively holograph-based *The White Devil*, we cannot be absolutely certain that their use in *The Duchess of Malfi* implies the compositors' deviation from their copy (or Crane's from his) rather than adherence to it, especially since same-line speeches recur in the most clearly Websterian parts of *Appius and Virginia* (1654) and in Webster, Rowley, and Heywood's *A Cure for a Cuckold* (1661). And the same caveat applies to *The Devil's Law-Case*.[21]

In our texts of *The White Devil* and *The Duchess of Malfi* we followed the long-standing editorial tradition of 'stepping' speeches to produce composite blank-verse lines whenever this seemed warranted. *The Devil's Law-Case* appears to us to call for a different approach, one that steers a middle course between those of two modern-spelling editors of the early 1970s, who tackled the Quarto's lineation in strikingly dissimilar ways, Shirley (1971) mostly deferring to the Quarto's arrangements and stepping speeches sparingly, Gunby (1972) very frequently relining the verse and making the stepping of adjacent speeches the norm. Brennan (1975) took Gunby's policy a stage further. She sees many instances of the kind of mislineation illustrated in the opening speech, where the Quarto has Prospero say to Romelio:

> YOU haue shewen a world of wealth;
> I did not thinke there had bene a Merchant
> Liv'd in Italy of halfe your substance. (I.i.1–3)

Clearly, this should be:

> YOU have shewen a world of wealth; I did not thinke
> There had bene a Merchant liv'd in Italy
> Of halfe your substance.

Romelio's reply begins in the Quarto:

> Ile giue the King of Spaine
> Ten thousand Duckets yearely, and discharge
> My yearely Custome. The Hollanders scarse trade
> More generally then I. (I.i.4–6)

Here Romelio's short first line completes Prospero's short last line: together they form a regular iambic pentameter with an 'epical caesura' or 'extra mid-line syllable'; the shared line forms an exact metrical counterpart to Romelio's third line ('My . . . trade').[22] Gunby and Brennan step Romelio's first line, while Shirley, despite relining Prospero's, does not.

More often Gunby's and Brennan's stepping creates much longer composite lines, as when the ending of Romelio's speech, 'In erecting a Lotterie' is followed by Prospero's 'I pray Sir, what doe you thinke'. The combination has five main stresses, but there are fifteen syllables. Since in this play Webster is capable of somewhat similar lines even within single speeches, Gunby's and Brennan's practice is defensible. So is stepping that leaves composite lines with fewer than ten syllables. However, it is clear that in *The Devil's Law-Case* Webster also often begins a speech with a metrically short line even when the preceding speech ends with a full pentameter, or ends a speech with a metrically short line when the following speech begins with a full pentameter. And the beginnings and endings of speeches are often only vaguely iambic, as though Webster were modulating between the two media, verse and prose. In *The White Devil* at least 70 per cent of stepped lines over which our edition is supported by same-line printing in the Quarto are regular iambic pentameters, with or without double endings, and many of the other shared lines can plausibly be scanned in terms of familiar variations. In contrast, in Brennan's edition of *The Devil's Law-Case* fewer than 20 per cent of stepped lines are regular, over half have twelve or more syllables, and in a very large proportion of the irregular shared lines the rhythms are prose-like.

There survives no manuscript in which an early modern English dramatist 'stepped' shared lines: the normal practice was to start every line at the left-hand margin, and seventeenth-century printed texts followed suit. The layout of the Quarto of *The White Devil*, with its small-capital same-line prefixes, is exceptional, though precedents had been set by Ben Jonson's *Sejanus* (1605) and *Volpone* (1606): both dramatists were dressing their plays as 'works' or 'poems', rivalling classical texts.[23]

The modern practice of stepping lines is 'by no means obligatory', and is eschewed by several nineteenth- and twentieth-century editors; it was developed as a means of making evident to readers and actors 'that the verse, though divided between speakers, is continuous'.[24] But since it is virtually impossible to hear as blank verse most of the shared 'lines' in Brennan's edition, and the structure of the verse in exchanges involving short speeches is so ambiguous, we have decided to revert to a policy of stepping only when this creates a regular iambic pentameter, or a line with no more than two of the standard variations, such as a 'feminine' or 'double' ending, a trochaic or anapaestic foot at the beginning of the line or after a mid-line pause, or an 'epical caesura'. Often the scansion necessitates elision of some such combination as 'You are' (pronounced as 'Y'are'), or the disyllabic pronunciation of an '-ion' ending. Even where the combining of speech endings and beginnings as stepped lines would be in accord with our general guidelines, we have not automatically imposed such an arrangement, but have felt obliged to justify to ourselves each individual instance. We have taken the wider context into account:

in some scenes, or portions of scenes, the verse is fairly regular and clusters of speeches suitable for dovetailing occur; in other passages the verse is rugged, close to prose, and potentially composite lines of the requisite degree of regularity are rare and seem more likely to have been produced by accident than by design; also, some characters appear more apt than others to complete a verse line begun by another speaker.

However editors decide to arrange the metrical fragments of separate speakers, they are faced with verse that seems mislined in the Quarto. One source of mislineation is probably compositorial: sometimes (as in the play's opening lines), unable to fit a longish verse line into his 90-millimetre measure, the compositor divided it after a clause or phrase; when the residue left plenty of space on the next line, he filled that with the first few words of the next line of his copy, and so on, until verse line and type line once again coincided. He was similarly tempted to fill some of the metrically incomplete lines with which certain speeches began. But the Quarto also contains passages that, though printed as verse, were almost certainly intended by the playwright as prose, and we have presented more of the dialogue as prose than previous editors. We have considered the possibility that Julio, Winifrid, and Sanitonella are consistently prose-speaking characters, but all appear to have *some* verse lines, and it is rather a matter of certain stretches of dialogue being wholly or basically prose. Characters differ, however, in the kind of verse they typically speak, the noble Ercole's speeches, for example, being much more controlled, in prosodic terms, than the merchant Romelio's.

The Duchess of Malfi also contains substantial stretches of prose that are set in the Quarto as verse. We postulated that Nicholas Okes's compositors were confused by Crane's habit of not beginning verse lines with majuscules.[25] In this Crane was by no means unusual. Hand D of *Sir Thomas More* seldom begins speeches, or sentences even, with majuscules, while at the same time liberally sprinkling the text with capital 'C', in particular. Indeed, the Melbourne Manuscript, a fragment of foul papers that may well be Webster's, is unusual in employing majuscules for verse and miniscules for prose.[26] If this was Webster's normal practice, the foul papers of *A Devil's Law-Case* should not have presented special difficulties, though where capitals coincidentally fell at the left-hand margin (because they began sentences or were names or other regularly or sporadically capitalized nouns) a compositor or scribe might be misled and take some time to realize his mistake. Of course, the more expansive the handwriting and the narrower the paper the more alike verse and prose would look on the page, regardless of capitalization practices.

Mislineation is such a common feature of sixteenth- and seventeenth-century dramatic quartos, many evidently printed from authorial papers, that *The Devil's Law-Case*'s blunders need occasion no surprise, whatever the printer's manuscript copy. But if Webster had originally submitted to Queen Anne's Men a fair copy of his play, while retaining his foul papers, he might well have commissioned a scribe to prepare a transcript for the printer: it was, after all, to be dedicated to Sir Thomas Finch. Webster had procured the services of Ralph Crane to transcribe—whether from foul papers or (more likely) the promptbook—*The Duchess of Malfi*, to be dedicated to George Harding, Baron Berkeley. Obviously, if *The Devil's Law-Case* was printed from a scribal transcript, the scribe was not Crane. But reliance on a transcript from foul papers, by somebody whose setting out of verse and prose was no less puzzling than Crane's, might explain the Quarto's mix of freedom from verbal muddle, authorial but service-able stage directions, and severe mislineation.

A possible pointer to the printer's use of scribal copy is the presence in the Quarto of nine instances of the '-en' ending in 'drawen' (twice), 'growen' (twice), 'knowen' (3 times), and 'showen' (twice).[27] These endings never appear in any other Webster text, and they are rare in con-temporary play quartos. The *LION: Drama* electronic database includes almost seven hundred plays first performed in the period 1576–1642, only two of which, apart from *The Devil's Law-Case*, have five or more such forms, and these both belong to the 1580s.[28] The past participle 'shewen' appears in the very first line of the play, where a compositor is perhaps most likely to reproduce the spelling of his copy. The '-en' endings are not characteristic of the other playtexts printed by Mathewes in 1622–4.[29] It is conceivable that Webster favoured such forms, but that they were all regularized in his other printed texts, or that they represent the preference of a compositor who did not work on the other Mathewes quartos, but it is perhaps more likely that they are scribal spellings. Also suggestive of a tampering scribe are the formulae ending Acts I, II, III, and IV, with their false Latin: *Finis Actus primi* (C2ʳ), *Explicit Actus secundi* (E2ᵛ), *Explicit Acti Tertij* (G3ᵛ), *Explicit Acti quarti* (K2ʳ). As Lucas points out, the genitives in the '*Explicit*' ('Here ends') formulae have arisen through confusion with the '*Finis*' ('The finish') formula. Such muddled Latin not only differentiates this Quarto from those of Webster's two Italian tragedies but makes it unique among Renaissance dramatic texts.[30]

Our conclusion must be tentative, like Brown's—that behind the Quarto lay a 'literary rather than a theatrical manuscript', which was probably a scribal transcript of Webster's foul papers.

SUBSEQUENT EDITIONS

The Quarto of 1623 was followed by the editions of Dyce (1830, 1857), Hazlitt (1857), and Lucas (1927). Dyce introduced scene divisions, made most of the desirable verbal emendations, and performed some useful relineation. Gunby's Penguin edition (1972) thoroughly overhauled the Quarto's versification, and was followed, with some modifications, by Brennan's New Mermaid (1975). Shirley's edition in the Regents Renaissance Drama series (1971) paid more deference to the Quarto's layout. Dollimore and Sinfield (1983) adopted Brennan's lineation in every detail. René Weis, including *The Devil's Law-Case* in his edition of four Webster plays (1996), supplements the Quarto's stage directions more liberally than his predecessors. All the modern editors benefited from Brown's collation of twenty copies of the Quarto, which revealed its press variants. Brennan, Shirley, and Dollimore and Sinfield recorded these. The above-mentioned editions have all been examined in the preparation of this one. *The Devil's Law-Case* is in Dyce's volume II, Hazlitt's III, and Lucas's II.

1. Greg, *Bibliography*, II, 388; STC 25173.
2. Though headed 'The Actors Names', like the list prefacing *The Duchess of Malfi*, this one differs in not actually including the names of the actors who played the roles.
3. Brown 1956, p. 122.
4. Since the text of the play begins on A3^r, the running title heads only the last three pages of sheet A. One cannot be sure, but that on A3^v probably recurs on B2^r (where it contributes to skeleton II), that on A4^r on B4^v (skeleton I), and that on A4^v recurs on B4^r (skeleton II).
5. For 'ssi' combinations see MacD. P. Jackson, '"A Curious Typesetting Characteristic" in Some Elizabethan Quartos', *The Library*, sixth series, II (1980), pp. 70–2.
6. There is perhaps a slight tendency for anomalies to be found near the start of the Quarto. For instance, 'Mistres' on B2^v and 'Mistresse' on B4^v are the only exceptions to 'Mistris' (16 times). A compositor might take a while to establish his preferences in setting a particular text.
7. Pages with both 'ith' and 'i'th' are F3^v, I2^v, K3^v, and L3^v. The contraction without the apostrophe also occurs on B1^v, B4^r, F4^r, H3^r, I3^r, L2^v, and L3^v.
8. The increase from F3^v onwards in uses of 'ith' without the apostrophe may be relevant, and also the slightly greater use up to F1^v of blank lines associated with stage directions. Also 'Deuil(l)' normally has a capital (eighteen times); five of the six occasions on which it is not capitalized fall on pages from F4^v onwards (D2^v, F4^r, H3^r, I3^v, L1^r, L2^v). The only exceptions to '-cke' endings occur in the first half of the Quarto: 'black' C2^r, 'Arithmatick' C4^v, 'chollerick' E2^r, 'musick' F1^r, and 'stuck' F1^v; but '-cke' endings greatly predominate over these earlier sheets.
9. Single words are turned over or under on C4^v, D4^r, E3^r, G3^r, H2^v, I2^r, and I4^r (as well as on F1^r), and two words are turned over on H1^r.

10. Brown 1956, pp. 122–3.

11. Ibid., p. 122.

12. The manuscript may, however, have read 'ith Margent o'th sheet' (or 'a'th sheet'); 'o'th sheet' might then be a 'first thought' that had been unclearly erased in the printer's copy; or, standing unaltered in the copy but bungled by the compositor's omission of 'o'th', the whole phrase may have been curtailed by Webster as he looked over the forme in the printing-house.

13. However, at least two of the other variants in inner G would be explicable in terms of authorial intervention. At IV.i.38 (G4ʳ) Ariosto calls Sanitonella, in the uncorrected state, 'sirrah Ignorance'. This is idiomatic, on the analogy of Shakespeare's 'Sir Prudence' (*The Tempest*, II.i.286) and 'Sir Valor' (*Troilus and Cressida*, I.iii.176), but it is corrected to 'sirrah Ignoramus', which is clearly authoritative. Tinkering by Webster himself is possible, but 'Ignorance' could be the compositor's substitution. Six lines later, at IV.i.44 (G4ʳ), Sanitonella, who claims, that while he has not studied Law at the University, he has 'Commenc't | In a Pewe of our Office', adds: 'I have been dry-foundred in't this foure yeares'. Here 'in't' is a correction of 'with't', and seems an improvement, but there is no obvious element in the context that might have provoked a compositor to substitute 'with't' if 'in't' were the reading of his copy. There may, however, have been deletions and replacements in the manuscript, the press-corrector recovering the author's true intention. Hammond and DelVecchio noted the coexistence in the Melbourne Manuscript, which may be an example of Websterian foul papers, of first and second thoughts, the latter inscribed over the former, in such a way that it would be difficult for a compositor or scribe to determine which represented the author's final intention (see 'The Melbourne Manuscript and John Webster: a Reproduction and Transcript', *SB* XLI [1988], pp. 1–32).

14. Brown 1954, p. 140.

15. Particularly influential have been Paul Werstine, 'Narratives about Printed Shakespeare Texts: "Foul Papers" and "Bad" Quartos', *SQ* XLI (1990), pp. 65–86, and 'McKerrow's "Suggestion" and Twentieth-Century Shakespeare Textual Criticism', *Renaissance Drama* XIX (1989), pp. 149–73; and William B. Long, 'Stage-Directions: a Misinterpreted Factor in Determining Textual Provenance', *Text* II (1985), pp. 121–37. In a paper contributed to the 1997 Shakespeare Association of America conference in Cleveland, 'Foul Papers: Narratives Old and New', T. H. Howard-Hill accepted Long's argument that early modern promptbooks might be less tidy than Greg and his contemporaries assumed, but exposed the flaws in Werstine's assault on New Bibliographical conceptions of foul papers.

16. Also, in his dedication to Sir Thomas Finch, Webster claims that 'the greatest of the *Cæsars* haue cheerefully entertain'd lesse Poems then this'. For discussion of Webster's distinction between 'poem' and 'presentment', see *Webster*, I, 35–42.

17. To the count of fifty one might reasonably add one example of a seven-word speech on L1ᵛ, because the words are so short that the total number of letters is only twenty-one.

18. There is no tendency for same-line speeches to fall within the second half of the page, so the space-saving is unlikely to have arisen from a need to compensate for miscalculations in casting-off of copy.

19. IV.i begins on I1ʳ and V.ii ends on M3ʳ.

20. Brown 1962, p. 64.

21. Greg, *Documents*, II, 207, notes that in theatre manuscripts speeches begin on separate lines and are separated by rules. So if the same-line speeches in *The Devil's Law-Case* are not *merely* products of the printing-house, they would furnish further evidence of non-theatrical manuscript copy.

22. The 'epical caesura' and other aspects of dramatic blank verse are well discussed by George T. Wright, *Shakespeare's Metrical Art* (London, 1988).

23. Jonson dedicated *Volpone* to the Universities of Oxford and Cambridge 'for their love and acceptance shew'n to his poeme in the presentation' (typography regularized), which foreshadows Webster's distinction between his 'poem' and its 'presentment'; see n. 16.

24. *Webster*, I, 43.

25. Ibid., I, 454.

26. Ibid., I, 126–8.

27. The '-en' endings predominate over the first half of the play, '-ne' endings over the second half, but the data are complex: 'drawen' B1^v, G1^r; 'growen' B2^r, C4^r; 'knowen' C3^r, F4^r, I1^v; 'shewen' A3^r, D1^v; 'drawne' I4^r, 'grown' G3^r; 'growne' H4^r; 'knowne' B1^r, F4^r, G1^r, G4^r, H2^r, I2^r, K1^v, K4^v. This means that up to the first half of G1^r the figures for '-en': '-n(e)' are 8:2, whereas for the rest of the play they are 1:10. But amalgamating figures for the four words makes the distinction between the earlier half of the play and the later seem sharper than it really is: the past participle for 'shew' or 'show' does not occur in any form after D1^v, while the figures for 'knowen': 'knowne' before and after the middle of G1^r are 2:2 and 1:6, and F4^r has both spellings, the '-ne' ending coming first. Nevertheless, the spelling of these words constitutes another scrap of evidence for a possible change of compositors, while doing nothing to clarify precisely where, if at all, it occurred. One compositor may have been more tolerant than another of his copy's '-en' endings, or a single compositor may have imposed his own preferences more firmly as he proceeded.

28. Robert Wilson's *The Three Lords and Ladies of London* (1590) has fourteen '-en' endings, including at least one instance of each of the four words. Christopher Marlowe's *1 Tamburlaine the Great* (1590) has 8 '-en' endings, all in 'drawen'. Five plays have four examples, but three belong to the 1580s and the latest is Thomas Middleton's *Michaelmas Term* (1607), which has only 'knowen'.

29. I have checked *A Fair Quarrel* (1622), *The Troublesome Reign of King John* (1622), *The Spanish Tragedy* (1623), and *The Tragedy of Nero* (1624).

30. Jackson 1999.

The Deuils Law-cafe.

OR,

When Women goe to Law, the Deuill is full of Bufineffe.

A new Tragecomædy.

The true and perfeƈt Copie from the Originall.

As it was approouedly well Aƈted by her Maiefties Seruants.

Written by IOHN WEBSTER.

Non quam diu, fed quam bene.

LONDON,

Printed by *A. M.* for *Iohn Grifmand*, and are to be fold at his Shop in Pauls Alley at the Signe of the Gunne. 1623.

4. Title-page of *The Devil's Law-Case* (1623).

[Dramatis personae (in order of appearance)]

The Scæne, NAPLES.

The Actors Names.

Romelio, a Merchant.
Prospero [a merchant].
Contarino, a Nobleman.
Leonora [a widow, mother of Romelio and Jolenta].
Ercole, a Knight of Malta.
Jolenta [Romelio's sister].   10
[*Winifrid*] A wayting Woman.
Crispiano, a Civill-Lawyer.
Sanitonella [Crispiano's clerk].
Julio [Crispiano's son].
Ariosto, an Advocate.
[*Baptista*, a merchant.]
A Capuchin.
[1 *Surgeon.*]
[2 *Surgeon.*]
Contilupo [a spruce lawyer].   20
[*Angiolella*, a nun.]
[*A Marshal.*]
[*A Herald.*]
[*Servants, Bellmen, Register and Officers of the Court, Judge, Lawyer.*]

1–24 (matter in square brackets)] *not in* Q; *for order of names, see Commentary.*
5 *Romelio*] *Romelia* Q
11 a wayting Woman] Qa; *aligned to left of column in* Qb

12 Civill-Lawyer.] Ciuill-Lawer Q
17 *Capuchin*] *Capouchin* Q
20 *Contilupo*] *Cantilupoe* Q

76

TO THE RIGHT
WORTHIE, AND
All-accomplisht Gentleman,
Sir THOMAS FINCH, Knight
BARONET.

SIR, let it not appeare strange, that I doe aspire to your Patronage. Things that taste of any goodnesse, love to bee shelter'd neere Goodnesse: Nor do I flatter in this (which I hate) onely touch at the originall Copy of your vertues. Some of my other Works, as *The White Devill, The Dutchesse of Malfi, Guise,* and others, you have formerly seene; I present this humbly   10 to kisse your hands, and to find your allowance. Nor doe I much doubt it, knowing the greatest of the *Cæsars,* have cheerefully entertain'd lesse Poems then this: and had I thought it unworthy, I had not enquired after so worthy a Patronage. Your selfe I understand, to bee all curtesie. I doubt not therefore of your acceptance, but resolve, that my election is happie. For which favour done mee, I shall ever rest

Your Worships humbly devoted,
JOHN WEBSTER.

9 *White*] *white* Q

TO THE JUDITIOUS
READER.

I *hold it, in these kind of Poems with that of* Horace; Sapientia prima, stultitia caruisse; *to bee free from those vices, which proceed from ignorance; of which I take it, this Play will ingeniously acquit it selfe. I doe chiefly therefore expose it to the Judicious*: Locus est, & pluribus Umbris, *others have leave to sit downe, and reade it, who come unbidden. But to these, should a man present them with the most excellent Musicke, it would delight them no more, then* Auriculas Citharæ collecta sorde dolentes. *I will not further insist upon the approovement of it, for I am so farre from praising my selfe, that I have not given way to divers of my Friends, whose unbeg'd Commendatory Verses offered themselves to doe me service in the Front of this Poeme. A great part of the grace of this (I confesse) lay in Action; yet can no Action ever be gracious, where the decency of the Language, and Ingenious structure of the Scæne, arrive not to make up a perfect Harmony. What I have fayl'd of this, you that have approoved my other Workes, (when you have read this) taxe me of. For the rest,* Non ego Ventosæ Plebis, Suffragia venor.

10

The Devil's Law–Case.
OR,
When Women goe to Law, the Devill is full of Businesse.

[I.i]

Enter ROMELIO, *and* PROSPERO.

Prospero. YOU have shewen a world of wealth; I did not thinke
    There had bene a Merchant liv'd in Italy
    Of halfe your substance.
Romelio.   Ile give the King of Spaine
    Ten thousand Duckets yearely, and discharge
    My yearely Custome. The Hollanders scarse trade
    More generally then I: my Factors wives
    Weare Shaperoones of Velvet, and my Scriveners
    Meerely through my imployment, grow so rich,
    They build their Palaces and Belvidears
    With musicall Water-workes: Never in my life   10
    Had I a losse at Sea. They call me on th'Exchange,
    The fortunate Youngman, and make great suite
    To venture with me: Shall I tell you Sir,
    Of a strange confidence in my way of Trading,
    I reckon it as certaine as the gaine
    In erecting a Lotterie.
Prospero. I pray Sir, what doe you thinke
    Of Signiour *Baptista's* estate?
Romelio. A meere Begger:
    Hee's worth some fiftie thousand Duckets.   20
Prospero. Is not that well?
Romelio. How, well? For a man to be melted to snow water,
    With toyling in the world from three and twentie,   [A3ᵛ]
    Till threescore, for poore fiftie thousand Duckets.

1 YOU] YOu Q   22 How,] ~ₐ Q
18 *Baptista's*] Dyce 1; *Baptisto's* Q

Prospero.   To your estate 'tis little I confesse:
    You have the Spring-tide of Gold.
Romelio.   Faith, and for Silver,
    Should I not send it packing to th'East Indies,
    We should have a glut on't.

                   Enter Servant.

Servant.   Here's the great Lord *Contarino.*   [*Exit.*]
Prospero.   Oh, I know his busines, he's a suitor to your sister.   30
Romelio.   Yes Sir, but to you,
    As my most trusted friend, I utter it,
    I will breake the alliance.
Prospero.   You are ill advised then;
    There lives not a compleater Gentleman
    In Italy, nor of a more ancient house.
Romelio.   What tell you me of Gentrie, 'tis nought else
    But a superstitious relique of time past:
    And sift it to the true worth, it is nothing
    But ancient riches: and in him you know
    They are pittifully in the wane; he makes his colour   40
    Of visiting us so often, to sell land,
    And thinkes if he can gaine my sisters love,
    To recover the treble value.
Prospero.   Sure he loves her intirely, and she deserves it.
Romelio.   Faith, though shee were
    Crookt shoulderd, having such a portion,
    Shee would have noble Suitors; but truth is,
    I would wish my noble Venturer take heed,
    It may be whiles he hopes to catch a Gilt head,
    He may draw up a Gudgeon.   50

                 Enter CONTARINO.

Prospero.   Hee's come: Sir, I will leave you.   [*Exit.*]
Contarino.   I sent you the Evidence of the peece of land
    I motioned to you for the Sale.
Romelio.   Yes.
Contarino.   Has your Counsell perus'd it?
Romelio.   Not yet my Lord: Doe you intend to travell?
Contarino.   No.
Romelio.   Oh then you loose

That which makes man most absolute.

Contarino.   Yet I have heard   60
Of divers, that in passing of the Alpes,   [A4ʳ]
Have but exchang'd their vertues at deare rate
For others vices.

Romelio.   Oh my Lord, lye not idle;
The chiefest action for a man of great spirit,
Is never to be out of action: we should thinke
The soule was never put into the body,
Which has so many rare and curious pieces
Of Mathematicall motion, to stand still.
Vertue is ever sowing of her seedes: 70
In the Trenches for the Souldier; in the wakefull study
For the Scholler; in the furrowes of the sea
For men of our Profession, of all which
Arise and spring up Honor. Come, I know
You have some noble great Designe in hand,
That you levy so much money.

Contarino.   Sir, Ile tell you,
The greatest part of it I meane to imploy
In payment of my Debts, and the remainder
Is like to bring me into greater bonds,
As I ayme it.   80

Romelio.   How Sir?

Contarino.   I intend it for the charge of my Wedding.

Romelio.   Are you to be married, my Lord?

Contarino.   Yes Sir; and I must now intreat your pardon,
That I have concealed from you a businesse,
Wherein you had at first been call'd to Counsell,
But that I thought it a lesse fault in Friendship,
To ingage my selfe thus farre without your knowledge,
Then to doe it against your will: another reason
Was, that I would not publish to the world,   90
Nor have it whispered scarce, what wealthy Voyage
I went about, till I had got the Myne
In mine owne possession.

Romelio.   You are darke to me yet.

Contarino.   Ile now remove the cloud. Sir, your sister and I

---

63 others] *as* Brennan 1975 (others'); other Q

Are vowed each others, and there onely wants
Her worthy mothers, and your faire consents
To stile it marriage: this is a way,
Not onely to make a friendship, but confirme it
For our posterities. How doe you looke upon't?   [A4ᵛ]

Romelio.   Beleeve me Sir, as on the principall Colume   100
          To advance our House: why you bring honour with you,
          Which is the soule of Wealth. I shall be proud
          To live to see my little Nephewes ride
          O'th upper hand of their Uncles; and the Daughters
          Be ranckt by Heraulds at Solemnities
          Before the Mother: all this deriv'd
          From your Nobilitie. Doe not blame me sir,
          If I be taken with't exceedingly:
          For this same honour with us Citizens,
          Is a thing we are mainely fond of, especially   110
          When it comes without money, which is very seldome,
          But as you doe perceive my present temper,
          Be sure I am yours, [*aside*] fierd with scorne and laughter,
          At your over confident purpose, [*aloud*] and no doubt,
          My mother will be of your mind.

Contarino.   Tis my hope sir.   *Exit Romelio.*
          I doe observe how this *Romelio*,
          Has very worthy parts, were they not blasted
          By insolent vaine glory: there rests now
          The mothers approbation to the match,
          Who is a woman of that State and bearing,   120
          Tho shee be Citie-borne, both in her language,
          Her Garments, and her Table, shee excels
          Our Ladies of the Court: shee goes not gawdy,
          Yet have I seene her weare one Diamond,
          Would have bought twenty gay ones out of their clothes,
          And some of them, without the greater grace,
          Out of their honesties.

                    Enter LEONORA.
                    Shee comes, I will trie
          How she stands affected to me, without relating

---

113 SD] Dyce 2; *not in* Q   **115** SD] *placed as* Dyce 1; *after* mind. Q
114 SD] This ed.; *not in* Q   **127** SD] *placed as* Dyce 2; *after* trie Q

My Contract with her Daughter.
Leonora.   Sir, you are nobly welcome, and presume   130
    You are in a place that's wholly dedicated
    To your service.
Contarino.   I am ever bound to you for many speciall favours.
Leonora.   Sir, your fame renders you most worthy of it.
Contarino.   It could never have got a sweeter ayre to fly in,   [B1ʳ]
    Then your breath.
Leonora.   You have bin strange a long time, you are weary
    Of our unseasonable time of feeding:
    Indeed th'Exchange Bell makes us dine so late;
    I thinke the Ladies of the Court from us   140
    Learne to lye so long a bed.
Contarino.   They have a kind of Exchange among them too;
    Marry, unlesse it be to heare of newes, I take it,
    Theirs is like the New Burse, thinly furnisht
    With Tyers and new Fashions. I have a suite to you.
Leonora.   I would not have you value it the lesse,
    If I say, Tis granted already.
Contarino.   You are all Bounty,
    Tis to bestow your Picture on me.
Leonora.   Oh sir, shaddowes are coveted in Summer,   150
    And with me, tis Fall o'th Leafe.
Contarino.   You enjoy the best of Time;
    This latter Spring of yours, shewes in my eye,
    More fruitfull and more temperate withall,
    Then that whose date is onely limitted
    By the musicke of the Cuckow.
Leonora.   Indeed Sir, I dare tell you,
    My Looking-glasse is a true one, and as yet
    It does not terrifie me. Must you have my Picture?
Contarino.   So please you Lady, and I shall preserve it   160
    As a most choyce Object.
Leonora.   You will enjoyne me to a strange punishment:
    With what a compeld face a woman sits
    While shee is drawing! I have noted divers,
    Either to faine smiles, or sucke in the lippes,

---

142 kind∧] ~, Q   too;] ~, Q   150 shaddowes∧] ~, Q
143 Marry,] ~∧ Q   unlesse∧] vnlesse, Q   154 witʠall] Qb; (*turned h*) Qa
144 Theirs∧] ~, Q

To have a little mouth; ruffle the cheekes,
To have the dimple seene, and so disorder
The face with affectation, at next sitting
It has not been the same; I have knowne others
Have lost the intire fashion of their face,   170
In halfe an houres sitting.
Contarino.   How!
Leonora.   In hote weather,   [B1ᵛ]
The painting on their face has been so mellow,
They have left the poore man harder worke by halfe,
To mend the Copie he wrought by: but indeed,
If ever I would have mine drawne to'th life,
I would have a Paynter steale it, at such a time,
I were devoutly kneeling at my prayers,
There is then a heavenly beautie in't, the Soule   180
Mooves in the Superficies.
Contarino.   Excellent Lady,
Now you teach Beautie a preservative,
More then 'gainst fading Colours; and your judgement
Is perfect in all things.
Leonora.   Indeed Sir, I am a Widdow,
And want the addition to make it so:
For mans Experience has still been held
Womans best eyesight. I pray sir tell mee,
You are about to sell a piece of Land
To my sonne, I heare.   190
Contarino.   Tis truth.
Leonora.   Now I could rather wish,
That Noble men would ever live ith Countrey,
Rather then make their visit's up to'th Citie
About such businesse: Oh Sir, Noble Houses
Have no such goodly Prospects any way,
As into their owne Land: the decay of that,
Next to their begging Churchland, is a ruine
Worth all mens pitie. Sir, I have forty thousand crownes
Sleepe in my Chest, shall waken when you please,   200
And flie to your commands. Will you stay supper?
Contarino.   I cannot, worthy Lady.
Leonora.   I would not have you come hither sir, to sell,
But to settle your Estate. I hope you understand

84

Wherefore I make this proffer: so I leave you.   *Exit.*

Contarino.   On what a Treasury have I pearch'd! I hope
    You understand wherefore I make this proffer.
    Shee has got some intelligence, how I intend to marry
    Her daughter, and ingenuously perceived,
    That by her Picture, which I begged of her,   [B2ʳ]
    I meant the faire *Jolenta*: here's a Letter,   211
    Which gives expresse charge, not to visit her
    Till midnight:
    [*reads*] *Faile not to come, for tis a businesse*
    That concernes both our honors.
                Yours in danger to be lost, Jolenta.
    Tis a strange Injunction; what should be the businesse?
    She is not chang'd I hope. Ile thither straight:
    For womens Resolutions in such deeds,
    Like Bees, light oft on flowers, and oft on weeds.   *Exit.*

[I.ii]

Enter ERCOLE [*with a letter*], ROMELIO, JOLENTA.

Romelio.   Oh sister come, the Taylor must to worke, to make your
    wedding Clothes.
Jolenta.   The Tombe-maker, to take measure of my coffin.
Romelio.   Tombe-maker? Looke you, the king of Spaine greets you.
                  [*Proffers her Ercole's letter.*]
Jolenta.   What does this meane, do you serve Proces on me?
Romelio.   Proces? Come, you would be wittie now.
Jolenta.   Why, what's this, I pray?
Romelio.   Infinite grace to you: it is a Letter from his Catholike Majestie,
    for the commends of this Gentleman for your Husband.
Jolenta.   In good season: I hope he will not have my Allegiance stretcht   10
    to the undoing of my selfe.
Romelio.   Undoe your selfe? He does proclaime him here—

---

205 SD] *placed as* Dyce 1; *Exit Leon. to right of*
  line 206 after pearch'd. Q
206 On what] Dyce 2; What Q   pearch'd!]
  ~. Q
214 SD] Dyce 2; *not in* Q
214–15 *Faile . . . honors*] roman *in* Q

I.ii] *as* Dyce 1; *not in* Q
0.1 *with a letter*] This ed.; *not in* Q
4.1 SD] *after* Lucas; *not in* Q
6 Come,] ~ₐ Q
12 here—] ~ₐ Q

Jolenta.   Not for a Traytor, does he?

Romelio.   You are not mad? For one of the Noblest Gentlemen.

Jolenta.   Yet Kings many times know meerly but mens outsides; was this
   commendation voluntary, thinke you?

Romelio.   Voluntary: what meane you by that?

Jolenta.   Why I do not thinke but he beg'd it of the King,
   And it may fortune to be out of's way:
   Some better suite, that woo'd have stood his Lordship   20
   In farre more stead: Letters of Commendations,
   Why tis reported that they are growen stale,
   When places fall i'th Universitie.   [B2ᵛ]
   I pray you returne his Passe: for to a Widdow
   That longs to be a Courtier, this Paper
   May doe Knights service.

Ercole.   Mistake not excellent Mistres, these commends
   Expresse, his Majestie of Spaine has given me
   Both addition of honour, as you may perceive
   By my habit, and a place heere to command   30
   Ore thirtie Gallies; this your brother shewes,
   As wishing that you would be partner
   In my good Fortune.

Romelio [*to Jolenta*].   I pray come hither, have I any interest in you?

Jolenta.   You are my Brother.

Romelio.   I would have you then use me with that respect,
   You may still keepe me so, and to be swayed
   In this maine businesse of life, which wants
   Greatest consideration, your Marriage,
   By my direction: Here's a Gentleman—   40

Jolenta.   Sir, I have often told you,
   I am so little my owne to dispose that way,
   That I can never be his.

Romelio.   Come, too much light
   Makes you Moone-eyed, are you in love with title?
   I will have a Herauld, whose continuall practise
   Is all in pedigree, come a wooing to you,
   Or an Antiquary in old Buskins.

Ercole.   Sir, you have done me
   The maynest wrong that ere was offred

14 mad?] ~; Q   34 SD] Weis; *not in* Q

86

To a Gentleman of my breeding.   50
Romelio.   Why sir?
Ercole.   You have led me
     With a vaine confidence, that I should marry
     Your sister, have proclaim'd it to my friends,
     Employd the greatest Lawyers of our State
     To settle her a joynture, and the issue
     Is, that I must become ridiculous
     Both to my friends and enemies: I will leave you,
     Till I call to you for a strict account
     Of your unmanly dealing.
Romelio.   Stay my Lord.   [B3ʳ]
     [*aside to Jolenta*] Doe you long to have my throat cut?
                              [*to Ercole*] Good my Lord,   61
     Stay but a little, till I have remooved
     This Court-mist from her eyes, till I wake her
     From this dull sleepe, wherein sheele dreame herselfe
     To a deformed Begger: [*to Jolenta*] you would marry
     The great Lord *Contarino.*
                         Enter LEONORA.
Leonora.   *Contarino*
     Were you talking of? He lost last night at Dice
     Five thousand Duckets; and when that was gone,
     Set at one throw a Lordship, that twice trebled
     The former losse.   70
Romelio.   And that flew after.
Leonora.   And most carefully
     Carried the Gentleman in his Carroch
     To a Lawyers Chamber, there most Legally
     To put him in possession: was this wisedome?
Romelio.   O yes, their credit in the way of gaming
     Is the mayne thing they stand on, that must be paid,
     Tho the Brewer bawle for's money; and this Lord
     Does shee preferre i'th way of marriage,
     Before our Choyce here, noble *Ercole.*
Leonora [*to Jolenta*].   Youle be advis'd I hope: Know for your sakes 80
     I married, that I might have children;

61 *aside to Jolenta*] Lucas; *not in* Q   *to Ercole*]   **79** Choyce here,] ~. Here‸ Q   *Ercole.*] ~, Q
     This ed.; *not in* Q   **80** SD] This ed.; *not in* Q
65 SD] Lucas; *not in* Q

87

And for your sakes, if youle be rul'd by me,
I will never marry agen. Here's a Gentleman
Is noble, rich, well featur'd, but 'bove all,
He loves you intirely; his intents are aymed
For an Expedition 'gainst the Turke,
Which makes the Contract cannot be delayed.

Jolenta.   Contract? You must do this without my knowledge;
Give me some potion to make me mad,
And happily not knowing what I speake,   90
I may then consent too't.

Romelio.   Come, you are mad already,
And I shall never heare you speake good sense,
Till you name him for Husband.

Ercole.   Lady, I will doe a manly Office for you,
I will leave you, to the freedome of your owne soule,
May it move whither heaven and you please.   [B3ᵛ]

Jolenta.   Now you expresse your selfe most nobly.

Romelio.   Stay sir, what doe you meane to doe?

Leonora [*kneeling*].   Heare me, if thou dost marry *Contarino*,
All the misfortune that did ever dwell   100
In a parents curse, light on thee.

Ercole.   Oh rise Lady, certainly heaven never
Intended kneeling to this fearefull purpose.   [*Leonora rises.*]

Jolenta.   Your Imprecation has undone me for ever.

Ercole.   Give me your hand.

Jolenta.   No sir.

Romelio.   Giv't me then: [*He takes her hand.*]
Oh what rare workmanship have I seene this
To finish with your needle, what excellent musicke
Have these strucke upon the Violl!   110
Now Ile teach a piece of Art.

Jolenta.   Rather a damnable cunning,
To have me goe about to giv't away,
Without consent of my soule.   [*She weeps.*]

Romelio.   Kisse her my Lord, if crying had been regarded, Maidenheads
had nere been lost, at least some appearance of crying, as an Aprill
showre i'th Sunshine.

---

99 SD] *as* Lucas; *not in* Q   **114** SD] This ed.; *not in* Q
103 SD] This ed.; *not in* Q   **117.1** SD] This ed.; *not in* Q
107 SD] Lucas; *not in* Q

[Ercole kisses Jolenta.]

Leonora.   Shee is yours.

Romelio [to Ercole].   Nay, continue your station, and deale you in dumbe
    shew; kisse this doggednesse out of her.   120

Leonora.   To be contracted in teares, is but fashionable.

Romelio.   Yet suppose that they were heartie.

Leonora.   Virgins must seeme unwilling.

Romelio.   Oh what else; and you remember, we observe the like in
    greater Ceremonies then these Contracts; at the Consecration of
    Prelates, they use ever twice to say nay, and take it.

Jolenta.   Oh Brother.

[He seizes her hand and lays it in Ercole's.]

Romelio.   Keep your possession, you have the dore bith ring,
    That's Livery and Seasin in England; but my Lord,
    Kisse that teare from her lip, youle find the Rose   130
    The sweeter for the dewe.

Jolenta.   Bitter as gall.

Romelio.   I, I, all you women,   [B4ᵛ]
    Although you be of never so low stature,
    Have gall in you most abundant, it exceeds
    Your braines by two ounces. I was saying somewhat;
    Oh doe but observe ith Citie, and youle finde
    The thriftiest bargaines that were ever made,
    What a deale of wrangling ere they could be brought
    To an upshot.

Leonora.   Great persons doe not ever come together—   140

Romelio.   With revelling faces, nor is it necessary
    They should; the strangenesse and unwillingnesse
    Weares the greater state, and gives occasion that
    The people may buzz and talke of't, tho the Bells
    Be tongue-tide at the Wedding.

Leonora.   And truely I have heard say,
    To be a little strange to one another,
    Will keepe your longing fresh.

Romelio.   I, and make you beget
    More children when yare maried: some Doctors   150
    Are of that opinion. You see my Lord, we are merry

---

119 SD] This ed.; *not in* Q   **127.1** SD] Lucas; *not in* Q
125 Contracts;] ~, Q   **140** together—] ~. Q

At the Contract, your sport is to come hereafter.
Ercole. I will leave you excellent Lady, and withall
    Leave a heart with you so entirely yours,
    That I protest, had I the least of hope
    To enjoy you, tho I were to wayt the time
    That Schollers doe in taking their degree
    In the noble Arts, 'twere nothing, howsoere
    He parts from you, that will depart from life,
    To doe you any service, and so humbly   160
    I take my leave.
Jolenta.   Sir, I will pray for you.   *Exit Ercole.*
Romelio. Why thats well, 'twill make your prayer compleat,
    To pray for your Husband.
Jolenta. Husband?
Leonora. This is the happiest houre that I ever arrived at.   [Exit.]
Romelio. Husband, I husband: come you peevish thing,
    Smile me a thanke for the paynes I have tane.
Jolenta. I hate my selfe for being thus enforst,
    You may soone judge then what I thinke of you   [B4ᵛ]
    Which are the cause of it.   170
            Enter [WINIFRID, *the*] *Wayting-woman.*
Romelio. You Lady of the Laundry, come hither.
Winifrid. Sir?
Romelio. Looke as you love your life, you have an eye upon your
    Mistresse; I doe henceforth barre her all Visitants: I do heare there are
    Bawds abroad, that bring Cut-works, and Man-toons, and convey
    Letters to such young Gentlewomen, and there are others that deale in
    Corne-cutting, and Fortune-telling; let none of these come at her on
    your life, nor *Dewes-ace* the wafer woman, that prigs abroad with
    Muskmeloons, and Malakatoones; nor the Scotchwoman with the
    Citterne, do you marke, nor a Dancer by any meanes, tho he ride on's   180
    foot-cloth, nor a Hackney Coachman, if he can speake French.
Winifrid. Why sir?

161 SD] *placed as* Dyce 1; *after* leave. Q
165 SD] Lucas; *not in* Q
170.1 WINIFRID, *the*] Lucas; *not in* Q;
  WINIFRED. Dyce 1 (*replacing* Q *Wayting-
  woman*)
172 *Winifrid*] *as* Dyce 1 (WIN.); *Wayt.* Q (*so
  to end of scene except for* Wait. *at line 209,* Wai.

at line 219, Wa. *at line 261*)
175 Cut-works, and] Qa; ~, & Qb   Man-
  toons] Qb; Man-oons Qa   and convey] &
  conuey Q
177 Corne-cutting] Qb; Cornecutting Qa
  Fortune-telling;] ~, Q
178 *Dewes-ace*] Dewes ace Q

Romelio. By no meanes: no more words; nor the woman with
Maribone puddings. I have heard strange jugling tricks have been
conveyd to a woman in a pudding: you are apprehensive?
Winifrid. Oh good sir, I have traveld.
Romelio. When you had a Bastard, you traveld indeed: but my precious
Chaperoonesse, I trust thee the better for that; for I have heard, there is
no warier Keeper of a Parke, to prevent Stalkers, or your Night-
walkers, then such a man, as in his youth has been a most notorious   190
Deare-stealer.
Winifrid. Very well sir, you may use me at your pleasure.
Romelio. By no meanes *Winifrid*, that were the way to make thee travell
agen: Come be not angry, I doe but jest; thou knowest, wit and a
woman are two very fraile things, and so I leave you.   *Exit.*
Winifrid. I could weepe with you, but tis no matter, I can doe that
at any time, I have now a greater mind to rayle a little: Plague of   [C1ʳ]
these unsanctified Matches; they make us lothe the most naturall desire
our grandame *Eve* ever left us. Force one to marry against their will;
why 'tis a more ungodly worke then inclosing the Commons.   200
Jolenta. Prethee peace;
         This is indeed an argument so common,
         I cannot thinke of matter new ynough,
         To expresse it bad enough.
                         Enter CONTARINO.
Winifrid. Heere's one I hope will put you out of't.
Contarino. How now sweet Mistris?
         You have made sorrow looke lovely of late,
         You have wept.
Winifrid. She has done nothing else these three dayes; had you stood
behinde the Arras, to have heard her shed so much salt water as I have   210
done, you would have thought she had been turn'd Fountaine.
Contarino. I would faine know
         The cause can be worthy this thy sorrow.
Jolenta [to Winifrid]. Reach me the Caskanet, *[to Contarino]* I am study-
         ing Sir,
         To take an Inventory of all that's mine.

188 Chaperoonesse] This ed.; Chaperoones
Q
194 jest;] ~, Q
195 woman∧] ~, Q
200 worke∧] ~, Q

204.1 SD] *placed as* Shirley; *follows line 205* Q
209 three] Qb; thee Qa
214 *to Winifrid] as* Weis; *not in* Q   *to
Contarino]* This ed.; *not in* Q

Contarino.   What to doe with it Lady?

Jolenta.   To make you a Deed of gift.

Contarino.   That's done already; you are all mine.

Winifrid.   Yes, but the Devil would faine put in for's share, in likenesse
    of a Separation.   220

Jolenta.   Oh sir, I am bewitcht.

Contarino.   Ha?

Jolenta.   Most certaine, I am forespoken,
    To be married to another: can you ever thinke
    That I shall ever thrive in't? Am I not then bewitcht?
    All comfort I can teach my selfe is this,
    There is a time left for me to dye nobly,
    When I cannot live so!

Contarino.   Give me in a word, to whom, or by whose meanes
    Are you thus torne from me?   230

Jolenta.   By Lord *Ercole*, my Mother, and my Brother.

Contarino.   Ile make his bravery fitter for a grave,   [C1ᵛ]
    Then for a wedding.

Jolenta.   So you will beget
    A farre more dangerous and strange disease
    Out of the cure; you must love him agen
    For my sake: for the noble *Ercole*
    Had such a true compassion of my sorrow.
    Harke in your eare, Ile shew you his right worthy
    Demeanour to me.

        [*She whispers in his ear, and they embrace.*]

Winifrid [*aside*].   Oh you pretty ones, I have seene this Lord many a time   240
    and oft set her in's lap, and talke to her of Love so feelingly, I doe
    protest it has made me run out of my selfe to thinke on't; oh sweet
    breath'd Monkey, how they grow together! Well, tis my opinion, he
    was no womans friend that did invent a punishment for kissing.

Contarino.   If he beare himselfe so nobly,
    The manliest office I can doe for him,
    Is to affoord him my pitie, since hee's like
    To faile of so deare a purchase: for your mother,
    Your goodnesse quits her ill; for your brother,

---

231 and my] Dyce 1; and by Q   **240** SD] Lucas; *not in* Q
239.1 SD] This ed.; *not in* Q

He that vowes friendship to a man, and prooves   250
A traytor, deserves rather to be hang'd,
Then he that counterfets money; yet for your sake
I must signe his pardon too. Why doe you tremble?
Be safe, you are now free from him.
Jolenta.   Oh but sir,
The intermission from a fit of an ague
Is grievous: for indeed it doth prepare us,
To entertaine torment next morning.
Contarino.   Why, hee's gone to sea.
Jolenta.   But he may returne too soone.
Contarino.   To avoyd which, we will instantly be maried.   260
Winifrid.   To avoid which, get you instantly to bed together, doe, and I
   thinke no Civill Lawyer for his fee can give you better Councell.
Jolenta.   Fye upon thee, prethee leave us.   [Exit Winifrid.]
Contarino.   Be of comfort sweet Mistris.   [C2ʳ]
Jolenta.   On one condition: we may have no quarrell about this.
Contarino.   Upon my life, none.
Jolenta.   None, upon your honour?
Contarino.   With whom? With Ercole?
You have delivered him guiltlesse.
With your Brother? Hee's part of your selfe.   270
With your complementall Mother?
I use not fight with women.
To morrow weele be married:
Let those that would oppose this union,
Grow nere so subtill, and intangle themselves
In their owne worke like Spiders, while we two
Haste to our noble wishes, and presume,
The hindrance of it will breed more delight,
As black copartaments shewes gold more bright.   Exeunt.
                    Finis Actus primi.

263 SD] as Lucas; not in Q   275 Grow] grow Q
265 condition:] ~∧ Q   279 shewes] Q; show Dyce I   Exeunt.] ~∧
266 life,] ~∧ Q   Q
267 None,] ~∧ Q

ACTUS SECUNDUS, SCENA PRIMA. [II.i]

Enter CRISPIANO [*disguised as a merchant*], SANITONELLA.

Crispiano. Am I well habited?

Sanitonella. Exceeding well; any man would take you for a Merchant:
but pray sir resolve me, what should bee the reason, that you being one
of the most eminent Civill Lawyers in Spaine, and but newly arrived
from the East Indies, should take this habit of a Marchant upon you?

Crispiano. Why my sonne lives here in Naples, and in's riot doth farre
exceed the exhibition I allowed him.

Sanitonella. So then, and in this disguise you meane to trace him.

Crispiano. Partly for that, but there is other businesse of greater consequence.   10

Sanitonella. Faith for his expence, tis nothing to your estate. What, to
Don Crispiano, the famous Corrigidor of Civill, who by his meere
practise of the Law, in lesse time then halfe a Jubile, hath gotten thirtie
thousand Duckets a yeare.

Crispiano. Well, I will give him line, let him run on in's course of spend-   [C2ᵛ]
ing.

Sanitonella. Freely?

Crispiano. Freely:
       For I protest, if that I could conceave
       My sonne would take more pleasure or content,   20
       By any course of ryot, in the expence,
       Then I tooke joy, nay soules felicitie
       In the getting of it, should all the wealth I have
       Waste to as small an atomy as Flies
       I'th Sunne, I doe protest on that condition,
       It should not moove mee.

Sanitonella. How's this? Cannot hee take more pleasure in spending it
ryotously, then you have done by scraping it together? O ten thousand
times more, and I make no question, five hundred yong gallants wil be
of my opinion.   30
       Why all the time of your Collectionship,

0.1 *disguised . . . merchant*] This ed.; *not in* Q;
     disguised Lucas
6 and] & Q
8 and] & Q

11 estate.] ~, Q   What,] ~ₐ Q
27 pleasure] Dyce 1; peasure Q
28 together?] ~,Q
30 opinion] opiniõ Q

94

Has bene a perpetuall Callender: begin first
With your melancholly studie of the Law
Before you came to finger the Ruddocks, after that
The tyring importunitie of Clyents,
To rise so early, and sit up so late,
You made your selfe halfe ready in a dreame,
And never prayed but in your sleepe: Can I thinke,
That you have halfe your lungs left with crying out
For Judgements, and dayes of Tryall. Remember sir,   40
How often have I borne you on my shoulder,
Among a shoale or swarme of reeking Night-caps,
When that your Worship has bepist your selfe,
Either with vehemency of Argument,
Or being out from the matter. I am merry.
Crispiano.   Be so.
Sanitonella.   You could not eat like a Gentleman, at leasure;
But swallow'd it like Flap-dragons, as if you had lived
With chewing the Cud after.
Crispiano.   No pleasure in the world was comparable too't.   50
Sanitonella.   Possible?
Crispiano.   He shall never taste the like, unlesse he study law.
Sanitonella.   What, not in wenching sir? Tis a Court game,   [C3ʳ]
Beleeve it, as familiar as Gleeke,
Or any other.
Crispiano.   Wenching? O fie, the Disease followes it:
Beside, can the fingring Taffaties, or Lawnes,
Or a painted hand, or a Brest, be like the pleasure
In taking Clyents fees, and piling them
In severall goodly rowes before my Deske?   60
And according to the bignesse of each heape,
Which I tooke by a leare: for Lawyers do not tell them,
I vayl'd my cap, and withall gave great hope
The Cause should goe on their sides.
Sanitonella.   What thinke you then
Of a good crie of Hounds? It has bene knowen
Dogs have hunted Lordships to a fault.

32 Callender:] ~, Q   48 swallow'd] Dyce 2; swallow Q
34 came] Dyce 2; come Q   54 Gleeke,] Qb; ~ₐ Qa
47 could not] Hazlitt; could Q

Crispiano.   Cry of Curres?
　　The noyse of Clyents at my Chamber doore,
　　Was sweeter Musicke farre, in my conceit,　　　　　　70
　　Then all the Hunting in Europe.
Sanitonella.   Pray stay sir,
　　Say he should spend it in good House-keeping.
Crispiano.   I marry sir, to have him keepe a good house,
　　And not sell't away, Ide find no fault with that:
　　But his Kitchin, Ide have no bigger then a Saw-pit;
　　For the smalnesse of a Kitchin, without question,
　　Makes many Noblemen in France and Spaine,
　　Build the rest of the house the bigger.
Sanitonella.   Yes, Mock-beggers.　　　　　　　　80
Crispiano.   Some sevenscore Chimneyes,
　　But halfe of them have no Tonnels.
Sanitonella.   A pox upon them, Cuckshawes that beget
　　Such monsters without fundaments.
Crispiano.   Come, come, leave citing other vanities;
　　For neither Wine, nor Lust, nor riotous feasts,
　　Rich cloathes, nor all the pleasure that the Devill
　　Has ever practis'd with, to raise a man
　　To a Devils likenesse, ere brought man that pleasure
　　I tooke in getting my wealth. So I conclude:　　　90
　　If he can out-vie me, let it flie to'th Devill.　　　[C3ᵛ]
　　　　Enter ROMELIO [*and*] JULIO [*talking*], ARIOSTO, BAPTISTA.
　　Yon's my sonne, what company keepes he?
Sanitonella.   The Gentleman he talks with,
　　Is *Romelio* the Merchant.
Crispiano.   I never saw him till now,
　　A has a brave sprightly looke, I knew his father,
　　And sojourn'd in his house two yeares together,
　　Before this young mans birth: I have newes to tell him
　　Of certaine losses happened him at Sea,
　　That will not please him.
Sanitonella [*indicating Ariosto*].   What's that dapper fellow　100
　　In the long stocking? I doe thinke 'twas he

83 them,] ~ Q
90 wealth.] ~: Q   conclude:] ~.
Q
91.1 ROMELIO [*and*] JULIO [*talking*]]

This ed.; *Rom.Julio* Q   SD] This ed. *for*
placing; right of lines 93–4 Q
100 SD] This ed.; *not in* Q   What's] Dyce 1;
What Q

Came to your lodging this morning.

Crispiano.   Tis the same,
There he stands, but a little piece of flesh,
But he is the very myracle of a Lawyer,
One that perswades men to peace, and compounds quarrels
Among his neighbours, without going to law.

Sanitonella.   And is he a Lawyer?

Crispiano.   Yes, and will give counsell
In honest causes gratis, never in his life   110
Tooke fee, but he came and spake for't, is a man
Of extreame practise, and yet all his longing
Is to become a Judge.

Sanitonella.   Indeed that's a rare longing with men of his profession. I
think heel prove the miracle of a lawier indeed.

Romelio.   Heere's the man brought word your father dyed i'th Indies.

Julio.   He died in perfect memory I hope, and made me his heyre.

Crispiano.   Yes sir.

Julio.   He's gone the right way then without question: Friend, in time of
mourning, we must not use any action, that is but accessary to the   120
making men merry, I doe therefore give you nothing for your good
tidings.

Crispiano.   Nor doe I looke for it sir.

Julio.   Honest fellow, give me thy hand, I doe not thinke but thou hast
carried New-yeares gifts to'th Court in thy dayes, and learndst there to
be so free of thy paynes taking.

Romelio.   Here's an old Gentleman sayes he was chamber-fellow to your   [C4ʳ]
father, when they studied the Law together at Barcellona.

Julio.   Doe you know him?

Romelio.   Not I, he's newly come to Naples.   130

Julio.   And what's his businesse?

Romelio.   A sayes he's come to read you good counsell.

Crispiano [*to Ariosto*].   To him, rate him soundly.   *This is spoke aside.*

Julio.   And what's your counsell?

Ariosto.   Why, I would have you leave your whoring.

Julio.   He comes hotly upon me at first: whoring?

Ariosto.   O yong quat, incontinence is plagued in all the creatures
of the world.

Julio. When did you ever heare, that a Cockesparrow had the French
poxe?   140

Ariosto. When did you ever know any of them fat, but in the nest? Aske
all your Cantaride-mongers that question; remember your selfe sir.

Julio. A very fine Naturallist, a Phisician, I take you by your round slop;
for tis just of the bignes, and no more, of the case for a Urinall: tis concluded, you are a Phisician. [*Ariosto doffs his hat.*] What doe you meane
sir? Youle take cold.

Ariosto. Tis concluded, you are a foole, a precious one, you are a meere
sticke of Sugar Candy, a man may looke quite thorow you.

Julio. You are a very bold gamester. [*Doffs his hat.*]

Ariosto. I can play at chesse, and know how to handle a rook.   150

Julio. Pray preserve your velvet from the dust.

Ariosto. Keepe your hat upon the blocke sir, 'twill continue fashion the
longer.

Julio. I was never so abused with the hat in the hand in my life.

Ariosto. I will put on [*replacing his hat*]; why looke you, those lands that
were the Clyents, are now become the Lawyers; and those tenements
that were the Countrey Gentlemans, are now growen to be his
Taylors.

Julio. Taylors?

Ariosto. Yes, Taylors in France, they grow to great abominable purchase,   [C4ᵛ]
and become great officers. How many Duckets thinke you he has   161
spent within a twelvemonth, besides his fathers allowance?

Julio. Besides my fathers allowance? Why Gentlemen, doe you thinke
an Auditor begat me? Would you have me make even at yeares end?

Romelio. A hundred duckets a month in breaking Venice glasses.

Ariosto. He learnt that of an English drunkard, and a Knight too, as I
take it. This comes of your numerous Wardrobe.

Romelio. I, and wearing Cut-worke, a pound a Purle.

Ariosto. Your daintie embroydered stockings, with overblowne Roses,
to hide your gowtie anckles.   170

Romelio. And wearing more taffaty for a garter, then would serve the
Gally dung-boat for streamers.

Ariosto. Your switching up at the horse-race, with the Illustrissimi.

Romelio. And studying a pusling Arithmatick at the cock-pit.

145 SD] *after* Lucas; *not in* Q   **150** and] & Q
146 sir?] ~, Q   **155** SD] *after* Brennan 1975; *not in* Q   on;]
148 you.] ~ᴧ Q   ~, Q
149 SD] *after* Lucas; *not in* Q   **162** Gentlemen] Hazlitt; Gentleman Q

Ariosto.   Shaking your elbow at the Tavle-boord.

Romelio.   And resorting to your whore in hir'd velvet, with a spangled
copper fringe at her netherlands.

Ariosto.   Whereas if you had staid at Padua, and fed upon Cow trotters,
and fresh beefe to Supper—

Julio [aside].   How I am bayted!   180

Ariosto [to Romelio].   Nay, be not you so forward with him neither, for tis
thought, youle prove a maine part of his undoing.

Julio [aside].   I thinke this fellow is a witch.

Romelio.   Who I sir?

Ariosto.   You have certaine rich citie Chuffes, that when they have no
acres of their owne, they will goe and plow up fooles, and turne them
into excellent meadow; besides some Inclosures for the first Cherries
in the Spring, and Apricocks to pleasure a friend at Court with. You
have Potecaries deal in selling commodities to yong Gallants, will put
foure or five coxcombs into a sieve, and so drumme with them upon   190
their Counter; theyle searse them through like Ginny Pepper, they   [D1ʳ]
cannot endure to finde a man like a payre of Tarriers, they would
undoe him in a trice.

Romelio.   May be there are such.

Ariosto.   O terrible exactors, fellowes with six hands, and three heads.

Julio.   I those are Hell-hounds.

Ariosto [to Julio].   Take heed of them, theyle rent thee like Tenter-
hookes. *[to Romelio]* Hearke in your eare, there is intelligence upon
you; the report goes, there has been gold conveyd beyond the Sea in
hollow Ancres. Farewell, you shall know mee better, I will doe thee   200
more good, then thou art aware of.   *Exit Ariosto.*

Julio.   Hee's a mad fellow.

Sanitonella.   He would have made an excellent Barber, he does so curry
it with his tongue.   *Exit.*

Crispiano.   Sir, I was directed to you.

Romelio.   From whence?

Crispiano.   From the East Indies.

Romelio.   You are very welcome.

Crispiano.   Please you walke apart, I shall acquaint you with particulars
touching your Trading i'th East Indies.   210

179 Supper—] ~. Q
180 SD] This ed.; *not in* Q
181 SD] This ed.; *not in* Q
183 SD] Lucas; *not in* Q

197 SD] This ed.; *not in* Q
198 SD] This ed.; *not in* Q
201 SD] *placed as* Lucas; *to right of line 202* Q

Romelio.   Willingly, pray walke sir.   *Exeunt Crispiano [and] Romelio.*
                          Enter ERCOLE.
Ercole.   Oh my right worthy friends, you have staid me long,
        One health, and then aboord; for all the Gallies
        Are come about.
                          Enter CONTARINO.
Contarino.   Signior *Ercole,*
        The wind has stood my friend sir, to prevent
        Your putting to Sea.
Ercole.   Pray why sir?
Contarino.   Onely love sir,
        That I might take my leave sir, and withall   220
        Intreat from you a private recommends
        To a friend in Malta, 'twould be delivered
        To your bosome, for I had no time to write.
Ercole.   Pray leave us Gentlemen.   *Exeunt [Julio and Baptista].*
                          Wilt please you sit?   *They sit downe.*
Contarino.   Sir, my love to you has proclaim'd you one,
        Whose word was still led by a noble thought,   [D1ᵛ]
        And that thought followed by as faire a deed:
        Deceive not that opinion, we were Students
        At Padua together, and have long
        To'th worlds eye shewen like friends,   230
        Was it hartie on your part to me?
Ercole.   Unfained.
Contarino.   You are false
        To the good thought I held of you, and now
        Joyne the worst part of man to you, your malice,
        To uphold that falsehood, sacred innocence
        Is fled your bosome. Signior, I must tell you,
        To draw the picture of unkindnesse truely,
        Is to expresse two that have dearly loved,
        And falne at variance; tis a wonder to me,
        Knowing my interest in the fayre *Jolenta,*   240
        That you should love her.
Ercole.   Compare her beauty, and my youth together,
        And you will find the faire effects of love
        No myracle at all.

211 SD] *Ex.Cris.Rom.* Q   224 SD] *as* Lucas; *Exeunt.* Q

Contarino.   Yes, it will prove prodigious to you.
    I must stay your Voyage.
Ercole.   Your Warrant must be mightie.
Contarino.   'Tas a Seale from heaven
    To doe it, since you would ravish from me
    What's there entitled mine: and yet I vow,   250
    By the essential front of spotlesse Vertue,
    I have compassion of both our youths:
    To approve which, I have not tane the way,
    Like an Italian, to cut your throat
    By practise, that had given you now for dead,
    And never frownd upon you.
Ercole.   You deale faire, sir.
Contarino.   Quit me of one doubt, pray sir.
Ercole.   Move it.
Contarino.   Tis this,
    Whether her Brother were a maine Instrument   260
    In her designe for Marriage.
Ercole.   If I tell truth, you will not credit me.   [D2ʳ]
Contarino.   Why?
Ercole.   I will tell you truth,
    Yet shew some reason you have not to beleeve me:
    Her Brother had no hand in't, ist not hard
    For you to credit this: for you may thinke,
    I count it basenesse to ingage another
    Into my quarrell; and for that take leave
    To dissemble the truth. Sir, if you will fight   270
    With any but my selfe, fight with her Mother,
    Shee was the motive.
Contarino [*rising*].   I have no enemy in the world then, but your selfe;
    You must fight with me.
Ercole [*rising*].   I will sir.
Contarino.   And instantly.
Ercole.   I will haste before you, poynt whither.
Contarino.   Why you speake nobly, and for this faire dealing,
    Were the rich Jewell which we vary for,
    A thing to be divided, by my life,   280

---

256 faire,] ~ Q   **275** SD] This ed.; *not in* Q
273 SD] This ed.; *not in* Q

I would be well content to give you halfe:
But since tis vaine to thinke we can be friends,
Tis needfull one of us be tane away,
From being the others enemy.
Ercole.   Yet me thinks, this looks not like a quarrell.
Contarino.   Not a quarrell?
Ercole.   You have not apparelled your fury well,
It goes too plaine like a Scholler.
Contarino.   It is an ornament makes it more terrible,
And you shall finde it   290
A weightie injury, and attended on
By discreet valour; because I doe not strike you,
Or give you the lye, such foule preparatives
Would show like the stale injury of Wine.
I reserve my rage to sit on my swords poynt,
Which a great quantitie of your best blood
Cannot satisfie.
Ercole.   You promise well to your selfe.
Shall's have no Seconds?
Contarino.   None, for feare of prevention.   300
Ercole.   The length of our weapons?   [D2ᵛ]
Contarino.   Weele fit them by the way:
So whether our time calls us to live or dye,
Let us doe both like noble Gentlemen,
And true Italians.
Ercole.   For that let me embrace you. [*Embraces Contarino.*]
Contarino.   Me thinks, being an Italian, I trust you
To come somewhat too neere me: but your Jelousie
Gave that embrace to trie if I were armed,
Did it not?   310
Ercole.   No, beleeve me,
I take your heart to be sufficient proofe,
Without a privie coat; and for my part,
A Taffaty is all the shirt of Mayle
I am armed with.
Contarino.   You deale equally.   *Exeunt.*
              Enter JULIO, [BAPTISTA,] *and Servant.*

301 weapons?] ~. Q   311 No,] ~ₐ Q
306 you.] ~: Q   SD] Shirley; *not in* Q
310 not?] ~. Q   316.1 BAPTISTA,] This ed.; *not in* Q

Julio.   Where are these Gallants, the brave *Ercole*, and noble *Contarino*?

Servant.   They are newly gone sir, and bade me tell you, that they will returne within this halfe houre.

Enter ROMELIO.

Julio.   Met you the Lord *Ercole*?   320

Romelio.   No, but I met the devill in villanous tydings.

Julio.   Why, what's the matter?

Romelio.   Oh I am powr'd out like water, the greatest Rivers i'th world are lost in the Sea, and so am I: pray leave me. Where's Lord *Ercole*?

Julio.   You were scarse gone hence, but in came *Contarino*.

Romelio.   *Contarino*?

Julio.   And intreated some private conference with *Ercole*, and on the sudden they have giv'ns the slip.

Romelio.   One mischiefe never comes alone: they are gone to fight.

Julio.   To fight?   330

Romelio.   And you be Gentlemen, doe not talke, but make haste after them.

Julio.   Let's take severall wayes then, and if't be possible for womens   [D3ʳ]
sakes, for they are proper men, use our endeavours, that the pricke doe not spoyle them.   *Exeunt.*

[II.ii]

Enter ERCOLE, CONTARINO.

Contarino.   Youle not forgoe your interest in my Mistris?

Ercole.   My sword shall answer that; come, are you ready?

Contarino.   Before you fight sir, thinke upon your cause,
   It is a wondrous foule one, and I wish,
   That all your exercise these foure dayes past,
   Had been imploy'd in a most fervent prayer,
   And the foule sinne for which you are to fight
   Chiefly remembred in't.

Ercole.   Ide as soone take
   Your counsell in Divinitie at this present,
   As I would take a kind direction from you   10
   For the managing my weapon; and indeed,

319.1 SD] *placed as Dyce 1; to right of line 319*   **II.ii**] *as Dyce 1; not in* Q
  Q

Both would shew much alike.
Come, are you ready?
Contarino. Bethinke your selfe,
How faire the object is that we contend for.
Ercole. Oh, I cannot forget it. *They fight. [Contarino wounds Ercole.]*
Contarino. You are hurt.
Ercole. Did you come hither only to tell me so,
Or to doe it? I meane well, but 'twill not thrive.
Contarino. Your cause, your cause sir:
Will you yet be a man of Conscience, and make   20
Restitution for your rage upon your death-bed?
Ercole. Never, till the grave gather one of us.
                    Fight. [Contarino wounds Ercole again.]
Contarino. That was faire, and home I thinke.
Ercole. You prate as if you were in a Fence-schoole.
Contarino. Spare your youth, have compassion on your selfe.
Ercole. When I am all in pieces. I am now unfit
For any Ladies bed; take the rest with you.
  [Ercole makes a final thrust.] Contarino wounded, fals upon Ercole.
Contarino. I am lost in too much daring: yeeld your sword.
Ercole. To the pangs of death I shall, but not to thee.
Contarino. You are now at my repayring, or confusion: 30
Begge your life.   [D3ᵛ]
Ercole. Oh most foolishly demaunded,
To bid me beg that which thou canst not give.
  Enter ROMELIO, PROSPERO, BAPTISTA, ARIOSTO, JULIO *[and Servants].*
Prospero. See both of them are lost; we come too late.
Romelio. Take up the body, and convey it
To Saint *Sebastians* Monastery.
Contarino. I will not part with his sword, I have won't.
Julio. You shall not:
Take him up gently: so, and bow his body,
For feare of bleeding inward.   40
Well, these are perfect lovers.
Prospero.   Why, I pray?
Julio. It has been ever my opinion,

13 Come,] ~ ₐ Q
15 *Contarino . . . Ercole.*] *after Gunby 1972; not in* Q
22.1 *Contarino . . . again.*] *after Lucas (Wounds Ercole. to right of line 23); not in* Q
26 pieces.] ~, Q
27.1 *Ercole . . . thrust.*] This ed.; *not in* Q
33.1 SD] This ed.; *Enter Romelio, Prosp. Bapt.Ario.Iulio.* Q

That there are none love perfectly indeed,
But those that hang or drowne themselves for love:
Now these have chose a death next to Beheading,
They have cut one anothers throats, brave valiant Lads.
Prospero.   Come, you doe ill, to set the name of valour
Upon a violent and mad despaire.
Hence may all learne, that count such actions well,
The roots of fury shoot themselves to hell.   *Exeunt.*   50

[II.iii]

Enter ROMELIO, ARIOSTO.

Ariosto.   Your losses I confesse, are infinite, yet sir, you must have patience.
Romelio.   Sir, my losses I know, but you I doe not.
Ariosto.   Tis most true, I am but a stranger to you, but am wisht by some of your best friends, to visit you, and out of my experience in the world, to instruct you patience.
Romelio.   Of what profession are you?
Ariosto.   Sir, I am a Lawyer.
Romelio.   Of all men living, you Lawyers I account the onely men to confirme patience in us, your delayes would make three parts of this   10
little Christian world run out of their wits else. Now I remember, you read Lectures to *Julio*, are you such a Leech for patience?   [D4ʳ]
Ariosto.   Yes sir, I have had some crosses.
Romelio.   You are married then I am certaine.
Ariosto.   That I am sir.
Romelio.   And have you studied patience?
Ariosto.   You shall find I have.
Romelio.   Did you ever see your wife make you Cuckold?
Ariosto.   Make me Cuckold?
Romelio.   I aske it seriously, and you have not seene that, your patience   20
has not tane the right degree of wearing Scarlet; I should rather take you for a Batchelor in the Art, then for a Doctor.
Ariosto.   You are merry.
Romelio.   No sir, with leave of your patience, I am horrible angry.
Ariosto.   What should moove you put forth that harsh Interrogatory, if these eyes ever saw my wife doe the thing you wot of?

II.iii] *as Dyce 1; not in* Q   **26** of?] of. Q
25 you‸] you? Q

Romelio. Why Ile tell you, most radically to try your patience, and the meere question shewes you but a Dunse in't. It has made you angry; there's another Lawyers beard in your forehead, you doe brissle.

Ariosto. You are very conceited: But come, this is not the right way to   30
cure you. I must talke to you like a Divine.

Romelio. I have heard some talk of it very much, and many times to their Auditors impatience; but I pray, what practise doe they make of't in their lives? They are too full of choller with living honest, and some of them not onely impatient of their owne sleightest injuries, but starke mad, at one anothers preferment: now to you sir, I have lost three goodly Carracks.

Ariosto. So I heare.

Romelio. The very Spice in them, had they been shipwrackt heere upon our coast, would have made all our Sea a Drench.   40

Ariosto. All the sicke horses in Italy would have been glad of your losse then.

Romelio. You are conceited too.   [D4ᵛ]

Ariosto. Come, come, come, you gave those ships most strange, most dreadfull, and unfortunate names, I never lookt they'd prosper.

Romelio. Is there any ill Omen in giving names to ships?

Ariosto. Did you not call one, *The Stormes Defiance*; another, *The Scourge of the Sea*; and the third, *The Great Leviathan*?

Romelio. Very right sir.

Ariosto. Very devillish names all three of them: and surely I thinke, they   50
were curst in their very cradles, I doe meane, when they were upon their Stockes.

Romelio. Come, you are superstitious, Ile give you my opinion, and tis serious: I am perswaded there came not Cuckolds enow to the first Launching of them, and 'twas that made them thrive the worse for't. Oh your Cuckolds hansell is praid for i'th Citie.

Ariosto. I will heare no more, give me thy hand, my intent of comming hither, was to perswade you to patience; as I live, if ever I doe visit you agen, it shall be to intreat you to be angry, sure I will, Ile be as good as my word, beleeve it.   60

Romelio. So sir: *Exit* [*Ariosto*].

[*Handbells and voice heard.*] *Enter* LEONORA.

How now? Are the Scritch-owles abroad already?

---

48 *Great*] great Q
61 SD] *to right of line 60 (Exit.)* Q
61.1 *Handbells and voice heard.*] This ed.; *not in*

Q; *Sound of a bell ringing repeatedly* Weis
Enter LEONORA.] *placed as* Shirley; *after* How
now? Q

Leonora.   What a dismall noyse yon bell makes, sure some great person's
   dead.
Romelio.   No such matter, it is the common Bell-man goes about, to
   publish the sale of goods.
Leonora.   Why doe they ring before my gate thus? Let them into'th
   Court, I cannot understand what they say.

                Enter two Belmen and a CAPUCHIN.

Capuchin.   For pities sake, you that have teares to shed,
   Sigh a soft Requiem, and let fall a Bead,   70
   For two unfortunate Nobles, whose sad fate
   Leaves them both dead, and excommunicate:
   No Churchmans prayer to comfort their last groanes,
   No sacred sodd of earth to hide their bones;   [E1ʳ]
   But as their fury wrought them out of breath,
   The Canon speakes them guiltie of their owne death.
Leonora.   What Noble men I pray sir?
Capuchin.   The Lord *Ercole,* and the noble *Contarino,*
   Both of them slaine in single combat.
Leonora.   O, I am lost for ever.   80
Romelio.   Denide Christian buriall, I pray what does that,
   Or the lazy dead march in the Funerall,
   Or the flattery in the Epitaphs, which shewes
   More sluttish farre then all the Spiders webs
   Shall ever grow upon it: what doe these
   Adde to our well being after death?
Capuchin.   Not a scruple.
Romelio.   Very well then;
   I have a certaine Meditation,
   If I can thinke of't, somewhat to this purpose,   90
   Ile say it to you, while my mother there
   Numbers her Beades.
      You that dwell neere these graves and vaults,
      Which oft doe hide Physicions faults,
      Note what a small Roome does suffice,
      To expresse mens good, their vanities
      Would fill more volume in small hand,
      Then all the Evidence of Church-land.
      Funerals hide men in civill wearing,

74 sodd] *as* Dyce 2 (sod); seed Q   90 of't,] Dyce 1; of‸ Q
82 lazy dead] This ed. (*conj.* Lucas); dead lazy   93-124] *only line 93 indented* Q
   Q   96 vanities‸] ~, Q

And are to the Drapers a good hearing, 100
Make the Heraulds laugh in their blacke rayment,
And all die Worthies die worth payment
To the Altar Offerings, tho their fame,
And all the charitie of their name,
'Tweene heaven and this yeeld no more light,
Then rotten trees, which shine i'th night.
Oh looke the last Act be the best i'th Play,
And then rest gentle bones, yet pray,
That when by the precise you are vewed,
A Supersedeas be not sued, 110
To remoove you to a place more ayrie,
That in your stead they may keepe chary [E1ᵛ]
Stockfish, or Seacole, for the abuses
Of sacriledge have turn'd graves to vilder uses.
How then can any Monument say,
Here rest these bones, till the last day,
When time swift both of foot and feather,
May beare them the Sexton kens not whither.
What care I then, tho my last sleepe,
Be in the Desart, or in the deepe, 120
No Lampe, nor Taper, day and night,
To give my Charnell chargeable light:
I have there like quantitie of ground,
And at the last day I shall be found.
 Now I pray leave me.
Capuchin. I am sorry for your losses.
Romelio. Um sir, the more spatious that the Tennis court is,
 The more large is the Hazard.
 I dare the spitefull Fortune doe her worst,
 I can now feare nothing. 130
Capuchin. Oh sir, yet consider,
 He that is without feare, is without hope,
 And sins from presumption; better thoughts attend you.
       Exit Capuchin [*with Bellmen*].
Romelio. Poore *Jolenta*, should she heare of this!
 Shee would not after the report keepe fresh,
 So long as flowers in graves.

---

102 payment∧] ~. Q   136.1 *with the Will*] This ed.; *not in* Q
133.1 SD] *as* Dyce 1; *Exit.Ca. at line 134* Q

Enter PROSPERO [*with the Will*].

How now *Prospero*.

Prospero.   *Contarino* has sent you here his Will,
Wherein a has made your sister his sole heire.

Romelio.   Is he not dead?   140

Prospero.   Hee's yet living.

Romelio.   Living? The worse lucke.

Leonora.   The worse? I doe protest it is the best,
That ever came to disturbe my prayers.

Romelio.   How?

Leonora.   Yet I would have him live
To satisfie publique Justice for the death
Of *Ercole*: [*to Prospero*] oh goe visit him for heavens sake.
I have within my Closet a choyce Relicke,
Preservative 'gainst swounding, and some earth,   150
Brought from the Holy Land, right soveraigne   [E2ʳ]
To staunch bloud: has he skilfull Surgeons, thinke you?

Prospero.   The best in Naples!

Romelio.   How oft has he been drest?

Prospero.   But once.

Leonora.   I have some skill this way:
The second or third dressing will shew clearely,
Whether there be hope of life: I pray be neere him,
If there be any soule can bring me word,
That there is hope of life.   160

Romelio.   Doe you prise his life so?

Leonora.   That he may live,
I meane, to come to his tryall, to satisfie the Law.

Romelio.   Oh, ist nothing else?

Leonora.   I shall be the happiest woman.   *Exeunt Leonora* [*and*] *Prospero.*

Romelio.   Here is cruelty appareled in kindnesse.
I am ful of thoughts, strange ones, but they'r no good ones.
I must visit *Contarino*, upon that
Depends an Engine shall weigh up my losses,
Were they sunke as low as hell; yet let me thinke,   170
How I am impayred in an houre, and the cause of't,
Lost in securitie: oh how this wicked world bewitches,

143 worse?] ~: Q   165 SD] *Exeunt Le.Pro.* Q
148 SD] This ed.; *not in* Q   167 strange] sträge Q
162 live,] ~; Q   171 an] Dyce 2; a Q

Especially made insolent with riches:
So Sayles with fore-winds stretcht, doe soonest breake,
And Piramides ath top, are still most weake.   *Exit.*

[II.iv]

Enter CAPUCHIN, ERCOLE *led betweene two.*

Capuchin.   Looke up sir, you are preserved beyond naturall reason; you
were brought dead out a'th field, the Surgeons ready to have
embalmed you.

Ercole.   I do looke on my action with a thought of terror;
To doe ill and dwell in't, is unmanly.

Capuchin.   You are divinely informed sir.

Ercole.   I fought for one, in whom I have no more right,
Then false executors have in Orphans goods,
They cozen them of; yet tho my cause were naught,
I rather chose the hazard of my soule,   10
Then foregoe the complement of a chollerick man.
I pray continue the report of my death, and give out,   [E2^v]
Cause the Church denyed me Christian buriall,
The Viceadmirall of my Gallies tooke my body,
With purpose to commit it to the earth,
Either in Cicil, or Malta.

Capuchin.   What ayme you at by this rumour of your death?

Ercole.   There is hope of life
In *Contarino*; and he has my prayers,
That he may live to enjoy what is his owne,   20
The faire *Jolenta*; where, should it be thought
That I were breathing, happily her friends
Would oppose it still.

Capuchin.   But if you be supposed dead,
The Law will strictly prosecute his life
For your murder.

Ercole.   That's prevented thus,
There does belong a noble Priviledge
To all his Family, ever since his father
Bore from the worthy Emperour *Charles* the fift,

II.iv] *as Dyce 1; not in* Q   **4** terror;] ~, Q
1 reason;] ~, Q   **28** father$_\wedge$] ~, Q

An answere to the French Kings challenge, at such time   30
The two noble Princes were ingag'd to fight,
Upon a frontier arme o'th sea in a flat-bottom'd Boat,
That if any of his Family should chance
To kill a man i'th Field, in a noble cause,
He should have his Pardon; now sir, for his cause,
The world may judge if it were not honest.
Pray helpe me in speech, tis very painfull to me.
Capuchin.   Sir I shall.
Ercole.   The guilt of this lyes in *Romelio,*
And as I heare, to second this good Contract,   40
He has got a Nun with child.
Capuchin.   These are crimes that either must make worke
For speedy repentance, or for the Devill.
Ercole.   I have much compassion on him,
For sinne and shame are ever tyde together,
With Gordion knots, of such a strong threed spun,
They cannot without violence be undone.   *Exeunt.*
          Explicit Actus secundus.

ACTUS TERTIUS, SCENA PRIMA. [III.i]   [E3ʳ]

Enter ARIOSTO, CRISPIANO [*disguised as a merchant*].
Ariosto.   Well sir, now I must claime your promise,
To reveale to me the cause why you live thus clouded.
Crispiano.   Sir, the King of Spaine
Suspects, that your *Romelio* here, the Merchant
Has discover'd some Gold-myne to his owne use,
In the West Indies, and for that employes me,
To discover in what part of Christendome
He vents this Treasure: Besides, he is informed
What mad tricks has bin plaid of late by Ladies.
Ariosto.   Most true, and I am glad the King has heard on't: 10
Why they use their Lords, as if they were their Wards;
And as your Dutchwomen in the Low-Countries,
Take all and pay all, and doe keepe their Husbands
So silly all their lives of their owne estates,

31 fight,] ~. Q   **0.1** *disguised as a Merchant*] This ed.; *not in* Q
47.1 *secundus.*] *secundi.* Q

That when they are sicke, and come to make their Will,
They know not precisely what to give away
From their wives, because they know not what they are worth:
So heare should I repeat what factions,
What Bat-fowling for Offices,
As you must conceive their Game is all i'th night,   20
What calling in question one anothers honesties
Withall what sway they beare i'th Viceroyes Court,
You'd wonder at it:
Twill doe well shortly, can we keepe them off
From being of our Councell of Warre.
Crispiano.   Well, I have vowed,
That I will never sit upon the Bench more,
Unlesse it be to curbe the insolencies
Of these women.
Ariosto.   Well, take it on my word then,   30
Your place will not long be emptie.   *Exeunt.*

[III.ii]

Enter ROMELIO *in the habit of a Jew.*
Romelio.   Excellently well habited, why me thinks,
That I could play with mine owne shaddow now,
And be a rare Italienated Jew;   [E3ᵛ]
To have as many severall change of faces,
As I have seene carv'd upon one Cherrystone;
To winde about a man like rotten Ivie,
Eate into him like Quicksilver, poyson a friend
With pulling but a loose haire from's beard, or give a drench,
He should linger of't nine yeares, and nere complaine,
But in the Spring and Fall, and so the cause   10
Imputed to the disease naturall; for sleight villanies,
As to coyne money, corrupt Ladies Honours,
Betray a Towne to'th Turke, or make a Bonefire
A'th Christian Navy, I could settle too't,
As if I had eate a Politician,

III.ii] *as* Dyce 1; *not in* Q   **8** With] with Q   from's] frō's Q   drench]
5 *one*] Dyce 1; *on* Q   drēch Q

And disgested him to nothing but pure blood.
But stay, I loose my selfe, this is the house.
Within there!

Enter two Surgeons.

1 Surgeon.	Now sir.
Romelio.	You are the men of Art, that as I heare,		20
	Have the Lord *Contarino* under cure.
2 Surgeon.	Yes sir, we are his Surgeons,
	But he is past all Cure.
Romelio.			Why, is he dead?
1 Surgeon.	He is speechlesse sir, and we doe find his wound
	So fester'd neere the vitals, all our Art
	By warme drinks, cannot cleare th'impostumation,
	And hee's so weake, to make incision
	By the Orifix were present death to him.
Romelio.	He has made a Will I heare.
1 Surgeon.	Yes sir.		30
Romelio.	And deputed *Jolenta* his heyre.
2 Surgeon.	He has, we are witnesse too't.
Romelio.	Has not *Romelio* been with you yet,
	To give you thanks, and ample recompence
	For the paines you have tane?
1 Surgeon.	Not yet.
Romelio.	Listen to me Gentlemen, for I protest,
	If you will seriously mind your owne good,
	I am come about a businesse shall convey
	Large legacies from *Contarino's* Will		40
	To both of you.
2 Surgeon.	How sir? Why *Romelio* has the Will and in that he has given	[E4ʳ]
	us nothing.
Romelio.	I pray attend me: I am a Phisician.
2 Surgeon.	A Phisician? Where doe you practise?
Romelio.	In Rome.
1 Surgeon.	O then you have store of Patients.
Romelio.	Store? Why looke you, I can kill my 20. a month
	And worke but i'th forenoones: you will give me leave
	To jest and be merry with you; but as I said,		50

18 there!] ~. Q		42 *Romelio*] *Rom.* Q	Will] wil Q	and] &
27 incision] Dyce 1; *not in* Q			Q
35 tane?] ~. Q

113

All my study has been Phisicke. I am sent
From a noble Roman that is neere a kinne
To *Contarino*, and that ought indeed,
By the Law of Alliance, be his onely heyre,
To practise his good and yours.
Both. How, I pray sir?
Romelio. I can by an Extraction which I have,
Tho he were speechlesse, his eyes set in's head,
His pulses without motion, restore to him
For halfe an houres space, the use of sense,   60
And perhaps a little speech: having done this,
If we can worke him, as no doubt we shall,
To make another Will, and therein assigne
This Gentleman his Heyre, I will assure you,
Fore I depart this house, ten thousand Duckets,
And then weele pull the pillow from his head,
And let him eene goe whither the Religion sends him
That he died in.
1 Surgeon. Will you give's ten thousand Duckets?
Romelio. Upon my Jewisme.   70
2 Surgeon. Tis a bargaine sir, we are yours:
CONTARINO *in a bed.*
Here is the Subject you must worke on.
Romelio. Well said, you are honest men,
And goe to the businesse roundly: but Gentlemen,
I must use my Art singly.
1 Surgeon. Oh sir, you shall have all privacy.
Romelio. And the doores lockt to me.
2 Surgeon. At your best pleasure. [*aside*] Yet for all this, I will not
trust this Jew.
1 Surgeon [*aside*]. Faith, to say truth, I doe not like him neither, he looks   [E4ᵛ]
like a rogue. This is a fine toy, fetch a man to life, to make a new Will,   81
there's some tricke in't. Ile be neere you Jew.   *Exeunt Surgeons.*
Romelio. Excellent, as I would wish: these credulous fooles
Have given me freely what I would have bought
With a great deale of money. —Softly, her's breath yet;
Now *Ercole*, for part of the Revenge,
Which I have vow'd for thy untimely death:

51 Phisicke.] ~, Q
71.1 SD] *to right of line 70* Q
76 privacy.] priuacy, Q

78 SD] Lucas; *not in* Q
80 SD] Lucas; *not in* Q
83 Excellent,] ~ₐ Q

114

Besides this politique working of my owne,
That scornes President. Why, should this great man live,
And not enjoy my sister, as I have vowed   90
He never shall, oh, he may alter's Will
Every New Moone if he please; to prevent which,
I must put in a strong Caveat. Come forth then
My desperate Steeletto, that may be worne
In a womans haire, and nere discover'd,
And either would be taken for a Bodkin,
Or a curling yron at most; why tis an engine,
That's onely fit to put in execution
Barmotho Pigs, a most unmanly weapon,
That steales into a mans life he knowes not how: 100
O that great *Cæsar*, he that past the shocke
Of so many armed Pikes, and poyson'd Darts,
Swords, Slings, and Battleaxes, should at length
Sitting at ease on a cushion, come to dye
By such a Shoo-makers aule as this, his soule let forth
At a hole, no bigger then the incision
Made for a wheale: uds foot, I am horribly angry,
That he should dye so scurvily: yet wherefore
Doe I condemne thee thereof so cruelly,
Yet shake him by the hand? Tis to expresse,   110
That I would never have such weapons used,
But in a plot like this, that's treacherous:
Yet this shall proove most mercifull to thee,
For it shall preserve thee
From dying on a publique Scaffold, and withall
Bring thee an absolute Cure, thus.   *Stabs him.*   [F1ʳ]
So, tis done: and now for my escape.
                    Enter Surgeons.
1 *Surgeon.*   You Rogue Mountebanke, I will try whether your inwards
     can indure to be washt in scalding lead.
Romelio.   Hold, I turne Christian.   120
2 *Surgeon.*   Nay prethee bee a Jew still; I would not have a Christian be
     guiltie of such a villanous act as this is.
Romelio.   I am *Romelio* the Marchant.

---

88 Besides‸] ~, Q   101 O that] Dyce 1; O Q
89 President. Why,] ~, ~‸ Q   109 cruelly,] ~? Q
91 shall,] ~? Q   alter's] Dyce 1; alters Q 110 hand?] ~, Q
     Will] will Q

1 Surgeon. *Romelio!* You have prooved your selfe a cunning Marchant indeed.

Romelio. You may reade why I came hither.

2 Surgeon. Yes, in a bloudy Roman Letter.

Romelio. I did hate this man, each minute of his breath
    Was torture to me.

1 Surgeon. Had you forborne this act, he had not liv'd this two houres. 130

Romelio. But he had died then,
    And my revenge unsatisfied: here's gold;
    Never did wealthy man purchase the silence
    Of a terrible scolding wife at a dearer rate
    Then I will pay for yours: here's your earnest
    In a bag of double Duckets.   *[Gives money.]*

2 Surgeon. Why looke you sir, as I do weigh this busines, this cannot be counted murder in you by no meanes. Why tis no more, then should I goe and choke an Irish man, that were three quarters drownd, with powring Usquebath in's throat. 140

Romelio. You will be secret?

1 Surgeon. As your soule.

Romelio. The West Indies shall sooner want gold, then you then.

2 Surgeon. That protestation has the musick of the Mint in't.

Romelio [aside]. How unfortunatly was I surpriz'd!
    I have made my selfe a slave perpetually
    To these two beggars.   *Exit.*

1 Surgeon. Excellent; by this act he has made his estate ours.

2 Surgeon. Ile presently grow a lazy Surgeon, and ride on my foot-cloth; Ile fetch from him every eight dayes a policy for a hundred 150 double Duckets; if hee grumble, Ile peach.

1 Surgeon. But let's take heed he doe not poyson us. [F1ᵛ]

2 Surgeon. Oh, I will never eate nor drinke with him, without Unicornes Horne in a hollow tooth.

Contarino. Oh!

1 Surgeon. Did he not groane?

2 Surgeon. Is the wind in that doore still?

1 Surgeon. Ha! Come hither, note a strange accident: his Steele has lighted in the former wound, and made free passage for the congealed blood; observe in what abundance it delivers the putrifaction. 160

2 *Surgeon.*   Me thinks he fetches his breath very lively.

1 *Surgeon.*   The hand of heaven is in't, that his entent to kill him should become the very direct way to save his life.

2 *Surgeon.*   Why this is like one I have heard of in England, was cured a'th Gowt, by being rackt i'th Tower. Well, if we can recover him, here's reward on both sides: howsoever, we must be secret.

1 *Surgeon.*   We are tyde too't; when we cure Gentlemen of foule diseases, they give us so much for the cure, and twice as much, that we doe not blab on't. Come, lets to worke roundly, heat the Lotion, and bring the Searing.   *Exeunt.*   170

[III.iii]

A Table set forth with two Tapers, a Deaths head, a
Booke, JOLENTA *in mourning* [*sits*], ROMELIO *sits by her.*

Romelio.   Why do you grieve thus? Take a Looking-glasse,
        And see if this sorrow become you; that pale face
        Will make men thinke you usde some Art before,
        Some odious painting: *Contarino's* dead.

Jolenta.   Oh that he should dye so soone!

Romelio.   Why, I pray tell me,
        Is not the shortest fever the best? And are not bad Playes
        The worse for their length?

Jolenta.   Adde not to'th ill y'ave done
        An odious slander; he stuck i'th eyes a'th Court,
        As the most choyce jewell there.

Romelio.   Oh be not angry;   10
        Indeed the Court to well composed nature
        Addes much to perfection: for it is, or should be,   [F2ʳ]
        As a bright Christall Mirrour to the world,
        To dresse it selfe; but I must tell you sister,
        If th'excellency of the place could have wroght salvation,
        The Devill had nere falne from heaven; he was proud.
        [*Jolenta rises and makes to leave.*] Leave us, leave us?
        Come, take your seat agen, I have a plot,

---

166 howsoever,] howsoeuer∧ Q

167 too't;] ~, Q

169 Come,] ~∧ Q

III.iii] *as* Dyce 1; *not in* Q

0.2 *mourning* [*sits*]] This ed.; *mourning* Q

5 soone!] ~. Q

12 is,] ~∧ Q

16 proud.] ~. Q

17 SD] *after* Lucas; *not in* Q

If you will listen to it seriously,
That goes beyond example, it shall breed 20
Out of the death of these two Noble men,
The advancement of our House.
Jolenta.   Oh take heed, a grave is a rotten foundation.
Romelio.   Nay, nay, heare me.
Tis somewhat indirectly, I confesse:
But there is much advancement in the world,
That comes in indirectly. I pray mind me:
You are already made by absolute Will,
Contarino's heyre: now, if it can be prooved,
That you have issue by Lord *Ercole,* 30
I will make you inherite his Land too.
Jolenta.   How's this?
Issue by him, he dead, and I a Virgin!
Romelio.   I knew you would wonder how it could be done,
But I have layd the case so radically,
Not all the Lawyers in Christendome,
Shall finde any the least flaw in't: I have a Mistris
Of the Order of Saint *Clare,* a beautious Nun,
Who being cloystred ere she knew the heat
Her blood would arrive to, had onely time enough 40
To repent, and idlenesse sufficient
To fall in love with mee; and to be short,
I have so much disordered the holy Order,
I have got this Nun with child.
Jolenta.   Excellent worke made for a dumbe Mid-wife!
Romelio.   I am glad you grow thus pleasant.
Now will I have you presently give out,
That you are full two moneths quickned with child
By *Ercole,* which rumour can beget
No scandall to you, since we will affirme, 50
The Precontract was so exactly done, [F2ᵛ]
By the same words usde in the forme of mariage,
That with a little Dispensation,
A money matter, it shall be registred
Absolute Matrimony.

34 knew] Dyce 2; know Q   45 Mid-wife!] ~. Q
39 heat‸] ~, Q

Jolenta.   So, then I conceave you,
    My conceaved child must prove your Bastard.
Romelio.   Right: for at such time
    My Mistris fals in labour, you must faine the like.
Jolenta.   Tis a pretty feat this, but I am not capable of it.   60
Romelio.   Not capable?
Jolenta.   No, for the thing you would have me counterfet,
    Is most essentially put in practise: nay, tis done,
    I am with child already.
Romelio.   Ha, by whom?
Jolenta.   By *Contarino.* Doe not knit the brow,
    The Precontract shall justifie it, it shall:
    Nay, I will get some singular fine Churchman,
    Or tho he be a plurall one, shall affirme,
    He coupled us together.
Romelio.   Oh misfortune!
    Your child must then be reputed *Ercoles.*   70
Jolenta.   Your hopes are dasht then, since your Votaries issue
    Must not inherit the land.
Romelio.   No matter for that,
    So I preserve her fame. I am strangely puzled:
    Why, suppose that she be brought abed before you,
    And we conceale her issue till the time
    Of your delivery, and then give out,
    That you have two at a birth; ha, wert not excellent?
Jolenta.   And what resemblance think you, would they have
    To one another? Twinnes are still alike:
    But this is not your ayme, you would have your child   80
    Inherite *Ercoles* Land,—Oh my sad soule,
    Have you not made me yet wretched ynough,
    But after all this frostie age in youth,
    Which you have witcht upon me, you will seeke
    To poyson my Fame?
Romelio.   That's done already.
Jolenta.   No sir, I did but faine it,   [F3ʳ]
    To a fatall purpose, as I thought.
Romelio.   What purpose?

56 So,] ~ₐ Q   **65** *Contarino.*] ~, Q
62 No,] ~ₐ Q   **85** Fame?] ~. Q

Jolenta.   If you had lov'd or tendred my deare honour,
        You would have lockt your ponyard in my heart,
        When I nam'd I was with child; but I must live   90
        To linger out, till the consumption
        Of my owne sorrow kill me.
Romelio [*aside*].   This will not doe; the Devill has on the sudden furnisht
    mee with a rare charme, yet a most unnaturall falshood: no matter so
    'twill take.
        Stay sister, I would utter to you a businesse,
        But I am very loath: a thing indeed,
        Nature would have compassionately conceal'd,
        Till my mothers eyes be closed.
Jolenta.   Pray what's that sir?
Romelio.   You did observe,   100
        With what a deare regard our mother tendred
        The Lord *Contarino*, yet how passionately
        Shee sought to crosse the match: why this was meerely
        To blind the eye o'th world; for she did know
        That you would marry him, and he was capable.
        My mother doated upon him, and it was plotted
        Cunningly betweene them, after you were married,
        Living all three together in one house,
        A thing I cannot whisper without horrour:
        Why, the malice scarse of Devils would suggest,   110
        Incontinence 'tweene them two.
Jolenta.   I remember since his hurt,
        Shee has bene very passionately enquiring,
        After his health.
Romelio.   Upon my soule, this Jewell,
        With a piece of the holy Crosse in't, this relicke,
        Vallewed at many thousand crownes,
        She would have sent him, lying upon his death-bed.
Jolenta.   Professing as you say,
        Love to my mother: wherefore did he make
        Me his heyre?   120
Romelio.   His Will was made afore he went to fight,   [F3ᵛ]
        When he was first a Suitor to you.
Jolenta.   To fight: oh well membred,

93 SD] Dyce 2; *not in* Q   105 capable.] ~ˌ Q

    If he lov'd my mother, wherefore did he loose
    His life in my quarrell?
Romelio.   For the affront sake, a word you understand not,
    Because *Ercole* was pretended Rivall to him,
    To cleare your suspition; I was gulld in't too:
    Should he not have fought upon't,
    He had undergone the censure of a Coward.   130
Jolenta.   How came you by this wretched knowledge?
Romelio.   His Surgeon over-heard it,
    As he did sigh it out to his Confessor,
    Some halfe houre fore hee died.
Jolenta.   I would have the Surgeon hang'd
    For abusing Confession, and for making me
    So wretched by'th report. Can this be truth?
Romelio.   No, but direct falshood,
    As ever was banisht the Court: did you ever heare
    Of a mother that has kept her daughters husband   140
    For her owne tooth?
    He fancied you in one kind, for his lust,
    And he loved our mother in another kind, for her money,
    The Gallants fashion right. But come, nere thinke on't,
    Throw the fowle to the Devill that hatcht it, and let this
    Bury all ill that's in't, shee is our mother.
Jolenta.   I never did find any thing ith world,
    Turne my blood so much as this: here's such a conflict,
    Betweene apparant presumption, and unbeleefe,
    That I shall dye in't.   150
    Oh, if there be another world i'th Moone,
    As some fantasticks dreame, I could wish all men,
    The whole race of them, for their inconstancy,
    Sent thither to people that. Why, I protest,
    I now affect the Lord *Ercoles* memory,
    Better then the others.
Romelio.   But were *Contarino* living?
Jolenta.   I doe call any thing to witnesse,
    That the divine Law prescribed us   [F4ʳ]
    To strengthen an oath, were he living and in health,   160
    I would never mary with him.

157 living?] liuing. Q

Nay, since I have found the world
So false to me, Ile be as false to it;
I will mother this child for you.

Romelio.   Ha?

Jolenta.   Most certainly it will beguile part of my sorrow.

Romelio.   Oh most assuredly, make you smile to thinke,
How many times ith world Lordships descend
To divers men, that might, and truth were knowne,
Be heyre, for any thing belongs to'th flesh,   170
As well to the Turkes richest Eunuch.

Jolenta.   But doe you not thinke
I shall have a horrible strong breath now?

Romelio.   Why?

Jolenta.   Oh, with keeping your counsel, tis so terrible foule.

Romelio.   Come, come, come, you must leave these bitter flashes.

Jolenta.   Must I dissemble dishonestie? You have divers
Counterfeit honestie: but I hope here's none
Will take exceptions; I now must practise
The art of a great bellyed woman, and goe faine   180
Their qualmes and swoundings.

Romelio.   Eat unripe fruit, and Oatmeale,
To take away your colour.

Jolenta.   Dine in my bed
Some two houres after noone.

Romelio.   And when you are up,
Make to your petticoat a quilted preface,
To advance your belly.

Jolenta.   I have a strange conceit now.
I have knowen some women when they were with child,
Have long'd to beat their Husbands: what if I,
To keepe decorum, exercise my longing
Upon my Taylor that way, and noddle him soundly,
Heele make the larger Bill for't.   190

Romelio.   Ile get one shall be as tractable too't as Stockfish.

Jolenta.   Oh my phantasticall sorrow, cannot I now
Be miserable enough, unlesse I weare
A pyde fooles coat? Nay worse, for when our passions   [F4ᵛ]

---

169 might,] ~ₐ Q   knowne,] ~ₐ Q   **194** coat?] ~: Q
173 now?] ~. Q

Such giddy and uncertaine changes breed,
We are never well, till we are mad indeed.   *Exit.*
Romelio.   So, nothing in the world could have done this,
But to beget in her a strong distaste
Of the Lord *Contarino:* oh Jelousie,
How violent, especially in women,   200
How often has it raisd the Devil up
In forme of a Law-case! My especiall care
Must be, to nourish craftily this fiend,
Tweene the mother and the daughter, that the deceit
Be not perceived. My next taske, that my sister,
After this supposed child-birth, be perswaded
To enter into Religion: tis concluded,
Shee must never marry; so I am left guardian
To her estate: and lastly, that my two Surgeons
Be waged to the East Indies: let them prate,   210
When they are beyond the Lyne; the Callenture,
Or the Scurvy, or the Indian Pox, I hope,
Will take order for their comming backe.
Enter LEONORA.
Oh heere's my mother: I ha strange newes for you,
My sister is with child.
Leonora.   I doe looke now for some great misfortunes
To follow: for indeed mischiefes,
Are like the Visits of Franciscan Fryers,
They never come to pray upon us single.
In what estate left you *Contarino?*   220
Romelio.   Strange, that you can skip
From the former sorrow to such a question!
Ile tell you, in the absence of his Surgeon,
My charitie did that for him in a trice,
They would have done at leasure, and been paid for't.
I have killed him.
Leonora.   I am twentie yeares elder since you last opened your lips.
Romelio.   Ha?
Leonora.   You have given him the wound you speake of,
Quite thorow your mothers heart.   230
Romelio.   I will heale it presently mother: for this sorrow

201 Devil] deuil Q   **202** Law-case] law-case Q

Belongs to your errour: you would have him live,   [G1ʳ]
Because you thinke hee's father of the child;
But *Jolenta* vowes by all the rights of Truth,
Tis *Ercole's*: it makes me smile to thinke,
How cunningly my sister could be drawen
To the Contract, and yet how familiarly
To his bed. Doves never couple
Without a kind of murmur.
Leonora.   Oh, I am very sicke.
Romelio.   Your old disease,   240
    When you are griev'd, you are troubled with the Mother.
Leonora.   I am rapt with the Mother indeed,
    That I ever bore such a sonne.
Romelio.   Pray tend my sister,
    I am infinitely full of businesse.
Leonora.   Stay, you will mourne for *Contarino*?
Romelio.   Oh by all meanes, tis fit, my sister is his heire.   *Exit.*
Leonora.   I will make you chiefe mourner, beleeve it.
    Never was woe like mine: oh that my care,
    And absolute study to preserve his life,
    Should be his absolute ruine. Is he gone then?   250
    There is no plague i'th world can be compared
    To impossible desire, for they are plagued
    In the desire it selfe: never, oh never
    Shall I behold him living, in whose life
    I lived farre sweetlier then in mine owne.
    A precise curiositie has undone me;
    Why did I not make my love knowne directly?
    T'had not been beyond example, for a Matron
    To affect i'th honourable way of Marriage,
    So youthfull a person: oh I shall runne mad,   260
    For as we love our youngest children best:
    So the last fruit of our affection,
    Where ever we bestow it, is most strong,
    Most violent, most unresistable,
    Since tis indeed our latest Harvest-home,
    Last merryment fore Winter; and we widdowes,
    As men report of our best Picture-makers,

We love the piece we are in hand with better,
Then all the excellent worke we have done before,
And my sonne has depriv'd me of all this. Ha, my sonne!   270
Ile be a fury to him, like an Amazon Lady,
Ide cut off this right pap, that gave him sucke,
To shoot him dead. Ile no more tender him,
Then had a Wolfe stolne to my teat i'th night,
And robb'd me of my milke: nay, such a creature
I should love better farre. —Ha, ha, what say you?
I doe talke to somewhat, me thinks; it may be
My evill Genius. Doe not the Bells ring?
I have a strange noyse in my head: oh, fly in pieces,
Come age, and wither me into the malice   280
Of those that have been happy; let me have
One propertie more then the Devill of Hell,
Let me envy the pleasure of youth heartily,
Let me in this life feare no kinde of ill,
That have no good to hope for: let me dye
In the distraction of that worthy Princesse,
Who loathed food, and sleepe, and ceremony,
For thought of loosing that brave Gentleman,
She would faine have saved, had not a false convayance,
Exprest him stubborne-hearted. Let me sinke,   290
Where neither man, nor memory may ever find me.   *Falls downe.*
                    [*Enter* CAPUCHIN *and* ERCOLE.]
Capuchin [*to Ercole*].   This is a private way which I command,
        As her Confessor. I would not have you seene yet,
        Till I prepare her.   [*Ercole withdraws.*]
                    Peace to you Lady.
Leonora.   Ha!
Capuchin.   You are wel imployd, I hope; the best pillow i'th World
        For this your contemplation, is the earth,
        And the best object heaven.
Leonora.   I am whispering to a dead friend.
Capuchin.   And I am come   300

270 Ha, my sonne!] ~ₐ ~ ~, Q
272 this] Qb; his Qa
289 convayance,] Qb; countenance. Qa
290 Exprest him stubborne-hearted.] Qb; *not*
     in Qa

291.1 SD] Dyce 1; *not in* Q
292 SD] This ed.; *not in* Q
294 SD] Lucas; *not in* Q; ERCOLE *retires.* Dyce
     2

> To bring you tidings of a friend was dead,
> Restored to life againe.
Leonora.   Say sir.
Capuchin.   One whom I dare presume, next to your children,
> You tendred above life.
Leonora.   Heaven will not suffer me utterly to be lost.
Capuchin.   For hee should have been
> Your sonne in Law, miraculously saved,   [G2ʳ]
> When Surgery gave him ore.
Leonora.   Oh, may you live
> To winne many soules to heaven, worthy sir,   310
> That your crowne may be the greater. Why my sonne
> Made me beleeve he stole into his chamber,
> And ended that which *Ercole* began
> By a deadly stabb in's heart.
Ercole [*aside*].   Alas, shee mistakes,
> Tis *Contarino* she wishes living; but I must fasten
> On her last words, for my owne safetie.
Leonora.   Where, oh where shall I meet this comfort?
Ercole [*coming forward*].   Here in the vowed consort of your daughter.
Leonora.   Oh I am dead agen, instead of the man,   320
> You present me the grave swallowed him.
Ercole.   Collect your selfe, good Lady,
> Would you behold brave *Contarino* living?
> There cannot be a nobler Chronicle
> Of his good then my selfe: if you would view him dead,
> I will present him to you bleeding fresh,
> In my penitency.
Leonora.   Sir, you doe onely live,
> To redeeme another ill you have committed,
> That my poore innocent daughter perish not,
> By your vild sinne, whom you have got with child.   330
Ercole [*aside*].   Here begin all my compassion: oh poore soule!
> Shee is with child by *Contarino*, and he dead,
> By whom should she preserve her fame to'th world,
> But by my selfe that loved her bove the world?
> There never was a way more honourable,

---

301 was] Qb; not in Qa
302 Restored] Qb; Reserued Qa
312 Made] Dyce 1; made Q
315 SD] Dyce 2; not in Q

319 SD] Dyce 2; *not in* Q   consort] Brennan
  1975 (*conj.* Lucas); comfort Q
331 SD] Gunby 1972; *not in* Q

To exercise my vertue, then to father it,
And preserve her credit, and to marry her.
[*to Leonora*] Ile suppose her *Contarino's* widdow, bequeath'd to me
Upon his Death: for sure shee was his wife,
But that the Ceremony a'th Church was wanting.　　　　　340
Report this to her, Madam, and withall,
That never father did conceave more joy
For the birth of an heyre, then I to understand,
Shee had such confidence in me. I will not now
Presse a Visit upon her, till you have prepar'd her:
For I doe reade in your distraction,　　　　　[G2ᵛ]
Should I be brought a'th sudden to her presence,
Either the hastie fright, or else the shame
May blast the fruit within her. I will leave you,
To commend as loyall faith and service to her,　　　　　350
As ere heart harbour'd— [*aside*] by my hope of blisse,
I never liv'd to doe good act but this.
Capuchin [*aside to Ercole*].　　Withall, and you be wise,
Remember what the mother has reveal'd
Of *Romelio's* treachery.　　　　　*Exeunt Ercole, Capuchin.*
Leonora.　　A most noble fellow, in his loyaltie
I read what worthy comforts I have lost
In my deare *Contarino*, and all addes
To my dispayre.—Within there.
　　　　　　Enter WINIFRID.
　　　　　　　　Fetch the picture
Hangs in my inner closet.　　　　　*Exit Winifrid.*
　　　　　　　　I remember,　　　　　360
I let a word slip of *Romelio's* practise
At the Surgeons: no matter, I can salve it,
I have deeper vengeance that's preparing for him,
To let him live and kill him, that's revenge
I meditate upon.
　　　　　Enter WINIFRID *and the Picture.*
　　　　　So, hang it up.

338 SD] This ed.; *not in* Q; *at line 341 Gunby*
1972
351 harbour'd—] ~, Qa; ~; Qb　SD] This
ed.; *not in* Q
353 SD] *as* Dyce 2; *not in* Q　Withall,] ~ₐ Q

356 fellow,] ~ₐ Q　loyaltieₐ] ~. Q
360 SD] *placed as* Dyce 2; *to right of line 361* Q
362 matter,] ~ₐ Q
364 him,] ~ₐ Q
365 So] Dyce 1; *Leo.* So Q

[*aside*] I was enjoyned by the partie ought that picture,
Fortie yeares since, ever when I was vext,
To looke upon that: what was his meaning in't,
I know not, but me thinkes upon the sudden,
It has furnisht me with mischiefe, such a plot,   370
As never mother dreamt of. Here begines
My part i'th play: my sonnes estate is sunke,
By losse at sea, and he has nothing left,
But the Land his father left him. Tis concluded,
The Law shall undoe him. [*to Winifred*] Come hither,
I have a weightie secret to impart,
But I would have thee first confirme to mee,
How I may trust, that thou canst keepe my counsell,
Beyond death.
Winifrid.   Why Mistris, tis your onely way,
To enjoyne me first that I reveale to you   380
The worst act I ere did in all my life:
So one secret shall bind another.   [G3ʳ]
Leonora.   Thou instruct'st me
Most ingenuously, for indeed it is not fit,
Where any act is plotted, that is nought,
Any of counsell to it should be good,
And in a thousand ils have hapt i'th world,
The intelligence of one anothers shame
Have wrought farre more effectually then the tye
Of Conscience, or Religion.
Winifrid.   But thinke not, Mistris,   390
That any sinne which ever I committed,
Did concerne you, for prooving false in one thing,
You were a foole, if ever you would trust me
In the least matter of weight.
Leonora.   Thou hast lived with me
These fortie yeares; we have growne old together,
As many Ladies and their women doe,
With talking nothing, and with doing lesse:

366 SD] This ed.; *not in* Q   the partie]
  thepartie Q
369 thinkes upon] thinkesvpon Q
370 mischiefe,] ~ₐ Q
371 of.] ~ₐ Q

375 SD] This ed.; *not in* Q
382 another] Hazlitt; one another Q
383 instruct'st] Dyce 1; instru'st Q
388 shameₐ] ~, Q

We have spent our life in that which least concernes life,
Only in putting on our clothes; and now I thinke on't,
I have been a very courtly Mistris to thee,   400
I have given thee good words, but no deeds, now's the time,
To requite all; my sonne has sixe Lordships left him.
Winifrid.   Tis truth.
Leonora.   But he cannot live foure dayes to enjoy them.
Winifrid.   Have you poysoned him?
Leonora.   No, the poyson is yet but brewing.
Winifrid.   You must minister it to him with all privacie.
Leonora.   Privacie? It shall be given him
In open Court, Ile make him swallow it
Before the Judges face: if he be Master   410
Of poore ten arpines of land fortie houres longer,
Let the world repute me an honest woman.
Winifrid.   So 'twill I hope.
Leonora.   Oh thou canst not conceive
My unimitable plot; let's to my ghostly Father,
Where first I will have thee make a promise
To keepe my counsell, and then I will employ thee
In such a subtill combination,   [G3ᵛ]
Which will require to make the practise fit,
Foure Devils, five Advocates, to one womans wit.   *Exeunt.*
                    Explicit Actus Tertius.

ACTUS QUARTUS, SCENA PRIMA. [IV.i]

Enter LEONORA, SANITONELLA [*with the brief and the foul copy*]
    at one doore, [*with*] WINIFRID, *Register: at the other* ARIOSTO.
Sanitonella [*to Register*].   Take her into your Office sir, shee has that in
her belly will drie up your inke I can tell you.
                         [*Exeunt Winifrid and Register.*]
    [*to Leonora*] This is the man that is your learned Councell,

---

415 Where] Dyce 1; Were Q
419 Advocates,] Advocats∧ Qb; Advocates∧
    Qa   one] Qb; a Qa
419.1 *Actus Tertius*] Lucas; *Acti Tertij* Q
0.1 *with...copy*] This ed.; *not in* Q

0.2 [*with*] WINIFRID] Brennan 1975;
    WINIFRID Q
1 SD] Lucas; *not in* Q
2 belly∧] Belly, Q
2.1 SD] *as* Lucas; *not in* Q
3 SD] Lucas; *not in* Q

A fellow that will trowle it off with tongue:
He never goes without Restorative powder
Of the lungs of Fox in's pocket, and Malligo Reasins
To make him long winded. [*to Ariosto*] Sir, this Gentlewoman
Intreats your Counsell in an honest cause,
Which please you sir, this Briefe, my owne poore labor
Will give you light of. [*Gives him the brief.*] 10
Ariosto. Doe you call this a Briefe?
Here's as I weigh them, some fourescore sheets of paper.
What would they weigh if there were cheese wrapt in them,
Or Figdates. [*Reads the brief.*]
Sanitonella. Joy come to you, you are merry;
We call this but a Briefe in our Office.
The scope of the businesse lyes i'th Margent.
Ariosto. Me thinks you prate too much.
I never could endure an honest cause
With a long Prologue too't. 20
Leonora [*to Sanitonella*]. You trouble him.
Ariosto. Whats here? Oh strange; I have lived this 60 yeres,
Yet in all my practise never did shake hands
With a cause so odious. Sirrah, are you her knave?
Sanitonella. No sir, I am a Clarke.
Ariosto. Why you whorson fogging Rascall,
Are there not whores enow for Presentations,
Of Overseers, wrong the will o'th Dead,
Oppressions of Widdowes, or young Orphans,
Wicked Divorces, or your vicious cause [G4ʳ]
Of *Plus quam satis*, to content a woman, 31
But you must find new stratagems, new pursenets?
Oh women, as the Ballet lives to tell you,
What will you shortly come to?
Sanitonella. Your Fee is ready sir.
Ariosto. The Devill take such Fees,
And all such Suits i'th tayle of them; see, the slave
Has writ false Latine: sirrah Ignoramus,

7 SD] *This ed.; not in* Q
10 SD] *as* Dyce 2; *not in* Q
14 SD] *as* Lucas; *not in* Q
17 i'th Margent] Qb; ith Margent sheet Qa
21 SD] *This ed.; not in* Q

30 Divorces] Qb; Diuerses Qa
32 pursnets?] ~, Qb; pursuits, Qa
37 them] Qb; thee Qa see,] ~ᴧ Q
38 Ignoramus] Qb; Ignorance Qa

    Were you ever at the Universitie?
Sanitonella.   Never sir: 40
    But tis well knowne to divers I have Commenc't
    In a Pewe of our Office.
Ariosto.   Where, in a Pew of your Office?
Sanitonella.   I have been dry-foundred in't this foure yeares,
    Seldome found Non resident from my deske.
Ariosto.   Non resident Subsumner:
    Ile teare your Libell for abusing that word,
    By vertue of the Clergie.   [*Tears the brief.*]
Sanitonella.   What doe you meane sir? It cost me foure nights labour.
Ariosto.   Hadst thou been drunke so long,   50
    Th'adst done our Court better Service.
Leonora.   Sir, you doe forget your gravitie, me thinks.
Ariosto.   Cry ye mercy, doe I so?
    And as I take it, you doe very little remember
    Either womanhood, or Christianitie: why doe ye meddle
    With that seducing knave, that's good for nought,
    Unlesse't be to fill the Office full of Fleas,
    Or a Winter itch, weares that spatious Inkehorne
    All a Vacation onely to cure Tetters,
    And his Penknife to weed Cornes from the splay toes   60
    Of the right worshipfull of the Office.
Leonora.   You make bold with me sir.
Ariosto.   Woman, yare mad, Ile swear't, and have more need
    Of a Physician then a Lawyer.
    The melancholly humour flowes in your face,
    Your painting cannot hide it: such vild suits
    Disgrace our Courts, and these make honest Lawyers   [G4ᵛ]
    Stop their own eares, whilst they plead, and thats the reason
    Your yonger men that have good conscience,
    Weare such large Night-caps; go old woman, go pray,   70
    For Lunacy, or else the Devill himselfe
    Has tane possession of thee; may like cause
    In any Christian Court never find name:
    Bad Suits, and not the Law, bred the Lawes shame.   *Exit.*

41 But tis] Qb; It is Qa   54 remember₌] ~, Q
44 in't] Qb; with't Qa   57 Unlesse't be] Vnlesse 'tbe Q
48 SD] Dyce 2; *not in* Q   63 and] & Q
51 Th'adst] T'hadst Q   68 plead, and] plead₌ & Q

Leonora.   Sure the old man's franticke.

Sanitonella.   Plague on's gowtie fingers,
    Were all of his mind, to entertaine no suits,
    But such they thought were honest, sure our Lawyers
    Would not purchase halfe so fast:

                    Enter CONTILUPO *a spruce Lawyer.*

                                    But here's the man,   80
    Learned Seignior *Contilupo,* here's a fellow
    Of another piece, beleeve't; I must make shift
    With the foule Copie.   [*Approaching Contilupo.*]

Contilupo.   Businesse to me?

Sanitonella.   To you sir, from this Lady.

Contilupo.   She is welcome.

Sanitonella.   Tis a foule Copy sir, youle hardly read it,
    There's twenty double duckets, can you reade sir?

Contilupo.   Exceeding well, very, very exceeding well.

Sanitonella [*aside*].   This man will be saved, he can read; Lord, Lord, to
    see what money can doe, be the hand never so foule, somewhat will be
    pickt out on't.

Contilupo.   Is not this *Vivere honeste?*   90

Sanitonella.   No, that's strucke out sir; and where ever you find *vivere*
    honeste in these papers, give it a dash sir.

Contilupo.   I shall be mindfull of it:
    In troth you write a pretty Secretary;
    Your Secretary hand ever takes best
    In mine opinion.

Sanitonella.   Sir, I have been in France, and there beleeve't your
    Court hand generally, takes beyond thought.

Contilupo.   Even as a man is traded in't.

Sanitonella [*aside*].   That I could not think of this vertuous Gentleman   100
    before I went to'th tother Hogg-rubber. Why this was wont to give
    young Clerkes halfe fees, to helpe him to Clyents. [*to Contilupo*] Your
    opinion in the Case sir?

---

74 bred] Qb; breds Qa
79 SD] *to right of* But . . . man, Q
81 piece,] ~ˌ Q   beleeve't;] ~, Q
82 SD] *after* Weis; *not in* Q
83 welcome] welcom Q
87 SD] Dyce 2; *not in* Q

88 see] ~, Q
94 Secretary;] ~, Q
100 SD] Dyce 2; *not in* Q
102 SD] This ed.; *not in* Q
103 sir?] ~. Q

Contilupo.   I am strucke with wonder, almost extaside,   [H1ʳ]
    With this most goodly Suite.
Leonora.   It is the fruit
    Of a most heartie penitence.
Contilupo.   Tis a Case
    Shall leave a President to all the world,
    In our succeeding Annals, and deserves
    Rather a spatious publike Theater,
    Then a pent Court for Audience; it shall teach   110
    All Ladies the right path to rectifie their issue.
Sanitonella.   Loe you, here's a man of comfort.
Contilupo.   And you shall goe unto a peacefull grave,
    Discharg'd of such a guilt, as would have layne
    Howling for ever at your wounded heart,
    And rose with you to Judgement.
Sanitonella.   Oh give me such a Lawyer, as wil think of the day of
    Judgment.
Leonora.   You must urge the businesse against him
    As spightfully as may be.   120
Contilupo.   Doubt not. What, is he summon'd?
Sanitonella.   Yes, and the Court will sit within this halfe houre. Peruse
    your Notes, you have very short warning.
Contilupo.   Never feare you that:
    Follow me worthy Lady, and make account
    This Suite is ended already.   *Exeunt.*

[IV.ii]

Enter Officers preparing seats for the Judges,
to them ERCOLE *muffled.*

1 Officer.   You would have a private seat sir?
Ercole.   Yes sir.
2 Officer.   Here's a Closset belongs to'th Court, where you may heare all
    unseene.
Ercole.   I thank you; there's money.

---

104 wonder?] ~ˌ Q   122 and] & Q
110 Audience] *as* Dyce; Audence Q   IV.ii] *as* Dyce 1; *not in* Q
121 What,] ~ˌ Q   1 sir?] ~. Q

2 Officer.   I give you your thanks agen sir.   [*Ercole withdraws.*]
     Enter CONTARINO [*disguised as a Dane*], *the Surgeons disguised.*
Contarino.   Ist possible *Romelio's* perswaded,
     You are gone to the East Indies?
1 Surgeon.   Most confidently.
Contarino.   But doe you meane to goe?   10
2 Surgeon.   How? Goe to the East Indies? And so many Hollanders gone
     to fetch sauce for their pickeld Herrings; some have bene pepperd
     there too lately; but I pray, being thus well recoverd of your wounds,
     why doe you not reveale your selfe?   [H1ᵛ]
Contarino.   That my fayre *Jolenta* should be rumor'd
     To be with child by noble *Ercole,*
     Makes me expect to what a violent issue
     These passages will come. I heare her brother
     Is marying the Infant shee goes with,
     Fore it be borne, as if it be a Daughter,   20
     To the Duke of *Austrias* Nephew; if a Sonne,
     Into the Noble ancient Family
     Of the *Palavasini*: Hee's a subtill Devill.
     And I doe wonder what strange Suite in Law,
     Has hapt betweene him and's mother.
1 Surgeon.   Tis whisperd 'mong the Lawyers, 'twill undoe him for ever.
          Enter SANITONELLA [*and*] WINIFRID.
Sanitonella.   Doe you heare, Officers? You must take speciall care, that
     you let in no *Brachigraphy* men, to take notes.
1 Officer.   No sir?
Sanitonella.   By no meanes. We cannot have a Cause of any fame, but   30
     you must have scurvy pamphlets, and lewd Ballets engendred of it
     presently. [*to Winifrid*] Have you broke fast yet?
Winifrid.   Not I sir.
Sanitonella.   'Twas very ill done of you: for this cause will be long a
     pleading; but no matter, I have a modicum in my Buckram bagg, to
     stop your stomacke.

6 SD] Shirley; *not in* Q; ERCOLE *goes into the* / *closet.* Dyce 2
6.1 SD] *placed as* Dyce 1; *to right of lines 3–5* / Q   *disguised as a Dane*] *after* Lucas; *not in* Q
8 Indies?] ~. Q
13 lately;] ~, Q
23 Palavasini] This ed.; Palavafini Q;

Pallavacini *conj.* Dyce 1
26.1 SD] *Enter Sanit.Win. to right of line 26* Q
27 heare,] ~ᴧ Q
30 meanes.] ~, Q
32 SD] This ed.; *not in* Q   Have] Dyce 1; / *San.* Haue Q
35 no] Dyce 1; not Q

134

Winifrid.   What ist? Greene ginger?

Sanitonella.   Greene ginger, nor Pellitory of Spaine neither, yet 'twill
    stop a hollow tooth better then either of them.

Winifrid.   Pray what ist?   40

Sanitonella.   Looke you, it is a very lovely Pudding-pye, which we
    Clerkes find great reliefe in.

Winifrid.   I shall have no stomacke.

Sanitonella.   No matter and you have not, I may pleasure some of our
    Learned Councell with't; I have done it many a time and often, when
    a Cause has prooved like an after-game at Irish.

> Enter CRISPIANO *like a Judge, with another Judge;*   [H2ʳ]
> CONTILUPO, *and another Lawyer at one Barre;* ROMELIO,
> ARIOSTO, *at another;* LEONORA *with a blacke vaile over*
> *her, and* JULIO.

Crispiano.   Tis a strange Suite: is *Leonora* come?

Contilupo.   She's here my Lord; make way there for the Lady.

Crispiano.   Take off her Vaile: it seemes she is ashamed
    To looke her cause i'th face.

Contilupo.   Shee's sicke, my Lord.   50

Ariosto.   Shee's mad my Lord, and would be kept more dark.
    [*to Romelio*] By your favour sir, I have now occasion to be at your
    elbow, and within this halfe houre shall intreat you to bee angry, very
    angry.

Crispiano.   Is *Romelio* come?

Romelio.   I am here my Lord, and call'd, I doe protest,
    To answer what I know not, for as yet
    I am wholly ignorant, of what the Court
    Will charge me with.

Crispiano.   I assure you, the proceeding
    Is most unequall then, for I perceive,   60
    The Councell of the adverse partie furnisht
    With full Instruction.

Romelio.   Pray my Lord, who is my accuser?

Crispiano.   Tis your mother.

Romelio [*aside*].   Shee has discovered *Contarino's* murder:
    If shee proove so unnaturall, to call

46.1 *another Judge;*] ~ ~, Q   **51** and] & Q
46.2 *Barre;*] ~, Q   **52** SD] *as* Dyce 2; *not in* Q
46.3 *another,* ~, Q   **56** call'd,] ~ₐ Q
47 Suite:] ~, Q   come?] ~. Q   **65** SD] Dyce 2; *not in* Q

My life in question, I am arm'd to suffer
This to end all my losses.

Crispiano.   Sir, we will doe you this favour,
You shall heare the Accusation,   70
Which being knowne, we will adjourne the Court,
Till a fortnight hence; you may provide your Counsell.

Ariosto.   I advise you, take their proffer,
Or else the Lunacy runnes in a blood,
You are more mad then shee.

Romelio.   What are you sir?

Ariosto.   An angry fellow that would doe thee good,
For goodnesse sake it selfe, I doe protest,
Neither for love nor money.

Romelio.   Prethee stand further, I shal gall your gowt else.

Ariosto.   Come, come, I know you for an East Indy Marchant,   [H2ᵛ]
You have a spice of pride in you still.   81

Romelio [to Crispiano].   My Lord, I am so strengthned in my innocence,
For any the least shaddow of a crime,
Committed gainst my mother, or the world,
That shee can charge me with, here doe I make it
My humble suite, onely this houre and place,
May give it as full hearing, and as free,
And unrestrain'd a Sentence.

Crispiano.   Be not too confident, you have cause to feare.

Romelio.   Let feare dwell with Earth-quakes,   90
Shipwracks at Sea, or Prodegies in heaven,
I cannot set my selfe so many fathome
Beneath the haight of my true heart, as feare.

Ariosto.   Very fine words I assure you, if they were
To any purpose.

Crispiano [to Romelio].   Well, have your intreatie:
And if your owne credulitie undoe you,
Blame not the Court hereafter: [to Contilupo] fall to your Plea.

Contilupo.   May it please your Lordship and the reverend Court,
To give me leave to open to you a Case
So rare, so altogether voyd of President,   100
That I doe challenge all the spacious Volumes,

72 hence;] ~, Q
82 SD] This ed.; *not in* Q
95 SD] This ed.; *not in* Q

97 SD] Brennan 1975; *not in* Q
98 Lordship and] Lordsh.& Q

Of the whole Civill Law to shew the like.
We are of Councell for this Gentlewoman,
We have receiv'd our Fee, yet the whole course
Of what we are to speake, is quite against her,
Yet weele deserve our fee too. There stands one,
Romelio the Marchant; I will name him to you,
Without either title or addition:
For those false beames of his supposed honour,
As voyd of true heat, as are all painted fires,   110
Or Glow-wormes in the darke, suite him all basely,
As if he had bought his Gentry from the Herauld,
With money got by extortion: I will first
Produce this *Æsops* Crow, as he stands forfeit
For the long use of his gay borrowed plumes,
And then let him hop naked: I come to'th poynt,
T'as been a Dreame in Naples, very neere
This eight and thirtie yeares, that this *Romelio*,   [H3ʳ]
Was nobly descended; he has rankt himselfe
With the Nobilitie, shamefully usurpt   120
Their place, and in a kind of sawcy pride,
Which like to Mushromes, ever grow most ranke,
When they do spring from dung-hills, sought to oresway,
The *Fieski*, the *Grimaldi*, *Dorii*,
And all the ancient pillars of our State;
View now what he is come to: this poore thing
Without a name, this Cuckow hatcht ith nest
Of a Hedge-sparrow.
Romelio.   Speakes he all this to me?
Ariosto.   Onely to you sir.   130
Romelio.   I doe not aske thee, prethee hold thy prating.
Ariosto.   Why very good, you will be presently
      As angry as I could wish.
Contilupo.   What title shall I set to this base coyne?
      He has no name, and for's aspect he seemes
      A Gyant in a May-game, that within

114 forfeit‸] ~, Q
119 descended;] ~, Q
124 *Fieski*] This ed.; Fliski Q; *Fieschi* Lucas
   (*conj.* Dyce 1)   *Dorii*] Dyce 2; *Dori* Q;
   Doria Lucas

134 coyne?] ~, Q
135 seemes‸] ~, Q

Is nothing but a Porter: Ile undertake,
He had as good have traveld all his life
With Gypsies: I will sell him to any man
For an hundred Chickeens, and he that buyes him of me, 140
Shall loose byth hand too.

Ariosto.   Loe, what you are come too:
You that did scorne to trade in any thing,
But Gold or Spices, or your Cochineele,
He rates you now at poore John.

Romelio.   Out upon thee,
I would thou wert of his side—

Ariosto.   Would you so?

Romelio.   The devill and thee together on each hand,
To prompt the Lawyers memory when he founders.

Crispiano.   Signior *Contilupo*, the Court holds it fit,
You leave this stale declaiming 'gainst the person,
And come to the matter.

Contilupo.   Now I shall my Lord. 150

Crispiano.   It showes a poore malicious eloquence,
And it is strange, men of your gravitie
Will not forgoe it: verely, I presume,   [H3ᵛ]
If you but heard your selfe speaking with my eares,
Your phrase would be more modest.

Contilupo.   Good my Lord, be assured,
I will leave all circumstance, and come toth purpose:
This *Romelio* is a Bastard.

Romelio.   How, a Bastard?
Oh mother, now the day begins grow hote 160
On your side.

Contilupo.   Why shee is your accuser.

Romelio.   I had forgot that; was my father maried
To any other woman, at the time
Of my begetting?

Contilupo.   That's not the businesse.

Romelio.   I turne me then to you that were my mother,
But by what name I am to call you now,
You must instruct me: were you ever marryed
To my father?

145 side—] ~, Q

Leonora.   To my shame I speake it, never.

Crispiano.   Not to *Francisco Romelio?*

Leonora.   May it please your Lordships,   170
    To him I was, but he was not his father.

Contilupo.   Good my Lord, give us leave in a few words,
    To expound the Riddle, and to make it plaine,
    Without the least of scruple: for I take it,
    There cannot be more lawfull proofe i'th world,
    Then the oath of the mother.

Crispiano.   Well then, to your proofes, and be not tedious.

Contilupo.   Ile conclude in a word:
    Some nine and thirtie yeares since, which was the time,
    This woman was maryed, *Francisco Romelio,*   180
    This Gentlemans putative father, and her husband,
    Being not married to her past a fortnight,
    Would needs goe travell; did so, and continued
    In *France* and the *Low-Countries* eleven monthes:
    Take speciall note o'th time, I beseech your Lordship,
    For it makes much to'th businesse: in his absence
    He left behind to sojourne at his house
    A Spanish Gentleman, a fine spruce youth
    By the Ladies confession, and you may be sure
    He was no Eunuch neither; he was one   [H4ᵛ]
    Romelio loved very dearely, as oft haps,   191
    No man alive more welcome to the husband
    Then he that makes him Cuckold.
    This Gentleman I say,
    Breaking all Lawes of Hospitalitie,
    Got his friends wife with child, a full two moneths
    Fore the husband returned.

Sanitonella [aside to Contilupo].   Good sir, forget not the Lambskin.

Contilupo [aside to Sanitonella].   I warrant thee.

Sanitonella [aside to Contilupo].   I wil pinch by the buttock, to put you in   200
    mind of't.

Contilupo [aside to Sanitonella].   Prethee hold thy prating.
    [*aloud*] What's to be practis'd now my Lord? Marry this,
    Romelio being a yong novice, not acquainted

---

169 *Francisco*] Dyce 1; *Franscisco* Q   **198, 199, 200, 202** SDs] *after* Lucas; *not in* Q
181 husband,] ₍ₐ₎Q   **203** SD] This ed.; *not in* Q

With this precedence, very innocently
Returning home from travell, finds his wife
Growne an excellent good Huswife, for she had set
Her women to spin Flax, and to that use,
Had in a study which was built of stone,
Stor'd up at least an hundreth waight of flaxe: 210
Marry such a threed as was to be spun from the flax,
I thinke the like was never heard of.

Crispiano.   What was that?

Contilupo.   You may be certaine, shee would lose no time,
In braging that her Husband had got up
Her belly: to be short, at seven moneths end,
Which was the time of her delivery,
And when shee felt her selfe to fall in travell,
Shee makes her Wayting woman, as by mischance,
Set fire to the flax, the fright whereof,   220
As they pretend, causes this Gentlewoman
To fall in paine, and be delivered
Eight weekes afore her reckoning.

Sanitonella [aside to Contilupo].   Now sir, remember the Lambeskin.

Contilupo.   The Midwife strait howles out, there was no hope
Of th'infants life, swaddles it in a flead Lambeskin,
As a Bird hatcht too early, makes it up
With three quarters of a face, that made it looke
Like a Changeling, cries out to *Romelio*,   [H4ᵛ]
To have it Christned, least it should depart   230
Without that it came for: and thus are many serv'd,
That take care to get Gossips for those children,
To which they might be Godfathers themselves,
And yet be no arch-Puritans neither.

Crispiano.   No more.

Ariosto.   Pray my Lord give him way, you spoile his oratory else: thus
would they jest were they fee'd to open their sisters cases.

Crispiano.   You have urged enough;
You first affirme, her husband was away
From her eleven moneths?

Contilupo.   Yes my Lord.

---

220 fright] Dyce 1; flight Q   **236** fee'dₐ] feed, Q
224 SD] *after* Lucas; *not in* Q   **239** moneths?] ~. Q

Crispiano. And at seven moneths end,					240
    After his returne shee was delivered
    Of this *Romelio*, and had gone her full time?
Contilupo.   True my Lord.
Crispiano.   So by this account this Gentleman was begot,
    In his supposed fathers absence.
Contilupo.   You have it fully.
Crispiano.   A most strange Suite this, tis beyond example,
    Either time past, or present, for a woman,
    To publish her owne dishonour voluntarily,
    Without being called in question, some fortie yeares		250
    After the sinne committed, and her Councell
    To inlarge the offence with as much Oratory,
    As ever I did heare them in my life
    Defend a guiltie woman; tis most strange:
    Or why with such a poysoned violence
    Should shee labour her sonnes undoing: we observe
    Obedience of creatures to the Law of Nature
    Is the stay of the whole world; here that Law is broke,
    For though our Civill Law makes difference
    Tween the base, and the ligitimate; compassionat Nature	260
    Makes them equall, nay, shee many times preferres them.
    [*to Romelio*] I pray resolve me sir, have not you and your mother
    Had some Suite in Law together lately?
Romelio.   None my Lord.
Crispiano.   No? No contention about parting your goods?
Romelio. Not any.								[11ʳ]
Crispiano.   No flaw, no unkindnesse?
Romelio.   None that ever arrived at my knowledge.
Crispiano.   Bethink your selfe, this cannot chuse but savour
    Of a womans malice deeply; and I feare,				270
    Y'are practiz'd upon most devillishly.
    [*to Leonora*] How hapt Gentlewoman, you reveal'd this no sooner?
Leonora.   While my husband lived, my Lord, I durst not.
Crispiano.   I should rather aske you, why you reveale it now?
Leonora.   Because my Lord, I loath'd that such a sinne
    Should lie smotherd with me in my grave; my penitence,

242 time?] ~. Q
253 life‸] ~, Q
256 sonnes] *as* Dyce 1 (son's); soones Q
257 Nature‸] ~, Q
262 SD] This ed.; *not in* Q
272 SD] This ed.; *not in* Q

Though to my shame, preferres the revealing of it
Bove worldly reputation.

Crispiano.   Your penitence?
Might not your penitence have beene as hartie,
Though it had never summon'd to the Court   280
Such a conflux of people?

Leonora.   Indeed I might have confest it,
Privately toth Church, I grant; but you know repentance
Is nothing without satisfaction.

Crispiano.   Satisfaction? Why your Husbands dead,
What satisfaction can you make him?

Leonora.   The greatest satisfaction in the world, my Lord,
To restore the land toth right heire, and thats my daughter.

Crispiano.   Oh shee's straight begot then?

Ariosto.   Very well, may it please this honourable Court, if he be a   290
bastard, and must forfeit his land for't, she has prooved her selfe a
strumpet, and must loose her Dower; let them goe a begging together.

Sanitonella.   Who shall pay us our Fees then?

Crispiano.   Most just.

Ariosto.   You may see now what an old house you are like to pull over
your head, Dame.

Romelio.   Could I conceive this Publication
Grew from a heartie penitence, I could beare
My undoing the more patiently; but my Lord,
There is no reason, as you sayd even now,   300
To satisfie me but this suite of hers
Springs from a devillish malice, and her pretence,
Of a grieved Conscience, and Religion,
Like to the horrid Powder-Treason in England,   [I1ᵛ]
Has a most bloody unnaturall revenge
Hid under it: Oh the violencies of women!
Why they are creatures made up and compounded
Of all monsters, poysoned Myneralls,
And sorcerous Herbes that growes.

Ariosto.   Are you angry yet?   310

Romelio.   Would man expresse a bad one,

---

281 people?] ~. Q
288 and] & Q
289 then?] ~. Q
292 Dower;] ~, Q

301 me‸] ~: Q
309 growes] Q; grow Dyce 1
311 man] Dyce 1; men Q

Let him forsake all naturall example,
And compare one to another; they have no more mercy,
Then ruinous fires in great tempests.

Ariosto.   Take heed you doe not cracke your voice sir.

Romelio.   Hard hearted creatures, good for nothing else,
But to winde dead bodies.

Ariosto.   Yes, to weave seaming lace with the bones of their Husbands
that were long since buried, and curse them when they tangle.

Romelio.   Yet why doe I   320
Take Bastardy so distastfully, when i'th world,
A many things that are essentiall parts
Of greatnesse, are but by-slips, and are father'd
On the wrong parties,
Preferment in the world a many times,
Basely begotten? Nay, I have observ'd
The immaculate Justice of a poore mans cause,
In such a Court as this, has not knowen whom
To call Father, which way to direct it selfe
For Compassion: but I forget my temper,   330
Onely that I may stop that Lawyers throat,
I doe beseech the Court, and the whole world,
They will not thinke the baselyer of me,
For the vice of a mother: for that womans sinne,
To which you all dare sweare when it was done,
I would not give my consent.

Crispiano.   Stay, heere's an Accusation,
But here's no proofe; [*to Contilupo*] what was the Spanyards name
You accuse of adultery?

Contilupo.   *Don Crispiano*, my Lord.   340

Crispiano.   What part of Spaine was he borne in?

Contilupo.   In Castile.

Julio [*aside*].   This may prove my father.

Sanitonella [*aside*].   And my Master, my Clyent's spoyl'd then.   [I2ʳ]

Crispiano.   I knew that Spanyard well: if you be a Bastard,
Such a man being your father, I dare vouch you
A Gentleman; and in that Signiour *Contilupo*,
Your Oratory went a little too farre.

---

324 parties,] ~. Q   **342** SD] Lucas; *not in* Q
326 begotten?] ~: Q   **343** SD] Lucas; *not in* Q
338 SD] This ed.; *not in* Q

When doe wee name *Don John* of *Austria*,
The Emperours sonne, but with reverence?
And I have knowne in divers Families,   350
The Bastards the greater spirits; but to'th purpose,
What time was this Gentleman begot?
And be sure you lay your time right.

Ariosto.   Now the mettall comes to the Touchstone.

Contilupo.   In *Anno* seventie one, my Lord.

Crispiano.   Very well, seventie one: the Battell of *Lepanto* was fought in't, a most remarkeable time, 'twill lye for no mans pleasure: And what proofe is there more then the affirmation of the Mother, of this corporall dealing?

Contilupo.   The deposition of a Wayting-woman served her the same   360
time.

Crispiano.   Where is shee?

Contilupo.   Where is our Solicitor with the Waiting-woman?

Ariosto.   Roome for the bagge and baggage.

Sanitonella.   Here my Lord, *Ore tenus*.

Crispiano.   And what can you say Gentlewoman?

Winifrid.   Please your Lordship, I was the partie that dealt in the businesse, and brought them together.

Crispiano.   Well.

Winifrid.   And conveyed letters betweene them.   370

Crispiano.   What needed letters, when tis said he lodg'd in her house?

Winifrid.   A running Ballad now and then to her Violl, for he was never well, but when he was fidling.

Crispiano.   Speake to the purpose; did you ever know them bed together?

Winifrid.   No my Lord, but I have brought him to the bed side.

Crispiano.   That was somewhat neere to the busines; and what, did you helpe him off with his shooes?

Winifrid.   He wore no shooes, an't please you my Lord.

Crispiano.   No? What then, Pumpes?   380

Winifrid.   Neither.

Crispiano.   Boots were not fit for his journey.   [I2ᵛ]

Winifrid.   He wore Tennis-court woollen slippers, for feare of creaking sir, and making a noyse, to wake the rest o'th house.

---

349 reverence?] ~: Q   374 purpose;] ~, Q
363 Waiting-woman] Waitingwoman Q

Crispiano.   Well, and what did he there, in his Tennis-court woollen
    slippers?

Winifrid.   Please your Lordship, question me in Latin, for the cause is
    very foule; the Examiner o'th Court was faine to get it out of me alone
    i'th Counting-house, cause he would not spoyle the youth o'th Office.

Ariosto.   Here's a Latin spoone, and a long one, to feed with the Devill.   390

Winifrid.   Ide be loth to be ignorant that way, for I hope to marry a
    Proctor, and take my pleasure abroad at the Commencements with
    him.

Ariosto.   Come closer to the businesse.

Winifrid.   I wil come as close as modesty will give me leave. Truth is,
    every morning when hee lay with her, I made a Caudle for him, by the
    appoyntment of my Mistris, which he would still refuse, and call for
    small drinke.

Crispiano.   Small drinke?

Ariosto.   For a Julipe.   400

Winifrid.   And said he was wondrous thirstie.

Crispiano.   What's this to the purpose?

Winifrid.   Most effectuall, my Lord; I have heard them laugh together
    extreamely, and the Curtaine rods fall from the tester of the bed, and
    he nere came from her, but hee thrust money in my hand; and once in
    truth, he would have had some dealing with mee, which I tooke he
    thought 'twould be the onely way ith world to make me keepe coun-
    sell the better.

Sanitonella [aside to Winifrid].   That's a stinger, tis a good wench, be not
    daunted.   410

Crispiano.   Did you ever find the print of two in the bed?

Winifrid.   What a questions that to be askt; may it please your Lordship
    tis to be thought he lay nearer to her then so.

Crispiano.   What age are you of, Gentlewoman?

Winifrid.   About six and fortie, my Lord.

Crispiano.   *Anno* seventie one, and *Romelio* is thirty eight: by that   [13ʳ]
    reckoning, you were a Bawd at eight yeare old: now verily, you fell
    to the Trade betimes.

Sanitonella [aside].   There ya're from the Byas.

Winifrid.   I doe not know my age directly; sure I am elder, I can remember   420

392 and] & Q   **412** askt;] ~, Q   Lordship] Lordsh. Q
403 Lord;] ~, Q   **414** of,] ~∧ Q
406 tooke∧] ~; Q   **419** SD] Lucas; *not in* Q
409 SD] *after* Lucas; *not in* Q

145

two great frosts, and three great plagues, and the losse of Callis, and the
first comming up of the Breeches with the great Codpiece, and I pray
what age doe you take me of then?

Sanitonella [aside].   Well come off agen.

Ariosto.   An old hunted Hare, she has all her doubles.

Romelio.   For your owne gravities,
  And the reverence of the Court, I doe beseech you,
  Rip up the cause no further, but proceed to Sentence.

Crispiano.   One question more and I have done:
  Might not this *Crispiano*, this Spanyard,   430
  Lye with your Mistris at some other time,
  Either afore or after, then ith absence of her husband?

Leonora.   Never.

Crispiano.   Are you certaine of that?

Leonora.   On my soule, never.

Crispiano.   That's well, he never lay with her,
  But in *anno* seventy one, let that be remembred.
  [to Winifrid] Stand you aside a while. *[to Leonora]* Mistris, the truth is,
  I knew this *Crispiano*, lived in Naples
  At the same time, and loved the Gentleman   440
  As my bosome friend; and as I doe remember,
  The Gentleman did leave his Picture with you,
  If age or neglect have not in so long time ruin'd it.

Leonora.   I preserve it still my Lord.

Crispiano.   I pray let me see't, let me see the face
  I then loved so much to looke on.

Leonora.   Fetch it.

Winifrid.   I shall, my Lord.

Crispiano.   No, no, Gentlewoman, I have other businesse for you.
                          [*Exit an Officer for the picture.*]

1 Surgeon [aside to Contarino].   Now were the time to cut *Romelio's*   450
  throat, and accuse him for your murder.

Contarino [aside to Surgeons].   By no meanes.

2 Surgeon [aside to Contarino].   Will you not let us be men of fashion, and   [I3ᵛ]
  downe with him now hee's going?

Contarino [aside to Surgeons].   Peace, lets attend the sequell.

Crispiano.   I commend you Lady,

---

424 SD] Lucas; *not in* Q
436 well,] ~ₐ Q
438 SDs] This ed.; *not in* Q

449.1 SD] *as* Shirley; *not in* Q; *Exit one for the
  picture.* Dyce 1
450, 452, 453, 455 SDs] *after* Lucas; *not in* Q

There was a maine matter of Conscience,
How many ills spring from Adultery!
First, the supreame Law that is violated,
Nobilitie oft stain'd with Bastardy,   460
Inheritance of Land falsly possest,
The husband scorn'd, wife sham'd, and babes unblest.
                [*Enter Officer with*] *the Picture.*
So, hang it up i'th Court; you have heard,
What has been urged gainst *Romelio.*
Now my definitive sentence in this cause,
Is, I will give no sentence at all.
Ariosto.   No?
Crispiano.   No, I cannot, for I am made a partie.
Sanitonella [*aside*].   How, a party? Here are fine crosse trickes, what the
   devill will he doe now?   470
Crispiano.   Signior *Ariosto,* his Majestie of Spaine,
   Conferres my Place upon you by this Patent,
   Which till this urgent houre I have kept
   From your knowledge: [*giving Ariosto the patent*]
                may you thrive in't, noble sir,
   And doe that which but few in our place doe,
   Goe to their grave uncurst.
Ariosto [*taking Crispiano's place*].   This Law businesse
   Will leave me so small leasure to serve God,
   I shall serve the King the worse.
Sanitonella [*aside*].   Is hee a Judge? We must then looke for all   480
   Conscience, and no Law; heele begger all his followers.
Crispiano [*to Romelio*].   Sir, I am of your Counsell, for the cause in hand
   Was begun at such a time, fore you could speake;
   You had need therefore have one speake for you.
Ariosto.   Stay, I doe here first make protestation,
   I nere tooke fee of this *Romelio,*
   For being of his Councell, which may free me,
   Being now his Judge, from the imputation
   Of taking a Bribe. Now sir, speake your mind.

462.1 SD] This ed.; *to right of line 463 (The*
   Picture.) Q; *The picture is brought in.* Dyce 1
469 SD] Lucas; *not in* Q
474 SD] This ed.; *not in* Q
477 SD] Weis; *not in* Q

480 SD] Lucas; *not in* Q
481 Law;] ~, Q
482 SD] Lucas; *not in* Q
488 from] This ed.; for Q; fro' Hazlitt

Crispiano.   I do first intreat, that the eyes of all here present,   490
    May be fixt upon this.
           [*Indicates the picture and removes his disguise.*]
Leonora [*aside*].   Oh, I am confounded: this is *Crispiano.*
Julio [*aside*].   This is my father—how the Judges have bleared him.   [I4ᵛ]
Winifrid [*aside*].   You may see truth will out in spite of the Devill.
Crispiano.   Behold, I am the shadow of this shadow,
    Age has made me so; take from me fortie yeares,
    And I was such a Summer fruit as this,
    At least the Paynter fayned so: for indeed,
    Painting and Epitaphs are both alike,
    They flatter us, and say we have been thus: 500
    But I am the partie here, that stands accused,
    For Adultery with this woman, in the yeare
    Seventie one: now I call you my Lord to witnesse,
    Foure yeares before that time, I went to'th Indies,
    And till this month, did never set my foot since
    In Europe; and for any former incontinence,
    She has vowed there was never any: what remaines then,
    But this is a meere practise 'gainst her sonne,
    And I beseech the Court it may be sifted,
    And most severely punisht.   510
Sanitonella [*aside*].   Uds foot, we are spoyled; why my Clyent's prooved
an honest woman.
Winifrid [*aside to Sanitonella*].   What doe you thinke will become of me
now?
Sanitonella [*aside to Winifrid*].   You'l be made daunce *lachrimæ* I feare at a
Carts tayle.
Ariosto.   You Mistris, where are you now? Your Tennis-court slippers,
and your tane drinke in a morning for your hote liver? Where's the
man, would have had some dealing with you, that you might keepe
counsell the better?   520
Winifrid.   May it please the Court, I am but a yong thing, and was
drawne arsie, varsie into the businesse.
Ariosto.   How, young! Of five and fortie?

491.1 SD] This ed.; *not in* Q   513, 515 SDs] *after* Lucas; *not in* Q
492 SD] Lucas; *not in* Q   517 slippers] Dyce 1; slips Q
493 SD] Lucas; *not in* Q   father—] ~, Q   518 liver?] liuer; Q
  bleared] Lucas; bleated Q   520 better?] ~. Q
494 SD] Lucas; *not in* Q   523 How,] ~ₐ Q
511 SD] Lucas; *not in* Q   spoyled;] ~, Q

Winifrid. Five and fortie! And shall please you, I am not five and twentie: shee made me colour my haire with Bean-flower, to seeme elder then I was; and then my rotten teeth, with eating sweet-meats: why, should a Farrier looke in my mouth, he might mistake my age. Oh Mistris, Mistris, you are an honest woman, and you may be asham'd on't, to abuse the Court thus.

Leonora. Whatsoere I have attempted,   [I4ᵛ]
    Gainst my owne fame, or the reputation   531
    Of that Gentleman my sonne, the Lord *Contarino*
    Was cause of it.

Contarino [aside]. Who I?

Ariosto. He that should have married your daughter?
    It was a plot belike then to conferre
    The land on her that should have bin his wife.

Leonora. More then I have said already, all the world
    Shall nere extract from me; I intreat from both
    Your equall pardons.   540

Julio [to Crispiano]. And I from you sir.

Crispiano. Sirrah, stand you aside,
    I will talke with you hereafter.

Julio [aside]. I could never away with after reckonings.

Leonora. And now my Lords, I doe most voluntarily
    Confine my selfe unto a stricter prison,
    And a severer penance, then this Court can impose,
    I am entred into Religion.

Contarino [aside]. I the cause of this practise! This ungodly woman,
    Has sold her selfe to falshood: I wil now   550
    Reveale my selfe.

Ercole [revealing himself, to Ariosto]. Stay my Lord, here's a window
    To let in more light to the Court.

Contarino [aside]. Mercy upon me! Oh, that thou art living
    Is mercy indeed!

1 Surgeon [aside to Contarino]. Stay, keepe in your shell a little longer!

Ercole. I am *Ercole.*

Ariosto. A guard upon him for the death of *Contarino.*

---

524 fortie! . . . you,] ~, . . . ~! Q
534 SD] Dyce 2; *not in* Q
541 SD] This ed.; *not in* Q
544 SD] This ed.; *not in* Q
549 SD] Dyce 2; *not in* Q   practise!] ~; Q

552 SD] Lucas; *not in* Q; *coming from the closet.*
   Dyce 2
554 SD] Dyce 2; *not in* Q
556 SD] Weis; *not in* Q

Ercole.   I obey the arrest o'th Court.
Romelio.   Oh sir, you are happily restored to life,   560
And to us your friends.
Ercole.   Away, thou art the Traytor
I onely live to challenge; this former suite,
Toucht but thy fame, this accusation
Reaches to thy fame and life: the brave *Contarino*
Is generally supposed slaine by this hand.
Contarino [aside].   How knowes he the contrary?
Ercole.   But truth is,
Having received from me some certaine wounds,
Which were not mortall, this vild murderer,   570
Being by Will deputed Overseer
Of the Noblemans Estate, to his sisters use,   [K1ʳ]
That he might make him sure from surviving,
To revoke that Will, stole to him in's bed, and kild him.
Romelio.   Strange, unheard of, more practise yet!
Ariosto.   What proofe of this?
Ercole.   The report of his mother delivered to me,
In distraction for *Contarino's* death.
Contarino [aside].   For my death? I begin to apprehend,
That the violence of this womans love to me,   580
Might practise the disinheriting of her sonne.
Ariosto.   What say you to this *Leonora?*
Leonora.   Such a thing I did utter out of my distraction:
But how the Court will censure that report,
I leave to their wisdomes.
Ariosto.   My opinion is,
That this late slaunder urged against her sonne,
Takes from her all manner of credit:
Shee that would not sticke to deprive him of his living,
Will as little tender his life.
Leonora.   I beseech the Court,   590
I may retire my selfe to my place of pennance,
I have vowed my selfe and my woman.
Ariosto.   Goe when you please: [*Exeunt Leonora and Winifrid.*]
[*to Ercole*] what should move you

562 Traytor‸] ~: Q   579 SD] Dyce 2; *not in* Q
567 SD] Dyce 2; *not in* Q   593 *Exeunt . . . Winifrid.*] *as* Dyce 2; *not in* Q
573 from] Qb; *not in* Qa   *to Ercole*] Lucas; *not in* Q

150

Be thus forward in the accusation?

Ercole.   My love to *Contarino.*

Ariosto.   Oh, it bore very bitter fruit at your last meeting.

Ercole.   Tis true: but I begun to love him,
When I had most cause to hate him, when our bloods
Embrac'd each other, then I pitied,
That so much valour should be hazarded   600
On the fortune of a single Rapier,
And not spent against the Turke.

Ariosto.   Stay sir, be well advised,
There is no testimony but your owne,
[*turning to Romelio*] To approve you slew him, therefore no other way
To decide it, but by Duell.

Contarino.   Yes my Lord, I dare affirme gainst all the world,
This Noble man speakes truth.

Ariosto.   You will make your selfe a party in the Duell.

Romelio.   Let him, I wil fight with them both, sixteen of them.   610

Ercole.   Sir, I doe not know you.   [K1ᵛ]

Contarino.   Yes, but you have forgot me, you and I have sweat
In the Breach together at Malta.

Ercole.   Cry you mercy, I have knowne of your Nation
Brave Souldiers.

Julio [*aside*].   Now if my father have any true spirit in him, Ile recover his
good opinion. [*to Contarino*] Doe you heare? Doe not sweare sir, for I
dare sweare, that you will sweare a lye, a very filthy, stinking, rotten lye:
and if the Lawyers thinke not this sufficient, Ile give the lye in the
stomacke, that's somewhat deeper then the throat; both here, and all   620
France over and over, from Marselys, or Bayon, to Callis Sands, and
there draw my Sword upon thee, and new scoure it in the gravell of
thy kidneys.

Ariosto.   You the Defendant charged with the murder,
And you Second there,
Must be committed to the custody
Of the Knight-Marshall; and the Court gives charge,
They be to morrow ready in the Listes
Before the Sunne be rissen.

Romelio.   I doe entreat the Court, there be a guard   630

605 SD] *as* Lucas, *placed as* Shirley; *not in* Q   616 SD] Dyce 2; *not in* Q
610 with them] ~ thẽ Q   617 SD] Lucas; *not in* Q
612 Yes,] ~ₐ Q

151

Placed ore my Sister, that shee enter not
Into Religion: shee's rich my Lords,
And the perswasions of Fryers, to gaine
All her possessions to their Monasteries,
May doe much upon her.

Ariosto. Weele take order for her.

Crispiano. There's a Nun too you have got with child,
How will you dispose of her?

Romelio. You question me, as if I were grav'd already,
When I have quencht this wild-fire   640
In *Ercoles* tame blood, Ile tell you.   *Exit.*

Ercole. You have judged to day
A most confused practise, that takes end
In as bloody a tryall, and we may observe
By these great persons, and their indirect
Proceedings, shaddowed in a vaile of State,   [K2ʳ]
Mountaines are deformed heaps, sweld up aloft;
Vales wholsomer, though lower, and trod on oft.

Sanitonella. Well, I will put up my papers, and send them to France for
a President, that they may not say yet but, for one strange Law-suite,   650
we come somewhat neere them.   *Exeunt.*

Explicit Actus quartus.

ACTUS QUINTUS, SCENA PRIMA. [V.i]

Enter JOLENTA, *and* ANGIOLELLA *great bellied.*

Jolenta. How dost thou friend? Welcome, thou and I
Were play-fellowes together, little children,
So small awhile agoe, that I presume,
We are neither of us wise yet.

Angiolella. A most sad truth on my part.

Jolenta. Why doe you plucke your vaile over your face?

Angiolella. If you will beleeve truth,
There's nought more terrible to a guiltie heart
Then the eye of a respected friend.

Jolenta. Say friend, are you quicke with child?   10

646 State,] ~. Q
650 yet‸ but,] ~, ~‸ Q
651.1 *Actus quartus*] Lucas; *Acti quarti* Q

8 heart‸] ~, Q
9 Then] *as* Dyce 2 (Than); As Q

152

Angiolella. Too sure.

Jolenta. How could you know
 Of your first child when you quickned?

Angiolella. How could you know, friend?
 Tis reported you are in the same taking.

Jolenta. Ha, ha, ha, so tis given out:
 But *Ercoles* comming to life againe, has shrunke,
 And made invisible my great belly; yes faith,
 My being with child was meerely in supposition,
 Not practise.   20

Angiolella. You are happy,
 What would I give, to be a Mayd againe?

Jolenta. Would you, to what purpose?
 I would never give great purchase for that thing
 Is in danger every houre to be lost: pray thee laugh.
 A Boy or a Girle for a wager?

Angiolella. What heaven please.   [K2ᵛ]

Jolenta. Nay, nay, will you venter
 A chaine of Pearle with me whether?

Angiolella. Ile lay nothing,   30
 I have ventur'd too much for't already, my fame.
 I make no question sister, you have heard
 Of the intended combate.

Jolenta.   O what else?
 I have a sweet heart in't, against a brother.

Angiolella. And I a dead friend, I feare; what good counsell
 Can you minister unto me?

Jolenta. Faith onely this,
 Since there's no meanes i'th world to hinder it,
 Let thou and I, wench, get as farre as we can
 From the noyse of it.   40

Angiolella. Whither?

Jolenta. No matter, any whither.

Angiolella. Any whither, so you goe not by sea:
 I cannot abide rough water.

Jolenta. Not indure to be tumbled? Say no more then,
 Weele be land-Souldiers for that tricke: take heart,
 Thy boy shall be borne a brave Roman.

Angiolella.   O you meane to goe to Rome then.
Jolenta.   Within there.

Enter a Servant.

Beare this Letter

To the Lord *Ercole.*   [*Exit Servant.*]

Now wench, I am for thee   50

All the world over.
Angiolella.   I like your shade pursue you.   *Exeunt.*

[V.ii]

Enter PROSPERO, *and* SANITONELLA.

Prospero.   Well, I do not thinke but to see you as pretty a piece of Law-
flesh.
Sanitonella.   In time I may; marry I am resolved to take a new way for't.
You have Lawyers take their Clients fees, and their backs are no sooner
turn'd, but they call them fooles, and laugh at them.
Prospero.   That's ill done of them.
Sanitonella.   There's one thing too that has a vild abuse in't.
Prospero.   What's that?
Sanitonella.   Marry this, that no Proctor in the Terme time be tollerated
to go to the Taverne above six times i'th forenoone.   10
Prospero.   Why man?
Sanitonella.   Oh sir, it makes their Clients overtaken, and become friends   [K3ʳ]
sooner then they would be.

Enter ERCOLE *with a letter, and* CONTARINO, *comming*
in Friers habits, as having bin at the Bathanites,
a Ceremony used afore these Combates.

Ercole.   Leave the Roome, Gentlemen. [*Exeunt Prospero and Sanitonella.*]
Contarino (speaks aside).   Wherefore should I with such an obstinacy,
Conceale my selfe any longer. I am taught,
That all the blood which wil be shed to morrow,
Must fall upon my head; one question
Shall fix it or untie it: [*to Ercole*] Noble brother,
I would faine know how it is possible,   20

---

49 SD] *placed as Dyce 2; to right of line 49* Q
50 SD] This ed.; *not in* Q
V.ii] *as Dyce 1; not in* Q
3 may;] ~, Q   resolved] Qb; resolned Qa
4 and] & Q

13.1 CONTARINO,] ~ₐ Q
14 SD] *after* Dyce 1; *not in* Q
15 SD] *to right of lines 16–17 (Con.speaks*
aside.) Q
19 SD] Lucas; *not in* Q

When it appeares you love the faire *Jolenta*
With such a height of fervor, you were ready
To father anothers child, and marry her,
You would so suddenly ingage your selfe,
To kill her brother, one that ever stood,
Your loyall and firme friend?

Ercole.   Sir, Ile tell you,
My love, as I have formerly protested
To *Contarino*, whose unfortunate end,
The traytor wrought: [*showing letter*] and here is one thing more,   30
Deads all good thoughts of him, which I now receiv'd
From *Jolenta*.

Contarino.   In a Letter?

Ercole.   Yes, in this Letter:
For having sent to her to be resolved
Most truely, who was father of the child,
Shee writes backe, that the shame she goes withall,
Was begot by her brother.

Contarino.   O most incestious villaine!

Ercole.   I protest,
Before, I thought 'twas *Contarinos* Issue,   40
And for that would have vail'd her dishonour.

Contarino.   No more.
Has the Armorer brought the weapons?

Ercole.   Yes sir.

Contarino.   I will no more thinke of her.

Ercole.   Of whom?

Contarino.   Of my mother, I was thinking of my mother.   [K3ᵛ]
Call the Armorer.   *Exeunt.*

[V.iii]

Enter [2] Surgeon, and WINIFRID.

Winifrid.   You doe love me sir, you say?

2 Surgeon.   O most intirely.

---

30 SD] This ed.; *not in* Q; *He shows him a
letter (at end of speech, line 32)* Weis
33 Letter?] Qb; ~. Qa
39 villaine!] ~. Q
40 Before,] ~ₐ Q

V.iii] *as* Dyce 1; *not in* Q
0.1 2] This ed.; *not in* Q
2 *2 Surgeon.*] This ed.; *Sur.* Q (*so to end of
scene*)

Winifrid. And you will marry me?

2 Surgeon. Nay, Ile doe more then that.
    The fashion of the world is many times,
    To make a woman naught, and afterwards
    To marry her: but I a'th contrary,
    Will make you honest first, and afterwards
    Proceed to the wedlocke.

Winifrid. Honest, what meane you by that?   10

2 Surgeon. I meane, that your suborning the late Law-suite,
    Has got you a filthy report: now there's no way,
    But to doe some excellent piece of honesty,
    To recover your good name.

Winifrid. How sir?

2 Surgeon. You shall straight goe, and reveale to your old Mistris,
    For certaine truth, *Contarino* is alive.

Winifrid. How, living?

2 Surgeon. Yes, he is living.

Winifrid. No, I must not tell her of it.   20

2 Surgeon. No, why?

Winifrid. For shee did bind me yesterday by oath,
    Never more to speake of him.

2 Surgeon. You shall reveale it then to *Ariosto* the Judge.

Winifrid. By no meanes, he has heard me
    Tell so many lyes ith Court, hee'l nere beleeve mee.
    What if I told it to the *Capuchin*?

2 Surgeon. You cannot think of a better; as for your yong Mistris,
    Who as you told me, has perswaded you,
    To runne away with her: let her have her humour.   30
    I have a suite *Romelio* left i'th house,
    The habit of a Jew, that Ile put on,
    And pretending I am robb'd, by breake of day,
    Procure all Passengers to be brought backe,
    And by the way reveale my selfe, and discover
    The Commicall event. They say shee's a little mad,
    This will helpe to cure her: goe, goe presently,
    And reveale it to the *Capuchin*.   [K4ʳ]

Winifrid.   Sir, I shall.   *Exeunt.*

28 as for] Dyce 1; for as Q   **28** Mistris,] Mʳⁱˢ· Q

[V.iv]

Enter JULIO, PROSPERO, *and* SANITONELLA.

Julio.   A pox ont, I have undertaken the challenge very foolishly: what if
I doe not appeare to answer it?

Prospero.   It would be absolute conviction
Of Cowardice, and Perjury; and the Dane,
May to your publike shame, reverse your Armes,
Or have them ignominiously fastned
Under his horse tayle.

Julio.   I doe not like that so well. I see then I must fight whether I will or
no.

Prospero.   How does *Romelio* beare himselfe? They say, he has almost   10
brain'd one of our cunningst Fencers, that practisd with him.

Julio.   Very certaine; and now you talke of fencing, doe not you remember the Welsh Gentleman, that was travailing to Rome upon returne?

Prospero.   No, what of him?

Julio.   There was a strange experiment of a Fencer.

Prospero.   What was that?

Julio.   The Welshman in's play, do what the Fencer could, hung still an
arse; he could not for's life make him come on bravely: till one night at
supper, observing what a deale of Parma cheese his Scholler devoured,
a goes ingeniously the next morning, and makes a spacious button for   20
his foyle, of tosted cheese, and as sure as you live, that made him come
on the braveliest.

Prospero.   Possible!

Julio.   Marry it taught him an ill grace in's play, it made him gape still,
gape as he put in for't, as I have seene some hungry Usher.

Sanitonella.   The tosting of it belike, was to make it more supple, had he
chanc'd to have hit him a'th chaps.

Julio.   Not unlikely. Who can tell me, if we may breath in the Duell?

Prospero.   By no meanes.

Julio.   Nor drinke?   [K4ᵛ]

Prospero.   Neither.   31

Julio.   That's scurvy, anger will make me very dry.

Prospero.   You mistake sir, tis sorrow that is very dry.

V.iv] *as* Dyce 1; *not in* Q   **20** a] Lucas; *not in* Q
6 ignominiously] Dyce 1; ignomiously Q   **21** foyle,] ~∧ Q
16 *Prospero*] *Pras.* Q

Sanitonella.   Not alwayes sir, I have knowne sorrow very wet.

Julio.   In rainy weather?

Sanitonella.   No, when a woman has come dropping wet out of a
    Cuckingstoole.

Julio.   Then twas wet indeed sir.

    Enter ROMELIO *very melancholly, and the* CAPUCHIN[, *severally*].

Capuchin [*aside*].   Having from *Leonoras* Wayting-woman,
    Deliver'd a most strange Intelligence   40
    Of *Contarino's* recovery, I am come
    To sound *Romelio's* penitence; that perform'd,
    To end these errours by discovering,
    What shee related to me. [*to Romelio*] Peace to you sir.
    [*to the others*] Pray Gentlemen, let the freedome of this Roome
    Be mine a little. [*to Julio*] Nay sir, you may stay.

                          Exeunt Prospero [*and*] *Sanitonella.*

    [*to Romelio*] Will you pray with me?

Romelio.   No, no, the world and I
    Have not made up our accounts yet.

Capuchin.   Shall I pray for you?   50

Romelio.   Whether you doe or no, I care not.

Capuchin.   O you have a dangerous voyage to take.

Romelio.   No matter, I will be mine owne Pilot:
    Doe not you trouble your head with the businesse.

Capuchin.   Pray tell me, do not you meditate of death?

Romelio.   Phew, I tooke out that Lesson,
    When I once lay sicke of an Ague: I doe now
    Labour for life, for life. Sir, can you tell me,
    Whether your Tolledo, or your Millain Blade
    Be best temper'd?   60

Capuchin.   These things you know, are out of my practice.

Romelio.   But these are things you know,
    I must practice with to morrow.

Capuchin.   Were I in your case,
    I should present to my selfe strange shaddowes.

Romelio.   Turne you, were I in your case,

35 weather?] ~. Q

38.1 *severally*] This ed.; *not in* Q

39 SD] Dyce 2; *not in* Q

44 SD] *as* Dyce 1; *not in* Q   sir.] ~, Q

45 SD] This ed.; *not in* Q

46 SD] *as* Dyce 1; *not in* Q

46.1 SD] *Exeunt Pro.San.* Q

47 SD] This ed.; *not in* Q

67 owne] *as* Dyce 1 (own); one Q

I should laugh at mine owne shadow.
Who has hired you to make me Coward?

Capuchin.   I would make you a good Christian.   [L1ʳ]

   Romelio.   Withall, let me continue   70
An honest man, which I am very certaine,
A coward can never be; you take upon you
A Phisicians place, rather then a Divines.
You goe about to bring my body so low,
I should fight i'th Lists to morrow like a Dormouse,
And be made away in a slumber.

Capuchin.   Did you murder *Contarino*?

Romelio.   That's a scurvy question now.

Capuchin.   Why sir?

   Romelio.   Did you aske it as a Confessor, or as a spie?   80

Capuchin.   As one that faine would justle the devill
Out of your way.

Romelio.   Um, you are but weakly made for't:
Hee's a cunning wrastler, I can tell you, and has broke
Many a mans necke.

Capuchin.   But to give him the foyle, goes not by strength.

Romelio.   Let it goe by what it will,
Get me some good victuals to breakfast, I am hungry.

Capuchin.   Here's food for you.   *Offering him a Booke.*

Romelio.   Pew, I am not to commence Doctor: 90
For then the word, Devoure that booke, were proper.
I am to fight, to fight sir, and Ile doo't,
As I would feed, with a good stomacke.

Capuchin.   Can you feed, and apprehend death?

Romelio.   Why sir? Is not Death
A hungry companion? Say? Is not the grave
Said to be a great devourer? Get me some victuals.
I knew a man that was to loose his head,
Feed with an excellent good appetite,
To strengthen his heart, scarce halfe an houre before.   100
And if he did it, that onely was to speake,
What should I, that am to doe?

Capuchin.   This confidence,
If it be grounded upon truth, tis well.

Romelio.   You must understand, that Resolution
Should ever wayt upon a noble death,

As Captaines bring their Souldiers out o'th field,
And come off last: for, I pray, what is death? [L1ᵛ]
The safest Trench i'th world to keepe man free
From Fortunes Gunshot; to be afraid of that,
Would prove me weaker then a teeming woman, 110
That does indure a thousand times more paine
In bearing of a child.
Capuchin.   O, I tremble for you:
For I doe know you have a storme within you,
More terrible then a Sea-fight, and your soule
Being heretofore drown'd in securitie,
You know not how to live, nor how to dye:
But I have an object that shall startle you,
And make you know whither you are going.
Romelio.   I am arm'd for't.

> Enter LEONORA *with two Coffins borne by her servants, and*
> *two Winding-sheets stucke with flowers, presents one to*
> *her sonne, and the other to Julio.*

Tis very welcome, this is a decent garment 120
Will never be out of fashion. I will kisse it.
    All the Flowers of the Spring,   *Soft Musicke.*
    Meet to perfume our burying:
    These have but their growing prime,
    And man does flourish but his time.
    Survey our progresse from our birth,
    We are set, we grow, we turne to earth.
    Courts adieu, and all delights,
    All bewitching appetites;
    Sweetest Breath, and clearest eye, 130
    Like perfumes goe out and dye;
    And consequently this is done,
    As shadowes wait upon the Sunne.
    Vaine the ambition of Kings,
    Who seeke by trophies and dead things,
    To leave a living name behind,
    And weave but nets to catch the wind.
O you have wrought a myracle, and melted
A heart of Adamant, you have compris'd

107 pray,] ~ₐ Q   122 SD] *to right of line 128* Q
122–37] *not indented* Q   137 wind.] ~: Q

In this dumbe Pageant, a right excellent forme   140
    Of penitence.
Capuchin.   I am glad you so receive it.
Romelio.   This object does perswade me to forgive   [L2ʳ]
    The wrong she has don me, which I count the way
    To be forgiven yonder: and this Shrowd
    Shewes me how rankly we doe smel of earth,
    When we are in all our glory. *(to his mother)* Will it please you
    Enter that Closet, where I shall confer
    Bout matters of most waightie consequence,
    Before the Duell.   *Exit Leonora.*
Julio.   Now I am right in the Bandileere for th' gallows. What a scurvy   150
fashion tis, to hang ones coffin in a scarfe!
Capuchin.   Why this is well:
    And now that I have made you fit for death,
    And brought you even as low as is the grave,
    I will raise you up agen, speake comforts to you
    Beyond your hopes, turne this intended Duell
    To a triumph.
Romelio.   More Divinitie yet?
    Good sir, doe one thing first, there's in my Closet
    A Prayer booke that is cover'd with guilt Vellom,   160
    Fetch it, and pray you certifie my mother,
    Ile presently come to her.
                 [Exit Capuchin. Romelio] lockes him into a Closet.
              So now you are safe.
Julio.   What have you done?
Romelio.   Why, I have lockt them up
    Into a Turret of the Castle safe enough
    For troubling us this foure houres; and he please,
    He may open a Casement, and whistle out to'th Sea,
    Like a Boson, not any creature can heare him.
    Wast not thou a weary of his preaching?
Julio.   Yes, if he had had an houre-glasse by him, I would have wisht him   170
he would have joggd it a little. But your mother, your mother's lockt in
to.

---

146 SD] *to right of lines 142–3* Q   **164** Why,] ~ₐ Q
162 *Exit Capuchin. Romelio*] This ed., *after*   **165** enoughₐ] ~, Q
    Dyce 1; *not in* Q   *lockes him into a Closet.*]
    to right of line 162 (Lockes) Q

Romelio.   So much the better, I am rid of her howling at parting.

[Knocking within.]

Julio.   Harke, he knocks to be let out and he were mad.

Romelio.   Let him knocke till his Sandals flie in pieces.

[Shouting within.]

Julio.   Ha, what sayes he? *Contarino* living?

Romelio.   I, I, he meanes he would have *Contarino's* living
 Bestowed upon his Monastery, 'tis that
 He onely fishes for. So, 'tis breake of day,   [L2ᵛ]
 We shall be call'd to the combate presently.   180

Julio.   I am sory for one thing.

Romelio.   What's that?

Julio.   That I made not mine owne Ballad: I doe feare I shall be roguishly
 abused in Meeter, if I miscarry. Well, if the young *Capuchin* doe not
 talke a'th flesh as fast now to your mother, as he did to us a'th spirit; if
 he doe, tis not the first time that the prison royall has been guiltie of
 close committing.

Romelio.   Now to'th Combate.   [*Exeunt.*]

[V.v]

Enter CAPUCHIN and LEONORA above at a window.

Leonora.   *Contarino* living?

Capuchin.   Yes Madam, he is living, and *Ercoles* Second.

Leonora.   Why has he lockt us up thus?

Capuchin.   Some evill Angell
 Makes him deafe to his owne safetie, we are shut
 Into a Turret, the most desolate prison
 Of all the Castle, and his obstinacy,
 Madnesse, or secret fate, has thus prevented
 The saving of his life.

Leonora.   Oh the saving *Contarino's*!
 His is worth nothing: for heavens sake call lowder.   10

Capuchin.   To little purpose.

Leonora.   I will leape these Battlements,
 And may I be found dead in time enough,

173.1 SD] *as* Weis; *not in* Q   V.v] *as* Dyce 1; *not in* Q
175.1 SD] This ed.; *not in* Q   9 *Contarino's*!] ~, Q
188 SD] Dyce 1; *not in* Q   12 in] This ed., *conj.* Dyce 2; *not in* Q

162

    To hinder the combate.
Capuchin.   Oh looke upwards rather,
    Their deliverance must come thence. To see how heaven
    Can invert mans firmest purpose! His intent
    Of murthering *Contarino*, was a meane
    To worke his safety, and my comming hither
    To save him, is his ruine: wretches turne
    The tide of their good fortune, and being drencht
    In some presumptuous and hidden sinnes,   20
    While they aspire to doe themselves most right,
    The devil that rules ith ayre, hangs in their light.
Leonora.   Oh they must not be lost thus; some good Christian
    Come within our hearing: ope the other casement
    That looks into the citie.
Capuchin.   Madam, I shall.   *Exeunt.*

[V.vi]

             The Lists set up [by Officers].   [L3ʳ]
   Enter the Marshall, CRISPIANO, *and* ARIOSTO *as Judges, they sit.*
       [Enter also SANITONELLA, *and a Herauld.]*
Marshall.   Give the Appealant his Summons, doe the like
    To the Defendant.   *Two Tuckets by severall Trumpets.*
      Enter at one doore, ERCOLE *and* CONTARINO, *at the*
           other, ROMELIO *and* JULIO.
    Can any of you alledge ought, why the Combate
    Should not proceed?
Combatants.   Nothing.
Ariosto.   Have the Knights weighed,
    And measured their weapons?
Marshall.   They have.
Ariosto.   Proceed then to the battell, and may heaven
    Determine the right.   10
Herauld.   *Soit le Battaile, et Victory a ceux que droit.*
                  [Trumpets sound a charge.]

---

14 thence.] ~: Q   heaven∧] ~, Q   **0.1** *by Officers*] This ed.; *not in* Q
15 purpose!] ~: Q   **0.3** SD] This ed.; *not in* Q
23 Christian] christian Q   **11.1** SD] This ed.; *not in* Q
V.vi] *as* Dyce 1; *not in* Q

Romelio. Stay, I doe not well know whither I am going:
    'Twere needfull therefore, though at the last gaspe,
    To have some Church mans prayer. [*to an Officer*] Run I pray thee,
    To Castle Novo; this key will release
    A *Capuchin* and my mother, whom I shut
    Into a Turret, bid them make hast, and pray; [*Exit Officer.*]
    I may be dead ere he comes. Now, *Victory a ceux que droit.*
All the Champ.   *Victory a ceux que droit.*   [*Trumpets sound another charge.*]
          The Combate continued to a good length, when
               enters LEONORA, *and the* CAPUCHIN.
Leonora.   Hold, hold, for heavens sake hold.   20
Ariosto.   What are these that interrupt the combate?
    Away to prison with them.
Capuchin.   We have been prisoners too long:
    [*to Ercole*] Oh sir, what meane you? *Contarino's* living.
Ercole.   Living!
Capuchin.   Behold him living.
                  [*Contarino removes his disguise.*]
Ercole [*to Contarino*].   You were but now my second, now I make you
    My selfe for ever.   [*They embrace.*]
Leonora.   Oh here's one betweene,
    Claimes to be neerer.
Contarino.   And to you deare Lady,
    I have entirely vowed my life.   30
Romelio.   If I doe not dreame, I am happy to.
Ariosto.   How insolently
    Has this high Court of Honor beene abused!
      Enter ANGIOLELLA *vail'd, and* JOLENTA, *her face colour'd like*   [L3ᵛ]
    a Moore [*and vail'd*], *the two Surgeons, one of them* [*2 Surgeon*] *like a Jew.*
    How now, who are these?
2 Surgeon.   A couple of strange Fowle, and I the Falconer,
    That have sprung them. This is a white Nun,
    Of the Order of Saint *Clare*; and this a blacke one,
    Youle take my word for't.   *Discovers Jolenta.*
Ariosto.   Shee's a blacke one indeed.

14 SD] This ed.; *not in* Q
17 pray;] ~ₐ Q   SD] This ed.; *Exit an
    Attendant (after* comes *in line 18)* Dyce 2
19 ceux] Dyce 1; *ceux* Q   SD] This ed.; *not in*
    Q
24 SD] This ed.; *not in* Q

26.1 SD] *as* Shirley; *not in* Q
27 SD] This ed.; *not in* Q
28 SD] Lucas; *not in* Q
33.2 and vail'd] This ed.; *not in* Q   2 Surgeon]
    This ed.; *not in* Q
34 How] Dyce 1; *Ario.* How Q

Jolenta.   Like or dislike me, choose you whether,   40
          The Downe upon the Ravens feather
          Is as gentle and as sleeke,
          As the Mole on *Venus* cheeke.
          Hence vaine shew, I onely care,
          To preserve my Soule most faire.
          Never mind the outward skin,
          But the Jewell that's within:
          And though I want the crimson blood,
          Angels boast my Sister-hood.
          Which of us now judge you whiter,   50
          Her whose credit proves the lighter,
          Or this blacke, and Ebon hew,
          That unstain'd, keeps fresh and true:
          For I proclaim't without controle,
          There's no true beauty, but ith Soule.
Ercole.   Oh tis the faire *Jolenta*; to what purpose
          Are you thus ecclipst?
Jolenta.   Sir, I was running away
          From the rumour of this Combate: I fled likewise,
          From the untrue report my brother spread   60
          To his politike ends, that I was got with child.
Leonora.   Cease here all further scruteny, this paper
          Shall give unto the Court each circumstance,
          Of all these passages.   *[Proffers paper.]*
Ariosto.   No more: attend the Sentence of the Court.
          Rarenesse and difficultie give estimation
          To all things are i'th world: you have met both
          In these severall passages: now it does remaine,
          That these so Comicall events be blasted
          With no severitie of Sentence: You *Romelio*,   70
          Shall first deliver to that Gentleman,   [L4ʳ]
          Who stood your Second, all those Obligations,
          Wherein he stands engaged to you,
          Receiving onely the principall.
Romelio.   I shall my Lord.
Julio.   I thanke you, I have an humour now to goe to Sea against the
    Pyrats; and my onely ambition, is to have my Ship furnisht with a rare

41–55] *not indented* Q   **64** SD] This ed.; *not in* Q
41 feather‸] ~, Q

consort of Musicke; and when I am pleased to be mad, they shall play
me *Orlando*.

Sanitonella. You must lay wait for the Fidlers, theyle flye away from the 80
presse like Watermen.

Ariosto [to Romelio]. Next, you shall marry that Nun.

Romelio. Most willingly.

Angiolella. Oh sir, you have been unkind;
> But I doe onely wish, that this my shame
> May warne all honest Virgins, not to seeke
> The way to Heaven, that is so wondrous steepe,
> Thorough those vowes they are too fraile to keepe.

Ariosto. *Contarino*, and *Romelio*, and [*to Ercole*] your selfe,
> Shall for seven yeares maintaine against the Turke, 90
> Six Gallies. *Leonora, Jolenta*,
> And *Angiolella* there, the beautious Nun,
> For their vowes breach unto the Monastery,
> Shall build a Monastery. Lastly, the two Surgeons,
> For concealing *Contarino's* recovery,
> Shall exercise their Art at their owne charge,
> For a twelvemonth in the Gallies: so we leave you,
> Wishing your future life may make good use
> Of these events, since that these passages,
> Which threatned ruine, built on rotten ground, 100
> Are with successe beyond our wishes crown'd.   *Exeunt Omnes.*

FINIS.

82 SD] This ed.; *not in* Q   89 SD] This ed.; *not in* Q
85 shame∧] ~, Q   92 there,] ~∧ Q
88 Thorough] Dyce 2; Through Q

Press variants

Symbols used to identify copies are those of the revised Wing *STC*. The copies collated (all known copies to which we had access) are listed below. Line numbers for G1^v and G2^r refer to copies in the corrected state.

C	Cambridge University Library
CH1	Huntington Library 79602
CH2	Huntington Library 79601
CK	King's College, Cambridge
CN	Newberry Library, Chicago
E	Edinburgh University
EC	Eton College
EN1	National Library of Scotland Bute 602
EN2	National Library of Scotland H.28.e.2(5)
IU	University of Illinois
L1	British Library 644.f.71
L2	British Library Ashley 2206
L3	British Library 82.c.26(2)
LC	Library of Congress
LU	University of London
LVD	Victoria and Albert Museum Dyce Collection
MB	Boston Public Library
MH	Harvard University Houghton Library
NN1	New York Public Library Berg copy 1
NN2	New York Public Library Berg copy 2
NNM	Pierpont Morgan Library, New York
O	Bodleian Library Malone 199(7)
PBL	Lehigh University, Bethlehem, Pennsylvania
PET	Petworth House, Sussex (Lord Egremont)
RHT	Robert H. Taylor Collection, Princeton University Library
TCU	Texas Christian University, Fort Worth
TU	University of Texas
WCL	Chapin Library at Williams College, Williamstown
WF	Folger Shakespeare Library
WU	University of Wisconsin
XPI	Robert S. Pirie Collection (by way of Harvard microfilm)
Y1	Yale University (Robert Herring copy)
Y2	Yale University
ZWT	Alexander Turnbull Library, National Library of New Zealand, Wellington

INNER A

First state: CH1, CN, LC, NNM, TU, ZWT
Second state: C, CH2, CK, E, EC, EN1, EN2, IU, L1, L2, L3, LU, LVD, MB, MH, NN1, NN2, O, PBL, PET, RHT, TCU, WCL, WF, WU, XPI, Y1, Y2

A1ᵛ (last line) *A wayting Woman. (beginning 15 mm to left of column of names)*] *A wayting Woman (in line with rest of column)*

OUTER B

First state: CH1, NNM
Second state: all other copies

B1ʳ (20) witﬂall] withall
B4ᵛ (9) and Man-oons] & Man-toons
B4ᵛ (11) Cornecutting] Corne-cutting

OUTER C

First state: E, EC, L1, L3, LU, TU, WCL, WF, XPI, ZWT
Second state: C, CH1, CH2, CK, CN, EN1, EN2, IU, L2, LC, LVD, MB, MH, NN1, NN2, NNM, O, PBL, PET, RHT, TCU, WU, Y1, Y2

C1ʳ (15) thee] three
C3ʳ (3) Gleeke‸] ~,

OUTER G

First state: MH
Second state: all other copies

G4ᵛ (8) breds] bred

INNER G

First state: C, CH1, CK, CN, EC, LU, MH, NN1, NN2, NNM, WCL, WF, Y1
Second state: CH2, E, EN1, EN2, IU, L1, L3, LC, LVD, MB, O, PBL, PET, RHT, TCU, WU, XPI, Y2, ZWT
Mixed: L2, TU (see below)

G1ᵛ (4) his] this
G1ᵛ (21) countenance.] conuayance,
G1ᵛ (22–3) Let] Expreſt him ſtubborne-hearted. | Let
G1ᵛ (32) not] was
G1ᵛ (33) Referued] Reſtored
G1ᵛ (catchword) When] Your
G2ʳ (1) Your ſonne in Law, miraculouſly ſaued, *(printed as last line of* G1ᵛ*)*] Your ſonne in Law, miraculouſly ſaued, *(printed as first line of* G2ʳ*)*

G2r (2) When Surgery gaue him ore. | *Leon.* Oh, may you liue] When Surgery gaue him
  ore. *Leon.* Oh, may you liue (*printed as one line*)
G3v (3) Aduocates to a] Aduocats to one
G3v (26) ith Margent ſheet] i'th Margent
G4r (1) Diuerſes] Diuorces
G4r (3) purſuits] purſnets
G4r (8) thee] them
G4r (9) Ignorance] Ignoramus
G4r (12) It is] But tis
G4r (15) with't] in't

OUTER K

First state: CN, E, EC, O, PBL, TCU, WCL, WF, XPI, Y1, ZWT
Second state: C, CH1, CH2, CK, EN1, EN2, IU, L1, L3, LC, LU, LVD, MB, MH, NN1,
NN2, NNM, PET, RHT, WU, Y2
Mixed: L2, TU (see below)

K1r (2) ſure] ſure from
K2v (18) ſalt] rough
K2v (30) reſolned] reſolued
K3r (25) Letter.] ~?

Brown records one further press variant at L4r (20), where he takes Harvard (MH) to read
'*Romelto*' for the correct '*Romelio*', which appears in all other copies. We think that the
appearance of the anomalous letter results from the effects of damage, dirt, or inking on
'i'. Other apparent variants, especially in punctuation, have similar causes, which include
slight loosening of the type within the chase. It is only after close examination of a large
number of copies that these illusory press variants can be distinguished from the genuine.
Copies L2 (British Library, Ashley) and TU (Texas) are anomalous. L2 has G1v–2r, K1r,
and K2v in the second state and G3v–4r and K3r in the first; TU has G1v–2r and K2v in the
first state and G3v–4r, K1r, and K3r in the second. L2 is evidently a composite copy, with
some leaves stolen from L3 (which is therefore defective, K1r being the only variant page
that it lacks) and others from another copy. The University of Texas also has a few dis-
bound Quarto leaves, which have been checked but are too fragmentary to warrant tabu-
lation of variants. The University of Chicago copy for which Brown records relevant
details is non-existent: his collation was presumably of the Newberry Library copy.

Lineation

For the conventions used here see pp. xiii–xiv.

I.i

1–3a] *as* Dyce 1; . . . wealth; | . . . Merchant | Q

60–3] *as* Dyce 1; *prose* Q

79–80] *as* Dyce 1; *one line* Q

127] *as* Dyce 1; *two lines* . . . honesties. | Q

148–9] *as* Dyce 1; . . . your | Q

213–14] *as* Lucas; *one line* Q

I.ii

1–2] *verse* . . . worke, | Q

4] *verse* . . . you, | Q

8–9] *verse* . . . Letter | . . . commends |

10–11] *verse* . . . my | Q

14] *verse* . . . mad? | Q

15–16] *verse* . . . times | . . . commendation | Q

102–3] *as* Dyce 1; . . . Intended | Q

115–17] *as* Q (*but* Q *capitalizes* Of *at the beginning of a line*)

124–6] *verse* . . . the | . . . Contracts; | . . . ever | Q

173–81] *verse* . . . eye | . . . her | . . . abroad, | . . . Letters | . . . others | . . . Fortune-telling; | . . . life, | . . . abroad | . . . Malakatoones; | . . . marke, | . . . foot-cloth, | Q

183–5] *verse* . . . words; | . . . heard | . . . woman | Q

187–91] *verse* . . . indeed: | . . . Chaperoonesse, | . . . heard, | . . . Parke | . . . Night-walkers, | . . . been | Q

192] *verse* . . . sir, | Q

193–5] *verse* . . . way | . . . angry, | . . . woman | Q

196–200] *verse* . . . matter, | . . . now | . . . these | . . . lothe | . . . us | . . . 'tis | Q

212–13] . . . this | Q

219–20] *as* Brennan; *verse* . . . share, | Q

240–4] *verse* . . . ones, | . . . oft | . . . Love | . . . me | . . . breath'd | . . . opinion | . . . invent | Q

261–2] *verse* . . . together, | . . . fee | Q

II.i

6–7] *verse* . . . riot | Q

9–10] *verse* . . . businesse | Q

11–14] *as* Dyce 1; *ambiguously printed* . . . estate. | . . . Civill, | . . . lesse | . . . thirtie | (*last three lines unjustified but uncapitalized*) Q

15–16] *verse* . . . line, | Q

53–5] . . . sir | . . . it, | Q

117] *verse* . . . hope, | Q

119–22] *as* Dyce 1; *verse* . . . question: | . . . action, | . . . merry, | Q

137–8] *verse* . . . plagued | Q

139–40] *verse* . . . Cockesparrow | Q

152–3] *as* Dyce 1; *verse* . . . sir, | Q

154] *as* Dyce 1; *verse* . . . hand | Q

155–8] *verse* . . . you, | . . . become | . . . were | . . . growen | Q

160–2] *as* Dyce 1; *verse* . . . great | . . . officers. | . . . spent | Q

163–4] *as* Dyce 1; *verse* . . . allowance? | . . . me? | Q

166–7] *as* Dyce 1; *verse* . . . drunkard, | . . . it. | Q

169–70] *as* Dyce 1; *verse* . . . stockings, | Q

176–7] *as* Dyce 1; *verse* . . . velvet, | Q

188 and . . . with] *as* Dyce 1; *set as one line of verse* Q

195] *as* Dyce 1; *verse* . . . hands, | Q

203–4] *as* Dyce 1; *verse* . . . Barber, | Q

209–10] *verse* . . . apart, | . . . particulars | Q

212–14] *as* Dyce 1; *prose* Q

308–10] . . . me: | . . . trie | Q

317] *verse* . . . Ercole, | Q

318–19] *verse* . . . sir, | . . . returne | Q

323–4] *verse* . . . greatest | . . . Sea, | . . . me. | Q

327–8] *verse* . . . Ercole, | Q

329] *verse* . . . alone: | Q

331-2] *verse* . . . Gentlemen, | Q

333–5] *verse* . . . then, | . . . sakes, | . . . endeavours, | Q

II.ii

46] *as* Dyce 1; *two lines* . . . throats, | Q

II.iii

1–2] *verse* . . . infinite, | Q

4–6] *verse* . . . but am | . . . visit you, | . . . world, | Q

9–12] *verse* . . . living, | . . . men | . . . delayes | . . . world | . . . else. | . . . *Julio*, | Q

20–2] *verse* . . . that, | . . . degree | . . . you | Q

25–6] *verse* . . . you | . . . eyes | Q

27–9] *verse* . . . you, | . . . patience, | . . . in't. | . . . beard | Q

30–1] *verse* . . . conceited: | . . . cure you. | Q

33–7] what . . . Carracks.] *verse* . . . lives? | . . . honest, | . . . impatient | . . . mad, | . . . sir, | Q

39–40] *verse* . . . them, | . . . coast, | Q

41–2] *verse* . . . Italy | Q

44–5] *verse* . . . come, come, | . . . dreadfull, | Q

47–8] *verse* . . . *Defiance*; | . . . third, | Q

50–2] *verse* . . . names | . . . thinke, | . . . meane, | Q

53–6] *verse* . . . superstitious, | . . . serious: | . . . enow | . . . them, | . . . for't | Q

57–60] *verse* . . . more, | . . . hither, | . . . live, | . . . agen, | . . . will, | Q

61–2] *verse* . . . now? | Q

63–4] *verse* . . . makes, | Q

65–6] *verse* . . . matter, | . . . about, | Q

67–8] *verse* . . . thus? | Q

III.i

1–2] *as* Q; . . . claime | . . . cause | Dyce 1

III.ii

42–3] *verse* . . . sir? | Q; . . . Will | Dyce 1

78–9] *verse* . . . pleasure. | Q

80–2] *verse* . . . truth, | . . . rogue. | . . . life, | . . . in't. | Q

98–9] *as* Dyce 1; . . . Pigs, | Q

118–19] *verse* . . . Mountebanke, | . . . indure | Q

121–2] *verse* . . . still; | . . . guiltie | Q

124–5] *verse* . . . selfe | Q

130] *verse* . . . liv'd | Q

137–40] *verse* . . . busines, | . . . meanes. | . . . choke | . . . drownd, | Q

145–7] *as* Dyce 1; *prose* Q

153–4] *verse* . . . him, | Q

158–60] *verse* . . . accident: | . . . wound, | . . . blood; | Q

162–3] *verse* . . . in't, | . . . become | Q

164–6] *verse* . . . England, | . . . Tower. | . . . reward | Q

167–80] *verse* . . . too't; | . . . diseases, | . . . as much, | . . . roundly, | Q

III.iii

32–3] *as* Dyce 1; *one line* Q

91–2] *as* Dyce 1; . . . owne | Q

93–5] *as* Q; *verse* . . . doe; | . . . mee | . . . unnaturall | Dyce 1

116–17] *as* Shirley; *prose* Q; . . . him, | Dyce 1

141–3] . . . kind, | . . . loved | Q

176] *as* Dyce 1; *two lines* . . . come, come, | Q

181b–2a] *as* Dyce 2; *prose* Q; . . . away | Dyce 1

182b–3a] *as* Dyce 2; *one line* Q

192–4] *as* Dyce 1; . . . sorrow, | . . . enough, | . . . coat? | Q

201–3] *as* Dyce 1; *two lines* . . . Law-case! | Q

240b–1] . . . griev'd, | Q

256–9] . . . I not | . . . been | . . . Matron Q; . . . I not | . . . been | . . . affect Lucas

290–1] *as* Dyce 1; . . . stubborne-hearted. | . . . man, | Qb (Exprest him stubborne-hearted *not in* Qa)

296–7] *as* Dyce 1; . . . i'th | Q

320–1] *as* Dyce 1; *prose* Q

359b–60a] *as* Dyce 1; *one line* Q

IV.i

1–2] *as* Dyce 1; *ambiguously printed* . . . her | Belly . . . (*first line justified*) Q; . . . Belly | Hazlitt

13–14] *as* Dyce 1; . . . cheese | Q

49] *two lines* . . . sir? | Q

87–9] *verse* . . . Lord, Lord, | . . . foule, | Q

91–2] *verse* . . . sir; | . . . papers, | Q

97–8] *verse* . . . France, | . . . generally, | Q

100–3] *verse* . . . Gentleman | . . . Hogg-rubber. | . . . fees, | Q

105b–6a] *as* Dyce 1; *one line* Q

106b–7] *as* Dyce 1; *one line* Q

IV.ii

3–4] *verse* . . . Court, | Q

11 How . . . Indies?] *as* Dyce 1; *verse* Q

19–20a] *as* Dyce 1; *one line* Q

26] *verse* . . . Lawyers, | Q

27–8] *verse* . . . Officers? | . . . in | Q

30–2] *verse* . . . meanes. | . . . fame, | . . . Ballets | . . . presently. | Q

34–6] *verse* . . . you: | . . . matter, | . . . bagg, | Q

38–9] *verse* . . . neither, | Q

41–2] *verse* . . . you, | . . . Pudding-pye, | Q

44–6] *verse* . . . pleasure | . . . it | . . . Cause | Q

94–5] *as* Dyce 1; *one line* Q

144b–5a] *as* Dyce 1; *one line* Q

159–61a] *as* Dyce 1; . . . mother, | Q

162–4a] *as* Dyce 1; *prose* Q

237–8a] . . . From her | Q

290–2] *verse* . . . Court, | . . . for't, | . . . loose | Q

294–5] *verse* . . . house | Q

356] *verse* . . . one: | Q

357–9] *ambiguously printed* . . . pleasure: | And . . . of the | Mother . . . *(justified as prose)* Q

367–8] *as* Dyce 1; *verse* . . . dealt | Q

372–3] *as* Dyce 1; *verse* . . . Violl, | Q

376] *as* Dyce 1; *verse* . . . Lord, | Q

377–8] *as* Dyce 1; *verse* . . . busines; | Q

383–4] *as* Dyce 1; *verse* . . . slippers, | . . . noyse, | Q

385–6] *as* Dyce 1; *verse* . . . there, | Q

387–9] *as* Dyce 1; *verse* . . . Latin, | . . . Court | . . . Counting-house, | Q

390] *as* Dyce 1; *verse* . . . one, | Q

391–3] *as* Dyce 1; *verse* . . . way, | . . . abroad | Q

395–8] *as* Dyce 1; *verse* . . . leave. | . . . her, | . . . appoyntment | . . . refuse, | Q

403–4 Most . . . bed,] *as* Dyce 1; *verse* . . . Lord; | . . . extremely, | Q

416–18] *verse* . . . one, | . . . reckoning, | . . . verily | Q

420–1 I . . . plagues,] *as* Dyce 1; *ambiguously printed* . . . elder, | I . . . *(first line almost full, second full)* Q

421–3 and the . . . then?] *as* Dyce 1; *verse* . . . up | . . . Codpiece, | Q

449] *two lines* . . . Gentlewoman, | Q

450–1] *verse* . . . throat, | Q

453–4] *verse* . . . fashion, | Q

469–70] *verse* . . . trickes; | Q

480–1] *verse* . . . Judge? | . . . Law; | Q

511–12] *verse* . . . spoyled; | Q

517–20] *verse* . . . now? | . . . drinke | . . . man, | . . . might | Q

521–2] *as* Dyce 1; *verse* . . . thing, | Q

524–9] *as* Dyce 1; *verse* . . . you, | . . . twentie: | . . . Bean-flower, | . . . teeth, | . . . Farrier | . . . age. | . . . woman, | Q

550–1] *as* Dyce 1; *one line* Q

616–23] *verse* ... father | ... recover | ... sir, | ... a lye, | ... rotten lye: | ... sufficient, | ... stomacke, | ... throat; | ... over, | ... Sands, | ... thee, | Q

649–51] *verse* ... papers, | ... President, | ... strange | Q

V.i

6] *as* Shirley; *two lines* ... vaile | Q

21–2] ... give, | Q

V.ii

3 In ... for't] *as* Dyce 1; *verse* ... may; | Q

9 Marry this,] *as* Dyce 1; *as verse in unjustified line* Q

12–13] *as* Dyce 1; *verse* ... overtaken, | Q

39b–40] *as* Dyce 1; *one line* Q

V.iii

16–17] *as* Dyce 1; ... old | Q

V.iv

8–9] *verse* ... well. | Q

10–11] *verse* ... say, | ... Fencers, | Q

12–13] *verse* ... fencing, | ... Gentleman, | Q

17–22] *verse* ... could, | ... life | ... supper, | ... cheese | ... ingeniously | ... button | ... live, | Q

24–5] *verse* ... play, | ... for't, | Q

26–7] *verse* ... belike, | ... chanc'd | Q

28] *verse* ... me, | Q

36–7] *verse* ... wet | Q

150–1] *ambiguously printed* ... gallows. | What ... (*both lines justified*) Q; *as verse* Dyce 1

170–2] *verse* ... him, | ... little. | Q

173] *verse* ... better, | Q

183–7] *verse* ... feare | ... Meeter, | ... *Capuchin* | ... mother, | ... doe, | ... royall | Q

V.v

23–5b] *as* Dyce 1; *prose* Q

V.vi

32–3] *as* Dyce 1; ... Honor | Q

76–9] *verse* ... you, | ... Sea | ... ambition, | ... consort | ... mad, | Q

80–1] *verse* ... Fidlers, | Q

Commentary

TITLE-PAGE

8 her Majesties Servants Queen Anne's Men. This company, which had performed *WD* at the Red Bull (cf. *WD* title-page, 10n), and was probably playing at the Cockpit in Drury Lane (also known as the Phoenix) when *DLC* was first presented, was dissolved at the death of the Queen in March 1619; see p. 3.

10 *Non . . . bene* As Lucas notes, an abbreviated quotation from Seneca, *Ad Lucilium Epistolae Morales*, 77: 'Quomodo fabula, sic vita non quam diu, sed quam bene acta sit, refert.' Translated, it reads in full: '(As with a play, so with life it matters) not how long, but how good (the performance is).'

12 *A.M.* Augustine Matthewes, printer, 1619–53. See p. 59.

12 *John Grismand* Active as a bookseller and typefounder 1618–38.

DRAMATIS PERSONAE

Dramatis personae This list is based on Q, but recast to present characters in order of appearance. Additions are in square brackets. We preserve Q's incidentals of punctuation, capitalization, spelling, and use of roman and italics, except where alterations are collated. All characters listed separately have speaking roles, and among those grouped together at the end one Servant and two Officers also speak. Q names characters in the following order: Romelio, Contarino, Crispiano, Ercole, Ariosto, Prospero, Julio, A Capuchin, Contilupo, Sanitonella, Leonora, Jolenta, Winifrid. Male roles precede female, and for both there is a rough correlation between position on the list and the size of the part.

9 a Knight of Malta i.e. a member of the Knights of St John of Jerusalem. See I.ii.0.1n, and *Webster*, I, 88 and *WD* IV.iii.9n.

17 *A Capuchin* The Capuchin friars broke away from the Franciscan order *c.* 1528 to effect a renewed observance of the austerities of St Francis; cf. *WD* V.i.15–16. The robe is grey, with a large cowl (capuche). Q here has '*Capouchin*', and both spellings occur in the play. We have normalized throughout to **Capuchin**, and although the name is preceded in Q by an indefinite article here, at II.iii.67.1, and V.vi.15, and by a definite article at V.iii.27 and 38, and V.iv.38.1 and 184, we have treated it as a proper name, as we did *DM*'s Cardinal, who also has a principal role.

DEDICATION

4 SIR THOMAS FINCH (*c.* 1575–1629) was the second son of Sir Moyle Finch and grandson of Sir Thomas Heneage (d. 1595), Vice-Chamberlain of Queen Elizabeth's household. He was M.P. for Winchelsea 1621–2, and lived in Drury Lane, close to the Phoenix (or Cockpit) Theatre where the Queen's Men may have first performed *DLC* (see pp. 46–7). As Weis notes, 'W's tentative tone suggests that he and Finch had not met, but that W was hoping to enlist him as a patron.'

8 touch . . . Copy 'reach out to the ultimate source'; so Weis, who suggests an allusion to the Platonic ideal.

10 *Guise* Little is known of this play, now lost. Presumably written after *DM*, it is tentatively dated *c.* 1614–18. From late seventeenth-century play-lists we learn both that it was printed and (inconclusively) that it was a tragedy. See *Webster*, I, 11.

12–13 the greatest . . . then this Dent compares the dedication to *DM* 16–18. Gaius Julius Caesar Octavianus, named 'Augustus' (63 B.C.–A.D. 14), was the nephew of Julius Caesar, and first Emperor (27 B.C.). The Augustan age is generally regarded as the high point of Latin literature.

12 lesse 'lesser' (Weis).

15 election 'judicious selection' (*OED* 2b).

TO THE JUDITIOUS READER

2 *that of* Horace A seventeenth-century Latinism (*OED* that 8), based on construction of the type 'illud Solonis'—'that saying of Solon' (Cicero, *De Senectute*, xiv.50).

3–4 Sapientia prima . . . caruisse 'To have got rid of folly is the beginning of wisdom' (Horace, *Epistolae*, I.i.41–2).

6 Locus . . . Umbris 'There is room, too, for a number of shades [i.e. unbidden guests]' (Horace, *Epistolae*, I.v.28).

8–9 Auriculas . . . dolentes Translated in full, this abbreviated quotation from Horace reads: '[To one with fears and cravings, house and fortune give as much pleasure as painted panels to sore eyes, warm wraps to the gout, or] citherns to ears that suffer from secreted matter' (*Epistolae*, I.ii.53). (Lucas notes that strictly **Citherae** should be 'Citharae'.)

12 *in Action* In the Epilogue to *WD*, W pays tribute to the actors; see also pp. 49–50, and *Webster*, I, 98.

15 *approoved* 'tried, tested' (*OED* approve 8). Cf. *1H4* IV.i.9.

16 Non ego . . . venor 'I am not one to hunt for the votes of a fickle public' (Horace, *Epistolae*, I.xix.37). Dent notes Dekker's use of this tag in *The Magnificent Entertainment* (1604, line 64), modified with an initial 'Nunc' rather than 'Non'.

ACT I, Scene i

0.1 ROMELIO Presumably (1) dressed very richly, but (2) in a fashion appropriate to a merchant. He is thirty-eight (see IV.ii.117–18, 416). Prospero is no doubt more modestly dressed, also in merchant style.

1–3 YOU . . . substance That Romelio's companion, who speaks so eloquently of the merchant's wealth, should be named Prospero is a literary irony only, since an audience will not learn his name until II.iii.137.

4–10 Ile . . . Water-workes Romelio's account of his prosperity is in the form of a rising hyperbole, climaxing in the preposterous claim that his **Scriveners** are **so rich** that they can **build their Palaces . . . | With musicall Water-workes**.

4–5 discharge . . . Custome 'Spain ruled Naples in accord with the Treaty of Cateau Cambrésis (1559) and collected taxes or custom duties' (Shirley). As Lucas notes, Romelio's point is that if he gave the King of Spain 10,000 ducats a year, that would be about equivalent to the customs duties he pays annually, and hence indicates the scale on which he is trading.

5 The Hollanders As Lucas notes, 'English sympathy with the Netherlands as the victims of Spain had changed by this time to jealous alarm at the growth of their trade, especially in the East Indies.' From 1616 anti-Dutch feeling was fuelled by conflict in and over the Spice Islands (the Moluccas), involving periodic skirmishes and the confiscation of ships. In November 1618 Dutch negotiators were in London to attempt to resolve the question of trading rights in the East Indies. King James also wanted to address the continuing problem of the cloth trade, the relative value of the currencies, and the Atlantic herring fisheries. Cf. IV.ii.11–13n. Hostilities continued in the Spice Islands until March 1620 (see Gardiner, III, 171–9).

7 Shaperoones i.e. 'chaperons', a kind of fashionable hood, which in 1620 Dekker mentions (*Dekker his Dreame*, E3ʳ) as worn by 'gay women' (Lucas).

9 Belvidears i.e. 'belvederes'; 'a summer house erected on an eminence in a garden or pleasure-ground, for the purpose of viewing the surrounding scene' (*OED* 1).

10 musicall Water-workes artificial cascades, fountains, and streams of water contrived to make imitation birds sing, etc. Lucas compares Sidney, *Arcadia*, I.xiv (*Works*, I, 92): 'The table was set neere to an excellent water-worke', including 'birds also made so finely, that they did not onely deceive the sight with their figure, but the hearing with their songs; which the watrie instruments did make their gorge deliver'; also Nashe, *The Unfortunate Traveller* (*Works*, II, 282): 'a summer banketting house belonging to a merchaunt, that was the meruaile of the world'.

10–11 Never . . . Sea In fact, as Crispiano reveals at II.i.97–9, Romelio has recently lost several ships, though he does not yet know it.

11 Exchange 'a building where merchants assemble to transact business' (*OED* 10a). The Burse, or Exchange, built in London by Sir Thomas Gresham in 1566, received from Queen Elizabeth the name of Royal Exchange. Cf. 139n and 144n.

14 a strange confidence Along with pride, confidence is a key feature in the characterization of Romelio. Both are challenged early in the trial scene (see IV.ii.81 and 89).

16 Lotterie Although earlier lotteries, from their inception in England in 1569 to the grand lottery granted by King James in 1612 for the benefit of the colony in Virginia, were for specific projects, by 1620 they were regarded as primarily money-making schemes, and were suspended by order in Council. Wiggins (pp. 372–3) notes 'the repeated rumours of corrupt administration' surrounding the Virginia Lottery, and suggests that W is giving an early indication of the 'probable shadiness' of Romelio's dealings.

22 For a man . . . snow water Dent compares *MonC* (Lucas), 109–10: 'O Greatnesse! what shall we compare thee to? | To Giants, beasts, or Towers fram'd out of Snow', noting a possible source in Matthieu, *Henry IV*, Xx3ᵛ: 'Your greatnesses are but heapes of snow, which we see melt into water'. Cf. *DM* V.v.112–16 and n.

26   Spring-tide   The very high tide coinciding with a new or full moon; hence, figuratively, a copious flow or flood, an appropriate metaphor for a merchant.

28.1   *Servant*   It is possible the *Servant* gives Romelio the document Contarino refers to at 57–8: 'the Evidence of the peece of land | I motioned to you for the Sale'. An immediate exit for the *Servant* seems most likely.

34–9   There . . . riches   Though both bourgeois, Prospero and Romelio present opposing views of the aristocracy, one conservative, the other radical.

36–7   What . . . time past   As Sykes notes, from Sir Thomas Overbury, *A Wife* (1615), B3ᵛ: '*Gentry* is but a *relique* of Time-past.' Cf. *DM* Dedication, 13–14.

38–9   it is nothing . . . riches   'W's source is clearly Burghley's *Certaine Precepts* (1617), A6ᵛ, "that Gentleman that selles an Acre of Land, looseth an ounce of C[r]edite: for *Gentilitie is nothing but ancient Riches*: So that if the Foundation doe sinke, the Building must needes consequently fall"' (Dent).

40–1   colour . . . land   i.e. 'he makes a wish to sell land a pretext (*OED* colour *n.*¹ 12a) for visiting us' (Lucas).

46   portion   'pronounced here as a trisyllabic word' (Weis).

48   Venturer   (1) 'adventurer' (*OED* 1), and (2) figuratively, 'merchant-venturer' (*OED* 2), in that he is risking the sale of land in the hope of gaining 'treble value' (47).

49   Gilt head   Probably, as Lucas suggests, *Crenilabrus melops*, otherwise known as the Golden Maid, but with a pun (which Lucas does not note) on 'gold coin' (*OED* gilt *n.*¹ 3).

50   Gudgeon   Small fish, easily caught; hence in common usage = 'credulous person, gull'.

50.1   *Enter* CONTARINO   Presumably Contarino's dress will signal and justify the description of 'the great Lord *Contarino*' (29); his bearing will be more problematic (see pp. 39–41).

52   Evidence   'title-deeds' (*OED* 8).

53   motioned   'proposed' (see *OED* motion *v.*1).

54–7   Yes . . . No   The abruptness of Romelio's answer, and the apparent inconsequence of his question about travel, appear to leave Contarino briefly nonplussed.

55   Counsell   'legal adviser' (*OED* 8b).

59   absolute   'complete, finished, perfect' (*OED* 4).

61   passing of the Alpes   The setting being Italy, Contarino must be talking of travel to Northern Europe. The audience would, however, see the comment in the context of English warnings against travel south of the Alps, to Italy. Dent compares Burghley's *Certaine Precepts* (1617), A7ʳ: 'Suffer not your Sonnes to passe the *Alpes*: for they shall exchange for theyr forraine trauell (vnlesse they goe better fortified) but others vices for thyr owne vertues, *Pride, Blasphemy*, and *Atheisme*, for *Humility, Reuerence*, and *Religion*.'

63   others   (= others') W's texts never use the apostrophe in the plural possessive of this word. Emending Q's 'other' gives a much more pointed antithesis (**their vertues** . . . **others vices**) and is supported by the source cited at 61n.

65–6   The chiefest . . . of action   From Matthieu, 'Continuation', p. 1019: 'The cheefe action is neuer to bee without action' (Dent).

67–9 The soule ... stand still Sykes proposes a source in Sidney, *Arcadia*, I.ix (*Works*, I, 58): 'the gods would not have delivered a soule into the body, which hath armes & legges, only instruments of doing, but that it wer intended the mind should imploy them'. Dent, however, suggests a supplementary source, as used by Dekker in *The Seven Deadly Sinnes of London* (1606), D4ᵛ–E1ʳ:

> Man (doubtlesse) was not created to bee an idle fellow ... he was not set in this Vniuersall Orchard to stand still as a Tree ... And to haue him remember this, he carries certaine Watches with Larums about him, that are euer striking: for all the Enginous Wheeles of the Soule are continually going ... euerie member of his body (if it could speake would chide him) if they were put to no vse ... at the end of the armes, are two beautifull Mathematicall Instruments, with Fiue seuerall motions in each of them, and thirtie other mouing Engines, by which they stirre both.

curious = 'made with care, elaborately wrought' (*OED* 7a). **Mathematicall** = 'rigorously exact' (*OED adj.* 2a); cf. *WD* I.ii.87.

70 Vertue ... seedes Cf. Montreux, *Honours Academie*, Bb3ᵛ: 'Vertue soweth her seeds, in trauaile, and trouble' (Dent).

79 bonds Contarino's primary meaning is the bonds of matrimony (*OED n.*¹ 7b), but he is punning here on legal obligation (9a): 'A deed by which A ... binds himself ... to pay a certain sum of money to B.' The pun is precisely that used by Shakespeare in *MV*, where the bonds of love, exemplified in Antonio and Portia, are contrasted with legal and financial bonds, exemplified in Shylock.

83 Are you to be married Romelio is dissembling, since he is already aware of Contarino's suit.

87–9 I thought ... will From Sidney, *Arcadia*, I.xiii (*Works*, I, 86): '(thinking it a lesse fault in friendship to do a thing without your knowledge, then against your wil) to take this secret course' (Lucas). Dent notes that W uses the preceding sentence at V.i.8–9.

91 wealthy Voyage Contarino's metaphor unwittingly takes up Romelio's earlier reference to him as a 'Venturer' (53).

92–3 Myne ... mine Cf. Donne, 'To his Mistress Going to Bed': 'My myne of precious stones' (29). Donne's reference to 'my America' (27) makes plain that he has the West Indies in mind. See also 'The Sunne Rising' (17): 'both the'India's of spice and Myne'. Lucas notes that the same quibble probably occurs at *DM* I.i.415.

96 Her worthy mothers This reference, and 119, make it clear that Romelio and Jolenta's father is dead.

97–9 this is ... posterities 'From Sidney, *Arcadia*, II.vi (*Works*, I, 187): "Her [his sister] he had given in mariage to *Dorilaus*, Prince of *Thessalia*, not so much to make a frendship, as to confirm the frendship betwixt their posteritie"' (Dent).

100–14 Beleeve ... purpose In the theatre it would be plain from the outset that Romelio's speech is bitterly ironic. The aside at 113–14 reinforces this, as does a likely sarcasm at 110–11 (**especially ... seldome**) and an equally likely equivocation at 112–13 (**But ... yours**).

103–4 ride ... Uncles Weis glosses **O'th upper hand** as 'i.e. on a coat of arms', but

ride suggests a more literal meaning: that the **little Nephewes** will take precedence over their **Uncles** in formal procession, just as 'the Daughters [will] | Be ranckt . . . at Solemnities | Before the Mother' (104–6).

110 mainely 'very, exceedingly' (*OED* 2c).

115 *Exit Romelio* Q prints the *Exit* to right of 'mind', prior to Contarino's final words to him; followed exactly, this staging would emphasize the abruptness of Romelio's departure ('insolent vaine glory', 118). More likely, however, Contarino's words act as, in effect, a polite farewell, with Romelio leaving after **Tis my hope sir**.

116–18 I doe . . . vaine glory However fallible Contarino may in time appear, his assessment of Romelio holds good; cf. Antonio's assessment of Bosola (*DM* I.i.69–71).

119–27 The mothers . . . honesties Contarino's encomium, praising her **Tho shee be Citie-borne**, serves to place Leonora immediately prior to her entry. It also distinguishes her from Romelio. That Contarino's praise of Leonora is reminiscent of, though of course less passionate than, Antonio's encomium on the Duchess (*DM* I.i.175–93) may be a first, highly oblique pointer towards the eventual pairing of Leonora and the spendthrift aristocrat.

126 without . . . grace 'into the bargain (i.e. without requiring an extra favour)', but given 'Out of their honesties' (134), with the implications, as Dollimore and Sinfield suggest, of 'without the grace of God'. Cf. Middleton, *The Revenger's Tragedy*, I.iii.13–16: 'That maid in the old time, whose flush of grace | Would never suffer her to get good clothes. | Our maids are wiser, and are less asham'd; | Save Grace the bawd, I seldom hear grace nam'd!'

127 trie 'attempt to find out' (*OED* 12), but with the sense also of 'test' (7a).

127.1 *Enter* LEONORA Presumably her 'State and bearing', 'language', and 'Garments' (120–2) will match Contarino's description; what he will not have noticed, but which may be evident to the audience, is Leonora's attraction to him. Given that Romelio is thirty-eight, Leonora must be in her fifties at least (cf. III.iii.394–9). As a widow (cf. I.ii.83n) she presumably wears black.

128 stands affected 'having an affection (formerly *affect*), disposition, or inclination of any kind; disposed, inclined' (*OED* II.1).

130 presume i.e. 'you may take for granted' (*OED* 4).

130–6 Sir . . . breath This opening exchange establishes Leonora's capacity for a politesse equal to Contarino's, in strong contrast to Romelio's earlier abruptness. Contarino's compliment (135–6) takes the exchange to a point at which Leonora will begin to misinterpret his intentions.

135–6 It could . . . breath From Sidney, *Arcadia*, II.vi (*Works*, I, 183–4): 'his fame could by no meanes get so sweete & noble an aire to flie in, as in your breath' (Dent). Cf. *MonC* (Lucas), 222. A kiss of salutation may have been exchanged.

137 strange 'distant, reserved' (*OED* 11).

137–41 You . . . a bed Leonora's speech both reinforces social differences and coyly invites Contarino to deny that he is **weary | Of** [their] **unseasonable time of feeding**.

139 th'Exchange Bell The Exchange 'was a four-storied building with a bell-tower'

(Sugden, p. 185). The bell-tower can be clearly seen in Visscher's 'View of London' (1616), and in similar panoramic views of London. Peter Eisenberg, who published an itinerary in 1614, says that the merchants met at the Exchange from eleven till twelve and from five till six (see William Brenchley Rye, *England as Seen by Foreigners in the Days of Elizabeth and James the First* [London, 1865], p. 171). The hours may have varied at different periods. Here it is clearly from eleven till twelve. Cf. Middleton, *Your Five Gallants*, ed. C. Lee Colegrove (New York and London, 1979), 2159–61 (IV.v): 'Why how now sirrah, vpon twelve of the clock, & not the cloth laide yet—must we needs keepe Exchange time still?' Similarly Harrison, 'Description', I, 171: 'With vs the nobilitie, gentrie, and students, doo ordinarilie go to dinner at eleuen before noone. . . . The merchants dine . . . seldome before twelue at noone' (after Lucas).

140 **from us** 'with emphasis on **us**; for one would naturally have expected the bourgeoisie to copy the Court, not vice versa'; so Lucas, who on the late rising of citizens' wives compares Dekker and George Wilkins, *Jests to Make You Merie* (1607), F2v: ''tis growne a fashion amongst them to eate their breakfasts in their beds and not to be ready till halfe an houre after noone, about which time, their husbands are to returne from the Bursse and they make it their dinner time'.

140–5 **I thinke . . . Fashions** Contarino responds to Leonora's comments on Court ladies' indolence with a critique of their life style, given over to gossip (**to heare of newes**) and **Tyers and new Fashions**.

144 **the New Burse** The New Exchange was built by the Earl of Salisbury in the Strand and opened by James in 1609 as a rival to the Old Exchange erected by Gresham on Cornhill in 1566–7 (see 11n). It is described as 'being furnished with shops on both sides the walls, both below and above the stairs for milleners, sempstresses, and other trades, that furnished dresses'. It did not flourish at first (cf. 'thinly furnisht') and soon after the date of this play there was talk of selling it: 'Lady Hatton is saide to have bought Britains burse or the new exchaunge . . . for £6000 and meanes to make yt her dwelling house, I presume but the upper part, for the nether can be put to no better use then to make £320 a yeare rent' (Chamberlain, *Letters*, 20 December 1623 [II, 535]) (after Lucas). Cf. 11n and 139n.

145 **Tyers** 'apparel' (*OED* tire *n.*[1] 2).

149 **bestow . . . Picture** Contarino's allusion to Jolenta as Leonora's **Picture** ('a person so strongly resembling another as to seem a likeness of her', *OED* 2g) is the source of the confusion which ensues. Presumably he must be portrayed as self-absorbed in not detecting Leonora's misunderstanding (see 160–1).

150–6 **shaddowes . . . Cuckow** With Contarino the emphasis is on the spring; with Leonora on autumn (**Fall**). But Contarino praises her **latter** (second; cf. *WD* V.i.205 and n) **Spring** above spring itself. The reference to **the Cuckow**, a bird associated with the spring, carries with it implications of cuckoldry which are to have ironic echoes when Leonora sets out to prove that when young she cuckolded her husband. Leonora puns on **shaddowes** as (1) 'shade' (*OED n.* 1a), and (2) 'a portrait as contrasted with the original' (*OED* 6b). Cf. *TGV* IV.ii.125 (of Silvia's portrait): 'And to your shadow will I make true love', and *WD* III.ii.146 and n.

155 **onely limitted** 'exclusively circumscribed' (*OED* only *adv.* 1, fixed *ppl.a.* 2).

159–61 Must . . . Object Contarino's reference to the **Picture** as **it**, rather than 'her', allows the misunderstanding to continue.

163 compeld 'constrained, forced' (*OED* 1).

164 drawing 'being drawn'.

174 mellow 'soft' (with the implication here of juicy over-ripeness).

181 Mooves in the Superficies 'lives in the outward form' (of the face), suggesting God as the 'mover of the universe' (*OED* move *v*. 2b, 19).

181–8 Excellent . . . eyesight Contarino's praise of Leonora's **judgement** draws from her a disclaimer that she lacks **the addition** (of a man's, a husband's, experience) to make it **perfect**. She also conveys, through her use of **want** (as both 'lack' [*OED* 2a] and 'desire' [5a]), her interest in marrying again. Cf. *DM* I.i.368.

187–8 For mans . . . eyesight From Sidney, *Arcadia*, III.v (*Works*, I, 380): 'mans experience is womans best eie-sight' (Dent).

193–4 Countrey . . . Citie 'Repeated attempts were being made at this time to make the nobility and gentry stay in their country homes instead of flocking to London' (Charles H. McIlwain, ed., *The Political Works of James I* [Cambridge, Mass., 1918], p. 343). McIlwain quotes a speech of King James to Star Chamber on 20 June 1616: 'It is the fashion of *Italy*, especially of *Naples* (which is one of the richest parts of it) that all the Gentry dwell in the principall Townes, and so the whole countrey is emptie: even so now in *England*, all the countrey is gotten into *London*; so as with time, *England* will onely be *London*, and the whole countrey be left waste.' The issue was still alive in 1623, when Chamberlain wrote to Carleton (5 April): 'Here is a third strict proclamation come foorth for gentlemen of qualitie to avoyde this towne . . . Yt is nothing pleasing to all, but least of all to the women' (Chamberlain, *Letters*, II, 487).

194 visit's Lucas eliminates the apostrophe, but apostrophes in plurals other than possessives are sufficiently common in seventeenth-century texts to be considered spelling variants.

196–7 Prospects . . . Land Cf. Overbury, *Characters* (1614), 'Newes from my Lodging' (by 'B. R.'), F8^r: 'the best prospect is to looke inward' (Lucas).

198 Next . . . Churchland i.e. soliciting land that has been confiscated from the Church is the most demeaning of all acts. This is not, as Lucas thinks, an allusion to 'the greedy appropriation of Church-property at the Reformation' but to a current controversy over the continued pillaging of **Churchland** by the laity. An Act of 1604 forbade further alienation, but made no move to ensure the restitution of lands and incomes which members of Queen Elizabeth's court had acquired. It was in protest against this situation, and to argue 'the duety, iustice and necessity' of restitution that in 1613 Sir Henry Spelman published *De Non Temerandis Ecclesiis, A Tract of the Rights and Respect due unto Churches*. A second, enlarged, edition appeared in 1616. In his book Spelman comments on the 'many in this Kingdom, that became vnfortunate after they medled with Churches, and Church-liuings' (2nd ed. p. 99). See D. C. Gunby, 'Webster's "Begging Churchland": a Note', *Uttar Pradesh Studies in English*, II (1982), pp. 55–8.

203–5 I would . . . proffer Leonora comes here as close as decorum allows to declaring her availability.

206 On what . . . pearch'd i.e. 'on what a veritable storehouse of wealth have I alighted'. **On**, not in Q, was added by Dyce. Lucas, however, is followed by most modern editors in retaining Q, taking **pearch'd** to be a rare sixteenth- and seventeenth-century spelling of 'pierc'd', here meaning 'penetrated, broached'. But use of so violent a verb is improbable, and the spelling recorded by *OED* extremely rare. Emendation seems required, and omission of a two-letter preposition is marginally more likely than the alternative conjectured but rejected by Lucas—that 'purchased' was intended ('pearch'd' being presumed a scribal or compositorial aberration, perhaps provoked by **Treasury** with its 'rea' and 'ur'). Dyce's emendation is supported by a search of *LION: Drama*, which uncovers fifty-three other examples of 'pearch' and its inflexions, in all but two of which the verb or noun 'perch', meaning 'roost', is intended; the two exceptions being an unusual spelling of 'parched' and an instance of the measurement of length.

208–11 Shee . . . Jolenta Contarino's self-congratulatory obtuseness here is both remarkable and dramatically necessary. For the child/portrait conflation cf. *Son.* 16, 9–14.

209 ingenuously i.e. 'ingeniously'. 'Ingenious' and 'ingenuous' were frequently confused in the seventeenth century.

211–15 here's a Letter . . . Jolenta The **Letter** suggests here what is later confirmed: that Jolenta already knows that Romelio intends not only to prevent her marrying Contarino, but also to marry her to someone of his own choosing. The reason for her specific injunction about **midnight** is never made clear, but adds to the sense of urgency and conspiracy.

217 not chang'd I hope Indicative of Contarino's lack of confidence in Jolenta—or in himself as the object of her affections.

217 Ile thither straight i.e. to a specific location, as 'to Jolenta's room', or 'to Jolenta'; but **thither** may also have a purposive sense (*OED* 3b: 'To or towards that end, purpose, result or action'). Cf. *AYLI* I.i.172–3, 'Nothing remains but that I kindle the boy thither.'

219–20 Resolutions . . . weeds A cynical 'sentence' which will prove to have an ironic application to Contarino himself. Such *sententiae* often conclude scenes: cf. *WD* To the Reader, 16n and II.ii.55–6 and n.

ACT I, Scene ii

0.1 Enter ERCOLE Presumably dressed as richly as Contarino, his rival; and including perhaps the insignia of an order of chivalry (see 29–30 and n and 44n). He may be wearing the Maltese cross and black cloak of a Knight of St John (see p. 41). He probably carries the letter that Romelio then proffers to Jolenta (see 4.1 and n), so that it is seen to be his (so York 1980).

1 Oh sister come Possibly summoning Jolenta (= 'O sister, come forth'); more likely, remonstrative (= 'Oh come now, sister'), since it becomes immediately apparent that Jolenta is aware that her marriage is envisaged to someone other than Contarino. Cf. I.i.211–15n.

3 Tombe-maker Cf. *DM* IV.ii.137.

4 king . . . greets you If the dialogue is taken at face value, the King of Spain has written a letter to Jolenta recommending Ercole for her husband (see 8–10). Lucas, however, takes it to be Ercole's commission to command the 'thirtie Gallies' (31), which Romelio simply treats 'as if it were a letter addressed to her in person'. But there seems no reason to disbelieve its identification by Romelio, Jolenta, and Ercole as a letter of commendation (see 21–3n), even should it not be personally to Jolenta. The King may extend a greeting to whomever it may concern, and include both a general introduction and praise of 'one of the Noblest Gentlemen' (14) as well as specific mention of Ercole's 'addition of honour' (29) and his position of command over the galleys.

4.1 *Proffers her Ercole's letter* Lucas and most subsequent editors supply a stage direction for Romelio to give the letter to Jolenta at this point, with only Shirley properly leaving it uncertain whether or not Jolenta accepts the proffered document. Her refusal to take it would reinforce her bitter jibe that Romelio is serving 'Proces' on her (6), and build up a stage picture of her active resistance to Romelio's plan. It would also explain why Romelio keeps telling her what is in the letter (8–10, 12, 14). At 12 his 'here' may imply that he is holding it, and this sense is reinforced by Ercole's statement 'this your brother shewes' (31), just as his request that she recognize his 'addition of honour' (29) by his 'habit' (30) implies that she has not read the letter.

5 serve Proces Jolenta's bitter wit, early established, is in evidence throughout the scene. A **Proces** is a summons or writ requiring a person to appear before a court of justice (*OED* process 7b).

8 grace 'favour' (*OED* 6a).

8 his Catholike Majesty 'a title given to the kings of Spain' (*OED* catholic 7c).

12–13 proclaime . . . a Traytor 'stock phrase for announcing that a person was enemy to a state' (Shirley).

19–21 it may . . . stead A somewhat obscure statement which seems to mean that the 'commendation' (16) which Jolenta says Ercole 'beg'd . . . of the King' (18) may turn out (**fortune**, *OED v.* 3b) to be fruitless, because outside his scope (**out of's way**, *OED* way 38d), and that a **better suite** (a suit directed elsewhere) would have been more to his advantage (**that woo'd have stood . . . In farre more stead**). See D. C. Gunby, 'Webster's *The Devil's Law-Case*', *Explicator* LIV (1996), pp. 213–15. An alternative is not only to drop Q's colon after **way** but also to emend **be** to 'bear(e)', giving: 'And it may fortune to bear out of's way | Some better suite, that woo'd haue stood his Lordship | In farre more stead'. In the emended text Jolenta would be saying that the King's commendation of Ercole to her may chance to deprive Ercole of a more advantageous suit elsewhere. See MacD. P. Jackson, 'John Webster's *The Devil's Law-Case*, I.ii.27–29: an Emendation', *N&Q*, n.s. XLVI (1999), pp. 258–60.

21–3 Letters of Commendations . . . Universitie 'i.e. "even for filling places in the University such letters have ceased to carry weight". Such letters were naturally disliked by the Universities themselves: thus in 1579 the Vice-Chancellor of Cambridge and the Heads of Colleges wrote to Lord Burghley "complaining of the frequency of letters mandatory from the Queen for the admission of Fellows and Scholars in Colleges, whereby the right of free election was taken away, and the scholars were induced to look for preferment to the favour of courtiers, rather than to diligence and proficiency in their studies" (Charles Henry Cooper, *Annals of Cambridge*, vol. II [Cambridge, 1843], p. 368)' (Lucas).

23 fall 'become vacant' (*OED* 41b).

24 return his Passe Her mocking implication is that the paper is no more than 'a written permission to go' (*OED* pass *n.*[2] 8; cf. *DM* III.ii.206). If Jolenta has been holding it (see 4.1n), she presumably returns it to Romelio now.

26 Knights service 'good service' (*OED* knight-service 2); cf. the still current 'yeoman service'. 'There is also a hit at the proverbial frequency of weddings between wealthy widows wanting rank and poor knights wanting money' (so Lucas, comparing W. Fennor, The *Compters Common-wealth* (1617), D2ᵛ–D3ʳ: 'with more feruency and protestation wooe . . . then many decayed Knights will rich widdowes to inherit their possessions'.

27–8 commends Expresse Presumably 'these commendations [*OED* commend *n.* 2] specify [*OED* express 8a] that'. Dollimore and Sinfield note the possibility that **Expresse** is adjectival (= 'explicit', *OED adj.* 3a), modifying **commends**.

29–30 addition of honour . . . habit All editors gloss **addition** as 'rank, title', which it may figuratively mean, perhaps derived from 'something annexed to a man's name, to show his rank' (*OED* 4), or from 'something added to a coat of arms, as a mark of honour' (*OED* 5); if so, **of honour** is adjectival. The whole phrase may, however, mean more literally 'an augmentation to the honours' held by Ercole. In either case, he is displaying the visual evidence of his apparel (**habit**), perhaps simply costume itself (so Shirley), or more likely the insignia of an order of chivalry. The premier Spanish order, and one with which W was familiar and the company may have had in its stock (cf. *WD* IV.iii.10n), was the Order of the Golden Fleece.

34 come hither Romelio calls her apart from Ercole to remonstrate with her. By the time Ercole interjects at 48, their volume or gestures may further indicate Jolenta's refusal. Alternatively Ercole may approach during the argument.

34 interest in you 'influence due to personal connection' (*OED* 6) with you. But Romelio's trade and personality alike make the term ambiguous, as with 'maine businesse' (38).

42–3 I am . . . his Presumably Jolenta puns, meaning both 'I have already given myself to another, emotionally, so am unavailable', and (bitterly) 'I have so little say in what I am to do that I cannot make myself his.'

43–4 too much light . . . Moone-eyed 'too much gazing on the glitter of worldly greatness has dazzled and half blinded you' (Lucas). Cf. *DM* IV.i.41. **Moone-eyed** is a farrier's term applied to horses suffering from 'moon-eye', an intermittent blindness attributed to the moon's influence (*OED* 1). Lucas compares G. Markham, *Markhams Maister-peece* (1610), Hh4ʳ: 'Now they be called moone eyes, because if the Farrier do obserue them, he shall perceiue that at some times of the moone, the horse will see very prettily, and at some times of the moone, he will see nothing at all.' A rival explanation, that the eye seems sometimes covered with white, like a moon, sometimes clear, is provided by Topsell, *Historie*, p. 358.

44 in love with title This implies that Ercole, unlike Contarino, is merely a 'Gentleman' (40); but at 60, Romelio calls him 'my Lord', and at IV.ii.608 he is described as a 'Noble man'.

47 Antiquary . . . Buskins i.e., like the 'Herauld' (45), a student or recorder of antiquities, here imagined as grotesquely dressed in the high thick-soled boot of classical tragedy (not the common riding boots also known as buskins). *OED* (antiquary 2) cites *Pliny, Nat. Historie*: 'another antiquarie or heralt at armes of Rome'. Cf. Earle, *Microcosmographie*, C3ʳ, 'An Antiquary': 'His very atire is that which is the eldest out of fashion, and you may picke a Criticism out of his Breeches. He never lookes vpon himselfe till he is gray hair'd, and then he is pleased with his owne Antiquity.'

49 maynest 'greatest'.

52–8 You . . . . enemies Ercole's speech suggests that, though she has only recently learned of it (see I.i.213–15), his marriage to Jolenta has been arranged for some time—long enough for the legal aspects to be settled—and widely spoken of.

56 joynture 'a competent livelyhood of freehold for the wife, of lands and tenements; to take effect, in profit and possession, presently after the death of the husband; for the life of the wife at least' (Edward Coke, *Commentary upon Littleton*, quoted in Paul S. Clarkson and Clyde T. Warren, *The Laws of Property in Shakespeare and the Elizabethan Drama* [New York, 1968], p. 81.)

58–60 I will leave . . . dealing Ercole makes to leave, but is stayed by Romelio at 60–1. Although Ercole clearly intends challenging Romelio to a duel, Romelio's aside to Jolenta, 'Doe you long to have my throat cut?', suggests either that he expects rather to be murdered, or, comically, that he sees no distinction between duelling and murder.

63 Court-mist 'delusion emanating from the court through Contarino. The phrase probably puns on "courting", i.e. wooing and romantic love' (Weis).

66.1 *Enter* LEONORA Her unexpected and unmotivated appearance at the mention of Contarino's name underlines Leonora's interest in him.

67–70 He lost . . . money The reasons for Contarino's indebtedness (I.i.77–8) are here spelt out, contrasting strongly with the virtues of Ercole.

72 Carroch Luxurious coach used by the noble and wealthy; cf *WD* I.ii.8n.

79 our Choyce Clearly Leonora has been involved in ensuring that Jolenta marries Ercole, her motives presumably involving self-interest.

83 never marry agen Leonora is lying, since she has made it as plain to Contarino as she can that she would marry him. Cf. the Duchess's lie (or equivocation) on the same point ('I'll never marry—') and the Cardinal's cynical response: 'So most Widowes say' (*DM* I.i.288); also W's 'A vertuous Widdow' 2–3 : 'For her Childrens sake she first marries, for she married that she might have children, and for their sakes she marries no more', and 'An ordinarie Widdow' 2–3: 'The end of her husband beginnes in teares; and the end of her teares beginnes in a husband.'

86 an Expedition . . . Turke Though defeated at Lepanto in 1571 by Don John of Austria (cf. IV.ii.348n and 356n), the Ottoman Empire was still a major sea power in the Mediterranean, and a continuing threat to Spain.

94–6 Lady . . . please Ercole's attitude contrasts strongly not only with Romelio's and Leonora's, but also with Contarino's, and draws from Jolenta a first recognition of his worth.

99–101 Heare me . . . ever The parallels with the situation in *WD* (I.ii.276–85) are strong, but the contrasts stronger. Like Cornelia, Leonora kneels to reinforce a mother's curse. Unlike Vittoria, however, Jolenta does not. And where Brachiano declares Cornelia 'mad', Ercole remonstrates positively. Leonora's action in kneeling to her son Romelio is more dramatic and extreme than it might appear to a modern audience, since she is inverting the convention whereby even adult children were expected to kneel to receive a parental blessing, and to remain either kneeling or standing in their parents' presence. Lawrence Stone, *The Family, Sex and Marriage in England 1500–1800* (London, 1977), p. 171, cites Aubrey, *Brief Lives*: 'Gentlemen of thirty and forty were to stand like mutes and fools bare-headed before their parents, and the daughters (grown Woemen) were to stand at the cupboard-side during the whole time of their proud Mother's visit.'

105–7 your hand ... Giv't me Jolenta refuses her hand to Ercole but Romelio seizes it; if he takes her hand again at 127, she perhaps snatches it back at 112 (but see 128–9n). The two men may now be either side of Jolenta; cf. *WD* I.i.29–30n, and *DM* I.i.279–316 and n, where Ferdinand and the Cardinal catechize the Duchess.

116–17 at least ... i'th Sunshine Cf. Tilley L92a: 'To laugh and cry at once (like rain in sunshine)'. This comment is probably a cynical supplement to 'if crying had been regarded', but could possibly be in apposition to it.

117.1 *Ercole kisses Jolenta* This action, which Romelio called for at 115 ('Kisse her my Lord'), is required to justify Leonora's 'Shee is yours' at 118. Cf. Flamineo's 'Stop her mouth with a sweet kisse, my Lord' (*WD* IV.ii.189). There are situational similarities also. For as Flamineo and Zanche encourage Brachiano to kiss and so win over the angry Vittoria, so Romelio and Leonora likewise encourage Ercole to woo Jolenta.

119–20 continue your station ... kisse Romelio's **Nay** may be prompted by Ercole discreetly separating from Jolenta. Romelio urges Ercole to maintain his 'position assigned to a man on duty, or in games' (*OED* station 7). Lucas, followed by other editors, thinks 'station' refers to the appointed playing place for a medieval pageant wagon, relating here to the theatrical metaphor of Ercole wooing **in dumbe shew** with silent kisses, but this specialist medieval sense was no longer current.

122 that they were heartie Lucas takes **they** to refer to 'Virgins' (123) rather than 'teares' (121); hence, 'What would happen if virgins were cheerful at the prospect of marriage?' (Brennan 1975). Romelio may, however, be continuing his 'Aprill showre' metaphor: 'Even if the tears are heartfelt [*OED* hearty 4a], maidens will, once married, be "The sweeter for the dewe" (131)'.

126 Prelates ... take it Cf. Tilley M34 ('Maids say nay and take it'). Dent suggests that for the comparison with prelates, W may be indebted to More, *Richard III*, p. 80: 'And menne must sommetime for the manner sake not bee a knowen what they knowe. For at the consecracion of a bishop, euery man woteth well by the paying for his bulles, yt he purposeth to be one, & though he paye for nothing elles. And yet must he bee twise asked whyther he wil be bishop or no, and he muste twyse say naye, and at the third tyme take it as compelled ther unto by his owne wyll.'

128–9 possession ... Livery and Seasin 'Livery of seisin' was, legally, 'the delivery of property into the corporal possession [seisin] of a person; in the case of a house, by giving him the ring, latch, or key of the door' (*OED* livery 5c). Ercole metaphorically has the door by the **ring** ('circular knocker upon a door' *OED* n.¹3a]). Dent compares Barry, *Ram-Alley* (1611), H1ʳ: 'Short tale to make, I fingered haue your daughter, | I haue tane liuery and season of the wench' (Dent). For Ercole to **Keep** his **possession**, either he is still embracing Jolenta (so Brennan 1975; cf. 117.1n and 119–20n), or Romelio '*seizes her hand and lays it in Ercole's*' (so Lucas, at 127.1).

133–51 I, I . . . merry As the 'dumbe shew' (119–20) of Ercole and Jolenta progresses, Romelio and Leonora's commentary becomes increasingly satiric.

143 Weares . . . state i.e. 'presents the greater splendour' (*OED* state 17).

153–8 I will . . . nothing Ercole's steady devotion contrasts strongly with Contarino's lack of trust (I.i.218–20).

156–7 time . . . degree Ercole's reference to **the noble Arts** suggests that he is referring to the quadrivium, the study of which (leading to the award of the MA) took a further three years following the four-year trivium of the BA.

161–3 I will . . . Husband By a proleptic irony, she is doing what Romelio says.

164 Husband? Whether interrogative or exclamatory, the repeated word indicates Jolenta's shock that she has been 'enforst' (168) to a form of betrothal.

165 This is . . . happiest houre Whether or not Leonora speaks this as direct address to the audience, it is clear that Romelio and Jolenta pay it no attention. Q does not mark Leonora's exit, but this seems the most likely place.

166 peevish 'froward, headstrong' (*OED* 4a). Cf. *DM* III.2.25.

167 a thanke i.e. 'a thank-you' (*OED* thank 4c).

168–70 I hate . . . cause of it 'From Sidney, *Arcadia*, III.i (*Works*, I, 355): "Assure thy selfe, I hate my selfe for being so deceived; judge then what I doo thee, for deceiving me"' (Dent). Given her eventual marriage to Ercole, it is significant that Jolenta does not reinforce her refusal to marry him with an oath, as later (III.iii.158–61) she does her vow not to marry Contarino.

170.1 WINIFRID Her entry brings with it a significant change in the register of Romelio's speeches, which also become noticeably more idiomatic and metrically irregular.

171 Lady of the Laundry As Lucas notes, laundresses had a poor reputation for virtue. Cf. *WD* IV.i.89n, and *AQL* (Lucas) II.i.42. At the trial Winifrid is addressed as 'Gentlewoman' (IV.ii.365, 414, 449), suggesting a waiting gentlewoman; but as Romelio's jocular comment implies, her social status in the play is lower rather than higher. Her age is 'About six and fortie' (IV.ii.415), and she has served Leonora 'these fortie yeares' (III.iii.395).

173–85 Looke as . . . pudding The source, as Lucas pointed out, is Jonson, *The Devil Is an Ass*, II.i.160–7:

> Be you sure, now,
> Yo' haue all your eyes about you; and let in
> No lace-woman; nor bawd, that brings French-masques,
> And cut-works. See you? Nor old croanes, with wafers,
> To conuey letters. Nor no youths, disguis'd
> Like country-wiues, with creame, and marrow-puddings.
> Much knauery may be vented in a pudding.
> Much bawdy intelligence: They'are shrewd ciphers.

That the play was not published until 1631, though first performed in 1616, argues that W may have had access to it in MS. There are further borrowings at II.i.155–8, and 167–79.

175 Cut-works Fabric or garments such as ruffs and bands cut and embroidered into an open-work pattern, rather than woven like lace; as at II.i.168 and *WD* I.i.51, regarded as an expensive Italian speciality.

175 Man-toons Probably 'mantuas' (= silks made in Mantua), or 'mantua gowns' (also 'manto', 'manteau'), although they are not referred to as being worn in England until the second half of the century. The *OED* identification as '? a large cloak' gives this as the only example, and seems unlikely. The hyphen and press correction may suggest the compositor was setting an unfamiliar word.

178 *Dewes-ace* 'two and one (i.e. a throw that turns up deuce with one die and ace with the other); hence, a poor throw, bad luck, mean estate, the lower class' (*OED* deuce *n.*[1] 5).

178 wafer woman 'a seller of thin cakes and confectionery. As a class they were notorious go-betweens.' So Lucas, who compares Fletcher and Rowley, *The Maid in the Mill*, I.iii.9–12: 'am I not able (cosen) | At my years and discretion, to deliver | A Letter handsomly! is that such a hard thing? | Why every wafer-woman will undertake it.'

178 prigs 'haggles over prices as she moves about town' (Shirley). **prigs** is slang, meaning (1) 'cheats', (2) 'haggles', or (3) 'rides' (Partridge 1984, p. 724). As Lucas notes, sense (3) fits with **abroad**, but not with a woman on foot, so (2) may be the sense here.

179 Muskmeloons 'The name seems to have originally belonged to an oriental melon which has a musky scent, and to have been transferred to the common melon by mistake' (*OED*). See *DM* II.i.130n. Gerard's *Herball* (1597), p. 772, suggests that they are 'usually eaten of the Italians and the Spaniards, rather to represse the rage of lust, than any other Physicall vertue'.

179 Malakatoones i.e. melocotons, a late variety of peach. So Nares, *Glossary* (p. 540): 'MALE-COTOON, or MELICOTTON. A sort of late peach, *Malum cotoniatum*, a cotton apple, from the rough coat'. See also Jean de la Quintinie, *The Compleat Gard'ner*, tr. John Evelyn (London, 1693), p. 150: 'This *Yellow Latter Admirable Peach*, is also called the *Apricock-Peach*, and the *Sandalie*: It is a *Malacotoon*.' Presumably because both '*Admirable*' and 'late', **Malakatoones** were a delicacy, like **Muskmeloons**, which helped '*Dewes-ace*' the wafer-woman' (178) gain entry to the homes of 'young Gentlewomen' (176).

180 Citterne i.e. 'cittern', a stringed instrument similar to a lute, but with wire strings and a flat back.

181 foot-cloth An ornamented horse cloth, a mark of dignity or state, that hangs down to the ground on either side to protect the rider's feet from mud or dust. See III.ii.149–50 and *WD* I.ii.47n.

181 Hackney Coachman ... French 'Romelio means that a French-speaking coachman is more likely to be an insinuating . . . rogue than a plain-dealing fellow speaking [the] vernacular' (Weis).

183 no more words This may simply be emphatic; but Winifrid has only been allowed to speak three words since her entry, so comic business may be hinted at here (e.g., each 'Nor' by Romelio, including that in the next line, pre-empting an attempt by Winifrid to expostulate).

184   Maribone i.e. 'marrow-bone', supposedly an aphrodisiac. Lucas compares Middleton: 'her wanton pamphlets, as *Hero and Leander*, *Venus and Adonis*; oh, two luscious mary-bone pies for a young married wife' (*A Mad World, My Masters*, ed. Standish Henning [London, 1965], I.ii.43–5).

185–6   apprehensive . . . traveld Romelio's question if Winifrid is **apprehensive** simply asks if she understands, but she picks up its additional sense of 'quick to learn' (*OED* 4), and responds that she has **traveld**. Since 'travel' and 'travail' were originally the same word (cf. *WD* I.ii.49), and spelled interchangeably, she puns that she has (1) 'journeyed', much discussed as educative, and (2) 'travailed, laboured' to learn. Romelio responds with the well-worn pun on an illegitimate pregnancy leading to both 'travel' to an obscure location so that her pregnancy will not become known, and the 'travail' of childbirth.

187   but my precious As is more explicit at 194–5, Romelio first teases, then mollifies, Winifrid. Her silent reactions will be integral to the comedy; cf. 183n.

188   Chaperoonesse i.e. 'chaperoness', a nonce-form of 'chaperon(e)', an older woman who protects (like a 'chaperon', or hood; see I.i.7n) a young unmarried woman. W's use is over a century earlier than the first *OED* citation. Lucas added an 's' to Q's 'Chaperoones' to indicate the number of syllables, clarify the pronunciation, and distinguish the word from 'Shaperoones' (I.i.7). We have altered Q's '-nes' to '-nesse', which, unlike the modern '-ness', is an ending favoured by W.

188–91   there . . . Deare-stealer Lucas compares Chaucer's 'Physician's Tale', lines 83–5—'A theef of venysoun, that hath forlaft | His likerousnesse and al his olde craft, | Kan kepe a forest best of any man'—but Dent considers direct indebtedness improbable. Cf. Tilley D191, 'The greatest deer-stealers make the best park-keepers.' **Stalkers** = 'poachers' (*OED* 3).

192   Very well . . . pleasure This appears to be an example of W expecting the comic actor to play 'in front of the fiction'; in this case, the actor knowingly making a bawdy double entendre which his character is then affronted at (see David Mann, *The Elizabethan Player: Contemporary Stage Representation* [London and New York, 1991], p. 57).

194–5   thou knowest . . . things Cf. Overbury, *Characters* (1614), 'Newes from Court' (E7^v): '*Wit* and a *Woman*, are two frayle things' (Dent).

195   so I leave you Here Romelio's joke is to omit the mollification of Winifrid, and, by his exit, to deprive her of a chance to respond (cf. 187n).

198–200   unsanctified Matches . . . Commons Forced marriages are not only being decried as **unsanctified** and **ungodly**, but also compared to the widely condemned enclosures of common land, frequent at this time, which brought both criticism and local peasant revolts. Cf. *WD* I.ii.89–90n.

204.1   *Enter* CONTARINO Presumably this is the visit sought by Jolenta in her letter (I.i.211–15). What follows has something in common both with the Duchess's wooing of Antonio (*DM* I.i.348 ff.) and the love scenes between Vittoria and Brachiano (*WD*

I.ii and IV.ii); cf. 209–10n, 214–15n, and 238–44n. Q places the SD at 204.1, but it is almost certain Winifrid's line is in reaction to seeing him enter; there is no basis for thinking she has kept Contarino hidden until Romelio has left, and now produces him, though her loyalties, despite Romelio's instructions to prevent visitors, would not make such a staging impossible (so York 1980).

209–10 stood ... Arras As Cariola does during the Duchess's wooing of Antonio (*DM* I.i.347 SD; cf. also *WD* I.ii.43n).

214 Caskanet i.e. 'casket'. *OED* suggests the word was formed by confusion of 'casket' and 'carcanet' (an ornamental collar or necklace, the more common meaning).

214–15 studying ... Inventory Cf. the Duchess's 'I am making my will' (*DM* I.i.362).

223 forespoken 'previously spoken for'. *OED* includes the sense of prior speech, but not, as is clearly involved here, of 'bespoken, or claimed'.

227–8 There ... live so From Sidney, *Arcadia*, III. xxvii (*Works*, I, 508): 'for then would be the time to die nobly, when you can not live nobly'. Cf. Seneca, *Epistolae*, 17.5: 'si quid te vetat bene vivere, bene mori non vetat' (Dent).

232–3 Ile ... wedding From Jonson's *Sejanus*, I.568–70: 'my sword | Shall make thy brau'rie fitter for a graue, | Then for a triumph' (Dent). **bravery** = 'display, ostentation, splendour' (*OED* 3) and hence, by extension, 'finery, gay apparel'. This may be taken either as the first inkling of what will eventuate—a duel with Ercole—or as a more general, and less honourable, threat.

233–5 So ... cure Proleptically ironic, since Contarino will be dangerously wounded, and then 'cured' by Romelio's attempt to murder him.

238–44 Harke in your eare ... kissing Subsequent dialogue confirms that Jolenta has indeed whispered in Contarino's ear the gist of Ercole's gentlemanly conduct, but Winifrid's commentary to the audience makes it clear that amorous embraces are at least as important. In this it is more reminiscent of Flamineo and Zanche's commentary during the Vittoria–Brachiano love scenes (see 242–3n, and *WD* I.ii. and IV.ii), which likewise serve to distance us somewhat from the lovers, than of the earlier 'dumbe shew' with Ercole which is commented on by Romelio and Leonora at 133–51.

242–3 sweet breath'd ... grow together The **Monkey** is clearly Jolenta: it is a common term of endearment or playful contempt for girls and women (*OED* 2b, citing, e.g., *Oth.* IV.i.127, 'This is the monkey's own giving out. She is persuaded I will marry her'), and appropriate from the older Winifrid (so Shirley). Furthermore, as Lucas points out, **sweet breath** was contributed by the monkey among the gifts from the beasts to woman in Sidney's *Arcadia*, I, First Eclogues (*Works*, I, 135). Despite this, Lucas believes Contarino is intended. Brennan 1975 draws attention to the association of the monkey with lechery (e.g., *Oth.* III.iii.403). Winifrid's **how they grow together!** echoes Zanche's 'See now they close' (*WD* I.ii.198).

244 no womans friend ... kissing Lucas notes that '*Cato* put out of the Senate, also, one [*Manilius*] ... onely because he kissed his wife too louingly in the day time, and before his daughter: and reprouing him for it, he told him, his wife neuer kissed him, but when it thundered' (North's Plutarch [1612 ed.], p. 345).

248 purchase 'acquisition, gain' (*OED* 3).

249 quits her ill Either **ill** is a noun, in which case Contarino means 'absolves, acquits' or 'balances' (*OED* quit 2b, 11b) her evil (with perhaps a sense of 'releases' her [*OED* 1]); or **ill** is adverbial, the phrase meaning 'does not succeed in acquitting, absolving her' (Lucas) or 'is an inappropriate return (*OED* 11b) for her evil'.

250–2 He that . . . money Perhaps suggested by Guazzo, *Civile Conversation*, E5ᵛ, of flatterers: 'the Philosopher counteth him worse then a forger of monie, for that there can bee no friendship, where there is counterfeiting' (Dent).

253 you tremble Perhaps a proleptic response to Ercole's danger.

255–7 The intermission . . . morning Dent compares Sidney, *Arcadia*, II.xx (*Works*, I, 282): 'our restraints were more, or lesse, according as the ague of her passion was either in the fit, or intermission'. Cf. *DM* V.iv.67–8 and n.

260–1 To avoid . . . together Winifrid's suggestion is sound, since consummation would reinforce a marriage *per verba de presenti* such as in essence Contarino proposes (see *DM* I.i.462n). In *DM*, the Duchess and Antonio, married *de presenti*, declare their intention only to lie chastely together (*DM* I.i.481–4), whereas here Winifrid bawdily urges consummation without a formal exchange of vows.

262 Civill Lawyer i.e. a lawyer who undertakes only civil (as opposed to criminal) cases. There may be a play on **Civill** = 'humane, kind' (*OED* 11).

262 fee . . . Councell Cf. *WD* I.ii.81 ('This is my counsell and I aske no fee for't') and n.

265–7 one condition . . . honour This exchange, in which Jolenta stipulates that there should be no **quarrell** between Contarino and the others, is important in laying the ground for the denouement, in which Ercole is the appropriate husband for Jolenta. Contarino here swears both on his **honour** and his **life** not to quarrel with Ercole or Romelio, so certainly his duel in II.ii against Ercole is dishonourable, and possibly that in V.v against Romelio.

271 complementall 'accomplished' (*OED* 5). Cf. *DM* I.i.264n.

272 use not 'am not accustomed to'.

274–6 Let . . . Spiders From Montaigne, *Essayes*, III.xiii (p. 635), where the mind 'vncessantly goeth turning, winding, building and entangling her selfe in hir owne worke, as doe our silke-wormes'. Cf. *WD* I.ii.179–80 where, Dent comments, 'the self-entangler is, more appropriately, the silkworm'.

276–8 we . . . wishes Cf. Flamineo's urging Brachiano to 'Pursew your noble wishes' (*WD* I.ii.4).

279 copartaments 'compartments', probably here referring to painted divisions on a heraldic shield (*OED* compartment 3).

279 *Exeunt* Presumably they leave by different doors.

ACT II, Scene i

0.1 Crispiano Since he was a friend of Leonora's husband, and 'went to'th Indies' (IV.ii.504) four years before Romelio was born, Crispiano is in his fifties or sixties.

1 **well habited** Comic reinforcement of Sanitonella's explanation that Crispiano is in disguise would be possible by, e.g., having an element of his gentleman's attire still visible, by an incongruous 'habit of a Marchant' (6), or by his still disguising himself as he comes on stage.

4 **Civill Lawyers** See I.ii.262n. Lucas notes the possible play upon **Civill** = Seville; cf. 12 (and n).

6 **riot** 'debauchery, dissipation, extravagance' (*OED* 1a).

7 **exhibition** 'living allowance' (see *OED* 2a).

9–10 **other . . . consequence** Crispiano later tells Ariosto that the King of Spain has sent him to investigate an illegal gold mine of Romelio's, and to 'curbe the insolencies' of women (III.i.4–8, 28–9); and he reveals during the trial that he has also been sent with Ariosto's patent appointing him a judge (IV.ii.471–4). We hear nothing further about the mine, but his central role in the play is indeed, as it turns out, to defeat Leonora at law.

12 **Corrigidor of Civill** 'corregidor of Seville', i.e. a magistrate or 'corrector' (*OED*); cf. Kyd, *The Spanish Tragedy*, III.xiii.58: 'To plead in causes as Corrigidor'. Since Crispiano has spent the last forty-two years in the East Indies (IV.ii.504–6), **of Civill** must, as Lucas notes, mean 'born in Seville' rather than 'Chief Justice of Seville', unless W is deliberately or carelessly giving him two incompatible careers. See also 4n.

13 **lesse . . . Jubile** i.e. less than twenty-five years. Brennan 1975 comments that 'the period of jubilee was generally thought of as 50 years', though originally it was more, and in 1450 it had been halved. See *WD* I.ii.91n.

14–17 **line . . . Freely** The metaphor is from angling.

20–3 **pleasure . . . getting of it** Aubrey reports, of the famous lawyer and judge Sir Edward Coke, that 'Sir John Danvers, who knew him, told me that he had heard one say to him, reflecting on his great scraping of wealth, that his sonnes would spend his Estate faster than he gott it; he replyed, They cannot take more delight in the spending of it then I did in the getting of it' (*Aubrey's Brief Lives*, ed. Oliver Lawson Dick [Harmondsworth, 1972], pp. 226–7).

24 **atomy** 'minute particle'; cf. *WD* IV.ii.41.

25 **on that condition** i.e. 'in those circumstances' (*OED* condition 9b).

27–30 **Cannot . . . opinion** The point is the usual one of the spendthrift heir spending his father's hard-earned wealth.

31–49 **all the time . . . after** Clearly Sanitonella has shared Crispiano's long and successful legal career in the East Indies.

31 **Collectionship** Not in *OED*, nor elsewhere in English Renaissance drama, but presumably meaning, as Lucas conjectured, 'accumulation, collecting of wealth', and referring to 'the whole period of Crispiano's amassing a fortune at the bar'. Alternatively, it might refer to 'collection' as mental activity and composure (*OED* 5, 6). It is just possible that the compositor mistook 'Correctionship', referring to 'Corrigidor' (corrector); see 12 and n.

32 **perpetuall Callender** A calendar which 'remains valid for all time to come'

(because it can be adjusted 'for any year or for many years' [*OED* perpetual 1c]); hence, here, every year (with perhaps also the sense of every day of the year) has been the same hard work.

34   came (Lucas; Q 'come') Although, as Lucas remarks, Q's 'present tense might just possibly stand, with its more general tone', a mistake is more likely; Q's 'come' may have been provoked by the presence of three other instances of 'o' within the same sequence of a mere twelve letters.

34   Ruddocks 'in pl. money, gold; esp. gold money' (Partridge 1984, p. 995).

37   made ... halfe ready 'half dressed yourself' (see *OED* ready 13b).

42   Night-caps i.e. 'lawyers', from the coif or skullcap worn by sergeants at law. See *DM* II.i.4n and 19n.

45   out from the matter 'off the point, having lost your thread' (Lucas), based on *OED* out *adv*. 20, 'at a loss from failure of memory or self-possession' (as lawyers and actors).

47   could not eat Q's 'could eat' might be defended as meaning 'could have eaten, had the means to eat (but chose not to)', but Sanitonella's point seems better served by Hazlitt's insertion of the negative.

48   swallow'd it like Flap-dragons i.e. very fast, at a gulp. **Flap-dragons** were raisins or other small objects put into burning brandy, and quickly swallowed while still alight. *OED* cites *WT* III.iii.97–8: 'to make an end of the ship, to see how the sea flap-dragon'd it!'

48–9   as if ... after i.e. 'as if it had been your habit to chew the cud later'.

53   Court game i.e. a game popular at court.

54   Gleeke A card-game for three, popular in the seventeenth century (*OED* gleek *n.*[1]), but there may be, as Lucas suggested, a play on **Gleeke** = an 'ogle' (OED *n.*[2] 2). Cf. Jonson, *Cynthia's Revels*, Palinode 10: 'coy glaunces, glickes, cringes, and all such simpring humours'. Lucas further notes that 'there *may* also be a particular point in "*familiar* as Gleeke": for its terminology, as given in Cotton's *The Compleat Gamester* (1674), is "familiar" in the extreme: "The Ace is called *Tib*, the Knave *Tom*, the four of Trumps Tiddy . . . the fifth Towser, the sixth Tumbler"' (G5ᵛ–G6ʳ).

57   Taffaties, or Lawnes 'light glossy silks, or very fine linens'. Both would be employed in fashionable or showy women's garments, and **fingring** such thin material has a clearly erotic tone.

58   painted hand Whether **painted** refers to nail polish or, more likely, to skin cosmetics (e.g., to whiten the **hand**) is uncertain. Cosmetic decoration, like 'Wenching' (58), may imply courtesans or whores, or simply vanity; cf. John Williams, *A Sermon of Apparell* (preached before King James in 1619; pub. 1620), on the hypocrisy of women who 'come into a church . . . holding up to God a pair of painted hands' (cited by Kate Aughterson, *Renaissance Women: Constructions of Femininity in England: A Sourcebook* [London, 1995], p. 78).

60   before my Deske The type of **Deske** meant here is not the modern combination of table top and storage space, but a small, portable writing box, with a sloping top, hinged to allow the storage of papers and writing implements underneath (see *OED*

1b). The 'Clyents fees' (59) are on the table in front of the **Deske**. Cf. Earle, *Microcosmographie*, C4ʳ, of an attorney: 'two Deskes, and a quire of paper set him up, where he now sits in state for all commers'.

62–3 tooke . . . vayl'd my cap Potential for comic mimic gesture is evident. He calculated (*OED* take *v.* 32b) with 'a side glance: a look or roll of the eye expressive of slyness' (*OED* leer *n.*²), and doffed his cap as a sign of respect (*OED* vail *v.*² 2). **tell** = 'count'.

66 crie 'pack' (*OED* cry *n.*13).

67 hunted . . . fault A **fault** is a break in the scent (*OED* 8), and **to a fault** = 'excessively' (*OED* 3c), the point being that by their passion for hunting, landowners have ruined their estates.

68 Curres Crispiano's use of the derogatory **Curres**, rather than 'Hounds' (66), carries with it contempt for such recreation as hunting.

70 conceit 'personal opinion, judgement' (*OED* 4).

77–9 For . . . bigger Dent compares *Char.* (Lucas), 'A French Cooke', 11–12: 'He is the prime cause why noblemen build their Houses so great, for the smalnesse of the Kitchin, makes the house the bigger.' Cf. also Tilley K111: 'A little kitchen makes a large house.' The precise import of these statements is unclear, but seems to be that stinting on hospitality, as French cooks are clearly believed to do, frees up funds for enlarging a house, or that heavy expenditure on building necessitates stinting on hospitality. There may possibly, however, be architectural implications. Sir Henry Wotton, in *The Elements of Architecture* (1624), notes the Italian practice of putting the Kitchen and other offices underground, 'which besides the Benefit of removing such *Annoyes* out of sight, and the gayning of so much more roome above, doth also by elevation of the *Front*, add *Maiesty* to the whole *Aspect*' (p. 70). He compares the situation in England, where 'by the naturall *Hospitalitie* of *England*, the *Buttrie* must be more visible, and wee need perchance for our *Raunges*, a more spacious and luminous *Kitchin* than the foresaid *Compartition* will bear' (p. 71). Cf. 80–4n.

80–4 Mock-beggers . . . fundaments With **Mock-beggers** Sanitonella puns on inhospitable houses, whose deceptively fine appearance would mock a beggar (*OED* mock *v.* 5), and, as Lucas noted, on 'bigger' (79). There was a trend in sixteenth-century England to elaboration and display in chimneys, and also to the building of false chimneys, lacking **Tonnels** (i.e. 'tunnels, flues'). Sanitonella's condemnation of false chimneys as **monsters without fundaments** (i.e. 'anuses' [*OED* 3a]) embodies widespread contemporary concern about the decline of hospitality; cf. Arnold Davenport's comprehensive note on Hall, *Virgidemiarum*, V.ii.67 ff. (*The Collected Poems of Joseph Hall* [Liverpool, 1949], pp. 242–3) for complaints about smokeless (and hence inhospitable) houses. Satire on such 'vanities' (85), however, seems to overwhelm Crispiano's logic. He wants his son to 'keepe a good house' (74), meaning (as customarily at this time) 'provide liberally for . . . visitors or guests' (*OED* keep 18b); but since he also wants Julio to avoid the expensive ostentation of houses in 'France and Spaine' (78) with **sevenscore Chimneyes** of which **halfe . . . have no Tonnels**, he should not see as desirable the small kitchen 'no bigger then a Saw-pit' (76) which proverbially accompanies such extravagant building.

83   Cuckshawes   i.e. 'kickshaws': 'a fantastical, frivolous person' (*OED* 3: French *quelque-chose*, 'trifles, [little] somethings'). Cf. Milton (*Of Education*), who speaks of youths returning from France 'transformed into Mimicks, Apes, and Kicshoes' (*The Works of John Milton*, ed. F. A. Paterson et al. [New York, 1931–8], IV, 290).

88–9   raise . . . likenesse   The meaning appears to be 'to induce an individual to behave like a devil', but **raise** = 'to cause a spirit to appear by means of incantations' (*OED v.*[1] 21), so there is here an ironic reversal of the usual situation, in which the necromancer raises devils. There is a further irony inasmuch as taking on the **Devils likenesse** involves debasement, not raising.

91   out-vie me   i.e. if Julio can get greater pleasure in spending his father's wealth than Crispiano enjoyed in accumulating it.

91.1   SD   Julio is likely to be identifiable by the foppish extremes of fashion which are described at 167 ff., and which will justify his father's remarks at 6 about his 'riot'. The clothing and appearance of the 'old Gentleman' (127), the 'dapper' (100) Ariosto, are of considerable importance in the scene: see notes to 101, 104, 143–4, 151, and pp. 41–2. Baptista has no lines, but is required later in the scene as one of Ercole's 'right worthy friends' (see 212 and n); assuming he is the Baptista discussed earlier, he is a prosperous merchant aged sixty or more (I.i.17–24).

96–8   I knew . . . birth   A comment which sets up as plausible Leonora's charge.

98   losses . . . at Sea   How Crispiano knows of this is not clarified. Although it may be related to the investigation of Romelio's trading illegally in gold (see 9–10 and n), its importance is for theme rather than plot.

100   dapper   'a little person who is trim or smart in his ways and movements' (*OED* 1b); cf. 104 and n.

101   long stocking   Whether or not Ariosto wears a lawyer's gown, he evidently wears very old-fashioned long tailored stockings reaching from the foot up to the thigh, where they attach to his 'round slop' (143–4 and n), the small pumpkin-shaped stuffed trunk hose of Elizabeth's reign. See pp. 41–2.

102   Came to your lodging   This and the encomium which follows clearly indicate that Crispiano and Ariosto knew each other of old.

104   little piece of flesh   This suggests W knew that the actor who would play this role was small, which is of relevance at 143–4; see n.

106   compounds   'settles, composes' (*OED* 6a); cf. *Char.* (Lucas), 'An ordinary Fencer', 14: 'Hee Compounds quarrels among his Scholers.'

110   honest causes gratis   This refers to the practice of giving free legal representation to those who appeared *in forma pauperis* (literally 'in the character of a pauper'). 'Every poor person desirous of bringing an action who could swear that he had not property worth £5, except his wearing apparel and the subject matter of the intended action, was to be allowed to bring an action without payment of the court fees, and was to have assigned to him an attorney and counsel who acted for him without payment' (Jowitt, p. 949).

112   extreame practise   'with a large practice' (Shirley).

114   rare . . . profession   While the basis for payment of judges varied according to which court they presided over (some being salaried, some receiving fees, and some unpaid but undertaking the duties in hope of future promotion), the point here is another satiric cut at what were regarded as the exorbitant fees charged by lawyers.

116 Heere's the man i.e. Crispiano; evidently Romelio has met him, or knows of him.

120 but accessary 'even contributory' (see *OED* but *adv*. 6, and accessory *adj*. 1, 2).

124–6 thou . . . paynes taking At the Jacobean court **New-yeares gifts** to those in public office or with political influence were often bribes in all but name. In the Star Chamber proceedings against the Lord Treasurer, Thomas Howard, Earl of Suffolk, and his wife in October 1619, Suffolk admitted 'taking gifts both in plate and cash. Thus Sir Allen Apsley testified that he gave Suffolk £100 or plate of that value every year "but with no contract," i.e. as a free gift . . . Accused of taking £300, a cup of gold worth £100 and other rewards "for favors to be done" Suffolk replied that he had received no monies but confessed he had accepted a cup of gold as a New Year's gift' (Linda Levy Peck, *Court Patronage and Corruption in Early Stuart England* [London, 1990], p. 182). Those who made such gifts but received no benefit as a result might feel aggrieved; cf. Nashe, *Pierce Pennilesse* (*Works*, I, 161): 'those that stand most on their honour, haue shut vp their purses, and shifte vs off with court-holie-bread' (i.e. 'fair words or flattery without performance' [*OED*]).

127 Here's an old Gentleman Romelio draws Julio's attention to Ariosto, who may be standing apart until after Crispiano's aside to him at 133.

133 rate 'scold, criticize severely'.

136 He comes . . . upon me This is the first of several occasions when it is impossible to know whether Julio addresses his stage audience of Baptista and initially Romelio, the theatre audience in aside, or both. Cf. 154–5, 180, 183.

137 quat 'pimple'; hence a term of contempt, applied particularly to a young person (see *OED n.*[1] 1, 2). Cf. *Oth.* V.i.11–12: 'I have rubb'd this young quat almost to the sense | And he grows angry.'

139–40 When . . . poxe 'Probably from Overbury, *Characters* (1618), "Newes from the very Country" (signed I. D., and usually attributed to Donne), P2ᵛ: "That intemperance is not so vnwholsome heere; for none euer saw Sparrow sicke of the poxe"' (Dent).

142 Cantaride-mongers i.e. 'rakes, whoremongers'; traffickers in *Cantharis vesicatoria* (Spanish fly), an aphrodisiac. Cf. *WD* II.i.283n.

143–4 Phisician . . . Urinall Responding to Ariosto's tart retort about the 'Cocke-sparrow' (139), Julio first labels him a **Naturallist** (*OED* 3a: 'One who studies . . . natural science'), and then a **Phisician**. Julio jests at Ariosto's **round slop** (cf. 101n) as small enough to just hold a **Urinall**, the glass flask used to collect urine samples for medical inspection (a universally recognized conventional symbol of the **Phisician**). His point is not that Ariosto is small ('dapper' [100], 'a little piece of flesh' [104]), but that he is wearing long-out-of-fashion small trunk hose rather than fashionable baggy breeches such as Julio himself is undoubtedly wearing. See Carnegie and Gunby.

144–7 tis concluded . . . Tis concluded Ariosto presumably mimics Julio. Cf. also 90.

145 *Ariosto doffs his hat* We cannot be certain of the extent of the business here. It seems that Ariosto mocks Julio with an exaggerated gesture of salutation to accompany his sharp criticism; this may be what Julio means by 'You are a very bold gamester' (149).

147 precious 'out and out, arrant' (*OED adj.* 4a).

147–8 you . . . thorow you Cf. *DM* III.i.42–3: 'He's a meere sticke of sugar-candy, | You may looke quite thorough him.'

149 gamester i.e. 'antagonist'. A **gamester** might be a competitor in wrestling or other games (*OED* 1), an opponent in a game of chance, 'a gambler' (*OED* 3), or what Jonson called 'Such petulant, geering, gamsters that can spare | No argument or subiect from their iest' (*Every Man in His Humour* [1616], I.i.108–9; cited in *OED* 4). For ***Doffs his hat*** cf. 145n, and 151–5.

150 play . . . rook Responding to the metaphor of 'gamester' (149 and n), Ariosto is able to score off Julio by punning on **rook** as (1) a **chesse** piece, (2) 'a cheat' in gaming (*OED* rook *n.*¹ 2b), and (3) 'a gull, or simpleton' (*OED n.*¹ 2c). Lucas compares Chapman, *May Day*, III.i.154–5: 'An arrant Rooke by this light; . . . a man may carry him vp and down by the eares like a pipkin.'

151 preserve . . . dust Julio's point is that Ariosto should put his **velvet** hat on again, rather than letting it trail in the **dust**.

152 blocke . . . fashion The shape of the wooden **blocke** on which a hat was made determined its **fashion**; Ariosto manages to satirize Julio's addiction to fashion and the no doubt extreme style of his particular hat, as well as suggesting he is a blockhead. Julio's foppish costume is an essential element of the following exchanges, especially 168–72; see p. 41.

154 hat in the hand Since 'hat in hand' indicates 'the head uncovered in respect' (*OED* hat 5), Julio is probably sharing his astonishment with his companions, or the audience, at the contrast between Ariosto's sharp criticism and his courteous gestures.

155 put on The primary sense is clearly 'put my hat on' (*OED* put 47b) but given the satiric comments which follow, there may well be also the subordinate sense of 'push on', 'proceed' (47i). Presumably Julio will also **put on** his hat.

155–8 those lands . . . Taylors As Dent notes, from Jonson, *The Devil Is an Ass*, II.iv.33–7:

> the faire lands,
> That were the *Clyents*, are the *Lawyers* now:
> And those rich Mannors, there, of good man *Taylors*,
> Had once more wood vpon 'hem, then the yard,
> By which they were measur'd out for the last purchase.

160 purchase 'acquisitions, wealth, property' (see *OED* 5, 8, 11); cf. *DM* III.i.28.

163 Gentlemen (Hazlitt) Q reads **Gentleman**, but Ariosto has in the previous speech appealed to the others present ('thinke you' 161) as if they were a jury, and he and Julio may have been doing this from the start of the sequence. The general appeal would invite Romelio's entry into the baiting in the following speech.

164 make even 'balance the accounts' (having no debt) (see *OED* even 10a).

165–80 A hundred duckets . . . bayted! Lucas points out the structural similarities to other scenes in this and earlier W plays, 'where two characters alternately break in upon each other in baiting and rating a third'; see I.ii.105–7n. Here there is the additional irony of Romelio's participation leaving him the more exposed as a target for Ariosto at 181 ff. **duckets** were Italian coins worth, as W understood it, approximately five shillings (see *WD* IV.iii.133n); 100 ducats was therefore about £25, a huge sum of money.

165 breaking Venice glasses The extravagant fashion of smashing one's glass after a toast would be even more costly if fine **Venice glasses** were used.

166 English . . . Knight Cf. *Oth.* II.iii.76–85, where Iago tells Cassio that the English 'are most potent in potting' and able to out-drink the Danes, Germans, and Dutch, thought of stereotypically (by the English) as drunkards. The force of **a Knight too** presumably depends on the popular disrepute into which the rank had fallen following James's sale of knighthoods (cf. the satiric description of Sir Petronel Flash, himself a drunkard, in Jonson, Chapman, and Marston, *Eastward Ho*, IV.i.178: 'I ken the man weel, hee's one of my thirty pound knights').

167–79 This comes . . . Supper Noting that 'Jonson's content explains Ariosto's sudden mention of food at lines 178–9', Dent compares two passages from *The Devil Is an Ass*:

Tissue gownes,
Garters and roses, fourescore pound a paire,
Embroydred stockings, cut-worke smocks, and shirts,
More certaine marks of lechery, now, and pride,
Then ere they were of true nobility!   (I.i.126–30)

and

This comes of wearing
Scarlet, gold lace, and cut-works! your fine gartring!
With your blowne roses, Cousin! and your eating
Phesant, and *Godwit*, here in *London*! haunting
The *Globes*, and *Mermaides*! wedging in with *Lords*,
Still at the table! and affecting lechery,
In veluet! where could you ha' contented your selfe
With cheese, salt-butter, and a pickled hering,
I'the Low-countries; there worne cloth, and fustian!   (III.iii.22–30)

This = Julio's financial embarrassment.

168 Cut-worke . . . Purle Probably 'a ruff or band of **Cut-worke** [see I.ii.175n] worth a pound for each pleat or fold' (*OED* purl *n.*[1] 3). Lucas compares Jonson, *Every Man out of His Humour*, IV.vi.89–91: 'it [a sword] graz'd on my shoulder, takes me away six purles of an *Italian* cut-worke band I wore (cost me three pound in the exchange, but three daies before)'. Shirley's gloss, 'a loop of embroidery, often of silver or gold wire thread', is less likely, and presumably derives from Linthicum (pp. 139–42), who takes Romelio to be referring to an individual space in the cutwork embroidered with purl wire (see also *OED* 2, 'each of the minute loops . . .'). Both purl-embroidered cutwork and purl lace, however, seem always to be referred to by measure (length or weight), not by individual working.

169 overblowne Roses Large silk, lace or embroidered rosettes on the shoes (on costliness and size, see *WD* V.iii.103n). **overblowne** = 'oversize, excessive', since 'blown' roses have already reached full blossom.

170 gowtie 'swollen' (as with gout; *OED* gouty 3).

171 taffaty . . . garter Elegant glossy silk sashes for tying in a bow below the knee to secure the stocking, and for display; they might cost a pound or more a pair, and are often listed with roses (see 169 and n). For **taffaty** cf. II.i.57n.

172 Gally dung-boat A **Gally** is a 'large open row-boat' (*OED* galley 3). Lucas compares Cowley, 'An Answer to an Invitation to Cambridge' (*The English Writings of Abraham Cowley*, ed. A. R. Waller, 2 vols. [Cambridge, 1905–6], II, 66):

> I shall contemne the troubled *Thames*,
> On her chiefe *Holiday*, even when her streames,
> Are with rich folly guilded, when
> The *quondam Dungboat* is made gay,
> Just like the bravery of the men,
> And graces with fresh paint that day.

173 switching . . . Illustrissimi i.e. 'galloping up with the best society' (Lucas), based on **switching** as 'whipping (a horse) with a switch', and **Illustrissimi** as Italian nobility ('most illustrious').

174 pusling . . . cock-pit 'perplexing (puzzling) calculations (of the betting odds) on cockfighting'.

175 Shaking . . . Tavle-boord 'playing at dice' (see *OED* **elbow** *n*. 4e). A tavel-board, or table-board, is a board for playing dice on (see *OED* tavel *n*., and table-board, where this citation is misplaced). Lucas and other modern editors erroneously read 'Taule-boord'.

176 hir'd velvet 'belongs to the whore, not the youth' (Lucas).

176–7 spangled . . . fringe Spangles were small discs of shining metal sewn onto garments as decoration, but **fringe** implies pendent reflective (**spangled**) copper lace, unless the choice of word is for its associations with the physical (and moral) border of the underskirt or petticoat. Lucas is probably right that **copper** is 'imitating gold lace'.

177 netherlands i.e. 'lower (genital) regions' (see Partridge 1984, p. 787); with an additional quibble upon the reputedly numerous Dutch whores in London.

178 Padua The university, one of the oldest and most famous in Europe. Cf. 228–9, and *WD* I.ii.304.

178 Cow trotters i.e. an inexpensive meat.

180 *aside* Here, as at 183 and possibly 196, Julio is most likely to be seeking sympathy direct from the audience, though it would be possible for him to speak to Baptista. Cf. 136n.

181–93 Nay . . . trice Having shared with him in the denunciation of Julio's spendthrift behaviour, Ariosto suddenly turns on Romelio. This satire on knaves who exploit young gentlemen is clearly a warning to Romelio (cf. V.vi.72–4n) as much as Julio; since Romelio replies at 194, this is probably all addressed to him. Cf. 197–8n.

185 rich citie Chuffes i.e. 'prosperous (possibly usurious) fat citizens'. *OED* defines 'chuff as either 'a rustic, boor, clown' (*n.*[1] 1; clearly not the sense for a **citie** man), or as general opprobrium, sometimes specifically 'a close avaricious man' (*n.*[1] 2). The latter meaning has been adopted by previous editors, but the citations relating to the wealthy (e.g. 'An old, stradling Vsurer . . . a fat chuffe it was' [Nashe, *Pierce Penilesse* (*Works*, I, 161–2)]) seem related to the adjectival sense of 'swollen or puffed out with fat' (*a.*[1]), itself derived from *n.*[2], 'a cheek swollen or puffed with fat'. Cf. *NHo* V.i.136, 'your fat Citty chuffes', and *1H4* II.ii.88–9, 'gorbellied knaves . . . ye fat chuffs'. It seems most likely that *OED* has failed to distinguish adequately between the two senses of (1) boor, and (2) fat person, and has, under *n.*[1] 2, inadvertently associated City moneymaking with coarseness rather than overfeeding.

187–8 cherries . . . Court Cf. Bosola's gift of **Apricocks** to the Duchess (*DM* II.i.123–4). Ariosto here continues the image of ruthless City con men who 'plow up fools' (186), although 'Inclosures' (187; and cf. I.ii.198–200n) are now literal, for orchards which will provide delicacies (cf. 'Malakatoones', I.ii.179n). But both **cherries** and **Apricocks** have complex bawdy associations as well. Rubinstein (p. 48) glosses cherry as 'maidenhead, vulva' and cites the common association with cherry-pit, a 'child's game of rolling pits into a small hole, sometimes with less innocent meaning, as in Herrick [p. 19], "Cherry Pit": "Julia and I . . . playing for sport at Cherry-pit . . . I got the pit, and she the stone"'. **Apricocks**, as Dale Randall notes, had long had sexual connotations: 'As early as the 1570s, Rembart Dodoen's *Nieuwe Herball* informed English readers of Dioscurides' warning about the fruit: "[B]eing ripe, they loose the belly, and engender noughtie humours"' ('The Rank and Earthy Background of Certain Physical Symbols in *The Duchess of Malfi*', *Renaissance Drama*, n.s. XVIII [1987], p. 710).

189 selling commodities A common confidence trick; see *WD* IV.i.49n.

191 Counter With a play on **Counter** = 'debtor's prison' (*OED n.*[3] 7). Cf. *AV* III.ii.25: 'for we kennell him i'th'counter'.

191 searse 'sift' (*OED* searce, citing George Turberville, *The Booke of Faulconrie or Hauking* [1575], p. 301: 'beate it into fine pouder, which they serce through a fine cloth'). Hence 'drumme' (203).

191 Ginny Pepper An early name for 'Cayenne pepper' (*OED* guinea pepper, citing Gerard, *Herball*, II.lxvi.293: 'Guinie pepper hath the taste of pepper, but not the power or vertue').

192 Tarriers i.e. 'tarrying-irons, puzzle-rings', an elaborate mechanical puzzle which requires one to 'tarry' (see *OED* tiring-irons). The point here is that the avaricious 'Potecaries' (189) are impatient: rather than **finde a man like a payre of Tarriers** (i.e. slowly and painstakingly), they prefer to ruin him instantly (**would undoe him in a trice**). Cf. Overbury, *Characters* (K5[r]), 'A meere Petifogger', 4–5.

195 exactors 'extortioners' (*OED* 2).

195–6 three heads . . . Hell-hounds Cerberus, the monstrous dog who guarded the gates of Hell in classical mythology, had three heads.

197 I . . . Hell-hounds This may be aside to the audience (see 180n) even though it is heard by Ariosto.

197–8 rent . . . Tenter-hookes i.e. 'tear you as tenterhooks would'. **Tenter-hookes** were the hooks used to hold newly-woven cloth for stretching, and the word came to be associated with both the pain of sharp hooks and the suffering of being stretched. Lucas compares Overbury, *Characters* (C5ᵛ), 'A Golden Asse': 'Knaues rent him like Tenter-hookes'; and 'A Creditor' (N4ᵛ): 'Euery Tearme hee sets vp a *Tenters* in Westminster Hall vpon which he racks and stretches *Gentlemen* like English *broad cloth*'.

198 Hearke in your eare Presumably Ariosto draws Romelio apart for the rest of this speech.

198–9 intelligence upon you i.e. 'an informer has reported on you'.

199 gold . . . Sea For such an offence see *WD* V.iii.82n. Lucas notes Gardiner's account (III, 323) of the 1619 Star Chamber trial of foreign merchants, mainly Dutch, for smuggling gold out of England. Heavy fines were imposed.

203–4 Barber . . . curry Sanitonella puns on **curry** as 'to comb' (*OED v.*¹ 1), as 'scratch' (2) or 'to give a drubbing to' (3). Barbers were, Weis suggests, notorious for gossip; hence **tongue**.

204 SD The Q *Exit* for Sanitonella has no evident motivation.

211.1 ERCOLE His imminent departure may well be signalled by his wearing a sea gown or cloak (see MacIntyre, pp. 186–7).

212 worthy friends i.e. Julio and Baptista, the only ones left.

212 staid me 'waited for me' (see *OED* stay *v.*¹ 19). Cf. Fletcher, *Monsieur Thomas*, V.vi.51: 'Get you afore, and stay me at the Chappell.'

214 come about i.e. 'facing the opposite way' (because the wind has changed direction—see 216–17—and is now favourable for departure); see *OED* about *adv.* 6b. Cf. *DM* I.i.139–40. Weis and Brennan 1975 gloss as 'have returned to port', but do not explain.

215 Signior Ercole That Contarino and Ercole know each other only emerges here, to be explained at 228–30 ('Students . . . friends').

221–3 private . . . bosome By means of this invention, Contarino makes it clear he wishes to be left alone with Ercole.

224 *They sit downe* This is an unusual SD with no plot function, and is already signalled in the dialogue. Perhaps W was concerned to emphasize the friendship and civility with which the quarrel is carried on, in contrast to the baiting scene just past. Stools seem to have been generally available on the stage. The men must be standing again to 'embrace' (306), but may well stand earlier when they agree to fight (274–7; so York 1980). See pp. 42–3.

226–7 whose word . . . deed 'From Sidney, *Arcadia*, I.v (*Works*, I, 31), of Argalus: "his worde ever ledde by his thought, and followed by his deede"' (Dent).

231 hartie 'heartfelt, sincere' (*OED adj.* 4a).

238 expresse 'delineate, depict' (*OED* 5a).

242–4 Compare . . . all 'From Sidney, *Arcadia*, V (*Works*, II, 186): "Let her beawtie be compared to my yeares, and such effectes will be found no miracles"' (Dent).

THE DEVIL'S LAW-CASE [II.i]

245 Yes ... prodigious Contarino is making the point that, like a 'myracle' (244), 'the faire effects of love' (243) will for Ercole prove a prodigy, i.e. 'portentous, unnatural, amazing' (*OED* 1, 2, 3).

248 Seale ... heaven Presumably, given his love for Jolenta, Contarino claims he is betrothed to her in the eyes of God (*OED* seal *n.*[2] 1b: 'a symbol of a covenant'). The outcome proves otherwise.

251 essential front Contarino is presumably vowing by the essence (*OED* essential *adj.* 1a) of **spotlesse Vertue** which the face (*OED* front *n.* 2) reveals.

254–6 Italian ... frownd 'I have not arranged for you to be murdered in the devious fashion characteristic of Italians. If I had, you would now be dead and I would not have bothered to confront you' (Weis).

255 practise 'treachery' (*OED* 6a).

261 her designe for Marriage Not a **designe** approved by Jolenta, of course, but rather Romelio's plan for her **Marriage**, with **designe** carrying the implications of Dr Johnson's definition, 'A scheme formed to the detriment of another' (cf. *OED* 1b).

272 motive 'promoter, instigator' (*OED* 5). Lucas comments: 'Though Ercole denies that he is influenced by the chivalrous desire not to transfer the blame and the quarrel to Romelio's shoulders, that appears to be in fact his only motive for deceiving Contarino.'

275 *rising* It is uncertain when, precisely, they stand (after '*They sit downe*' at 224), but this seems to be the point at which the emotional dynamic beween them changes most markedly.

279 vary for 'quarrel about' (*OED* 5b), and possibly 'contend for' (see *OED* 5c).

293 give you the lye 'accuse you of lying'. Brennan 1975 notes that 'Striking or giving a man the lie was a formal method of leading up to a duel and Elizabethan and Jacobean gentlemen were punctilious in the observation of the rules of quarrelling. The theory of the honourable quarrel, seriously expounded in such works as *Vincentio Saviolo his Practise* (1595) and Sir William Segar's *The Booke of Honor and Armes* (1590) and *Honor, Military and Ciuill* (1602), is mocked by Touchstone in *AYLI* V.iv.48–97.' Cf. 318n.

294 stale injury of Wine i.e. 'tiresome and unfashionable challenge arising from quarrelsome drunkeness' (see OED stale *a.*[1] 3).

300 prevention 'being forestalled' (see *OED* 4a). Not only was duelling illegal, but the government and King James himself conducted a vigorous campaign against it in the period 1613–18; see Brian Parker, '*A Fair Quarrel* (1617), the Duelling Code, and Jacobean Law', in *Rough Justice*, ed. M. L. Friedland (Toronto, 1991), pp. 52–75, esp. 55–63.

302 fit them i.e. 'make sure they match for length'; cf. *WD* V.i.200. The 'weapons' (301) will be the rapiers they are already wearing, which are unlike the traditional military swords for the later judicial combat (see V.vi.5–6n).

302 by the way 'as we go, in passing' (cf. *OED* by 12a).

303–5 So whether ... Italians Cf. *DM* III.ii.70–1: 'whether I am doom'd to live, or die, | I can doe both like a Prince'.

306 embrace The stage picture of the two duellists embracing adds comic or poignant force to Ercole's summation, 'This looks not like a quarrell' (285).

307 being an Italian 'An allusion to the secretly vindictive character which Jacobean Englishmen attributed to Italians' (Brennan 1975). Cf. 253–5 and 305.

309 trie 'ascertain, test, determine' (*OED* 5).

312 sufficient proofe (1) 'satisfactorily impenetrable' (as of armour; *OED* proof 10a), and (2) 'evidence enough' (*OED* 1a).

313 privie coat 'a coat of mail worn under the ordinary dress' (*OED* privy *adj.* 8b), contrary to the laws of duelling because it constituted an unfair advantage. Cf. *CC* III.i.86–8. Lucas compares a passage in one of Fynes Moryson's unpublished chapters dealing with Italy (*Shakespeare's Europe*, ed. C. Hughes [London, 1903], p. 159): 'myselfe haue seene young Gentlemen, for feare of those with whome they had some quarrells, weare continually an yron Coate of male of 30 pounds weight, next aboue their shirts'.

314 Taffaty i.e. taffeta shirt (cf. 57n).

316.1 BAPTISTA Baptista must re-enter with Julio (so York 1980) to permit Romelio's plural form of address at 331, 'And you be Gentlemen', since clearly the Servant is not a gentleman. Prospero could come on as well or instead, but Baptista, though also only a merchant, is very wealthy (see I.i.20), and already associated with Julio (see 212n). Although the stage being briefly clear might indicate the start of a new scene, the action is probably continuous: as soon as Ercole and Contarino have left by one door, Julio and Baptista enter from the other and meet the Servant who has been sent back (and who may even have been previously on stage, and briefly exited with his master, Ercole or Contarino). If it were a new scene, and time were imagined to have elapsed, the Servant might enter with Julio and Baptista, but this action would serve the dramaturgy less well.

321 met the devill . . . tydings i.e. 'the bad news I received was like meeting the devil'.

323–4 the greatest . . . am I See Eccles. 1: 7, and Tilley R140: 'All Rivers run into the sea.'

324 pray leave me Romelio's request for solitude is perhaps intended as a reinforcement of the melancholy caused by his losses; if so, there may be a psychological link to checking up on his last asset, Ercole.

329 One . . . alone Dent compares Montreux, *Honours Academie*, Rr3^r: 'One mischiefe neuer commeth alone', and de Serres, *General Inventorie*, p. 264: 'One mischiefe comes neuer alone.' But the phrase is proverbial; see Tilley M1012 and M1004, and cf. III.iii.216–17 and *WD* III.iii.65–6.

334–5 proper . . . spoyle Besides meaning 'admirable' (*OED* 8a), 'of good character' (8b) and 'well-made, handsome' (9), **proper** also means 'complete' (*OED* 7), in the sexual sense, the pun matching **pricke** as (1) 'sword' (*OED* 15), (2) 'puncture' (i.e. 'wound'), and (3) 'penis'. Similarly, **spoyle** means 'inflict serious bodily injury upon', or even 'destroy' (*OED v.*[1] 10), but also seems here to employ sexual innuendo as 'to injure to such an extent as to render unfit' (*OED* 11). Cf. II.ii.26–7.

ACT II, Scene ii

2–3 ready? . . . Before you fight Ercole must discard his cloak (see II.i.211.1n) and probably has his **sword** drawn at **are you ready?** Contarino's action here will do much to govern the tone of the dialogue. If he now also draws and prepares to duel, then stops to speak, he is likely to reinforce a comic view of two friends unable to get down to the business of fighting (this would prepare for a comic repetition of the preparation and interruption before 13; so York 1980). If the actors seek a more serious effect, however, Contarino's speeches here and at 13–14 may be a final plea prior to the fight, meaning (1) repent your immoral cause, or (2) repent because you are to die, or (3) relinquish your unjust claim on Jolenta so that we need not fight.

3–4 cause . . . foule Contarino's is in fact the **foule cause**, given his undertaking to Jolenta not to quarrel with Ercole (I.ii.265–9).

8–13 Ide . . . ready? At V.iv.56–60 Romelio similarly rejects **counsell in Divinitie** from the Capuchin.

16 You are hurt Again Contarino pauses to talk, and again the effect could be comic or chivalric (see 2–3n).

18 I meane well . . . thrive i.e. 'I am doing my best, but not succeeding', possibly an aside. The duel may have resumed after **doe it**, with Ercole's wound preventing him from fighting well. If so, a further pause, with yet another exhortation from Contarino, probably follows.

23 faire, and home i.e. 'a clean thrust that fully reached its mark'.

27 take the rest 'receive my final venture (i.e. the last sword thrust of which I am capable)'. This is the point at which Contarino is wounded. In the game of primero, the **rest** is the reserve stake, whose loss terminates the game; hence, figuratively, one's final throw or hazard (*OED* rest *n.*^{2} 6).

27.1 SD Contarino, unscathed to this point, is now dangerously wounded by Ercole's final lunge (see 27n), and collapses on top of him. If seeing both men, apparently mortally wounded but arguing about who has won the duel, is intended to be comic (or grotesque), the SD *fals upon Ercole* will assist the effect (so York 1980); cf. 37n.

30 at my . . . confusion 'at my mercy to kill or spare'. For 'repair' = 'save' cf. R. Southwell, *Mary Magdalens Funeral Teares* (1591), F6^r: 'Could thy loue repaire thee from his rage?'

33.1 SD The entry of all the characters from II.i, and Prospero (perhaps reinforcing the possibility that he may have entered with Baptista at II.i.316.1; see n), will provide dramatic public reaction to the duel. The *Servants*, whom Romelio and Julio seem to be instructing (see 35–9n), are needed to remove the bodies.

35–9 the body . . . gently Romelio is presumably occupied with Ercole, who gives no sign of life in the text; but Contarino is still talking at 37, and Julio replies, so Julio's concern about preventing 'bleeding inward' (40) probably refers to him (so York 1980). Here **bow** means 'to force into a curved shape' (*OED v.*^{1} 9), and is pronounced as in 'bow down'.

36 Saint *Sebastians* 'The saint recovered after being left for dead' (Weis).

37 I have won't Evidently Contarino, before lapsing into unconsciousness, has managed to wrest from Ercole **his sword**, hence 'won it' as signifying victory; cf. 29.1n. Dessen and Thomson cite Brome, *The Lovesick Court*, 142, '*They struggle, and both fall down, still striving to hold each other's sword.*'

49–50 Hence . . . hell That **all** should **learne** from what has happened clearly indicates that this concluding 'sentence' is directed at the audience as well as those on stage.

50 *Exeunt* Since Romelio and Ariosto have to enter at the start of the next scene, it is most likely that they have already exited, Romelio perhaps accompanying Ercole's body, and that the dialogue between Julio and Prospero at 42–50 has the function of providing a pause before the re-entry.

ACT II, Scene iii

2 patience The extent of Romelio's loss of **patience** at his losses will be in part evident from his bearing and whether or not his costume is dishevelled (a sign of distraction). The word is beaten on like a drum by Romelio between here and 33.

10 delayes Complaints about the law's **delayes** were frequent. Cf. *Ham.* III.i.71: 'the law's delay'; also *MonC* (Lucas), 164: 'in court delaies'.

11 little Christian world Presumably **little** in the sense of 'endearingly familiar' (*OED* 3); cf. *DM* IV.ii.121: 'the world is like her little turfe of grass'.

12 Leech for patience 'a doctor who cures by administering patience' (Brennan 1975).

21–2 degree . . . Scarlet . . . Doctor The holder of an Oxford or Cambridge **degree** of **Doctor** of Civil Law might, on occasion, wear **Scarlet** (unlike a mere **Batchelor**); see *WD* III.ii.71–4n.

29 Lawyers beard . . . brissle Ariosto's evident indignation (*OED* bristle *v.*[1] 2) leads to the pun on his beard (*OED* bristle *n.* 2), but the reference to a **Lawyers beard** is more obscure. Possibly Ariosto wears a forked beard, as old-fashioned as his clothes (see II.i.143–4n), and Romelio jests that he has a second forked beard on his **forehead**, like a cuckold's horns; or perhaps the upright hair suggested by **brissle** is sufficient to imply horns.

30 conceited The primary meaning is presumably 'fanciful' (*OED* 4), as in poetry full of witty conceits, but this shades over into 'ingenious, clever' (*OED* 1b).

30–1 right . . . Divine Unconsciously proleptic, in that the **cure** comes after **talke** by the Capuchin (V.iv).

32–3 I . . . impatience Lucas compares *WD* V.vi.67–71. **it** = 'patience' (6 and 24), on which so many sermons were preached. Cf. Herbert, 'The Church Porch', LXXII (*The Works of George Herbert*, ed. F. E. Hutchinson [Oxford, 1941], p. 23):

> Judge not the preacher; for he is thy Judge:
> If thou mislike him, thou conceiv'st him not.
> God calleth preaching folly. Do not grudge
> To pick out treasures from an earthen pot.
> The worst speak something good: if all want sense,
> God takes a text, and preacheth patience.

37 Carracks 'large merchant vessels, galleons'.

39–40 Spice . . . Drench Lucas notes mention by G. Markham of such ingredients in drenches. Thus in *Markham's Maister-peece* (1610) T4ᵛ: 'take a quart of malmsey, of cloues, pepper, cinamon, of each halfe an ounce . . . annoynt all his flankes with oyle de bay, or oyle of Spike'.

43 conceited Taking up Ariosto's remark at 30.

45 unfortunate names For the widespread superstition about hubristic names cf. *The Observations of Sir Richard Hawkins Knight, In His Voyage into the South Sea* (1622), A1ᵛ–A2ʳ: 'Yet advise I all persons ever (as neere as they can) by all meanes, and in all occasions, to presage vnto themselves the good they can, and in giving names to terrestriall Workes (especially to Ships), not to giue such as meerly represent the celestiall Character; for, few have I knowne, or seen, come to a good end, which have had such attributes.' Hawkins then cites the *Revenge*, whose career was one long chapter of mishaps; the *Thunderbolt*, which 'had her Mast cleft with a Thunderbolt, upon the Coast of *Barbary*', then had her poop mysteriously blown up at Dartmouth, and was finally 'burned with her whole Companie in the River of Bourdieux' (after Lucas). Brennan 1975 notes that 'Hawkins' own ship, "The Repentance", had bad luck, and in William Kidley's poem, *Hawkins* (1624) the hero is represented as protesting against this choice of name, made by his mother.'

51–2 cradles . . . Stockes Ariosto puns on 'cradle', which has the same nautical meaning as 'stock': 'the framework on which a ship rests during construction' (*OED* cradle *n.* 9).

56 hansell 'the first money taken by a trader in the morning' (*OED* handsel 3) was an especially good omen from a fool (cf. *Bartholomew Fair*, II.ii.139: 'a fooles handsell is lucky') or, according to Lucas, a cuckold. Romelio therefore probably means that the mere presence of more cuckolds would have been good omen enough: but he might be referring to good luck gifts (*OED* 2).

57–9 my intent . . . angry Having assessed Romelio's state of mind, Ariosto abandons his earlier efforts at instilling patience, and recognizes that only by making him **angry** will he be rescuable. See IV.ii.52–4 and 132–3, and pp. 26–7.

61.1 Handbells and voice Despite the singular 'bell' at 63, the entry of '*two Belmen*' at 68.1 clearly requires two **Handbells** (cf. 63–6n) to be heard. Leonora also says before they enter 'I cannot understand what they say' (68), so she evidently hears at least one *voice*: presumably the Capuchin, possibly accompanied by the Bellmen, either praying or perhaps chanting the dirge they are about to deliver on stage (69–76).

62 How now . . . Scritch-owles Romelio's surprised **How now** is probably reaction to seeing or hearing Leonora, since it must be her he refers to as a screech owl. Although **Scritch-owles** were thought of as harbingers of death (cf. *WD* V.iii.19, *DM* IV.ii.166–8n), and no doubt introduced by W for this reason, Romelio may be using the word as a satiric term of opprobrium for 'screeching' women, or possibly responding to a cry of alarm from Leonora as she enters. As Brennan 1975 notes, what follows echoes *DM* IV.ii.160 ff. 'both in tone and in specific references to the bellman and the screech-owl as well as in the use of a formal dirge'.

63–6 yon bell . . . goods Leonora recognizes the ringing as that of a handbell for the dead (having the same function as the passing bell rung from the church tower, defined by Johnson as 'The bell which rings at the hour of departure, to obtain prayers for the passing soul'). W would have known at first hand the spiritual task of the **Bell-man**, since his father was a witness to the charitable provision, in 1605, of a bellman to bring spiritual exhortation to condemned prisoners in Newgate; see *DM* IV.ii.160–2n. Romelio, however, demonstrates his indifference to spiritual matters by interpreting **yon bell** as that of **the common Bell-man**, or town-crier, announcing **the sale of goods**. Concerning such notices of sale, Lucas cites Holinshed (1577), III.1209: 'Certeine houses in cornehill, being first purchased by the citizens of London, were in the moneth of Februarie cried by a belman and afterward sold.'

69–76 This passage in rhyming couplets and end-stopped lines may be accompanied by the handbells; cf. Bosola's dirge (*DM* IV.ii.165–82).

70 Bead 'prayer' (*OED* 1a). Lucas compares Herrick (p. 68), 'Corinna's going a Maying' (27–8): 'be brief in praying: | Few Beads are best, when once we goe a Maying'.

72 excommunicate Because canon law treated death by duelling as tantamount to suicide, those dying in duels were, like heretics, the unbaptized, the excommunicate, and suicides, excluded from Christian burial (hence 'No Churchman's prayer to comfort their last groanes, | No sacred sodd of earth to hide their bones' [73–4]). See Richard Burn, *The Ecclesiastical Law*, 9th ed. (London, 1842), I, 265, which includes 'persons killed in *duels, tilts* or *tournaments*' amongst those 'anciently' refused burial.

74 sodd Emendation of Q's 'seed' to **sodd** (Dyce's 'sod') is required by the context: 'e/o' and 'e/d' misreadings of secretary hand are common, and **sodd** is a seventeenth-century spelling. Although all twentieth-century editors except Lucas and Gunby 1972 retain 'seed' (which Shirley tentatively glosses as 'small particles strewn about'), the idea of **bones** being hidden by 'seed of earth' is bizarre.

76 Canon 'rule, law, or decree of the Church' (*OED* canon *n.*[1] 1). Cf. 72n.

80 lost for ever Cf. *WD* V.iii.35 and n. Romelio says at 92 that Leonora 'Numbers her Beades', so she may here fall to her knees with her rosary (so York 1980).

82 lazy dead march Lucas is surely right in conjecturing that Q's 'dead lazy march' is a transpositional error. *OED*'s first example of a **dead march** is dated 1603, but stage directions calling for dead marches, in association with funerals, are common in plays of the period, beginning as early as Kyd's *The Spanish Tragedy*, Marlowe's *The Massacre at Paris*, and *1H6*, all plays first performed in the late 1580s or early 1590s.

83–4 Epitaphs . . . Spiders Cf. *WD* V.vi.154–5.

89 a certaine Meditation Cf. Bosola's meditation, similarly introduced (*DM* II.i.40). His later dirge (*DM* IV.ii.165–82) resembles Romelio's (93–124) in content and four-stress rhyming couplet form, and may similarly be chanted or sung, possibly accompanied by a bell (cf. *DM* IV.ii.164n and 165–82n).

92 Numbers her Beades i.e. 'counts, tells over' her rosary beads; = 'prays using her rosary' (see *OED* number *v.* 3).

93–4 You that dwell . . . faults Cf. Tilley D424: 'If the Doctor cures, the sun sees it, but if he kills, the earth hides it.'

95 small Roome Cf. *DM* IV.ii.169–70 (and n): '*Much you had of Land and rent, | Your length in clay's now competent.*'

98 Evidence of Church-land i.e. title-deeds and other documents. The Church's ownership of land was very fully documented.

99–101 Funerals . . . rayment The **Funerals** of the nobility and gentry were strictly controlled by the College of Heralds, who determined the number and rank of mourners. They and their servants were outfitted in mourning attire at the expense of the deceased's estate, with the quality and quantity of cloth likewise prescribed by the College (see Phillis Cunnington and Catherine Lucas, *Costume for Births, Marriages and Deaths* [London, 1972], p. 283). Clare Gittings notes that the yardage of black cloth needed frequently exceeded that which a single merchant could supply, and that the cost of such cloth (**civill wearing**: i.e. 'decent or grave attire' [see *OED* civil 10, wearing *vbl. n.*[1] 1]) could be very large indeed: 'of the £1,977 paid for Robert Cecil's burial [1612] no less than £1,544 was spent on black cloth' (*Death, Burial and the Individual in Early Modern England* [London, 1984], p. 181). Such **Funerals** thus brought **Drapers a good hearing** (i.e. 'pleasant news' [see *OED* hearing 5]), and since the College of Heralds took fees at many stages in the proceedings, **Heraulds** might well **laugh**.

102–3 Worthies . . . Offerings i.e. 'all will be called **Worthies** who die having enough money to pay **Altar Offerings**' (*OED* offering *vbl. n.* 2: 'Something presented to God; e.g. money'). The satiric sense of **Worthies** is clear.

105–6 yeeld . . . night Cf. Hall, *Characters*, 'Hypocrite', p. 76: 'In briefe, hee is . . . a rotten sticke in a darke night' (Dent).

107 last Act . . . Play Romelio's concerns in this speech are located within the tradition of the *ars moriendi* (i.e. the craft of dying well). Handbooks, such as William Perkins's *A Salve for a Sicke Man* (1597), and George Strode's *The Anatomie of Mortalitie* (1618), differed in their theological bases, but all included prayers and exhortations, affirmations of faith and means of overcoming deathbed temptations, traditionally identified as unbelief, despair, impatience, spiritual pride, and avarice. Preparation for a good death was seen as the concern of the living and the sick as well as the terminally ill and dying. See Nancy Lee Beaty, *The Craft of Dying: A Study of the Literary Tradition of the Ars Moriendi in England* (New Haven, 1970). For further dramaturgical comment from Romelio, see III.iii.7–8.

109 precise . . . vewed The **precise** are 'precisians, Puritans'; cf. *DM* II.iii.64n; 'vewe' is listed by *OED* as a seventeenth-century spelling of 'view'.

110 Supersedeas Literally, 'a Writ commanding the stay of legal proceedings which ought otherwise to have proceeded' (*OED* 1), but here figurative, 'something which stops, stays, or checks' (*OED* 2), the point being that the dead will have their last rest interrupted. Lucas compares *The Workes of . . . Gervase Babington* (1615), p. 165: 'Sweet Death is a Supersedeas for all.' Cf. also *AQL* (Lucas) II.i.121. The legal meaning is what Romelio satirically intends: the Puritans, wanting a charnel-vault for business purposes, will not hesitate to take legal action to achieve their ends.

112 chary i.e. 'charily, carefully'. Cf. Shakespeare, *Son.* 22, 11–12: 'which I will keep so chary | As tender nurse her babe from faring ill'.

113 Seacole i.e. 'coal' (as opposed to charcoal) (*OED* 2).

114 vilder uses Lucas compares Marston, *Sophonisba*, IV.i.157–60: 'Where tombes and beauteous urns of well dead men | Stoode in assured rest, the shepheard now | Unloads his belly: Corruption most abhord | Mingling it self with their renowned ashees.'

117 foot and feather Traditionally, time was represented as fleeting through the emblem of winged feet. Cf. Tilley T327, 'Time flees away without delay (has wings)'; also Michael Drayton, *Poly-Olbion*, X.cccxxii (*Works*, IV, 209): 'wing-footed Time them farther off doth beare'.

118 Sexton 'a church officer having the care of the fabric of a church and its contents, and the duties of ringing the bells and digging graves' (*OED* 1). There is perhaps the implication here of '*even* the Sexton', given that he would be more likely to know the location of graves, which were at this time generally unmarked, or of bones, since an additional responsibility was the periodic removal of bones displaced by later burials from churchyard to charnel-house. See Vanessa Harding, 'Burial Choice and Burial Location in Later Medieval London', in *Death in Towns: Urban Responses to the Dying and the Dead, 100–1600*, ed. Steven Bassett (Leicester, 1992) pp. 119–35.

119–24 What care . . . found 'W might have found the suggestion for these lines in countless places. Cf., for example, Seneca, *Epist*. xcii.34–5 (tr. Lodge, ed. 1620, p. 388): "But as we neglect the haires that be shauen from the beard; so that diuine soule being to depart out of the bodie, supposeth that it concerneth her in no sort what shall become of hir case or couer, (whether the fire burne it vp, or the beasts pluck it asunder, or the earth couer it) no more then the secondines [i.e. secundines, afterbirth] pertaine to an infant new borne. As much is it to her whether it be cast for a prey to the birds, or deuoured in the Sea by Dogge-fishes. What is this to her?" Or Guevara, *Diall*, P1ʳ: "I wyll sweare, that at this daye all the deade do sweare, that they care lytell, if their bodyes be buried in the depe Seas, or in the golden tombes, or that the cruell beastes haue eaten them, or that they remayne in the fieldes withoute a graue: so that their soules maye be amonge the celestiall companies"' (Dent). Cf. *WD* V.iv.103–4.

122 Charnell 'A mortuary chapel, a charnel house' (*OED* 1b).

122 chargeable 'expensive' (*OED* 4; cf. *DM* I.i.319).

128 the Hazard For the frequent quibble on the hazards, or openings in the sides of Jacobean tennis-courts, as 'peril', see *WD* V.i.71n.

132–3 He . . . presumption Cf. *DM* IV.ii.350–1n.

139 a 'he'. On the ellipsis of the nominative 'he' see Abbott, Sect. 402.

143 The worse? At York 1980 Leonora's sudden reinvolvement in the dialogue was emphasized by her getting up from prayer (see 80n) only at this point.

146–7 Yet . . . Justice Leonora's desperation to retrieve her slip at 143–4 is akin to Juliet's (*Rom*. III.v.80 ff.). **Yet** = 'still' (*OED conj*. 2a), with, as Lucas points out, an emphatic echo of Prospero's 'He's yet living' (141).

148–59 visit him . . . bring me word Presumably all spoken to Prospero.

150 swounding 'swooning, fainting' (*OED*).

151 soveraigne 'excellent, outstanding'.

154 How . . . drest? i.e. 'how often has his wound been dressed?'

157–8 second . . . life i.e. any deadly infection will show up at this point.

165 *Exeunt* Presumably together, to fetch Leonora's remedies (so York 1980).

169 Engine . . . weigh up An **Engine** is a 'mechanical contrivance' (*OED* 4), in this case to **weigh up**, i.e. 'raise (a sunk ship, gun, etc.) from the bottom of the water'

(*OED* 6). Romelio's figurative usage is that his **Engine** ('device, plot, snare'; *OED* 3) will retrieve his 'sunke' (170) hopes of money.

172 in securitie On the theological dangers of **securitie**, see *DM* V.ii.328–9n.

174 fore-winds 'favourable winds, that blow a ship forward on its course' (see *OED*).

175 Piramides . . . weake Cf. *DM* V.v.75–8 (and n): 'That thou, which stood'st like a huge Piramid | Begun upon a large, and ample base, | Shalt end in a little point, a kind of nothing.'

ACT II, Scene iv

0.1 ERCOLE *led betweene two* Presumably Ercole will give indication that even standing, like speech, is 'very painfull' (37). At York 1980 he almost immediately collapsed.

1 Looke up sir Presumably to heaven, in acknowledgement of a miracle.

5 dwell in't 'persist in it, unrepentantly' (Lucas).

6 informed 'instructed, enlightened' (*OED ppl. a.* 2). Cf. *Cor.* V.3.70–2: 'The God of soldiers . . . inform | Thy thoughts with nobleness.'

9 naught 'worthless, bad' (*OED adj.* 1).

10 hazard 'risking, peril' (*OED* 3).

11 foregoe the complement i.e. 'abstain from [*OED* 6] the observance of ceremony' (of quarrelling) (*OED* complement 8b; cf. 'to keep complement: to observe ceremony').

16 Cicil Lucas alters to 'Sicil', but Q's spelling (as an abbreviated form of Sicily) was common at the time; 'Cicillia' occurs repeatedly in, e.g., *The Thracian Wonder*.

22 happily 'haply, perchance'.

27–35 Priviledge . . . Pardon Transparently a dramatic device, this combines, as Lucas notes, an allusion to the famous and abortive exchange of cartels in 1528 between Francis I and Charles V, who had accused the French King of violating the Treaty of Madrid, and to another challenge at a Papal Consistory in 1536. There Charles V rose and said (in the words of Montaigne, *Essayes*, I.16, p. 26): 'he had challenged the king (Francis I) to fight with him, man to man in his shirt, with Rapier and Dagger in a boate'.

42–3 These . . . Devill 'From Overbury, *Characters* (1615), G1ʳ, "Newes of my Morning worke": "That sinne makes worke for repentance or the Deuill"' (Dent).

46 Gordion knots Cf. *DM* I.i.463–4 (and n): 'this sacred Gordian, which, let violence | Never untwine'. Lucas emends to 'Gordian', but *OED* records **Gordion** as a sixteenth-century spelling, and *LION: Drama* and *LION: Poetry* turn up several other seventeenth-century instances.

47.1 *Explicit Actus secundus* 'Here ends the second act.' As Lucas notes, Q's genitive '*secundi*' has resulted from confusion with the alternative Latin formula, *Finis Actus secundi* ('the end of the second act'). We have corrected the same mistake at the ends of Acts III and IV. See p. 70.

ACT III, Scene i

2 thus clouded 'thus obscured' (*OED* 3a), probably with a gesture to Crispiano's disguise; cf. II.i.1n.

5–9 Gold-myne . . . Ladies For the first explanation no evidence is ever forthcoming, although W may have intended to develop extraterritorial treason in order to invoke the jurisdiction of the High Court of Chivalry later in the play (see IV.ii.622–7n, and Carnegie, pp. 261–2). The second—**mad tricks . . . plaid of late by Ladies**—is central to the play's concerns, as witness the sub-title, 'When Women goe to Law, the Devill is full of Businesse'. Cf. II.i.9–10.

8 vents Probably 'sells, vends' (see *OED v.*³ 1, and Jonson, *Volpone*, II.ii.5–6: 'They are quack-salvers, | Fellowes, that live by venting oyles, and drugs'). Lucas and Brennan 1975 gloss as 'spends' (*OED v.*² 7c); but since the King of Spain wants to apprehend Romelio in an illegal transaction, 'sells' is much more likely, especially as it was common usage at the time. An alternative might be 'to put (coins, etc.) in circulation' (*OED v.*² 8b). Wiggins's suggestion (p. 373) of 'a metaphorical variation on *OED vent v.*² 11', meaning 'removes from the earth', seems unlikely.

11 Lords . . . Wards i.e. the 'Ladies' (10) treat their husbands (*OED* lord 4) as if they were minors under their guardianship: the point being that they control their husbands' assets and income. Cf. 11–17. As Lucas points out, an audience would naturally take 'the King' (10) to mean King James.

12–13 Dutchwomen . . . pay all i.e. they control the household finances, both income and outgoings. See Tilley A203: 'Take All and pay all' (1601), and cf. *WHo* I.ii.105: 'thou art faine to take al, and pay all'. Lucas compares Moryson, *Itinerary*, p. 288: 'The wiues of *Holland* buy and sell all things at home, and vse to saile to *Hamburg* and into *England* for exercise of traffique . . . And the Women not onely take young Men to their Husbands, but those also which are most simple and tractable: so as by the foresaid priuiledge of Wiues to dispose goods by their last will . . . they keepe their Husbands in a kind of awe, and almost alone, without their Husbands intermedling, not onely keepe their shops at home, but exercise trafficke abroad. My selfe haue heard a Wife make answere to one asking for her Husband, that he was not at home, but had newly asked her leaue to goe abroad . . . I may boldly say, that the Women of these parts, are aboue all other truly taxed with this vnnatural dominering ouer their Husbands.'

14 silly 'ignorant' (*OED* 3a).

16–17 give away from i.e. 'leave to someone other than'. It is not altogether clear whether this is a standard use of **away from**, or a testamentary disposition **from** ('denoting qualitative remoteness', *OED* 8b) **their wives**.

18 So heare Either 'therefore if here and now (I told you)', or 'it is the same here'.

19 Bat-fowling 'swindling'. Literally, 'the catching of birds at night when at roost' by 'dazing them with a light, and knocking them down' with a bat; hence 'victimizing the simple' (*OED*). Lucas notes a lengthy account of the 'sport' in Gervase Markham, *Hungers Prevention* (1600).

20 conceive 'understand' (*OED* 9).

20 Game . . . i'th night i.e. women are manoeuvring darkly behind the scenes to secure lucrative employment for their husbands. Their **Game**, being **all i'th night**, presumably involves sexual favours.

26–9 vowed . . . women Crispiano bears out his promise at the IV.ii trial, though ironically he is also one of the victims of Leonora's **insolencies**.

ACT III, SCENE ii

III.ii Distinguishing between verse and prose is a particularly acute problem in this scene. Q prints III.ii entirely as verse, but the Surgeons, despite intermittent iambic rhythms, seem to drop into prose after 32. With Romelio the converse appears to be the case and, problematic lines notwithstanding (e.g. 48–50), his speeches have been allowed to stand as verse.

0.1 *habit of a Jew* This SD implies an immediately recognizable stage costume, quite possibly the 'Jewish gaberdine' referred to by Shylock (*MV* I.iii.112). We may expect that Shylock, Barabas (from *The Jew of Malta*; cf. 3n), and other stage Jews provided a model (and theatrical stock) of clothing and other features (such as a large nose and red beard; see 3n) on which Romelio could base his disguise.

1 well habited Romelio shows off his costume, no doubt with physical energy appropriate to playing 'with mine owne shaddow' (2). At York 1980 his disguise had passed its first test as Crispiano and Ariosto, exiting from the previous scene, passed him without recognizing him.

2 shaddow Cf. *R3* I.i.26–7: 'to see my shadow in the sun | And descant on mine own deformity'. Romelio may refer to the shape he makes in his disguise clothing, or possibly to a large false nose (see 3n).

3 Italienated Jew 'It seems clear that W had here in mind *The Jew of Malta*, and its Machiavellian villain Barabas (cf. "Betray a Towne to'th Turke" [13])'. So Lucas, who compares William Rowley's *A Search for Money* (1609), C2ᵛ, describing a usurer: 'his visage (or vizard) like the artificiall Jewe of Maltaes nose . . . vpon which nose, two casements were built, through which his eyes had a little ken of vs'. Attaching glasses to a false nose to hold it on is still common. ('Casement' in this figurative sense is not recorded in *OED*.) A red beard and wig are also likely.

5 carv'd . . . Cherrystone Presumably already a well-known curiosity, though the first reference *OED* gives (cherry-stone 1) is dated 1677. Although Q's 'on' is a possible spelling of **one**, the omission of 'e' is here more likely to be due to the influence of the immediately preceding **upon**.

6 rotten The clear transferred meaning here, that the ivy rots that which it clings to and strangles, is not recorded in *OED*.

7 Quicksilver 'mercury'; cf. *WD* V.ii.158n.

7–8 poyson . . . beard Cf. Lodovico's 'T'have poison'd his praier booke, or a paire of beades, | The pummell of his saddle, his looking-glasse, | Or th' handle of his racket, ô that, that!' (*WD* V.i.66–8).

8 drench 'large (poisonous) draught or potion' (*OED n.* 2).

11 disease naturall Not a specific **disease**, but one caused by things **naturall** (the humours, weather, spirits, etc.), as opposed to things non-natural (foul air, affections, food, etc.), or things against nature (sickness, causes of sickness, accident). The point is that the victim will seem to be suffering from a natural condition (perhaps = old age), aggravated by seasonal change ('Spring and Fall', 10), rather than unnatural poison. On this standard Galenic schema concerning the origins of disease, see Hoeniger, p. 45.

11   sleight   i.e. 'slight', but with, presumably, an ironic pun on **sleight** = 'cunning, crafty' (*OED* 1), and 'expert' (*OED* 2), given the villainies Romelio lists.

13   Betray ... to'th Turke   A self-consciously theatrical reference to Barabas in *The Jew of Malta* (see III.ii.3 and n). Richard Perkins, the actor probably cast as Romelio, certainly acted Barabas later in his career, and it is just possible that he is here mocking a role he already plays; see pp. 49–50.

15   Politician   'one skilled in politics' (*OED* 2); but, as frequently, with the additional sense of 'a crafty plotter or intriguer' (*OED* 1).

16   disgested ... blood   Strictly impossible, since digestion (**disgested** = 'digested') resulted not only in the formation of blood, but also in waste material that had to be eliminated. Romelio's point, however, is that politicians feed on others' blood.

17   loose myselfe   i.e. 'become deeply absorbed (in acting my disguise role)'.

18 Within there!   Romelio may knock (so Lucas) as well as calling.

18.1   *Surgeons*   Costume will partly determine the extent of low comedy in this scene. Surgeons were often barbers as well, known as 'checkered apron' men (C. Willett and Phillis Cunnington, *Handbook of English Costume in the Sixteenth Century*, rev. ed. [London, 1973], p. 195), no doubt in jocular reference to bloodstains spattering their aprons (so Bristol 1989). Aprons were not universal, however, and wealthier surgeons might be indistinguishable from physicians in dress, merely adding a long gown (see Cunnington and Lucas, pp. 302–3) to fashionable clothing; W ensures we are told they are surgeons.

20 ff.   Romelio's impersonation of a Jew may well include an assumed accent.

20 Art   'professional skill' (*OED* 4); see 25 and V.vi.94–7.

26   warme drinks   Frequently prescribed as part of medical treatment; 'these might soothe the patient, but as the best surgeons of W's time knew, never cure an abcess' (David Hoeniger, communicated privately). Cf. *DM* IV.ii.333.

26 impostumation   Either 'festering, suppuration' (*OED* 1) or 'abcess' (*OED* 2).

27   incision   (Dyce; not in Q) 'An almost certain conjecture' (Lucas), since it occurs again at III.iii.106.

28   Orifix   i.e. 'orifice'. Cf. G. Markham, *Cheape and Good Husbandry* (1614), A7ʳ: '*Orifice* is the mouth, hole, or open passage, of any wound or vlcer.'

31 deputed   'appointed' (*OED* depute *v.* 1).

42 How sir?   This may well be an exclamation, not a question.

42   Will   Q has 'wil', but the fact that the word appears within a tight line that includes the abbreviations '*Rom.*' and '&' warrants regularizing to the '–ll' ending. Capitalization of the noun is also normal in Q.

47 store   'abundant supply' (*OED* 4a) because of the crime and vice prevalent in Rome.

48–9 I can . . . forenoones 'cf. Jonson, *Volpone*, II.ii.59–62: *"These . . . rogues . . . are able, very well, to kill their twentie a weeke, and play"'* (Dent). The first of several borrowings from *Volpone* in this scene.

49 you will give me leave Perhaps a hurried response to an unamused reaction by the Surgeons.

54 Law of Alliance Not a legal term *per se*. A legal definition of **Alliance** is 'relation by marriage, or relation by any form of kindred' (so Jowitt, p. 88). **By the Law of Alliance** could thus be paraphrased as 'because of the expectations of such a relationship'.

55 practise 'bring about, accomplish' (*OED* 8).

57 Extraction Romelio may produce a phial containing the **Extraction** (= extract, active principal), or make a great show of having it safely tucked away, to point the speech. Cf. *Volpone*, II.ii.94–5: *'this rare extraction . . . hath . . . power to disperse all malignant humours'*.

65 ten thousand Duckets About £2,500; see II.i.165–80n.

66 pull the pillow Sykes compares Jonson, *Volpone*, II.vi.87–8 ('Tis but to pull the pillow, from his head, | And he is thratled'), and Dent Donne, *Biathanatos*, II.vi.7: 'that ordinarily . . . women which are desperate of sick persons' recovery use to take the pillow from under them, and so give them leave to dye sooner'.

70 Upon my Jewisme 'an oath as false as Romelio's assumed disguise' (Brennan 1975). Romelio will be well aware that in his mouth this affirmation has even less validity than a Jacobean audience might expect of it anyway.

71.1 in a bed The Surgeons may, as Lucas added, *'draw the traverse, discovering'* Contarino; but it is equally possible that he is thrust forth or carried on in a bed. See Dessen and Thomson, 'bed'.

74 roundly 'briskly, promptly' (*OED* 7).

81 toy Either 'a fantastic notion' (*OED n.* 4), or 'a piece of nonsense' (*OED* 5).

82 neere i.e. 'close to', both physically and figuratively; cf. Middleton, *A Chaste Maid in Cheapside*, I.i.195: 'You'll steal away some man's Daughter: am I near you?' (*OED adv.*[2] 16).

82 *Exeunt Surgeons* Subsequent events make it clear that they now observe Romelio from hiding, perhaps from behind a stage hanging (cf. III.iii.292–4n).

91 Will It is possible that Romelio displays the will; cf. 126–7n.

93 put in . . . Caveat 'a process in court to suspend proceedings' (*OED* 1), here used figuratively with the sense of prevention by pre-emption.

93–4 Come forth . . . Steeletto A stiletto is 'a little sharpe dagger' (*OED* 1, quoting Coryat's *Crudities* [1611], p. 275), particularly associated with Italian murder. Romelio's speech implies that the stiletto he now draws has been hidden on his person, not worn openly in the usual manner of a dagger.

96 Bodkin Romelio puns on (1) 'a long ornamental hairpin', (2) 'dagger, stiletto' (*OED* 1), and possibly (3) 'a frizzling iron' (*OED* 3b). *OED* (frizzling) quotes Coryat's *Crudities* [1611], p. 261), 'A frisling or crisping pinne of iron'.

97 engine 'instrument used in warfare' (*OED* 5, which cites reference to a rapier as late as 1676). For the associated sense of 'contrivance', see II.iii.169n.

99 Barmotho Pigs The Bermudas were as famous for pigs as for tempests. Cf. S. Jourdan, *A Discovery of the Bermudas* (1610), B4ᵛ: 'The country affordeth great abound-ance of hogs, as that there hath beene taken by Sir George Sommers, who was the first that hunted for them, to the number of two and thirty at one time.' Cf. *AQL* (Lucas) V.i.350–60 (after Lucas).

101 O that great *Cæsar* The addition of **that** (Dyce) is required by sense and metre. The syntax is 'O, that great *Cæsar* (i.e. Julius Caesar, assassinated in 44 B.C.) . . . should . . . come to dye'; cf. III.iii.5.

101 past the shocke i.e. 'endured the military encounter' (*OED* pass *v.* 32, shock *n.*³ 1).

107 wheale 'pimple, pustule' (*OED* wheal 1).

109–10 thee . . . him The syntax is not clear. Lucas is surely right that **thee** is direct address to the stiletto, but **shake him by the hand** seems to refer to holding the handle of the stiletto. Such an abrupt switch from first-person to third-person address may imply a sudden very broad aside to the audience.

113 this . . . thee Here it is clear that Contarino is being addressed: 'this stiletto shall prove merciful to you'. Cf. 109–10n.

116 absolute Cure Proleptically ironic, in that Romelio means death, but in fact cures Contarino.

118–19 inwards . . . lead While **washt** may indicate that he will have to drink the **lead** (as Bartervile is forced to drink molten gold in Dekker's *If This Be Not a Good Play, the Devil Is In It*, V.iv.49–51: 'it scaldes,—it scaldes,—it scaldes,—it scaldes'), one of the victims in Dekker's torture scene is Ravaillac, who assassinated Henri IV of France in 1610. Contemporary pamphlets describe in grisly detail the tortures to which he was subjected. These included pouring into his wounds 'scalding Oyle, Rosen, Pitch, & Brimstone, melted together', and also a torture involving **lead**: 'they put vpon his Navell a rundle of clay, very hard, with a hole in the midst, and into the same hole poured they moulten lead, till it was filled, yet reauealed he nothing' (*The Terrible and Deserved Death of Francis Ravilliack, Shewing the Manner of his Strange Torments at his Execution* [1610], B1ᵛ–2ᵛ). This particular torture could conceivably be what W had in mind for the Surgeon's threat to Romelio. Cf. *WD* V.vi.138–41, which seems to draw on Dekker. Wiggins, however, argues (pp. 373–4) that reference is to the infamous Henrician penalty for poisoners, death by boiling either in water or lead, and that 1 Surgeon's 'try' (118) both reinforces the judicial context and plays on the Barber Surgeons' right to the bodies of four executed criminals each year for experimental purposes.

120 I turne Christian Probably throwing off his disguise here, though York 1980 delayed it until 124. Cf. V.iii.31–2.

124 Marchant The standard meaning of 'merchant' as trader included connotations of cheating in such phrases as 'play the merchant' (*OED* 1c); the word could also mean 'fellow' (*OED* 3, citing G. Carleton, *Jurisdiction Regall, Episcopall, Papall* [1610], Z2ᵛ: 'The King to hold fast this slippery Merchant, required all the Bishops to set their approbation, and seales to those Lawes').

126–7 reade . . . bloudy Roman Letter Romelio's pun on **reade** = 'discover the meaning or significance of' (*OED* 2a) is capped by the Surgeon's pun on **Roman Letter** as handwriting. But while the pun is evident, it is not clear what Romelio might actually offer the Surgeons to **reade**, unless it is Contarino's will.

136 double Duckets W understood the single ducat (probably a silver coin) to be worth about five shillings (see II.i.165–80n), so **double Duckets** (probably gold) were worth nearly ten shillings. Cf. *MV* II.viii.18–19: 'A sealed bag, two sealed bags of ducats, | Of double ducats'.

137 weigh this busines 'No doubt, as he speaks, the Surgeon weighs also the bag of ducats in his hand' (Lucas).

139 drownd With the implication also, it seems, of 'drunk', though *OED* does not record this usage, only the figurative sense of killing oneself through drink (*OED* drown *v*. 3b).

141 Usquebath i.e. 'usquebaugh, whiskey'.

144 musick of the Mint At York 1980 the Surgeon jingled the bag of ducats loudly.

149–50 foot-cloth A horsecloth; see I.ii.181n. Lucas notes that this 'sign of affluence [was] especially affected by physicians'.

150 policy The usage here is unclear. In English at this time **policy** usually meant a 'policy of assurance, insurance policy' (*OED n.*² 1a), and in a general figurative sense 2 Surgeon may mean that Romelio has provided him with a policy on which 2 Surgeon can, as it were, make a full claim 'every eight dayes'. But this reading will not sustain close examination, given that 2 Surgeon wants money or its equivalent, not a contractual obligation, so Lucas may be right that **policy** = 'bill, bond', based on the Italian *polizza*, although *OED* does not record this usage in English.

151 peach 'to inform against an accomplice' (*OED* 2).

154 Unicornes Horne Supposedly efficacious against poison; cf. *WD* II.i.14n.

155–6 Oh . . . groane Contarino's **Oh** is in effect a direction for a **groane**; cf. *WD* V.ii.14, 15n. The Surgeon may address the question to the audience to increase comedy (so Bristol 1989).

157 Is the wind in that doore still? Proverbial (Tilley W419), the modern equivalent being 'Is the wind in that quarter?' or 'Is that the way the wind blows?' Cf. *1H4* III.iii.88–9: 'is the wind in that door, i'faith? must we all march?'

158 Come hither Whether Contarino is centrally placed in a bed or in a discovery space (see 71.1n), the Surgeons have been talking at some distance from him on stage (or at York 1980 nonchalantly sitting on the end of his bed). 1 Surgeon, who has crossed first to Contarino, seems the more active throughout the scene.

158–60 Steele . . . congealed blood 'According to the ancients, usually with reference to Jason of Pherae, the dagger of a would-be assassin saved the tyrant's life by piercing an abscess. The story, told or referred to in Pliny, Cicero, Seneca, Valerius Maximus, Plutarch, etc., is mentioned by innumerable Elizabethan authors. But W probably drew upon a more contemporary history, as found in one of his sources for *DM*; cf. Goulart's *Admirable and Memorable Histories* (tr. Grimeston, 1607), p. 289—"An extraordinarie Cure": "A Certaine Italian hauing had a quarrell with another, fell so grieuously sicke, as they did not hope for life of him. His enemie hearing thereof, came to his lodging, and inquires of his seruant, where his master was. The seruant answered him, hee is at the point of death, and will not escape this day. The other grumbling to himselfe, replied, he shall die by my hands: whereupon he enters into the sicke mans chamber, giues him certaine stabbes with his dagger, and then flies. They binde vp this poore sicke mans wounds, who by the meanes of so great a losse of blood, recoured his health. So hee recoured his health and life by his meanes who sought his death"' (Dent, crediting Lucas). Cf. *DM* IV.ii.39–43n.

160   blood; observe Presumably a stage effect visible to the audience; cf. *WD* V.vi.235–6n, and *R3* I.ii.55–6.

160 delivers 'discharges'.

162–3 his entent . . . his life i.e. Romelio's and Contarino's.

165 rackt i'th Tower 'A topical allusion current about 1603, but perhaps suggested to W by Jonson, *Volpone*, IV.vi.32–3: "I haue heard, | The racke hath cur'd the gout"' (Dent).

167–8 foule diseases Presumably venereal.

170 Searing i.e. 'searing iron, cauterizing iron' (*OED* does not list this meaning, but cf. searing *vbl. n.* 1b).

170 *Exeunt* Contarino on his bed must be dragged or carried in by the Surgeons or stage attendants, unless he has remained in a discovery space throughout and simply needs a traverse curtain drawn across to hide him from view. The Second Surgeon may take up Romelio's Jewish disguise (cf. 120 and n), since he is identified as using it in Act V (see V.iii.31 and V.vi.33.2).

ACT III, Scene iii

0.1–.2 *Tapers . . . mourning* The props on the *Table* all signify melancholy, as will Jolenta's black *mourning* garments. See p. 42.

1 Looking-glasse It is possible that Romelio supports this speech by using an actual mirror from the table; for the emblematic potential of such action see *DM* III.ii.69 SD and n.

4 painting It is possible that hitherto the actor playing Jolenta has applied colour, or that a white makeup is applied for this scene.

7 shortest fever the best Cf. *MonC* (Lucas), 131: 'Of all, the shortest madnesse is the best.'

7–8 bad Playes . . . length Cf. II.iii.107 for previous dramaturgical advice from Romelio.

9 stuck *OED* does not give a usage precisely as here, but the sense appears to be that of *OED* stick *v.*[1] II, 'to remain fixed'.

11–13 Court . . . Mirrour Cf. *DM* I.i.11–13: 'Considring duely, that a Princes Court | Is like a common Fountaine, whence should flow | Pure silver-droppes in generall'; and *DM* I.i.192–3: 'Let all sweet Ladies break their flattring Glasses, | And dresse themselves in her.'

15 wroght i.e. 'wrought'. Q's spelling is not listed in *OED* after the sixteenth century, but occurs in, e.g., the 1625 Quarto of Middleton's *A Game at Chess* (G3^v).

17 **Jolenta rises and makes to leave** Jolenta rises in anger (so Lucas), given her reaction at 8–10, and no doubt Romelio rises to force her back down (so York 1980); he may remain in the more dominant standing position. Cf. *WD* V.vi.1–3 for a similar instance of brother detaining sister.

28 **absolute Will** i.e. 'unconditionally, by the terms of the will'.

35 **radically** 'thoroughly'.

38 **Order of Saint *Clare*** The Order of Poor Clares, known in England as the Minoresses, was founded *c.* 1215 by St Clare of Assisi (*c.* 1194–1253), and was characterized by poverty and austerity. See also V.i.0.1n.

45 **dumbe Mid-wife** i.e. one whose affliction will enable her to keep the secret.

51–5 **Precontract ... Matrimony** Romelio's intention is to confirm the betrothal of I.ii, though since it was entered into without Jolenta's consent ecclesiastical approval will need to be bought.

56 **So, then** The comma has been added to Q because this is an example of 'W's common use of *so* as an interjection' (Lucas).

56–7 **conceave ... conceaved** From **conceave** = 'apprehend, understand' (*OED* conceive 9), Jolenta develops a double pun, where **conceaved** has the meaning of 'devised' (*OED* 7) as well as the usual gynaecological sense.

63 **essentially** 'in essence, really' (*OED* 1).

66 **Precontract ... justifie it** Jolenta here turns Romelio's argument at 50–3 neatly against him, claiming that she and Contarino were contracted to marry but also that she will get a priest to affirm (corruptly) that he married them.

67 **singular** 'Above the ordinary; special' (*OED* 10), but used here for the play on 'plurall' (68).

68 **plurall** 'holding two or more benefices at the same time' (*OED* 1); a widely condemned abuse. Cf. *AQL* (Lucas) V.i.125–8.

71 **Votaries** 'nun's'.

79 **still** 'invariably, always' (*OED adv.* 3a).

83 **frostie ... youth** i.e. full of cares, such as turn the hair white (cf. *OED adj.* frosty 4).

84 **witcht upon me** i.e. 'have forced on me by witchcraft' (see *OED* witch *v.*[1] 2). There is presumably also a homonymic pun on 'wished'.

94 **falshood** Romelio is of course unaware that this **falshood** (that Leonora loves Contarino) is true, though the alleged plot is not.

101 **tendred** i.e. 'acted tenderly (or was solicitous) towards' (see *OED* tender *v.*[2] 3).

105 **and he was capable** 'if he were fit' (Brennan 1975), taking **and** in its conditional sense (*OED* C), with **capable** reminding us of the duel, and throwing doubt on Contarino's current capability. It is just possible, however, that the phrase should be glossed as 'and, furthermore, he was capable of undertaking such a thing', with **capable** conveying in addition to its usual sense that of susceptibility (*OED* 4a).

110 **malice ... Devils** Ironic, in that Romelio is suggesting what he claims **Devils** would scarcely do.

115–17 **this relicke ... sent him** At II.iii.165 Leonora and Prospero exited to fetch the 'choyce Relicke' (II.iii.149) for Contarino. Logic suggests that for Romelio to have it now he either prevented Leonora sending it or, more likely, retrieved it from Contarino when he stabbed him, and is now lying to Jolenta. An audience is unlikely to ponder the matter.

125 my quarrell i.e. 'a quarrel on my behalf'.

127 pretended 'alleged' (*OED* 2); the usual connotation of denying the validity of the description is in this case assigned to Contarino rather than Ercole.

128 To cleare your suspition i.e. 'to clear up any suspicion you might have formed that he was not really in love with you' (Lucas).

130 censure of i.e. 'adverse judgement, hostile criticism, as . . .' (cf. *OED* 4).

138 direct falshood i.e. 'no, it is as downright [*OED* direct 5] dishonesty as ever brought expulsion from court'. Having brought Jolenta to believe his story that Leonora and Contarino 'plotted | Cunningly' (106–7) to satisfy their mutual love under the cover of Jolenta's marriage ('Can this be truth?' 137), Romelio now says the story is untrue: no mother would act so, and Contarino's 'love' for Leonora masks his avarice. Romelio thus plants suspicion in Jolenta's mind and strengthens it by unconvincing retraction. There may be a satiric jibe at the prevalence of Court dishonesty.

144 right 'exactly, to the full' (*OED* right *adv.* 5). Cf. *WD* II.i.367.

145 fowle A pun on 'bird' and 'foul'; Brennan 1975 suggests it is 'a variant of the proverb (Tilley B376) "An ill Bird lays an ill egg"'.

145 Devill Ironically, Romelio himself.

148 Turne my blood An obscure phrase, which seems to have a meaning similar to 'turn thy complexion' (*Oth.* IV.ii.62); the point being that the impact of strong emotions was believed to make the blood rush from the heart to the extremities, and therefore the face, or the opposite, causing the face to be pale. So perhaps 'turns me cold and pale' (David Hoeniger, private communication).

149 apparant 'manifest, evident' (*OED* apparent 3).

151 world i'th Moone Cf. *DM* II.iv.16–19: 'We had need goe borrow that fantastique glasse | Invented by *Galileo* the Florentine, | To view an other spacious world i'th' Moone, | And looke to find a constant woman there.'

152 fantasticks 'those with fanciful ideas' (*OED n.* 1).

155 affect 'prefer, am drawn to' (*OED v.*[1] 2).

158–61 witnesse . . . mary with him A solemn oath which, though sworn as a result of Jolenta's being misled by Romelio, will carry weight, and help prepare us for her eventual marriage to Ercole.

168–71 Lordships . . . Eunuch Richard Knolles's widely-read *Generall Historie of the Turkes* (1603) provides examples of astonishing Ottoman wealth going to eunuchs: '*Amurath* had heretofore taken *Hassan Bassa* the Eunuch out of the Serraglio, from the charge he had there to serue in the queens Court, and at her instance sent him as Bassa to CAIRE the great citie of ÆGYPT. Which great office, beside the honour belonging vnto it, is also beneficiall to them whose good hap it is to be aduanced thereunto: the riches the multitude of people inhabiting therein being so great, that it seemeth to be not one citie, but rather to containe within the large circuit thereof many cities' (p. 980).

170 for any ... flesh 'for aught that physical relationship has to do with it' (Lucas).

173–5 Breath ... foule 'Cf. Guazzo, *Civile Conversation*, D6ʳ: "we should imitate the Greeke, who as one told him his mouthe stunke, answered, that the cause of it was the many secrets which he suffred to mould and vinew [grow mouldy] within it"' (Dent).

180–1 faine ... swoundings At York 1980 Jolenta acted out a feigned swoon and fell to the stage.

181–2 unripe ... colour The **unripe fruit** will presumably induce stomach pains, and hence pallor; cf. the Duchess's reaction to apricots (*DM* II.i). **Oatmeale** was regarded likewise: see Gerard, *Herball*, p. 69: 'Otemeale is good for to make a faire and well-coloured maide to looke like a cake of tallow, especially if she take next her stomacke a good draught of strong vineger after it.' Oatmeal could also be used to whiten the face: cf. the pretended deathbed makeup of Poore, 'some meale now | To make a white man of mee & a sickly' ('The Part of Poore', perf. *c.* 1615; in *Collections*, xv, Malone Society [Oxford, 1993], lines 1523–4).

184 preface 'something preliminary or introductory' (*OED* 4: which does not, however, include the physical sense intended here).

185 advance 'push out' (Weis).

188 keepe decorum 'behave with propriety'; here doubly ironic, since pregnancy, itself improper for an unmarried woman, will be affirmed by unseemly behaviour which will be regarded as normal eccentricity.

189 noddle 'beat (on the head?)' (*OED v.*¹).

191 Stockfish Cf. Peter Martyr, *The Decades of the Newe Worlde or West India* (tr. R. Eden, 1555), Zzziʳ, where stockfish are defined as 'haddockes or hakes indurate and dryed with coulde, and beaten with clubbes or stockes, by reason whereof the Germayns caule them stoke-fysshe'. Also Tilley S867: 'To beat one like a Stockfish'.

194 pyde fooles coat Either the motley (particoloured, pied) coat of the fool or jester universally recognizable from graphic tradition as an emblem of Folly (cf. *AYLI* II.vii.13: 'A motley fool'), or possibly the long motley coat which seems to have been adopted by English stage clowns early in the seventeenth century (see David Wiles, *Shakespeare's Clown* [Cambridge, 1987], pp. 182–91, and Fig. 9).

197–9 nothing ... Contarino i.e. 'nothing in the world but begetting in her a dislike for Contarino could have done this'.

199–203 Jelousie ... fiend Romelio's point is that the **Law-case** itself is a **Devil** which he has 'hatcht' (145) and **raisd**; hence **nourish craftily this fiend**. Lucas compares *DM* I.i.298 in arguing against Deighton's proposed emendation of **fiend** to 'feud', although he accepts that 'Tweene [204] is certainly awkward after fiend', and would more naturally follow Deighton's emendation. Romelio's statement is proleptic, in part, of the case Leonora brings. Q's 'devil' and 'law-case' are set in a single line too full to accommodate the upper-case initial letters.

210 waged to the East Indies i.e. 'hired to go there' (Lucas), but with the sense of 'bribed' (*OED* 7c).

211 beyond the Lyne i.e. south of the equator, hence in the tropics; cf. *WD* III.iii.25.

211 Callenture 'A disease incident to sailors within the tropics, characterized by delirium in which the patient, it is said, fancies the sea to be green fields, and desires to leap into it' (*OED* calenture 1). Cf. Nashe, *Christ's Teares Over Jerusalem* (1613), *Works*, II, 92: 'Then (as the possessed with the Calentura) thou shalt offer to leape.'

212 Indian Pox Whether syphilis, the **Pox**, was brought to Europe by Columbus's men from the West Indies is still debated. W's use of the term **Indian Pox** is slightly unusual, as the disease was more commonly known as simply 'the pox' or, more scientifically, as *morbus gallicus*, the French disease. It was also popularly associated with Naples and Spain. See Johannes Fabricius, *Syphilis in Shakespeare's England* (London, 1994) and Claude Quétel, *History of Syphilis* (London, 1990).

213 take order for '"see to"; here, ensure against' (Weis).

217–19 mischiefes . . . single Franciscans and other orders of friars were required to travel in pairs; hence perhaps the Italian proverb cited by Dent from Florio's 'Giardino di Ricreatione' in *Second Frutes* (1591), Aa2ʳ: 'Un male & un frate, rare volte soli' [An evil-doer and a friar rarely go about alone]. See also II.i.329 and n. Lucas notes the quibble on **pray** and 'prey'. Cf. *WD* V.iii.129 ff., where the pair of false Capuchins torment the dying Brachiano.

220 estate 'state, condition' (*OED* 1a).

224 My charitie Cf. *WD* V.iii.169–70 for a similarly ironic use of the term.

227 I am . . . lips Cf. *WD* V.iv.47–8: 'Your reverend mother | Is growne a very old woman in two howers.'

229–30 wound . . . heart 'Cf. Sidney, *Arcadia*, III.ii (*Works*, I, 361), where Pamela laments the absence of love-wounded Musidorus, "having given the wound to him through her owne harte"'. (So Dent, who compares *CC* IV.ii.25: 'Oh you have struck him dead thorough my heart').

231 presently 'now, immediately'.

231–2 this . . . errour Romelio has earlier discerned Leonora's 'deare regard' (101) for Contarino, so here he must be deceiving her into thinking he (Romelio) is deceived.

234 rights 'justifiable claims' (*OED n.*¹ 7). A pun on 'rites' is possible.

236 cunningly . . . drawen i.e. 'how much cunning Jolenta showed in (apparently) requiring to be led'.

238–9 Doves . . . murmur Dent compares Jonson, *Catiline*, II.325–6: 'Doues, they say, will bill, | After their pecking, and their murmuring.'

241 Mother i.e. 'hysteria'. Cf. *DM* II.i.108n.

242–3 rapt . . . sonne This is probably an aside (so Lucas), but it could be a direct retort to Romelio. **rapt** = 'carried away, spellbound'.

247 chiefe mourner (1) 'with pride of place at the funeral', and (2) 'with most cause to rue Contarino's death'.

251–3 plague . . . desire it selfe 'From Sidney, *Arcadia*, II.iv (*Works*, I, 174): "it is the impossibilitie that dooth torment me: for, unlawfull desires are punished after the effect of enjoying; but unpossible desires are punished in the desire it selfe"' (Dent).

252 they 'i.e. they who desire the impossible' (Lucas).

256 precise curiositie 'over-exact' (*OED* 2) 'niceness of behaviour' (*OED* 2a).

258–60 Matron . . . youthfull Such marriages did occur, but were often the subject of censure or ridicule, and particularly so if differences in rank were involved, as in the case of Frances Brandon, Duchess of Suffolk, who married her groom, Adrian Stokes. In 1559, when their joint portrait was painted by Hans Eworth, she was thirty-six and he twenty-one. The age gap is considerably greater here, with Leonora about sixty, and Contarino presumably in his twenties.

261 we . . . best Cf. Delamothe, *The Treasure of the French Toung* (1615), p. 26: 'The children borne the last, be often loued the best' (Dent).

265 latest Harvest-home Not just the completion of the harvest, but the associated festivities (cf. 'merryment', 266); **latest** = 'last'.

271 fury i.e. one of the classical goddesses of vengeance; cf *WD* I.ii.230n. There may here be a hint of the style of acting to be associated with Leonora's distraction that follows; cf. *WD* II.i.244n.

271–2 Amazon . . . pap The legendary Amazons, who first appear in Homer, were reputed to have their right breasts removed to facilitate their archery.

273 tender 'regard, care for' (*OED v.*² 3).

274–5 Wolfe . . . milke The wolf's traditional association with greed, lust, viciousness, and ruthlessness (Joseph D. Clark, *Beastly Folklore* [Metuchen, N.J., 1968], pp. 117–24) is being invoked by Leonora to emphasize what she sees as her unfilial betrayal by Romelio.

276 ff. Ha, ha, what say you? This laughter or exclamation initiates an increasing distraction (signalled at 260, 'I shall runne mad') that culminates at 291 in the physical image of collapse towards earth, the element associated with grief (cf., e.g., Kyd, *The Spanish Tragedy* I.iii.8–14). The actor may also employ other conventional indications of distraction, such as loosened hair or dishevelled garments.

277 talke to somewhat i.e. to 'some thing of unspecified nature' (*OED* somewhat *n.* 1b), to her 'evill Genius' (278).

279 fly in pieces Cf. *DM* III.v.101–2: 'like to a rusty ore-charg'd Cannon, | Shall I never flye in peeces?'

282 propertie 'special, or distinctive quality' (*OED* 5).

284–5 feare . . . hope for 'Possibly based on Jonson, *Sejanus*, IV.i.7: "Let me not feare, that cannot hope"' (Dent).

285–90 dye . . . stubborne-hearted Lucas notes the legend that the Earl of Essex, awaiting execution for his failed coup, sent Queen Elizabeth (**that worthy Princesse**) a ring, given by her with a promise that if he ever sought pardon the ring would assure it. The ring failed to reach the Queen, owing to its **false convayance** (i.e. wrong delivery) to the Countess of Nottingham, and in the absence of any other suit from **that brave Gentleman, | She would faine have saved**, Elizabeth had to assume he was **stubborne-hearted**. According to the legend, the Countess made a death-bed confession, whereupon the Queen took to her bed, and shortly died. As Lucas notes, W's allusion to the ring episode seems to be the 'earliest evidence of a popular belief in the story sufficiently widespread to make a reference like this intelligible'.

291 Falls downe Cf. 276n. When she gets up is not indicated; perhaps after 304–5 (so York 1980).

292–4 private way . . . [Ercole withdraws] Ercole *withdraws* sufficiently for the audience to accept that Leonora does not see him, but presumably remains visible to the audience for his speech at 315–17. Use of a stage hanging would be appropriate to suggest a concealed **private way**, and could also be used to partly conceal Ercole. Ercole may, by gait, bandages, or other means, still give evidence of his convalescent state.

304–5 One . . . You tendred Leonora takes this to be Contarino, as Ercole recognizes, 315–17. Cf. 101.

309 gave him ore i.e. 'pronounced him incurable' (see *OED* give 63e).

316–17 fasten . . . safetie Presumably Ercole means that concentrating on Leonora's revelation (that Romelio has murdered Contarino) will be essential, either as a defence against a charge of killing Contarino, or possibly so as to be wary of Romelio, or have a hold over him should one be needed.

319 vowed consort i.e. 'betrothed partner'. Q's 'comfort' is probably a simple misreading of 'confort' under the influence of 'comfort' at the end of the previous line. *OED*'s citations under comfort *n.* 5c ('A person or thing that affords consolation: a source or means of comfort') all retain elements of the abstraction, as in the biblical 'My fellow workers . . . which have beene a comfort unto me' (1611). One is a comfort *to*, not *of*, another. From the early fifteenth century onwards **consort** means 'partner, companion, mate'. Although *OED*'s first record (*n.* 3) of the specific meaning 'spouse' is dated 1634, the 'partner' sense shaded into it at least as early as 1606, when in Chapman's *Sir Gyles Goosecappe, Knight* Lord Furnifall offers Captain Fowlewether loyal mateship in compensation for his disappointment in love: 'Ile marrie thee, | For while we liue, thou shalt my consort be' (V.ii.327–8). If Q's 'comfort' were retained, the sense would be 'devoted (or 'betrothed') comforter' (*OED* vowed 1b, 1c, comfort *n.* 5c).

331–8 aside . . . to Leonora Ercole must speak aside, either to the audience or the Capuchin, until at least 335, since Leonora is not to hear. Resumption of speech to Leonora is most likely to be at 336, since 'Report this' at 341 seems to need an antecedent ('and withall' indicates an addition to 'this' rather than an explanation). See also 342–4n.

338–40 widdow . . . Church At I.ii.260 Contarino proposes marriage, and Winifrid recommends (261–2) that they consummate it. This would have resulted in a valid marriage. Hence, though Leonora calls Jolenta's supposed pregnancy a 'vild sinne' (350), Ercole agrees to 'preserve her credit' (357). Cf. *DM* IV.ii.242 and I.i.462n.

342–4 never father . . . confidence Ercole's careful ambiguity avoids disabusing Leonora, but will convey to Jolenta that he will accept her publication of him as father of her child by Contarino.

351–2 by my hope . . . this This aside may be spoken to the audience, or to the Capuchin, who seems to reply.

353 and 'if'.

362 salve 'account for, explain away' (see *OED* $v.^2$ 2a, b).

365 hang it up Since the indoor Cockpit had no structural stage posts, the picture is presumably hung against the tiring-house facade. Cf. IV.ii.463, and p. 42.

366–8 enjoyed . . . looke The reason for Crispiano's admonition, and what he meant, are never clarified, though presumably he intended his image to induce calm and virtue. Perhaps we are meant to take the comment ironically, given that looking at the picture gives Leonora the inspiration for her plot.

366 the partie ought i.e. 'the person who owned' (see *OED* ought 1a).

371–2 Here ... play Another self-reflexively theatrical comment; cf. 7–8 and II.iii.107, and pp. 49–50.

376–82 weightie secret ... another 'Possibly suggested by Alexander, *Jul. Caes.* IV.i (Y3ʳ): "I thought no creature shuld my purpose know | But he whose intrest promisde mutuall cares, | Of those to whom one would his secrets show, | No greater pledge of trust than to know theirs' (Dent).

382 another (Hazlitt; Q 'one another') As Lucas remarks, Q creates 'rather a queer phrase: and if *each* revealed a secret, there would be two secrets, not one'. Transposition of the two words would have much the same effect on the meaning and improve the line metrically (if Winifrid is indeed speaking verse, as we have hesitantly followed Q in indicating her to be doing). But 'another one' is a rare collocation in the period.

384 ingenuously 'ingeniously'; cf. I.i.209n.

385 nought 'wicked, immoral, naught' (*OED adj.* 1).

389 have The plural verb form presumably derives from 'one anothers', or possibly from 'intelligence' and 'shame'.

394–9 Thou hast lived ... clothes The intimate tone of this often-remarked speech was emphasized at York 1980 by Leonora sitting Winifrid down and holding her hands as she spoke.

401 words ... deeds Cf. Matthieu, *Henry IV*, K4ʳ: 'he said, *I haue euer giuen him good wordes, but no deeds*' (Dent). Here **courtly** seems to be an ironic glance at the niggardliness of courtiers as employers.

402 Lordships 'estates, manors' (*OED* 2a).

411 arpines i.e. 'arpents', a French measure of land equal to approximately an acre. **ten arpines** is therefore about 4 hectares.

414 ghostly Father 'spiritual advisor, father confessor' (*OED* ghostly 1c).

419 Foure ... wit Leonora's point is that **one womans wit** equals that of **Foure Devils** and **five Advocates**. **Foure** is frequently used as a general number indicative of several (cf. *DM* IV.i.9 and n). Qb's change from Qa **Advocates** to **Advocats** was made merely to accommodate the correction of **a** to **one** within a full line.

419.1 Explicit Actus Tertius An immediate re-entry follows for Leonora and Winifrid, suggesting that the act ending indicated here is theatrical, not just literary.

ACT IV, SCENE i

0.1 brief and the foul copy The **brief** will be of comic dimensions; see 11–14. The 'foule Copie' (82) may be at least as big. No doubt Sanitonella carries both in his 'Buckram bagg' (IV.ii.35), a standard lawyer's appendage. Cf. *WD* III.ii.47 and n. He also wears a 'spatious Inkehorne' (58). See p. 39, and Fig. 5.

0.2 *at one doore . . . at the other* Leonora, Sanitonella, Winifrid, and the Register (= Registrar; cf. *WD* III.i.0.1) all enter in a group ***at one doore***, and Ariosto alone ***at the other***.

2 belly . . . inke Presumably playing on the idea of 'gall' (*OED n.*³), especially oak-galls, as a constituent of **inke**, and 'gall' as bile, a bitter secretion in the **belly**, and hence on the 'bitterness, rancour' (*OED n.*¹ 3a) of what Winifrid will depose. There may also be a sexual innuendo on Winifrid absorbing all the Register's **inke**; cf. *MV* V.i.237: 'I'll mar the young clerk's pen.'

3 This i.e. Ariosto. He is apart from them until greeted by Sanitonella at 7.

4 trowle it i.e. 'utter nimbly or rapidly; recite in a full rolling voice' (*OED* troll 12).

6 lungs of Fox 'Fox lung was recommended to cure breathing difficulties and to strengthen and preserve the lungs. There is a discernible sympathetic association here between the drug and the condition it was said to cure' (Joan Lane and Melvin Earles, *John Hall and His Patients: The Medical Practice of Shakespeare's Son-in-Law* [Stratford-upon-Avon, 1996], p. 183). The Stratford physician prescribed fox lung for cases of breathing difficulties. On the preparation of dried fox lung Lucas cites *Pharmacopoea Londinensis* (1618), p. 180 which, as translated by Nicholas Culpeper in *A Physicall Directory* (1649), reads: 'Take of Fox lungues being fresh the Aspera Arteria being taken away, wash them diligently with white Wine, wherein Hysop and Scabious have been boyled, dry it gently in an oven but burn it not, then lay it up wrapped in Wormwood, Horehound or Hysop dried' (p. 343).

6 Malligo Reasins i.e. 'Malaga raisins', identified with the Spanish sea-port. For the medical use of raisins, cf. Gerard, *Herball*, p. 729: 'They are good for the chest, lungs, winde pipe, and are good against hoarsnesse, shortnesse of breath, or difficultie in breathing' (as Lucas).

11 Briefe 'A summary of the facts of a case . . . drawn up for the instruction of counsel' (*OED* 7, which lists no example prior to 1631). Sanitonella's **Briefe** is far from brief; cf. 0.1n.

14 Figdates i.e. 'fig-dotes'. The point presumably is that they are 'an inferior kind of fig' (*OED*), and like cheese (13), cheap.

17 scope . . . Margent As Ariosto reads the tedious brief, Sanitonella may generate comic business of peering over his shoulder and indicating the notations in the **Margent** (= 'margin') of the **scope** (= 'main purpose, argument' [*OED n.*² 3a]).

21 You trouble him Leonora's need to distract Sanitonella may indicate that comic business of Sanitonella pestering Ariosto has not stopped. It also allows Ariosto to reclaim audience focus dramatically at 'Whats here?' (22).

23–4 shake hands With 'meet'. 'Cf. *3H6*, I.iv.102: "Till our King Henry had shook hands with death". Contrast the sense "say farewell to" as in *DM* III.ii.135: "shooke hands with Reputation"' (Lucas).

24 knave 'servant'.

26 fogging Presumably 'pettifogging', i.e. 'acting as a rascally attorney; mean, shifty, quibbling' (*OED*).

27 whores enow . . . Presentations i.e. 'enough whores for (there to be a great many) legal complaints'. **Presentations** = 'presentments', statements on oath made to a judicial authority by a constable or magistrate (*OED* 2b).

28 Overseers, wrong i.e. 'executors (enough) who wrong'. Technically, an 'overseer' was not an executor, but 'appointed by a testator to supervise or assist the executor or executors of the will' (*OED* 1b; cf. *DM* I.i.369); Ariosto is therefore implying connivance.

31 *Plus quam satis* 'more than enough'; seemingly a comic variation of the legal tag *nunquam satis* used to annul marriages on the grounds of impotence, and meaning 'by no means enough' (Lucas/Brennan 1975).

32 pursnets i.e. 'purse-nets', bag-shaped nets, with a neck drawn tight by a cord (*OED* 1). Used largely for catching rabbits, hence by extension 'traps' (especially for gulls).

33 Oh women . . . you No such ballad (**Ballet**) is now known, but Lucas notes possible allusion to it in T. May, *The Heir* (1622), H2^r: 'O women, monstrous women'. Lucas notes also a letter from Chamberlain to Carleton on 12 February 1620: 'Our Pulpits ring continually of the insolence and impudence of Women; and to help forward, the Players have likewise taken them to task, and so to the Ballads and Ballad-Singers: so that they can come nowhere but their ears tingle' (Chamberlain, *Letters*, II, 289).

35 Your Fee is ready Sanitonella may make much of producing the money to propitiate Ariosto's anger.

37–8 see . . . false Latine Ariosto must be addressing his indignation to either Leonora or, more likely, the audience.

38–9 Ignoramus . . . Universitie The legal term **Ignoramus** (= 'we do not know', used by a Grand Jury when they considered the prosecution evidence insufficient to warrant a case going forward) came to be applied satirically to lawyers as a result of Charles Ruggle's play *Ignoramus*. It achieved notoriety by depicting the character of Ignoramus as closely resembling Sir Edward Coke, the Chief Justice, at two performances before King James at Cambridge in 1615, so reference here to **the Universitie** may be deliberate. See p. 39, and Fig. 1.

41 Commenc't (1) 'begun' (with a possible pun on legal suits; see *OED* 1), and (2) 'taken a Master's or Doctor's degree' (see *OED* 4; cf. Marlowe, *Dr Faustus*, I.i.31: 'Having commenc'd, be a Divine in shew'). Cf. 38–9n, and V.iii.90.

42 Pewe 'a raised seat or bench' (*OED* n.^{1} 3a); cf. John Evelyn: 'The Palais (as they call it above) was built in the time of Philip the faire, noble and spacious; and the greate Hall annex'd to it bravely arch'd with stone, having a range of Pillars in the middle, round which, and at the sides, are shops of kinds; especialy bookesellers; the other side is full of pewes for the Clearkes of the Advocates, which (as ours at Westminster [Hall]) swarme here' (3 February 1644; *The Diary of John Evelyn*, ed. E. S. De Beer [Oxford, 1955], II, 98).

44 dry-foundred i.e. 'foundered', a term applied to horses fallen lame or collapsed, usually from overwork (see *OED* founder v. 4, n.^{6} 1).

45–8 Non resident . . . Clergie 'Ariosto is outraged by Sanitonella's application of pompous professional and ecclesiastical language to himself—a mere lawyer's hack, a "sub-summoner"' (Lucas). **Non resident** is a term of contempt for clergy who held several livings or benefices and were culpably non-resident in all but one of them (see *OED* 1a). The actor may decide to pause slightly after **Non resident** so that the reference to it of **that word** will be clear. (Q4 inserted a comma, presumably for this reason.) **Subsumner** (not in *OED*) is clearly a contemptuous derogation from 'sumner', 'one who is employed to summon persons to appear in court; *esp.* a summoning officer in an ecclesiastical court' (*OED*). **Libell** = (1) 'the plaintiff's written charges' which institute a suit (see *OED* libel 3a, b), and (2) 'defamatory matter'; i.e. the '*brief*' (see 48n, and cf. *DM* II.iii.41–2n). Lucas suggests an ironic stress on **vertue**, given the grave scandal of **Non resident Clergie**. He also suggests a play on 'by benefit of clergy', used of those who escaped the death sentence for a capital felony by reading their 'neck-verse' (generally Psalm 51: 1), proving that they were 'clerks' (i.e. able to read, and therefore **Clergie**).

48 *Tears the brief* With 'fourescore sheets of paper' (12), it is likely that many of the pages are simply scattered (perhaps giving Sanitonella considerable business picking them up; so York 1980); but Ariosto's action must be sufficiently devastating to force Sanitonella to 'make shift | With the foule Copie' (81–2) with Contilupo.

52 forget your gravitie A further hint at how much this scene may rely on physical comic business.

58 Winter itch Presumably chilblains.

58 weares that spatious Inkehorne See Fig. 5.

59 Vacation 'period when the law courts are closed'.

59 Tetters Skin eruptions, such as eczema, impetigo, or ringworm; cf. *IndMP* (Lucas) 66 and *DM* II.i.74. Lucas notes that the efficacy of ink as a remedy was due to the presence of tannic acid from the oak-galls used in its manufacture. Cf. IV.i.1–2n.

60 weed 'remove' (*OED* 3c).

65 melancholly . . . face Cf. *DM* I.i.71n. and 148n.

70 Night-caps 'lawyers'; cf. II.i.42n.

73 never find name Legal procedure until the nineteenth century depended upon conformity to the *forms of action*, whereby a writ (or *action*) could not be lodged unless it was in the proper *formula*, which in practice meant that it had a precedent. There was thus a distinction made between *actiones nominatae*, writs for which there were precedents, and *actiones innominatae*, for which there were not (Jowitt, p. 41). Etymologically at least, this suggests the perhaps more colloquial **never find name**. Ariosto would be thus telling Leonora that he hopes that suits such as hers will always fall into the latter category, and so never be heard in a court of law.

74 bred Either past tense of 'breed', or more likely an alternative spelling of the present tense: cf. *WD* IV.ii.217 'a worme breds i'th teeth of't'.

75 franticke Leonora may well mean 'mad' (*OED* 1), but the meaning shades over into 'insanely foolish' and 'frenzied' (*OED* 3b). This reinforces earlier hints that Ariosto is acted in a physically comic style.

79 purchase 'acquire possessions, become rich' (*OED* 5b).

80–2 Learned Seignior . . . foule Copie Various options of address are possible here. **Learned Seignior** may well be a salutation (to *Contilupo*), although it could be description (to Leonora or the audience). Similarly, **here's . . . foule Copie** may be to Leonora or, more likely, partly or wholly to the audience.

81 Of another piece i.e. 'of a different kind' (cf. 'of a piece').

82 foule Copie Sanitonella's compendious 'Buckram bagg' (IV.ii.35) must be capacious indeed, since it holds the rough draft (**foule Copie**), perhaps even bigger than the fair copy of the brief which Ariosto tore up (cf. 48n). There may follow business such as bowing or presenting the papers to Contilupo.

83 welcome Q's 'welcom' is a variant spelling occurring nowhere else in the play, and was only needed here as the last word in a full line.

84 hardly i.e. 'only with difficulty'.

85–6 reade . . . exceeding well Contilupo's gesture of weighing the money, like the Second Surgeon's (see III.ii.137 and n), will probably make clear the assistance it gives his mental capacities.

87–9 saved . . . pickt out Contilupo may be **saved** by 'benefit of clergy' (cf. IV.i.45–8n), but perhaps with connotations also of salvation through reading the Bible. Sanitonella puns further on **hand . . . pickt out** = (1) 'however bad the handwriting (*OED* hand 16), something of the meaning will be made out', and (2) 'however **foule** (evil) the **hand** that wrote it, some gain will be forthcoming'. It would be possible to play the entire speech to Leonora, but this seems both less likely and less comic than playing to the audience.

90 *Vivere honeste* 'to live honestly (chastely)' (Latin).

92 Give it a dash i.e. 'strike it out' (*OED* dash 7a).

94 Secretary The standard English handwriting of the sixteenth century for nearly all business, correspondence, records, and literary composition. During the seventeenth century secretary hand was gradually supplanted by the italic hand for most purposes.

95 takes i.e. 'wins favour, gains acceptance' (*OED* 10a); cf. 98.

98 Court hand 'The style of handwriting in use in English law-courts until the reign of George II' (*OED* court). 'In the course of time certain law courts and government offices developed each its own peculiar variety of court hand, which its clerks were required to learn and use' (Giles E. Dawson and Laetitia Kennedy-Skipton, *Elizabethan Handwriting 1500–1650: A Manual* [New York, 1966], p. 10). There were, in addition, separate legal hands, so ample material is available for these pedantic and mutually congratulatory exchanges about handwriting.

98 takes See 95n; with the punning implication, perhaps unintentional on Sanitonella's part, of bribery and corruption.

98 beyond thought 'beyond imagining'.

99 traded in't 'skilled, practised, experienced' (*OED* traded 2). Lucas compares Nashe (*Works*, III, 317), speaking of Sir John Cheke as 'supernaturally traded in al' tongs'. Cf. 98n for the need to practise.

101 Hogg-rubber Clearly a term of opprobrium, though *OED*'s 'one who rubs hogs' (*OED* hog *n.*[1] 13) is mystifying; perhaps the meaning is 'one who rubs up against, mingles with, hogs', which would imply 'a rustic' (so Brennan 1975), but this does not seem appropriate here. There is possible confusion and transference with 'hog-grubber', meaning 'a mean or sneaking fellow'. OED quotes Jonson, *Bartholomew Fair*, V.iv.175 ff., '*Goodman Hogrubber o' Pickt-hatch*' where, as Lucas points out, this form of address leads to blows.

107 President i.e. 'precedent'.

108–10 deserves . . . Audience A nice theatrical joke, intensified by the statement that such a theatre setting would enable the trial to 'teach | All ladies the right path to rectifie their issue' (110–11). Unlike Vittoria's appeal (*WD* III.ii.13–21) to a popular audience in a **publike Theater**, Contilupo's ideal, possibly accompanied by a gesture to the audience, is expressed in a **pent** ('confined'; *OED ppl. a.* 1) indoor playhouse; see pp. 45–6.

110 Audience (Q 'Audence') *OED* gives 'audenes' as a fifteenth-century spelling, but provides no citation, and electronic databases afford no seventeenth-century instance of Q's spelling, so a misprint is probable.

111 rectifie their issue i.e. 'put right' (*OED* rectify 1b, 2b) the matter of their children's proper status.

112 Loe you As likely to be to the audience as to Leonora; cf. 117–18.

116–18 Judgement . . . Judgment While both references to judgement are clearly eschatological in meaning, the second also carries the legal sense. Sanitonella's line is probably to the audience; cf. 112.

121 What . . . summon'd? Stage business may alert Contilupo to the imminence of the trial; perhaps a musical flourish, or the entry of the Officers '*preparing seats for the Judges*' (IV.ii.0.1).

125 make account 'consider, expect' (*OED* account 13).

ACT IV, Scene ii

0.1 *Officers preparing seats* These **Officers** may be legal officers (cf. *WD* III.ii.0.2n), but more likely serve as both attendants and guards. There are probably only two. The **seats** for the two judges will be chairs rather than stools, probably on a dais (cf. *WD* III.i.0.1n). The Officers no doubt also place the two bars; see IV.ii.46.2n and pp. 50–1.

0.2 ERCOLE *muffled* i.e. with the face 'wrapped or covered up' (*OED* 1), not fully disguised.

3 Closset i.e. 'private room; inner chamber' (*OED* closet 1a). On stage this hidden position for Ercole is probably conventional and in view of the audience, though possibly partly hidden behind a tiring-house door or stage hanging.

6.1 *Dane . . . disguised* Contarino's disguise must be recognizably Danish, since Ercole identifies his 'Nation' at 614 and Prospero describes him as 'the Dane' at V.iv.4. Danish costume was evidently distinctive enough on stage for Henslowe to list 'ij Danes sewtes, and j payer of Danes hosse' (Henslowe, *Diary*, p. 318). Contemporary references to elaborately stuffed and slashed Danish military fashion may indicate that Contarino is now foolishly extravagant in appearance, like Julio; see p. 39. One of the

Surgeons later in the play disguises himself in the 'habit of a Jew' (V.iii.32), so their disguise here must be different. In both cases the audience's enjoyment depends on recognizing the characters beneath the disguises.

11–13 Hollanders . . . lately This appears to refer to specific and, at the time, recent hostilities between the Dutch and the English in the East Indies, but no precise dating is certain (see Lucas, II, 214). **sauce** for **pickeld Herrings** (seen as a Dutch national dish) would include pepper from the East Indies: hence the pun on **pepperd** = (1) 'provided with pepper for pickling herring', and (2) 'bombarded with shot'. Control of the Atlantic herring fisheries was a concern of King James when the Dutch negotiators visited London in November–December 1618. Cf. I.i.5n.

17 expect 'wait to see' (*OED* 2b).

18 passages 'incidents, events' (*OED* 13a).

21 Duke of *Austrias* Nephew References to Don John of Austria (348) and to his famous victory at Lepanto (356) may lie behind this suggestion of an illustrious marriage, although no individual matches this description.

23 *Palavasini* Q ('Palavafini') has misread or mis-set an 'fi' ligature as 'fi'. As Lucas suggests, the reference is probably to the Italian noble family of the Pallavicini, one of whom, Sir Horatio Palavicino, lent vast sums to Queen Elizabeth. Lucas's suggestion that W may have encountered the name 'in connection with *WD*, since it was in their palazzo on Lake Garda that the Bracciano of history died' may be discounted, since none of the sources that W seems to have used refers to this.

27.1 SD Presumably Contarino and the Surgeons find inconspicuous places as Sanitonella enters and shows off to Winifrid his familiarity with the court.

28 *Brachigraphy* men i.e. stenographers, writers of shorthand. The allusion is to the practice of unscrupulous publishers in hiring *Brachigraphy* **men** to take down plays (and sermons) surreptitiously, so that they could be pirated. Lucas cites Heywood's complaint, in the 'Epistle' to *The Rape of Lucrece* (1614), of plays of his 'coppied onely by the eare' (A2ʳ), and the prologue to the 1639 edition of *1 If You Know Not Me You Know Nobody*: 'Some by Stenography, drew | The Plot: put it in print, scarce one word true' (A2ʳ). Lucas notes that modern shorthand begins with the *Characterie* of Dr Timothy Bright in 1588, followed by Peter Bale's *Writing Schoolemaster* (1590), and J. Willis's highly successful *Art of Stenographie* (1602).

31 Ballets 'ballads'.

35–41 Buckram bagg . . . Pudding-pye The length of time taken before Sanitonella's **Looke you** (41) implies, yet again, considerable comic business with the lawyer's enormous **Buckram bagg**.

36 stop your stomacke i.e. fill it up (cf. *OED* stop *v.* 4a).

37 Greene ginger i.e. the fresh root, not powdered ginger.

38 Pellitory of Spaine A small Mediterranean plant, the root of which contains an oil which was used to treat toothache. Gerard, *Herball*, p. 619, refers to its 'hot and fierie taste', and says that it 'easeth the paine of the teeth, especially if it be stamped with a little Staphifagria, and tied in a small bagge, and put into the mouth, and there suffered to remaine a certain space'. The point here, however, seems to be that both 'Greene ginger' and **Pellitory of Spaine** serve also to dull the pangs of hunger.

41 Pudding-pye 'A meat-pudding baked in a dish. Doubtless the point of this some-what slender episode was the unexpected production of this object from a bag appar-ently bulging with its weight of legal erudition' (Lucas). If the pie is very large, it will both point 'modicum' (35) and explain Winifrid's reaction.

46 after-game at Irish A form of backgammon, **Irish** is described in Charles Cotton, *The Compleat Gamester* (1674), pp. 154–5, as an **after-game**, or second game played to retrieve a first, which tended to be particularly lengthy. Cf. Beaumont and Fletcher, *The Scornful Lady*, V.iv.81–2: 'longer bearing then ever after-game at *Irish* was' (after Lucas).

46.1 *like a Judge* Crispiano is no longer habited as a merchant (cf. II.i.1–3), but now as a *Judge*, which he is. Presumably something like the splendid full dress of an English judge is indicated: a scarlet robe and shoulder cape edged with white fur, a full furred hood of miniver, a ruff at the neck, and the traditional white coif and black skullcap over which is worn a limp black 'cornered' cap (see W. N. Hargreaves-Mawdsley, *A History of Legal Dress in Europe* [Oxford, 1963], pp. 59–60). See Fig. 1. An element of disguise, perhaps a false beard, probably remains, to be removed at 492.

46.2 *at one Barre . . . at another* This arrangement of two bars, presumably physically opposed to each other, is highly unorthodox but dramatically effective. See pp. 50–1.

46.3 *blacke vaile* The *vaile*, probably of transparent *blacke* cypress, would suggest mourning, but is also the first of several uses of veils to suggest real or apparent shame. Cf. V.i.7–8 and V.vi.33.1–.2, and p. 37.

46.4 JULIO Since he is not a party to the law-case, and takes no active role until 616, he presumably stands or sits well aside.

47–8 *Leonora . . .* make way Contilupo (or W) has stage-managed affairs so that Leonora advances to be revealed only after the court has settled; cf. Brachiano's entrance to the trial in *WD* (III.ii.1 and n). **make way there** suggests she is having to pass through a crowded area of the stage, perhaps through onlookers bunched near one of the tiring-house doors.

48–51 Vaile . . . dark Presumably Crispiano's instruction to 'Take off her Vaile' is carried out, though Contilupo's excuse at 50 and Ariosto's joke at 51 could indicate the con-trary. Confinement in the dark was a standard treatment for the mad; cf. Malvolio's incarceration in *TN* IV.ii. This is the first of a series of exchanges in which Ariosto sup-ports and echoes Crispiano's sardonic scepticism about Leonora's case.

52–4 By . . . angry Ariosto is not Romelio's lawyer (see lines 75 and 79), but wishes to take this opportunity to entreat him to be angry. **I have now occasion** and **within this halfe houre** both serve through their prescience to point up Ariosto's special role (cf. II.iii.57–9 and n).

60 unequall 'unfair, inequitable' (*OED* 4a).

61–2 furnisht . . . Instruction The conspicuous 'foule Copie' (IV.i.84) provided by Sanitonella.

63–4 accuser . . . mother Since Romelio has to ask, presumably Leonora is not stand-ing with 'Councell of the adverse partie' (61) at his '*Barre*' (46.2); see pp. 50–1.

65 discovered 'revealed' (*OED* 2), not 'found it out', since, as Lucas notes, Romelio had himself told her.

66–7 call . . . question 'i.e. to charge me with an offence punishable by death' (Brennan 1975).

72 provide 'prepare, arrange beforehand' (*OED* 3).

74 runnes in a blood i.e. 'runs in the family'. Cf. Tilley B464.

78 for love nor money Cf. Tilley L484: 'I could not get any, neither for Love nor money.'

79 gall your gowt i.e. 'irritate your gout'. Although **gowt** may be used here primarily for its alliterative value, and to emphasize Ariosto's age (cf. IV.i.76, 'Plague on's gowtie fingers'), it may also indicate the physical playing of age, and possible stage business with, e.g., Romelio threatening to bang his stick on Ariosto's feet (so Wellington 1995).

81 spice of pride Ariosto puns on the 'East Indy' (80) trade in pepper. He also seems to be retorting to Romelio's jibe about the disabilities of age ('gowt', 79) by a further pun on **spice**: (1) the usual idiomatic sense of 'a dash or flavour of' (*OED* 5b), and (2) 'a touch of some physical malady' (*OED* 5a, citing North's Plutarch [1612 ed.], p. 481: 'A paine and numnesse in his legges . . . a spice of gout').

93 as feare i.e. 'as to fear'.

94–5 Very fine . . . purpose Dent notes North's Plutarch (1612 ed.), p. 54: 'Friend, thou speakest many good words, but to litle purpose.'

96 have your intreatie i.e. 'have it as you have solicited' (see *OED* entreaty 4).

98 fall to your Plea The absence of further form of address to Contilupo may indicate that he has been ostentatiously ready to begin before now (particularly, perhaps, following 96).

100 President i.e. 'precedent' (cf. IV.i.107).

108 title or addition i.e. 'style of address'; a typical Contilupo repetition.

109–11 false beames . . . darke Cf. *WD* V.i.38–9, and *DM* IV.ii.133–4: 'Glories, like glowe-wormes, a farre off, shine bright | But look'd to neere, have neither heate, nor light.'

112 bought . . . Herauld 'The relaxing of standards by the heralds was dramatized by the revelation in 1616 that Sir William Segar, Garter King of Arms, had been tricked by the York Herald into selling arms (for 22 shillings) to that overworked man, Gregory Brandon, the common hangman of London' (Stone, *Crisis*, p. 68). Even without trickery, however, the sale of knighthoods and titles was one of the most notorious scandals of the Jacobean court, the poverty and lack of gentility of many of the new knights becoming the subject of popular derision. Cf. II.i.166n.

114 Æsops Crow In Aesop's fable, the crow adorned himself with feathers fallen from the peacocks, but was then humiliated by the peacocks and ostracized by his own flock. Modern versions usually refer to a jackdaw; but cf. Robert Greene's reference to Shakespeare as 'an vpstart Crow, beautified with our feathers' (*Greenes Groats-worth of Witte* [1592], F1ᵛ).

116 I come to'th poynt Possibly reacting to some show of impatience by Crispiano; cf. 151–3.

117 Dreame i.e. 'unreal vision' (cf. *OED* n.² 2).

119–25 rankt himselfe . . . State 'W has casually shifted to Naples the Genoese civil disorders of the late sixteenth century. His source was probably some such account as that in Bodin's *Six Bookes of a Commonweale*, tr. Knolles (1603), pp. 712–13: "The sedition [in Genoa] happened for the qualitie of their nobilitie: for after that Andrew Doria had setled the state (as I haue said) & excluded the Plebeians from being Dukes of Genes, the gentlemen of the antient houses (which were but foure, the Dorias, the Spinolas, the Grimoaldes, and the Fiesques) caused their genealogies to be drawne and registred in publicke acts, diuiding themselues by this meanes from the Plebeians that were newly ennobled; who disdaining thereat, and finding themselues the greater number and the stronger, they haue chased away the antient houses, and if they be not soone reconciled, the people in the end will expell them all." Bodin's preceding paragraph refers to "John Flisco" being chosen Duke of Genoa in mid-century. Perhaps a similar juxtaposition in W's source accounts for his having "Fliski" rather than "Fieschi"' (Dent). Since '*Fliski*', however, is certainly erroneous, we have emended to *Fieski*, which is an acceptable seventeenth-century phonetic spelling of '*Fieschi*'.

121–3 pride . . . dung-hills Cf. *WD* III.iii.41–2: 'so many earlie mushromes, whose best growth sprang from a dunghill'.

124 The *Fieski* . . . *Dorii* For these great families of Genoa, see 119–25n. Dyce's Latinate plural, *Dorii* (corresponding to Knolles's 'Dorias'; see 119–25n), is a slightly more plausible emendation of Q's 'Dori' than is Lucas's 'Doria'. Cf. *FMI* II.iv.77, a section of the play attributed to W: 'The Family of the *Baptisti*'.

127–8 Cuckow . . . Hedge-sparrow 'A common image'; so Dent, who compares *1H4* V.i.59–64: 'And being fed by us you us'd us so | As that ungentle gull, the cuckoo's bird, | Useth the sparrow; did oppress our nest, | Grew by our feeding to so great a bulk.'

129–31 Speakes . . . thee Romelio's rhetorical question is not to Ariosto (**I doe not aske thee**), therefore presumably either to the court at large or to the audience.

134 base 'worthless' (*OED* 14).

135 aspect 'appearance'.

136–7 Gyant . . . Porter Cf. Barnabe Riche, *Opinion Diefied* [*sic*] (1613) C4^{r-v}: 'the *Giants* that are accustomed at *London* once a yeare, to march before the *Lord Mayors Pageantes*, that outwardly do make semblance to be men of great might and valiance, but inwardly are nothing else but Lathes, towe and ragges' (Dent). **Porter** is here both a literal description of the hidden man who carries the **Gyant**, and also a social slur on Romelio.

140 Chickeens i.e. 'chequeens' (It. *zecchino*), Italian gold coins worth about nine shillings (*OED*).

141 byth hand Lucas, in a lengthy and valuable note, points out that the *OED* definition, 'expeditiously, readily, straightaway' ('hand', *n.* 26c, drawing only on a 1659 example) makes no sense here, and suggests 'by the deal, by the bargain', comparing Henry Fitzjeffrey, *Notes from Blackfriars* (1617), who says (F2^r) of a prostitute: 'Let her alone! What ere she giues to stand, | Shee'l make her selfe a gayner, *By the Hand*' (with presumably a sexual imputation also). Cf. *AV* IV.i.206–8: 'see they bring the maid | In her most proper habit, bond-slave like, | And they will save by th' hand too'. Just conceivably an adjuration is intended in all these cases; cf. *OED* 6 and *DM* II.ii.59, 'By this hand'.

141–4 Loe . . . poore John Ariosto is continuing his campaign (cf. 132–3) to make Romelio angry. **poore John** is a term of disparagement (*OED* 1b), apparently based on the primary meaning 'hake salted and dried for food; a type of poor fare' (*OED* 1a). Cf. *Rom.* I.i.30–1: "Tis well thou art not fish; if thou hadst, thou hadst been poor-John.' Lucas also compares Massinger, *The Renegado*, I.i.26, and *AV* III.iv.29.

143 Cochineele i.e. 'cochineal', the scarce and costly red dye the Spanish brought to Europe from Mexico in the early sixteenth century, for which explorers and merchants constantly sought new sources.

147 founders 'stumbles, breaks down'; cf. IV.i.44n.

158 Bastard Consternation on stage will emphasize this as the first of several turning points in the scene.

162 I had forgot that Possibly aside.

165 turne . . . mother If Romelio does literally **turne**, it reinforces the likelihood that Leonora is not standing with Contilupo; see 63–4n.

169 *Francisco* Since this is how the name appears (correctly) at 180, we have followed Lucas in assuming that Q's '*Franscisco*' exemplifies dittography rather than constituting an intended variant spelling.

171 his father Gesture towards Romelio will clarify Leonora's meaning: that her husband, Francisco Romelio, was not Romelio's father.

174 Without . . . scruple An unconscious irony, as Lucas notes, since Contilupo means 'without the least doubt', but his words point up his own unscrupulousness. **scruple** = 'doubt or uncertainty as to a matter of fact or allegation' (*OED n.*² 2).

181 This Gentlemans Again, gesture towards Romelio will ensure clarity.

192–3 welcome . . . Cuckold Dent notes that though Tilley (C888, 'Cuckolds are kind to those that make them so') cites no example before 1696, the idea was probably proverbial in W's day. This part of the speech might well be to the audience.

205 precedence Either (1) 'antecedent [event]' (*OED* 2), or (2) 'the foregoing facts' (*OED* precedent 1a).

207–8 Huswife . . . spin Flax In describing ordinary domestic activities, Contilupo may imply that she had been keeping a bawdyhouse. Punning on **Huswife** as 'loose woman' (*OED* 2) is commonplace, Lucas comparing *Oth.* II.i.112: 'Players in your huswifery, and huswives in your beds'. For the connection with **spin** cf. *TN* I.iii.93–104, where Sir Andrew's hair is described as hanging like 'flax on a distaff', and Sir Toby hopes 'to see a huswife take [him] between her legs and spin it off'. Rubinstein (p. 249) glosses **spin** as slang for coition, 'spinster' as a whore of either sex, and says '"spinning houses" were houses of correction for loose women'.

209 study Used in a wider sense then than now, of any private room of the master of the house (Lucas).

211 threed i.e. 'intrigue'.

220 fright Q's 'flight', though emended by all editors, is not perhaps impossible—the physical exertion of fleeing the fire could have caused Leonora to 'fall' (222) and have hastened labour—but one might have expected it to be followed by 'wherefrom' rather than **whereof**.

224 Lambeskin Sanitonella may well 'pinch by the buttock' (200) as he promised.

227 makes it up i.e. 'prepares it'. It is not clear whether **makes up** here means (1) 'attire' (so Lucas; see *OED* make *v.*[1] 96i (a)), (2) 'disguising his features by means of false hair, cosmetics etc.' (*OED* 96i (b); but the earliest instance is a theatrical citation of 1809), or (3) 'to arrange (the features) so as to produce a particular expression' (*OED* 96i (d); first citation is 1641). How the baby could be made to appear to have only 'three quarters of a face' (228) simply by the use of clothing or wrappings around its face is hard to imagine, so either the distortion of its features or the use of cosmetics may well be intended.

229 Changeling 'a child (usually stupid or ugly) supposed to have been left by fairies in exchange for one stolen' (*OED* 3).

231 that it came for i.e. 'salvation' (Brennan 1975).

232–4 Gossips . . . arch-Puritans A Church of England canon forbade parents becoming godparents (*OED* gossip 1c) to their own children. The **Puritans**, however, objected that it was precisely the child's parents who ought to be most responsible for its religious training; and argued for the Genevan form of baptism, where the parents (or other responsible persons) recite the Creed as representing the faith in which they mean to bring up the child (so Lucas).

236 cases With a double entendre on 'vagina'. Cf. Fletcher, *The Chances*, IV.iii.98, where the Bawd offers to 'shew your mastership my case'.

248 time past, or present i.e. 'in times past or present' (*OED* 3b).

251–2 Councell . . . inlarge i.e. 'and (it is beyond example) for her counsel to set forth at length' (see *OED* enlarge 2b).

254 Defend . . . woman i.e. 'defend a guilty woman with' (Lucas).

257–8 Obedience . . . world Cf. Richard Hooker, *Of the Lawes of Ecclesiasticall Politie* (1594), E3[r]: 'See we not plainly that obedience of creatures vnto the lawe of nature is the stay of the whole world?' (Dent).

259–61 Civill Law . . . equall From Matthieu, 'Continuation', p. 1027: 'for although the Law doth distinguish Bastards from them that are lawfully begotten, yet nature makes no difference'. Cf. *DM* IV.i.35–7.

265 parting 'dividing into parts' (cf. *OED* part *v.* 1).

267 flaw With the sense both of 'rift' (*OED* n.[1] 4) and 'sudden uproar or tumult' (*OED* n.[2] 2); cf. *WD* I.ii.55 and n.

272 hapt 'came it about'.

283–4 repentance . . . satisfaction The division of repentance into the three stages of contrition, confession, and satisfaction, noted by Weis, is traditionally Catholic, but was scorned by Protestants. They emphasized the importance of faith in repentance, and rejected auricular confession; that Leonora refers to this Catholic practice is confirmed by her saying that she might have 'confest it, | Privately toth Church' (282–3).

292 loose her Dower In English law Leonora would have been liable to lose her dowry only if she had gone to live with her lover (so Lucas, citing 13 Edw. I, c. 34: 'And if a Wife willingly leave her Husband, and go away, and continue with her Advouterer, she shall be barred for ever of Action to demand her Dower, that she ought to have of her

Husband's Lands, if she be convict thereupon, except that her Husband willingly, and without Coertion of the Church, reconcile her, and suffer her to dwell with him; in which Case she shall be restored to her Action' [*The Statutes of the Realm* (London, 1810; repr. 1963), I, 87]).

293–4 Who . . . Most just Presumably Sanitonella's line is to the audience (although it could be to Contilupo), and Crispiano's in reply to Ariosto.

295–6 old house . . . head Proverbial; cf. Tilley H756 and *WHo* V.iv.147.

297 Publication i.e. 'making publicly known'.

302–4 malice . . . Powder-Treason The view that the 1605 Gunpowder Plot had been motivated by **malice** was sustained by the official prayers for 5 November, which called on God to 'scatter our enemies that delight in blood. Infatuate and defeat their counsels, abate their pride, assuage their malice, and confound their devices' (quoted in David Cressy, *Bonfires and Bells: National Memory and the Protestant Calendar in Elizabethan and Stuart England* [Berkeley, 1989], p. 142). Lucas notes that Thomas Percy, one of the leading conspirators, nursed 'a personal grudge against James I as having duped him when, in 1602, he was sent to Scotland on behalf of the English Catholics to ask toleration for them in return for their support of James'.

306–30 violencies . . . temper Ariosto's ironic **Are you angry yet?** (310) emphasizes the requirement here for the actor of Romelio to suit his action to the emotional extremity of the language.

309 growes Abbott, Sect. 334 notes the frequency with which the third-person plural form in '–s' occurs in Shakespeare: cf. *MV* I.iii.161–2: 'Whose own hard dealings teaches them suspect | The thoughts of others'. Nevertheless, a compositorial slip under the influence of **sorcerous Herbes** would have been easy enough.

311 expresse 'delineate, describe' (*OED v.*[1] 5a, 9b).

312 forsake . . . example 'i.e. to do justice to the infamy of women one must give up comparing them with anything else in Nature, such as the traditional Hyrcanian tigers, crocodiles, pestilences and the like—a precept which the speaker proceeds himself to infringe two lines lower' (Lucas).

317 winde dead bodies As Cornelia does Marcello's: see *WD* V.iv.59.3 and n.

318 seaming lace i.e. lace used to cover seams. Cf. F. M. Palliser, *A History of Lace* (1875), p. 289 n.: '"Seaming" lace and spacing lace appear to have been generally used at this period to unite the breadths of linen, instead of a seam sewed. We find them employed for cupboard cloths . . . shirts etc. throughout the accounts of King James and Prince Charles.'

318 bones 'bobbins made of bones for weaving "bone-lace"' (*OED* 5c, citing *TN* II.iv.45: 'And the free maids that weave their thread with bones').

323 by-slips 'bastards' (*OED* 2).

325–6 Preferment . . . begotten Cf. Bosola's bitter comment on his own preferment to the 'Provisor-ship o'th horse': 'Say then my corruption | Grew out of horse-doong' (*DM* I.i.273–4).

332 Court . . . world As at 129, Romelio seems to include the theatre audience in his address; cf. also IV.i.108–10n.

334–6 sinne . . . consent Somewhat obscure. The simplest reading seems to be (following Dent's suggested source in Machiavelli's *Florentine History*) 'as for Leonora's sin, which you are all prepared to swear to the timing of, I did not give my agreement (was not an accessory—because I was not yet alive)'. Lucas believes **consent** means 'agreement with your opinion' (*OED* 4), hence 'I would never admit it to be true.'

343 my Master As Lucas pertinently asks, 'How could this statement of Contilupo's come as a surprise to Sanitonella, when he had himself drawn up the brief which is Contilupo's sole source of information?'

343 spoyl'd 'irremediably damaged' (see *OED* spoil $v.^1$ 12).

344 I knew that Spanyard Crispiano may well share this joke with the audience, since only they and Sanitonella can appreciate the irony.

348 *Don John* of *Austria* Bastard son of Emperor Charles V, acknowledged by his father in a codicil to his will, and officially recognized by Philip II in 1559. He commanded the Imperial fleet which defeated the Turks at the Battle of Lepanto (see 356n).

351 Bastards the greater spirits Thomas Milles, *The Treasurie of Auncient and Moderne Times* (1613), pp. 723–4, observes that bastards are commonly 'ingenious [and] of sprightly judgement' because they 'are begot in more heat and vigour of love, with more agreeable conformity of willes, and farre sweeter Union of the spirites then the most part of our Legitimate Children'. Cf. also, e.g., *Lr.* I.ii.10–15.

353 lay 'assign, describe' (*OED* 26c).

355 *Anno* seventie one i.e. 'the year 1571'.

356 Battell of *Lepanto* Fought on 7 October 1571, this sea battle, celebrated throughout Christian Europe, marked a turning point in the struggle against Ottoman expansion in the Mediterranean. See 348n.

358–9 corporall dealing i.e. 'sexual commerce', **corporall** meaning 'of or belonging to the human body; bodily' (*OED adj.* 1). For the double entendre on **dealing** (not recorded in this sense in *OED*) see Henke 1975, II, 130 '"Dealings": Business transactions with innuendo of both copulations and pandering'. Cf. Dekker, *The Honest Whore, Part Two*, IV.iii.75, where the bawd, Mistress Horseleech, comments: 'Your Prentices know my dealings well.'

363 Waiting-woman Q omits the hyphen (and possibly changes the more common 'y' spelling of 360) in an exceptionally tight line.

364 bagge and baggage Idiomatically, 'all belongings' (*OED* bag 20); suggested here by Winifrid as **baggage** = 'a woman of disreputable or immoral life' (*OED* 6). Ariosto completes the joke by metonymic reference to Sanitonella and his buckram **bagge**. Ariosto's cry of **Roome** may imply a bustle and confusion as Winifrid makes her way from amongst other onlookers to a central part of the stage; cf. Contilupo's 'make way there' (47–8 and n) for Leonora.

365 *Ore tenus* Although *OED* gives the literal meaning as 'by word of mouth' (medieval Latin legal phrase), the context here requires something like 'ready to give oral testimony'. 'Deposition' (360) may refer to the written statement Winifrid gave to the Register (IV.i.1–2), if his ink did not prove insufficient for the task, or to the oral testimony she is about to give.

372 running 'of a smooth, easy or rapid character' (*OED ppl. a.* 11, citing Nashe, *Christ's Teares over Jerusalem* [*Works*, II, 73] 'merry-running Madrigals').

372 Violl With a double entendre. Henke 1975, II, 308, noting a 'play on . . . the viol de gamba, a string instrument held between the legs of the player while being played', cites Middleton, *A Trick to Catch the Old One*, I.i.164–6: 'the voice between her lips, and the viol between her legs—she'll be fit for a consort very speedily'. Cf. 373n.

373 fidling With a double entendre; see Henke 1975, II, 153 'Fiddle': 'To play sexually with a woman; to take sexual liberties with her', citing Chapman, *Bussy D'Ambois* [*Bussy I*], III.ii.257–8: 'tis my chastity, which you shall neither riddle nor fiddle'. Throughout this speech Winifrid may be playing mainly to the audience.

378–83 shooes . . . slippers Slippers covered only the front part of the foot; pumps were close-fitting low-cut indoor footwear with no inner sole; shoes such as 'corks' (see 383n) covered the foot to the ankle or above; and anything extending to the calf or above was a boot (Linthicum, pp. 241 ff.).

383 Tennis-court . . . creaking The felt-soled **slippers** for playing in an indoor **Tennis-court** would avoid the notorious **creaking** of cork-soled shoes (cf. 378–83n, and *WHo* II.ii.64–6: 'why prettie soule tread softlie, and come into this roome: here be rushes, you neede not feare the creaking of your corke shooes'.

387 question me in Latin Appropriate if the subject matter is scandalous (and particularly sexual); cf. Monticelso's response to Vittoria's request to be questioned in English (*WD* III.ii.22–3). A serving-woman with a knowledge of Latin is somewhat of a surprise, but cf. 391.

390 Here's . . . Devill Proverbial: 'He must have a long Spoon that will eat with the devil' (Tilley S771). Lucas notes a pun on **Latin** and 'latten' = 'brass', and Dyce quotes an anecdote (thought apocryphal) of Shakespeare's making this pun. After much doubt what to give to his godchild, Jonson's little boy, at last Shakespeare decided: 'I' faith Ben: I'le e'en give him a douzen good Lattin Spoones, and thou shalt translate them' (Roger L'Estrange, *Merry Passages and Jeasts* [1650–5], ed. H. F. Lippincott [Salzburg, 1974], p. 19). Ariosto's interjection may be for the benefit of Crispiano, or for the audience.

391 ignorant that way i.e. of Latin. Cf. 387n.

392 Proctor . . . Commencements Given the courtroom setting, and Winifrid's earlier dealings with the Register and Sanitonella, **Proctor** is generally assumed to have its legal sense of 'one whose profession is to manage the causes of others in a court administering civil or canon law; corresponding to an attorney or solicitor in courts of equity and common law' (*OED* 4). This assumption no doubt lies behind Lucas's statement that **Commencements** refers to the start of the law terms. *OED* offers no support for this, however, defining 'Commencement' as the granting of higher degrees at the end of the academic year, especially at Cambridge, and the public ceremony and celebrations surrounding it (see *OED* 2 and V.iv.90n). That women attended Cambridge commencements as an attraction is confirmed by Thomas Tomkis's play, *Lingua: or the Combat of the Tongue and the Five Senses* (perf. Cambridge 1602, pub. 1607), IV.ii (H3ʳ): 'we should come to a Commedy, as gentlewomen to the commencement, only to see men speake' (cited by Gurr 1992, p. 102). Why a proctor should take his wife to Cambridge for an outing is not clear, and raises the possibility that there is a joke here about Winifrid confusing a law proctor with the **Proctor** who was an officer of the university (*OED* 3).

396–400 Caudle . . . Julipe A **Caudle** is a warm alcoholic drink made of gruel with wine or ale, sweetened and spiced, and given to the sick, and their visitors, whereas **small drinke** is either 'of low alcoholic strength' or 'non-alcoholic' (*OED* small 12). Cf. T. Phaer, *The Regiment of Lyfe* (1560), fol. lxxix: 'To abstayne from all kynds of wyne and to use him selfe to small drynke'. A **Julipe** (i.e. julep) is a sweet drink, but here used in its figurative sense of 'something to cool or assuage the heat of passion' (*OED* 1b). Cf. Massinger, *The Parliament of Love*, III.i.11: 'A courser iulip may well coole his worship.'

404 tester 'the wooden or metal framework supporting the canopy and curtains over a bed' (cf. *OED* tester[1] 1).

406 dealing For the double entendre see 358–9n.

409 stinger 'a pungent or crushing argument' (*OED* 3). It seems likely Sanitonella is close enough to Winifrid to talk aside to her, though possibly he plays to the audience in approval; cf. 419.

416 *Anno* seventie one i.e. '1571'; cf. 355.

418 betimes 'early in life'.

419 from the Byas The 'bias' in bowls is not only the off-centre weight in the ball, but also, as here, the oblique path it follows as a result (*OED* 2); Winifrid is therefore off her planned (oblique) course. Cf. the substantial bowls imagery, including 'bias', at *WD* I.ii.61–3 and n. As at 409, Sanitonella speaks aside to Winifrid or the audience.

421 two great frosts . . . Callis As Lucas notes, Winifrid, in 'trying to extricate herself from the difficulties she has created by [stating she is] only forty-six: and . . . pretending that she did not really know her own age', 'chooses her chronological data very cunningly, so that they gradually get earlier and earlier'. The **two great frosts** were probably those of 1564 and 1607–8, when the Thames froze hard (see Stow, *Annales*, pp. 658 and 892), while the **three great plagues** were probably those of 1563, 1592–4, and 1603 (see Chambers, I, 329 and IV, 346 ff.). For the **losse of Callis** (Calais, captured by the French on 5 January 1558) Lucas compares Chapman, *Monsieur d'Olive*, IV.2.99–100, where that boastful personage says his own embassage will become so famous a landmark that 'the losse of *Calice* and the winning of *Cales*, shal grow out of vse'. That Winifrid is actually 'About six and fortie' (415) there is no reason to question, though Leonora says that they have lived together 'These fortie yeares; we have growne old together' (III.iii.395).

422 comming up . . . Codpiece Since the **great Codpiece** was introduced about 1520 (cf. *WD* V.iii.100n), and ceased to be fashionable about 1570 (codpieces were abandoned entirely by about 1600; cf. *DM* II.ii.36n), Winifrid is now claiming to be a centenarian. Brennan 1975 finds a double entendre in **comming up** (*OED* come 74e 'to come into use, become the fashion').

425 Hare . . . doubles A double is 'a sharp turn in running, as of a hunted hare' (*OED* 6).

426 gravities 'dignities (relating to office)' (see *OED* 3).

428 Rip up 'slash open, search into' (*OED* v.[2] 3a, 4a).

433 Never This is the first time Leonora has spoken out for herself at the trial, and thus marks a significant new phase.

445–6 face . . . on A reserved second meaning suggests pleasure in looking in the mirror.

447–9 Fetch . . . No, no A gesture from Crispiano will stop Winifrid (possibly then blocked by a court Officer) from going for the picture, and reinforce the previous instruction to an Officer to fetch it.

449–56 Gentlewoman . . . Lady Crispiano reserves Winifrid for dealing with later, and now turns his attention to Leonora.

453–4 Will . . . going? 2 Surgeon is voicing the common belief that courtiers and men of fashion are fair-weather friends only. **downe with** = 'put down', reduce to humiliation (see *OED* down *adv*. 25b).

463 hang it up The words repeat Leonora's earlier, and presumably the picture will be hung at the same place on the theatre's tiring-house facade (see III.iii.365 and n), where it will now be alongside Crispiano so that comparison can be made by the audience.

465–6 sentence . . . no sentence Expectation and possible formality such as standing to deliver sentence (cf. V.vi.65, and *WD* III.ii.263n) allow Crispiano to manipulate the suspense.

469 How, a party? Since at 343 Sanitonella recognized that his 'Master' was a party to the case, the only plausible explanation for his surprise here must be that, as Lucas suggested, he had not recognized the judge to be Crispiano.

469 fine crosse trickes i.e. 'a fine red herring'—**crosse trickes** being tricks which cut irrelevantly across the progress of the main issue (Lucas).

477 *taking Crispiano's place* Crispiano may have descended from his place at some point after 468 to present the document of appointment ('Patent', 472) to Ariosto, who has certainly mounted to the judge's chair by 485. At York 1980 Crispiano also gave Ariosto his robe; at Bristol 1989, his judge's wig.

478–9 God . . . King Cf. *H8* III.ii.455–7: 'Had I but serv'd my God with half the zeal | I serv'd my king, He would not in mine age | Have left me naked to mine enemies.'

480–1 all . . . Law Cf. Dent 1984, L110.11 ('To have neither Law nor conscience'), who cites, e.g., Jonson, Chapman, and Marston, *Eastward Ho*, III.iii.54 ff. (Q1 in cancel): 'we shall haue no more Law then Conscience, and not too much of either'.

482–9 Sir . . . Bribe Crispiano, it seems, takes Ariosto's place as Romelio's counsel, but despite Ariosto's protestation that he **nere tooke fee of this *Romelio* | For being of his Councell**, it is not clear that Ariosto was ever acting for Romelio; indeed Romelio is irritated by his presence (see IV.ii.75–9).

488 from Q's 'free . . . for' is not idiomatic, and W never uses 'for' to mean 'from' in this way. Hazlitt emended to 'fro', which was adopted by Shirley and Brennan 1975, but this form does not appear elsewhere in the W canon. The mistaken setting or writing of one common pronoun for the other would have been very easy, especially since 'For' begins the previous line.

491.1 picture ... disguise Crispiano evidently draws the eyes of everyone in the court (and in the audience) to 'be fixt upon this' (491): either his face or the picture. Either way, the point is the identification of him undisguised (perhaps removing a false beard) with the portrait.

493 bleared him i.e. 'deceived, "thrown dust in his eyes"' (so Lucas; see *OED* blear *v*.[1] 3). Despite the syntax, **him** can only refer to Contilupo, not to Julio's **father** Crispiano, so a gesture may be called for to make this clear. Q's 'bleated', accepted by Dyce, Hazlitt, and Shirley, no doubt because it might apply to Crispiano, makes no sense, and is unsupported by *OED*. The setting of 't' for 'r' (and vice versa) is common in seventeenth-century printed texts, probably most often because of foul case.

494 truth ... Devill A conflation, it seems, of Tilley T566, 'Speak the truth and shame the devil', and T591 'Truth will come to light.'

495 shadow ... shadow i.e. merely a vestige of the figure in the portrait (see *OED* shadow 6b; cf. *WD* III.ii.146n).

504–6 Foure ... Europe On a possible contradiction concerning Crispiano's career, see II.i.12n.

511 spoyled 'ruined'; cf. 343n.

512 honest (1) 'law-abiding', (2) 'chaste' (*OED* 3c, b).

515 daunce *lachrimæ* A common phrase for being whipped. Lucas compares *FMI* IV.ii.239: 'twice sung *Lacrymæ* to the Virginalls of a carts taile'; cf. Tilley L15: 'To sing Lachrymæ'. The phrase derives from John Dowland's most famous composition, a lute pavan that occurs in various printed and manuscript sources in the 1590s and then in a vocal version ('Flow, my tears') in Dowland's *Second Book of Songs or Ayres* (1600). In 1604 Dowland published a set of consort variations on the tune as *Lachrimæ or Seaven Teares Figured in Seaven Passionate Pavans*. 'Lachrymæ' is alluded to in many plays of the period, including Beaumont's *The Knight of the Burning Pestle* (ante 1611), Middleton's *No Wit, No Help Like a Woman* (1613), Fletcher's *The Bloody Brother* (*c.* 1617), Massinger's *The Maid of Honour* (1621), Jonson's *Time Vindicated* (1624) and Massinger's *The Picture* (1629). See M. C. Boyd, *Elizabethan Music and Musical Criticism*, 2nd ed. (Philadelphia, 1962), pp. 167 ff.

517–18 Your ... liver Ariosto seems to be using **Your** simply as the possessive: the **Tennis-court slippers** are 'Your' in as much as they were part of Winifrid's (false) testimony. Hence **your tane drinke** = 'the drink that you said you took [to Crispiano]' and **your hote liver** = 'the lust which you implied you assuaged in bringing Crispiano "small drinke" (398)'. In the latter case, however, **your** may also carry the associated sense discussed by Abbott, Sect. 221: the use of **your** 'to appropriate an object to a person addressed'. Cf. Jonson, *Volpone*, II.i.86: 'But he could read and had your languages' (i.e. 'the languages which you know are considered important'). The **liver** was believed to be the seat of passion, and particularly of lust; hence a **hote liver** was a sign of unbridled sensuality. Cf. *Luc.* 46–7: 'with swift intent he goes | To quench the coal which in his liver glows'; also *AV* IV.i.224.

517 slippers Q's 'slips' is a slip on the part of compositor or scribe; **slippers** are specified at 383–5, and Ariosto is here mockingly repeating Winifrid's testimony. There is no known instance of 'slips' as an abbreviated form.

522 arsie, varsie 'backside foremost, upside down' (*OED*) but here with the sense of 'pushed into it'.

525 Bean-flower i.e. 'bean flour'; cf. Vittoria looking 'as if she had sinn'd in the Pastrie', *WD* V.iii.118 (and 117n). See also III.iii.181–2n.

527 Farrier . . . age 'the surest way to know a Horses age, is to looke in a Horses mouth' (Markham, *Cavelarice* [1607], E2ᵛ).

529 abuse 'deceive' (*OED* 4a).

532–3 Contarino . . . cause That Leonora is in love with Contarino will not be apparent to those in court. Cf. Contarino's aside, 579–81.

539 from both i.e. from Romelio and Crispiano.

544 away with after reckonings i.e. 'put up with, tolerate [*OED* away 16a] final accounts'.

549 practise 'intrigue' (*OED* practice 6b).

552 revealing himself (Lucas) Since Ercole is not disguised, merely '*muffled*' (0.2), he only needs to uncover himself; presumably he also advances to a central position.

558–9 guard . . . obey Given the importance of Ercole's involvement to the end of the scene, the **guard** may be more a formal instruction to the Officers than active restraint; possibly Ercole surrenders his sword (so York 1980). For the absence of other actors as guards, see pp. 49–50.

563 challenge 'accuse, impeach, call to account, defy' (see *OED* 1, 2, 7).

564 fame 'reputation' (*OED n.*[1] 2a).

567 How . . . contrary? Contarino assumes that Ercole knows he is alive, whereas Ercole is preparing to say that Romelio killed him.

569–74 Having . . . kild him Syntactically compressed, at times misleadingly so, Ercole's lines may be paraphrased thus: 'Contarino having been wounded by me, though not mortally, this murderer (Romelio), acting as executor (cf. 'overseer', IV.i.28n) of Contarino's estate on Jolenta's behalf, in order to ensure that Contarino did not survive to change his will, went secretly to his bedside, and killed him.'

588–9 living . . . life The ultimate source is Ecclus. 34: 22, 'He that taketh away his neighbour's living, slayeth him'. Cf. *DM* V.i.11–13 (and n).

594 forward 'eager'.

597–9 I begun . . . pitied Lucas and all modern editors except Weis strengthen the punctuation after **hate him**. Wiggins (p. 374), however, argues for 'the inherent doubleness of the moment', and against 'two distinct grammatical units'. Following Wiggins, Weis retains the comma after 'hate him' in favour of strengthening the punctuation after **each other**.

605 approve 'prove, demonstrate' (*OED* 1).

613 Malta 'The Turks were repulsed at Malta in 1565. W may, however, be thinking of later skirmishes between the Turks and the Knights of Malta who were sometimes joined by young adventurers like Contarino, because a date of 1565 would render Contarino and Ercole too old' (Weis).

614   your Nation Danish, as would appear clearly enough to an audience by Contarino's dress; cf. 6.1n. Lucas suggests that this tribute to Denmark slightly supports a dating of the play prior to the death of Anne of Denmark, the patron of the acting company, on 2 March 1619, but whether it is a compliment needs to be judged in the context of Danish costume that may be intended to look foolish.

619–20   give . . . throat 'to lie in the throat' is an intensification of 'to lie' (Sykes compares *Ham.* II.ii.574–5: 'gives me the lie i'th'throat | As deep as to the lungs?'); Julio's **in the stomacke** provides further, comic, intensification.

621   Marselys 'Marseilles'.

621   Bayon 'Bayonne'.

621   Callis Sands Calais (then pronounced **Callis**) was a favourite duelling-ground for Englishmen, as the nearest place beyond the jurisdiction of the English laws against duelling. Cf. *CC* I.ii.90.

622   gravell Julio puns on (1) 'sand' for cleaning a sword (*OED* gravel 1), and (2) renal calculus, 'aggregations of urinary crystals' (*OED* 4).

626–7   custody . . . Knight-Marshall The **Knight-Marshall** is an officer of the court of King's Bench, or of the royal household, responsible for the custody of prisoners (cf. *OED* marshal 4a, 6b, and marshalsea 1). The title derives from being a deputy to the Earl (or Lord) Marshal, who presides over the judicial combat at V.vi, but he himself seems to have been called the Knight-Marshall on occasion (see Young, p. 83). W may even be conflating the two positions. Cf. also Selden, *Duello* (p. 28), 'The defendant committed to the Marshals custody'. The High Constable and the Marshal are identified by Selden (p. 36) as the two royal officers supervising the Court of Chivalry.

629   rissen i.e. 'risen'. Q's is one of many possible forms of the past participle, appearing, for example, in Middleton's *The Witch*: 'The King's now rissen' (MSR, 46).

639   grav'd 'buried' (*OED*).

640–1   quencht . . . blood Cf. *DM* II.v.47–8: ''Tis not your whores milke, that shall quench my wild-fire, | But your whores blood.' **tame** = 'submissive, meek, poor-spirited, pusillanimous, servile' (*OED* 4).

642   You have judged Ercole seems to address the theatre audience as much as the other characters, especially as he becomes overtly sententious from 644 (see 647–8n). This speech may cover the departure of most of the court (so York 1980).

643   practise Cf. 549n.

645   indirect 'devious'; cf. *WD* I.ii.337–8.

646   shaddowed 'obscured' (*OED* 3), but with the additional sense of 'disguised, veiled' (7a).

646   vaile of State i.e. 'state affairs acting as a cloak or mask' (see *OED* veil *n.*[1] 5).

647–8   Mountaines . . . on oft 'Condensed from Alexander, *Alex. Trag.* V.ii (O3ᵛ): "Thus though the mountaines make a mighty show, | They are but barren heapes borne vp aloft, | Where plaines are pleasant still, though they lie lowe, | And are most fertile too, though troad on oft"' (Dent). Cf. *DM* III.v.140 and n.

649 put up 'stow away, parcel up' (*OED* put *v.*[1] 56 n [*a*]). More comic business with the vast quantity of papers may be implied here.

649–51 papers . . . neere them Sanitonella and Contilupo both expressed interest in **France** and precedents (**President**) at IV.i.97–111. Sanitonella's point here is that his **papers** relating to the law-suit will demonstrate that, though they have nothing else in common, where a **strange Law-suite** is concerned Naples (for which read England) can **come somewhat neere** France. Ercole's rhyming couplet *sententia* at 647–8 carries the formality that usually closes a scene, so Sanitonella's comment here is almost certainly a comic afterword to the audience (so York 1980).

649–50 France . . . Law-suite No plausible suggestion has been made as to a particular French **Law-suite**, but the comment suggests a topical reference.

ACT V, Scene i

0.1 ANGIOLELLA *great bellied* The visual oxymoron of a pregnant nun will be comic; this effect may be heightened if Angiolella hides her great belly until she answers Jolenta's query at 10. The habit of a nun of the 'Order of Saint *Clare*' (III.iii.38) would be grey or brown, with a black veil (cf. V.v.36–7n); for discussion of the Poor Clares and their costume, see Andrew Gurr, '*Measure for Measure*'s Hoods and Masks: the Duke, Isabella, and Liberty', *ELR* XXVII, 1 (Winter 1997), pp. 89–105.

5–21 sad . . . happy From the outset, Angiolella's sadness is challenged by Jolenta's determination to laugh at serious matters.

6 vaile i.e. her black nun's veil; for discussion of costume, see p. 37. Plucking the veil over the face suggests a strongly stylized acting gesture of shame; cf. IV.ii.46.3n.

8–9 There's . . . friend From Sidney, *Arcadia*, I.xiii (*Works*, I, 86): 'there is nothing more terrible to a guilty hart, then the eie of a respected friend' (Dent). This source supports Lucas's emendation of Q's 'As' to **Then**, old spelling for Dyce's 'Than'. Q has muddled the alternative constructions, 'as . . . as' and 'more . . . than'.

10 quicke with child i.e. pregnant; perhaps with the sense of 'in the stage of pregnancy at which the motion of the fœtus is felt' (*OED* quick *adj.* 4a). Cf. 12–13n.

11 Too sure Probably comic, given the great belly; see 0.1n.

12–13 How . . . quickned This question has puzzled editors. The Q reading, retained here, appears to mean 'How did you know (this being your first child) that you were pregnant?' Brennan 1975's colon after **child** results in the meaning 'What did you feel as the first sign of pregnancy: movement (quickening)?' (cf. 10n). Dyce, followed by Lucas and others, posits a transposition error and reads 'first of your child'; the meaning thus becoming 'How did you first know you were expecting a child?' The emended word order results, however, in improbable syntax.

15 taking 'Condition, situation, state, plight' (*OED* 4a, citing Pepys, 'the poor boy was in a pitiful taking and pickle'; see Pepys, *Diary*, IV, 13).

17–18 shrunke . . . great belly Stage business of Jolenta removing her 'quilted preface' (III.iii.184) at this point (so Wellington 1995) increases the low comedy, but is not justified by the text.

20 practise 'practice, action, reality'.

24–5 thing . . . lost i.e. 'virginity'; the jest was common at the time.

28 venter i.e. 'venture', in the sense of 'hazard, risk, or stake' (*OED* 1), as with 'ventur'd' (31).

45 tumbled With a double entendre on 'copulate, play amorously' (Partridge 1955, p. 210). Henke 1975, II, 301, cites *The Jew of Malta*, IV.iv.28–9: 'Love me little, love me long, let musicke rumble, | Whilst I in thy incony [fine, pretty] lap doe tumble.' For a similar punning debate on land transport ('your Cittizens wiues loue iolting') as an alternative to the salacious 'go by water', see *WHo* II.iii.68–78 and Hoy 1980 on the passage.

46 for that tricke Probably **tricke** is continuing the nautical metaphors, meaning 'the time alloted to the man on duty at the helm; a spell; a turn', although the first written citation is not until 1669 (*OED* 9). Lucas believes the sense of a 'hand, round' at cards is intended (*OED* 11), which is possible (especially given 'venter' at 28), but Shirley's gloss of 'clever expedient' seems unlikely.

47–8 brave Roman . . . Rome Jolenta is presumably citing Romans as the quintessential 'land-Souldiers' (46), with the added sense of classical Roman virtues, especially courage; cf. *AV* IV.ii.32: 'Bravely like *Roman* Leaguerers'. Angiolella's response may only pun on literally travelling from Naples to Rome, or may be played to the audience as a jibe at conversion to the Church of Rome.

49 Letter Jolenta probably has this letter to Ercole with her when she enters, but might write it during the course of the scene.

52 shade 'shadow'.

ACT V, Scene ii

7–12 abuse . . . friends Lucas is probably right that **Marry this**, which seems to herald a description of the **vild abuse**, actually leads into Sanitonella's proposed cure: a prohibition on Proctors inadvertently losing cases as a result of going to the **Taverne** with **Clients**, since they, when **overtaken** ('drunk', *OED* 9), **become friends** with their adversaries. Since anti-lawyer satire is the essence of the exchange, it hardly matters what the abuse is perceived to be. Weis takes Sanitonella's concern for ethics seriously, suggesting that the prohibition on drinking is an abuse of justice because it prevents more cases being settled out of court. If one wishes to read the prohibition as the abuse, it is more likely that Sanitonella thinks it an abuse of law clerks, who would otherwise get free drinks (cf. *CC* IV.i.101–4). He then explains why lawyers abuse their clerks so: for fear of losing business.

13.1 with a letter Sent by Jolenta in the previous scene.

13.2 Friers habits . . . Bathanites Despite wide-ranging research, no reference to such an order has been traced. Lucas suggests 'the name . . . is doubtless a corruption, perhaps of Bethlemites'. This makes little difference, however, since W's source for such a custom has not been found. It is clear, nevertheless, that the special costume, and perhaps ceremonial, would emphasize the preparations for judicial combat. Books of conduct for trial by combat urge that participants confess and be shriven before they put their bodies and souls to the test (see, e.g., Christine de Pisan, *The Book of Fayttes of Armes and of Chyvalrye*, tr. William Caxton, ed. A. T. P. Byles, E.E.T.S. [Oxford, 1932], pp. 280–1).

28 protested 'solemnly or publicly asserted' (*OED* 1).

38 begot by her brother Apparently confessing incest, Jolenta really means that the 'shame' (37) was 'occasioned' (*OED* beget 4) by Romelio.

41 vail'd i.e. 'veiled, concealed', but with an obvious irony given the veiled but pregnant Angiolella in the previous scene.

45–6 thinke of her . . . mother Comically, Contarino, speaking of Jolenta, has to lie in order to maintain his disguise role.

ACT V, Scene iii

0.1 [2] Surgeon Although Q does not identify, either in the entry SD or speech prefixes, which Surgeon this is (Brennan 1975, thinking it does not matter, identifies him as 1 Surgeon), *2 Surgeon* here reveals the plan and disguise for which he takes credit during the final discovery at V.vi.35–8. See also 34n.

6 naught 'morally bad, wicked' (*OED* 2), but with sexual implications deriving associatively from **naught** = o = vagina.

10 Honest Contrary to the usual double entendre, the apparent slur on her chastity against which Winifrid reacts so strongly is not the primary meaning here.

11 suborning Although the primary sense may be, as Lucas suggests, simply 'supporting, aiding' (see *OED* suborn 5), it seems certain that the negative legal connotations of perjury and conspiracy are also intended (see *OED* 1, 2).

31 suite Romelio abandoned this 'habit of a Jew' (32) after his attempt on Contarino; see III.ii.120 and n.

34 Procure 'cause' (*OED* 4d).

34 Passengers 'travellers, foot-passengers' (*OED* 1b). Given 2 Surgeon's reference to himself as a 'Falconer' at V.vi.35, there may also be a play on 'passenger falcon', which is 'an adult hawk caught on its migration; also, a name for the Peregrine falcon' (*OED* 5b).

35 discover 'reveal' (*OED* 4), but here with the added theatrical sense. Cf. V.iv.43.

36 Commicall event Cf. Ariosto's 'Comicall events' (V.vi.69). A proleptic reference, this serves to alert us to a comic rather than tragic outcome.

36–7 mad . . . cure her Possibly, for comic effect, aside to the audience; on curing by laughter, cf. *DM* IV.ii.39–44.

ACT V, Scene iv

0.1 SD Both the approaching judicial combat and Julio's comic cowardice may be emphasized by business during the scene with swords (so Wellington 1995).

4 Perjury Presumably because Julio swore an oath in court. See IV.ii.617 ff.

4 Dane Contarino is still in disguise as a Dane.

5–7 reverse . . . horse tayle Turning an escutcheon upside down was a traditional heraldic indication of dishonour (see *OED* reverse *v.*¹ 3c). Selden's *Duello* says that if one of the parties 'on the Duell day . . . without iust cause hide his head, it is sufficient conuiction, and without all hope of restitution is his honor attainted; wherevpon . . . some appelants carrie the pictures of such dastards about them with exprobration, or their coate-armour reversed, or ignominiously fastened vnder their horses tayle or with such like disgrace' (p. 41). Although *OED* records late sixteenth-century uses of the shortened form 'ignomious', W's reliance on Selden supports Lucas's emendation of Q's 'ignomiously' to **ignominiously**, which is also metrically superior.

8 I . . . so well Julio may, with this and similar lines in this scene, be playing to the audience for laughs.

13   upon returne A reference (not in *OED*) 'to the curious custom practised by Elizabethan travellers of gambling on their risks—a kind of inverted insurance. The traveller paid down a certain sum at his departure; if he failed to return, the agent kept it; if he did return, he received the amount of his deposit several times over'. So Lucas, who compares Jonson, *Every Man out of His Humour*, II.iii.243–8: 'I doe intend . . . to trauaile: and . . . I am determined to put forth some fiue thousand pound, to be paid me, fiue for one, vpon the returne of my selfe, my wife, and my dog, from the *Turkes* court in *Constantinople*.' Lucas adds that 'it grew common among "bankerruts, stage-players, and men of base condition" to travel abroad merely to make money in this way', citing Barnabe Riche, *Faultes Faults and Nothing Else but Faultes* (1606), C4ʳ: 'those whipsters, that having spent the greatest part of their patrimony in prodigality, will give out the rest of their stocke, to be paid two or three for one, upon their returne from *Rome*, from *Venice*, from *Constantinople*, or some other appoynted place'. As Lucas observes, 'The odds given seem to imply that the probability of non-return was incredibly high.'

17–18 hung still an arse 'held back, hesitated' (Partridge 1984, p. 527).

19–22 cheese . . . braveliest 'For this ancient jest' Lucas compares Fletcher, *The Pilgrim*, IV.iii.90, where there is a joke on a Welshman who 'run mad because a rat eate up's cheese'. Cf. also *Char.* (Lucas), 'A drunken Dutch-man resident in England', 12–14: 'He loves a Welch-man extreamely for his Dyet and Orthography; that is, for plurality of Consonants and Cheese. Like a Horse, hee's onely guided by the mouth.'

20 a goes Q lacks **a**, which Lucas supplied, declaring: 'Some pronoun is needed.' There are three other instances of the colloquial **a** for 'he' in the play (II.i.96, 132, II.iii.139), and its accidental omission here would have been very easy.

25 put in for't i.e. 'made his thrusts' (see *OED* put B 1d).

25 hungry Usher 'ushers at a feast who, without partaking, have to watch the guests as they dine' (Weis).

27 chaps 'jaws, chops' (*OED* chap *n.*² 2).

28 breath i.e. 'breathe, pause, take breath' (*OED* breathe 5).

32–3 anger . . . sorrow . . . dry 'with reference to the doctrine of humours' (so Lucas, who compares Robert Burton, *The Anatomy of Melancholy* (1624), C1ʳ: 'Choler, is hot and drie . . . Melancholy, cold and drie'). Dent compares Tilley S656: 'Sorrow is dry (thirsty).'

37 Cuckingstoole 'An instrument of punishment formerly in use for scolds [and] disorderly women . . . consisting of a chair . . . in which the offender was fastened and . . . conveyed to a pond or river and ducked' (*OED*).

38.1 very melancholly Since Romelio is at 89 offered a book, that standard prop to indicate **melancholly** is evidently not used here. The most likely visual signal of his state will therefore be clothing (perhaps black or dishevelled) and conventional action (probably 'Musing and sighing, with [his] arms across' [*JC* II.i.240]). Cf. *DM* I.i.22n.

40 Deliver'd i.e. 'had related, narrated' (*OED* 11a).

40 Intelligence 'news, tidings' (*OED* 7a).

43 discovering 'revealing' (*OED* discover 4). Cf. IV.ii.65.

46 to Julio Since he takes no further part in the scene until the entry of Leonora, Julio presumably stands apart observing. (At York 1980 he knelt facing upstage, praying.)

55 meditate of death The Capuchin is perhaps referring to the techniques of Ignatian meditation, central to Counter-Reformation affective devotion, which had been absorbed into the English *ars moriendi* tradition via Robert Persons's *The First Booke of the Christian Exercise, Appertayning to Resolution* (1582) and its pirated, Protestant version, R. P., *A Booke of Christian Exercise Appertaining to Resolution*, 'Perused' by Edmund Bunny (1585). Cf. II.iii.107 ff. and n.

56 tooke out 'learnt' (*OED* take 87f).

61–3 practice . . . practice The Capuchin's point is that knowledge of sword blades is not part of his profession (*OED n.* 5), while for Romelio **practice** means 'make use of, employ' (*OED v.* 7).

64–7 Were I . . . shadow Given **present to my selfe**, the Capuchin may, by **shaddowes**, mean 'reflected images' (*OED* 5a), but Romelio's response uses **shadow** in its now usual meaning. Cf. III.ii.1–2, where Romelio imagines 'That I could play with mine owne shaddow now' (also *DM* V.ii.31–40, where Ferdinand, fearing his shadow, tries to throttle it). Romelio uses **Turne you** in the sense of 'reversing your proposition' (see *OED* turn 10b), continuing the debate structure of the exchanges. **case** = 'situation, plight'.

71–2 honest . . . coward Cf. *Char.* (Lucas), 'A worthy Commander in the Warres', 7–8: 'He holds it next his Creed, that no coward can be an honest man.'

75–6 Dormouse . . . slumber The **Dormouse** was a by-word for both cowardice and torpidity: cf. *TN* III.ii.17, 'thy dormouse valour', and *DM* I.i.269–70 (and n), 'a pollitique dormouse . . . halfe a sleepe'.

84–5 Hee's . . . necke Cf. Eph. 6: 12, 'For we wrestle not against flesh and blood, but against principalities, against powers, against the rulers of the darkness of this world, against spiritual wickedness in high places.' This is developed by Sir Thomas More, *Dialogue of Comfort*, II.ix: 'there is in this world set vpp as it were a game of wrestelyng, wherin the people of god come in on the tone side, & on the tother side come mighty strong wrestelers & wily, that is to wit, the devilles the cursid prowd dampnid sprites. For it is not our flesh alone that we must wrestell with, but with the devill to' (*The Complete Works of St Thomas More*, vol. XII, ed. Louis L. Martz and Frank Manley [New Haven, 1976], p. 101). Cf. also perhaps the death of Camillo, *WD* II.ii.

86 give him the foyle In wrestling, to almost throw an opponent, or to throw him, although without achieving a fall (see *OED* foil *n.*[2] 1); more generally, to give 'a repulse; a baffling check' (*OED n.*[2] 2).

88   Get me . . . victuals   Not only countering the Capuchin's argument about the source of strength, but also contemptuously ordering him about as if he were a menial.

89   *a Booke*   A conventional as well as specific offering of religious guidance; cf. *WD* V.vi.1n. Romelio evidently rejects it with 'Pew' at 90.

90   commence Doctor   i.e. graduate with a doctorate. More associated with Cambridge than with Oxford, although relevant to both; cf. Harrison, 'Description', I, 149: 'In Oxford this solemnitie is called an Act, but in Cambridge they vse the French word Commensement.' See also IV.i.41n and IV.ii.392n.

91   word   'command' (*OED* 7).

94   apprehend   i.e. 'feel the force of, understand' (*OED* 7, 8), and perhaps also 'antici-pate' (*OED* 10).

95–7   Death . . . devourer?   Dent 1984 (D138.1: 'Death devours all things') cites Henry Chettle, *Hoffman* (1602; pub. 1631), III.i (E4^v): 'But rich or fair or strong, death swal-lowes all.' Cf. also G425.11 ('As unsatiate as the grave'), where Dent cites Massinger, *A New Way to Pay Old Debts*, I.ii.46: 'His stomach's as insatiate as the grave'.

98–100   I knew . . . before   Possibly a reference to the execution of Raleigh, which took place in 1618. Gardiner (III, 151) writes: 'As the hour for his execution approached, Raleigh took his breakfast, and smoked his tobacco as usual . . . [then on the scaffold] he knelt down, and laid his head upon the block. Some one objected that he ought to lay his face towards the east: "What matter," he said, "how the head lie, so the heart be right?"'

101   speake   It was customary for prisoners to make a speech before execution. Raleigh (see 98–100n) made a carefully prepared speech on the scaffold.

102–3   confidence . . . truth   The Capuchin's point is that Romelio's **confidence** is carnal 'securitie' (115): i.e. self-satisfaction and unconcern for the hereafter. Cf. 113–16, II.iii.172 and n, and *DM* V.ii.328 and n.

110   teeming   'pregnant'.

113   storme   Cf. *WD* IV.iii.100–1: 'thou'rt a foule blacke cloud, and thou do'st threat | A violent storme', and V.vi.243–4: 'My soule, like to a ship in a blacke storme, | Is driven I know not whither.'

117   I have an object   Clearly the Capuchin and Leonora have prepared beforehand for Romelio's intransigence. **object** has the usual seventeenth-century sense of 'something presented to the sight' (*OED* 3a).

119.1–.3   SD   The emblematic meaning of Leonora's elaborate *memento mori* in 'dumbe Pageant' (140) is immediately clear to Romelio. Cf. Jolenta's *mementi mori* at III.iii, and *WD* V.iv.59 ff. Music may well accompany the entry.

119.2–120   *presents* . . . garment   Both the action here and Julio's later comment (150–1) make clear that the ***Winding-sheets*** are handed to Romelio and Julio. It is possible the two men are draped in them, as at Wellington 1995, where the top ends were already tied up to place over their heads, so that they resembled the well-known engraving of John Donne in his winding sheet, tied like a cracker; cf. *WD* V.iv.59.3n. In Thomas Goffe's university play *The Couragious Turke* (perf. 1619) two nobles enter to the penitent

Aladin 'with a winding sheet, Aladin puts it on' (1374; IV.iv), and in the next scene 'Aladin, his Wife, two Children, all in white sheets kneele downe to Amurath' (The Raging Turke and The Couragious Turke, MSR, 1399–1401; V.i).

122–37 All the Flowers . . . wind Although Romelio has a moralizing 'Meditation' at II.iii.93 ff. which is also in rhyming couplets in an octosyllabic metre changed from the blank verse norm, here the verse (or song; note the SD for **Soft Musicke**) serves the function of the stanza under a printed emblem, explaining and elaborating on the visual image. The function is so similar to that of Bosola's dirge in DM IV.ii.165–82, accompanying the presentation of a coffin, that Lucas raises, before dismissing, the possibility that this verse is misassigned to Romelio, and should be spoken or sung by the Capuchin or Leonora.

122 Soft Musicke i.e. a string consort, probably viols. The relatively quiet string music probably accompanied the entire passage (123–37); but Q's placing in the margin opposite 128 could indicate a deliberate intention to start when 'Courts' and 'delights' are mentioned.

127 set 'planted'.

131 goe out 'are extinguished' (OED go 85d).

132 consequently Probably 'in sequence' (OED 1b; so Brennan 1975), or possibly 'as a consequence' (OED 2; so Lucas).

133 wait upon i.e. 'escort, accompany' (OED wait v.[1] 10, 14k).

134 ambition The tetrameter of the meditation requires tetrasyllabic pronunciation.

137 weave . . . wind Cf. Tilley W416: 'He catches the Wind in a net.'

139 compris'd 'brought together, included; summed up' (see OED 3a, b).

140 dumbe Pageant 'dumb show', but with the additional sense of 'tableau' (OED pageant 3).

142 object Cf. 117n. Leonora's servants may exit with the coffins at this point (so York 1980).

144 yonder Gesture will emphasize the sense of 'heaven, the other world'; cf. WD III.ii.313 and n.

147 Closet 'private room'. In this case, unlike IV.ii.3 (and see n), the **Closet** is imagined to be offstage, and a tiring-house door apparently 'lockt' (171) to keep them in; cf. WD I.ii.168–78.

150–1 Bandileere . . . scarfe These comments, probably to the audience, seem to depend on topical satire now lost. Julio's winding sheet is evidently over one shoulder and across his breast like a bandoleer or scarf, either having been placed there during the presentation (119.2–.3), or because he is now engaging in 'some by-play' (Lucas), perhaps struggling out of its entanglement (so Wellington 1995). Lucas also suggests that Julio thinks he now looks like 'a felon bound for the **gallows** and wearing his halter'. Wymer declares that his reaction 'is jokingly to wrap the winding sheet round his neck in the form of a hangman's halter' (p. 82), but he does not explain the bandoleer reference. What Julio means by hanging one's **coffin** in a scarf is obscure, though clearly based on the association of the winding sheet and the coffin it arrived

with. Possibly the use of bandoleers or scarves to support swords was becoming fashionable at this time, in which case **coffin** may be intended in a figurative sense, 'that
which may bring death' (though no such usage is recorded in OED). See also
119.2–120n.

160 guilt Vellom i.e. 'gilt vellum', literally 'parchment that has been gilded with gold
leaf'.

161 certifie 'assure, inform certainly' (OED 3b).

162 presently 'at once, directly' (OED 3).

162 Closet i.e. the door by which Leonora left; see 147n.

165 safe 'secured, unable to escape' (OED 10).

166 and 'if' (cf. Abbott, Sect. 101).

168 Boson i.e. 'bosun, boatswain', 'whose duty it is to summon the men to their duties
with a whistle' (OED boatswain 1); cf. 'whistle out to'th Sea' (167).

173 howling at parting Cf WD V.iii.36–7. Here **parting** figuratively means 'death'
(see OED vbl. n. 4).

173.1 Knocking within Just when the Capuchin starts his frantic knocking behind the
'lockt' door (171) is not specified, but the noise is commented on by Julio at 174; the
Capuchin will need to stop knocking (and shouting; see 175.1–6) by about 180 in
order to have time to get up to the upper level by V.v.0.1.

174 and 'as if' (OED C conj. conditional 3). Abbott, Sect. 104, rejects the view that 'an't
were' (or 'and') = 'as if', but this seems clearly to be the meaning here.

178–9 'tis that He onely i.e. 'it is only that he' (fishes for); so Lucas, who compares
DM I.i.31–2: 'where onely the reward | Of doing well, is the doing of it' for a similar
word order.

179 So . . . day Cessation of offstage noise may help mark the transition of time and
mood here.

183 mine owne Ballad Lucas notes 'perpetual allusions to the doggerel ballads which
the condemned criminal had to face'. Sykes compares Massinger and Fletcher, The
Lover's Progress V.iii.24–6: 'I have penn'd mine owne ballad | Before my condemnation,
in feare | Some rimer should prevent me.'

184 miscarry i.e. 'meet with my death, perish' (see OED 1), with perhaps the secondary sense of 'behave amiss' (OED 2).

184–5 Well . . . spirit i.e. 'well, [it will be surprising] if the young Capuchin does not
talk of the flesh as zealously [OED fast adv. 1c] now to your mother, as he did to us of
the spirit'. The reference to the Capuchin as **young** is the only indication in the play
that he is not the traditional elder advisor of the drama, and suggests either W's awareness of likely casting, or a deliberate generational dynamic to set against Leonora and
Ariosto.

187 close committing Julio puns, as (1) 'strictly confined, imprisoned', and (2) 'committing adultery or fornication' (see OED close 3, 17, and commit 3, 16). Cf. Lr.
III.iv.81–2: 'commit not with man's sworn spouse'.

ACT V, Scene v

0.1 *above at a window* The terrace acting level was often referred to in plays for both public and private playhouses as a *window* (see Gurr 1992, pp. 147, 159–62, and Dessen and Thomson); the Inigo Jones design for the Phoenix shows a full-height arched opening 1.2 metres wide. See also 24n and p. 46.

2 **he** i.e. Romelio.

7 **secret fate** The Capuchin seems to imply an element of predestination here, given **secret** = 'beyond ordinary apprehension' (*OED* 1g) and **fate** = 'predestined or appointed lot; destiny' (*OED* 3b and 4a). Cf. 14–17n.

10 **call lowder** Possibly the Capuchin has been shouting for help from time to time.

11 **leape … Battlements** The upper level was often imaginatively thought of as battlements high enough to be suicidal; cf. *Jn.* IV.iii.

12 **in time** (Dyce) Q lacks **in**, which, though not absolutely necessary, improves both sense and metre, and so seems likely to have been accidentally omitted.

14–17 **heaven … ruine** The Capuchin here affirms what he implied at 7, that divine providence is directing events, though now in ways which **invert mans … purpose**. Hence his recognition of his own powerlessness as an instrument of **heaven**, and his reliance on prayer ('look upwards' [15]).

20 **presumptuous** Cf. 'sins from presumption' (II.iii.132–3).

21–2 **aspire … light** Proverbial; cf. *DM* II.i.89–90: 'the Divell, that rules i'th'aire, stands in your light'.

23 **Christian** Q's 'christian' is the last word of a full line, and the only uncapitalized example in Q.

24 **other casement** Presumably another window imagined as being on the other side of the building. Despite the reference to **casement** here and at V.iv.167, there is no need to postulate a practicable opening and closing window in the upper acting space; see 0.1n and Leslie Thomson, 'Window Scenes in Renaissance Plays: a Survey and Some Conclusions', *Medieval and Renaissance Drama in English* v (1990), pp. 225–43.

ACT V, Scene vi

0.1 *Lists set up* The **Lists** are the 'pallisades or other barriers' enclosing the space set apart for the judicial tournament (cf. *OED n.*² 9). See pp. 51–2 and Fig. 3.

0.1 *Officers* Presumably the two court Officers from IV.ii undertake similar roles as attendants and guards; cf. IV.ii.0.1n.

0.2 CRISPIANO, *and* ARIOSTO *as Judges* As in IV.ii (see 46.1n), the apparel of the *Judges* will be a reminder that the trial by combat takes place in a 'high Court of Honor' (33). If staging imitated actual judicial combats, they would have raised seating (perhaps above in the theatre). The *Marshall* will not sit, since he is in charge of the lists; see pp. 51–2 and Fig. 3.

0.3 SANITONELLA, *and a Herauld* Both have speaking parts, so an entry is necessary. The *Herauld*, needed almost immediately, is under the direction of the Marshal and

Ariosto. Sanitonella was last seen with Julio, Prospero, and Romelio, so probably enters now as a spectator.

2 Tuckets . . . Trumpets The judicial combat in *R2* (I.iii) similarly has **Tuckets** (trumpet flourishes) by **severall Trumpets**, one for the defendant and one for the appellant. Probably the two tuckets are different, identifying the parties separately (see J. S. Manifold, *Music in English Drama from Shakespeare to Purcell* [London, 1956], pp. 26–8). It is not clear here whether the trumpeters are offstage, one behind each stage door (2.1–.2), or if **Trumpets** refers to musicians who enter before the combatants (cf. *Lr.* V.iii.117.2–.3 [quarto SD] '*Enter Edgar . . . a trumpet before him*').

2.1–.2 SD The two pairs of characters, entering at opposite sides of the stage, are formally prepared and armed for the combat (cf. 2n and 6–7).

3–4 alledge . . . not proceed? Cf. Selden, *Duello* (p. 43), 'Vppon sound of a Trumpet the Apellant and Defendant are seuerally demaunded; who in person present, the Register to their procurators [asks] *Vous Parains saches rien dire en empeachment del combat?*' The *Parains* (modern Fr. *parrains*) are the procurators, or seconds, who speak on behalf of the combatants in the full judicial procedure. For W's use of Selden, see p. 260.

5–6 weighed . . . weapons Cf. Selden, *Duello* (p. 43), 'Search is made . . . of equality of their weapons.' Unlike the duel fought with modern rapiers in II.ii, the High Court of Chivalry specified '*Auncient, Vsuall, and Military*' weapons. The actors therefore probably used bastard swords, heavy traditional swords with blades over a metre long; see pp. 42–3, and Charles Edelman, *Brawl Ridiculous* (Manchester, 1992), esp. pp. 25–7.

11 Soit . . . droit In modern French, *Que le combat soit, et victoire à ceux qui ont le droit de leur côté* ('Let the combat begin, and victory to those whose cause is just'). Cf. Selden, *Duello* (p. 44), 'an Herehault pronouncing *soiet la battaile grauntus & victorie a ceux que droit*'. W's use of Selden justifies retaining Q's English spelling of **Victory**, and the antique French.

11.1 Trumpets . . . charge A *charge* is 'a signal for the attack'; cf. 2n, *WD* V.iii.0.1 and n, and the trumpet signal for the combat in *R2* I.iii.117. Cf. Selden, *Duello* (p. 44), 'Vppon the sound of the alarme the battell begins.'

12 Stay . . . going We must assume that the tableau in V.iv has had an effect, and that Romelio's carnal 'securitie' (see V.iii.115n) has been shattered. Cf. *WD* V.vi.106, 244n, and *DM* V.ii.280. The sudden **Stay** will be a *coup de théâtre* as it disrupts the carefully-built formality and tension leading to the fight. It also has comic potential.

18 Victory . . . droit See 11n and 11.1n.

19 Champ Technically 'A field. *champ clos, champ of battle*: the ground set apart for a judicial duel, single combat, or tourney' (*OED n.*[1] 1), but here, by extension, as Lucas notes, the combatants on the field.

19.1 Combate . . . length Not only is enough imaginative time needed for a messenger to run to Castle Novo and back, but W no doubt intends to demonstrate Romelio's dictum 'looke the last Act be the best i'th Play' (II.iii.107). Cf. the elaborate and lengthy fighting at barriers in *WD* V.iii.

24 Oh sir Although Ercole is the most logical recipient of Leonora's information, it is just possible that she speaks to Ariosto.

THE DEVIL'S LAW-CASE [V.vi

28–9 *They embrace . . .* **neerer** Stage business may be intended about Leonora coming **betweene** (so Bristol 1989), and **neerer** Contarino.

30–1 Lady . . . life Contarino becomes aware of Leonora's passion for him during the trial (see IV.ii.549–50 and 579–81), and at V.ii.45 determines to put Jolenta out of his thoughts. When (or if) he **vowed** his **life** to Leonora is unclear; what matters is his commitment to her now.

31 happy i.e. 'fortunate, lucky' (*OED* 3), because Contarino is alive, and the murder charge no longer stands.

33.1, .2 *vail'd* i.e. with their veils pulled across their faces (cf. V.i.6 and n). Jolenta must remain veiled until 2 Surgeon '*Discovers*' her at 38.

33.1–.2 *colour'd like a Moore* This overtly symbolic makeup is reminiscent of, e.g., morality play action such as Idleness blackening Wyt's face in John Redford's *Wyt and Science*, 802–25 (in J. Q. Adams, ed., *Chief Pre-Shakespearean Dramas* [Cambridge, Mass., 1924]). Painting actors black is discussed in Eldred Jones, *Othello's Countrymen* (London, 1965), pp. 120–3, and Annette Drew-Bear, *Painted Faces on the Renaissance Stage* (Lewisburg, London, and Toronto, 1994), pp. 33–57.

33.2 *one of them like a Jew* 2 Surgeon in Romelio's disguise (see 35–6 and V.iii.0.1n and V.iii.31–2).

35 I the Falconer 2 Surgeon's self-conscious role as captor, and the balanced presentation of opposite images, suggest a symmetrical staging with the women on either side of him (so York 1980). W makes frequent use of such symmetry: cf. I.ii.105–7n and II.i.165–81. On **Falconer** see V.iii.34n.

36 sprung i.e. 'caused (a bird) to rise from cover' (cf. *OED* spring *v.*[1] 18, which cites Lyly, *Midas*, IV.iii.47–8: 'thou shouldest say, start a hare, rowse the deere, spring the partridge' (*Works*, III, 148).

36–7 white Nun . . . blacke Despite the stage and pictorial tradition of *MM* (in particular Holman Hunt's 'Claudio and Isabella'), there is no historical evidence to suggest that the Poor Clares ever wore white habits (see V.i.0.1n). The contrast here, which 2 Surgeon tells us to take his word for (38) until he unveils Jolenta, seems to be of skin colour only. See p. 37.

38 *Discovers Jolenta* Presumably removes her veil from her face.

40–55 Jolenta's change of metre emphasizes the self-consciously presentational mode of her moralizing. Cf. II.iii.93–124 and V.iv.122–37.

43 Mole . . . cheeke Cf. Tilley V31: 'Venus was choice, yet a wart (mole) on her cheek'; also Lyly, *Euphues* (*Works*, I, 179): 'Venus [was painted] cunningly, yet with hir Mole.'

48 crimson blood i.e. 'blood whose redness is visible' (as it is in 'the red cheeks of the white races' [Lucas]).

49 Sister-hood With a pun, given their attire, on the specialized religious sense (*OED* 2a).

50 Which . . . whiter Angiolella's veil has been removed at some point (cf. 38n) for her pale skin to be compared with Jolenta's black face.

51 credit . . . lighter Here **credit** carries, besides its usual meaning of 'reputation, honour' (*OED* 5b), a clear sexual implication not included in *OED*; cf. III.iii.337 and

338–40n. **lighter** = 'the more wanton, unchaste' (see *OED a.*[1] 14b), with of course a pun on lightness of complexion.

52 **Ebon** i.e. 'ebony'.

53 **unstain'd** 'with no moral taint', punning on the dye or colour of black skin. A joke, theatrically, in that her skin is stained black (see 33.1–.2n).

54 **without controle** 'unconstrainedly, freely' (*OED* control 2).

55 **There's . . . Soule** Though this sounds proverbial, Tilley records no instance.

56 **tis . . . *Jolenta*** Appropriately, Ercole is the first to recognize her.

57 **ecclipst** Ercole puns, seeing Jolenta as both 'obscured' (in her disguise) and 'darkened', the pun visually supported by Jolenta's blackened features.

62–3 **Cease . . . Court** Leonora's offer of the **paper** to Ariosto (or, if he is on the upper level, possibly to the Marshal or other officer of the **Court**) returns audience focus to Ariosto.

64 **passages** Cf. IV.ii.18; see also 68 and 99.

65 **No more** Ariosto may or may not reject Leonora's paper; he seems to indicate that he has no need to read it.

65 **attend . . . Court** Ariosto's formal delivery of **Sentence** may include adopting a formal posture (cf. *WD* III.ii.263n).

66 **Rarenesse . . . estimation** As Dent notes, from Montaigne, *Essayes*, II.xv (p. 357): '*Rarenes and difficultie giveth esteeme vnto things*'. **Rarenesse** = 'the fact of occurring seldom or in few instances' (*OED* 3), but *OED* 4 seems apposite also ('unusual or exceptional character, especially in respect of excellence') given **estimation** 'appreciation, valuation in respect of excellence or merit' (*OED* 1b).

67–8 **you . . . passages** Ariosto may well include the audience in this summation; see 'so we leave you' (97).

71–2 **that Gentleman . . . Second** i.e. Julio.

72–4 **Obligations . . . principall** Since Romelio is to receive only the original sum lent (**principall**), it is clear that the **Obligations** were contracts or bonds 'under seal containing a penalty with a condition annexed' (*OED* 2).

73 **engaged** Cf. *DM* III.ii.168. The primary sense is doubtless 'pledged', or 'contracted' (*OED* 4a) but there may well be the additional sense of 'entangled, ensnared' (11a, 13a).

76 **I thanke you** Since Romelio has just formally replied to Ariosto, Julio's thanks here are also more likely to Ariosto than to Romelio.

78–9 **consort . . . *Orlando*** Sanitonella's mention of **Fidlers** implies that Julio's company of musicians will be a violin **consort**, a specifically dance group. *Orlando Furioso* ('Orlando **mad**') was one of the most used texts for madrigal settings, but there may be a now lost topical reference here. A further reference to music composed by Orlando Gibbons is also possible.

80–1 **flye . . . Watermen** Cf. *Char.* (Lucas), 'A Water-man', 17–18: 'nothing but a *great Presse*, makes him flye from the River'. **presse** = 'the impressing of men for service in the navy' (*OED n.*[2] 1).

85 this my shame Angiolella gestures to her great belly, and perhaps directs the warning for 'all honest Virgins' (86) to the audience.

87 Thorough It seems worth following Dyce in adopting this spelling, rather than Q's 'Through', for the sake of the metre. There are clear instances of 'thorough' as metrical variants in *AV* II.ii.164 and *CC* IV.ii.25 (parts of these plays we attribute to W).

93 vowes breach The **vowes** which Leonora and Angiolella breached are clear: the former is to marry after declaring her intention to enter a monastery (IV.ii.545–8) and the latter broke her vows of chastity (III.iii.37–44). The only vow Jolenta has broken is that to marry Contarino (I.i.94–5), but this has been superseded by a further vow (III.iii.158–61) never to marry him. 'The dealing out of punishments at the end', Weis suggests, 'might be viewed as a satire on judicial whimsicality'. This seems unlikely, however, given Ariosto's role throughout. Moreover, the penalties imposed here are entirely in keeping with the conventions which bring comic resolution to a tragicomedy.

96 Art . . . charge i.e. work at their 'profession' (*OED* art 9) as ship's doctors; Ariosto's rider that they will get no pay may well provoke comic bathos from the Surgeons.

97 we leave you If **we** is taken as Ariosto and Crispiano, then **you** is the remainder of the characters on stage. But **we** can equally be read as a valedictory from the characters (and players) to the audience (so Bristol 1989), with a wish that the latter may 'make good use | Of these events' in their 'future life' (98–9).

101 beyond our wishes The signification of **our wishes** is similarly multiple, as (1) Ariosto and Crispiano's, (2) all of the characters', (3) all of the players', and (4) all of these plus the audience's. **beyond** = 'surpassing' (*OED* 6).

Sources

As Lucas notes, 'There is no source known for the plot as a whole; and it is perhaps Webster's own invention.'[1] On the other hand there is evidence of a variety of sources, more or less likely, for particular incidents in *The Devil's Law-Case*.

Of these sources the most nearly certain is that which lies behind Romelio's unintended saving of Contarino's life. Gerard Langbaine first noted the close resemblance of this ironic reversal to an episode reported in Goulart's *Histoires Admirables et Memorables*. Headed 'An Extraordinarie Cure', the story runs thus in Edward Grimeston's 1607 translation:

> A Certaine Italian hauing had a quarrell with another, fell so grieuously sicke, as they did not hope for life of him. His enemie hearing thereof, came to his lodging, and inquires of his servant, where his master was. The servant answered him, hee is at the point of death, and will not escape this day. The other grumbling to himselfe, replied, he shall die by my handes: whereupon he enters into the sicke mans chamber, gives him certaine stabbes with his dagger, and then flies. They binde vp the poore sicke mans wounds, who by the meanes of so great a losse of blood, recouered his health. So hee recouered his health and life, by his meanes who sought his death. R. Solenander, *lib. 5 of his Counsels.* 15. *Cons.* 9. *Sect.*[2]

As Langbaine noted, a similar story is told of Jason, tyrant of Pherae, by Valerius Maximus,[3] but given Webster's undoubted borrowings from Grimeston in *The White Devil* and *The Duchess of Malfi* there seems little reason to doubt that his translation of Goulart is the source of this incident in *The Devil's Law-Case*.

Almost as strong is the likelihood that throughout this episode Romelio's behaviour mimics that of Barabas in Marlowe's *The Jew of Malta*. As Lucas notes, Marlowe's villain boasts that 'Being young I studied Physicke, and began | To practise first upon the Italian' (II.iii.181–2), while Romelio, disguised as a Jewish physician, descants on his ability to 'be a rare Italienated Jew' (3) and boasts that amongst 'sleight villanies' that might be practised, he could 'Betray a towne to'th Turke' (13). Lucas lists further parallels, noting

> how both merchants boast poetically of their vast wealth and their scorn of mere silver; how Romelio promises his sister, as Barabas his daughter, to two rival suitors, whose friendship is thereby ended in a dual fatal (though only apparently so in Webster) to both alike; how Romelio plans to put out of the way the two surgeons who know his guilt, as Barabas the two friars; [and] how both villains mock religions and friardom, and show, when brought to bay, a courage that redeems their avarice from mere meanness.[4]

Less certain than either of the above is the source of the central episode in *The Devil's Law-Case*, the attempt by Leonora to disgrace and disinherit her son by accusing him of bastardy. The tale of the mother whose attempt falsely to disown her son is discovered and punished by a wise judge is, as Lucas notes,[5] found in two fifteenth- and sixteenth-century texts, Bernardo Giustiniani's *De Origine Urbis Gestisque Venetorum* (1492) and

Joannes Magnus's *De omnibus Gothorum Sueonorumque Regibus* (1554), which copies Giustiniani verbatim.

It seems unlikely, however, that either Magnus or Giustiniani is the immediate source of *The Devil's Law-Case*, but rather that Webster found the play's central episode in the anonymous *Lust's Dominion* (pub. 1657), generally attributed to Dekker, Haughton, and Day on the assumption that it is identical with *The Spanish Moor's Tragedy*, for which Henslowe records a part payment of £3 on 13 February 1600.[6] The history of *Lust's Dominion* is complex, to say the least, Hoy's judicious summation being that it represents a working-over, in part (first) by Marston and then by Dekker, assisted by Haughton and Day, of a play dating from the early 1590s.[7] In the reworking some aspects of the original plot have been obscured or confused, but the situation at issue here, thus summarized by Stoll, remains clear:

> A widow [Eugenia, the Queen Mother of Spain] revenges upon her son injuries done the man she loves by spreading abroad a report that he, though her own son, is a bastard. By this she hopes to injure his fame and deprive him of his inheritance. On the pretense of scruples of conscience she goes into a public assembly to avow it, giving all the particulars of proof in the most shameless way, and naming the father [Cardinal Mendoza]. All this is pure invention and is denied by the father named.[8]

Though the Queen Mother's public avowal differs in one significant respect from that of Leonora in *The Devil's Law-Case*, in that Mendoza is at first willing to vouch for her story and only denies it when it becomes clear that she is seeking his death, the resemblances between the two incidents are striking, and strongly suggest that it was in *Lust's Dominion* ('that grotesque play' as Lucas labelled it)[9] that Webster found the plot element which was to provide both the title of *The Devil's Law-Case* and its finest scene.

One minor source remains to be noted, John Selden's *The Duello, or Single Combat* (1610), a handbook of duelling and trial by combat, which supplies Webster with both wording and procedures for the judicial combat in V.vi (see Carnegie).

1. Lucas, II, 217.
2. Simon Goulart, *Admirable and Memorable Histories*, tr. Edward Grimeston (1607), p. 289; see also Stoll, *Periods*, pp. 153–4.
3. See Stoll, *Periods*, pp. 153–4.
4. Lucas, II, 218.
5. Ibid., II, 219.
6. Henslowe, *Diary*, p. 131.
7. Hoy 1980, IV, 59–61.
8. Stoll, *Periods*, p. 154.
9. Lucas, II, 219.

A CURE FOR A CUCKOLD

Date

'A Wedding, or a *Cure for a Cuckold*, by Webster, allowed July 26th. 1624, for the Princes Company I *li* [£1]': so runs the entry in the register of the Master of the Revels, Sir Henry Herbert, unnoticed until the publication in 1996 of N. W. Bawcutt's edition of all Herbert's surviving records.[1]

A *terminus a quo* for the writing of *A Cure for a Cuckold* cannot be established with the same certainty, but two pieces of internal evidence point towards a likely period of composition. One is the reference at IV.i.116 to the notorious Griffin Flood, informer, blackmailer, and murderer, who was pressed to death at Newgate on 18 January 1624. No 'Ballad of Flood' has come to light, but Lucas discovered a pamphlet on the subject which tells a variant version of the story alluded to in *A Cure for a Cuckold*.[2] The other item, noted by Lucas,[3] is the reference at V.i.171–2 to the fine of twelvepence for swearing introduced during the Parliament of 19 February to 29 May 1624. It is, of course, possible that Webster, Rowley, and Heywood were working on their collaborative venture prior to Flood's death, and that the reference to him is a later interpolation, but it seems plausible to assume that the dramatists were engaged upon *A Cure for a Cuckold* in the period January to July 1624.

1. Bawcutt, p. 153.
2. Lucas, III, 3–4.
3. Ibid., III, 4.

Critical introduction

DAVID GUNBY

The Introduction to *The Devil's Law-Case* noted the relative paucity of critical discussion of Webster's tragicomedy. There is even less relating to *A Cure for a Cuckold*, the tragicomedy written in collaboration with William Rowley and Thomas Heywood (see pp. 299–300), but what there is, while revealing greater agreement over meaning than that relating to *The Devil's Law-Case*, displays a similarly mixed response to the dramaturgy.

The first significant critical comment on *A Cure for a Cuckold* is that, in 1885, of Edmund Gosse. Praising the main plot, where he singled out for particular note the duel scene (III.iii), 'a scene, in our estimation, finer than any out of the two great tragedies, and second to few in them',[1] and the final scene, which he considered 'would be extremely effective' on the stage,[2] he was nonetheless unhappy with the Compass plot:

> Webster's characters are noble, sententious, gentleman-like; Rowley's are ribald, vulgar, ignoble. This is seen to perfection in the cases of Woodroff, Luce, and Franckford, who are supposed to bear the mutual relationship of brother, sister, and husband. Woodroff, whose action is confined to the upper section of the play, is a serene and virtuous figure in Webster's finest style. His sister Luce and her husband, whose station is almost wholly in the lower section, are coarse and vulgar.[3]

To rid *A Cure for a Cuckold* of this vulgarity, Gosse suggested that the main plot alone be published, and—drawing no doubt on an exchange between Clare and Lessingham at I.i.15–18—suggested it be entitled 'Love's Graduate'. S. E. Spring-Rice took up the suggestion and *Love's Graduate* appeared in the same year, Gosse, in his introduction, emphasizing that 'Webster's comedy is presented to the reader without any of Rowley's mud adhering to it.'[4]

In his distaste for the broad comedy of the sub-plot, rich in sexual innuendo, Gosse reflects late Victorian values. But since Lucas, at least, who praised Compass as 'so alive and genuine that we feel Dickens himself might have enjoyed him, in an expurgated form',[5] opinion has been firmly in favour of the sub-plot, on grounds neatly summarized by Peter B. Murray:

Gosse felt that the characters of the main plot are noble and those of the subplot are 'ribald', and that therefore the two plots conflict with each other. But his ideas of nobility were hopelessly conventional. No one could be more ignoble than Clare and Lessingham, nor more truly noble than the 'ribald' Mr. Compass.[6]

Gosse's enthusiasm for the main plot, likewise, has not always been echoed. Lucas, for instance, finds the motivation obscure, adding:

But there is more amiss than that. The main weaknesses of the play may be said to be three—that several of its chief characters are obscure, that two, in particular, Clare and Lessingham, are improbable; and that Lessingham, above all, is utterly ignoble.[7]

This being so, Lucas finds the ending of *A Cure for a Cuckold* unsatisfactory: indeed he finds it 'as monstrous as the end of *The Two Gentlemen of Verona* or *Measure for Measure*' in allowing Lessingham to enjoy 'a happy marriage, as quite a good fellow after all'.[8] Una Ellis-Fermor's objections are more general; she feels that the fifth act is destroyed by 'frivolous complications of plot and contradictions of character',[9] while Margaret Loftus Ranald, though considering *A Cure for a Cuckold* an 'underrated play',[10] in which Webster 'reaches his peak as a collaborative writer of tragicomedy',[11] takes wider exception to the main plot, labelling it 'singularly complicated and preposterous'.[12]

Charles Forker, too, is unhappy, concluding that in *A Cure for a Cuckold* Webster is 'writing against his natural tragic bent, for the web of misunderstandings, withheld information, verbal ambiguities, and shifting attitudes that holds the play together produces an effect dangerously close to moral absurdity'.[13] Forker concedes that 'the labyrinthine complexity of the dramatic procedure confuses us partly because it is meant to convey the experience of emotional and moral confusion',[14] but concludes that despite being one of Webster's 'most ambitious and original experiments', *A Cure for a Cuckold* 'as a totality leaves us with a sense of failure and disappointment', since 'Webster and his collaborator[s] toy with issues that are too profound, or at least too complex, to be satisfactorily explored within the Fletcherian framework.'[15]

What Forker calls 'the Fletcherian framework' is a problem for other critics. Elmer E. Stoll, for instance, finds 'Webster's two tragi-comedies are puzzles in plot and character': like the plays of Beaumont and Fletcher, they 'depict ladies and gentlemen, and unfold marvelous events and complications. They, too, present lay-figures instead of fresh, original characters. They, too, seek stage-effectiveness. And at a like cost in truth of character and circumstance.'[16] Ranald also finds this aspect of the ancestry of *A Cure for a Cuckold* unsatisfactory: for her the play presents 'critical problems because of the contrasting, even clashing approaches endemic to tragicomedy'.[17]

For Jacqueline Pearson, however, 'clashing tones' and 'tragicomic discords'[18] are part of the dramatists' techniques in *A Cure for a Cuckold*, and the play, dealing constantly in riddles and paradoxes, sets the confusion and disorienting shifts of the main plot against the securely comic sub-plot, resolving all in the final moments of the play. Noting Ellis-Fermor's objections, Pearson acknowledges that in the fifth act the mode changes: the play 'is becoming more blatantly aware of its own theatricality, presenting its extreme antitheses not so much in terms of convincing emotions but obviously, even parodically, fictional terms'.[19] This, however, is seen as integral to the dramatists' purposes.

To some extent Murray shares Pearson's view of Act V as demonstrating a 'clever comic artifice', in that 'the more seriously the characters take themselves in their passions, the more the psychological improbability of their sudden jealousy detaches us from them and makes us see that they certainly do not deserve to be taken seriously'. 'In a serious play and even in many comedies,' Murray continues, 'such inconsistency of character would be fatal, but here I think the writers knew what they were doing, for the idea that the passions of these people do not deserve to be taken seriously . . . is pretty much what the play is about.'[20]

In a sense, it seems, judgements of Act V depend on whether it is seen as deliberately becoming 'comical in its farcicality'[21] or whether the renewed and reconfigured complications of the last act are adjudged to be a Fletcherian *coup de théâtre*.

But whichever Act V is adjudged to be, an analysis of the plot structure shows that the complications of the final act are needed. For in this structurally orthodox play, eschewing the cyclic structure of Webster's two tragedies and *The Devil's Law-Case*, and depending on the customary plot and sub-plot, distinguished both by social status and by intricacy and seriousness, more dramatic action is required than the two plots alone can generate.

Interestingly, *A Cure for a Cuckold* takes its title from the straightforwardly comic sub-plot, in which the seaman, Compass, thought lost at sea, returns after four years to find his wife, Urse, has very recently had a child by the wealthy merchant Franckford. Immediately forgiving her, and expressing his delight at the fact that they at last have a child, Compass defeats an attempt by Franckford to deprive him of the boy and then takes up a suggestion by Raymond, one of the play's Gallants, concerning a means of wiping the slate clean, ridding himself of the name of cuckold, and Urse of the stain of adultery. Each 'dies', to be reborn immediately, and as widower and widow, to remarry.

But being so straightforward, the sub-plot of *A Cure for A Cuckold* is limited in its dramatic potential. Because Compass immediately forgives his wife her lapse and wishes to make her child by Franckford his own, there can be no extensive handling of his return or the discovery of the child's existence. Complications are provided when Franckford, whose wife Luce is childless, resists Compass's move to recover the child from the nurse who is rearing him at Franckford's charge, but this development too is limited in its extent, and the entire sub-plot is handled in four scenes.

There are problems of scale, too, in what might be described as the main element of the tragicomic romance plot: that involving the two couples, Bonvile and Annabel, and Lessingham and Clare. Though the establishment of the central situation takes two scenes, there is nothing for Annabel and Clare to do once Bonvile and Lessingham have gone to Calais but await the men's return, and then to resolve, in some fashion or other, whether Clare and Lessingham will marry. Without the complications introduced by Rochfield, indeed, the tragicomic plot would comprise five or at most six scenes. The problem is analogous to that in *The Merchant of Venice*, where, faced with the limitations of the bond and casket plots, Shakespeare introduces in Act II a subsidiary action involving Jessica's elopement with Lorenzo, thus delaying the climax of the casket plot, the correct choice of Bassanio. Webster, Rowley, and Heywood handle the problem differently, in that they involve Rochfield directly in the main action, his attempted robbery of Annabel leading to his incorporation into the extended family and social group centred on Woodroff and his daughter, and providing first a diversion, in the privateering venture in which Rochfield distinguishes himself, and then, in V.i, further complication when Lessingham seeks to convince Woodroff and Bonvile that Rochfield and Annabel are having an affair. Nonetheless, the rationale for introducing Rochfield seems closely akin to that for giving over Act II of *The Merchant of Venice* to Jessica's elopement with Lorenzo.

The structure of *A Cure for a Cuckold*, then, is determined to a considerable extent by the dimensions of the plots which the three dramatists selected as a vehicle for their purposes. The Compass sub-plot, of limited extension, starts late, in II.ii, is developed in III.ii and IV.i, and reaches its comic climax in IV.iii, when Compass demolishes his opponents' legal arguments as to ownership of the child. A brief celebratory linking of this plot with the main action in the last moments of the play apart, the Compass plot is thus concluded, leaving the fifth act entirely to the solving of the complications in the main plot.

The Rochfield component of the tragicomic action, likewise, starts in Act II and provides complicating interest during the absence of Lessingham and Bonvile, supplying II.i and ii, and most of II.iv, as well as, in the account of Rochfield's heroism, III.iii. This ensures that the main action, set in motion in I.i and ii, can be largely ignored until III.iii, the scene on Calais sands, and then is not focussed upon significantly until IV.ii, when the two men return. In that scene all could be resolved, with Bonvile and Annabel reunited, and Lessingham and Clare love's graduates, and indeed Pearson comments that 'by the end of Act IV it looks very much . . . as if the happy ending were about to take place'.[22] But the dramatists reconfigure the dynamics, as it were, and in the lengthy single scene which comprises Act V, complicate matters. Lessingham becomes a melancholiac, bent on revenge, and stirring up discord by falsely charging Annabel with infidelity, fooling neither Rochfield nor Woodroff, but poisoning Bonvile's mind temporarily, while Clare, reformed, seeks to bring reconciliation, and Rochfield, who has been made the object of suspicion, finally clears up all confusion, enabling harmony to be restored.

Clearly, the confusions of Act V have not only a structural purpose, in prolonging the action, and providing it with a fresh impetus, but also in some sense a clarifying one: testing of the various characters takes place, with Clare and Rochfield emerging with full credit, and Woodroff and his daughter Annabel not much less. Bonvile, however, and Lessingham need to be reclaimed from jealousy and vengefulness before harmony is fully restored and the play can end with an enlargement, through the remarriage of Compass and Urse, of the matrimonial celebrations interrupted in Act I.

What of the leading figures who undergo these in some cases startling character reversals in Act V? Stoll's dismissal of them as 'lay figures' is in a sense true, but this severely underrates their thematic and theatrical potential. Woodroff may be no more than a Jacobean *senex*, jovial, lively, and hospitable, and Bonvile, until his brief bout of jealousy, entirely virtuous, and, in his willingness to put the claims of friendship ahead of those of love, a paragon, though (in his unexplained desertion of Annabel on their wedding day) a somewhat thoughtless one. But Annabel, while in some respects a type of the loving, trusting, honest and long-suffering wife, displays her individuality in the strength, wit and generosity of her dealings with Rochfield (see p. 289). Rochfield, likewise, is more than just the prodigal younger son, since he learns quickly from Annabel, and in Act V proves himself an exemplar of true friendship, morally as well as physically courageous (see p. 287).

Of Lessingham and Clare more needs to be said. Lucas describes them as 'improbable', and though he was clearly thinking in terms of a realism which is somewhat beside the point, he nonetheless highlights difficulties in reading and interpreting them more severe than with any other characters in the play.

A Cure for a Cuckold opens briskly, with Lessingham making his love for Clare plain immediately, and declaring that if they do not follow the example set by Bonvile and Annabel they will 'be held | Meer Trewants in Loves school' (I.i.15–16). Clare's rebuff, 'That's a study | In which I never shall ambition have | To become graduate' (16–18), makes her position equally plain, and what follows before her departure at line 63 follows a pattern which would have been familiar to playgoers in the 1620s: the lover who has neglected everything—parents, friends, studies—in his passion for a woman who displays a cool disregard for his feelings. Lessingham voices the question which the audience might ask: 'Whence might this distaste arise?' (43), offering three possible explanations. That the terms in which they are cast, with her 'perverse and peevish will' (49) offered as the only possible explanation if the other two options—'dislike' engendered perhaps by 'calumny or scandal' (47), or 'Some late received Melancholy' (48) in Clare—are rejected by her as untrue, means that once she refuses to explain we are led to suspect the latter. The gnomic comment which follows—

> In all these travels, windings, and indents,
> Paths, and by-paths which many have sought out,
> There's but one onely road, and that alone
> To my fruition   (I.i.53–6)

—adds to the sense of mystery, while the conclusion of Clare's statement, that she will marry only if a suitor 'findes out' that 'onely road', gives it a fairy-tale colouring: she is the prize to be won only by the suitor who solves a mystery. Rightly, Lessingham declares himself 'in a Labyrinth' (59), and Clare's promise to let him know 'by my Maid' (62) how he may be guided in his quest for her hand only adds to the sense of mystery.

The advent of the Gallants adds to the speculation about Clare's behaviour, Lyonel noting 'her present melancholly' (75), and Grover speculating that 'her so sudden discontent' (77) is caused by envy of the bride.

That in a sense it is we do not learn until IV.ii, when she tells Lessingham of her passion for Bonvile, Webster and his collaborators choosing to hold back any explanation of Clare's behaviour, though letting us know in III.iii that Lessingham had misunderstood Clare's injunction that he should '*Prove all thy friends, finde out the best and nearest,* | *Kill for my sake that Friend that loves thee dearest*' (I.i.101–2). No blame, clearly, can attach to Lessingham for failing to intuit what Clare intends. And if blame is to be levelled at him for taking up the challenge which Clare issues by her letter, it has to be in terms of the play, and of Lessingham's debate with himself about Clare's letter, and possible responses to her injunction.

Lessingham's soliloquy opens with a quotation in Latin, a free version of Cicero's praise of friendship in *De Amicitia*. This prefaces a discussion of friendship as the greatest of Nature's bounties, and of the monstrousness of violating it by killing a friend, and particularly a best friend. Lessingham is, clearly, a man with a developed moral sense. But he is also in thrall to Clare, who 'ha's a power of me | Beyond all vertue—vertue, almost grace' (I.ii.11–12). We are given no explanation for this: it is a *donnée* common enough in tragicomedy. And Lessingham, having tried to speculate on alternative meanings—as that in 'these last and worser times' (II.ii.23) friendship no longer exists—can take his 'troubled brest | Distemper'd with a thousand fantasies' (25–6) no further than a decision to prove 'If such a thing there be' (28) as a true friend, and then to see which triumphs within him: Love or Friendship.

Once again the Gallants are introduced, to demonstrate the fickleness of fair weather friends as they marshal the weakest of excuses for not acting as Lessingham's second at Calais. Comic though they are, they supply a contrast with Bonvile, who unhesitatingly places friendship ahead of all other considerations. Lessingham, having tried to dissuade him, accepts the offer, and in the speech which concludes the scene, makes it clear that the fight between Love and Friendship has already been won by Love.

> Was ever known
> A man so miserably blest as I?
> I have no sooner found the greatest good,
> Man in this pilgrimage of Life can meet,
> But I must make the womb where 'twas conceived,
> The Tomb to bury it, and the first hour it lives,
> The last it must breath!   (I.ii.191–7)

Yet in the couplet with which Lessingham concludes we find, as in tragicomedy we will, the implicit reassurance that all, ultimately, will be well:

'Yet there's a Fate | That sways and governs above womans hate' (197–8). How the death of Bonvile is to be avoided is unclear. That it is, we may now feel confident.

The first scene of Act III brings the climax of the tragicomic romance plot, and the resolution of the conundrum: how Lessingham is to fulfil Clare's injunction, and yet not kill Bonvile. Again, the mode has much in common with fairy tale: the magic formula which enables the resolution of the apparently irresolvable. But the solution is provided by Bonvile, not Lessingham, who remains 'fettered in a womans proud Command' (III.i.66), who can acknowledge what he describes as Clare's 'malice' (69), yet cannot free himself of a compulsion to carry out her instruction, even though he feels it is given as an 'impossible task' (80) which is set to rid her of him. Bonvile's solution is delayed, however, until a crucial moment, when Lessingham has to decide whether to kill a man who will not defend himself, and we never find out whether he would have done so or not.

There may, perhaps, be some indication of what Lessingham's choice would have been in his response to Bonvile's invitation to him to fight as enemies (III.i.128–30). The move is dictated by Bonvile's sense of honour, but his opponent responds with equal punctilio, and with a modicum of humour:

> 'Twould appear ill in either of us to fight:
> In you unmanly; for believe it Sir,
> You have disarmed me already, done away
> All power of resistance in me; it would show
> Beastly to do wrong to the dead: to me you say,
> You are dead for ever, lost on *Callis-sands*,
> By the cruelty of a woman.   (III.i.138–44)

The duel scene has often been praised, as by Gosse. Like the duel between Contarino and Ercole in *The Devil's Law-Case*, it deals with the gentlemanly code of honour, but unlike the scene in the earlier tragicomedy, it does not need the participants to fight and (apparently) die. In *A Cure for a Cuckold* the potentially tragic outcome is never a serious possibility, and it is possible for the duel scene to end with an exchange which combines wit and punctilio with a serious edge:

> *Lessingham.*   . . . remember
> You had a noble friend, whose love to you
> Shall continue after death. Shall I go over
> In the same Barque with you?
> *Bonvile.*   Not for yon town
> Of *Callis*; you know 'tis dangerous living
> At Sea, with a dead body.

> Lessingham.   Oh you mock me,
> May you enjoy all your noble wishes.
> Bonvile.   And may you finde a better friend then I,
> And better keep him.   (III.i.144–52)

We next encounter Lessingham in IV.ii, when the expected meeting with Clare takes place. He has come to claim his reward: he has 'done ill | At a womans bidding' (3–4), and expects Clare to give herself to him. Instead he finds that she had intended otherwise, his 'Ye did not wish I hope, | That I should have murder'd you?' drawing from her the gnomic 'You shall perceive | More of that hereafter' (17–19). We have been privy since II.iv to the fact that Lessingham misconstrued Clare's letter, her 'Lessingham's mistaken, quite out o'th way | Of my purpose too' (II.iv.34–5) making this plain. But there has been a great deal of puzzlement, even to the point of textual emendation, over just what Clare intended, and it is necessary here to examine her words and actions earlier in the play before trying to sort out, in IV.ii, just what she did intend, particularly as it relates to her discussion with Bonvile.

The immediate and powerful impression of Clare in I.i is of a woman deeply unhappy, and both Lessingham and Lyonel describe her as melancholy (48, 75). Our sense of her is immeasurably darkened, however, by the letter she sends Lessingham, with its order to '*Kill for my sake that Friend that loves thee dearest*' (102). Like Lessingham, we take it at face value as an instruction to find and kill his best friend. That this is not what she intends is held back until II.iv, and even then we are only apprised of the fact that Lessingham has misread her intentions. What she does make clear, however, is her guilt at Bonvile's absence, and her regret:

> I fear my self most guilty for the absence
> Of the Bridegroom: what our wills will do
> With over rash and headlong peevishness,
> To bring our calm discretions to repentance!   (II.iv.30–3)

For the remainder of the scene, however, Clare resumes her taciturnity, and no further insight or explanation is forthcoming until III.iii, where in an aside she not only berates 'fool *Lessingham*' for mistaking her injunction 'utterly' (9–10), but also, and more importantly, reveals something of her own feelings:

> I am mad, stark mad
> With my own thoughts, not knowing what event
> Their going or'e will come too; 'tis too late

> Now for my tongue to cry my heart mercy,
> Would I could be senceless till I hear
> Of their return: I fear me both are lost.   (III.iii.11–16)

As Carnegie and Jackson point out, it is significant that Clare fears 'both are lost', since the phrase provides 'an alert audience [with] the first indication that Clare does not want either man dead: an important clue that the generic expectations of (tragi-) comedy may be fulfilled in respect of Clare and Lessingham'.[23] It also explains the brief episode (III.iii.21–31) in which Raymond tries to court Clare, only to be summarily rejected. Forker suggests that this 'demonstrates Clare's powers of attraction',[24] but as Carnegie and Jackson note, it has a more important function, since 'It demonstrates to the audience, just at the moment she indicates concern for Lessingham, that she is not interested in alternative suitors.'[25] Hence, when we next see her, with Lessingham in IV.ii, we may seek further signs of her concern. Instead we find, at first, only complication, as Clare, having failed fully to confirm Lessingham's dawning awareness that she might have intended him to kill her, goes on to ask, in horror, who he has 'sacrificed to [his] fury | And to my fatal sport, this bloody Riddle?' (IV.ii.22–3).

Being told that Bonvile is the victim draws from Clare an interesting two-fold reaction:

> Oh you have struck him dead thorough my heart,
> In being true to me, you have proved in this
> The falsest Traitor: oh I am lost forever:
> Yet wherefore am I lost? Rather recovered
> From a deadly witchcraft, and upon his grave
> I will not gather Rue, but Violets
> To bless my wedding strewings.   (IV.ii.25–31)

Grief at Bonvile's death has given way, almost at once, to a relief which she herself explains in her speech at 42–66: that her love for Bonvile was 'beyond reason' (56), and that when he married she 'fell into despair' (60), and intended Lessingham to realize that she was his 'onely friend i'th world' (62) and hence the one he should kill:

> You urging your Suit to me, and I thinking
> That I had been your onely friend i'th world,
> I heartily did wish you would have kill'd
> That friend your self, to have ended all my sorrow,
> And had prepared it, that unwittingly
> You should have don't by poison.   (IV.ii.61–6)

As Carnegie and Jackson note:

> the plot requires a divergence between what Lessingham, the audience, and in due course Bonvile think it means ('test your male friends, and, in order to win my love, kill the most loyal one'), and what, we find later, Clare intends it to mean ('think hard about whom you love, and who will love you for killing her [which you will understand after the event]'). Her intention is to send a riddle which will both explain her suicide and exculpate him once she is dead. Naturally, however, Lessingham and the audience take the message to involve the sort of romance test of 'Kill Claudio', or the closely related intrigue of Massinger's *Parliament of Love*.[26]

Clare's motivation, thus explained, is reinforced by her subsequent explanation to Bonvile, and by the second, delayed letter, which she gives him with the comment: 'had you known this which I meant to have sent you | An hour 'fore you were married to your wife, | The Riddle had been construed' (IV.ii.130–2). Lucas finds Clare's explanation of her motives 'not only improbable, but impossible',[27] and postulates problems of collaboration or faulty revision on Webster's part as the reason for motivational incoherence. But Carnegie and Jackson demonstrate that 'Clare's statement that she intended her initial riddling letter to direct Lessingham's thoughts to her, and that she would engineer events so that he unwittingly poisoned her, is consistent with her words, intentions, and characterisation.'[28]

This said, however, there remains the fact that there has been widespread confusion about the motivation of Clare. Why is this? Carnegie and Jackson identify the problem 'not in plot or character, but in the particular language chosen to extend the equivocation while maintaining divergent plot and character consistency', and see a dominance of plot considerations in what follows.[29] Certainly the shifts in position are dizzying in their rapidity, beginning as they do almost immediately Clare has explained herself to Lessingham. She is now willing to marry him, while he is caught, as he explains in a lengthy aside, between his love for Clare, who 'has bewitched me here, | For I cannot chuse but love her' (IV.ii.83–4), and 'guilt of conscience' (89). He rejects Clare, but what seems a victory for conscience is rapidly revealed as a complete about-face, with Lessingham in his disillusionment determining to wreck Bonvile's relationship:

> I will do somewhat
> To make as fatal breach and difference
> In *Bonviles* love as mine, I am fixt in't,
> My melancholly and the devil shall fashion't.   (IV.ii.97–100)

Where Clare's love-melancholy turns suicidal, Lessingham's has here become, instantly, a vicious nihilism, intent on destruction.

Clare, by contrast, now repents, recognizing that she is 'every way lost' (107), and accepting that she suffers 'Deservedly' (110). In the remainder of IV.ii she passes two tests of her virtue by Bonvile. The first is the temptation of an apparent willingness on his part to entertain a liaison with her. The second, more oblique, involves a series of shifts in position, apparent and real, in which Bonvile praises Lessingham, in order, he says, that Clare might 'fall in love and league with him' (174); for

> what worse office can I do i'th world
> Unto my enemy, than to endeavor
> By all means possible to marry him
> Unto a Whore? (IV.ii.175–8)

Clare's response, vehement denial ending in branding Bonvile a liar, achieves two ends. First, with her passion for him gone, Bonvile can now 'love [her] . . . With a noble observance' (187–8), and second, he can truly urge Lessingham's case and 'work reconcilement 'tween you' (194). A further twist, in which Clare, still smarting from his comment about marrying Lessingham to a whore, rejects Bonvile's offer, completes his revaluation of her, and ours. Bonvile feels her 'repentance and compassion now | May make amends' (200–1), and urges her to 'disperse this melancholly, | And on that turn of Fortunes Wheel depend, | When all Calamities will mend, or end' (201–3).

With Clare's virtue and constancy proven, and Lessingham's villainous intentions declared, Webster and his collaborators have established the terms of reference for the intrigues and reversals which constitute Act V. Lessingham's opening speech, a lengthy aside, restates his villainy in Machiavellian terms, but a Machiavellianism which comes comically close to parody:

> I am grown big with project: Project, said I?
> Rather with sudden mischief; which without
> A speedy birth fills me with painful throwes,
> And I am now in labor. (V.i.22–5)

Like classic Machiavels, such as Barabas and Richard of Gloucester, Lessingham considers 'occasion' gives him 'fit ground to work upon' in the evident affection of Rochfield and Annabel, but his attempt to sow discord is at once seen through by Rochfield, who plans countermeasures. A similar attempt with Woodroff also fails in its primary purpose, which is to convince the latter of his daughter's infidelity, but succeeds at one remove when Bonvile, told of Lessingham's allegations, reacts jealously.

This abrupt reversal is followed by another, as Annabel, hitherto a type of patience, reacts angrily to Bonvile's jealousy, and complication follows complication as not one but two duels threaten. In *A Cure for a Cuckold*, however, there is no place for a final duel, let alone one '*continued to a good length*', as in *The Devil's Law-Case*. Here all that threatens disaster amongst the men is averted when Rochfield confesses how he attempted to rob Annabel, and relates what followed, while discord on Annabel's part is dispersed by Clare, who, acknowledging that she was 'first cause | Of the wrong, which he has put upon you both' (V.i.276–7), clarifies offstage 'this toyl | Of a supposed and causeless Jealousie' (280–1). All is thus cleared in time for the two couples to join Compass and Urse as they remarry.

The denouement of the tragicomic romance plot is neatly enough handled, then, but not entirely satisfying. The reversals of Act V have about them too much contrivance. Like Bonvile's jealousy, Lessingham's brief essay into Machiavellian villainy is unprepared for, and the complications which ensue seem somewhat manipulated. The reconciliation between Clare and Lessingham is spelt out, with the latter asking forgiveness for 'wilde distractions [which] | Had overturned my own condition, | And spilt the goodness you once knew in me' (V.ii.76–8), and Clare acknowledging that 'It was my cause | That you were so possest, and all these troubles | Have from my peevish will original' (80–2). Lessingham may now claim that 'all's now as at first | It was wisht to be' (85–6), and since the reconciliation of Bonvile and Annabel has presumably taken place mutely, staging signalling their happiness, there is general celebration. Yet the comedic closure which has been attained by an all-embracing forgiveness and which is in a sense presided over by Compass and his widow–wife, leaves question-marks, not least as to the weight of significance to be attached to the outcome of the tragicomic plot.

Critics have sought to explain the gyrations of Act V in various ways. Murray, for instance, comments:

> The more seriously the characters take themselves in their passions, the more the psychological improbability of their sudden jealousy detaches us from them and makes us see that they certainly do not deserve to be taken seriously. In a serious play and even in many comedies such inconsistency of character would be fatal but here I think the writers knew what they were doing, for the idea that the passions of these people do not deserve to be taken seriously has been developed in other ways too, and is pretty much what the play is about.[30]

'The actors', he adds,

> must play their passions in a farcical fashion, making it obvious to the audience that they are inwardly laughing at the characters they portray, even if the characters are not

laughing at themselves. In this way Act V will end not only in a fusion of the two stories of the play but also in a fusion of *tone* between the two stories, the romantic story finally becoming comical in its farcicality.[31]

Murray requires the actors to subvert the roles they play, a dangerous ploy theatrically. Pearson, however, offers a reading more likely to succeed on stage. In Act V, she argues, 'the play returns temporarily to the ambiguous and riddling mode of the early scenes', and briefly 'it seems we have been swept back into the danger and ambiguity of the play's third act'.[32] 'This sense of danger, though, is undercut and shortlived', since the audience knows that the threats to harmony are groundless, the rapid resolution of the quarrels and misunderstandings occasions no difficulty, 'the rapid, balletic changes of combination in the quarrels, and the speed of the untidy exits and entrances, all give the scene a strong leaning towards comedy and parody, which resists the tragicomic danger of riddles and equivocations'.[33]

If Murray and Pearson disagree on how the bulk of Act V should be read and played, however, they do agree that the uniting of the main action and the Compass plot effects a satisfying comic closure. The device by which the sub-plot is united with the main action is mechanical. Franckford, whose child Urse has borne, is also Annabel's uncle, so that his presence at the closure of both plots is appropriate, while the Gallants feature in both actions also, with Raymond not only attempting to woo Clare (and thus providing a clue to her developing interest in Lessingham) but also suggesting to Compass the means by which the latter may cure himself of cuckoldry. But the links between the two plots are much more substantial than the presence in the two plots of several of the minor characters. For, as critics have noted, the story of Compass, and his struggle to keep the child that his wife has borne, is related significantly, both in theme and language, to the main action. Murray notes, for instance, that Compass is in a sense the teacher in the school of love,[34] his capacity for forgiveness, and ability to make good out of ill, reflecting on the incapacity of several of the major characters. More significant, however, is the way in which his very name relates to a repeated use of the word 'compass' in the main action; the latter in itself part of a significant linguistic and thematic structure relating to what might be described as 'the path of life'.

One of the key elements in this structure is the central metaphor of the 'way' or 'path', first found in the opening scene, where Clare riddlingly informs Lessingham that

> In all these travels, windings, and indents,
> Paths, and by-paths which many have sought out,

There's but one onely road, and that alone
To my fruition.   (I.i.53–6)

Lessingham's response—'Oh name it, Sweet. | I am already in a
Labyrinth | Until you guide me out' (58–60)—neatly links the 'path'
metaphor with the labyrinthine intricacies of the plot, and of motivation,
in which the two are caught until in the last act the repentant Clare can
lead not only Lessingham but also Annabel out of the labyrinth of misunderstanding:

> I do protest my self first cause
> Of the wrong, which he has put upon you both,
> Which please you to walk in, I shall make good
> In a short relation; come Ile be the clew
> To lead you forth this Labyrinth, this toyl
> Of a supposed and causeless Jealousie.   (V.i.276–81)

The same 'path' metaphor is found recurring in the Annabel–Rochfield
scenes in Act II, where Rochfield, forced by want to become a highway-
man, acknowledges that 'The old road, | The old high-way 't must be,
and I am in't' (II.i.15–16), and Annabel enters, literally lost, ordering her
servant to go on ahead:

> Ile make the best speed after that I can,
> Yet I am not well acquainted with the path:
> My fears I fear me will misguide me too.   (II.i.43–5)

But Rochfield bungles robbing her, and is led by Annabel back to the
path to honesty, while she, escorted by him back to the wedding feast,
explains her absence in terms which seem to describe also her recovery
from anxiety over Bonvile's absence. 'I was in fear when first I saw him
[Rochfield]' (II.iv.79), says Annabel punningly,

> I had quite lost my way
> In my first amazement, but he so fairly came
> To my recovery, in his kinde conduct,
> Gave me such loving comforts to my fears.   (II.iv.80–3)

But Rochfield, Annabel and Clare are not the best guides in *A Cure for
a Cuckold*: that honour clearly belongs to Compass. And the dramatists
link the metaphor of the 'path' to him through a punning use of
'compass' in various contexts. This is signalled well in advance of the
mariner's first appearance, and of our understanding of the joke, when
Luce alludes to her husband's illegitimate child:

> *Luce.*   Well, well brother,
> Though you may taunt me that have never yet

>Been blest with issue, spare my husband pray,
>For he may have a By-blow, or an Heir
>That you never heard of—
>*Franckford [aside].*   Oh fie wife,
>Make not my fault too publick.
>*Luce.*   —yet himself
>Keep within compass.   (I.i.153–9)

In Act IV we find a more crucial use of the term, when Bonvile, having tested Clare's virtue, considers her worthy of Lessingham, whom he praises as having borne 'his steerage true in every part, | Led by the Compass of a noble heart' (IV.ii.165–6). The following scene, in which Compass and Urse meet as widow and widower, each finding in the other qualities which they knew in their 'dead' spouses, provides reinforcement for this use of 'compass', when, as Murray notes, 'Compass talks about the way land people need to learn from those who know the sea, especially the lesson that they should not be jealous lovers, which is of course the very thing the play's romantic lovers most need to learn.'[35] Murray continues:

>In stating Compass's thesis that landsmen should be guided by seamen, Rowley cannot resist emphasizing the significance of the speaker's name by having him first box the compass (IV.iii.77–102) and then say that anyone who dares to call him a cuckold will be committing an act 'without compass of the general pardon' (IV.iii.124–5).[36]

The topical reference is to the general pardon issued by King James in 1624, but the play ends with just such a 'general pardon', encompassing all, and subsuming the tragicomic action in a cheerful comedic closure.

There is another strand of metaphor, however, which also contributes throughout the play, and reinforces the ending, and this involves death and rebirth. In Act I Lessingham relates this to the metaphor of the path in referring to 'this pilgrimage of Life' (I.ii.194), and at the beginning of II.i Rochfield punningly reflects on how mothers 'love to groan [in giving birth], although the Gallows eccho | And groan together for us' (11–12), adding, 'From the first | We travel forth, t'other's our journeys end' (12–13). In IV.i this conjunction of birth and death is given a telling comic twist when Compass and Urse agree to 'die' briefly, then revive to marry as strangers (IV.i.209–22), and in the following scene, as Murray notes,[37] there is another death and rebirth when Clare's heart dies on learning of Bonvile's 'death', and is then born anew (IV.ii.25–31). This paradoxical process continues as Bonvile, whom she thinks dead, reappears, and having suffered 'death' as Lessingham's best friend, is now prepared to 'work reconcilement' between Clare and Lessingham as 'his noblest enemy' (IV.ii.193–4).

The comic equivalent of this, in IV.iii, sees Compass and Urse meet as widower and widow, and ends in anticipation of the morrow's wedding celebrations. Before this can be celebrated, however, Lessingham must himself be reborn out of the despair into which he has sunk, while the rift between Bonvile and Annabel, which as Murray notes, is 'the final result of Clare's originally "peevish will"',[38] comes to a head in a quarrel over wills (V.i.232–54), resolved only when Rochfield explains all. The contrast with the sub-plot, where Franckford, having accepted that Compass keep the child, acts generously in not altering his will and disinheriting the child, is marked, and demonstrates yet again that it is in what Gosse labelled the 'ignoble' sub-plot that we find true nobility.

The complications of the fifth act unravelled, '*Soft Musick*' is heard off. Bonvile sees it as chiming '*Io pæan*' to the wedding of Lessingham and Clare, and once they have sought each other's forgiveness, the entry of Compass and the wedding party can subsume all into a comic conclusion, demonstrating the generosity which has made it possible, generosity which like the '*Soft Musick*' now permeates the main action, as Woodroff's concluding speech demonstrates: 'One Wedding we have yet to solemnize, | The first is still imperfect. Such troubles | Have drown'd our Musick: but now I hope all's friends' (V.ii.145–7).

A Cure for a Cuckold is not a profound play. Its thematic concerns are straightforward and in no way new. But in presenting their account of the conflicting claims of love and friendship, of the damage that can be done by a 'peevish will', and the healing that can occur if there is sufficient generosity of spirit, Webster, Rowley, and Heywood have created what Weis calls 'a riveting piece of theatre which still addresses the human condition'.[39] It is to be hoped that professional productions demonstrating this will follow the greater critical exposure *A Cure for a Cuckold* is now receiving.

1. Gosse, pp. 68–9.
2. Ibid., p. 69.
3. Ibid., p. 66.
4. S. E. Spring-Rice, ed., *Love's Graduate* (Oxford, 1885), p. iv.
5. Lucas, III, 19.
6. Murray, p. 217.
7. Lucas, III, 22.
8. Ibid.
9. Una Ellis-Fermor, *The Jacobean Drama: An Interpretation* (London, 1936), p. 183.
10. Ranald, p. 97.
11. Ibid.
12. Ibid., p. 96.

13. Forker, p. 172.
14. Ibid.
15. Ibid., p. 187.
16. Stoll, *Periods*, p. 175.
17. Ranald, p. 97.
18. Pearson, p. 121.
19. Ibid., p. 127.
20. Murray, p. 232.
21. Ibid., p. 235.
22. Pearson, p. 127.
23. Carnegie and Jackson, p. 18.
24. Forker, p. 183.
25. Carnegie and Jackson, p. 18.
26. Ibid., pp. 17–18.
27. Lucas, III, 21.
28. Carnegie and Jackson, p. 19.
29. Ibid., p. 19.
30. Murray, p. 232.
31. Ibid., p. 235.
32. Pearson, p. 129.
33. Ibid.
34. Murray, p. 217.
35. Ibid., p. 231.
36. Ibid.
37. Ibid.
38. Ibid., p. 232.
39. Weis, p. xxvii.

Theatrical introduction

David Carnegie

THE PATTERN OF THE PLAY

THE SCRIPT

At approximately 2,400 lines, *A Cure for a Cuckold* is comfortably towards the shorter end of the spectrum of average length for a play at the time, and may therefore have been performed uncut.[1] The printed text is largely actable as it stands.

PRODUCTION

Although the social range of characters depicted in this play is not as wide as in Webster's tragedies, or in *The Devil's Law-Case*, nevertheless costume will be a significant element in performance for distinguishing class, wealth, age, and occupation. Lessingham and Bonvile, for instance, are young gentlemen, well-dressed and wearing swords. They are easily placed beside the four 'Gallants' (although the Gallants may have an air of foppery about them; cf. the 'perfum'd Gallants' referred to at *WD* V.i.156), and Rochfield (whose poverty as a younger son may be apparent in his clothing, despite his social standing as a gentleman). Woodroff and Franckford, by contrast, may well wear the long robes appropriate to successful mercantile men of mature years. Another prosperous figure, Franckford's wife Luce, will presumably display her wealth in her dress and jewellery, in contrast, perhaps, to Compass's wife Urse (though presents from Franckford might provide an incongruous contrast to the rest of Urse's attire). Occupation will also be identified by costume for a number of characters, none more importantly than the seafaring Compass. While specific detail on sailors' costume is tantalisingly difficult to establish, there can be no doubt that it was distinctive. Elements may have included 'baggy breeches gathered in below the knee, a loose waist-length coat . . . and a shaggy brimless hat or cap'.[2] The breeches and coat were probably made of canvas, possibly coated with tar (hence 'tarpaulin'). Monmouthshire or other sailors' hats were evidently distinctive: cf., in *Twelfth Night*, III.iv.330, Antonio's attempt at anonymity by not wearing his 'sea-cap'. In a modern production, such as Wellington 1997, sea-boots, oilskins and sou'westers can serve the same purpose. And Jacobean mariners may have carried a knife, as Chaucer's Shipman did: 'A daggere hangynge on a laas hadde he | Aboute his nekke, under his arm adoun'.[3] The Sailor who makes two brief appearances in association with Woodroff's privateering expedition will no doubt be similarly identifiable. Lawyers, too, have their own distinctive garb and accoutrements (see Fig. 5 and p. 39).

The visual dramaturgy also includes important wedding costume. Annabel's first appearance at I.i.111.1 is as a bride, quite possibly in white and with her hair down and arranged with powder and jewels (cf. *WD* V.i.0.1–.3n). Probably both she and the wedding guests will wear or carry sprigs of rosemary, and may well wear favours.[4] Towards the end of the play Compass's instruction to Urse to 'change your Clothes too, do ye hear, widow' (IV.i.215–16) for their remarriage suggests that she may change into widow's black for the re-wooing in IV.iii; or they both may change at that point into the wedding finery whose further significance will appear at the very end of the play, when their marriage becomes one of several.

Costumed actors are sufficient for most of the visual story, so the dramaturgical demands on the playhouse structure are minimal. There is no evident need for trap door, terrace, or discovery. Whereas most of the play relies on imaginative space defined principally by exits (the establishment of Annabel's journey from her house and ambush by Rochfield being a particularly clear example), the setting of IV.i in the Three Tuns tavern is, by contrast, specific in its demands for seats and tables. Here, too, small properties are important: not only drinks for everyone, but presumably buckram bags, writing materials, and the volumes of paper that form part of Websterian and Jacobean visual satire whenever lawyers are introduced. Just as in *The Devil's Law-Case*, it is safe to assume that the lawyers here have mountains of documents and letters.

Letters, indeed, and their interpretation and misinterpretation, form an indispensable part of the plot mechanism, and one that critics have not always found easy. There is first of all the riddling letter in I.i from Clare to Lessingham which he misinterprets, with near-tragic consequences, as an instruction to kill his dearest friend Bonvile. A Quarto stage direction

5. Ignoramus, a lawyer, with pen-box and inkhorn (1630 engraved frontispiece from *Ignoramus* by George Ruggle).

indicates that his entry at I.ii is to be '*sad, with a Letter in his hand*'; the same letter, presumably so that he can show it to the audience again before he reaches his decision to challenge Bonvile. The letter reappears in III.i, given to Bonvile by Lessingham to justify his action. Bonvile on his return shows it to Clare, who to explain herself gives Bonvile another letter 'which I meant to have sent you | An hour 'fore you were married to your wife' (IV.ii.130–1). This letter of Clare's finally confirms what she told Lessingham a few minutes earlier: that because of hopeless love for Bonvile, she intended to make Lessingham the ignorant agent for her suicide.[5]

Yet another letter is important, that received by Annabel in III.iii from Bonvile and containing his will in case he should die in the duel. When Lessingham is successful in stirring jealousy between Bonvile and Annabel in V.i, she is summoned to bring the will to Bonvile, who then threatens to disinherit her (incidentally provoking Annabel's father, Woodroff, to determine on a tit-for-tat changing of his will so as to disinherit Bonvile).

Almost as important to the plot as Clare's riddling letter, and more visually striking, are the 'Carckanet and Bracelets' (I.ii.179) worn by Annabel. A wedding gift from Bonvile, they are richly jewelled enough to be a tempting prize for Rochfield, but locked about her neck and wrists. Annabel herself draws joking attention to her similarity to a fettered prisoner ('my Neck and Arms | Are still your Prisoners' [184–5]), and it is her reported freeing of herself from the constraints of marriage which provokes Bonvile's jealousy. The most visually striking episode of the 'Carckanet' occurs when Annabel offers her neck to Rochfield for him to try to violate the lock for which he has no key. His unwillingness to hurt her reinforces the sense of her virtuous willingness to wear her husband's chain, while at the same time demonstrating her physical and moral courage in allowing Rochfield the opportunity to take the jewelled chain. This is, of course, extended by her willingness to ransom her jewels, and the ransom of gold coins has its significance extended when Rochfield is persuaded to deposit all these coins back in Woodroff's hands for the privateering venture.

Unlike jewellery, swords are remarkable in this play for never being put to full use. The Gallants refuse the duel (Grover even excusing himself on the basis of the wrong category of sword having been chosen). Rochfield's sword is his 'Book' (II.ii.39), but Annabel proves him 'A bad Clerk' (54) when she steals his sword from him. Neither can use it. Lessingham and Bonvile can, presumably, use their swords, but the moment one of them advances his sword at Calais the other finds a reason to back off and talk. The repeated tension and anticlimax are likely to add considerably to the edgy comedy of the false duel. Finally, Woodroff draws his sword (V.i.183) against Lessingham in defence of Annabel's honour, but once again a threatened duel is evaded rather than engaged upon.

It is Woodroff, too, who draws attention to the role of music in the play. The '*Soft Musick*' (V.ii.72) that announces Compass's remarriage at the end has been heard earlier at Annabel's wedding: her father complains to his wedding guests that 'within | The Musick playes unto the silent walls' (I.i.125–6), and later that 'The Musick ceased' (II.iv.59). The interruption to the music underlines the disruption of the wedding, but it is Woodroff who notes the renewed wedding music at the end of the play (V.ii.87–8). This framing of the play with marriages and attendant music reinforces the sense of harmonious resolution in a typical Jacobean manner. A '*Soft Musick*' is a string consort, usually viols, but given the emphasis on dancing at the wedding it may in this case be a violin consort. If so, Rafe's appearance at the Three Tuns '*like a Musician*' (IV.i.56.1) with a fiddle may be an ironic variation on a theme. In addition, entr'acte music would presumably have been played between each of the five acts into which the play's performance is divided.[6]

ACTING

Of the seven young gentlemen in the play, Lessingham provides the greatest acting challenge. He is a romantic lover at the start but is almost immediately driven into tragicomic obsession by Clare's letter instructing him to kill '*that Friend that loves thee dearest*' (I.i.98). First the conflicting demands of honour, friendship, and love nearly lead to a tragic duel with Bonvile; then Clare's admission in IV.ii that she loved Bonvile turns Lessingham (until the final reconciliation) into a jealous and vengeful misogynist bent on destroying Bonvile and Annabel's marriage. Lessingham must, through all the brittle and extreme plot convolutions, retain enough audience sympathy to remain the desired and inevitable partner for Clare as the play achieves comedic closure. Much of this sympathy is likely to be based on Lessingham's frequent direct address to the audience as he shares his dilemmas with them.

Of the other young gentlemen, Bonvile is a more straightforward lover, mainly honourable and generous to a fault, with only a brief lapse into jealousy in Act V. The actors playing Bonvile and Lessingham face a particularly tricky question of tone in the aborted duel of III.i, since the potential for comedy in the overwrought debate about honour needs careful consideration and control. By contrast, the four Gallants—Raymond, Eustace, Lyonel, and Grover—seem deliberately undifferentiated, as if designed as a collective foil of comic shallowness against which Lessingham and Bonvile will stand out.

Rochfield is a more complex and serious character. He enters the play, though, with a section of solo comedy. The actor thus starts with the advantage of audience sympathy, which is maintained by the further comedy of his self-deprecating incompetence as a thief and his quaking terror of being found out when he is taken home by Annabel. The intelligence and seriousness of the character needs scope as well, however, initiated by the mock debate with Annabel over the terms 'Honest' and 'Thief' (II.ii.7–31), and continued by his acceptance of Annabel as his tutor and guide. He learns her lessons in trust and generosity well, and by the end of the play demonstrates qualities of true friendship by thwarting Lessingham's final plot and calming Annabel's father. Being the hero of a sea victory over the Spanish would have further endeared him to a 1624 audience as well as to Woodroff.

Woodroff is a simple, sanguine man whose generous amiability marks him as Annabel's father. A merchant who has risen in the world to be a justice of the peace, and have his daughter marry a gentleman, he is part of the fluid social milieu close to London that joins the characters of the Compass comedy plot with the young men and women of the tragicomic romance plot. Woodroff's brother-in-law Franckford is even more pivotal in this respect, married to Woodroff's sister Luce yet keeping Compass's wife Urse as his mistress. And despite his role as Compass's antagonist (which offers a variety of acting approaches), he shares the genial predisposition to generosity and reconciliation which characterizes the comedy plot.

Compass himself is a wonderful comic creation, presumably written by Rowley as if for himself even if he knew the play was for another company. The role invites huge comic energy and gusto, whether deflecting the 'plaguy boys' (II.iii.36), pretending to threaten the Nurse with seduction, terrifying and bearing down Franckford and his wife, or engaging in a bravura verbal (and perhaps physical) sailor's set piece about the winds from the four corners of the compass (IV.iii.83–93). As a character he is often playing a role (e.g., mock anger with Urse at II.iii.115–17), and the unexpectedness of his responses (e.g., delight at returning after four years to find his wife with a young baby) adds to the comic engagement with the audience that is central to any clown's performance. His robust comic language, too, provides a vivid low comedy contrast with the strained rhetoric of honour and friendship in the romance plot. Linguistic comedy of a different sort, quite possibly designed to be directed straight at lawyers and Inns of Court students in the audience, derives from Compass's ability continually to confuse the legal context within which the lawyers operate. In IV.i Compass carries on a conversation with his lawyer, Pettifog, in which, quite apart from sexual and other puns, and general anti-lawyer satire based on their love of jargon and legal complexities, there seems to be developed an elaborate set of contradictions about whether or not 'Civil Law' (see IV.i.75n) can be involved in Compass's case against Franckford. Common law rather than Civil law usually applied in English courts, but W. J. Jones cites a 1606 case, for instance, 'where the civil and common law prescribed different modes for the legitimization of children'.[7] The role of 'Atorneys in *Guild-hall*' (77–8) may be invoked precisely because of the anomalous jurisdictions of the London courts sitting at Guildhall. In the legal debate between Franckford and Compass, the Councellor starts with issues of ecclesiastical law (illegitimacy [151] and the role of the parish [153]), but seems to switch to common law when he invokes 'reason, upon which | The Law is grounded' (157–8). Compass, however, triumphantly betters the Councellor's civil-law arguments (in a country where it is understood by lawyers but does not apply), and then overwhelms the common-law argument (which probably has no standing in this case) with his energetic barnyard analogy (171–6). If, as appears to be the case, a section of over a hundred lines of this scene is comedy based on the intricacies of legal jurisdictions, it seems likely that this identifies an important segment of the audience the playwrights had in mind (understandably if written for the Blackfriars, but surprisingly if for the Red Bull; see below, p. 291). It also suggests an overt complicity with the audience—both lawyers and non-lawyers—to indulge in private jokes and satire for the knowledgeable. The actors of Pettifog, Dodge, and the Councellor act as straight men for Compass to play the comedy direct to the audience.

The other roles to be played by hired men—Sailor, the Drawer, and '*another*' (V.ii.86.2) at Compass's second wedding—are undemanding, but the boys of the company were provided some interesting challenges.

Of the female roles played by the boys, that of Clare is the most complex; critics from Rupert Brooke to Charles Forker have found the question of her motivation intractable. The critical problems, however, have been both overstated and misconceived, and Clare's motivation and characterization can be demonstrated to be entirely consistent (see pp. 273–4). Nevertheless, there are problems facing any actor of Clare. How is she to retain sympathy when it is revealed that plot contrivance has required her to mislead the audience as well as Lessingham about her intentions in her letter to him? How is she to be credible in her sudden transformations from deep melancholy (for love of Bonvile) to evident promises to Lessingham, to despair at Bonvile's apparent death, to 'extasied' (IV.ii.40) affection for Lessingham, back to love for Bonvile, then another 'strange alteration' (182) in which Bonvile's description of her as a 'Whore' (178) kills her love for him (as he intends). For the rest of the play she is an active agent of reconciliation between Annabel and Bonvile, as well as, in due course, a willing bride for Lessingham. In performance, the actor of Clare needs to decide whether her 'strange alteration' leads her to indicate acceptance of Bonvile's proffered friendship immediately, so that the audience see them leave the stage in harmony; or whether a slower or more complex transition—the last of her 'strange changes' (38)—is called for.

By comparison with Clare, Annabel is relatively straightforward, but not without interest. Although initially seen simply as a loving and trustful new wife to Bonvile, in her encounter with Rochfield she reveals physical and moral courage allied to a quick wit and mocking but kindly humour. Far from remaining a pallid adjunct of Bonvile, she displays herself as an astonishingly independent teacher and mentor of Rochfield (not least in her secure faith in Bonvile). Despite her brief flare of jealousy in Act V, her role quickly returns to its pattern as an agent of reconciliation, and an example of the love and trust of ideal friendship and marriage.

The two boys who played Clare and Annabel may, in the original production, have played Rafe and Jack, and certainly those two roles also have scope for actors of talent. Physical by-play can be expected between them as they encounter Compass to mockingly inform him of his cuckoldry, or provide pert repartee and bad music at the Three Tuns in IV.i. Similarly, the roles of Luce and Urse and the Nurse, small though they are in lines, offer considerable scope for comic business and reaction to what is happening on stage.

STAGE HISTORY

THE ORIGINAL PRODUCTIONS

The 1661 Q1 title-page of *A Cure for a Cuckold* announces that it 'hath been several times Acted with great Applause', and Francis Kirkman claims that '*several persons remember the Acting of it, and say that it then pleased generally well*' ('The Stationer, to the Judicious Reader', 20–1). The play's composition has long been thought to be about 1624–5, and it is now known that it was allowed for performance in July 1624: 'A Wedding, or a *Cure for a Cuckold*, by Webster, allowed July 26th. 1624, for the Princes Company I *li* [£1]'.[8]

Quite apart from introducing a new alternative (or possibly primary) title, *A Wedding*, Herbert's allowance of the play for the 'Princes Company' (i.e., Prince Charles's (I) Company, possibly at that time playing at the Red Bull)[9] is puzzling because William Rowley had by 1623 joined the King's Men. His collaboration with Fletcher on *The Maid in the Mill* was licensed by Herbert on 29 August 1623, and he regularly appears in King's Men documents as a leading member from then until his death in February 1626 (although his name appears anomalously as a Prince's man in the 1625 warrant for black cloth for King James's funeral).[10]

The explanation may be that Rowley was allowed to separate his acting duties from his writing from the time he left the Prince's company for the King's. Prior to 1622 his writing seems to have been for the company for which he acted, the Prince's; during their time at Beeston's Cockpit (or Phoenix) in Drury Lane (1619–?22) his plays included *All's Lost By Lust* (?1619–20), *The World Tossed at Tennis* (with Middleton; 1619–20), and *The Witch of Edmonton* (with Dekker and Ford; 1621). In 1622 he had a main hand in *The Birth of Merlin* for the same company, now removed to the Curtain.[11] This same year, however, saw Rowley and Middleton's *The Changeling* licensed for Lady Elizabeth's company (now at the Cockpit), and there is no evidence that Rowley ever played for them. After his collaboration on *The Maid in the Mill* for the King's company the only other two plays that can be attributed to him with any confidence—*A Cure for a Cuckold*, and *The Late Murder of the Son Upon the Mother, or, Keep the Widow Waking*—were both written for the Prince's Men (by now at the Red Bull) while Rowley continued as a member of the King's Men.[12] Whether or not Rowley had an arrangement with the King's Men that he could collaborate on plays for other companies, it seems to be the case that all the plays in which we can securely identify his hand after the 1619 move to the Cockpit were, with the single exception of *The Maid in the Mill*, for the King's, acquired by Christopher Beeston and remained in the repertoire of his various companies.[13]

The most significant questions this raises in regard to *A Cure for a Cuckold* are whether or not Rowley wrote the role of Compass for himself; and the implications of first performance at the Red Bull. Rowley is known to have taken the role of the fat clown Plumporridge in Middleton's *Inner Temple Masque, or Masque of Heroes*, and probably played the fat bishop in Middleton's *A Game at Chess*.[14] Rowley seems likely to have been writing such roles for himself also in 'Jaques, a simple clownish Gentleman' in *All's Lost by Lust*, Cuddy Banks in *The Witch of Edmonton*, and Bustopha in *The Maid of the Mill*.[15] Was he, then, writing Compass for himself in *A Cure for a Cuckold*? We may presume he was, if we suppose that the authors hoped for acceptance of the play by Rowley's own company, the King's Men. In that case we can envisage the romantic tragicomic plot of Lessingham, Clare, Bonvile and Annabel being written for the taste of the Blackfriars audience, and Rowley tailoring the Compass plot to suit his own capacities as a comic actor in the company.

In the event, the play was licensed to the Prince's company, then playing at the more populist Red Bull (about which Webster was presumably no more enthusiastic in 1624 than he had been when *The White Devil* failed there in 1612; see *Webster*, I, 97). Perhaps Beeston was able to block performance by the King's Men, or to insist on Rowley's terms of contractual obligation; if so, the play may still have been written with the Blackfriars, and Rowley as Compass, in prospect (looking, perhaps, to the precedent of *The Maid of the Mill*). But if it was always intended for the Prince's Men (or for Lady Elizabeth's; Rowley had been acting at the Cockpit for three years, and knew its conditions well), then Rowley presumably did not expect ever to enact Compass. Nevertheless, that need not have prevented him putting himself, as it were, into the writing; the part is a fine comic role for any actor of gusto and girth playing at the Red Bull.

The general characteristics of the Red Bull are discussed in *Webster*, I, 100, and *A Cure for a Cuckold* would have made no special demands on that or any other theatre of the period.

The Prince's company would presumably have had no difficulty filling the ten principal named roles in the play; and six or even fewer hired men could easily cover, with a small amount of doubling, Pettifog, Dodge, the Councellor, the two Clients, Annabel's servant, the Sailor, the Drawer, and '*another*' who appears at V.ii.86.2. The six female and two boys' roles could be undertaken by as few as five boys if Rafe and Jack were doubled with Clare and Annabel, and the Waiting-woman from I.i also doubled. Thus the acting resources required, in both men and boys, would put no strain at all upon a London acting company of the time.[16] But if the boys playing Clare and Annabel did in fact double

Rafe and Jack, the theatricality of such a pairing would reinforce the delight in artifice and intrigue which seems central to the tone of the romance plot.

Joseph Harris adapted *A Cure for a Cuckold* as *The City Bride, or The Merry Cuckold* (pub. 1696). There is no record of subsequent professional performance.

A student production at Victoria University of Wellington in 1997 used a quasi-Elizabethan stage arrangement with audience on three sides both below the stage and on upper galleries. The surrounding presence of the audience was acknowledged at all times, and direct address to them was adopted whenever possible. The gallery above the stage provided a further acting area which was particularly useful for, e.g., the Gallants at Annabel and Bonvile's wedding observing the strange behaviour of their friends Clare and Lessingham, and for Rochfield as a highwayman lying in wait to rob Annabel.

The tragicomic romance plot was driven by the moody, self-destructive impulses of Clare. Lessingham's obsessive desire to satisfy her ever more erratic wishes maintained audience attention and understanding despite the brittle convolutions of the plot before the final reconciliation and double wedding. The decision to address so many lines direct to the audience helped sustain the artificial and at times arbitrary plot by ensuring audience complicity in it.

The Compass plot introduced real gusto on stage, as well as a thematic counterpoise to the overheated jealousies of the romance plot. With a view to theatricalizing and contextualizing both Jacobean male casting of female roles and late twentieth-century gender politics, Compass was played by a powerful actress, and Urse, his wife, by a young male actor. Compass's energetic low comedy lines, delivered by a female actor, were both funny and problematized. Although neither cross-dressed actor played for easy laughs, the theatricality of the choices suited both the immediate fun of the Compass plot and the wider thematic implications in the play about sexual jealousy, tolerance, true friendship, and reasonable behaviour.

A different kind of comedy developed in the minor plot of Rochfield. His conversion by Annabel from highwayman back to gentlemanly younger son, and hero of a sea battle against Spain, demonstrated how much amusement is to be gained not only from her unexpected disarming of him, but even more from her teasing him, and gently playing on his fear of betrayal. If his virtue at the end of the play seems just too convenient, he has at least earned it, and from a Jacobean heroine with more self-reliance, independence, and gumption than may appear on the page.

Overall, the production demonstrated that the play is much more stageworthy than may be immediately apparent, that romance plot and Compass plot successfully link in thematic terms, and that both the high tragicomedy and the low comedy of Compass provide satisfying theatre.[17]

1. See Andrew Gurr, 'Maximal and Minimal Texts of Shakespeare', *Shakespeare's Globe Research Bulletin* 4 (April 1998).
2. Cunnington and Lucas, p. 56.
3. *The Canterbury Tales*, General Prologue, 392–3, in *The Poetical Works of Chaucer*, ed. F. N. Robinson (Cambridge, Mass., 1933).
4. See Dessen and Thomson, 'wedding', and MacIntyre, p. 146.
5. See Carnegie and Jackson.
6. See Taylor.
7. W. J. Jones, *The Elizabethan Court of Chancery* (Oxford, 1967), p. 400, n. 2.
8. Bawcutt, p. 153. This entry is not recorded by Bentley; nor was it known to Lucas. They both suggested, however, on the basis of topical references, composition about 1624–5. Bentley notes elsewhere (IV, 806) that £1 was the standard fee.
9. Bentley, I, 205–9.
10. Bawcutt, p. 144, Bentley, II, 557.
11. Bawcutt, p. 136; this date was not known to Bentley.
12. Rowley and Middleton appear to have collaborated with Ford and Dekker on *The Spanish Gypsy* of 1623, but the extent of Rowley's share has proved difficult to determine; see Gary Taylor and MacD. P. Jackson, 'Thomas Middleton and *The Spanish Gypsy*: Protocols for Attribution in Cases of Multiple Collaborators' (forthcoming). Whether Rowley had a share in Massinger's *The Parliament of Love* of 1624 is even more uncertain. Both plays were for Lady Elizabeth's company. See also David Gunby, 'William Rowley', *The New Dictionary of National Biography* (forthcoming). On what little is known of the contractual obligations of playwrights, see G. E. Bentley, *The Profession of Dramatist in Shakespeare's Time* (Princeton, 1971), pp. 111–26, and, on Rowley's collaborations, pp. 215–18.
13. Bentley, I, 204, Gurr 1996, p. 419.
14. Gurr 1996, p. 374.
15. Bentley, II, 556.
16. For the assumptions made here about standard doubling practices, see *Webster*, I, 98–100, 426–7.
17. A somewhat fuller description of this production may be found in *Research Opportunities in Renaissance Drama* XXXIX (2000), pp. 171–3.

Textual introduction

MacDonald P. Jackson

A Cure for a Cuckold was first printed in a quarto of 1661, which collates A^2 B–H^4.[1] There were two issues, the first naming Thomas Johnson as printer and Francis Kirkman as bookseller, and the second, with a new title leaf, 'to be sold by *Nath. Brook . . . Francis Kirkman . . . Tho: Johnson . . . and Henry Marsh*'. Also in 1661, Kirkman issued a few copies of the edition in conjunction with *The Thracian Wonder*, under the general title *Two New Playes*. Neither play was entered in the Stationers' Register, and *A Cure for a Cuckold* was not reprinted until Dyce included it among *The Works of John Webster* (1830).

Examination and measurement of the headlines reveals that the Quarto was printed throughout by the two-skeleton method. No headline ever appears in both the inner and outer formes of the same sheet, but the two skeletons are not preserved as completely separate entities: the pattern of composition, presswork, and distribution was evidently such that a single headline from one skeleton forme might be incorporated into the alternate skeleton forme for the printing of the subsequent sheet.

This pattern affords no grounds for conjecture about the number of compositors who set the text. There are, however, some indications in the spelling and typography that a new workman took over within sheet E. The speech prefixes for certain characters are suggestive. The play proper begins on B1^r. Raymond is always '*Raym.*' in B1^v–D3^r (18 times), but '*Ray.*' in E2^v–G2^v (20 times). Annabel begins as '*Anna.*' on B2^v (twice), becomes '*An.*' in C1^v–C3^v (23 times), reverts to '*Anna.*' in D2^r–D3^v (12 times), and then switches to '*Ann.*' in E2^v–H2^r (15 times), before ending, as she began, as '*An.*' on H2^r–H2^v (4 times).[2] Franckford changes from '*Franck.*' in B2^v–E2^r (20 times) to '*Fr.*' in E2^r–H4^v (9 times), though there are three deviations into '*Fran.*' on B3^r, which also contains three instances of the longer form, and E2^r has the sequence '*Franck.*'

(twice), '*Fr.*' (once), '*Franck.*' (once), '*Fr.*' (3 times). Thus the prefixes for Raymond undergo a decisive shift between D3^r and E2^v, those for Annabel between D3^v and E2^v, and those for Franckford within E2^r. A few spellings reinforce this evidence. The conjunction 'than' was usually spelt 'then' in seventeenth-century playscripts but the modern spelling also occurs. In the Quarto, the ratio of 'than' to 'then' is 12:2 in B–D, and 4:9 in E–H.[3] Examples of 'bin' (for 'been') and 'tho' (for 'though') fall almost exclusively in the second half of the Quarto.[4] The proportion of colons to semicolons also changes markedly: 104:51 in B–D, 59:65 in F–H; on some pages of E the ratio is more like that for B–D and for others it is more like that for F–H.[5] Taken together, these various data suggest that one compositor was largely responsible for sheets B–D and for E1^v–2^r and E4^r–4^v (where the ratio of colons to semi-colons is 27:7), and that another was largely responsible for the sheets F–H and for E1^r and E2^v–3^v (where the ratio is 14:12), but that E2^r may have been shared.[6]

Some variations may, however, have originated in the printer's manuscript copy of this collaborative play. The reversion of the speech prefixes for Annabel to the short form '*An.*' in H2^r, for example, coincides with her re-entry '*with a Will*' at V.i.241.1; before that, on the same page, she had once been '*Ann.*' Yet the same playwright, namely Webster, seems to have written the material either side of this point, and, in general, there is no correspondence between sections delineated by the orthographical variants noted above and the authorial shares as Lucas and others have determined them. Likewise puzzling is the liberal use of dashes (21 times altogether) on B3^v, B4^v, and C1^r, and their total absence from the rest of the Quarto. The pages affected all belong to I.ii, but so, of course, does B4^r, and its dialogue is of the same kind. The natural conclusion is that a different compositor set the deviant pages, but there is no confirmatory evidence from other variables, unless it be the understandable sparseness of colons and semicolons where dashes prevail. Fluctuations in the availability of the various sorts of type are a possible cause of such oddities.[7]

Shortages of '*I*' and '*W*' led to the makeshift use of '*I*' on D2^v, D3^r, G3^r, and G4^r, and, sporadically, of '*VV*' within H1^v–H4^r, but the pattern of substitution allows no easy inferences about whether typesetting was by formes or seriatim. It is clear, however, that the compositors were anxious to accommodate the text within eight sheets. The play finishes on H4^v with just enough space left on the page for Kirkman's brief advertisement. This neat fit was achieved through the setting of most of the play's verse as prose, and through an increasing tendency to begin a speech within a line on which another ends. In sheets B and C only short speeches, confined to the single part-line, are set in this way, but in D–H several longer speeches are similarly treated. The printing of most entry directions to the right of the dialogue, and sometimes in very small italic type, may also have been a space-saving device. But this feature is rather more likely to have derived from the underlying manuscript.

Before turning to the question of what kind of manuscript this may have been, we may consider the implications for the handling of the text of the above findings about printing-house practices. In fact, although the evidence that at least two compositors set the Quarto provides some basis for investigation of authorship (discussed below), it has little relevance to the actual editing. Though some orthographical differences between the earlier and later sheets are probably compositorial, we have been obliged to reproduce the variable spellings of our Quarto copy. In the same spirit, we have taken over the spate of dashes in B3^v–C1^r. Old-spelling editions inevitably reflect the 'instability' of seventeenth-century printing. Even the Quarto pattern of choice between colons and semicolons (with colons greatly prevailing in the earlier sheets but not in the later sheets), though influenced by compositorial whim, is perpetuated in our edition, but when replacing commas with heavier stops we have selected colons or semicolons according to our own sense of seventeenth-century usage, not according to the contrasting preferences of the two compositors. Our treatment of the Quarto's mislineation—much of which evidently originated in the printing-house—demands a section to itself.

PRINTER'S COPY

The nature of the manuscript obtained by Kirkman for his printer cannot confidently be determined, but it may have been a theatre playbook. The play is divided into acts, but not scenes. Yet the disposition of entry directions appears to imply that scenes were distinguished in some way in the manuscript. All entries that begin scenes, even short entries, are centred, whereas almost all others are set flush with the right margin, as are exits and the three indications of action: '*She draws his sword*' on C2^v, '*They sit down, Pettifog pulls out papers*' on E4^r, and '*Gives her a Letter. She gives him another*' on F4^r. Exceptions to the right-hand placing of entry directions within scenes occur on D2^r (II.iv), E4^v (IV.i), F1^v (IV.i), H2^r (V.i), H2^v (V.ii), H3^r (V.ii), and H4^r (V.ii), while '*Manent Rochfield solus*' (*sic*) is centred on D2^v (in II.iv): the faulty Latin is of a piece with '*Finis Actus secundus*' on D3^v at the end of II.iv. All but one of these exceptions to the rule (that on H2^r) fall within scenes that most scholars have ascribed to William Rowley.[8] Signs of the composite character of the manuscript copy thus show through the printed text.

The first of the right-set entries (on B1^v) is boxed on three sides by rules, and there is one more such entry on B4^v. This might suggest a book-keeper's hand—though there are examples in Heywood's manuscript of *The Captives*, and Heywood is the probable author of the first act of *A Cure for a Cuckold*—and most of the right-set entries are placed a few lines before the character or characters are observed by those on stage and are addressed or speak. 'Anticipatory' directions of this kind have traditionally been considered pointers to a playscript's having been prepared for theatrical use. Entries are exceptionally close to being complete. Raymond has five speeches towards the end of IV.i (F2^r–F2^v) without having entered in the Quarto, but this is the only omission. Ambiguities attend the comings and goings of the two Boys and their relation to the Drawer within E3^v–F1^v (IV.i.0.1–131), and the entry of Bonvile on F3^v (IV.ii.112.1)[9]. But the Quarto furnishes an unusually full guide to performance. The few descriptive touches in stage directions are of the kind that, while probably originating with the author, remain helpful for the actors. Lessingham enters '*sad*' on B3^r, Rochfield is characterized on his first entry as '*a young Gentleman*' (C1^v), and occupations are added to names for '*Pettifog the Attorney*' (E3^v) and '*Mr. Dodge a Lawyer*' (E4^r).

The call for '*Soft Musick*' on H3^v might be a book-keeper's, but the same direction occurs in *The Devil's Law-Case*, in Rowley's *A Shoemaker a Gentleman*, and in two of Rowley's collaborations, *Wit at Several Weapons* and *The Birth of Merlin*. There is no direction for music in the first scene of the Quarto of *A Cure for a Cuckold*, where music is clearly required. We have added '*Music within*' to the opening entry (see I.i.125–6n).

In short, there is insufficient evidence to identify the kind of manuscript that served as printer's copy, but there are uncertain signs that it had been prepared for the theatre, and it may conceivably have been used as a promptbook.

LINEATION

The Quarto prints most of the play's verse as prose. As explained above, the compositors seem to have been intent on saving space, and little of the mislineation is likely to have inhered in the manuscript from which they were working, though that manuscript may sometimes have confused them. Patches of correctly lined verse, fairly substantial in Act I, become shorter and more sporadic within Acts II–IV, and longer and more frequent again within Act V. Some prose, including much of Compass's in IV.iii, is set as verse. In places it is unclear whether the compositor intended verse or prose. Compass's speech on G2^r illustrates this point:

> Comp.   Durst confess? Why whom do you fear? here's none
> but honest Gentlemen my friends; let them hear, and
> Never blush for't.   (IV.iii.102–3)

The first of these lines stops a little short of the right-hand margin, the second well short. The second line begins with a lower case letter, the third with an upper case one, despite the fact that 'never' is never capitalized elsewhere unless it heads a line or a sentence. If 'but' were 'But' we could assume that the compositor thought, wrongly, that he was dealing with verse. As it is, we cannot be sure what he believed.

The Quarto's very first page of dialogue (B1^r) prints verse as prose, but retains a few uncertain vestiges of the original arrangement. Lessingham's fourth speech begins:

> Less.   True Lady, and a noble president
> me thinks for us to follow: why should these out-strip us in our
> loves, that have not yet out-gone us in our time.   (I.i.10–13)

The first of these three lines is an iambic pentameter, printed as such in the present edition. Yet the second is uncapitalized and fills the prose measure. The third, also uncapitalized, stops well short of the right-hand margin, but the remainder of the speech is set as two full lines of prose. Similarly, Lessingham's next speech begins:

> Less.   Lady, you are sad:
> this Jovial Meeting puts me in a spirit to be made such.   (I.i.18–20)

The first four words do in fact—in Dyce's arrangement, which we follow—complete a blank-verse line. The second, uncapitalized, leaves some twelve millimetres of white space at the end of the line, though the true verse-line division is 'spirit | To'. The speech finishes with three lines set unequivocally as prose.

Although such ambiguities create difficulties for the collation of editorial departures from the Quarto's lineation, and although the Quarto fails so conspicuously to differentiate between the play's verse and prose, there is little disagreement among editors over the correct setting out of *A Cure for a Cuckold*'s dialogue. Our own deliberations have resulted in decisions closely matching those by Dyce in 1830. The verse, even in scenes clearly

Webster's, is more regular than that of *The Devil's Law-Case* and the prose more definitely recognizable as prose. Correcting the Quarto's chaotic lineation is not an unduly complex task.

AUTHORSHIP

The title-page declares the play to be a collaboration between John Webster and William Rowley. Several early critics were reluctant to credit Webster with more than a very small share in the writing, but his significant presence was demonstrated by Stoll and Sykes and accepted by Lucas.[10] A complication was introduced by Gray, who argued that Heywood had been a third collaborator.[11] The question of the authorship of *A Cure for a Cuckold* is thus linked to that of the authorship of *Appius and Virginia*, which was printed as Webster's but thought by Gray and others to be partly, even largely, Heywood's.[12] Both plays can be dated to the last phase of Webster's playwriting career and both, as Lucas acknowledged, show 'strong marks of Heywood's style'.[13] Lucas wondered whether, in each case, (a) Webster was imitating Heywood, or (b) Webster was collaborating with Heywood, or (c) one playwright was revising the other's work. He suspected that the same answer would hold for both plays.

Lucas's own analyses persuaded him that Heywood had collaborated with Webster in *Appius and Virginia* and with Webster and Rowley in *A Cure for a Cuckold*. Jackson has since vindicated both these conclusions.[14] From careful inspection of their undoubted and unaided plays, he compiled contrasting 'linguistic profiles' for Webster, Rowley, and Heywood, consisting of their practices in regard to contractions, connectives, expletives, and other minutiae. The findings were then applied to the various scenes of the two doubtful plays. Lucas had categorized scenes and part-scenes of *A Cure for a Cuckold* as written by Webster, Rowley, Heywood and Webster jointly, or Rowley and Webster jointly. Jackson showed that these four kinds of material exhibited significantly different linguistic preferences, in line with those of the alleged authors. For example, Webster's distinctive 'of't' is confined to passages that Lucas attributed to Webster, while 'I'm', which Rowley favoured, Webster avoided, and Heywood employed rarely, is found only in scenes wholly or largely attributed by Lucas to Rowley. The 'Heywood and Webster' material is marked by a complete absence of Webster's and Rowley's favourite forms, a Heywoodian preference for 'betwixt' over 'between', and a proportion of 'hath' and 'doth' to 'has' and 'does' that can be matched in Heywood's plays but not in Webster's or Rowley's. The likelihood is that Heywood's hand is overwhelmingly predominant in this portion of the play. The authorial units substantiated by such variables are unrelated to the probable compositorial stints. The contrasting preferences of the playwrights are quite distinct from those of the compositors.

Jackson further confirmed Heywood's involvement in *A Cure for a Cuckold* by means of a comprehensive investigation, with the help of electronic databases, of phrasal parallels between Act V and the plays of Heywood, Webster, and Rowley. Lucas saw Act V as falling into three sections, dominated by each playwright in turn. Striking Heywood parallels could be shown to cluster within the portion assigned to Heywood, Webster parallels within the portion assigned to Webster, and Rowley parallels within the portion assigned to Rowley.

Rowley appears to have been mainly responsible for the Compass and Rochfield–Annabel plots, while the Lessingham–Clare–Bonvile story was handled by Heywood and Webster. To Webster can be attributed the bulk of III.i, III.iii.1–31, IV.ii, and V.i.112.1–283, to Heywood the bulk of I.i, I.ii, III.iii.31.1–107, and V.i.1–112, and to Rowley the bulk of what remains: II.i, II.ii, II.iii, II.iv, III.ii, IV.i, IV.iii, and V.ii. But several scenes were doubtless of mixed authorship.[15]

SUBSEQUENT EDITIONS

In 1830 Dyce corrected the Quarto's faulty lineation and a handful of misprints, and in 1857 he added several stage directions. Hazlitt (1857) contributed little of consequence, but Lucas made most of the further alterations and supplementations that we have adopted, besides providing the first detailed commentary. *A Cure for a Cuckold* is in Dyce's volume III, Hazlitt's IV, and Lucas's III. Weis's modern-spelling edition further augmented the Quarto's stage directions, and is the first to note the important press-variant that corrects all previous readings of the text at II.iii.104. Our collation of all available copies has revealed only one other variant.

Joseph Harris's adaptation of *A Cure for a Cuckold* as *The City Bride, or, The Merry Cuckold* (1693) adheres closely to the structure and order of scenes of Webster, Rowley, and Heywood's play, though it omits the Bonvile–Clare encounter in IV.ii, interpolates some songs and dances, and renames several characters. The dialogue, presented as prose, intermingles sentences and phrases taken verbatim from *A Cure for a Cuckold* with paraphrase and rough summary. Since *The City Bride* is not an edition of *A Cure for a Cuckold*, we have ignored it in the collation notes, but Harris anticipated Dyce's correction of a few obvious literals, such as the speech prefix '*Nuase*' at III.ii.5, and Lucas's provision of stage directions in the struggle between Rochfield and Annabel in II.ii. In 1885 Stephen Spring-Rice published *Love's Graduate: A Comedy by John Webster*, a version of *A Cure for a Cuckold* from which all material relating to the Compass plot had been excised. He based his text on Dyce, 'with a few slight verbal alterations, and many of punctuation'. None of the 'slight verbal alterations' is of editorial significance.

1. Greg, *Bibliography*, II, 817; Wing, W1220–21, W1225.
2. Figures exclude the catchwords '*An.*' on C2ᵛ, '*Anna.*' on D2ʳ, and '*Ann.*' on H1ᵛ. Besides five instances of '*Ann.*', E2ᵛ has one of '*An.*' in a full line, where is has been used to aid justification.
3. The spelling 'than' appears on B1ʳ, B1ᵛ, B3ʳ, B4ᵛ, C2ᵛ, C3ʳ, C3ᵛ, C4ʳ, C4ᵛ, D1ᵛ, D2ʳ, D2ᵛ, F1ᵛ, F4ᵛ, and G2ᵛ (twice); while 'then' is used on B1ᵛ (twice), E1ʳ, E2ᵛ, E3ᵛ, F2ʳ, F3ʳ, G1ᵛ (twice), H1ʳ, and H3ʳ. These figures relate only to the conjunction.
4. The spelling 'bin' occurs on B3ʳ (where it rhymes with 'sin'), E2ᵛ, E3ʳ, F3ᵛ (twice), and H4ᵛ; 'tho' is used on C3ᵛ, F1ᵛ, F3ʳ, and F3ᵛ.
5. The ratios of colons to semicolons per page in E are: E1ʳ 7:4, E1ᵛ 7:0, E2ʳ 7:3, E2ᵛ 2:3, E3ʳ 3:2, E3ᵛ 2:3, E4ʳ 4:2, E4ᵛ 9:2. It must be conceded that there is considerable variation among pages in sheets B–D and F–H.
6. Thus E1ʳ has 'then' and 4 semicolons; E2ᵛ not only has 'then' and 'bin' but strongly exemplifies the shift to '*Ann.*' (5 times) and '*Ray.*' (8 times), while preferring semicolons to colons; E3ʳ has 'bin', 3 instances of the new prefix '*Ann.*' and a 3:2 ratio of colons to semicolons; and E3ᵛ has 'then' and more semicolons than colons. On E2ʳ the evidence is ambiguous, since both '*Franck.*' and the new prefix '*Fr.*' occur, there are none of the less common spellings, and the proportion of colons to semicolons (7:3) reveals little.
7. It is perhaps worth mentioning that the anomalous spelling 'Rochfeild' occurs only on E2ᵛ and E3ᵛ, both instances falling within III.iii.
8. In addition to those noted above, there are two entry directions set in the position of speech prefixes, and probably intended to serve as prefixes as well as entries: '*Enter boy*' on E4ᵛ (IV.i) and '*Enter Bonvile*' on F3ᵛ (IV.ii). IV.i is a 'Rowley and Webster' scene, and IV.ii a Webster scene. See note 9 below.
9. See Commentary on IV.i.0.1–.2, IV.i.22.1–.3, IV.i.53.1, and IV.ii.113.
10. Stoll, *Periods*; H. D. Sykes, 'Webster's Share in *A Cure for a Cuckold*', *N&Q*, eleventh series, IX (1914), pp. 383–4, 404–5, 443–5, 463–4.
11. H. D. Gray, '*A Cure for a Cuckold* by Heywood, Rowley and Webster', *MLR* XXII (1927), pp. 389–97.
12. H. D. Gray, '*Appius and Virginia*: by Webster and Heywood', *Studies in Philology* XXIV (1927), pp. 279–89. See pp. 498–9 for further details.
13. Lucas, III, 12.
14. Jackson 1985; 'Late Webster and His Collaborators: How Many Playwrights Wrote *A Cure for a Cuckold*?', *PBSA* XCV (2001), pp. 295–313.

15. One typographical feature of the Quarto appears to have an association with author-
    ship. Parentheses (round brackets) occur 15 times in portions of the play that Lucas
    attributes to Rowley alone (7 times) or to Rowley working with Webster (8 times),
    and only 4 times elsewhere: twice in sections that Lucas attributes to Webster and
    twice in sections that he attributes to Heywood and Webster jointly. Rowley used
    many more parentheses than Middleton in plays on which the two men collaborated.
    Webster seems to have been sparing in his employment of parentheses (Ralph Crane
    was responsible for those in *The Duchess of Malfi*), while Heywood's usage was vari-
    able; see MacD. P. Jackson, *Studies in Attribution: Middleton and Shakespeare* (Salzburg,
    1979), pp. 124–31, 185–8.

A CURE FOR A CUCKOLD.

A PLEASANT COMEDY,

As it hath been several times Acted
with great Applause.

Written by JOHN WEBSTER *and*
WILLIAM ROWLEY.

Placere Cupio.

London, Printed by *Tho. Johnson*, and are to be sold by *Francis Kirkman*, at his Shop at the Sign of *John Fletchers Head*, over against the Angel-Inne, on the Back-side of St. *Clements*, without *Temple-Bar*. 1661.

6. Title-page of *A Cure for a Cuckold* (1661).

The Stationer, to the Judicious Reader.

Gentlemen,

It was not long since I was onely a Book-Reader, and not a Book-seller, which Quality (my former Employment somewhat failing, and I being unwilling to be idle) I have now lately taken on me. It hath been my fancy and delight (ere since I knew any thing) to converse with Books; and the pleasure I have taken in those of this nature, (viz. Plays) *hath bin so extraordinary, that it hath bin much to my cost; for I have been (as we term it) a Gatherer of* Plays *for some years, and I am confident I have more of several sorts than any man in* England, *Book-seller, or other. I can at any time shew* 700 *in number, which is within a small matter all*   10 *that were ever printed. Many of these I have several times over, and intend as I sell, to purchase more; All, or any of which, I shall be ready either to sell or lend to you upon reasonable Considerations.*

In order to the increasing of my Store, I have now this Tearm *printed and published three, viz. This called* A Cure for a Cuckold, *and another called,* The Thracian Wonder; *and the third called,* Gammer Gurtons Needle. *Two of these three were never printed, the third, viz.* Gammer Gurtons Needle, *hath bin formerly printed, but it is almost an hundred years since. As for this* Play, *I need not speak any thing in its Commendation, the Authors names,* Webster *and* Rowley, *are (to knowing men) sufficient to declare its worth: several persons*   20 *remember the Acting of it, and say that it then pleased generally well; and let me tell you, in my judgement it is an excellent old* Play. *The Expedient of Curing a Cuckold (after the maner set down in this* Play) *hath bin tried to my knowledge, and therefore I may say* Probatum est. *I should, I doubt, be too tedious, or else I would say somewhat in defence of this, and in Commendation of* Plays *in general, but I question not but you have read what abler Pens than mine have writ in their Vindication. Gentlemen, I hope you will so incourage me in my beginnings, that I may be induced to proceed to do you service, and that I may frequently have occasion in this nature, to subscribe my self*

Your Servant,   30
Francis Kirkman.

Dramatis Personae

[in order of appearance].

Lessingham a Gentleman in love with *Clare.*
Clare, Lessingham's Mistriss.
Raymond,
Eustace, } Gallants invited to the Wedding.
Lyonel, and
Grover,
A Waiting-woman [to *Clare*].
Woodroff, a Justice of the Peace, Father to *Annabel.*   10
Annabel the Bride, and Wife to *Bonvile.*
Bonvile a Gentleman, the Bridegroom and Husband to *Annabel.*
Franckford a Merchant, Brother in Law to *Woodroff.*
Luce Wife to *Franckford,* and Sister to *Woodroff.*
Nurse [employed by *Franckford*].
[*Servant.*]
Rochfield, a young Gentleman, and a Thief.
Two Boys [*Rafe* and *Jack*].
Compass, a Sea-man.
Urse, Wife to *Compass.*   20
A Saylor.
Pettifog, and }
Dodge,   } two Attorneys.
[*Drawer.*]
Two Clients.
A Councellor.

2–24 (matter in square brackets)] *not in* Q; *for*
   order of names, see Commentary

A CURE for a CUCKOLD.

ACT I. SCENE I. [I.i]

Enter LESSINGHAM *and* CLARE. [*Music within.*]

Lessingham.   This is a place of feasting and of joy,
    And as in Triumphs and Ovations, here
    Nothing save state and pleasure.
Clare.   'Tis confest.
Lessingham.   A day of Mirth and solemn Jubile.
Clare.   For such as can be merry.
Lessingham.   A happy Nuptial,
    Since a like pair of Fortunes suitable,
    Equality in Birth, parity in years,
    And in affection no way different,
    Are this day sweetly coupled.
Clare.   'Tis a Marriage.
Lessingham.   True, Lady, and a noble president   10
    Me thinks for us to follow: why should these
    Out-strip us in our loves, that have not yet
    Out-gone us in our time? If we thus loose
    Our best, and not to be recovered hours
    Unprofitably spent, we shall be held
    Meer Trewants in Loves school.
Clare.   That's a study
    In which I never shall ambition have
    To become graduate.
Lessingham.   Lady, you are sad:
    This Jovial Meeting puts me in a spirit
    To be made such. We two are Guests invited,   20
    And meet by purpose, not by accident;
    Where's then a place more opportunely fit,
    In which we may solicite our own Loves,
    Than before this example?

Clare.   In a word,
    I purpose not to marry.
Lessingham.   By your favor,
    For as I ever to this present hour
    Have studied your observance, so from henceforth
    I now will study plainness: I have loved you
    Beyond my self, mis-spended for your sake
    Many a fair hour, which might have been imployed   30
    To pleasure, or to profit, have neglected
    Duty to them from whom my being came,
    My parents; but my hopeful studies most.
    I have stol'n time from all my choice delights,
    And robb'd my self, thinking to enrich you.   [B1ᵛ]
    Matches I have had offered, some have told me
    As fair, as rich, I never thought 'em so,
    And lost all these in hope to finde out you.
    Resolve me then for Christian charity:
    Think you an Answer of that frozen nature   40
    Is a sufficient satisfaction for
    So many more then needful services?
Clare.   I have said, Sir.
Lessingham.   Whence might this distaste arise?
    Be at least so kinde to perfect me in that:
    Is it of some dislike lately conceived
    Of this my person, which perhaps may grow
    From calumny and scandal? If not that,
    Some late received Melancholy in you?
    If neither, your perverse and peevish will,
    To which I most imply it.   50
Clare.   Be it what it can, or may be, thus it is,
    And with this Answer pray rest satisfied.
    In all these travels, windings, and indents,
    Paths, and by-paths which many have sought out,
    There's but one onely road, and that alone
    To my fruition; which who so findes out,
    'Tis like he may enjoy me: but that failing,
    I ever am mine own.

28 plainness:] ~, Q   39 charity:] ~. Q
38 you.] ~, Q   48 you?] ~: Q

Lessingham.   Oh name it, Sweet.
    I am already in a Labyrinth
    Until you guide me out.
Clare.   Ile to my Chamber;   60
    May you be pleased, unto your mis-spent time
    To adde but some few minutes, by my Maid
    You shall hear further from me.
Lessingham.   Ile attend you.   *Exit* [*Clare*].
    What more can I desire, than be resolv'd
    Of such a long suspence? Here's now the period
    Of much expectation.
      Enter RAYMOND, EUSTACE, LYONEL, *and* GROVER, *Gallants.*
Raymond.   What? You alone retired to privacy,
    Of such a goodly confluence, all prepared
    To grace the present Nuptials?
Lessingham.   I have heard some say,
    Men are ne're less alone then when alone,   70
    Such power hath meditation.
Eustace.   Oh these choice Beauties
    That are this day assembled! But of all,
    Fair Mistriss *Clare*, the Bride excepted still,
    She bears away the prize.
Lyonel.   And worthily;   [B2ʳ]
    For, setting off her present melancholly,
    She is without taxation.
Grover.   I conceive
    The cause of her so sudden discontent.
Raymond.   'Tis far out of my way.
Grover.   Ile speak it then:
    In all estates, professions, or degrees
    In Arts or Sciences, there is a kinde   80
    Of Emulation; likewise so in this:
    There's a Maid this day married, a choice Beauty.
    Now Mrs. *Clare*, a Virgin of like Age,
    And Fortunes correspondent, apprehending
    Time lost in her that's in another gained,

---

60 Chamber;] ~, Q
62 minutes,] ~. Q
63 SD] *as* Dyce 2; *Exit. after* me. Q
65 suspence?] ~. Q

66.1 SD] *placed as* Dyce 1; *set in box to right of*
    lines 66–7 Q
70 alone∧] ~, Q

May upon this—for who knows womens thoughts?—
Grow into this deep sadness.

Raymond.   Like enough.

Lessingham.   You are pleasant, Gentlemen, or else perhaps,
Though I know many have pursued her Love—

Grover.   And you amongst the rest, with pardon Sir,   90
Yet she might cast some more peculiar eye
On some that not respects her.

Lessingham [*aside*].   That's my fear
Which you now make your sport.

> *Enter Wayting-woman* [*with a letter*].

Wayting-woman [*to Lessingham*].   A Letter, Sir.

Lessingham.   From whom?

Wayting-woman.   My Mistriss.

Lessingham [*aside*].   She has kept her promise,
And I will read it, though I in the same
Know my own death included.

Wayting-woman.   Fare you well, Sir.   *Exit.*

Lessingham [*reading letter*].   *Prove all thy friends, finde out the best and nearest,*
    Kill for my sake that Friend that loves thee dearest.
Her servant, nay her hand and character,
All meeting in my ruine! Read agen,   100
    Prove all thy Friends, finde out the best and nearest,
    Kill for my sake that Friend that loves thee dearest.
And what might that one be? 'Tis a strange difficulty,
And it will ask much councel.   *Exit Lessingham.*

Raymond.   Lessingham
Hath left us on the sudden.

Eustace.   Sure the occasion
Was of that Letter sent him.

Lyonel.   It may be
It was some Challenge.

Grover.   Challenge? Never dream it:
Are such things sent by women?

86 this—] ~. Q   thoughts?—] ~ΛΛ Q
87 sadness.] ~? Q
89 Love—] ~, Q
90 ΛAnd] (~ Q   rest,] ~) Q
92 her.] ~, Q   SD] This ed.; *not in* Q
93 SD] *placed as* Dyce 1; *to right of lines* 92–3
  Q   *with a letter*] Weis; *not in* Q

93, 94, 96 *Wayting-woman*] *as* Dyce 1; *Wom.*
  Q
93 SD] *after* Weis; *not in* Q
94 SD] Dyce 2; *not in* Q
97 SD] *after* Dyce 1; *not in* Q
102 *thee*] Dyce 1; *the* Q
107 Challenge?] ~, Q

Raymond.   'Twere an Heresie
   To conceive but such a thought.
Lyonel.   Tush, all the difference   [B2ᵛ]
   Begot this day, must be at night decided   110
   Betwixt the Bride and Bridegroom.
         Enter WOODROFF, ANNABEL, BONVILE, FRANCKFORD,
               LUCE, [*Servant*,] *and Nurse.*
                              Here both come.
Woodroff.   What did you call the Gentleman we met
   But now in some distraction?
Bonvile.   *Lessingham*:
   A most approv'd and noble friend of mine,
   And one of our prime Guests.
Woodroff.   He seemed to me
   Somewhat in minde distemper'd. What concern
   Those private humors our so publick Mirth
   In such a time of Revels? Mistriss *Clare*,
   I miss her too. Why Gallants, have you suffered her
   Thus to be lost amongst you?
Annabel.   Dinner done,   120
   Unknown to any, she retir'd her self.
Woodroff.   Sick of the *Maid* perhaps, because she sees
   You Mistriss Bride, her School- and Play-fellow
   So suddenly turned Wife.
Franckford.   'Twas shrewdly guest.
Woodroff [*to Servant*].   Go finde her out: [*Exit Servant.*]
                              Fie Gentlemen, within
   The Musick playes unto the silent walls,
   And no man there to grace it: when I was young,
   At such a Meeting I have so bestir'd me,
   Till I have made the pale Green-sickness Girls
   Blush like the Rubie, and drop pearls apace   130
   Down from their Ivory fore-heads: In those days
   I have cut Capers thus high. Nay, in, Gentlemen,
   And single out the Ladies.

111 SD] *to right of lines 107–8* Q   ANNABEL]
    Anabel Q   *Servant*] *as* Weis; *not in* Q
117 our] Dyce 1; ours Q

125 *to Servant*] Weis; *not in* Q   *Exit Servant.*]
    as Weis; *not in* Q
132 in,] ~ₐ Q

311

Raymond.   Well advised.
    Nay Mrs. Bride, you shall along with us;
    For without you all's nothing.
Annabel.   Willingly,
    With Mr. Bridegrooms leave.
Bonvile.   Oh my best Joy,
    This day I am your servant.
Woodroff.   True, this day;
    She his, her whole life after, so it should be:
    Onely this day a Groom to do her service,
    For which the full remainder of his age   140
    He may write Master. I have done it yet,
    And so I hope still shall do. Sister *Luce*,
    May I presume my brother *Franckford* can
    Say as much, and truly?
Luce.   Sir, he may,
    I freely give him leave.
Woodroff.   Observe that, brother,
    She freely gives you leave; but who gives leave,   [B3ʳ]
    The Master or the servant?
Franckford.   You 'r pleasant,
    And it becomes you well, but this day most;
    That having but one Daughter, have bestowed her
    To your great hope and comfort.
Woodroff.   I have one: 150
    Would you could say so, Sister; but your barrenness
    Hath given your husband freedom, if he please,
    To seek his pastime elsewhere.
Luce.   Well, well brother,
    Though you may taunt me that have never yet
    Been blest with issue, spare my husband pray,
    For he may have a By-blow, or an Heir
    That you never heard of—
Franckford [*aside*].   Oh fie wife,
    Make not my fault too publick.
Luce.   —yet himself
    Keep within compass.

145 that,] ~ₐ Q
147 You 'r] You 're Dyce 1; You are Dyce 2
157 of—] ~. Q   SD] Hazlitt; *not in* Q
158 —yet] ₐYet Q

Franckford [aside].   If you love me, Sweet.
Luce.   Nay I have done.
Woodroff.   But if he have not, Wench,   160
    I would he had, the hurt I wish you both.
    [to Luce] Prithee, thine ear a little.   *[They speak apart.]*
Nurse [to Franckford].   Your boy grows up, and 'tis a chopping Lad,
    A man even in the Cradle.
Franckford.   Softly Nurse.
Nurse.   One of the forwardst infants, how it will crow
    And chirrup like a Sparrow! I fear shortly
    It will breed teeth, you must provide him therefore
    A Corral, with a Whistle and a Chain.
Franckford.   He shall have any thing.
Nurse.   He's now quite out of Blankets.
Franckford [giving coin].   There's a Piece,   170
    Provide him what he wants, onely good Nurse
    Prithee at this time be silent.
Nurse.   A Charm to binde
    Any Nurses tongue that's living.
Woodroff [coming forward with Luce].   Come, we are mist
    Among the younger Frye, Gravity oft-times
    Becomes the sports of youth, especially
    At such Solemnities, and it were sin
    Not in our Age to show what we have bin.   *Exeunt.*

                        [I.ii]

    Enter LESSINGHAM *sad, with a Letter in his hand [and a book].*
Lessingham.   *Amicitia nihil dedit natura majus nec rarius,*
    So saith my Author. If then powerful Nature
    In all her bounties showred upon mankinde,
    Found none more rare and precious than this one
    We call Friendship, oh to what a Monster
    Would this trans-shape me, to be made that he

---

159 SD] Hazlitt; *not in* Q
162 *to Luce]* Lucas; *not in* Q   *They speak*
    apart.] after Weis; *not in* Q
163 SD] Dyce 2; *not in* Q
164 Nurse.] ~: Q

170 SD] *after* Dyce 2; *not in* Q
173 SD] Weis; *not in* Q
I.ii] *as* Dyce 1; *not in* Q
0.1 *and a book]* This ed.; *not in* Q

To violate such goodness! To kill any
Had been a sad Injunction, but a Friend!
Nay, of all Friends the most approved! A Task,
Hell till this day could never parallel: 10
And yet this woman ha's a power of me
Beyond all vertue—vertue, almost grace.   [B3ᵛ]
What might her hidden purpose be in this?
Unless she apprehend some fantasie
That no such thing ha's being:—and as kinred
And claims to Crowns are worn out of the world,
So the name Friend? 'T may be 'twas her conceit.
I have tryed those that have professed much
For coin, nay sometimes slighter courtesies,
Yet found 'em cold enough,—so perhaps she,   20
Which makes her thus opinion'd.—If in the former,
And therefore better days, 'twas held so rare,
Who knows but in these last and worser times,
It may be now with justice banisht th' earth?
I 'm full of thoughts, and this my troubled brest
Distemper'd with a thousand fantasies.
Something I must resolve. I'le first make proof
If such a thing there be; which having found,
'Twixt Love and Friendship 'twill be a brave Fight,
To prove in man which claims the greatest right.   30
            Enter RAYMOND, EUSTACE, LYONEL, *and* GROVER.
Raymond. What, Master *Lessingham*!
You that were wont to be compos'd of mirth,
All spirit and fire—Alacrity it self,
Like the lustre of a late bright shining Sun,
Now wrapt in clouds and darkness!
Lyonel.   Prithee be merry,
Thy dulness sads the half part of the house,
And deads that spirit which thou wast wont to quicken,
And, half spent, to give Life too.
Lessingham.   Gentlemen,
Such as have cause for sport, I shall wish ever
To make of it the present benefit   40

12 vertue—] ~, Q   26 fantasies.] ~, Q
19 coin,] ~; Q   33 fire—] ~ —. Q
24 earth?] ~. Q   38 And,] ~ₐ Q spent,] ~ₐ Q

314

While it exists.—Content is still short breathed,
When it was mine I did so. If now yours,
I pray make your best use on't.
Lyonel.   Riddles and Paradoxes:
Come, come, some Crotchet's come into thy pate,
And I will know the cause on't.
Grover.   So will I,
Or I protest ne're leave thee.
Lessingham.   'Tis a business
Proper to my self,—one that concerns
No second person.
Grover.   How's that? Not a friend?
Lessingham.   Why, is there any such?
Grover.   Do you question that? What do you take me for?   50
Eustace.   I Sir, or me? 'Tis many moneths ago
Since we betwixt us interchang'd that name,   [B4^r]
And of my part ne're broken.
Lyonel.   Troth, nor mine.
Raymond.   If you make question of a Friend, I pray
Number not me the last in your accompt,
That would be crown'd in your opinion first.
Lessingham.   You all speak nobly. But amongst you all
Can such a one be found?
Raymond.   Not one amongst us,
But would be proud to wear the character
Of noble Friendship. In the name of which,   60
And of all us here present, I intreat,
Expose to us the grief that troubles you.
Lessingham.   I shall, and briefly: If ever Gentleman
Sunk beneath scandal, or his reputation,
Never to be recovered, suffered, and
For want of one whom I may call a Friend,
Then mine is now in danger.
Raymond.   I'le redeem't,
Though with my lifes dear hazard.
Eustace.   I pray Sir,
Be to us open-breasted.

44 Crochet's] as Dyce 1; Crochets Q   64 reputation,] ~∧ Q
46 SP] as Dyce 1; Eust. Q

315

Lessingham. Then 'tis thus: 70
    There is to be performed a Monomachy,
    Combat, or Duel—Time, Place, and Weapon
    Agreed betwixt us. Had it toucht my self,
    And my self onely, I had then been happy;
    But I by composition am engag'd
    To bring with me my Second, and he too,
    Not as the Law of Combat is, to stand
    Aloof and see fair play, bring off his friend,
    But to engage his person; both must fight,
    And either of them dangerous.
Eustace. Of all things,
    I do not like this fighting.
Lessingham. Now Gentlemen, 80
    Of this so great a courtesie I am
    At this instant meerly destitute.
Raymond. The time?
Lessingham. By eight a clock to morrow.
Raymond. How unhappily
    Things may fall out! I am just at that hour
    Upon some late conceived Discontents,
    To atone me to my father, otherwise
    Of all the rest you had commanded me
    Your Second, and your Servant.
Lyonel. Pray, the Place?
Lessingham. Callis-Sands. 90
Lyonel. It once was fatal to a friend of mine,
    And a near kinsman, for which I vowed then,
    And deeply too, never to see that ground:
    But if it had been elsewhere, one of them
    Had before nine been worms-meat.
Grover. What's the weapon?
Lessingham. Single-sword.
Grover. Of all that you could name,
    A thing I never practis'd,—Had it been [B4ᵛ]
    Rapier—or that and Ponyard, where men use

70 Monomachy,] *as* Dyce 1; Monamachy- Q   89 Pray,] ~ₐ Q
71 Duel—] ~, Q   95 nine] Dyce 1; mine Q
82 time?] ~. Q   98 that̠] ~, Q
84 out!] ~, Q

Rather sleight than force, I had been then your Man;
Being young, I strained the sinews of my arm,   100
Since then to me 'twas never serviceable.

Eustace.   In troth Sir, had it been a money-matter,
I could have stood your friend, but as for fighting
I was ever out at that.

Lessingham.   Well, farewel Gentlemen.   *Exeunt Gallants.*
But where's the Friend in all this? Tush, she's wise,
And knows there's no such thing beneath the moon:
I now applaud her judgement.

                              Enter Bonvile.

Bonvile.   Why how now friend, this Discontent which now
Is so unseason'd, makes me question what
I ne're durst doubt before, your Love to me;   110
Doth it proceed from Envy of my Bliss
Which this day crowns me with? Or have you been
A secret Rival in my happiness,
And grieve to see me owner of those Joys,
Which you could wish your own?

Lessingham.   Banish such thoughts,
Or you shall wrong the truest faithful Friendship
Man e're could boast of. Oh mine honor, Sir,
'Tis that which makes me wear this brow of sorrow:
Were that free from the power of Calumny—
But pardon me, that being now a dying   120
Which is so near to man, if part we cannot
With pleasant looks.

Bonvile.   Do but speak the burthen,
And I protest to take it off from you,
And lay it on my self.

Lessingham.   'Twere a request,
Impudence without blushing could not ask,
It bears with it such injury.

Bonvile.   Yet must I know't.

Lessingham.   Receive it then.—But I intreat you sir,

103 fighting] Dyce 1; sighting Q   110 me;] ~, Q
104 Gentlemen.] ~, Q   SD] *placed as* Dyce   113 happiness,] ~? Q
       1; *to right of* that. Q   117 of.] ~, Q
107.1 SD] *placed as* Dyce 1; *in a box to right of* 119 Calumny—] ~. Q
       lines 104–6 Q

317

Not to imagine that I apprehend
A thought to further my intent by you,
From you 'tis least suspected.—'Twas my fortune   130
To entertain a Quarrel with a Gentleman,
The Field betwixt us challeng'd,—place and time,
And these to be performed not without Seconds.
I have rely'd on many seeming friends,
But cannot bless my memory with one   [C1ʳ]
Dares venter in my Quarrel.

Bonvile.   Is this all?

Lessingham.   It is enough to make all temperature
Convert to fury.—Sir, my Reputation
(The life and soul of Honor) is at stake,
In danger to be lost—the word of *Coward*   140
Still printed in the name of *Lessingham.*

Bonvile.   Not while there is a *Bonvile.*—May I live poor,
And die despised, not having one sad friend
To wait upon my Hearse, if I survive
The ruine of that Honor.—Sir, the time?

Lessingham.   Above all spare me that—for that once known,
You'l cancel this your promise, and unsay
Your friendly proffer.—Neither can I blame you;
Had you confirmed it with a thousand Oathes,
The Heavens would look with mercy, not with justice   150
On your offence, should you enfringe 'em all.
Soon after Sun-rise upon *Callis-sands,*
To morrow we should meet—now, to deferre
Time one half hour, I should but forfeit all.
But Sir, of all men living, this alas
Concerns you least;—For shall I be the man
To rob you of this nights felicity,
And make your Bride a Widow,—her soft bed
No witness of those joys this night expects?

Bonvile.   I still preferre my friend before my pleasure,   160
Which is not lost for ever—but adjourned
For more mature employment.

Lessingham.   Will you go then?

Bonvile.   I am resolved I will.
Lessingham.   And instantly?
Bonvile.   With all the speed celerity can make.
Lessingham.   You do not weigh those inconveniences
    This Action meets with.—Your departure hence
    Will breed a strange distraction in your friends,
    Distrust of Love in your fair vertuous Bride,
    Whose eyes perhaps may never more be blest
    With your dear sight: since you may meet a grave,   170
    And that not amongst your noble Ancestors,
    But amongst strangers, almost enemies.
Bonvile.   This were enough to shake a weak resolve,
    It moves not me. Take horse as secretly
    As you well may: my Groom shall make mine ready   [C1ᵛ]
    With all speed possible, unknown to any.
                 Enter ANNABEL.
Lessingham.   But Sir, the Bride.
Annabel.   Did you not see the Key that's to unlock
    My Carckanet and Bracelets? Now in troth
    I am afraid 'tis lost.
Bonvile.   No Sweet, I ha't: 180
    I found it lye at random in your Chamber,
    And knowing you would miss it, laid it by:
    'Tis safe I warrant you.
Annabel.   Then my fear's past:
    But till you give it back, my Neck and Arms
    Are still your Prisoners.
Bonvile.   But you shall finde
    They have a gentle Jaylor.
Annabel.   So I hope.
    Within y'are much enquired of.
Bonvile.   Sweet, I follow.   [*Exit Annabel.*]
    Dover?
Lessingham.   Yes, that's the place.
Bonvile.   If you be there before me, hire a Barque,   190
    I shall not fail to meet you.   *Exit.*
Lessingham.   Was ever known

---

164 the speed] thespeed Q   **187** SD] Dyce 1; *not in* Q
173 *Bonvile.*] *Bon,* Q   **191** SD] Dyce 1; *Exeunt.* Q

A man so miserably blest as I?
I have no sooner found the greatest good,
Man in this pilgrimage of Life can meet,
But I must make the womb where 'twas conceived,
The Tomb to bury it, and the first hour it lives,
The last it must breath! Yet there's a Fate
That sways and governs above womans hate.   *Exit.*
                    Explicit. Act. 1.

                    Actus secundus. Scena prima. [II.i]

                    Enter ROCHFIELD *a young Gentleman.*
Rochfield.   A Younger Brother! 'Tis a poor Calling
    (Though not unlawful) very hard to live on;
    The elder fool inherits all the Lands,
    And we that follow, Legacies of Wit,
    And get 'em when we can too. Why should Law
    (If we be lawful and legitimate)
    Leave us without an equal divident?
    Or why compels it not our Fathers else
    To cease from getting, when they want to give?
    No sure, our Mothers will ne're agree to that,   10
    They love to groan, although the Gallows eccho
    And groan together for us. From the first
    We travel forth, t'other's our journeys end.
    I must forward, to beg is out of my way,
    And borrowing is out of date: The old road,   [C2ʳ]
    The old high-way 't must be, and I am in't,
    The place will serve for a yong beginner,
    For this is the first day I set ope shop;
    Success then sweet *Laverna*, I have heard
    That Thieves adore thee for a Deity.   20
    I would not purchase by thee, but to eat,
    And 'tis too churlish to deny me meat.
                    Enter ANNABEL *and a Servant.*
    Soft, here may be a booty.   [*He stands apart.*]

---

193 have] Dyce 1; have have Q   **22.1** SD] *to right of lines 20–1* Q   *Servant*]
4 follow,] ~ₐ Q   *servant* Q

Annabel.   Hors'd, sayest thou?
Servant.   Yes Mistriss, with *Lessingham.*
Annabel.   Alack, I know not what to doubt or fear,
     I know not well whether't be well or ill:
     But sure it is no custom for the Groom
     To leave his Bride upon the Nuptial day.
     I am so yong and ignorant a Scholar,
     Yes, and it proves so: I talk away perhaps   30
     That might be yet recovered. Prithee run,
     The fore-path may advantage thee to meet 'em,
     Or the Ferry which is not two miles before,
     May trouble 'em until thou comest in ken,
     And if thou dost, prithee enforce thy voice
     To overtake thine eyes, cry out, and crave
     For me but one word 'fore his departure.
     I will not stay him, say, beyond his pleasure;
     Nor rudely ask the cause, if he be willing
     To keep it from me. Charge him by all the love—   40
     But I stay thee too long. Run, run.
Servant.   If I had wings I would spread 'em now, Mistriss.   *Exit.*
Annabel.   Ile make the best speed after that I can,
     Yet I am not well acquainted with the path:
     My fears I fear me will misguide me too.   *Exit.*
Rochfield [*coming forward*].   There's good moveables I perceive, what ere
     the ready Coin be; who ever owns her, she's mine now: the next
     ground has a most pregnant hollow for the purpose.   *Exit.*

                          [II.ii]

     Enter Servant running over [*and exit*]. *Enter* ANNABEL, *after her* ROCHFIELD.
Annabel.   I'm at a doubt already where I am.
Rochfield.   Ile help you, Mistriss, well overtaken.
Annabel.   Defend me goodness! What are you?
Rochfield.   A man.
Annabel.   An honest man, I hope.

23 SD] This ed.; *not in* Q; *He hides* Weis   **II.ii**] *as* Dyce 1; *not in* Q
40 love—] ~. Q   0.1 *and exit*] Dyce 2; *not in* Q
46 SD] Weis; *not in* Q   3 goodness!] ~. Q
47 be;] ~, Q

Rochfield.   In some degrees hot, not altogether cold,
  So far as rank poison, yet dangerous
  As I may be drest: I am an honest thief.
Annabel.   Honest and Thief hold small affinity,
  I never heard they were a kin before,
  Pray Heaven I finde it now!
Rochfield.   I tell you my name.   [C2ᵛ]
Annabel.   Then honest thief, since you have taught me so,   11
  For Ile enquire no other, use me honestly.
Rochfield.   Thus then Ile use you: First then to prove me honest,
  I will not violate your Chastity,
  (That's no part yet of my profession)
  Be you Wife or Virgin.
Annabel.   I am both, Sir.
Rochfield.   This then it seems should be your Wedding-day,
  And these the hours of interim to keep you
  In that double state. Come then, Ile be brief,
  For Ile not hinder your desired *Hymen*:   20
  You have about you some superfluous Toys,
  Which my lanck hungry pockets would containe
  With much more profit, and more privacy;
  You have an idle Chain which keeps your Neck
  A Prisoner, a Mannacle I take it,
  About your wrist too. If these prove Emblems
  Of the combined Hemp to halter mine,
  The Fates take their pleasure! These are set down
  To be your Ransom, and there the Thief is proved.
Annabel.   I will confess both, and the last forget;   30
  You shall be onely honest in this deed.
  Pray you take it, I intreat you to it,
  And then you steal 'em not.
Rochfield.   You may deliver 'em.
Annabel.   Indeed I cannot:
  If you observe, Sir, they are both lock'd about me,
  And the Key I have not; happily you are furnisht
  With some instrument, that may unloose 'em.
Rochfield.   No in troth, Lady, I am but a Fresh-man,

---

10 now!] ~. Q   28 pleasure!] ~, Q
22 containe] *as* Dyce 2; contrive Q

I never read further than this Book you see,   [*He draws his sword.*]
And this very day is my beginning too: 40
These picking Laws I am to study yet.
Annabel.   Oh, do not show me that, Sir, 'tis too frightful:
Good, hurt me not, for I do yield 'em freely:
Use but your hands, perhaps their strength will serve
To tear 'em from me without much detriment,
Somewhat I will endure.
Rochfield [*sheathing his sword*]. Well, sweet Lady,
Y' are the best Patient for a young Physician,
That I think e're was practis'd on. Ile use you
As gently as I can, as I'm an honest Thief.

                              [*He tries to force off the carcanet.*]
No? Wil't not do? Do I hurt you, Lady?
Annabel.   Not much, Sir.   50
Rochfield.   I'd be loath at all, I cannot do't.   *She draws his sword.*
Annabel.   Nay then you shall not, Sir. You a Thief,   [C3^r]
And guard your self no better? No further read?
Yet out in your own book? A bad Clerk, are you not?
Rochfield.   I, by Saint *Nicholas*, Lady, sweet Lady.
Annabel.   Sir, I have now a Masculine vigor,
And will redeem my self with purchase too.
What money have you?
Rochfield.   Not a cross, by this foolish hand of mine.
Annabel.   No money. 'Twere pity then to take this from thee: 60
I know thou'lt use me ne're the worse for this,
Take it agen, I know not how to use it: [*She returns his sword.*]
A frown had taken't from me, which thou hadst not.   [*She kneels.*]
And now hear and believe me, on my knees
I make the Protestation: Forbear
To take what violence and danger must
Dissolve, if I forgo 'em now; I do assure
You would not strike my head off for my Chain,
Nor my hand for this, how to deliver 'em

---

39 SD] Lucas (*to right of line 41*); *not in* Q
46 SD] *after* Lucas; *not in* Q
49.1 SD *after* Lucas (*bracelet*); *not in* Q
50 Wil't] Dyce 1; Wilt Q
55 I,] ~$_\wedge$ Q

62 SD] *after* Weis (*at line 61.1*); *not in* Q
63 SD] *after* Weis (*at line 64 after* believe me,);
    not in Q
65 Protestation:] ~, Q
67 now;] ~, Q

Otherwise I know not. Accompany
Me back unto my house, 'tis not far off;
By all the Vows which this day I have tyed
Unto my wedded husband, the honor
Yet equal with my Cradle puritie
(If you will tax me), to the hoped joys,
The blessings of the bed, posterity,
Or what ought else by woman may be pledg'd,
I will deliver you in ready Coin,
The full and dearest esteem of what you crave.

Rochfield. Ha! Ready money is the prize I look for,
It walks without suspition any where,
When Chains and Jewels may be stayed and call'd
Before the Constable: But—

Annabel [*rising*]. But? Can you doubt?
You saw I gave you my advantage up:
Did you e're think a woman to be true?

Rochfield. Thought's free. I have heard of some few, Lady,
Very few indeed.

Annabel. Will you adde one more to your belief?

Rochfield. They were fewer than the Articles of my Belief;
Therefore I have room for you, and will believe you.
Stay: you'l ransom your Jewels with ready Coin,
So may you do, and then discover me.

Annabel. Shall I reiterate the Vows I made
To this injunction, or new ones coyn?

Rochfield. Neither, Ile trust you: if you do destroy
A Thief that never yet did Robbery,
Then farewel I, and mercy fall upon me.
I knew one once fifteen years Courtier, owld,
And he was buried e're he took a Bribe:
It may be my case in the worser way.
Come, you know your path back?

Annabel. Yes, I shall guide you.

Rochfield. Your arm, Ile lead with greater dread than will,
Nor do you fear, tho in thiefs handling still. *Exeunt.*

70 not.] ~; Q
71 off;] ~, Q
75 me),] ~)ᴧ Q   joys,] ~ᴧ Q
80 Ha!] ~, Q

83 But—] ~, Q   SD] Weis; *not in* Q
97 owld] Lucas; owl'd Q; old Dyce 1
100 back?] ~. Q

[II.iii]

Enter two Boys, [RAFE, *and* JACK] *with a childe in his arms.*

Rafe.   I say 'twas fair play.

Jack.   To snatch up stakes! I say you should not say so, if the childe were
out of mine arms.

Rafe.   I, then thou'dst lay about like a man, but the childe will not be out
of thine arms this five years, and then thou hast a prentiship to serve to
a boy afterwards.

Jack.   So sir, you know you have the advantage of me.

Rafe.   I'm sure you have the odds of me, you are two to one.

Enter COMPASS. [*Boys stand apart.*]

But soft, *Jack*, who comes here? If a Point will make us friends, we'l
not fall out.   10

Jack.   Oh the pity, 'tis Gaffer *Compass*! They said he was dead three years
ago.

Rafe.   Did not he dance the *Hobby-horse* in *Hackney*-Morrice once?

Jack.   Yes, yes, at *Green-goose Fayr*, as honest and as poor a man.

Compass [*weeping*].   *Black-wall*, sweet *Black-wall*, do I see thy white
cheeks again? I have brought some Brine from sea for thee: tears that
might be tyed in a True-love Knot, for they'r fresh salt indeed. Oh
beautiful *Black-wall*! If *Urse* my wife be living to this day, though she
die to morrow, sweet Fates!

Jack.   Alas, let's put him out of his dumps for pity sake: [*coming forward*]   20
Welcome home, Gaffer *Compass*, welcome home, Gaffer.

Compass.   My pretty youths, I thank you. Honest *Jack*! What a little man
art thou grown since I saw thee! Thou hast got a child since, methinks.

Jack.   I am fain to keep it, you see, whosoever got it, Gaffer: it may be
another mans case as well as mine.

Compass.   Say'st true, *Jack*: and whose pretty knave is it?

Jack.   One that I mean to make a younger brother if he live to't, Gaffer.
But I can tell you news: You have a brave Boy of your own wifes: oh tis
a shot to this pig.

II.iii] *as* Dyce 1; *not in* Q
0.1 RAFE, *and* JACK] *after* Weis; *one* Q
1 *Rafe*] *as* Weis; *1 Boy* Q (*so to end of scene*)
2 *Jack*] *as* Weis; *2 Boy* Q (*so to end of scene*)
2 stakes!] ~: Q
4 I,] ~∧ Q

8.1 *Enter* COMPASS.] *placed as* Dyce 1; *to right of line 6* Q
8.1 *Boys stand apart.*] This ed.; *not in* Q
9 soft,] ~∧ Q
15 SD] This ed.; *not in* Q
20 SD] This ed.; *not in* Q

Compass.   Have I *Jack*? Ile ow thee a dozen of Points for this news.   30

Jack.   Oh 'tis a chopping Boy! It cannot chuse you know, Gaffer, it was   [C4ʳ]
so long a breeding.

Compass.   How long, *Jack*?

Jack.   You know 'tis four year ago since you went to sea, and your childe
is but a Quarter old yet.

Compass [*aside*].   What plaguy boys are bred now adays!

Rafe.   Pray Gaffer, how long may a childe be breeding before 'tis born?

Compass.   That is as things are and prove, childe; the soyl has a great
hand in't too, the Horizon, and the Clime; these things you'l understand when you go to sea. In some parts of *London* hard by, you shall   40
have a Bride married to day, and brought to Bed within a moneth
after, sometimes within three weeks, a fortnight.

Rafe.   Oh horrible!

Compass.   True as I tell you Lads: in another place you shall have a
couple of Drones, do what they can, shift Lodgings, Beds, Bed-
fellows, yet not a childe in ten years.

Jack.   Oh pitiful!

Compass.   Now it varies agen by that time you come at *Wapping*,
Radcliff, *Lymehouse*, and here with us at *Black-wall*, our children come
uncertainly, as the winde serves: sometimes here we are supposed to be   50
away three or four year together, 'tis nothing so; we are at home and
gone agen, when no body knows on't: if you'l believe me, I have been
at *Surrat* as this day, I have taken the Long-boat (a fair Gale with me),
been here a bed with my wife by twelve a Clock at night, up and gone
agen i'th morning and no man the wiser, if you'l believe me.

Jack.   Yes, yes Gaffer, I have thought so many times, that you or some
body else have been at home; I lye at next wall, and I have heard a
noise in your chamber all night long.

Compass.   Right, why that was I, yet thou never sawst me.

Jack.   No indeed, Gaffer.   60

Compass.   No, I warrant thee, I was a thousand leagues off e're thou
wert up. But *Jack*, I have been loath to ask all this while for discomforting my self, how does my wife? Is she living?

Jack.   Oh never better, Gaffer, never so lusty, and truly she wears better

---

30 news.] ~∧ Q

36 SD] This ed.; *not in* Q

39 Clime] Dyce 1; Cilme Q

43 horrible!] ~. Q

47 pitiful!] ~. Q

49 children] Dyce 1; chilrden Q

53 me),] me)∧ Q

56 times,] ~∧ Q

57 home;] ~, Q

clothes than she was wont in your days, especially on Holidays, fair
Gowns, brave Petticoats, and fine Smocks, they say that have seen 'em;
and some of the neighbors reports that they were taken up at *London*.   [C4ᵛ]

Compass.   Like enough: they must be paid for, *Jack.*

Jack.   And good reason, Gaffer.

Compass.   Well *Jack*, thou shalt have the honor on't, go tell my wife the   70
joyful tidings of my return.

Jack.   That I will, for she heard you were dead long ago.   *Exit.*

Rafe [*to Jack*].   Nay sir, Ile be as forward as you, by your leave.   *Exit.*

Compass.   Well wife, if I be one of the Livery, I thank thee, the Horners
are a great Company, there may be an Alderman amongst us one day,
'tis but changing our Copy, and then we are no more to be called by
our old Brother-hood.

Enter Compass his wife [U<small>RSE</small>].

Urse.   Oh my sweet *Compass*, art thou come agen?

Compass [*weeping*].   Oh *Urse*, give me leave to shed, the fountains of
Love will have their course; though I cannot sing at first sight, yet I can   80
cry before I see. I am new come into the world, and children cry
before they laugh, a fair while.

Urse.   And so thou art, sweet *Compass*, new born indeed;
For Rumor laid thee out for dead long since,
I never thought to see this face agen.
I heard thou wert div'd to th' bottom of the sea,
And taken up a Lodging in the Sands,
Never to come to *Black-wall* agen.

Compass.   I was going indeed wife, but I turn'd back: I heard an ill
report of my neighbors, Sharks and Sword-fishes, and the like, whose   90
companies I did not like: come kiss my tears now sweet *Urse*, sorrow
begins to ebb.

Urse.   A thousand times welcome home, sweet *Compass*. [*They embrace.*]

Compass.   An Ocean of thanks, and that will hold 'em: and *Urse*, how
goes all at home? Or cannot all go yet? Lanck still? Will 't never be full
Sea at our Wharf?

Urse.   Alas, husband.

Compass.   A lass or a lad, wench, I should be glad of both: I did look for
a pair of Compasses before this day.

68 *Jack.*] ~: Q

72 *Exit.*] ~ₐ Q

73 SD] This ed.; *not in* Q

77.1 U<small>RSE</small>] Dyce 2 (*Enter* U<small>RSE</small>.); *not in* Q

78 *Urse.*] Dyce 2; *Wife.* Q (*so to end of scene*)

79 SD] This ed.; *not in* Q   fountains] Dyce
1; fountain Q

93 SD] This ed.; *not in* Q

Urse. And you from home? 100

Compass. I from home? Why though I be from home, and other of our neighbors from home, it is not fit all should be from home, so the town might be left desolate, and our neighbors of *Bowe* might come further from the *Hams*, and inhabit here.

Urse. I'm glad y'are merry, sweet husband. [D1ʳ]

Compass. Merry? Nay, Ile be merrier yet, why should I be sorry? I hope my boy 's well, is he not? I lookt for another by this time.

Urse. What boy, husband?

Compass. What boy? Why the boy I got when I came home in the Cock-boat one night, about a year ago! You have not forgotten't, I 110 hope? I think I left behinde for a boy, and a boy I must be answer'd: I'm sure I was not drunk, it could be no girl.

Urse. Nay then I do perceive my fault is known.
Dear man, your pardon.

Compass. Pardon! Why thou hast not made away my boy, hast thou? Ile hang thee if there were ne're a whore in *London* more, if thou hast hurt but his little toe.

Urse. Your long absence, with rumor of your death,
After long battery I was surprized.

Compass. Surprized? I cannot blame thee: *Black-wall*, if it were double 120 black-walled, can't hold out always, no more than *Lymehouse*, or *Shadwell*, or the strongest Suburbs about *London*, and when it comes to that, woe be to the City too.

Urse. Pursued by gifts and promises I yielded:
Consider husband, I am a woman,
Neither the first nor last of such Offenders,
'Tis true, I have a childe.

Compass. Ha' you? And what shall I have then I pray? Will not you labor for me as I shall do for you? Because I was out o'th way when 'twas gotten, shall I loose my share? There's better Law amongst the 130 Players yet; for a fellow shall have his share though he do not play that day: if you look for any part of my four Years wages, I will have half the boy.

Urse. If you can forgive me, I shall be joyed at it.

---

104 *Hams*] Hams Qb; *Itacus* Qa
115 Pardon!] ~. Q
121 *Lymehouse*] *Lyme- | house* Q (*hyphen at end of line*)

128 Ha'] Dyce 1; ~, Q
132 four] Dyce 1; fours Q; foure Lucas

Compass.   Forgive thee, for what? For doing me a pleasure? And what is
   he that would seem to father my childe?
Urse.   A man sir, whom in better courtesies
      We have been beholding too: the Merchant, Mr. *Franckford.*
Compass.   Ile acknowledge no other courtesies: for this I am beholding
   to him, and I would requite it if his wife were young enough. Though   140
   he be one of our Merchants at Sea, he shall give me leave to be Owner
   at home. And where 's my boy? Shall I see him?
Urse.   He's nurst at *Bednal-green*: 'tis now too late,   [D1ᵛ]
      To morrow Ile bring you to it, if you please.
Compass.   I would thou couldst bring me another by to morrow. Come,
   we'l eat and to bed, and if a fair Gale come, we'l hoist sheets, and set
   forwards.
      Let fainting fools lie sick upon their scorns,
      Ile teach a Cuckold how to hide his horns.   *Exeunt.*

[II.iv]

Enter WOODROFF, FRANCKFORD, RAYMOND, EUSTACE, GROVER,
               LYONEL, CLARE, LUCE.
Woodroff.   This wants a president, that a Bridegroom
      Should so discreet and decently observe
      His Forms, Postures, all customary Rites
      Belonging to the Table, and then hide himself
      From his expected wages in the bed.
Franckford.   Let this be forgotten too, that it remain not
      A first example.
Raymond [*aside to other Gallants*].
                   Keep it amongst us,
      Lest it beget too much unfruitful sorrow:
      Most likely 'tis that love to *Lessingham*
      Hath fastened that on him, we all denied.   10
Eustace [*aside*].   'Tis more certain than likely. I know 'tis so.
Grover [*aside*].   Conceal it then: the event may be well enough.
Woodroff.   The Bride my daughter, she's hidden too:
      This last hour she hath not been seen with us.

II.iv] *as* Dyce 1; *not in* Q
6 remain] Dyce 2; remains Q
7 SD] *after* Lucas; *not in* Q; *aside* Lucas

10 that] Lucas; *not in* Q
11 SD] Lucas; *not in* Q
12 SD] Lucas; *not in* Q   it] Lucas; *not in* Q

Raymond. Perhaps they are together.

Eustace. And then we make too strict an inquisition;
Under correction of fair modesty,
Should they be stoln away to bed together,
What would you say to that?

Woodroff. I would say, Speed 'em well, 20
And if no worse news comes, Ile never weep for't.

Enter Nurse.

How now, hast thou any tidings?

Nurse. Yes forsooth, I have tidings.

Woodroff. Of any one that's lost?

Nurse. Of one that's found agen, forsooth.

Woodroff. Oh, he was lost, it seems then?

Franckford. This tidings comes to me, I guess Sir.

Nurse. Yes truly does it, sir. [*They speak apart.*]

Raymond. I, has old Lads work for young Nurses?

Eustace. Yes, when they groan towards their second infancy.

Clare [*aside*]. I fear my self most guilty for the absence 30
Of the Bridegroom: what our wills will do [D2ʳ]
With over rash and headlong peevishness,
To bring our calm discretions to repentance!
Lessingham's mistaken, quite out o'th way
Of my purpose too.

Franckford [*to Nurse*]. Return'd?

Nurse. And all discover'd.

Franckford. A fool! Rid him further off. Let him not come near the
child.

Nurse. Nor see't, if it be your charge. 40

Franckford. It is, and strictly.

Nurse. To morrow morning, as I hear, he purposeth to come to *Bednal-green*, his wife with him.

Franckford. He shall be met there; yet if he fore-stall my coming, keep
the childe safe.

Nurse. If he be the earlier up, he shall arive at the proverb. *Exit Nurse.*

---

16 inquisition;] ~, Q
20.1 SD] *placed as Dyce 1; to right of line 19* Q
27 SD] *after* Weis; *not in* Q; *They whisper together.* Lucas
30 SD] Dyce 2; *not in* Q

31 Bridegroom] Bride- | groom Q (*hyphen at end of line and page*)
36 SD] This ed.; *not in* Q
38 fool!] ~ₐ Q

Enter ROCHFIELD *and* ANNABEL.

Woodroff.   So, so,
　　There's some good luck yet, the Bride 's in sight agen.
Annabel.   Father, and Gentlemen all, beseech you
　　Entreat this Gentleman with all courtesie,   50
　　He is a loving kinsman of my *Bonviles*,
　　That kindly came to gratulate our Wedding;
　　But as the day falls out, you see alone
　　I personate both Groom and Bride;
　　Onely your help to make this welcome better.
Woodroff.   Most dearly.
Raymond.　　　　　　　To all, assure you sir.
Woodroff.   But where's the Bridegroom, Girl?
　　We are all at a *non-plus* here, at a stand, quite out,
　　The Musick ceased, and dancing surbated,
　　Not a light heel amongst us; my Cousin *Clare* too   60
　　As cloudy here as on a washing-day.
Clare.   It is because you will not dance with me,
　　I should then shake it off.
Annabel.　　　　　　　'Tis I have cause
　　To be the sad one now, if any be:
　　But I have question'd with my meditations,
　　And they have rend'red well and comfortably
　　To the worst fear I found: Suppose this day
　　He had long since appointed to his foe
　　To meet, and fetch a Reputation from him
　　(Which is the dearest Jewel unto man.)   70
　　Say he do fight, I know his goodness such,
　　That all those Powers that love it are his guard,
　　And ill cannot betide him.
Woodroff.　　　　　　　Prithee peace,
　　Thou'lt make us all Cowards to hear a woman
　　Instruct so valiantly. Come, the Musick,
　　Ile dance my self rather than thus put down,
　　What, I can rise a little yet.
Annabel.　　　　　　　Onely this Gentleman   [D2ᵛ]
　　Pray you be free in welcome too, I tell you
　　I was in a fear when first I saw him.

77 can rise] *conj.* Lucas; am rife Q　　　79 SD] Dyce 2; *not in* Q
　Gentlemanₐ] ~, Q

331

Rochfield [*aside*].   Ha! She'l tell.

Annabel.   I had quite lost my way   80
    In my first amazement, but he so fairly came
    To my recovery, in his kinde conduct,
    Gave me such loving comforts to my fears
    ('Twas he instructed me in what I spake)
    And many better than I have told you yet;
    You shall hear more anon.

Rochfield [*aside*].   So, she will out with 't.

Annabel.   I must, I see, supply both places still:
    [*to the guests*] Come, when I have seen you back to your pleasure,
    [*to Rochfield*] I will return to you, Sir: we must discourse
    More of my *Bonvile* yet.

Omnes.   A noble Bride, 'faith.   90

Clare [*aside*].   You have your wishes, and you may be merry,
    Mine have over-gone me.   *Exeunt. Manet Rochfield solus.*

Rochfield.   It is the tremblingst trade to be a Thief,
    H'ad need have all the world bound to the peace;
    Besides the bushes, and the phanes of houses,
    Every thing that moves he goes in fear of 's life on.
    A furr-gown'd Cat, and meet her in the night,
    She stares with a Constables eye upon him;
    And every Dog, a Watch-man; a black Cowe
    And a Calf with a white face after her,   100
    Shows like a surly Justice and his Clerk;
    And if the Baby go but to the bag,
    'Tis ink and paper for a *Mittimus*:
    Sure I shall never thrive on't, and it may be
    I shall need take no care, I may be now
    At my journeys end, or but the Goals distance,
    And so to'th t' other place: I trust a woman
    With a secret worth a hanging, is that well?
    I could finde in my heart to run away yet.
    And that were base too, to run from a woman;   110

83 fears∧] ~: Q
85 yet;] ~, Q
86 SD] Dyce 2; *not in* Q
88 SD] This ed.; *not in* Q
89 SD] This ed.; *not in* Q

90 Bride,] ~∧ Q
91 SD] Lucas; *not in* Q
92 *Manet*] Hazlitt; *Manent* Q
94 peace;] ~, Q
95 houses,] ~; Q

I can lay claim to nothing but her Vows,
And they shall strengthen me.

                Enter ANNABEL [*with money*].

Annabel.   See sir, my promise,
There's twenty Pieces, the full value I vow,
Of what they cost.

Rochfield.   Lady, do not trap me
Like a Sumpter-horse, and then spur-gall me
Till I break my winde: if the Constable
Be at the door, let his fair staff appear,
Perhaps I may corrupt him with this Gold.

Annabel.   Nay then, if you mistrust me: [*calling*] Father, Gentlemen,
Mr. *Raymond, Eustace*!   120

      Enter all as before [WOODROFF, FRANCKFORD, RAYMOND, EUSTACE,
          GROVER, LYONEL, CLARE, LUCE], *and a Saylor.*

Woodroff.   How now, what's the matter, Girl?   [D3ʳ]

Annabel.   For shame, will you bid your Kinsman welcome?
No one but I will lay a hand on him.
Leave him alone, and all a revelling!

Woodroff.   Oh, is that it? [*to Rochfield*] Welcome, welcome heartily. I
thought the Bridegroom had been return'd. But I have news, *Annabel*:
this fellow [*indicating the Sailor*] brought it. [*to Rochfield, shaking his
hand*] Welcome Sir. Why you tremble methinks, Sir.

Annabel.   Some agony of anger 'tis, believe it,
His entertainment is so cold and feeble.   130

Raymond.   Pray be cheer'd, Sir.

Rochfield.   I'm wondrous well, sir, 'twas the Gentlemans mistake.

Woodroff.   'Twas my hand shook belike, then you must pardon Age, I
was stiffer once. But as I was saying, I should by promise see the Sea to
morrow, 'tis meant for Physick, as low as *Lee* or *Margets*: I have a Vessel
riding forth, Gentlemen, 'tis called the *God-speed* too; though I say't, a
brave one, well and richly fraughted; and I can tell you she carries a

---

112 *with money*] This ed.; *not in* Q
119 Nay then,] ~? ~ₐ Q   SD] This ed.; *not
in* Q
120 *Eustace*!] ~. Q
120.1–.2 SD] *placed as* Dyce 1; *to right of lines
119–20* Q WOODROFF . . . LUCE] *as* Weis;
not in Q;
122 shame,] ~ₐ Q welcome?] ~: Q
123 him.] ~, Q

124 revelling!] ~. Q
125 it?] ~. Q SD] This ed.; *not in* Q; Greets
   Rochfield Weis heartily.] ~, Q
127 *indicating the Sailor*] This ed.; *not in* Q
127–8 *to Rochfield, shaking his hand*] This ed.;
  not in Q
128 Sir. Why] ~, why Q
135 Physick,] ~ₐ Q
136 too;] ~, Q

Letter of Mart in her mouth too, and twenty roaring Boys on both sides on her, Star-board and Lar-board. What say you now, to make you all Adventurers? You shall have fair dealing, that Ile promise you. 140

Raymond [giving money]. A very good motion; sir I begin, there's my ten pieces.

Eustace [giving money]. I second 'em with these.

Grover [giving money]. My ten in the third place.

Rochfield [giving money]. And Sir, if you refuse not a proffer'd love, take my ten Pieces with you too.

Woodroff. Yours, above all the rest, Sir.

Annabel. Then make 'em above, venter ten more.

Rochfield. Alas Lady, 'tis a younger brothers portion, and all in one Bottom. 150

Annabel. At my encouragement, Sir, your credit (if you want, Sir) shall not sit down under that sum return'd.

Rochfield. With all my heart, Lady. *[again giving Woodroff money]* There Sir. *[aside]* So, she has fisht for her Gold back, and caught it; I am no thief now.

Woodroff. I shall make here a pretty Assurance.

Rochfield. Sir, I shall have a suit to you.

Woodroff. You are likely to obtain it then, Sir.

Rochfield. That I may keep you company to Sea, and attend you back; I am a little travell'd. 160

Woodroff. And heartily thank you too, sir. [D3ᵛ]

Annabel. Why, that's well said: *[to Rochfield]* Pray you be merry; though your Kinsman be absent, I am here, the worst part of him, yet that shall serve to give you welcome: to morrow may show you what this night will not, and be full assured,

Unless your twenty Pieces be ill lent,

Nothing shall give you cause of Discontent.

There's ten more, Sir. *[She gives him money.]*

Rochfield [aside]. Why should I fear? Fouter on't, Ile be merry now spite of the Hang-man. *Exeunt.* 170

Finis Actus secundi.

---

141 SD] *as* Dyce 2 *(after* begin,); *not in* Q
motion;] ~, Q
143, 144, 145 SDs] *as* Dyce 2; *not in* Q
151 want,] ~ₐ Q
153 *Rochfield.*] Dyce 1; *Eoch.* Q SD] *after*
Dyce 2; *not in* Q

154 Sir.] ~: Q SD] *as* Dyce 2; *not in* Q
162 SD] This ed.; *not in* Q merry;] ~, Q
168 SD] *after* Dyce 2 *(before* There's)
169 SD] Dyce 2; *not in* Q
170.1 *secundi*] Lucas; *secundus* Q

ACT 3. SCENE I. [III.i]

Enter LESSINGHAM *and* BONVILE.

Bonvile.   We are first i'th field: I think your Enemy
Is staid at *Dover*, or some other Port,
We hear not of his landing.
Lessingham.   I am confident
He is come over.
Bonvile.   You look methinks fresh coloured.
Lessingham.   Like a red Morning, friend, that still foretels
A stormy day to follow: But methinks
Now I observe your face, that you look pale,
There's death in't already.
Bonvile.   I could chide your error,
Do you take me for a Coward? A Coward
Is not his own friend, much less can he be   10
Another mans. Know, Sir, I am come hither
To instruct you by my generous example,
To kill your enemy, whose name as yet
I never question'd.
Lessingham.   Nor dare I name him yet,
For dis-heartning you.
Bonvile.   I do begin to doubt
The goodness of your Quarrel.
Lessingham.   Now you hav't;
For I protest that I must fight with one
From whom in the whole course of our acquaintance,
I never did receive the least injury.
Bonvile.   It may be the forgetful Wine begot   20
Some sudden blow, and thereupon this Challenge;
Howe're, you are engaged; and for my part
I will not take your course, my unlucky friend,
To say your Conscience grows pale and heartless,
Maintaining a bad Cause: fight as Lawyers plead,
Who gain the best of reputation
When they can fetch a bad Cause smoothly off:
You are in, and must through.

21 this Challenge;] *as* Dyce 2; 'tis ~, Q   23 not∧] ~, Q
22 Howe're,] ~∧ Q

335

Lessingham.   Oh my friend,   [D4ʳ]
    The noblest ever man had: when my fate
    Threw me upon this business, I made trial   30
    Of divers had profest to me much love,
    And found their friendship like the effects that kept
    Our company together, Wine and Riot,
    Giddy and sinking. I had found 'em oft
    Brave Seconds at pluralities of Healths,
    But when it came to'th proof, my Gentlemen
    Appeared to me as promising and failing
    As cozening Lotteries; but then I found
    This Jewel worth a thousand Counterfeits:
    I did but name my Engagement, and you flew   40
    Unto my succor with that chearfulness,
    As a great General hastes to a Battel,
    When that the chief of the adverse part
    Is a man glorious, but of ample fame:
    You left your Bridal-bed to finde your Death-bed,
    And herein you most nobly exprest,
    That the affection 'tween two loyal friends
    Is far beyond the love of man to woman,
    And is more near allied to eternity.
    What better friends part could be showed i'th world?   50
    It transcends all! My father gave me life,
    But you stand by my honor when 'tis falling,
    And nobly under-prop it with your sword.
    But now you have done me all this service,
    How, how shall I requite this? How return
    My grateful recompence for all this love?
    For it am I come hither with full purpose
    To kill you.
Bonvile.   Ha!
Lessingham.   Yes: I have no opposite i'th world
    But your self: There, read the Warrant for your death.   60
                    [Gives him Clare's letter.]

33 Riot,] ~: Q
34 sinking.] ~ₐ Q oftₐ] ~, Q
44 but] Q; and Dyce 1
53 under-prop] Dyce 1; under-propt Q
55 How,] ~? Q

59 world] Dyce 1; would Q
60.1 SD] Lucas (*to right of lines 60–1 ending
   death and* hand); *Giving letter* (*before* There)
   Dyce 2

Bonvile.   'Tis a womans hand.

Lessingham.   And 'tis a bad hand too:
The most of 'em speak fair, write foul, mean worse.

Bonvile.   Kill me! Away, you jest.

Lessingham.   Such jest as your sharp-witted Gallants use
To utter, and loose their friends. Read there how I
Am fettered in a womans proud Command:
I do Love madly, and must do madly:
Deadliest Hellebore or vomit of a Toad
Is qualified poyson to the malice of a woman.

Bonvile.   And kill that friend? Strange!

Lessingham.   You may see, Sir,   70
Although the Tenure by which Land was held
In Villenage be quite extinct in *England*,
Yet you have women there at this day living,
Make a number of slaves.

Bonvile.   And kill that friend? She mocks you
Upon my life, she does Equivocate:
Her meaning is, you cherish in your breast
Either self-love, or pride, as your best friend,
And she wishes you'd kill that.

Lessingham.   Sure her Command
Is more bloody; for she loathes me, and has put,   [D4ᵛ]
As she imagines, this impossible task,   80
For ever to be quit and free from me;
But such is the violence of my affection,
That I must undergo it. [*He draws.*] Draw your sword,
And guard your self; though I fight in fury,
I shall kill you in cold blood, for I protest
'Tis done in heart-sorrow.

Bonvile.   Ile not fight with you,
For I have much advantage; the truth is,
I wear a privy Coat.

Lessingham.   Prithee put it off then, if thou bee'st manly.

Bonvile.   The defence I mean, is the justice of my Cause   90
That would guard me, and fly to thy destruction:
What confidence thou wearest in a bad cause!

65 friends.] ~; Q
83 SD] This ed.; *not in* Q
84 self;] ~, Q

89 thou] Dyce 1; then Q
92 cause!] ~, Q

337

I am likely to kill thee if I fight,
And then you fail to effect your Mistriss bidding,
Or to enjoy the fruit of 't.
I have ever wisht thy happiness, and vow
I now so much affect it in compassion
Of my friends sorrow; make thy way to it.

                              [*He submits himself to Lessingham.*]

Lessingham.   That were a cruel Murder.
Bonvile.   Believ't 'tis ne're intended otherwise,   100
    When 'tis a womans bidding.
Lessingham.   Oh the necessity of my fate!
Bonvile.   You shed tears.
Lessingham.   And yet must on in my cruel purpose:
    A Judge methinks looks lovelyest when he weeps,
    Pronouncing of deaths Sentence: how I stagger
    In my resolve! Guard thee, for I came hither
    To do, and not to suffer; wilt not yet
    Be perswaded to defend thee? Turn the point,
    Advance it from the ground above thy head,   110
    And let it underprop thee otherwise,
    In a bold resistance.
Bonvile.   Stay! Thy injunction was,
    Thou shouldst kill thy friend.
Lessingham.   It was.
Bonvile.   Observe me,
    He wrongs me most, ought to offend me least,
    And they that study man, say of a friend,
    There's nothing in the world that's harder found,
    Nor sooner lost: thou camest to kill thy friend,
    And thou mayest brag thou hast don't; for here for ever
    All friendship dyes between us, and my heart
    For bringing forth any effects of love,   120
    Shall be as barren to thee as this sand
    We tread on; cruel, and inconstant as
    The Sea that beats upon this Beach. We now

---

94 Mistriss] Mrs. Q   98.1 SD] *after* Lucas; *not in* Q
95 't.] ~; Q   102 fate!] ~. Q
98 sorrow;] ~, Q   112 Stay!] ~. Q

Are severed: thus hast thou slain thy friend,
And satisfied what the Witch thy Mistriss bad thee.
Go and report that thou hast slain thy friend.
Lessingham.   I am served right.
Bonvile.   And now that I do cease to be thy friend,
I will fight with thee as thine enemy,
I came not over idly to do nothing.   130
Lessingham.   Oh friend!   [E1ʳ]
Bonvile.   Friend?
The naming of that word shall be the quarrel.
What do I know but that thou lovest my wife,
And faind'st this plot to divide me from her bed,
And that this Letter here is counterfeit?
Will you advance Sir?
Lessingham.   Not a blow;
'Twould appear ill in either of us to fight:
In you unmanly; for believe it Sir,
You have disarmed me already, done away   140
All power of resistance in me; it would show
Beastly to do wrong to the dead: to me you say,
You are dead for ever, lost on *Callis-sands*,
By the cruelty of a woman; yet remember
You had a noble friend, whose love to you
Shall continue after death. Shall I go over
In the same Barque with you?
Bonvile.   Not for yon town
Of *Callis*; you know 'tis dangerous living
At Sea, with a dead body.
Lessingham.   Oh you mock me,
May you enjoy all your noble wishes.   150
Bonvile.   And may you finde a better friend then I,
And better keep him.   *Exeunt.*

125 Mistriss] Mrs. Q   146 death.] ~: Q
137 Sir?] ~. Q   148 Callis;] ~, Q
141 me;] ~, Q   152 Exeunt.] Dyce 1; Exenut. (turned ᴉ) Q

[III.ii]

Enter Nurse, COMPASS, *and his Wife* [URSE].

Nurse. Indeed you must pardon me, Goodman *Compass,* I have no authority to deliver, no not to let you see the Childe: to tell you true, I have command unto the contrary.

Compass. Command! From whom?

Nurse. By the father of it.

Compass. The father! Who am I?

Nurse. Not the father, sure. The Civil Law has found it otherwise.

Compass. The Civil Law! Why then the Uncivil Law shall make it mine agen; Ile be as dreadful as a *Shrove-tuesday* to thee, I will tear thy Cottage but I will see my Childe. 10

Nurse. Speak but half so much agen, Ile call the Constable, and lay Burglary to thy charge.

Urse. My good husband, be patient. And prithee Nurse let him see the Childe.

Nurse. Indeed I dare not: the father first delivered me the Childe, he pays me well, and weekly for my pains, and to his use I keep it.

Compass. Why thou white Bastard-breeder, is not this the mother?

Nurse. Yes, I grant you that.

Compass. Dost thou? And I grant it too: And is not the Childe mine own then by the wifes Coppy-hold? 20

Nurse. The Law must try that.

Compass. Law? Dost think Ile be but a Father in Law? All the Law [E1ᵛ] betwixt *Black-wall* and *Tuttle-street,* and there's a pretty deal, shall not keep it from me, mine own flesh and blood! Who does use to get my children but my self?

Nurse. Nay, you must look to that, I ne're knew you get any.

Compass. Never? Put on a clean Smock and try me, if thou darest, three to one I get a Bastard on thee to morrow morning between one and three.

Nurse. Ile see thee hangd first! 30

Compass. So thou shalt too!

III.ii] *as* Dyce 1; *not in* Q
0.1 URSE] Dyce 2 (*replacing* Q *his Wife*); *not in* Q
4 Command!] ~. Q
5 *Nurse*] Dyce 1; *Nuase* Q
6 father!] ~. Q
7 father,] ~ₐ Q

8 Law!] ~: Q
24 me,] ~ₐ Q
30 first!] ~. Q
31 too!] ~. Q
31.1 SD] *placed as* Dyce 1; *to right of lines 30–1* Q

Enter FRANCKFORD *and* LUCE.

Nurse.   Oh here's the father, now pray talk with him.

Franckford.   Good morrow Neighbor: morrow to you both.

Compass.   Both! Morrow to you and your wife too.

Franckford.   I would speak calmly with you.

Compass.   I know what belongs to a Calm and a Storm too. A cold word with you: You have tyed your Mare in my ground.

Franckford.   No, 'twas my Nag.

Compass.   I will cut off your Nags tayl, and make his rump make Hair-buttons, if e're I take him there agen.   40

Franckford.   Well sir, but to the Main.

Compass.   Main! Yes, and Ile clip his Main too, and crop his ears too, do you mark? And back-gaul him, and spur-gaul him, do you note? And slit his Nose, do you smell me now, Sir? Unbritch his Barrel, and discharge his Bullets: Ile gird him till he stinks, you smell me now I'm sure.

Franckford.   You are too rough neighbor, to maintain—

Compass.   Maintain? You shall not maintain no childe of mine, my wife does not bestow her labor to that purpose.

Franckford.   You are too speedy: I will not maintain—   50

Compass.   No marry shall you not.

Franckford.   —the deed to be lawful: I have repented it, and to the Law given satisfaction, my purse has paid for't.

Compass.   Your purse! 'Twas my wifes purse. You brought in the Coin indeed, but it was found base and counterfeit.

Franckford.   I would treat colder with you, if you be pleased.

Compass.   Pleased? Yes I am pleased well enough, serve me so still: I am going agen to sea one of these days, you know where I dwell, yet you'l but loose your labor, get as many children as you can, you shall keep   [E2ʳ] none of them.   60

Franckford.   You are mad.

Compass.   If I be horn-mad, what's that to you?

Franckford.   I leave off milder phrase, and then tell you plain you are a—

Compass.   A what? What am I?

Franckford.   A Coxcomb.

Compass.   A Coxcomb? I knew 'twould begin with a C.

42 Main!] ~. Q   **54** SP] Dyce 1; *Bomp.* Q   purse!] ~: Q
47 maintain—] ~. Q   **60** them.] ~, Q
50 maintain—] ~ₐ Q   **63** a—] ~ₐ Q
52 —the] ₐThe Q

Franckford.   The childe is mine, I am the father of it;
        As it is past the deed, 'tis past the shame,
        I do acknowledge it, and will enjoy it.

Compass.   Yes, when you can get it agen; is it not my wifes labor? I'm   70
    sure she's the mother, you may be as far off the father as I am; for my
    wife's acquainted with more Whore-masters besides your self, and
    crafty Merchants too.

Urse.   No indeed husband, to make my offence
        Both least and most, I knew no other man,
        He's the begetter, but the childe is mine,
        I bred and bore it, and I will not loose it.

Luce.   The childe 's my husbands, Dame, and he must have it:
        I do allow my sufferance to the deed,
        In lieu I never yet was fruitful to him,   80
        And in my barrenness excuse my wrong.

Compass.   Let him dung his own ground better at home, then. If he
    plant his Reddish roots in my garden, Ile eat 'em with bread and Salt,
    though I get no Mutton to 'em; what tho your husband lent my wife
    your distaff, shall not the yarn be mine? Ile have the head, let him carry
    the spindle home agen.

Franckford.   Forebear more words, then; let the Law try it: mean time
    Nurse keep the childe, and to keep it better, here take more pay
    beforehand. There's money for thee.   [*Gives money.*]

Compass.   There's money for me too, keep it for me, Nurse: give him   90
    both thy dugs at once: I pay for thy right dug.   [*Gives money.*]

Nurse.   I have two hands you see. Gentlemen this does but show how
    the law will hamper you: even thus you must be used.

Franckford.   The law shall show which is the worthier Gender: a School-
    boy can do't.

Compass.   Ile whip that School-boy that declines the childe from my
    wife and her heirs: do not I know my wifes case the *Genetive Case*, and
    that's *Hujus*, as great a case as can be.

Franckford.   Well, fare you well, we shall meet in another place. Come
    Luce.   *Exit* [*with Luce*].   100

Compass.   Meet her in the same place agen if you dare, and do your worst:

---

69 acknowledge it] This ed.; acknowledge Q
70 agen;] ~, Q
82 then.] ~∧ Q
87 then;] ~∧ Q
88 better,] ~∧ Q

89, 91 SDs] This ed.; *not in* Q
92 see.] ~, Q
100 *with Luce*] Hazlitt; *not in* Q; *Exeunt*
    Franckford and Lucy. Dyce 1

must we go to law for our Children now a days? No marvel if the   [E2ᵛ]
Lawyers grow rich; but e're the Law shall have a Lymb, a Leg, a Joynt,
a Nayl,
    I will spend more then a whole childe in getting,
    Some win by play, and others by by-betting.   *Exeunt.*

[III.iii]

Enter RAYMOND, EUSTACE, LYONEL, GROVER, ANNABEL
[*with a Letter and a Will*], CLARE.

Lyonel.   Whence was that Letter sent?
Annabel.   From *Dover*, Sir.
Lyonel.   And does that satisfie you what was the cause
    Of his going over?
Annabel.   It does: yet had he onely
    Sent this [*showing the Will*] it had bin sufficient.
Raymond.   Why, what's that?
Annabel.   His Will wherein he has estated me
    In all his land.
Eustace [*aside to other Gallants*].   He's gone to fight.
Lyonel [*aside to other Gallants*].   *Lessinghams*   second,
    certain.
Annabel.   And I am lost, lost in't for ever.
Clare [*aside*].   Oh fool *Lessingham*,
    Thou hast mistook my injunction utterly,   10
    Utterly mistook it, and I am mad, stark mad
    With my own thoughts, not knowing what event
    Their going or'e will come too; 'tis too late
    Now for my tongue to cry my heart mercy,
    Would I could be senceless till I hear
    Of their return: I fear me both are lost.
Raymond [*to other Gallants*].   Who should it be *Lessinghams* gone to fight
    with?
Eustace [*to other Gallants*].   Faith I cannot possibly conjecture.

---

102 Children now] Childrennow Q
105 by∧] ~, Q   by-betting] by betting Q
III.iii] as Dyce 1; *not in* Q
0.2 *with a Letter and a Will*] This ed.; *not in* Q
4 SD] This ed.; *not in* Q

5 Will] Qb; will Qa
7 SDs] *after* Lucas (*aside*); *not in* Q   second,]
   ~∧ Q
9 SD] Dyce 1; *not in* Q

Annabel.   Miserable creature! A Maid, a Wife,
    And Widow in the compass of two days.   20
Raymond [to Clare].   Are you sad too?
Clare.   I am not very well, Sir.
Raymond [holding her].   I must put life in you.
Clare.   Let me go, Sir.
Raymond.   I do love you in spight of your heart.
Clare.   Believe it
    There was never a fitter time to express it;
    For my heart has a great deal of spight in't.
Raymond.   I will discourse to you fine fancies.
Clare.   Fine fooleries, will you not?
Raymond.   By this hand I love you, and will court you.
Clare.   Fie,
    You can command your tongue, and I my ears
    To hear you no further.
Raymond [aside].   On my reputation,   30
    She's off o'th hindges strangely.
            Enter WOODROFF, ROCHFIELD, *and a Saylor.*
Woodroff.   Daughter, good news.
Annabel.   What, is my husband heard of?
Woodroff.   That's not the business; but you have here a Cousin
    You may be mainly proud of, and I am sorry
    'Tis by your husbands kindred, not your own,
    That we might boast to have so brave a man
    In our Allyance.   [E3ʳ]
Annabel.   What, so soon return'd?
    You have made but a short voyage; howsoever,
    You are to me most welcome.
Rochfield.   Lady thanks,
    'Tis you have made me your own creature;   40
    Of all my being, fortunes, and poor fame,
    If I have purchas'd any, and of which

17, 18 SDs] This ed.; *not in* Q; *aside* Lucas
21 SD] Weis; *not in* Q
22 SD] *after* Weis; *not in* Q
30 SD] Dyce 1; *not in* Q
31.1 SD] *placed as* Dyce 1; *to right of lines 30–1*
    Q   ROCHFIELD, *and a Saylor*] Rochfeild, *and
    a saylor* Q

32 What,] ~ₐ Q
37 What,] ~ₐ Q
38 howsoever,] ~ₐ Q
40 creature;] ~, Q
41 being, fortunes,] ~ₐ ~ₐ Q

I no way boast, next the high providence,
    You have bin the sole creatress.
Annabel.   Oh deer Cousin,
    You are grateful above merit, what occasion
    Drew you so soon from Sea?
Woodroff.   Such an occasion,
    As I may bless Heaven for, you thank their bounty,
    And all of us be joyful.
Annabel.   Tell us how.
Woodroff.   Nay daughter, the discourse will best appear
    In his relation; where he fails, Ile help.   50
Rochfield.   Not to molest your patience with recital
    Of every vain, and needless Circumstance,
    'Twas briefly thus: Scarce having reacht to *Margets*,
    Bound on our voyage, suddenly in view
    Appeared to us three Spanish men of War;
    These having spied the English Cross advance,
    Salute us with a piece to have us strike;
    Ours better spirited and no way daunted,
    At their unequal oddes, though but one bottom,
    Returned 'em fire for fire: the fight begins,   60
    And dreadful on the sudden, still they proffered
    To board us, still we bravely beat 'em off.
Woodroff.   But daughter, mark the Event.
Rochfield.   Sea room we got, our ship being swift of sayl,
    It helpt us much, yet two unfortunate shot,
    One struck the Captains head off, and the other
    With an unlucky splinter laid the Master
    Dead on the hatches; all our spirits then failed us.
Woodroff.   Not all, you shall hear further, daughter.
Rochfield.   For none was left to manage, nothing now   70
    Was talkt of but to yeild up ship and goods,
    And mediate for our peace.
Woodroff.   Nay Cous, proceed.
Rochfield.   Excuse me, I intreat you, for what's more,
    Hath already past my memory.
Woodroff.   But mine it never can: Then he stood up,

And with his oratory made us agen
To recollect our spirits so late dejected.
Rochfield.   Pray Sir!
Woodroff.   Ile speak't out; by unite consent
Then the command was his, and 'twas his place
Now to bestir him, down he went below,   [E3ᵛ]
And put the Lin-stocks in the Gunners hands,   81
They ply their ordinance bravely, then agen
Up to the decks; courage is there renewed,
Fear now not found amongst us: within less
Then four hours fight two of their ships were sunk,
Both foundered, and soon swallowed: not long after
The third begins to wallow, lyes on the Lee
To stop her leakes, then boldly we come on,
Boarded and took her, and she's now our prize.
Saylor.   Of this we were eye witness.   90
Woodroff.   And many more brave boys of us besides,
My self for one; never was, Gentlemen,
A Sea fight better mannaged.
Rochfield.   Thanks to Heaven
We have saved our own, dammaged the enemy,
And to our Nations glory, we bring home
Honor and profit.
Woodroff.   In which Cousin *Rochfield*,
You as a venturer have a double share,
Besides the name of Captain, and in that
A second benefit, but most of all,
Way to more great employment.
Rochfield [to Annabel].   Thus your bounty   100
Hath been to me a blessing.
Raymond.   Sir, we are all
Indebted to your valor; this beginning
May make us, of small venturers, to become
Hereafter wealthy Merchants.
Woodroff.   Daughter and Gentlemen,

---

78 Sir!] ~. Q
87 third] Dyce 1; three Q
91 us₍ₐ₎] ~, Q   besides,] ~₍ₐ₎ Q
96 *Rochfield*] *Rochfeild* Q

100 SD] *as* Dyce 1 (*to right of line 100*); *placed*
        as Dyce 2
102 valor;] ~, Q
103 us,] ~₍ₐ₎ Q

This is the man was born to make us all,
Come enter, enter; we will in and feast,
He's in the Bridegrooms absence my chief guest.   *Exeunt.*
                              Finis Actus Tertii.

ACT. 4. SCENE I. [IV.i]

Enter COMPASS, *Wife* [URSE], LYONEL, *and* PETTIFOG *the Attorney*
          [*with papers*], *and one Boy* [JACK. *Tables set out*].

Compass.   Three Tuns do you call this Tavern? It has a good neighbor of
   Guild-hall, Mr. *Pettifog.* Show a room, boy.
Jack.   Welcome Gentlemen.
Compass.   What? Art thou here *Hodge!*
Jack.   I am glad you are in health, sir.
Compass.   This was the honest *Crack-roap* first gave me tidings of my
   wifes fruitfulness. Art bound Prentice?
Jack.   Yes, Sir.
Compass.   Mayest thou long jumble Bastard most artificially, to the
   profit of thy Master, and pleasure of thy Mistriss.   10
Jack.   What Wine drink ye, Gentlemen?
Lyonel.   What Wine rellishes your pallate, good Mr. *Pettifog?*   [E4ʳ]
Pettifog.   Nay, ask the woman.
Compass.   Ellegant for her, I know her Diet.
Pettifog.   Believe me, I con her thank for't, I am of her side.
Compass.   Marry, and reason, sir, we have entertain'd you for our
   Atorney.
Jack.   A Cup of neat Allegant?
Compass.   Yes, but do not make it speak Welch, boy.
Jack.   How mean you?   20
Compass.   Put no Metheglin in't, ye rogue.
Jack.   Not a drop, as I am true Britain.   [*Exit.*]
          They sit down, Pettifog pulls out papers.

---

105 to] Dyce 1; to to Q   **3** *Jack.*] *Boy.* Q (*so to line 22*)
0.1 URSE] Dyce 1 (*replacing Q Wife*); *not in* Q   **22** SD] Dyce 2; *not in* Q
0.2 *with papers*] This ed.; *not in* Q   **22.1** SD] *placed as* Dyce 1; *to right of lines 20–1*
0.2 JACK. *Tables set out*] *after* Weis; *not in* Q   Q
2 room,] ~ₐ Q

Enter FRANCKFORD, EUSTACE, [RAYMOND,] LUCE, *and* MR. DODGE
a Lawyer to another Table, and a Drawer.

Franckford. Show a private room, Drawer.

Drawer. Welcome Gentlemen.

Eustace. As far as you can from noise, boy.

Drawer. Further this way then, sir; for in the next room there are three
or four Fish-wives taking up a brabling business.

Franckford. Let's not sit near them by any means.

Dodge. Fill Canary, sirrah.   *[Exit Drawer. They sit.]*

Franckford. And what do you think of my Cause, Mr. *Dodge*?   30

Dodge. Oh we shall carry it most indubitably: you have money to go
through with the business, and ne're fear it but we'l trownce 'em; you
are the true Father.

Luce. The mother will confess as much.

Dodge. Yes Mistriss, we have taken her Affidavit. Look you sir, here's
the Answer to his Declaration.

Franckford. You may think strange, sir, that I am at charge
    To call a Charge upon me: but 'tis truth,
    I made a Purchase lately, and in that
    I did estate the Childe, 'bout which I'm sued,   40
    Joynt-purchaser in all the Land I bought:
    Now that's one reason that I should have care,
    Besides the tye of blood, to keep the Childe
    Under my wing, and see it carefully
    Instructed in those fair Abilities
    May make it worthy hereafter to be mine,
    And enjoy the Land I have provided for't.

Luce. Right, and I councel'd you to make that Purchase;
    And therefore Ile not have the Childe brought up
    By such a Coxcomb as now sues for him,   50
    He'd bring him up onely to be a Swabber:
    He was born a Merchant and a Gentleman,
    And he shall live and die so.
            [Enter Drawer, fills glasses, and exit.]

Dodge. Worthy Mistriss, I drink to you: you are a good woman, and but   [E4ᵛ]
few of so noble a patience.

22.2 RAYMOND,] *as Lucas; not in* Q
29 SD] *This ed.; not in* Q; DRAWER *fills their*
  glasses, and then exit. Dyce 2
32 'em;] ~, Q

53.1 SD] *This ed.; not in* Q
55.1 SD] *This ed.;* Enter 2 Boy. (*to right of line*
  55 Q)

Enter JACK [*and fills glasses at Compass's table*].

Jack [*calling*].   Score a quart of Allegant t'oth' *Woodcock*.   [*Exit.*]

Enter RAFE *like a Musician.*

Rafe.   Will you have any musick, Gentlemen?

Compass.   Musick amongst Lawyers? Here's nothing but discord. What,
   Rafe! Here's another of my young Cuckoes I heard last *April*, before I
   heard the Nightingale: no musick, good *Rafe:* here boy, your father   60
   was a Taylor, and methinks by your leering eye you should take after
   him. A good boy, make a leg handsomly, scrape your self out of our
   company.   [*Exit Rafe.*]
   [*to Pettifog*] And what do you think of my Suit, sir?

Pettifog.   Why, look you, sir: The Defendant was arrested first by *Latitat*
   in an Action of Trespass.

Compass.   And a Lawyer told me it should have been an Action of the
   Case, should it not wife?

Urse.   I have no skill in Law, sir: but you heard a Lawyer say so.

Pettifog.   I, but your Action of the Case is in that point too ticklish.   70

Compass.   But what do you think, shall I overthrow my adversary?

Pettifog.   Sans question: The childe is none of yours: what of that? I
   marry a widow is possest of a Ward, shall not I have the tuition of that
   Ward? Now sir, you lye at a stronger Ward; for *partus sequitur ventrem,*
   says the Civil Law: and if you were within compass of the four Seas, as
   the common Law goes, the childe shall be yours certain.

Compass.   There's some comfort in that yet. Oh your Atorneys in *Guild-
   hall* have a fine time on't.

Lyonel.   You are in effect both Judge and Jury your selves.

Compass.   And how you will laugh at your Clients when you sit in a   80
   Tavern, and call them Coxcombs, and whip up a Cause, as a Barber
   trims his Customers on a Christmass Eve, a snip, a wipe, and away.

Pettifog.   That's ordinary, sir: you shall have the like at a *Nisi Prius.*

Enter 1 Client.

   Oh you are welcome, Sir.

1 Client.   Sir, you'l be mindful of my Suit?

Pettifog.   As I am religious; Ile drink to you.

56 SP] This ed.; *Enter boy.* Q   *calling*] *after*
   Weis; *not in* Q   *Exit.*] This ed.; *not in* Q
56.1 RAFE] This ed.; *1 Boy* Q; SECOND BOY
   Dyce 1
57 SP] This ed.; *1 Boy.* Q; SEC. BOY. Dyce 1
63 SD] This ed.; *Exit Second Boy.* Dyce 1
64 SD] This ed.; *not in* Q
65 *Latitat*] Dyce 1; *Latitate* Q
69 SP] Dyce 2; *Wife.* Q
83.1 SD] *placed as* Dyce 1; *to right of line 84* Q
85 Suit?] ~. Q
86 religious;] ~, Q

1 Client. I thank you. [*to Urse*] By your favor, Mistriss. [*giving Pettifog money*] I have much business and cannot stay; but there's money for a quart of Wine.

Compass. By no means.   [F1ʳ]

1 Client. I have said, Sir.   *Exit.*   91

Pettifog. He's my Client sir, and he must pay; this is my tribute. Custom is not more truly paid in the *Sound* of *Denmark.*

Enter 2 Client.

2 Client. Good sir, be careful of my business.

Pettifog. Your Declaration's drawn, sir: Ile drink to you.

2 Client. I cannot drink this morning; but there's money for a pottle of Wine.   [*Gives money.*]

Pettifog. Oh good sir!

2 Client. I have done, sir. Morrow, Gentlemen.   *Exit.*

Compass. We shall drink good cheap, Mr. *Pettifog.*   100

Pettifog. And we sate here long you'd say so. I have sate here in this Tavern but one half hour, drunk but three pints of wine, and what with the offering of my Clients in that short time, I have got nine shillings clear, and paid all the Reckoning.

Lyonel. Almost a Councellors Fee.

Pettifog. And a great one as the world goes in *Guild-hall*; for now our young Clerks share with 'em, to help 'em to Clients.

Compass. I don't think but that the Cucking-stool is an enemy to a number of brables, that would else be determined by Law.

Pettifog. 'Tis so indeed, sir: My Client that came in now, sues his neighbor for kicking his Dog, and using the defamatory speeches, *Come out Cuckolds curr!*   110

Lyonel. And what, shall you recover upon this speech?

Pettifog. In *Guild-hall* I assure you; the other that came in was an Informer, a precious knave.

Compass. Will not the Ballad of *Flood* that was prest, make them leave their knavery?

Pettifog. Ile tell you how he was served: This Informer comes into *Turnball-street* to a Victualling-house, and there falls in league with a Wench—   120

87 *to Urse*] as Weis; *not in* Q
87–8 *giving Pettifog money*] This ed.; *not in* Q
93.1 SD] *placed as* Dyce 1; *after line 91* Q
97 SD] This ed.; *not in* Q
98 sir!] ~. Q

112 *curr!*] ~. Q
113 what,] ~ₐ Q
114 you;] ~, Q
120 Wench—] ~. Q

Compass.   A *Tweak*, or *Bronstrops*, I learnt that name in a Play.

Pettifog.   —had belike some private dealings with her, and there got a
   Goose.

Compass.   I would he had got two, I cannot away with an Informer.

Pettifog.   Now sir, this fellow in revenge of this, informs against the
   Bawd that kept the house, that she used Cannes in her house; but the
   cunning Jade comes me into'th Court, and there deposes that she gave
   him true *Winchester* measure.

Compass.   Marry, I thank her with all my heart for't.   [F1ᵛ]

Enter Drawer.

Drawer.   Here's a Gentleman, one Justice *Woodroff*, enquires for Mr.   130
   Franckford.   [*Exit.*]

Franckford.   Oh, my brother and the other Compremiser come to take
   up the business.

Enter Councellor and WOODROFF.

Woodroff.   We have conferred and labored for your peace,
      Unless your stubborness prohibit it;
      And be assured, as we can determine it,
      The Law will end, for we have sought the Cases.

Compass.   If the Childe fall to my share, I am content to end upon any
   conditions, the Law shall run on head-long else.

Franckford.   Your purse must run by like a Foot-man then.   140

Compass.   My purse shall run open mouth'd at thee.

Councellor [*to Compass*].   My friend, be calm, you shall hear the reasons:
      I have stood up for you, pleaded your Cause,
      But am overthrown, yet no further yielded
      Than your own pleasure; you may go on in Law
      If you refuse our Censure.

Compass.   I will yield to nothing but my Childe.

Councellor.   'Tis then as vain in us to seek your peace,
      Yet take the reasons with you: This Gentleman [*indicating Woodroff*]
      First speaks, a Justice, to me, and observe it: 150
      A childe that's base and illegitimate born,
      The father found, who (if the need require it)
      Secures the charge and dammage of the Parish
      But the father? Who charged with education

---

122 —had] ∧Had Q
124 Informer.] ∼∧ Q
127 into'th] into 'th Q
130 *Woodroff,* ∼∧ Q

131 SD] Lucas; *not in* Q
142 SD] This ed.; *not in* Q
149 SD] This ed.; *not in* Q
150 Justice,] ∼∧ Q   it:] ∼, Q

But the father? Then by clear consequence
He ought for what he pays for, to enjoy.
Come to the strength of reason, upon which
The Law is grounded: the earth brings forth,
This ground or that, her Crop of Wheat or Rye,
Whether shall the Seeds-man enjoy the sheaf,   160
Or leave it to the earth that brought it forth?
The summer tree brings forth her natural fruit,
Spreads her large arms, who but the lord of it
Shall pluck the Apples, or command the lops?
Or shall they sink into the root agen?
'Tis still most cleer upon the Fathers part.
Compass.   All this Law I deny, and will be mine own Lawyer. Is not the
earth our Mother? And shall not the earth have all her children agen? I
would see that Law durst keep any of us back, she'l have Lawyers and
all first, tho they be none of her best children. My wife is the mother,   170
and so much for the Civil-law. Now I come agen, and y'are gone at
the Common-law: suppose this is my ground, I keep a Sow upon it, as
it might be my wife, you keep a Boar, as it might be my adversary here;   [F2ʳ]
your Boar comes foaming into my ground, jumbles with my Sow, and
wallowes in her mire, my Sow cryes *week*, as if she had Pigs in her
belly, who shall keep these Pigs? He the Boar, or she the Sow?
Woodroff.   Past other alteration, I am changed,
The Law is on the Mothers part.
Councellor.   For me, I am strong in your opinion,
I never knew my judgement erre so far,   180
I was confirmed upon the other part,
And now am flat against it.
Woodroff [*to Franckford*].   Sir you must yeild,
Believe it there's no Law can relieve you.
Franckford.   I found it in my self: [*to Compass*] well sir,
The childe 's your wifes, Ile strive no further in it,
And being so neer unto agreement, let us go
Quite through to't; forgive my fault, and I
Forgive my charges, nor will I take back
The inheritance I made unto it.
Compass.   Nay, there you shall finde me kinde too, I have a pottle of   190

164 pluck the] Dyce 1; pluck Q   **184** SD] This ed.; *not in* Q
182 SD] Weis; *not in* Q

Claret, and a Capon to supper for you; but no more Mutton for you, not a bit.

Raymond.　Yes a shoulder, and we'l be there too, or a leg opened with Venison sawce.

Compass.　No legs opened by your leave; nor no such sawce.

Woodroff.　Well brother, and neighbor, I am glad you are friends.

Omnes.　All, all joy at it.

　　　Exeunt Woodroff, Franckford, [Eustace, Councellor, Luce,] and Lawyers.

Compass.　*Urse,* come kiss, *Urse,* all friends.

Raymond.　Stay sir, one thing I would advise you, 'tis Councel worth a Fee, tho I be no Lawyer, 'tis Physick indeed, and cures Cuckoldry, to keep that spightful brand out of your forehead, that it shall not dare to meet or look out at any window to you, 'tis better then an Onion to a green wound i'th left hand made by fire, it takes out scar and all.　200

Compass.　This were a rare receipt, Ile content you for your skill.

Raymond.　Make here a flat divorce between your selves, be you no husband, nor let her be no wife, within two hours you may salute agen, wooe, and wed afresh, and then the Cuckold's blotted. This medicine is approved.

Compass.　Excellent, and I thank you: *Urse,* I renounce thee, and I renounce my self from thee; thou art a Widow, *Urse,* I will go hang my self two hours, and so long thou shalt drown thy self, then will we meet agen in the Pease-field by *Bishops-Hall,* and as the Swads and the Cods shall instruct us, we'l talk of a new matter.　210

　　　　　　　　　　　　　　　　　　　　　　　　　　　　　　　　[F2ᵛ]

Urse.　I will be ruled, fare you well, sir.

Compass.　Farewel widdow, remember time and place; change your Clothes too, do ye hear, widow?　　　　　　　　*Exit Wife [Urse].*
Sir, I am beholding to your good Councel.

Raymond.　But you'l not follow your own so far I hope? You said you'd hang your self.

Compass.　No I have devised a better way, I will go drink my self dead for an hour, then when I awake agen, I am a fresh new man, and so I go a wooing.　220

Raymond.　That's handsome, and Ile lend thee a dagger.

Compass.　For the long Weapon let me alone then.　　　　　　*Exeunt.*

197.1 *Woodroff, Franckford,*] *Wood.Fr.* Q
　Eustace, Councellor, Luce,] This ed.; *not in*
　Q; *Lucy* Dyce 1; LUCE Dyce 2
198 kiss,] ~ₐ Q
200 and] & Q

214 SP] Dyce 2; *Wife.* Q
215 place;] ~, Q
216 SD] *placed as* Weis; *to right of line 214* Q
　Wife [Urse]] This ed.; *wife* Q; URSE Dyce 2

[IV.ii]

Enter LESSINGHAM *and* CLARE.

Clare.   Oh sir, are you return'd? I do expect
    To hear strange news now.
Lessingham.   I have none to tell you,
    I am onely to relate I have done ill
    At a womans bidding, that's I hope no news:
    Yet wherefore do I call that ill, begets
    My absolute happiness? You now are mine,
    I must enjoy you solely.
Clare.   By what warrant?
Lessingham.   By your own condition; I have been at *Callis*,
    Performed your will, drawn my revengful sword,
    And slain my neerest and best friend i'th world   10
    I had, for your sake.
Clare.   Slain your friend for my sake?
Lessingham.   A most sad truth.
Clare.   And your best friend?
Lessingham.   My chiefest.
Clare.   Then of all men you are most miserable,
    Nor have you ought further'd your suit in this,
    Though I enjoyn'd you to't, for I had thought
    That I had been the best esteemed friend
    You had i'th world.
Lessingham.   Ye did not wish I hope,
    That I should have murder'd you?
Clare.   You shall perceive
    More of that hereafter: But I pray sir tell me,
    For I do freeze with expectation of it,   20
    It chills my heart with horror till I know
    What friends blood you have sacrificed to your fury
    And to my fatal sport, this bloody Riddle?
    Who is it you have slain?
Lessingham.   *Bonvile* the Bridegroom.
Clare.   Say?
    Oh you have struck him dead thorough my heart,
    In being true to me, you have proved in this
    The falsest Traitor: oh I am lost for ever:

IV.ii] *as* Dyce 1; *not in* Q   8 condition;] ~, Q

Yet wherefore am I lost? Rather recovered
From a deadly witchcraft, and upon his grave
I will not gather Rue, but Violets   30
To bless my wedding strewings; good sir tell me,
Are you certain he is dead?

Lessingham.   Never, never
To be recovered.

Clare.   Why now sir, I do love you,   [F3ʳ]
With an entire heart, I could dance methinks,
Never did wine or musick stir in woman
A sweeter touch of Mirth; I will marry you,
Instantly marry you.

Lessingham [*aside*].   This woman has strange changes. [*to Clare*] You are
    ta'ne
Strangely with his death.

Clare.   Ile give the reason
I have to be thus extasied with joy: 40
Know sir, that you have slain my deerest friend,
And fatalest enemy.

Lessingham.   Most strange!

Clare.   'Tis true,
You have ta'ne a mass of Lead from off my heart,
For ever would have sunk it in despair;
When you beheld me yesterday, I stood
As if a Merchant walking on the *Downs*,
Should see some goodly Vessel of his own
Sunk 'fore his face i'th Harbor, and my heart
Retained no more heat then a man that toyles,
And vainly labors to put out the flames   50
That burns his house to'th bottom. I will tell you
A strange concealement, sir, and till this minute
Never revealed, and I will tell it now,
Smiling and not blushing; I did love that *Bonvile*,
(Not as I ought, but as a woman might
That's beyond reason,) I did doat upon him,
Tho he neare knew of't, and beholding him
Before my face wedded unto another,

35 woman∧] ~, Q
36 Mirth;] ~, Q
38 aside] Dyce 2; *not in* Q   to Clare] *as* Weis;
    not in Q

54 *Bonvile*] *Bonvyle* Q
57 neare] This ed.; near Q; ne'er Lucas

And all my interest in him forfeited,
I fell into despair, and at that instant   60
You urging your Suit to me, and I thinking
That I had been your onely friend i'th world,
I heartily did wish you would have kill'd
That friend your self, to have ended all my sorrow,
And had prepared it, that unwittingly
You should have don't by poison.

Lessingham.   Strange amazement!

Clare.   The effects of a strange Love.

Lessingham.   'Tis a dream sure.

Clare.   No 'tis real sir, believe it.

Lessingham.   Would it were not.

Clare.   What sir, you have done bravely, 'tis your Mistriss
That tells you, you have done so.

Lessingham.   But my Conscience   70
Is of Councel 'gainst you, and pleads otherwise:
Vertue in her past actions glories still,
But vice throwes loathed looks on former ill.
But did you love this *Bonvile*?

Clare.   Strangely sir,
Almost to a degree of madness.

Lessingham [*aside*].   Trust a woman?
Never henceforward, I will rather trust
The winds which *Lapland* Witches sell to men;
All that they have is feign'd, their teeth, their hair,
Their blushes, nay their conscience too is feigned;   [F3ᵛ]
Let 'em paint, load themselves with Cloth of Tissue,   80
They cannot yet hide woman, that will appear
And disgrace all. The necessity of my fate!
Certain this woman has bewitched me here,
For I cannot chuse but love her. Oh how fatal
This might have proved; I would it had for me,
It would not grieve me, tho my sword had split
His heart in sunder, I had then destroyed
One that may prove my Rival; oh but then
What had my horror bin, my guilt of conscience!

75 SD] Dyce 2; *not in* Q   79 feigned;] ~, Q
77 men;] ~, Q   85 proved;] ~, Q

I know some do ill at womens bidding   90
I'th Dog-days, and repent all the Winter after:
No, I account it treble happiness
That *Bonvile* lives, but 'tis my chiefest glory
That our friendship is divided.
Clare.   Noble friend,
Why do you talk to your self?
Lessingham.   Should you do so,
You'd talk to an ill woman; fare you well,
For ever fare you well. [*aside*] I will do somewhat
To make as fatal breach and difference
In *Bonviles* love as mine, I am fixt in't,
My melancholly and the devil shall fashion't.   100
Clare.   You will not leave me thus?
Lessingham.   Leave you for ever,
And may my friends blood whom you loved so deerly,
For ever lye impostumed in your breast,
And i'th end choak you. Womans cruelty
This black and fatal thread hath ever spun,
It must undo, or else it is undone.   *Exit.*
Clare.   I am every way lost, and no meanes to raise me,
But blest repentance: what two unvalued Jewels
Am I at once deprived of! Now I suffer
Deservedly, there's no prosperity settled,   110
Fortune plays ever with our good or ill,
Like Cross and Pile, and turns up which she will.
                    Enter BONVILE [*with Clare's letter*].
Bonvile.   Friend!
Clare.   Oh you are the welcomest under heaven:
Lessingham did but fright me, yet I fear
That you are hurt to danger.
Bonvile.   Not a scratch.
Clare.   Indeed you look exceeding well, methinks.
Bonvile.   I have bin Sea-sick lately, and we count
That excellent Physick. How does my *Annabel*?
Clare.   As well sir, as the fear of such a loss   120
As your esteemed self, will suffer her.

---

96 woman;] ~, Q   *prefixes* Q   *with Clare's letter*] This ed.; *not*
97 well.] ~; Q   SD] *as* Dyce 2; *not in* Q   *in* Q
112.1 *Enter* BONVILE.] *aligned with speech*   113 *Bonvile.*] *as* Dyce 1; *not in* Q

Bonvile.   Have you seen *Lessingham* since he returned?
Clare.   He departed hence but now, and left with me
    A report had almost kill'd me.
Bonvile.   What was that?
Clare.   That he had kill'd you.
Bonvile.   So he has.   [F4ʳ]
Clare.   You mock me.
Bonvile.   He has kill'd me for a friend, for ever silenc't
    All amity between us; you may now
    Go and embrace him, for he has fulfilled
    The purpose of that Letter.   *Gives her a Letter.*
Clare.   Oh I know't.   *She gives him another.*
    And had you known this which I meant to have sent you   130
    An hour 'fore you were married to your wife,
    The Riddle had been construed.
Bonvile.   Strange! This expresses
    That you did love me.
Clare.   With a violent affection.
Bonvile.   Violent indeed; for it seems it was your purpose
    To have ended it in violence on your friend:
    The unfortunate *Lessingham* unwittingly
    Should have been the Executioner.
Clare.   'Tis true.
Bonvile.   And do you love me still?
Clare.   I may easily
    Confess it, since my extremity is such
    That I must needs speak or die.
Bonvile.   And you would enjoy me   140
    Though I am married?
Clare.   No indeed not I sir:
    You are to sleep with a sweet Bed-fellow
    Would knit the brow at that.
Bonvile.   Come, come, a womans telling truth makes amends
    For her playing false. You would enjoy me?
Clare.   If you were a Batchelor or Widower,
    Afore all the great Ones living.
Bonvile.   But 'tis impossible
    To give you present satisfaction,

129 *another.*] ~ˌ Q

358

For my Wife is young and healthful; and I like
The summer and the harvest of our Love,   150
Which yet I have not tasted of, so well,
That, and you'l credit me, for me her days
Shall ne're be shortned: let your reason therefore
Turn you another way, and call to minde
With best observance, the accomplisht graces
Of that brave Gentleman whom late you sent
To his destruction: A man so every way
Deserving, no one action of his
In all his life time e're degraded him
From the honor he was born too; think how observant   160
He'l prove to you in a nobler request, that so
Obeyed you in a bad one: and remember
That afore you engaged him to an act
Of horror, to the killing of his friend,
He bore his steerage true in every part,
Led by the Compass of a noble heart.

Clare.   Why do you praise him thus? You said but now
He was utterly lost to you: now 't appears
You are friends, else you 'd not deliver of him   [F4ᵛ]
Such a worthy commendation.

Bonvile.   You mistake,   170
Utterly mistake that I am friends with him,
In speaking this good of him: To what purpose
Do I praise him? Onely to this fatal end,
That you might fall in love and league with him.
And what worse office can I do i'th world
Unto my enemy, than to endeavor
By all means possible to marry him
Unto a Whore? And there I think she stands.

Clare.   Is Whore a name to be beloved? If not,
What reason have I ever to love that man   180
Puts it upon me falsely? You have wrought
A strange alteration in me: were I a man,
I would drive you with my sword into the field,
And there put my wrong to silence. Go, y'are not worthy
To be a womans friend in the least part

152 That,] ~ˬ Q   161 a] This ed.; *not in* Q

359

    That concerns honorable reputation;
    For you are a Liar.
Bonvile.   I will love you now
    With a noble observance, if you will continue
    This hate unto me: gather all those graces
    From whence you have faln, yonder, where you have left 'em   190
    In *Lessingham*, he that must be your husband;
    And though henceforth I cease to be his friend,
    I will appear his noblest enemy,
    And work reconcilement 'tween you.
Clare.   No, you shall not,
    You shall not marry him to a Strumpet; for that word
    I shall ever hate you.
Bonvile.   And for that one deed,
    I shall ever love you. Come, convert your thoughts
    To him that best deserves 'em, *Lessingham*.
    It's most certain you have done him wrong,
    But your repentance and compassion now   200
    May make amends: disperse this melancholly,
    And on that turn of Fortunes Wheel depend,
    When all Calamities will mend, or end.   *Exeunt.*

[IV.iii]

Enter COMPASS, RAYMOND, EUSTACE, LYONEL, GROVER.

Compass.   Gentlemen, as you have been witness to our Divorce, you
    shall now be evidence to our next meeting, which I look for every
    minute, if you please Gentlemen.

Raymond.   We came for the same purpose, man.

Compass.   I do think you'l see me come off with as smooth a forehead,
    make my Wife as honest a woman once more, as a man sometimes
    would desire, I mean of her rank, and a teeming woman as she has
    been. Nay surely I do think to make the Childe as lawful a childe too,   [G1ʳ]
    as a couple of unmarried people can beget; and let it be begotten when
    the father is beyond Sea, as this was: do but note.   1ᴄ

Eustace.   'Tis that we wait for.

190 faln,] ~₍ Q   **IV.iii**] *as* Dyce 1; *not in* Q
196 SP] Dyce 1; *Less.* Q

Enter Wife [URSE].

Compass. You have waited the good hour: see, she comes, a little room
  I beseech you, silence and observation.

Raymond. All your own, sir.   [*Gallants stand apart.*]

Compass. Good morrow fair Maid.

Urse. Mistaken in both sir, neither fair, nor Maid.

Compass. No? A married woman.

Urse. That's it I was sir, a poor widdow now.

Compass. A widdow? Nay then I must make a little bold with you; 'tis a
  kin to mine own case, I am a wiveless husband too. How long have   20
  you been a widow pray? [*Urse weeps.*] Nay, do not weep.

Urse. I cannot chuse, to think the loss I had.

Compass. He was an honest man to thee it seems.

Urse. Honest quoth a, oh!

Compass. By my feck, and those are great losses, an honest man is not to
  be found in every hole, nor every street. If I took a whole parish in
      Sometimes I might say true,
      For stincking Mackarel may be cried for new.

Raymond [*aside to other Gallants*]. Some what sententious.

Eustace [*to Raymond*]. Oh, silence was an Article enjoyned.   30

Compass. And how long is it since you lost your honest husband?

Urse. Oh the memory is too fresh, and your sight makes
      My sorrow double.

Compass. My sight? Why, was he like me?

Urse. Your left hand to your right, is not more like.

Compass. Nay then I cannot blame thee to weep; an honest man I
  warrant him, and thou hadst a great loss of him; such a proportion, so
  limb'd, so coloured, so fed.

Raymond [*to other Gallants*]. Yes faith, and so taught too.

Eustace [*to Raymond*]. Nay, will you break the Law?   40

Urse. Twins were never liker.

Compass. Well, I love him the better, whatsoever is become of him; and
  how many children did he leave thee at his departure?

11.1 SD] *to right of line 10* Q   URSE] Dyce 2
  (*replacing* Q *Wife*); *not in* Q
14 SD] *This ed.; not in* Q; *They withdraw a
  little.* Lucas
16 *Urse.*] Dyce 2; *Wife* Q (*so to end of scene*)
19 you;] ~, Q
20 too.] ~, Q
21 SD] *after* Lucas (*to right of line 22*); *not in* Q
22 chuse,] ~, Q

24 quoth,] ~, Q oh!] ~. Q
26 street.] ~, Q
29 SD] *after* Weis; *not in* Q
30 SD] *after* Weis; *not in* Q
34 Why,] why, Q
36 weep;] ~, Q
39 SD] *after* Weis; *not in* Q
40 SD] *after* Weis; *not in* Q
42 him;] ~, Q

Urse.   Onely one sir.

Compass.   A Boy, or a Girl?

Urse.   A Boy, Sir.

Compass.   Just mine one case still: my wife, rest her soul, left me a Boy   [G1ᵛ]
too, a chopping Boy I warrant.

Urse.   Yes if you call 'em so.

Compass.   I, mine is a chopping Boy, I mean to make either a Cook or a   50
Butcher of him, for those are your chopping Boys. And what profession was your husband of?

Urse.   He went to Sea, sir, and there got his living.

Compass.   Mine own faculty too; and you can like a man of that profession well?

Urse.   For his sweet sake whom I so deerly loved,
More deerly lost, I must think well of it.

Compass.   Must you? I do think then thou must venter to Sea once
agen, if thoul't be rul'd by me.

Urse.   Oh Sir, but there's one thing more burdensome   60
To us, then most of others wives, which moves me
A little to distaste it. Long time we endure
The absence of our husbands, sometimes many years,
And then if any slip in woman be,
As long vacations may make Lawyers hungry,
And Tradesmen cheaper pennyworths afford,
(Then otherwise they would for ready coin)
Scandals fly out, and we poor souls are branded
With wanton living, and incontinency,
When alas (consider) can we do withal?   70

Compass.   They are fools, and not saylors that do not consider that; I'm
sure your husband was not of that minde, if he were like me.

Urse.   No indeed, he would bear kinde and honestly.

Compass.   He was the wiser. Alack your land and fresh-water men never
understand what wonders are done at Sea; yet they may observe a
shore, that a Hen having tasted the Cock, kill him, and she shall lay
Eggs afterwards.

Urse.   That's very true indeed.

54 too;] ~, Q

62 it.] ~, Q

66 pennyworths] penny- | worths Q (*hyphen
at end of line*)

68 are] Dyce 1; *not in* Q

71 that;] ~, Q

74 wiser.] ~, Q

Compass. And so may women, why not? May not a man get two or
three children at once? One must be born before another, you know.   80

Urse. Even this discretion my sweet husband had:
       You more and more resemble him.

Compass. Then if they knew what things are done at sea, where the
Winds themselves do copulate, and bring forth issue, as thus: In the
old world there were but four in all, as Nor, East, Sou, and West: these
dwelt far from one another, yet by meeting they have ingendred Nor-   [G2ʳ]
East, Sou-East, Sou-West, Nor-West, then they were eight; Of them
were begotten Nor-Nor-East, Nor-Nor-West, Sou-Sou-East, Sou-
Sou-West, and those two Sows were Sou-East and Sou-Wests daughters, and indeed there is a family now of 32 of 'em, that they have fill'd   90
every corner of the world, and yet for all this, you see these baudy
Bellows-menders when they come ashore, will be offering to take up
Womens coats in the street.

Urse. Still my husbands discretion!

Compass. So I say, if your Land-men did understand that we send
Windes from Sea, to do our commendations to our wives, they would
not blame you as they do.

Urse. We cannot help it.

Compass. But you shall help it. Can you love me, widow?

Urse. If I durst confess what I do think, sir,   100
       I know what I would say.

Compass. Durst confess? Why whom do you fear? Here's none but
honest Gentlemen my friends; let them hear, and never blush for't.
                                              [*Gallants come forward.*]

Urse. I shall be thought too weak, to yeild at first.

Raymond. Tush, that's niceness; come, we heard all the rest; the first
true stroke of love sinks the deepest; if you love him, say so.

Compass. I have a Boy of mine own, I tell you that afore-hand, you shall
not need to fear me that way.

Urse [*to Raymond*]. Then I do love him.

Compass. So here will be man and wife to morrow then; what though   110
we meet strangers, we may love one another ne'r the worse for that.
Gentlemen, I invite you all to my Wedding.

Omnes. We'l all attend it.

89 Sou-Wests] This ed.; Sou-West Q; sou-
   west' Dyce 1; Sou-West's Lucas
103.1 SD] *after* Weis (*after line 104*); *not in* Q
104 weak,] ~ₐ Q

105 rest;] ~, Q
106 the] Dyce 1; thee Q   deepest;] ~, Q
109 SD] This ed.; *not in* Q
110 then;] ~, Q

Compass. Did not I tell you, I would fetch it off fair? Let any man lay a Cuckold to my charge, if he dares now.

Raymond. 'Tis slander who ever does it.

Compass. Nay, it will come to *Petty Lassery* at least, and without compass of the general pardon too, or I'le bring him to a foul sheet, if he has ne're a clean one, or let me hear him that will say I am not father   [G2ᵛ]
to the childe I begot!   120

Eustace. None will adventure any of those.

Compass. Or that my wife that shall be, is not as honest a woman, as some other mens wives are!

Raymond. No question of that.

Compass. How fine and sleek my brows are now!

Eustace. I, when you are married, they'l come to themselves agen.

Compass. You may call me Bridegroom if you please now, for the Guests are bidden.

Omnes. Good Master Bridegroom.

Compass. Come Widow then, ere the next Ebb and Tide,   130
      If I be Bridegroom, thou shalt be the Bride.   *Exeunt.*
              Finis Actus quarti.

ACT. 5. SCENE I. [V.i]

Enter ROCHFIELD *and* ANNABEL.

Rochfield. Believe me, I was never more ambitious,
      Or covetous, if I may call it so,
      Of any fortune greater than this one,
      But to behold his face.

Annabel.   And now's the time;
      For from a much feared danger as I heard,
      He's late come over.

Rochfield.   And not seen you yet?
      'Tis some unkindness.

Annabel.   You may think it so;
      But for my part, sir, I account it none:
      What know I but some business of import
      And weighty consequence, more near to him   10
      Than any formal Complement to me,

114 fair?] ~, Q
120 begot!] ~. Q

126 I,] ~ₐ Q
130.1 quarti] Lucas; quartii Q

May for a time detain him? I presume
No jealousie can be asperst on him,
For which he cannot well Apology.

Rochfield.   You are a Creature every way compleat,
As good a Wife, as Woman; for whose sake
As I in duty am endeer'd to you,
So shall I owe him service.

Enter LESSINGHAM [*unseen*].

Lessingham [*aside*].   The ways to Love, and Crowns, lye both through
    blood,
For in 'em both all Lets must be removed,   20
It could be stiled no true ambition else.
I am grown big with project: Project, said I?
Rather with sudden mischief; which without
A speedy birth fills me with painful throwes,   [G3ʳ]
And I am now in labor. Thanks Occasion
That givest me a fit ground to work upon.
It should be *Rochfield*, one since our departure
It seems ingrafted in this Family:
Indeed the Houses Minion, since from the Lord
To the lowest Groom, all with unite consent   30
Speak him so largely. Nor as it appears
By this their private Conference, is he grown
Least in the Brides opinion. A foundation
On which I will erect a brave Revenge.

Annabel [*to Rochfield*].   Sir, what kinde Offices lyes in your way
To do for him, I shall be thankful for,
And reckon them mine own.

Rochfield.   In acknowledgement
I kiss your hand, so with a gratitude
Never to be forgot, I take my leave.

Annabel.   I mine of you, with hourly expectation   40
Of a long-lookt-for husband.

Rochfield.   May it thrive
    According to your wishes.   *Exit* [*Annabel*].

---

12 him?] ~: Q
14 cannot] Dyce 1; cannor Q
18.1 *unseen*] This ed.; *not in* Q
19 SD] Dyce 2; *not in* Q
25 Occasion] occasion Q
26 upon.] ~, Q

35 SD] Weis; *not in* Q   what] What Q
41 long-lookt-for] long-lookt for Q
42 *Exit* [*Annabel*].] *as* Dyce 2; *Exit.* (*to right of*
    husband. *in line 41*) Q   aside] Dyce 2; *not*
    in Q

Lessingham [*aside*].   Now's my turn.
    [*advancing*] Without offence, Sir, may I beg your name?
Rochfield.   'Tis that I never yet denied to any,
    Nor will to you that seem a Gentleman:
    'Tis *Rochfield.*
Lessingham.   *Rochfield?* You are then the man
    Whose nobleness, vertue, valor, and good parts,
    Have voice'd you loud. *Dover* and *Sandwich,*
    Marget, and all the Coast is full of you:
    But more, as an Eye-witness of all these,   50
    And with most truth, the Master of this house
    Hath given them large expressions.
Rochfield.   Therein his love
    Exceeded much my merit.
Lessingham.   That's your modesty:
    Now I as one that goodness love in all men,
    And honoring that which is but found in few,
    Desire to know you better.
Rochfield.   Pray your name?
Lessingham.   *Lessingham.*
Rochfield.   A friend to Mr. *Bonvile?*
Lessingham.   In the number
    Of those which he esteems most dear to him,
    He reckons me not last.
Rochfield.   So I have heard.   60
Lessingham.   Sir, you have cause to bless the lucky Planet   [G3ᵛ]
    Beneath which you were born, 'twas a bright star
    And then shined cleer upon you, for as you
    Are every way well parted, so I hold you
    In all designs mark't to be fortunate.
Rochfield.   Pray do not stretch your love to flattery,
    'T may call it then in question; grow I pray you
    To some particulars.
Lessingham.   I have observed
    But late your parting with the Virgin Bride,
    And therein some affection.
Rochfield.   How!
Lessingham.   With pardon,   70

43 SD] *after Weis; not in Q*

In this I still applaud your happiness,
And praise the blessed influence of your stars:
For how can it be possible that she,
Unkindly left upon the Bridal-day,
And disappointed of those Nuptial sweets
That night expected, but should take the occasion
So fairly offered? Nay, and stand excused
Aswell in detestation of a scorn,
Scarce in a husband heard of, as selecting
A Gentleman in all things so compleat,   80
To do her those neglected offices,
Her youth and beauty justly challengeth?
Rochfield [*aside*].   Some plot to wrong the Bride, and I now
Will marry Craft with Cunning; if he'l bite,
Ile give him line to play on: [*to Lessingham*] wer't your case,
You being young as I am, would you intermit
So fair and sweet occasion?
Yet mis-conceive me not, I do intreat you,
To think I can be of that easie wit,
Or of that malice to defame a Lady,   90
Were she so kinde so to expose her self,
Nor is she such a creature.
Lessingham [*aside*].   On this foundation
I can build higher still. [*to Rochfield*] Sir I beleiv't,
I hear you two call Cousins; comes your kindred
By the *Woodroffs*, or the *Bonviles*?
Rochfield.   From neither, 'tis a word of courtesie
Late interchanged betwixt us, otherwise
We are forreign as two strangers.
Lessingham [*aside*].   Better still.
Rochfield.   I would not have you grow too inward with me
Upon so small a knowledge; yet to satisfie you,   100
And in some kinde too to delight my self,
Those Bracelets and the Carckanet she wears,
She gave me once.   [G4ʳ]

---

74 Bridal-day] *as* Dyce 1; Bride-day Q
82 challengeth?] ~. Q
83 SD] Dyce 2; *not in* Q
84 Cunning;] ~, Q
85 SD] *after* Weis; *not in* Q   case,] ~ₐ Q

88 Yet] Dyce 1; *Less.* Yet Q   you,] ~; Q
92 SD] Dyce 2; *not in* Q
93 still.] ~, Q   SD] *after* Weis; *not in* Q
   ₐSir I beleiv't,] (sir ~ ~) Q
98 SD] Dyce 2; *not in* Q

Lessingham.   They were the first, and special Tokens past
     Betwixt her and her husband.
Rochfield.   'Tis confest:
     What I have said, I have said: Sir, you have power
     Perhaps to wrong me, or to injure her;
     This you may do, but as you are a Gentleman
     I hope you will do neither.
Lessingham.   Trust upon't.   *Exit Rochfield.*
     If I drown Ile sink some along with me;   110
     For of all miseries I hold that chief,
     Wretched to be, when none co-parts our grief.
                              Enter WOODROFF.
     Here's another Anvile to work on: I must now
     Make this my Master-piece; for your old Foxes
     Are seldom ta'ne in Springes.
Woodroff.   What, my Friend!
     You are happily returned; and yet I want
     Somewhat to make it perfect. Where's your Friend,
     My Son in Law?
Lessingham.   Oh sir!
Woodroff.   I pray sir resolve me;
     For I do suffer strangely till I know
     If he be in safety.
Lessingham.   Fare you well: 'Tis not fit   120
     I should relate his danger.
Woodroff.   I must know't.
     I have a Quarrel to you already, for enticing
     My Son in Law to go over: Tell me quickly,
     Or I shall make it greater.
Lessingham.   Then truth is,
     He's dangerously wounded.
Woodroff.   But he's not dead I hope?
Lessingham.   No sir, not dead;
     Yet sure your daughter may take liberty
     To chuse another.
Woodroff.   Why that gives him dead.
Lessingham.   Upon my life Sir, no; your son's in health
     As well as I am.

112.1 SD] *to right of line 110* Q

Woodroff.   Strange! You deliver Riddles.   130
Lessingham.   I told you he was wounded, and 'tis true,
     He is wounded in his Reputation.
     I told you likewise, which I am loth to repeat,
     That your fair Daughter might take liberty
     To embrace another. That's the consequence
     That makes my best Friend wounded in his Fame.
     This is all I can deliver.   [G4ᵛ]
Woodroff.   I must have more of't;
     For I do sweat already, and Ile sweat more;
     'Tis good they say to cure Aches, and o'th sudden
     I am sore from head to foot. Let me taste the worst.   140
Lessingham.   Know Sir, if ever there were truth in falshood,
     Then 'tis most true, your Daughter plays most false
     With *Bonvile*, and hath chose for her Favorite
     The man that now past by me, *Rochfield*.
Woodroff.   Say?
     I would thou hadst spoke this on *Callis-sands*,
     And I within my Sword and Ponyards length
     Of that false throat of thine. I pray sir, tell me
     Of what Kin or Alliance do you take me
     To the Gentlewoman you late mentioned?
Lessingham.   You are her Father.   150
Woodroff.   Why then of all men living, do you address
     This Report to me, that ought of all men breathing
     To have been the last o'th Rowl, except the husband,
     That should have heard of't?
Lessingham.   For her honor Sir,
     And yours; that your good Councel may reclaim her.
Woodroff.   I thank you.
Lessingham.   She has departed sir, upon my knowledge,
     With Jewels, and with Bracelets, the first Pledges,
     And confirmation of th' unhappy Contract
     Between her self and husband.   160
Woodroff.   To whom?
Lessingham.   To *Rochfield*.
Woodroff.   Be not abused: but now,
     Even now I saw her wear e'm.

---

140 foot.] ~, Q

Lessingham.   Very likely;
    'Tis fit, hearing her husband is returned,
    That he should re-deliver 'em.
Woodroff.   But pray sir tell me,
    How is it likely she could part with 'em,
    When they are lockt about her Neck and Wrists,
    And the Key with her husband?
Lessingham.   Oh sir, that's but practise;
    She has got a trick to use another Key
    Besides her husbands.
Woodroff.   Sirrah, you do lie;   [H1ʳ]
    And were I to pay down a hundred pounds   170
    For every Lie given, as men pay Twelve pence,
    And worthily, for Swearing, I would give thee
    The Lie, nay though it were in the Court of Honor,
    So oft, till of the Thousands I am worth,
    I had not left a hundred. For is't likely
    So brave a Gentleman as *Rochfield* is,
    That did so much at Sea to save my life,
    Should now on Land shorten my wretched days,
    In ruining my Daughter? A rank Lie!
    Have you spread this to any but my self?   180
Lessingham.   I am no Intelligencer.
Woodroff.   Why then 'tis yet a secret?
    And that it may rest so, Draw; Ile take order
    You shall prate of it no further.   *[He draws.]*
Lessingham.   Oh, my Sword
    Is enchanted, Sir, and will not out o'th Scabbard:
    I will leave you, sir; yet say not I give ground,
    For 'tis your own you stand on.
               Enter BONVILE *and* CLARE.
    [aside] *Clare* here with *Bonvile*? Excellent! On this
    I have more to work. This goes to *Annabel*,
    And it may increase the Whirlwinde.   *Exit.*
Bonvile.   How now, Sir?
    Come, I know this choler bred in you   190

164 he] Dyce 1; she Q
173 Honor,] ~ˌ Q
183 SD] *after* Lucas (*to right of line 182*)

186.1 *and*] & Q
187 SD] *as* Dyce 2; *not in* Q
189 *Bonvile*] *as* Dyce 1; *Bou.* Q

For the Voyage which I took at his entreaty;
But I must reconcile you.
Woodroff.   On my credit
There's no such matter. I will tell you Sir,
And I will tell it in laughter: The Cause of it
Is so poor, so ridiculous, so impossible
To be believed! Ha, ha, he came even now
And told me that one *Rochfield*, now a Guest
(And most worthy, Sir, to be so) in my House,
Is grown exceedingly familiar with my Daughter.
Bonvile. Ha!   200
Woodroff. Your wife, and that he has had favors from her.
Bonvile. Favors?
Woodroff. Love-tokens I did call 'em in my youth;   [H1ᵛ]
Lures to which Gallants spread their wings, and stoop
In Ladies bosoms. Nay, he was so false
To Truth and all good Manners, that those Jewels
You lockt about her Neck, he did protest
She had given to *Rochfield*! Ha! Methinks o'th sudden
You do change colour. Sir, I would not have you
Believe this in least part: My Daughter's honest,   210
And my Guess is a noble Fellow: And for this
Slander deliver'd me by *Lessingham*,
I would have cut his throat.
Bonvile.   As I your Daughters,
If I finde not the Jewels 'bout her.
Clare.   Are you returned
With the Italian Plague upon you, Jealousie?
Woodroff. Suppose that *Lessingham* should love my Daughter,
And thereupon fashion your going over,
As now your Jealousie, the stronger way
So to divide you, there were a fine Crotchet!
Do you stagger still? If you continue thus,   220
I vow you are not worth a welcome home
Neither from her, nor me.
                Enter ROCHFIELD *and* ANNABEL.
                See, here she comes.
Clare. I have brought you home a Jewel.

198 worthy,] ~ˏ Q
203 SP] Dyce 1; *not in* Q

222 SD] *to right of lines 220–1* Q ANNABEL.]
~ˏ Q

Annabel.   Wear it your self;
     For these I wear are Fetters, not Favors.
Clare.   I lookt for better welcome.
Rochfield [*to Bonvile*].   Noble sir,
     I must wooe your better knowledge.
Bonvile.   Oh dear sir,
     My Wife will bespeak it for you.
Rochfield.   Ha! Your Wife!
Woodroff.   Bear with him, sir, he's strangely off o'th hinges.
Bonvile [*aside*].   The Jewels are i'th right place; but the Jewel
     Of her heart sticks yonder. [*to Annabel*] You are angry with me   230
     For my going over?
Annabel.   Happily more angry
     For your coming over.
Bonvile.   I sent you my Will from *Dover*?
Annabel.   Yes Sir.
Bonvile.   Fetch it.
Annabel.   I shall Sir, but leave your Self-will with you.   *Exit.*   [H2ʳ]
Woodroff.   This is fine, the woman will be mad too.
Bonvile [*to Rochfield*].   Sir, I would speak with you.
Rochfield.   And I with you
     Of all men living.
Bonvile [*aside to Rochfield*].   I must have satisfaction from you.
Rochfield [*aside to Bonvile*].   Sir, it growes upon the time of payment.   240
Woodroff.   What's that? What's that? Ile have no whispering.

                 Enter ANNABEL *with a Will.*

Annabel.   Look you, there's the Pattent
     Of your deadly affection to me.   [*Gives him the Will.*]
Bonvile.   'Tis wellcome,
     When I gave my self for dead, I then made over
     My Land unto you, now I finde your love
     Dead to me, I will alter't.
Annabel.   Use your pleasure,
     A man may make a garment for the Moon,
     Rather then fit your Constancy.

---

225 SD] This ed.; *not in* Q   **231** over?] ~. Q
226 knowledge.] ~? Q   **237** SD] This ed.; *not in* Q
227 Wife!] ~. Q   **239** SD] This ed.; *not in* Q; *whispers* Weis
229 SD] Dyce 2; *not in* Q   **240** SD] This ed.; *not in* Q; *whispers* Weis
230 SD] *as* Weis; *not in* Q   **243** SD] This ed.; *not in* Q

Woodroff.   How's this?
    Alter your Will!
Bonvile.   'Tis in mine own disposing,
    Certainly I will alter't.
Woodroff.   Will you so my friend?   250
    Why then I will alter mine too.
    I had estated thee, thou peevish fellow,
    In forty thousand pounds after my death.
    I can finde another Executor.
Bonvile.   Pray sir, do,
    Mine Ile alter without question.
Woodroff.   Doest hear me?
    And if I change not mine within this two hours,
    May my Executors cozen all my kindred
    To whom I bequeath Legacies.
Bonvile.   I am for a Lawyer, sir.
Woodroff.   And I will be with one as soon as thy self,
    Though thou ridest poste to'th devil.   [*Exit Bonvile.*]   260
Rochfield.   Stay, let me follow, and cool him.
Woodroff.   Oh by no means,
    You'l put a quarrel upon him for the wrong,
    H'as done my Daughter.   [H2ᵛ]
Rochfield.   No believe it sir,
    He's my wisht friend.
Woodroff.   Oh come, I know the way of't;
    Carry it like a French quarrel, privately whisper,
    Appoint to meet, and cut each others throats
    With Cringes and Embraces, I protest
    I will not suffer you exchange a word
    Without I over hear't.
Rochfield.   Use your pleasure. *Exeunt Woodroff, Rochfield.*
Clare.   You are like to make fine work now.
Annabel.   Nay, you are like   270
    To make a finer buissiness of't.
Clare.   Come, come,
    I must sowder you together.

249 Will!] ~. Q
253 death.] ~, Q
260 SD] *as* Dyce 1 (*to right of line 258*); *placed
    as* Dyce 2; *not in* Q

261 Stay,] ~ₐ Q
265 whisper,] ~ₐ Q
269 *Exeunt*] Dyce 1; *Exit* Q

Annabel.   You? Why I heard
        A bird sing lately, you are the onely cause
        Works the division.
Clare.   Who? As thou ever lovedst me—
        For I long, though I am a Maid, for't.
Annabel.   *Lessingham.*
Clare.   Why then I do protest my self first cause
        Of the wrong, which he has put upon you both,
        Which please you to walk in, I shall make good
        In a short relation; come Ile be the clew
        To lead you forth this Labyrinth, this toyl   280
        Of a supposed and causeless Jealousie.
        Cankers touch choicest fruit with their infection,
        And Fevers seize those of the best complexion.   *Exeunt.*

                              [V.ii]

                    Enter WOODROFF *and* ROCHFIELD.
Woodroff.   Sir, have I not said I love you? If I have,
        You may believ't before an Oracle,
        For there's no trick in't, but the honest sence.
Rochfield.   Believe it, that I do, sir.
Woodroff.   Your love must then
        Be as plain with mine, that they may suit together:
        I say you must not fight with my son *Bonvile.*
Rochfield.   Not fight with him, sir?
Woodroff.   No, not fight with him, sir.
        I grant you may be wronged, and I dare swear
        So is my childe, but he is the husband, you know,   [H3ʳ]
        The womans lord, and must not always be told   10
        Of his faults neither. I say you must not fight.
Rochfield.   Ile swear it, if you please sir.
Woodroff.   And forswear, I know't,
        E're you lay ope the secrets of your valour;
        'Tis enough for me I saw you whisper,
        And I know what belongs to't.

274 me—] ~, Q   11 neither.] ~, Q
V.ii] *as* Dyce 1; *not in* Q   12 forswear, I know't,] ~ˬ ~ ~ˬ Q
7 not] Not Q   13 valour;] ~, Q

Rochfield.   To no such end, assure you.

                    Enter LESSINGHAM.

Woodroff. I say you cannot fight with him,
        If you be my friend, for I must use you—
        Yonder's my foe, and you must be my Second;
        [*to Lessingham*] Prepare thee Slanderer, and get another
        Better then thy self too; for here's my Second,   20
        One that will fetch him up, and fierk him too.
        Get your tools, I know the way to *Callis-sands*,
        If that be your Fence-school, hee'l show you tricks 'faith,
        Hee'l let blood your Calumny, your best guard
        Will come to a *Peccavi* I believe.

Lessingham.   Sir, if that be your quarrel, he's a party
        In it, and must maintain the side with me;
        From him I collected all those Circumstances
        Concern your Daughter, his own tongue's confession.

Woodroff. Who, from him?   30
        He will belie to do thee a pleasure then,
        If he speak any ill upon himself,
        I know he ne're could do an injury.

Rochfield.   So please you, Ile relate it, sir.

                    Enter BONVILE, ANNABEL, CLARE.

Woodroff. Before her husband then, and here he is
        In friendly posture with my Daughter too;
        I like that well. Son Bridegroom, and Lady Bride,
        If you will hear a man defame himself,
        (For so he must if he say any ill,)
        Then listen.

Bonvile.   Sir, I have heard this story,   40
        And meet with your opinion in his goodness,
        The repitition will be needless.

Rochfield.   Your father has not, Sir. Ile be brief   [H3ᵛ]
        In the delivery.

Woodroff.   Do, do then, I long to hear it.

Rochfield.   The first acquaintance I had with your Daughter,
        Was on the Wedding-Eve.

16 him,] ~. Q   19 SD] *as* Weis; *not in* Q   thee] Dyce 1; the Q
17 you—] ~, Q   27 me;] ~, Q
18 Second;] ~, Q   30 Who,] ~ₐ Q

Woodroff.   So, 'tis not ended
    Yet, methinks.
Rochfield.   I would have robb'd her.
Woodroff.   Ah, thief!
Rochfield.   That Chain and Bracelet which she wears upon her,
    She ransom'd with the full esteem in Gold,
    Which was with you my Venture.
Woodroff.   Ah, thief agen!   50
Rochfield.   For any attempt against her honor, I vow
    I had no thought on.
Woodroff.   An honest thief 'faith yet.
Rochfield.   Which she as nobly recompenc'd, brought me home,
    And in her own discretion thought it meet,
    For cover of my shame, to call me Cousin.
Woodroff.   Call a thief Cousin? Why, and so she might,
    For the Gold she gave thee, she stole from her husband,
    'Twas all his now, yet 'twas a good Girl too.
Rochfield.   The rest you know, sir.
Woodroff.   Which was worth all the rest,
    Thy valor Lad; but Ile have that in Print,   60
    Because I can no better utter it.
Rochfield.   Thus (Jade unto my Wants, and spurred by my
    Necessities) I was going, but by
    That Ladies councel I was staid; (for that
    Discourse was our familiarity.)
    And this you may take for my Recantation,
    I am no more a thief.
Woodroff.   A blessing on thy heart,
    And this was the first time, I warrant thee, too.
Rochfield.   Your charitable Censure is not wrong'd in that.
Woodroff.   No, I knew't could be but the first time at most;   70
    But for thee (brave Valor) I have in store,
    That thou shalt need to be a thief no more.   *Soft Musick.*
    Ha! What's this Musick?
Bonvile [to Lessingham].   It chimes an *Io pæan* to your Wedding, sir,
    If this be your Bride.

47 thief!] ~. Q
50 agen!] ~. Q
52 on] Q; on't Lucas

68 time,] ~ ^ Q   thee,] ~ ^ Q
74 SD] *This ed.; not in* Q   an *Io pæan*] Dyce
    1; a *Jopæan* Q

Lessingham [*to Clare*].   Can you forgive me? Some wilde distractions
    Had overturned my own condition,
    And spilt the goodness you once knew in me,
    But I have carefully recovered it,
    And overthrown the fury on't.

Clare.   It was my cause   80
    That you were so possest, and all these troubles   [H4ʳ]
    Have from my peevish will original:
    I do repent, though you forgive me not.

Lessingham.   You have no need for your repentance then,
    Which is due to it: all's now as at first
    It was wisht to be.

Woodroff.   Why, that's well said of all sides.
    Enter COMPASS *and the four Gallants* [RAYMOND, EUSTACE, LYONEL,
    GROVER], [URSE *as a*] *Bride between* FRANCKFORD *and another,* LUCE,
    Nurse, and Childe.
    But soft, this Musick has some other meaning:
    Another Wedding towards. Good speed, good speed!

Compass.   We thank you, sir.

Woodroff.   Stay, stay, our neighbor *Compass*, is't not?   90

Compass.   That was, and may be agen to morrow, this day Master
    Bridegroom.

Woodroff.   Oh! Give you joy. But sir, if I be not mistaken, you were
    married before now; how long is't since your wife died?

Compass.   Ever since yesterday, sir.

Woodroff.   Why, she's scarce buried yet then.

Compass.   No indeed, I mean to dig her grave soon, I had no leisure yet.

Woodroff.   And was not your fair Bride married before?

Urse.   Yes indeed, sir.

Woodroff.   And how long since your husband departed?   100

Urse.   Just when my husbands wife died.

Woodroff.   Bless us *Hymen*, are not these both the same parties?

Bonvile.   Most certain, sir.

---

76 SD] This ed.; *not in* Q
77 overturned] over- | turned Q (*hyphen at*
   end of line)
84 then,] ~ₐ Q
86.1–.3 SD] *after line 88* Q
86.1–.2 RAYMOND . . . GROVER] *as* Dyce 1;
  not in Q

86.2 URSE *as a*] This ed.; *not in* Q; URSE
  (*replacing* Bride) Dyce 2
88 towards.] ~, Q   speed!] ~, Q
99, 101 SPs] Dyce 2; *Wife.* Q

Woodroff.   What Marriage call you this?

Compass.   This is called *Shedding of Horns*, sir.

Woodroff.   How!

Lessingham.   Like enough, but they may grow agen next year.

Woodroff.   This is a new trick.

Compass.   Yes sir, because we did not like the old trick.

Woodroff.   Brother, you are a helper in this design too?   110

Franckford.   The Father to give the Bride, sir.

Compass.   And I am his son, sir, and all the sons he has; and this is his
Grand-childe, and my elder brother, you'l think this strange now.

Woodroff.   Then it seems he begat this before you?

Compass.   Before me? Not so sir, I was far enough off when 'twas done;
yet let me see him dares say, this is not my Childe, and this my father.

Bonvile.   You cannot see him here, I think sir.

Woodroff.   Twice married! Can it hold?

Compass.   Hold? It should hold the better, a wise man would think,
when 'tis ty'd of two knots.   120

Woodroff.   Methinks it should rather unloose the first, and between 'em   [H4ᵛ]
both make up one *Negative*.

Eustace.   No sir, for though it hold on the contrary, yet two *Affirmatives*
make no *Negative*.

Woodroff.   Cry you mercy, sir.

Compass.   Make what you will, this little *Negative* was my wifes laying,
and I *Affirm* it to be mine own.

Woodroff.   This proves the marriage before substantial, having this issue.

Compass.   'Tis mended now sir; for being double married, I may now
have two children at a birth, if I can get 'em. D' ye think Ile be five   130
years about one, as I was before?

Eustace.   The like has bin done for the loss of the Wedding-ring, and to
settle a new peace before disjoynted.

Lyonel.   But this indeed sir, was especially done, to avoid the word of
Scandal, that foul word which the fatal Monologist cannot alter.

Woodroff.   Cuckow!

Compass.   What's that, the Nightingale?

Woodroff.   A Night-bird, much good may it do you, sir.

Compass.   Ile thank you when I'm at Supper. Come Father, Childe, and
Bride; and for your part Father,   140

---

110 too?] ~. Q   136 *Cuckow*!] ~. Q
128 issue.] ~ₐ Q   138 it] Dyce 1; *not in* Q

Whatsoever he, or he, or t'other says,
You shall be as welcome as in my t'other wifes days.
Franckford.   I thank you, sir.
Woodroff.   Nay, take us with you, Gentlemen:
One Wedding we have yet to solemnize,
The first is still imperfect. Such troubles
Have drown'd our Musick: but now I hope all's friends.
Get you to Bed, and there the Wedding ends.
Compass.   And so good night, my Bride and Ile to bed:
He that has Horns, thus let him learn to shed.   *Exeunt.*   150

FINIS.

Press variants

Symbols used to identify copies are those of the revised Wing *STC*. The copies collated (all known copies to which we had access) are listed below:

A   Abbotsford, by Melrose, Scotland (Library of Sir Walter Scott)
CH1   Huntington Library 109543
CH2   Huntington Library KD 178
CLC   William Andrews Clark Memorial Library, UCLA
CN   Newberry Library, Chicago
EC   Eton College
EN1   National Library of Scotland Bute 606
EN2   National Library of Scotland H.28.e.2(5)
L   British Library 82.c.26(6)
LT   British Library, Thomason Collection 644.f.78
LVD   Victoria and Albert Museum Dyce Collection
MB   Boston Public Library
MH   Harvard University Houghton Library
NIC   Cornell University
NN1   New York Public Library
NN2   New York Public Library (*Two New Plays* copy)
NNM   Pierpont Morgan Library, New York
NNP   Carl H. Pforzheimer Library (now at University of Texas)
NP   Princeton University
O1   Bodleian Library Malone 188(1)
O2   Bodleian Library Douce WW66
OW   Worcester College, Oxford
SBT   Shakespeare Birthplace Trust, Stratford-upon-Avon
WF   Folger Shakespeare Library
Y1   Yale University (first issue, Ih W394 661b)
Y2   Yale University (second issue, Ih W394 661)
ZWT   Alexander Turnbull Library, National Library of New Zealand, Wellington

OUTER C

First state: all copies except NIC, Y2
Second state: NIC, Y2

C4^v (38) *Itacus*] Hams

OUTER E

First state: CLC, EN1, LT, MH, NNP, O1
Second state: A, CH1, CH2, CN, EC, EN2, L, LVD, MB, NIC, NN1, NN2, NNM, NP, OW, SBT, WF, Y1, Y2, ZWT

E2^v (11) will] Will

Sheet E is lacking in O2.

Some letters, particularly hyphens and punctuation marks, have failed to print in certain copies, but are faintly visible in others, and (in a few cases) fully visible in yet others. These variations have not arisen through any deliberate correction to the type.

Lineation

For the conventions used here see pp. xiii–xiv.

I.i

1–50] *as* Dyce 1; *prose* Q

58b–9] *as* Dyce 1; *prose* Q

67] *as* Dyce 1; *two lines* . . . alone | Q

69b–87] *as* Dyce 1; *prose* Q

88–9] *as* Dyce 1; Gentlemen, | Q

92b–6] *as* Dyce 1; *prose* Q

104b–5a] *as* Dyce 1; *one line* Q

105b–6a] *as* Dyce 1; *one line* Q

106b–7a] *as* Dyce 1; *one line* Q

113b–15a] *as* Dyce 1; *prose* Q

120b–1] *as* Dyce 1; *one line* Q

133b–56a] *as* Dyce 1; *prose* Q

157b–9a] *prose* Q; *verse* . . . not | . . . public. | Dyce 1

159b–62] *prose* Q; *verse* . . . if | . . . hurt | Dyce 1

166b–73a] *as* Dyce 1; *prose* Q

173b–5] *as* Dyce 1; *two lines* . . . Frye, | Q

I.ii

1–30] *as* Dyce 1; *prose* Q

33–5a] *as* Dyce 1; *prose (but line 33 begins as though continuing verse)* Q

38b–9] *as* Dyce 1; *one line* Q

45b–6a] *as* Dyce 1; *one line* Q

46b–53] *as* Dyce 1; *prose* Q

58b–101] *as* Dyce 1; *prose* Q

122b–36] *as* Dyce 1; *prose* Q

165–72] *as* Dyce 1; *prose* Q

178–87a] *as* Dyce 1; *prose* Q

187b–8] *as* Lucas; *prose* Q; *one line* Dyce 1

189–96] *as* Dyce 1; *prose* Q

II.i

1–20] *as* Dyce 1; *prose* Q

25–42] *as* Dyce 1; *prose* Q

II.ii

8–37] *as* Dyce 1; *prose* Q

46b–50] *as* Dyce 1; *prose* Q

56–85] *as* Dyce 1; *prose* Q

87b–91] *as* Dyce 1; *prose* Q

94–100] *as* Dyce 1; *prose* Q

II.iii

74–7] *as* Dyce 1; *verse* . . . thee, | . . . be | . . . changing | . . . called | Q

79–82] *as* Dyce 1; *verse* . . . Love | . . . sight. | . . . world, | Q

113–14] *as* Dyce 1; *prose* Q

124–7] *as* Dyce 1; *prose* Q

137–8] *as* Dyce 1; *prose* Q

145–7] *as* Dyce 1; *verse* . . . morrow. | . . . come, | Q

II.iv

1–12] *as* Dyce 1; *prose* Q

15–19a] *as* Dyce 1; *prose* Q

31–5] *as* Dyce 1; *prose* Q

38–9] *verse* . . . not | Q

47–8] *as* Dyce 1; . . . yet | Q

49–61] *as* Dyce 1; *prose* Q

63b–90] *as* Dyce 1; *prose* Q

93–114] *as* Dyce 1; *prose* Q

115–18] *as* Dyce 1; *prose* Q; . . . till | . . . door | . . . may | Lucas

119–20] *as* Dyce 1; . . . Father, | (*perhaps intended as prose*) Q

129–30] *as* Dyce 1; *prose* Q

III.i

1–74a] *as* Dyce 1; *prose* Q

74b–5] *as* Lucas; *prose* Q; . . . friend? | Dyce 1

76–88] *as* Dyce 1; *prose* Q

89] *as* Q (*though intending prose*); *two lines* . . . then, | Dyce 1

90–4] *as* Dyce 1; *prose* Q

95–7] *as* Lucas; *prose* Q; . . . ever | . . . now | (*emending* wisht *to* Wishèd) Dyce 1

98–152] *as* Dyce 1; *prose* Q

III.ii

67–9] *as* Dyce 1; *prose* Q

74–81] *as* Dyce 1; *prose* Q

III.iii

1–3a] *as* Dyce 1; *prose* Q

3b–4a] *as* Lucas; *prose* Q; . . . he | Dyce 1

5–6] *prose* Q; wherein | Dyce 1

9–107] *as* Dyce 1; *prose* Q

IV.i

37–53] *as* Dyce 1; *prose* Q

134–7] *as* Dyce 1; *prose* Q

142–6] *as* Dyce 1; *prose* Q

148–66] *as* Dyce 1; *prose* Q

177–85] *as* Dyce 1; *prose* Q

186–9] *as* Lucas; *prose* Q; . . . agreement, | . . . fault, | . . . will I | Dyce 1

IV.ii

1–18a] *as* Dyce 1; *prose* Q

18b–19] *as* Lucas; *prose* Q; . . . More | Dyce 1

20–4] For . . . Bridegroom *as* Dyce 1; *prose* Q

24–5 Say . . . heart,] *as* Lucas; *prose* Q; *one line* Dyce 1

26–70a] *as* Dyce 1; *prose* Q

74b–104] *as* Dyce 1; *prose* (*with* i'th . . . cruelty *possibly intended as one verse line*) Q

107–10] *as* Dyce 1; *prose* Q

114–43] *as* Dyce 1; *prose* Q

144–5] *as* Hazlitt; *prose* Q; . . . truth | Dyce 1

147b–64] *as* Dyce 1; *prose* Q

167–96a] *as* Dyce 1; *prose* Q

IV.iii

1–3] *as* Dyce 1; *verse* . . . Divorce, | . . . meeting, | Q

5–10] *as* Dyce 1; *verse* . . . smooth | . . . more, | . . . rank, | . . . I | . . . too, | . . . let | . . . this | Q

27–8 Sometimes . . . new.] *prose* Q; Dyce 1 *begins verse line 28 with* I might, Hazlitt *with* A whole

32–3] *as* Lucas; *prose (though with same line division)* Q

56–7] *as* Dyce 1; *prose* Q

60–70] *as* Dyce 1; *prose* Q

74–7] *as* Dyce 1; *verse* . . . men | . . . yet | . . . tasted | Q

83–93] *as* Dyce 1; *verse* . . . where | . . . issue, | . . . all, | . . . another, | . . . Sou-East, | . . . them | . . . Sou-Sou-East | . . . Sou-West's (Sou-West Q) | . . . 'em, | . . . for | . . . they | . . . coats | Q

102–3] *as* Dyce 1; *prose but dividing* . . . and | Never . . .

105–6] *verse* . . . rest; | . . . deepest; | Q

107–8] *as* Dyce 1] *verse* . . . afore-hand, | Q

110–12] *as* Dyce 1] *verse* . . . though | . . . another | . . . invite | Q

114–15] *as* Dyce 1] *verse* . . . any | Q

117–20] *as* Dyce 1] *verse* . . . without | . . . to a | . . . me | Q

127–8] *as* Dyce 1] *verse* . . . now, | Q

V.i

1–14] *as* Dyce 1; *prose* Q

19–22] *as* Dyce 1; *prose* Q

37b–8] *as* Dyce 1; *prose* Q

41b–7] *as* Dyce 1; *prose* Q

48–9] *prose* Q; *Marget,* | Dyce 1

50–3a] *as* Dyce 1; *prose* Q

58b–60a] *as* Dyce 1; *prose* Q

68b–82] *as* Dyce 1; *prose* Q

92b–3] *as* Dyce 1; *one line* Q

104–9a] *as* Dyce 1; *prose* Q

118b–20a] *as* Dyce 1; *prose* Q

121b–4a] *as* Lucas; *prose* Q; . . . already, | . . . over: | Dyce 1

124b–5] *as* Lucas; *one line* Q

126b–8a] *as* Dyce 1; *prose* Q

144b–5] *as* Dyce 1; *one line* Q

154b–5] *as* Weis; . . . yours; | Q

162b–3] *as* Dyce 1; *one line* Q

189b–90] *as* Dyce 1; *one line* Q

199] *as* Q; *two lines* . . . with | Dyce 1

225b–6] *as* Dyce 1; *one line* Q

231b–2a] *as* Lucas; *one line* Q

237b–8] *as* Lucas; *one line* Q

248b–9a] *as* Dyce 1; *one line* Q

263b–4a] *as* Dyce 1; *one line* Q

270b–1a] *as* Dyce 1; *one line* Q

271b–2a] *as* Dyce 1; *one line* Q

V.ii

26–9] . . . quarrel, | . . . maintain | . . . collected | . . . Daughter, | Q

39–40a] *as* Dyce 1; *one line* Q

40b–4a] *as* Dyce 1; *prose* Q

46b–7] So . . . methinks *as* Dyce 1; *one line* Q

48–50a] *as* Dyce 1; *prose* Q

51–2a] *as* Dyce 2; *prose but dividing* . . . no | Thought . . . Q

59b–65] *prose* Q; . . . Wants, | . . . going, | . . . staid; | Dyce 1

66–7a] *as* Dyce 1; *prose* Q

74–5] *as* Dyce 2; *prose* Q

76–88] *as* Dyce 1; *prose* Q

121–2] *verse* . . . first, | Q

132–3] *as* Q (*but* And *is capitalized at beginning of line*)

141–2] *as* Dyce 1; *prose* Q

Commentary

TITLE-PAGE

10 WILLIAM ROWLEY A leading actor, specializing in roles such as that of the fat clown, and a dramatist whose best work was done in collaboration with Middleton, Rowley (*c.* 1585–1626) collaborated with W, Dekker, and Ford in the lost *KWW* (1624), and contributed commendatory verses to *DM*.

11 *Placere Cupio* 'I wish to please' (Latin).

12 *Tho. Johnson* London printer, active *c.* 1658–77. His involvement with playtexts, in association with Kirkman, was confined to 1661–2.

12–13 *Francis Kirkman* Scrivener, author, and translator, who began a chequered career as London bookseller about 1656, publishing *Lust's Dominion* in 1657. His preface to *The English Rogue Continued* (1668), also sub-titled *The Second Part*, provides some autobiography. From boyhood an assiduous collector, he compiled two catalogues of extant plays (1661, 1671), reproduced and evaluated by Greg, *Bibliography*, III, 1338–56. Kirkman claimed to have published *A Cure for a Cuckold*, along with *The Thracian Wonder* and *Gammer Gurton's Needle* (all 1661), from his own collection, but in the same year he was involved in more dubious ventures. In 1662 1,400 playbooks were seized from Kirkman's shop, because his partners, Thomas Johnson, Nathaniel Brooke, and Henry Marsh, had flouted copyright. Kirkman did not resume business until 1666, after Marsh, who was heavily in debt to him, had died of plague and Kirkman had acquired his estate. His name disappears from the records after 1678.

13 Sign of *John Fletchers Head* Presumably John Fletcher the dramatist (d. 1625).

14–15 *Angel-Inne* ... St. *Clements* One of several London inns with this name, situated in the Strand, behind the church of **St. *Clements*** (i.e. St Clement Danes). See Sugden, pp. 18 and 121.

15 *Temple-Bar* A gate at the western end of Fleet Street, near the Inns of Court, marking the limit of the jurisdiction of the City of London. See Sugden, p. 505.

THE STATIONER, TO THE JUDICIOUS READER

4 *Employment somewhat failing* In *The English Rogue Continued*, Kirkman records that 'during the time of great buildings at the East part of *London*', where he dwelt, he 'gained much' as a scrivener, 'but that ceasing, and the tide of employment ebbing at th'East part', he decided in the year of the Restoration (1660) to move to the West and again set up shop as both scrivener and bookseller (A6^v–7^r).

5 *ere* Lucas emends to '*e'er*', but Q's phonetic spelling of the contraction for 'ever' is common in seventeenth-century texts.

6 *converse with* 'be familiar or conversant with, deal with' (*OED* converse 3).

10 *700 . . . printed* In his advertisement to his 1671 catalogue Kirkman said that his 1661 catalogue contained '690 several Playes' and the new one 806 (Greg, *Bibliography*, III, 1353). Greg showed that the true counts were 685 and 804 (p. 1355). There is no good reason to doubt that in 1661 Kirkman possessed, or had possessed, copies of the sixteenth- and seventeenth-century English plays he lists, or that his catalogue of those that had reached print was very nearly comprehensive.

15–16 The Thracian Wonder Attributed on its title-page, like *CC*, to W and Rowley; some copies were issued jointly with the 1661 Quarto of *CC* under the single-leaf general title *Two New Playes*. The play's most recent editor supports attribution to Rowley and Heywood (see Michael Nolan, ed., *The Thracian Wonder* [Salzburg, 1997]).

17 Gammer Gurton's Needle An English university comedy from the mid-sixteenth century of which the earliest surviving edition is 1575.

18 *almost an hundred years* Kirkman's second edition is dated 1661.

23 *hath bin tried* The primary implication seems to be that this cure for cuckoldry *hath bin tried* successfully in real life, but Weis may be right in suspecting 'a glancing allusion perhaps to *AQL* II.i.120–2 (*c.* 1621, and a probable Webster–Middleton collaboration), in which the idea of a homecoming sailor and a temporary divorce is mentioned'.

24 Probatum est 'It has been proven' (Latin).

26–7 *abler . . . Vindication* Presumably a reference to Heywood's *An Apology for Actors* (1612), to which W contributed a prefatory poem.

DRAMATIS PERSONAE

3 *Lessingham* As Lucas notes, the name occurs in Heywood's *The Four Prentices of London* (?1602), where 'Guy of Lusignan' becomes 'Guy of Lessingham'.

10 *Woodroff* By virtue of his commission as a **Justice of the Peace** Woodroff is an appropriate arbitrator of the dispute in IV.i.

12 *Bonvile* As Lucas notes, a name used by Heywood in *The Royal King and The Loyal Subject* (1637).

13 *Franckford* Again, as Lucas notes, Heywood used the name before, in *A Woman Killed with Kindness* (1603).

15 *Nurse* i.e. a wet nurse in charge of the infant.

20 *Urse* Cf. Ursula the pig woman in Jonson's *Bartholomew Fair*. It may be that she is meant to be fat, like Rowley, who presumably wrote the role of her husband, Compass, with himself in mind, although he could not have played it (see pp. 290–1).

ACT I, Scene i

0.1 LESSINGHAM *and* CLARE While they will probably both be richly dressed for the celebration they are attending, and to indicate that they, like the bridal couple, share 'a like pair of Fortunes suitable, | Equality in Birth, parity in years' (6–7, and cf. 88–90), it will be evident in the acting that Clare is 'melancholly' (75); cf. *DLC* V.iv.38.1n. They probably enter *'with Rosemary as from a wedding'* (Fletcher, *The Woman's Prize*, I.i.0.1–.2; see Dessen and Thomson, 'wedding'). For **Music**, cf. 125–6 and n.

1–3 This . . . pleasure The entry of two characters onto an empty stage marks their separation from the festivities Lessingham describes. At Wellington 1997 Annabel and Bonvile's wedding party was in progress in the background, emphasizing the contrast.

2 Triumphs and Ovations Both terms denote the Roman ritual processions held in honour of a victorious commander (**Ovations** being lesser **Triumphs**), but are linked here for their more general sense of 'joyful celebrations' (*OED* triumph 4; cf. *DM* I.i.351 and n) and 'exultation' (*OED* ovation 2; although not cited prior to 1649, this is the Latin root meaning).

3 state 'dignified observance of form or ceremony' (*OED* 17b). As with 'Triumphs and Ovations' (2), rank and wealth are implicit.

3 'Tis confest i.e. 'That's so' (see *OED* confessed 1). Clare's excessively brief responses draw attention to the difference between her 'sad' (18) mood and Lessingham's.

4 Jubile Used here not in the technical, religious sense (cf. *WD* I.ii.91n) but generally, as 'exultant joy, general or public rejoicing, jubilation' (*OED* 5a).

5 For such as can be merry A first voicing of Clare's unhappiness.

9 'Tis a Marriage Grudging in tone, this may also be implicitly satiric.

10 president i.e. 'precedent'.

11 these Possibly accompanied by a gesture to the offstage bridal couple (so Wellington 1997).

16 Trewants in Loves school A conventionally flirtatious image; cf. Heywood, *How a Man May Choose a Good Wife from a Bad* (1602), C2ᵛ: 'Neuer was such a trewant in Loues schoole, | I am asham'd that ere I was his Tutor.'

19 Jovial Perhaps not merely 'merry' (*OED* 6), but 'under the influence of . . . the planet Jupiter . . . regarded as the source of joy and happiness' (*OED* 5), implying that their love is fated (cf. 'purpose' [25]).

20 made such Not 'sad' (18), but a 'graduate' (18) in 'Loves school' (16), as a gesture towards offstage (to imply the bridal couple) can make clear (so Wellington 1997).

21 meet by purpose Both 'Guests invited' (20), they were bound to meet, but it may be that Lessingham implies also that their meeting is divinely appointed. Cf. 19n.

23 solicite 'conduct, manage, push forward' (*OED* solicit 8a).

24 before i.e. 'in presence of' (*OED prep.* 3a) **this example**.

27 your observance 'deference, dutiful service' (*OED* 3) to you. There may also be the senses of 'observant care' (*OED* 4) and, figuratively, 'performance of customary worship or ceremony' (*OED* 1b).

39 Resolve me i.e. 'give me a clear understanding' (see *OED* resolve 15a).

44 perfect me i.e. 'fully inform me' (see *OED* perfect *vb.* 4). Here pronounced with the accent on the first syllable.

48 received 'experienced' (*OED* 19a); or, more strongly, 'suffered' (*OED* 19b).

50 imply 'attribute' (*OED* 5b): the only example given of this sense of 'imply'.

53 windings, and indents 'the twists and recesses (of the road to Clare's heart)' (Weis). See *OED* indent *n.*[1], which cites *1H4* III.i.103: 'It [the Trent] shall not wind with such a deep indent.'

56 to my fruition 'to the enjoyment of me' (see *OED* fruition 1, and cf. 57).

61–2 May you ... minutes, i.e. 'If you will wait (you shall hear from me).' Q's comma after 'Chamber' (60) and full stop after 'minutes' give the nonsensical reading 'I'll to my chamber, (if you will waste some more time).'

65 period 'conclusion' (*OED* 5a).

66.1 Enter ... Gallants As is clear from 119 (and the Dramatis personae), *Gallants* is a description of the four young men who enter, not a direction for additional characters. They tend to function in the play more as a group than as individuated characters (see pp. 286–7). *Gallants* is probably authorial, as it would be superfluous in the playhouse; but playscripts prepared for the stage often have directions highlighted as in Q. The direction is set on two lines, the first running to the right-hand margin, and is enclosed in a rectangle composed of short rules and open at the right. This typographical feature recurs at 1.ii.103–4. See p. 297.

67 You alone An element of mockery or 'sport' (93) may inform all the comments of the Gallants; cf. 'You are pleasant' (87 and n).

68 confluence 'large gathering' (see *OED* 5).

70 Men ... alone Lucas compares Cicero (*De Rep.*, I.xvii.27 and *De Off.*, III.i.1); it is also proverbial (Tilley A228).

73 Fair Mistriss Clare While this may indicate no more than that Lessingham's courtship of Clare is common knowledge among his friends, an earlier entrance by the Gallants, in time to observe Clare leaving, would make the teasing more pointed (so Wellington 1997).

75 setting off i.e. 'taking away, setting aside' (see *OED* set *v.* 147a).

76 without taxation 'beyond censure' (*OED* without *prep.* 2b, taxation 3).

83 Mrs. An abbreviation of 'Mistress' (and then so pronounced), which could be prefixed to the name of either a married or unmarried woman (see *OED* Mrs. 1, mistress 14; and cf. 136n). We have retained the abbreviation where it is a title of courtesy, and consequently standard, but expanded it at III.i.94 and 125, where as a noun it occurs in the phrases 'your Mrs.' and 'thy Mrs.'; these latter are in passages set as prose in Q, so have probably been used by the compositor as aids to justifying the line of type.

84 Fortunes correspondent Probably, continuing the comparison, '(of) wealth equivalent (to Annabel's)', though just possibly Fortune's 'accomplice' (*OED* correspondent *n.* 2), or 'correlative' (*OED* 1).

86 who ... thoughts? A cynical apothegm, perhaps jokingly aside to the audience, related to Tilley W672: 'A woman's heart and her tongue are not relatives.'

88 pleasant ... or else Although Lessingham's statement is incomplete, it appears to be a warning that even though he is aware they are being **pleasant** ('facetious, jocular' [*OED a.* 3a]), he will take exception to further joking about Clare.

91 peculiar 'particular, special' (*OED* 3).

92 some 'someone' (*OED* 1a [a]).

92 some . . . respects her 'someone [*OED* some 1a (a)] who does not esteem, show respect for, her' (see *OED* respect 4). This, it turns out, is true.

92–3 Lessingham probably moves away from the Gallants as he delivers this aside, allowing them to observe and comment on the delivery of the letter from a distance.

97 *Prove* 'try, test' (*OED* prove 1a).

99 character 'handwriting' (*OED* 4c), repeating and intensifying the sense of **hand**. Lessingham is most likely displaying the letter to the audience.

102 *thee dearest* Q's '*the*' must be a misprint for ***thee***, as Lessingham read it the first time (98), not a correction meaning that the friend must be found who loves 'the ***dearest***' (one) = Clare, since the entire meditation on friendship at the start of I.ii depends not just on the injunction to a friend, but 'of all Friends the most approved' (I.ii.9). He makes no attempt to find out who loves Clare; his energies are all towards establishing who loves him ***dearest***. See pp. 273–4 and pp. 288–9.

104 *Exit* Lessingham's behaviour as he exits may signal his 'distraction' (113).

106–7 It . . . challenge A proleptic statement, from one not notably prescient.

108 Heresie Raymond is playing on the convention of woman-as-saint in the Petrarchan tradition. Cf. Jonson, *The New Inn* (1631), III.ii.211–13: 'Where have I liu'd, in heresie, so long | Out of the Congregation of Loue, | And stood irregular, by all his Canons?'

109–10 difference . . . decided A typical wedding jest, perhaps inspired by seeing the couple enter. **difference** = 'disagreement' (*OED* 3a); **decided** = 'resolved' (*OED* decide 1).

111.1–.2 SD This entry of the bridal couple, the jovial Woodroff, and their guests brings a bustle of real celebration onto the stage for the first time. For costuming, see pp. 282–3. Annabel may be identifiable as the bride by white dress and hair down (cf. *WD* V.i.0.1–.3n), and the guests probably all carry or wear rosemary or favours (cf. 0.1n, and MacIntyre, p. 146). Notwithstanding Compass's jocular suggestion that Luce is too old to be sexually attractive (II.iii.140), she is presented as of childbearing age, though barren (155–6). The wet nurse is 'young' (II.iv.28). The reference to 'the Gentleman we met | But now' (112–13) may imply that they have entered by the same door by which Lessingham exited, or even an early entrance so that they see him exit (so Wellington 1997).

116 distemper'd 'vexed, troubled' (*OED* 2).

119 miss her 'notice her absence' (Weis).

121 retir'd her self 'withdrew' (see *OED* retire 6). Her withdrawal was not in fact 'Unknown to any', since Lessingham was privy to it.

122 Sick of the *Maid* i.e. 'suffering from green-sickness' (*OED* maid *n.*[1] 8), 'an anaemic disease which mostly affects young women about the age of puberty, and gives a pale or greenish tinge to the complexion' (*OED* green-sickness). Since green-sickness was popularly supposed to be caused, in part at least, by a yearning for marriage (cf. *AV* III.iii.166–7), the pun on *Maid* (= tired of being unmarried) was very common. Cf. Henke 1988, pp. 116–17.

125–6 within The Musick playes Evidently **The Musick** (either a consort of musicians, or what they play) has been playing from the beginning of the scene (Wiggins, p. 375; so Wellington 1997).

129 Green-sickness Girls Cf. 122n.

130 pearls i.e. beads of perspiration. Woodroff's Petrarchist terminology characterizes him as old-fashioned in his gallantry.

132 cut Capers . . . high If Woodroff indicates an improbable height, or does a high dance scissors leap himself, the comic aspect of his character will be stressed.

134 Mrs. Abbreviation of 'Mistress' (and so pronounced); see 83n.

134 along with us These lines suggest the possibility of the Gallants exiting, with Bonvile and Annabel, after 137 (so Weis) or during Woodroff's subsequent speech (see 138n), thus justifying Woodroff's 'we are mist | Among the younger Frye' (173–4). On the other hand, Q provides no SD, and the more characters remain on stage, the greater the comic danger of 'publick' (159) embarrassment for Franckford during the rest of the scene.

136 Mr. An abbreviation of 'Master', a title of courtesy prefixed to the name of a man not entitled to be addressed as 'Sir' or 'Lord'. 'Master' may have been pronounced 'Mister' by this time, so **Mr.** may also have been pronounced either 'Master' or 'Mister' (*OED* Mr. 2a, master *n.*[1] 22, mister *n.*[2] 1; and cf. 83n). In the theatre, the more emphatic 'Master' (cf., e.g., 'Master *Lessingham*' at I.ii.31) is almost certain to have been retained; cf. the word play leading to 'Master' at 141.

137–41 This day . . . Master Playing on Annabel's reference to him as 'Mr. Bridegroom' (136), itself cued from Raymond's 'Mrs. Bride' (134), Bonvile styles himself **your servant**. This Petrarchist conceit, however, Woodroff reduces to a popular wedding jest: today Bonvile is Annabel's **Groom** (i.e. bridegroom [*OED* 6], with a pun on 'serving-man, man-servant' [*OED* 3]), but hereafter her **Master**. For pronunciation, see 83n and 136n.

138 She his Woodroff describes both bride and groom in the third person, suggesting that he has already turned to address Luce and Franckford. It is possible the bridal couple and the Gallants are leaving; see 134n.

141–2 I . . . do A somewhat obscure statement, whose primary purpose is to tease Franckford; Woodroff's probable meaning is that he will continue to be master in his own house. The absence of any reference to a wife suggests that he is a widower, but he is unlikely to be referring to hopes of remarriage.

151–3 your barrenness . . . elsewhere Woodroff seems to be asserting, jocularly, that Luce's sterility (or age; cf. II.iii.140) licenses her husband.

156 By-blow 'an illegitimate child; a bastard' (*OED* 3).

157, 159 *aside* The extent to which these comments are to Luce or to the audience (or both) may vary from one performance to another.

159 within compass 'within the bounds of moderation' (*OED* compass 2), with a teasing pun by Luce on Urse (Mistress Compass), whom he has indeed been **within** to father her child. Although we do not learn Urse's husband's name until II.iii, this double entendre is much more likely than the additional one Weis suspects on **compass** as 'circle' (*OED* 5) and hence 'vagina'.

160–1 But . . . both Both Lucas and Weis see Woodroff as continuing here his train of thought at 150–3, Lucas glossing as: 'If he has not had a natural child, I can only say I wish he had. It might be rather discreditable; still that "hurt" would be worth while putting up with for the sake of having an heir.' It is possible, however, that this is a simpler, rougher jest playing on 'I have done' (160) and **if he have not** ('done' [160]; see Partridge 1955, do, p. 103); i.e. if he has not impregnated you (in which case the **hurt** is the pain of childbirth rather than a wrong).

162 thine ear Because Woodroff here draws Luce apart, the Nurse is freed to approach Franckford.

163 Your boy The Nurse may speak deliberately loudly, since her intent seems to be to cajole Franckford into giving her more money through fear of public embarrassment. Cf. 170–3n.

163 chopping 'big and vigorous' (*OED*); cf. Heywood, *The Silver Age*, III.i (F2ᵛ): 'A fine chopping boy', and (F3ʳ): 'bravest chopping lad'.

167 breed teeth Cf. *DM* IV.ii.128.

168 Corral . . . Chain A single item combining the functions of toy, teething stick, and possibly charm. A **Corral** 'helpeth Children to breed their Teeth, their gums being rubbed therewith; and to that purpose they have it fastened at the ends of their Whistles' (William Cole, *Adam in Eden* [1657], p. 107). Pierre Erondelle's *The French Garden* (1605), includes (G8ᵛ) part of a dialogue between a mother and her child's nurse: 'You need not yet to give him his Corall with the small golden chayne, for I beleeve it is better to let him sleepe untill the after noon.' Scot (*Disc. Witchcraft*, p. 294) refers to the use of coral as a charm: 'The corall preserueth such as beare it from fascination or bewitching, and in this respect they are hanged about childrens necks.'

170–3 Piece . . . tongue Probably 172–3 is a triumphant aside to the audience: the Nurse will now be quiet, having achieved her objective of getting Franckford to buy her silence. The **Piece** is most likely the English gold coin worth 22 shillings, a substantial sum (see II.iv.113n).

174 Gravity i.e. the personification of 'Age' (177), to match 'youth' (175). Cf. *1H4* II.iv.294: 'What doth gravity out of his bed at midnight?'

ACT I, SCENE ii

0.1 sad 'my Author' (2) makes clear that Lessingham carries not only the **Letter**, but also a book, a common signifier of melancholy (cf. *WD* V.vi.1).

1 Amicitia . . . rarius 'Nature has given nothing greater or rarer than friendship.' The sentiment is from Cicero, *De Amicitia*, but not a direct quotation or paraphrase. Lessingham may, nevertheless, appear to be reading from the book; cf. 0.1n.

2 Author Probably Cicero; cf. 0.1n and 1n.

6 trans-shape 'transform' (*OED*).

7–8 kill . . . Friend By now Lessingham will be gesturing to the letter rather than the book.

9 approved 'tried, tested' (*OED* 1a).

14–15 apprehend . . . being i.e. 'considers [*OED* apprehend 9] that no such thing (as "the name of Friend" [17]) exists'.

15–16 kinred . . . world Perhaps 'just as rights deriving from descent [see *OED* kindred 1], and inherited rights to monarchy, are suffered to decay or fade [see *OED* wear *v.*¹] from the world'. A recent example was the loss by King James's son-in-law Frederick, Elector Palatine, of his lands and electoral title.

17 conceit Three meanings seem apropos: (1) 'idea, thought'; (2) 'personal opinion, judgement'; (3) 'ingenious notion or expression' (see *OED* 1, 4, 8).

18 tryed 'tested, put to the proof' (*OED* try 7a).

21–3 former . . . worser times Cf. La Primaudaye: 'the world hath had his infancie, next his youth, then his mans estate, & now he is in his old-age. For we see how all things decline daily, and continually waxe worse and worse, as it were approching to their end' (*The French Academie* [1618], p. 554, cited by Victor Harris, *All Coherence Gone* [London, 1949], p. 197).

24 justice . . . th' earth 'In classical mythology, Astraea, the goddess of justice, abandoned the earth after the golden age; here it is a banishment rather than a tactical withdrawal, adding a hint of tyranny to the original idea' (Weis). **It** = friendship.

29 'Twixt Love . . . right In personifying the conflict between **Love** and **Friendship**, Lessingham encapsulates in a couplet the central theme of the main plot.

31 What, Master *Lessingham* The greeting and mocking tone of the Gallants almost exactly repeat I.i.67 ff.

32–3 compos'd . . . fire Cf. *DM* I.i.112.

38 too i.e. 'to'. In seventeenth-century texts 'to' is a frequent spelling of modern 'too', and **too** of modern 'to', though the latter occurs mostly in contractions, such as 'too'th' (for 'to the'). 'Too' meaning 'to' occurs so often in Q (here, II.iii.138, II.iv.78, III.iii.13, IV.ii.160) that the spelling cannot always be due to scribal or compositorial misunderstanding. Besides, all instances end a clause: compare 'the honor he was born too' (IV.ii.160) with 'born to make us all' (III.iii.105). Hence we have not followed Lucas in regularizing.

39 sport 'amusement, diversion' (*OED n.*¹ 1a), with perhaps also senses of 'amorous dalliance' (*OED* 1b) and 'jesting' (at him) (see *OED* 4).

40 make . . . benefit i.e. 'take advantage of it'.

41–2 Content . . . did so i.e. 'Content has no stamina. When I was contented, I made the most ('present benefit' [40]) of it.'

44 Crotchet's i.e. crotchets: 'whimsical fancies; perverse conceits' (see *OED n.*¹ 9a).

46 *Lessingham* Q attributes 46–8 to Eustace, but the lines are clearly Lessingham's, whose short exchanges with the Gallants have muddled a compositor, or perhaps a scribe who added speech prefixes after writing out the dialogue.

50–5 question . . . Friend Each of the four Gallants in turn avows his friendship here, thus setting up Lessingham's opportunity for each in turn to deny him (82–104).

55 accompt 'estimation, esteem' (*OED* account 11).

69 open-breasted 'frank' (*OED* 2).

70 Monomachy 'single combat, duel' (*OED*); the word is a Heywood speciality, occurring in *The Rape of Lucrece* (1608), *Troia Britanica* (1609), and *The Golden Age* (1611). Both etymology and usage (as recorded by *OED* and *LION: Drama*) support Lucas's emendation of Q's 'Monamachy'.

74 composition 'mutual agreement' (*OED* 22).

75–8 Second . . . must fight The custom of seconds fighting was of long standing; cf. *Lr.* IV.vi.194: 'No seconds? All myself?' and Middleton and Rowley, *A Fair Quarrel*, III.i.46: 'do you but draw, we'll fight it for you'. By the seventeenth century, however, commentators and legislation condemned the fashion, arguing the need for seconds to act as witnesses and referees (see Kiernan, pp. 63–75). Lucas cites evidence for English observers believing the custom of seconds fighting to be French.

77 bring off 'bring away' (*OED* bring 19).

79 either of them i.e. 'both of them'.

79 dangerous i.e. 'ready to venture danger' (see *OED* 3, citing Tourneur, *The Atheist's Tragedy*, IV.ii.43–4: 'I doubt his life; | His spirit is so boldly dangerous').

79–104 Of all . . . out at that The four excuses in a row will inevitably have a comic aspect, as well as reinforcing the Gallants in the role of a generic, almost morality play, grouping (here, False Friendship; cf. Fellowship in *Everyman*, and New-guise, Nowadays, and Nought in *Mankind*).

82 meerly 'absolutely, altogether' (*OED* 2).

85 Upon . . . Discontents 'concerning [*OED* upon 22] some recent causes of dissatisfaction, grievance [*OED* discontent *n.*[1] 2]'. It is likely that the excuse is fabricated, but if not, the phrasing may imply, as Weis suggests, 'that Raymond's father's grievances against him are imaginary'.

86 atone me to i.e. 'be reconciled with, seek forgiveness from' (see *OED* atone 3b).

90 Callis-Sands i.e. Calais (then pronounced **Callis**) sands, a favourite duelling-ground, being the nearest place beyond the jurisdiction of the English laws against duelling; cf. *DLC* IV.ii.621.

96–9 Single-sword . . . force Just as 'single rapier' means 'the **Rapier** only, without **Ponyard**' (see *OED* single *a.* 17), so **Single-sword** means the sword only, without buckler or dagger. Grover's excuse is that with the slender **Rapier** designed for thrusting he could employ **sleight** ('dexterity'), but with the heavier **sword** designed for cutting he would need **force**. In a letter of 18 October 1580, Sidney urges his brother 'when you play at weapons . . . use as well the blow as the thrust; it is good in itself, and besides encreaseth your breath and strength, and will make you a strong man at the tourney and barriers. First, in any case practice with the single sword, and then with the dagger' (cited in *Shakespeare's England*, II, 395). Contemporary manuals of combat list single sword as a common form of fencing. Weis's definition of 'Single-sword' as 'a sword with only one cutting edge' (i.e. a back-sword) is unsupported by *OED*, which is uncertain as to definition.

104 out The sense of 'incompetent' required by context seems to derive from *OED* 20: 'at a loss from failure of memory or self-possession'.

104 *Exeunt Gallants* The manner of exiting may well reinforce their comic cowardice (so Wellington 1997).

108 how now friend This greeting will resonate ironically throughout the scene with the repetition of the now questionable term **friend**.

109 unseason'd i.e. 'unseasonable' (*OED* 3); or, as Weis glosses, 'inappropriate to the occasion (of his wedding day)'.

122 burthen (1) 'chief theme' (*OED* burden 11, although citing no example prior to 1649), and (2) 'load' (*OED* 1, 2), punning on 'take it off . . . lay it on myself' (123–4).

123 protest 'vow, promise' (*OED* 4).

128–9 Not to imagine . . . by you 'not to suppose that I have any idea of using you to help me' (Lucas).

130 suspected 'expected' (*OED* suspect 5).

130 fortune 'chance, luck' (*OED* 3a).

136 venter 'run risks' (*OED* venture 7).

137 temperature 'moderation' (*OED* 3a).

141 Still printed in 'forever [*OED* still 7b] impressed, stamped [*OED* printed 1a] upon'.

146 spare me that Dyce's insertion of **that** improves both sense and metre; the compositor presumably omitted it in error because **for that** immediately followed, and he had already set **that** in the previous line.

150 not with justice i.e. 'not with strict justice'.

153–4 now, to deferre . . . forfeit all i.e. 'if I postponed my arrival at Calais one half-hour, my honour would be lost' (Lucas).

161–2 adjourned . . . employment i.e. 'deferred until due [*OED* mature 5, 3] time for such an occupation'.

165–72 You do not . . . enemies It is not clear whether, here and earlier, Lessingham's stress on reasons Bonvile has for rejecting the duel are further tests, remorse at what he is doing, or an anguished mixture of both. Cf. 191–8.

167 distraction 'disorder or confusion' (*OED* 3b).

179 Carckanet and Bracelets The two crucial characteristics of the **Carckanet** ('an ornamental collar or necklace, usually of gold or set with jewels' [*OED* carcanet 1a]) and **Bracelets** are that they be richly jewelled (cf. 'those Jewels | You lockt about her Neck' [V.i.206–7]), and locked, needing a key to unfasten them. The **Carckanet** is several times referred to as a 'Chain' (e.g. by Rochfield, II.ii.24), so presumably on stage it was a gold chain hung with jewels; the word is derived from 'carcan', whose first meaning was 'an iron collar used for punishment' (*OED*), which reinforces the various senses of Annabel being a willing or unwilling prisoner throughout the play, especially in Act V. The plural **Bracelets**, and the image of fetters, imply one on each wrist; see p. 285.

181 at random 'neglected, untended' (*OED* random 3c).

182 laid it by 'put it away for safety' (see *OED* lay *v.*¹ 50c, though no example is cited until nearly a century later).

184–5 my Neck . . . Prisoners 'because she cannot remove the jewels he gave her' (Weis). The loving banter invites stage business of displaying the 'fettered' wrists, perhaps in an embrace (cf. *DM* V.ii.158–9: 'I'll disarme you, | And arme you thus').

188–91 follow . . . meet you Bonvile's deliberation in not following Annabel may be underlined by his exiting by the opposite door from her.

188 *Exit Annabel* While an exit here is most likely, Q's '*Exeunt*' following 187 would be possible if the two men spoke aside to each other before Bonvile joined Annabel to exit.

190 Barque Not (as later) a three-masted ship, but any small sailing vessel, such as a fishing smack, which they might hire to cross the Channel.

ACT II, Scene i

0.1 *Gentleman* That Rochfield is a *Gentleman* will be signalled not just by his clothes and manner, but also by his wearing a '*sword*' (II.ii.51). He is likely to be dressed for outdoors (cf. 22.1n).

1–16 Younger Brother . . . high-way Lucas notes the slightly later 'Character' by John Earle of 'A Younger Brother': 'Others take a more crooked path, yet the Kings high-way, where at length their vizzard is pluck't off, and they strike faire for Tiburne' (*Microcosmographie* [1628], C6ᵛ).

1–2 poor Calling . . . live on Q's parentheses imply that **Though not unlawful** qualifies **poor**. Wiggins argues (p. 375), and Weis punctuates, to have line 2 as a single syntactical unit which 'expands and explains "a poor calling"'.

5 get 'em . . . too Either (1) 'also beget cunning schemes ourselves when we are able to', or (2) 'secure the "Legacies of Wit" (4) as and how we can' (i.e. 'we can't even be sure of inheriting intelligence' = 'we may be as foolish as "the elder fool" [3]').

7 divident 'portion, share' (*OED* dividend 3a).

9 getting . . . give As the lines about 'Mothers' who 'love to groan' (10–11) make clear, the primary sense here of **getting** is 'begetting' (*OED* getting 3); but the pun on **want to give** (= 'lack the means to be generous') is based on the additional sense of **getting** = 'acquiring' (*OED* get 1c).

11–12 groan . . . together Rochfield puns in rather laboured fashion on 'Mothers' (10) who **groan** in childbirth (and perhaps also in the sexual act which brings about conception, since they **love to groan** [see Partridge 1955, p. 123]), and the **Gallows**, which **eccho** the mothers inasmuch as they **groan** beneath the weight of a condemned man. Hence **together**.

12–13 first . . . t'other's i.e. from the 'groan' (11) of childbirth to that of the 'Gallows' (11).

14–15 beg . . . date Rochfield is not only saying that for him begging is **out of** (his) **way** (i.e. not his way of doing things), but also that the other option, **borrowing**, is out of season (*OED* date *n.*² 4), presumably because he has exhausted his credit.

19 *Laverna* Heywood, citing Horace's *Epistles*, Book I, defines this Roman goddess of just and unjust gain in *Gynaikeion* (1624) (D2ᵛ): '*Lauerna* She is ouer theeues, who make supplication to her for good and rich booties, as that she would charme the houshold with sleepe, keepe the dogges from barking, and the doore hinges from creeking, to defend them from shame, and keepe them from the gallowes.'

21 purchase 'acquire, gain' (*OED* 4a).

22.1 Enter ANNABEL . . . Servant Since Rochfield does not immediately identify her as a bride in II.ii, Annabel is probably wearing a cloak, perhaps with a hood, over her bridal dress (see I.i.111.1–.2n), which will reinforce the sense that this scene takes place outdoors as she tries to overtake Bonvile on his way to Dover. Almost certainly the *Servant* is a man.

23 booty 'plunder, a prize' (*OED* 3).

26–31 I know not . . . Prithee run Annabel's doubts may well be shared with the audience before she turns back to instruct her Servant (so Wellington 1997).

29 Scholar i.e. in matters relating to marriage.

30–1 I talk . . . recovered i.e. 'I may be losing through talking that (which) could yet be recovered.'

32 fore-path Probably 'short cut' (Lucas), although conceivably it might refer to a path along the foreshore. Not in *OED*.

32 advantage Either 'give an advantage to' (*OED* 1a) or 'place advantageously' (*OED* 1b).

33 Ferry Presumably a ferry across to the south bank of the Thames and the main road to Dover; most probably that at Woolwich (about **two miles** [3.2 km] east of Blackwall), established since the fourteenth century.

34 in ken 'in sight'.

35–6 enforce . . . eyes i.e. 'strive [*OED* enforce 5] to make your voice heard as far as your eyes can see'.

38 stay 'detain' (*OED* 20).

46 moveables Rochfield notes Annabel's 'personal property' (*OED* movable *n.* 2): the jewelled carcanet and the bracelets (cf. I.i.179n).

47–8 next ground i.e. 'adjacent land'.

48 Exit Presumably Rochfield exits by the same door as Annabel, and before her the Servant; cf. II.ii.0.1n.

ACT II, Scene ii

0.1 running over . . . after her Spatial logic is best served if the Servant enters by the opposite door from which they all exited (see II.i.48n), and after **running over** the stage to exit by the other door, is followed by first Annabel and then **after her** Rochfield. They are now, therefore, at the 'next ground' (II.i.47–8). Annabel's journey is in the same direction across the stage as in II.i, and her house still behind her.

1 at a doubt 'uncertain' (see *OED* doubt 1b).

3 Defend me Annabel's words suggest that she starts in fear at Rochfield's unexpected appearance behind her. Cf. 'well overtaken' (2).

5–6 degrees hot . . . poison Anticipating the apparent contradiction of 'honest thief'

(7; and see 30–1n), Rochfield claims to have sufficient heat to counteract being as dangerously cold as **poison**: 'Classical writers on pharmacology had defined the qualities of both narcotics and poisons as very cold. Of the three that were mainly used in the Middle Ages and Renaissance—mandrake or *atropia mandragora*, opium, and hemlock—the first was regarded as safest because it was marked as cold in the third degree, not in the fourth and highest like the two others' (Hoeniger, p. 252).

7 drest 'addressed' (*OED* address 16), but as Lucas notes, with a play on **drest** = 'dressed (prepared) for cooking' (see *OED* dress 13a), with a possible continuation of the metaphor of 'poison' (i.e. herbs).

19 double state 'Wife' and 'Virgin' (16), like 'Honest and Thief' (11), 'hold small affinity' (8).

20 Hymen 'marriage' (*OED* n.¹ 2), which would not be complete until physically consummated (cf. 17–19).

21 Toys 'knick-knacks, trinkets' (*OED* 7a); clearly not, here, of 'little intrinsic value' (*OED*), but labelled **Toys** by Rochfield as indicating that they will be little missed by one who is wealthy, like Annabel.

22 containe Dyce's emendation to Q's almost incomprehensible 'contrive' implies simple misreading of 'r' as 'a' and 'n' as 'v' or, more probably, as 'u', which in this late-seventeenth-century Quarto was set as 'v', according to the modern convention; the more colourful 'consume' would fit neatly with the idea of **hungry pockets**, but is graphically less plausible, since 's/t' confusion is rare.

24 idle Chain Rochfield's **idle** continues the jocular diminution of Annabel's rich jewellery started at 21 with 'superfluous Toys'; the **Chain** is the carcanet, presumably gold with hanging jewels.

25–6 Mannacle . . . wrist Here and throughout this scene only one bracelet and one hand and wrist are referred to, though elsewhere in the play the plural is often used (cf. I.ii.179 and n). It is possible one prop is used to stand for both.

26–7 Emblems . . . halter mine Rochfield continues the play on 'Chain' and 'Mannacle' (24–5), acknowledging, fatalistically, that the bracelet and especially the carcanet for her 'Neck' (24) may prove to be **Emblems** (i.e. symbols *OED* 3b) of the hangman's noose made of **combined Hemp** which will hang him (*OED* **halter** *v.* 4) by his neck. For **combined** as 'conjoined in substance' (*OED* 1a), cf. *Ham.* I.v.18–19: 'Thy knotted and combined locks to part, | And each particular hair to stand an end'.

30–1 confess both . . . onely honest i.e. 'I shall accept that you are both "honest" and "thief" (8), but forget the term "thief"; this episode will demonstrate only your honesty.' This is the final stage in the mock debate in which Rochfield first proves himself 'honest' (13–14), then a 'Thief' (29); Annabel's willingness to participate in the repartee is an important pointer to Rochfield's rehabilitation. (Lucas and Weis gloss 'both' as the carcanet and bracelet, which misses the more important verbal play.)

32–4 take it . . . deliver 'em Annabel presumably approaches Rochfield to offer her neck or wrist, and his reply suggests a possibly comic embarrassment at her proximity, reversing the situation at the beginning of the scene.

35 If you observe Further indication of Annabel's continuing physical proximity, implying total confidence in Rochfield; cf. 32–4n.

38 Fresh-man 'novice', but with the particular sense of 'a student during his first year [or] term, at a University' (*OED* 1, 2), as becomes clear in the rest of the speech.

39 this Book i.e. his sword.

41 picking Laws On the one hand Rochfield, continuing the metaphor of **study** (see 38n), says he has not yet learned the skills needed to pick locks (such as those on Annabel's rich jewellery); on the other he presents the comic (and frightening) image of responding to her suggestion of using a pick-lock on the tiny locks ('some instrument, that may unloose 'em' [37]), with a large sword.

43 Good An abbreviated form of 'Good sir' or 'Good gentleman' (see *OED adj.* 2c, and Alexander Schmidt, *Shakespeare-Lexicon*, 3rd ed. [Berlin, 1902], subst. 1).

45–50 tear 'em . . . hurt you The final stage of Annabel's literally putting herself in Rochfield's hands is best served if he tries to **tear** off the carcanet (not the bracelet, as Lucas suggests in his SD); thus both her physical vulnerability and the potential that she may **endure** some **hurt** are emphasized. See also 50n.

50 Not much Annabel may be stoically submitting to pain, or speaking simple truth, or pretending in order to cover an already premeditated plan to seize Rochfield's sword.

51 at all 'in any way' (*OED* all 9b).

51 *She draws* The comic reversal may be achieved by Annabel's taking hold of the hilt of Rochfield's sword as he struggles with her jewellery, so that as he steps back the sword is left in her hand.

53–4 read . . . Clerk Annabel continues teasing Rochfield as an unread 'Fresh-man' (38 and n) who is **out** (= 'nonplussed' [*OED* 20]; cf. *DLC* II.i.46) even with his own **book** (= sword; cf. 39) and therefore a **bad** ('unlearned' as well as 'immoral') **Clerk** (= 'scholar' [*OED* 4; and cf. 55n]).

55 Saint *Nicholas* In Elizabethan slang, patron saint of thieves; but also an appropriate response to Annabel's 'bad Clerk' (54), since highway robbers were jokingly known as Saint Nicholas's clerks ('scholars'; see 53–4n). Cf. Dekker, *The Belman of London* (1608) (G4ᵛ): 'the High Law is nothing else but taking a purse by the *High-way side* . . . The theefe that commits the *Robbery*, and is cheife clerke to Saint *Nicholas*, is called the High *Lawyer*'; and *1H4* II.i.61–2, 'if they meet not with Saint Nicholas' clerks, I'll give thee this neck'.

57 with purchase Lucas glosses as 'with a profit into the bargain'. Cf. *OED* purchase 8a: 'That which is obtained . . . *esp.* that which is taken in . . . robbery or thieving; booty'.

59 cross 'coin' (*OED* 20). Cf. IV.ii.112n.

60 this i.e. Rochfield's sword.

65–7 Forbear . . . Dissolve 'Do not take (this jewellery) which can only be loosened [*OED* dissolve 5] by means of destructive force, and danger (to my person).' She goes on to specify the danger to her 'head' (68) and 'hand' (69).

67 assure i.e. 'feel certain' (*OED* 9b), 'assure myself'.

73–4 honor . . . Cradle puritie In the context of her 'Vows' (72) to her **husband**, and the 'joys . . . of the bed' (75–6), the **honor** Annabel swears by is 'chastity', here reinforced by the concept of **Cradle puritie**.

75 tax me 'call me to account' (see *OED* tax 6).

79 esteem 'estimated value' (*OED* 1b).

82–3 Chains . . . Constable Annabel's jewellery **may be stayed** (= 'detained' [*OED* stay *v.*¹ 20]) by the law; i.e. with her jewellery in his possession Rochfield would be in danger of arrest, whereas 'ready money' (80) can circulate freely 'without suspition' (81). This further disquisition on the difficulties of the thief's trade may, like II.i.1–22, be to the audience.

88 Articles of my Belief 'punning on the twelve articles of the Apostle's Creed' (Weis; see *OED* article 3). The ability to recite the Creed, the Lord's Prayer, and the Ten Commandments was a common test of godliness. For example, paupers seeking admission as pensioners into the College or Hospital of the Poor in the parish of St Saviour, Southwark, had to be 'honest and godly . . . None but such as can say the Lord's Prayer, the Articles of the Christian Faith or belief and the ten commandments of God in English' (cited in Jeremy Boulton, *Neighbourhood and Society: A London Suburb in the Seventeenth Century* [Cambridge, 1987], p. 144).

91 discover 'reveal, betray' (*OED* 6).

92–3 reiterate . . . injunction i.e. 'repeat the promises I made in urging you (to 'Forbear' [65] and to 'Accompany | Me back unto my house' [70–1]).

97–100 I knew . . . way i.e. 'I knew a man who served at the (corrupt) court for fifteen years, and grew old, (died) and was buried without ever accepting a bribe: I may (like a courtier) be assumed guilty (despite my innocence), and my fate will be worse (hanging).' As part of this anti-courtier satire, Rochfield may be jesting that the courtier did succumb to bribery after **he was buried**. The spelling **owld** (Q 'owl'd') for 'old' is common, occurring three times in Heywood's manuscript of *The Captives*, which also yields the only known instance, in the drama of W's time, of 'oul'd' (with an intrusive apostrophe). No parallel has, however, been found for Q's 'owl'd' as a spelling of 'old': it seems more likely to have arisen through misunderstanding or accident than to be an intentional and authentic variant. Lucas believed there was a play on the **Courtier** being only **fifteen years** of age (**owld**), but this seems unlikely.

102 handling (1) 'treatment, management' (*OED* 2), and (2) 'treatment in which the hands are . . . roughly used' (*OED* 1). Rochfield's pun is reinforced by the visual contrast between Annabel now decorously taking his arm, and both her earlier fear of being in a thief's hands, and her subsequent submission to his attempt to get the jewellery by very rough **handling**.

ACT II, SCENE iii

0.1 RAFE, *and* JACK Q's *two Boys* are only given speech prefixes as '1 *Boy*' and '2 *Boy*'. '2 *Boy*' is called '*Jack*' at 9 and elsewhere in this scene, and Compass identifies his companion as '*Rafe*' at IV.i.60.

0.1 childe Urse's son by Franckford, presumably a stage property babe in arms.

2 snatch up stakes 'grab what was wagered'.

2–6 childe . . . afterwards Rafe's joke seems to be that Jack has five years ahead of minding the **childe** as a full-time occupation, after which he will need to resume his delayed apprenticeship, by that time serving the child (**boy**) growing up as the master's heir. Rafe also puns on **childe** and **arms** as meaning Jack will have only a child's strength in his arms.

9 Point One of the laces, generally with a metal **Point**, for attaching the hose to the doublet (see *OED n.*¹ B 5). Usually referred to, and sold, in dozens (cf. 30), merely **a Point** implies a quarrel of no great seriousness (or impoverished boys).

11 Gaffer *Compass* The title **Gaffer** usually indicated rusticity, and might or might not be used respectfully (*OED* 1a, b). The boys stand apart to comment until they greet him at 20. **Compass** will presumably be distinctively dressed as a mariner; see pp. 282–3.

13–14 *Hobby-horse . . . Green-goose Fayr* Compass probably took the role of the '*Hobby-horse*' for Hackney's 'group of morris dancers' (*OED* morris *n.*¹ 2) who performed at the Goose Fair at Bow. The ***Hobby-horse*** is a role taken by one of the dancers, wearing the form of a horse strapped about his waist, and with a long foot-cloth hiding his own legs, as if he were riding the horse. The foolery and antics of representing a skittish horse—'my Reines my Carree'res, my Prannckers, my Ambles, my false Trotts' (William Sampson, *The Vow breaker* [1636] V.i [I3ʳ])—led to the more generalized meaning, perhaps glanced at here, 'a foolish fellow, buffoon' (*OED* 3). **Hackney** was then a village about three miles (5 km) northwest of Blackwall (see 15–16n), with Bow (see 103–4n) about halfway between. Lucas suggested that **Hackney-Morrice** indicated a morris dance at Hackney, which required him to postulate a ***Green-goose Fayr*** at Hackney. Contemporary references, however, all associate the fair with Bow; cf. Middleton, *A Chaste Maid in Cheapside*, I.i.80–3, and Taylor, *All The Workes of John Taylor the Water-Poet* (1630), p. 110: 'At Bowe the Thursday after Pentecost, | There is a Faire of Green Geese, ready rost.' As Wiggins points out (p. 376), 'What Lucas apparently overlooked is the geographical proximity of Bow and Hackney: there would be no more incongruity in the Hackney morris dancers performing at a fair in neighbouring Bow than there would be in a Blackwall man like Compass dancing with them.'

14 as honest and as poor a man i.e. 'as honest and as poor as can be' (so Lucas).

15–16 *Black-wall . . . white cheeks* Lying on the north bank of the Thames about four miles (6.4 km.) east of St Paul's, just downstream from the Isle of Dogs, at the mouth of the River Lea, Blackwall was a major port. Cf. Dekker, *Penny-Wise, Pound-Foolish* (1631), 'to *Black-wall* to see the Ships' (cited in Hoy 1980, II, 203). Compass plays on **Black-wall** in contrast to, presumably, the **white cheeks** of the local women.

16–17 tears . . . salt An obscure passage, though clearly punning on salt tears and 'Brine' (16). Lucas suggests that 'his tears might be tied in a true-love knot because, though salt, they are the expression of a constant and ever-fresh affection'. He also sees a quibble on **tears** as tears wept and as 'torn pieces' (see *OED n.*² 2), but an audience could not have heard it, as the pronunciation is different. More likely, aurally, is a pun on **tyed** as (1) 'tied up', and (2) '(**salt** water) tide'. Lucas also detects a quibble on **fresh** as (1) 'not stale' (*OED* 7a), and (2) 'not salted' (*OED* 4a).

18–19 If . . . Fates i.e. '(I shall be thankful to you,) sweet Fates, if she is still alive'.

23–5 got a child . . . mine This passage seems to rely on typical apprentice bawdy wit in response to Compass's assumption that Jack has **got** (fathered) **a child**. Jack says he will **keep** (mind/retain) the child whoever fathered it, and begins teasing Compass by pointing out that other men may be in the same **case** (= [1] 'situation', [2] 'vagina') of having children they did not father.

27 One ... live to't Jack's complicated syntax seems to signify: 'The child's father is a man for whom I intend to provide a younger brother to this child, if it lives' (i.e. I shall continue my affair with his wife and get her pregnant again, just as I produced this child). Jesting about apprentices getting children on their masters' wives is common: e.g. Beaumont, *The Knight of the Burning Pestle*, II.340–1. Jack uses this jesting as his springboard into baiting Compass with news of his wife's illegitimate child.

29 shot i.e. a 'shoat' or 'shote', a piglet that has only recently been weaned.

29 to 'in comparison with'.

31 cannot chuse i.e. 'it was bound to be'.

33 How long Although this makes grammatical sense (= 'What length of time?'), it is possible that Compass is saying 'How! "Long"?' (= 'Just a minute; why did you say that?').

36 plaguy 'pestiferous'; Compass comically admits his vexation to the audience.

40 hard by There is presumably a theatrical component to this joke: i.e. it is not merely in suburbs close to Blackwall where babies are born embarrassingly soon after marriage, but close to the theatre where *CC* was acted.

43 Oh horrible Presumably, like 'Oh pitiful' at 47, to each other and the audience, although Compass is aware of the tenor of the boys' reaction to his jovial hyperbole.

44–6 in another ... years There may be a specific allusion here, or a more general satiric comment on the inability of some couples to beget children. The comment also applies neatly to Franckford and Luce, save that, by a change in bed and bed-fellow, he has got a child.

48–9 *Wapping, Radcliff, Lymehouse* Compass is listing suburbs on the north bank of the Thames going east from London (Blackwall is the next in line, on the far side of the Isle of Dogs; cf. 15–16n). Lucas cites John Stow, *A Survey of London* (1598), on Wapping: 'a continuall streete, or rather a filthy straight [i.e. strait] passage, with Lanes and Allyes, of small Tenements inhabited by Saylors, and Uictuallers, along by the Riuer of Thames, almost to Rad[c]liffe, a good myle from the Tower' (p. 347). Sugden notes that the area opposite Ratcliff and Limehouse on the Thames was known as Cuckold's Haven (see pp. 140, 308).

50 uncertainly i.e. because husbands are absent at sea, but with a pun on uncertainty as to who the father is.

50 as ... serves i.e. 'depending how favourable the wind is'.

53 *Surrat* i.e. Surat, then a prosperous port on the west coast of India north of Bombay, in the hands of the East India Company from 1612 (see Sugden, p. 492).

53 Long-boat 'the largest boat belonging to a sailing vessel' (*OED*), and hence that which Compass would use to sail home half across the world in a night. Cf. 110n.

57 at next wall i.e. the 'nearest' (*OED* next 9a), and hence 'the intervening wall'.

60 No indeed Jack's knowing mockery will continue to be evident in the way this is spoken.

62–3 discomforting i.e. 'distressing' (see *OED* discomfort *v.* 2).

64 lusty (1) 'healthy, vigorous' (*OED* 5), (2) 'full of sexual desire' (*OED* 4).

66 they say . . . seen 'em Jack continues his lewd innuendo.

67 taken up 'bought, got' (*OED* take *v.* 93d [a]; cf. 'paid for' [68]), with a double entendre based on 'lifted, raised' (*OED* 93a). See Partridge 1955, p. 201; also *Shr.* IV.iii.162–3, 'Take up my mistress' gown to his master's use! | O fie, fie, fie!'

73 Nay sir . . . forward Rafe is evidently addressing Jack; his unwillingness to stay behind may indicate that he shares Jack's eagerness to be present when Urse learns of the return of Compass. It also continues the jokey rivalry with which they entered.

74–5 Livery . . . Company Compass imagines himself robed in the **Livery** of a London guild, in this case the 'renowned' (*OED* **great** 11a) **Company** of **Horners**, who made articles from horn, such as windows and hornbooks; the point being to pun on the very numerous (*OED* great 8b) community of cuckolded (horned) husbands.

75 there . . . one day A satiric jibe, the implication being that there are certainly aldermen who are cuckolded.

76 changing our Copy i.e. 'assuming another character (or style)' (see *OED* copy 11a). The point is that they will no longer be designated cuckolds.

77.1 *Compass his wife* [URSE] Urse's name suggests the possibility that she may be comically fat; see Dramatis personae 20n.

79 fountains Comic business may be implied by Compass weeping again, as when he first entered, and apparently delaying Urse's embrace until 91.

80–1 sing . . . see Compass quibbles that he cannot sing **at first sight** = (1) when he first has vision, (2) by sight-reading music, but he can **cry** = (1) 'weep', (2) 'cry out', before he can **see**.

81–2 cry before they laugh Lucas cites Pliny, *Nat. Historie*, Proem to Book VII, p. 152: '*And verily to no babe or infant is it given once to laugh before he be fortie daies old.*'

87 Sands Although literally meaning a 'sea bed' (*OED* *n.*[2] 1a) in the Indies, there is probably also a reference to 'sand-bank, shoal' (*OED* 1c), and perhaps specifically the Goodwin Sands, on which many mariners perished.

91 kiss . . . now This may imply that Urse has attempted to kiss him earlier, and been prevented by the full flood (cf. 'ebb', 92) of Compass's tears (cf. 79n).

94 that will hold 'em i.e. his tears.

95 goes . . . go Compass puns, with **goes** = 'fares' (see *OED* go 18a) and **go** = 'to be pregnant' (*OED* 7; cf. *Ant.* I.ii.63–4: 'let him marry a woman that cannot go'). Weis reads **go** as 'walk' (*OED* 1a): 'there are some people at home who are so young that they haven't yet learned to walk'.

95 Lanck 'loose from emptiness' (*OED* lank 1a), here because not pregnant. He is apparently either looking at or feeling her belly.

95–6 full Sea 'high tide' (*OED* 4), with a clear figurative sense of plenitude and pregnancy.

98 A lass Compass puns on Urse's 'Alas' (97), possibly mimicking her, before the comic addition of **a lad**.

99   pair of Compasses (1) two children bearing his name, (2) the mathematical instrument, frequently referred to as **a pair** because of its two equal legs (see OED compass
n.[1] 4a), and therefore here perhaps with a pun on the children (cf. Donne, 'A
Valediction forbidding mourning' [26]: 'stiff twin compasses'), and possibly (3) two
mariner's (magnetic) compasses for finding one's direction. Both kinds of compass are
appropriate to a seaman.

103–4 *Bowe . . . Hams* Bow (fully, Stratford-at-Bow) is about four and a half miles (7.25
km) northeast of St Paul's, and a mile and a half (2.5 km) north of Blackwall (cf.
15–16n); West Ham and East Ham lie to the east of Bow, further from Blackwall.
Wiggins (p. 376) suggests that Compass may be punning on 'ham' as meat, since Bow
was historically a centre of meat production, and therefore of a stench from which the
residents might wish to **come further**. The press variant 'Hams' is found only in the
Cornell copy and the Yale copy of the second issue. Qa's '*Itacus*' is presumably due to
misreading: although Qb's correction is not italicized, Qa's erroneous reading is, and
the place name was probably in italics in the MS. An italic form of 'H' (often used even
in predominantly cursive Secretary hands) can closely resemble 'It', if the crossbar projects to the right, while the three minims of 'm' are easily mistaken for 'cu'.
Alternatively, certain forms of Secretary 'h', written large as a capital, look like
Secretary 'I/J'.

110   Cock-boat 'a small ship's boat' (*OED*); cf. 53n. In relation to Urse's pregnancy,
Compass puns, of course on **Cock** = 'penis' (Partridge 1955, p. 88).

111   left behinde for Compass seems to indicate a purposive action prior to his departure; i.e. he **left behinde**, when he departed, that which would have the consequence
of, or obtain, a **boy** (see *OED* leave 6, 14a). The phrase sounds comically appropriate
to paying for goods ordered, or the reckoning at a tavern (see *OED* for 6, 9).

113   Nay . . . known Possibly spoken to the audience, just as up until now many of
Compass's jests may have been.

115–17 Pardon! . . . little toe The implication is that Urse is a whore and murderess,
but Compass deliberately undercuts the mock ferocity of his abuse with comic insistence that she cherish the child.

119 battery . . . surprized Urse's metaphor is of military siege: **battery** = 'bombard-
ment' (*OED* 3), and **surprized** = 'captured' (*OED* surprise 2b).

122 *Shadwell* Lying between Wapping and Ratcliff (cf. 48–9n), 'like most ports, it had an
unsavoury reputation' (Sugden, p. 463). Cf. Jonson, *The Magnetic Lady*, II.i.27–9: 'have
you an oare | I' the Cockboat, 'cause you are a Saylors wife | And come from
Shadwell?'

122 strongest Suburbs In punning, Compass both takes up Urse's fortress metaphor
(119 and n), with **strongest** = (1) 'most resolute, able to resist temptation' (see *OED*
strong 3a), and (2) 'most difficult to capture' (*OED* 8a), but also, given the implications
of **Suburbs** (as where the city's brothels are to be found), (3) 'strongest-smelling'
(*OED* 15a) and 'grossest' (*OED* 11e).

123 woe . . . City The surface meaning is that if the strongest suburbs, even those
'double . . . walled' (120–1), may fall to armed assault, the **City** will too. But as at 74–5,
there is also a cut at **City** merchants as cuckolds.

129 labor for me . . . you? Compass's point, punningly made as usual, is that since he laboured to earn a living for himself and Urse, the results of her **labor** in producing a child should likewise be shared.

131 Players . . . share Generally in a theatre company the ten or so principal **Players** 'shared the workload, the costs of investment and production, and the profits' (Gurr 1996, p. 97), unlike the 'hired men', musicians and others employed for wages. The role of Compass would certainly have been taken by a sharer (a **fellow**), so the comment is highly self-referential.

132 look for . . . wages As at 115–17 (see n), Compass uses comic mock aggression as delicate forgiveness.

138 too i.e. 'to'; cf. I.ii.38n.

138 Mr. Abbreviation of 'Master' (pronounced either 'Master' or 'Mister'; see I.i.136n).

141–2 Merchants . . . home 'he may be a merchant-venturer (trading in goods and, here, in illicit sex), but now that I am home I shall be the legitimate owner of my goods' (Weis).

143 *Bednal-green* i.e. 'Bethnal Green', a poor district about two and a half miles (4 km.) northwest of Blackwall, to the west of Bow (see 103–4n) and east of Shoreditch (see Sugden, pp. 59–60).

146–7 fair Gale . . . forwards The metaphor is nautical: 'if a favourable wind blow, we'll hoist the sails and set off (on a voyage)'. This use of **sheets** = 'sails' is, as *OED* points out (sheet *n.*[1] 4), not nautical, probably deriving from misuse of 'sheet' = 'rope attached to the lower corners of a sail' (*OED n.*[2]); the first *OED* citation is from Heywood in 1637. The error may be inadvertent by the playwrights, or deliberate by Compass; either way, it is for the sake of the sexual innuendo (cf. 'shaking the sheets'; *OED* sheet *n.*[1] 3b). In addition, **set** is frequently used in a sexual sense (see Henke 1975, II, 266 and Partridge 1955, pp. 185–6).

148 upon their scorns i.e. 'by reason of [*OED* upon 11c (a)] their cuckoldry'. This final couplet is likely to be a triumphant parting shot to the audience, whose expectations about a cuckold's reactions he has so thoroughly and jovially subverted.

ACT II, Scene iv

1 wants a president i.e. 'lacks a precedent'.

2 discreet i.e. 'discreetly' (see Abbott, Sect. 23).

3–4 Forms . . . Table Woodroff praises Bonvile's observance of 'decorum' (*OED* form 15) and his 'attitudes' (*OED* posture 1a: here, it seems, in the sense of 'behaviour', not recorded in *OED*). Having performed **all customary Rites | Belonging to the Table** (i.e. wedding feast), Bonvile is entitled to 'his expected wages in the bed' (5).

6 remain Thus Dyce (and Lucas). Q's 'remains' is just feasible as a variation on the subjunctive, but on balance it seems more likely that the final 's' is compositorial or scribal rather than authorial.

7–12 Keep it . . . Conceal it This consultation among the Gallants is typical of their tendency to operate on stage as a group; cf. I.i.66.1n.

9 **that** The addition of this word to Q is necessary for the sense and regularizes the metre. The meaning is that Bonvile's love for Lessingham has **fastened that on him** which **we all denied**, i.e. has made him feel an obligation that the other Gallants shirked. As Lucas notes, the pronoun 'probably dropped out through confusion with the *that* immediately above it in the previous line'. Cf. I.ii.146n.

12 **it** (Hazlitt; not in Q) Omissions often come in clusters, and, as with 9, the compositor may have been affected by the previous line, with its **'Tis . . . 'tis**.

28–9 **old Lads . . . infancy** i.e. 'Oh yes, do old men have reason to employ (wet-) nurses (for illegitimate children they have sired)? Yes, when they are as old and feeble as children.' There is possible punning on **work** = 'copulate' (Partridge 1955, p. 223), which would mean that the **old Lads** have impregnated the **Nurses** so that they **groan** in childbirth (or copulation; cf. II.i.11–12n). On **has** = 'have', see Abbott, Sect. 335.

34–5 **out . . . purpose** 'mistaken [*OED* way 37b] as to my intention'.

38 **A fool! . . . off** i.e. 'send [*OED* rid 6a] the **fool** away [*OED* further 4b]'; this is 'an order to the Nurse' (Lucas). Cf. Rowley, *The Birth of Merlin*, III.iii (E1ʳ), 'a witch, sister: rid him out of your company'. *LION: Drama* reveals that instructions to 'rid' a place of a fool are common. Without Lucas's emendation (the exclamation mark after 'fool'), the meaning might conceivably be '(may) a fool send him away'.

46 **the proverb** i.e. 'Early up and never the nearer' (Tilley E27). Cf. Nathan Field, *Amends for Ladies* (1618), F3ʳ: 'I have beene earely up, but as God helpe me, I was neuer the neere.' As Lucas points out, this is the opposite of 'The early bird catches the worm.'

52 **gratulate** 'congratulate' (*OED* 2), or perhaps 'express joy at' (*OED* 1).

53 **falls out** 'chances' (*OED* fall 94g).

56 **To all** i.e. Rochfield is 'welcome' (55) to all of them.

58 **at a *non-plus*** 'confounded, unable to proceed'.

58 **at a stand** 'unable to proceed in thought, speech, or action; a state of perplexity' (*OED* stand *n.*¹ 6), possibly punning on standing still after 'dancing' (59).

58 **out** 'perplexed, confused' (see *OED* out 5a).

59 **Musick** As earlier, either the band of musicians, or the music they play; cf. I.i.125–6n.

59 **surbated** 'foot-sore', in a figurative sense (*OED* 1c); i.e. the dancing has been given over (as though the dancers were weary).

61 **cloudy . . . washing-day** The phrase sounds proverbial, but is not recorded. Clare's excuse that Woodroff was unwilling to dance, comically implausible though it is (see 75, and I.i.132), indicates that she is trying to hide the agitation she revealed at 30–5.

66 **rend'red** 'answered' (see *OED* render 10).

68 **appointed to** i.e. 'arranged with' (see *OED* appoint 3).

69 **fetch a Reputation** 'go in quest of, and bring back, a reputation' (Weis).

75 **the Musick** See 59n. If this command is obeyed, the music will reinstate a festive atmosphere as in I.i (cf. I.i.125–6n).

76 put down i.e. '(be) surpassed, excelled' (see *OED* put 42f).

77 can rise i.e. 'am able to cut a caper, can dance', with some suggestion of lingering potency: Woodroff is still, in a diminished way, 'up to it' (on the dance floor and, by punning implication, in bed). Just as Woodroff may have 'cut Capers' (I.i.132 and n) in the earlier scene, so he may here, before Annabel returns attention to Rochfield. Lucas, in putting forward the conjecture adopted here, that Q's 'am rife' is a misreading of **can rise**, pointed out that **rise** 'goes rather well with *put down* just before' (76), and that in I.i.127–32 Woodroff claims that 'when I was young . . . I have cut Capers thus high'. *OED* (30c) cites a passage by Steele in the *Spectator*: 'I have seen him rise six or seven Capers together', and this association of rising with cutting capers has clear precedents in seventeenth-century drama: the manuscript tragedy *Ghismonda* (*c.* 1623) alludes to 'a stirring prince whose agitation | Can rise high capers from her' (*LION: Drama*, I.i.27–8), while Woodroff's transitive use of the verb is foreshadowed in Marston's *What You Will* (1607), III (E1ᵛ), where Laverdure, protesting that he is capable of attracting a woman, declares, 'Why I can rise high, a straight legge, a plumpe thighe'; again the boast seems to be of both sexual prowess and ability to dance. *OED* affords no sense of Q's 'rife' that fits the context. Although under *a.* 6 it lists 'disposed or inclined; ready, prompt; quick', Woodroff says in Q that he is **a little** rife ('I am rife a little yet'), whereas *OED* and *LION: Drama* instances of the adjective are invariably associated with excess. Limited rifeness is a contradiction in terms. Also, the adjective is usually followed by the preposition 'for', 'of', or 'to'. No parallel has been found to Q's usage here. Minim confusion could easily have led to the misreading of 'am' as 'can'; and 'f' and long 's' ('rife' and '**rife**') are barely distinguishable.

78 too i.e. 'to'; cf. I.ii.38n.

79 She'l tell Rochfield's aside makes clear that he has not realized that Annabel is teasing him, in a continuation of her witty responses to him in II.ii.

81 amazement 'bewilderment, perplexity' (*OED* 2).

82 To my recovery i.e. 'to my assistance (to regain my way and my composure)'.

84 what I spake 'i.e. in 67ff. above' (Lucas).

85 better 'i.e. better "comforts" (83)' (Lucas).

87 supply both places i.e. 'personate both Groom and Bride' (54). This is explained in the next two lines: after she has, as the bride, led her father and the guests ('you' [88]) back to the dancing as she did in I.i, she will return to finish welcoming Rochfield ('you' [89]), as Bonvile would do were he present.

92 over-gone me 'passed me by' (see *OED* overgo 11).

93–103 It is . . . *Mittimus* Lucas compares *The Unfortunate Traveller* (Nashe, *Works*, II, 319): 'A theefe, they saie, mistakes euerie bush for a true man', and *3H6* V.vi.12: 'The thief doth fear each bush an officer.' **tremblingst** may be a clue to a comic display of fear in this speech.

94 bound to the peace i.e. 'bound over (placed under a legal obligation) to keep the peace'. Rochfield, comically, would seek legal restraint on all that terrifies the criminal.

95 phanes 'vanes, weathercocks' (see *OED* vane 1).

97 and meet her 'if you meet her' (see Abbott, Sect. 101).

102–3 if the Baby … *Mittimus* i.e. 'if the "Calf with a white face" (100) goes to the udder (*OED* bag 10) it has the appearance of the pale "Clerk" being summoned by the "Justice" (101) to draw up a ***Mittimus*** (a warrant of commitment to prison)'.

106 Goals i.e. 'gaol's' (both spellings were current in the seventeenth century). Rochfield's point is that he 'may be now' (105) at the last stop (gaol) before his **journeys end**, hanging. Lucas sees a quibble on 'goal' and 'gaol', but does not explain, and death can hardly be seen as Rochfield's goal.

107 to'th t' other place i.e. to hell.

107 trust a woman Cf. *WD* V.vi.157.

113 twenty Pieces Probably £22, a substantial sum. Although 'piece' could refer to any coin (see *OED* 3c, 13a), the fact that these are 'Gold' (128) suggests reference to the '*unite*', an English gold coin first issued under James in 1604, and raised in 1612 to the value of 22 shillings (see *OED* 13b).

114 trap 'caparison, adorn with trappings' (*OED v.*² 1a).

115 Sumpter-horse 'pack horse, beast of burden' (*OED* sumpter 4b).

115 spur-gall 'gall or injure with the spur in riding' (*OED* 1). Cf. *R2* V.v.92–4 (Folio): 'I was not made a horse, | And yet I bear a burthen like an ass, | Spur-gall'd, and tir'd by jauncing Bullingbrook.'

116 break my winde i.e. 'drive me until I am broken-winded' (suffering from a disabling disease of the lungs caused by being ridden too hard).

117 fair staff i.e. his **staff** of office. Constables wore no uniform, but had as the badge of their office a white staff with the royal coat of arms (see Donald Rumbelow, *I Spy Blue: The Police and Crime in the City of London from Elizabeth I to Victoria* [London, 1971], p. 46).

119 *calling* Annabel's shouting, urgent enough to worry Woodroff (see 121), is actually to further tease Rochfield, but it will be apparent from his trembling (see 128) that he is terrified.

119 Mr. Abbreviation of 'Master' (pronounced either 'Master' or 'Mister'; see I.i.136n).

120.2 Saylor His profession will be evident from his costume (cf. pp. 282–3).

123 lay a hand Presumably 'shake hands (in welcome)' (so Weis), though *OED* does not record this usage. Certainly it prepares for Woodroff shaking hands (see 128, 133) with Rochfield, and thus discovering his trembling (see 128, and 119n), though here it may mean no more than that Annabel has been the only person to take his arm, and that he has had a stage position isolated from the rest.

129 agony of anger Annabel's teasing of Rochfield continues as she provides an excuse which she presumably knows is the opposite of the truth; cf. 119n.

130 entertainment 'reception' (*OED* 10).

132 Gentlemans mistake i.e. Woodroff's error (in thinking Rochfield trembled). Evidently Woodroff has moved away, and Raymond is now greeting Rochfield (perhaps silently followed by all the other Gallants—so Wellington 1997—since they tend to work as a group).

134 stiffer 'stronger' (see *OED* stiff 13a), in that formerly his hand would not have trembled.

135 'tis meant for Physick Lucas is surely correct in assuming that the **Physick** (*OED* 4b 'a cathartic or purge') involves being sea-sick (cf. IV.ii.118–19), and Weis astray in seeing it as a reference 'to the supposedly invigorating properties of sea-air'. (Sea air was actually regarded as a cause of illness; see Samuel Purchas, *Purchas His Pilgrimes* [1625], pp. 926–7).

135 as low . . . Margets Lucas glosses **low** as 'far down the river', with *Lee* (presumably Leigh in Essex, on the north bank of the Thames) and *Margets* (Margate, on the Isle of Thanet, in Kent) thought of as an extension of the Thames Estuary. Cf. III.iii.53 and V.i.48n. A similar association of these two ports is found in Act II of Thomas Drue's *The Duchess of Suffolk* (perf. 1624). Woodroff presumably means that he should get at least this far on his voyage by 'to-morrow' (134–5).

136 riding forth i.e. 'sailing forth' (see *OED* ride 8).

136 the *God-speed* On the significance of ships' names, see *DLC* II.iii.45n.

137 fraughted 'freighted', possibly with cargo (see 'goods' [III.iii.71 and n]), but certainly with supplies.

138 *Letter of Mart* 'a licence authorizing reprisals on the subjects of a hostile state' (see *OED* marque[1] 2). Letters of reprisal (as they were also known) for shipowners were at this time technically only available in peacetime, as a means of recouping specific loss, but in practice were often a legal fiction during the undeclared war between England and Spain from 1624. Cf. *Cal. S. P. Dom.* (James I), CLXXXIII, 36 (10 February 1625), 'authorizing Lord Buckingham to grant letters of marque and reprisal to such merchants as have been injured at sea by the Spanish Netherlanders or the Hollanders'. Letters of marque only subsequently developed into wartime licences to privateer (see N. A. M. Rodger, *The Safeguard of the Sea: A Naval History of Britain Volume One: 660–1649* [London, 1997], pp. 199–200).

138 in her mouth i.e. the '*Letter of Mart*' permits her to 'show her teeth'.

138 roaring Boys i.e. ships' guns, 'noisy swaggerers' (cf. *OED* boy *n*.[1] 6). 'Roaring Meg' was a name for a large gun (*OED*).

140 Adventurers 'speculators, participants in commercial ventures' (see *OED* 4).

142 pieces gold coins worth 22 shillings (see 113n).

147–8 above . . . above The first **above** expresses a courteous preference. Annabel picks this up and invites him to 'surpass' (*OED* above *adv*. B8) the others' ventures (after Weis).

148 venter 'venture, risk, stake' (see *OED* 1).

149–50 'tis . . . Bottom i.e. 'all invested in one ship (or, metaphorically, in one venture)'.

152 sit down under Metaphorically, Rochfield's credit will be 'allocated a place at table not less worthy than . . .'.

156 Assurance Several meanings may be involved: (1) 'securing title to a property' (*OED* 4; here, by extension, gaining prizes); (2) 'insurance' (in case property is lost; *OED* 5).

163 your Kinsman i.e. Bonvile. Annabel claimed this status for Rochfield at 51, so again she speaks in a way that has special meaning for him.

169 Fouter on't 'Fuck it' (French *foutre*; see Henke 1975, II, 160).

ACT III, SCENE i

0.1 *Enter* Both men are likely to wear boots, signifying travel (see Dessen, pp. 39–40), and possibly cloaks or sea gowns as well (see MacIntyre, pp. 186–7), which will help signal their arrival at Calais.

2 staid 'detained, hindered' (*OED* stay *v.*¹ 20), but possibly also with the legal sense of 'prevented, arrested' (*OED* 25) to stop the duel.

2 *Dover* Then as now the principal port for crossings to France.

4 fresh coloured i.e. 'with a healthy, ruddy complexion'.

5–6 red . . . stormy Cf. Tilley M1175: 'A red Morning foretells a stormy day.'

7–8 face . . . death in't Cf. *WD* V.iii.80.

9–10 A Coward . . . mans Though this sounds proverbial, it is not recorded as such.

15 For dis-heartning i.e. 'for fear of disheartening'.

20 forgetful 'causing forgetfulness' (see *OED* 3). Cf. *WD* IV.ii.166.

21 this (Q ''tis') Dyce's emendation allows Bonvile to suggest that 'Wine begot' (20) a 'blow' (21) and consequently, in retaliation, **this Challenge**. Q's ''tis' could stand only if **Challenge** were emended to 'Challenged'. However, although nouns are frequently capitalized in Q, verbs are not (cf. 'challeng'd' at I.ii.132 and 'challengeth' at V.i.82 with the noun 'Challenge' at I.i.107), so Q's capital 'C' probably begins a noun; from which it follows that the error lies in ''tis'.

23 take your course i.e. 'adopt your course of action' (see *OED* take 25b).

27 fetch . . . off i.e. 'rescue a difficult case' (see *OED* fetch 16).

28 You . . . through i.e. 'you are committed and must see it through'.

34 Giddy and sinking. i.e. **Giddy** from 'Wine' (33) and, as a result of 'Riot' (33), 'falling into ruin or decay' (*OED* **sinking** *ppl. a.* 2b; although the earliest citation is 1693, it is closely based on sink *v.* 14). Q's punctuation ('Riot: giddy and sinking I had') loses the relationship between the results and their causes.

35 pluralities of Healths i.e. 'at drinking large numbers (*OED* plurality 1b) of toasts'.

37–8 promising . . . Lotteries Cf. *DLC* I.i.16n.

40 Engagement Clearly this refers to the supposed duel, but the precise meaning is uncertain, and all the possible options are slightly earlier than any *OED* citations. It may mean 'single combat' (*OED* 8 [1665]), 'entangled condition' (*OED* 5 [1642]), 'piece of business requiring attention' (*OED* 6 [1665]), or possibly 'formal undertaking' (*OED* 2 [1624–47]).

44 glorious, but of ample fame i.e. the enemy challenged by the 'great General' (42) is **a man** 'eager for glory' (*OED* glorious 2); **a man** constituted 'absolutely' (*OED* but 6) of **ample** ('abundant, excellent' [*OED a.* 3]) **fame**. The phrasing is awkward, however, and Lucas may have been right to emend **but** to 'and'.

47–9 the affection . . . eternity Cf. Tilley L539: 'A perfect love does last eternally.' As in I.ii, Lessingham is echoing Cicero, *De Amicitia*.

53 under-prop 'support, sustain' (*OED* 2); cf. 111 and n. Q's illogical 'under-propt' is more likely to be a misprint under the influence of the immediately following 'it' than an example of a Renaissance English playwright's (W's, in this scene) cavalier way with tenses.

59 opposite 'opponent' (*OED* 3).

60 *Clare's letter* Bonvile retains the letter, and produces it at IV.ii.129.

61 bad hand Lessingham puns, meaning that both the handwriting (*OED* 16) and the individual that wrote it are **bad**.

62 fair . . . worse Cf. Tilley W702: 'Women are in church saints, abroad angels, at home devils.'

68 Hellebore Its qualities as a 'poyson' (69) were well known. William Coles (*Adam in Eden* [1657], p. 239) says it provokes 'extream vomiting', 'brings down the Courses, and kills the Child in the womb'; and John Gerard warns 'it is not to be giuen but to robustious and strong bodies' (*Herball* [1597], p. 827). Association with witchcraft is suggested by **vomit of a Toad**.

69 qualified . . . woman i.e. 'only moderate [*OED* qualified 8a] **poyson** compared to a woman's **malice**'.

72 Villenage i.e. 'villeinage', the 'Tenure by which land was held' (72) in medieval England and Europe from a lord by villeins (a class of peasants annexed either to a lord or to a piece of land, and barely better than 'slaves' [74]). See Jowitt, pp. 1865–6. 'Villein' was pronounced (and sometimes spelt) 'villain', and both senses of ignobility attach to Lessingham's view of what has been required of him by his lady.

75 Equivocate Cf. *DM* III.v.27–9 and n for a similarly equivocal letter.

76–8 Her meaning . . . kill that Bonvile is incorrect: Clare's true **meaning** only emerges when she talks to Lessingham in IV.ii.

79 put 'imposed' (*OED* 23a), or, more strongly, 'saddled me with' (*OED* 23c).

83 *He draws* Business with swords is integral to the scene. It seems most likely that Lessingham draws here. Bonvile may draw in response before lowering his point at 'Ile not fight' (86), or may keep his sword sheathed until offering it to Lessingham (see 97n). Both men must at some point divest themselves of their cloaks in preparation for duelling (cf. 0.1n; and see MacIntyre, pp. 150, 187).

87 much advantage i.e. both situationally and in knowing something that you do not (see *OED* advantage *v.* 1b).

88 privy Coat 'a coat of mail worn under the ordinary dress' (*OED* privy *adj.* 8b), against the laws of duelling because it constituted an unfair 'advantage' (87). Cf. *DLC* II.i.313 and n.

94 Mistriss (Q 'Mrs.') See I.i.83n.

97 *submits himself* Bonvile probably offers his undefended breast to Lessingham (cf. *R3* I.ii.174–8), possibly kneeling. Lucas's '*He offers his sword to Lessingham*' is also required if Bonvile has not yet drawn his sword (see 83n), since Lessingham speaks at 107–12 as if Bonvile is holding his sword but not guarding himself (see 111n).

107 Guard thee Lessingham resumes the *en garde* position, and from here to 126 urges Bonvile to do the same. The code of honour prevents Lessingham from attacking while his opponent is clearly unready.

111 underprop thee otherwise Lessingham puns: 'instead of leaning on your sword, advance it to support your cause' (cf. 53n).

112 Stay Whether or not Bonvile has acceded to Lessingham's demand that he 'Advance' his sword (110; and see 107n), the further substitution of talking for fighting has, like the much-delayed duel in *DLC* II.ii, potential for either tension or comedy. See pp. 52–3.

114 ought '*who* ought' (Lucas).

115–17 friend . . . lost Cf. Tilley F695 'A friend is not so soon gotten as lost.'

125 Mistriss (Q 'Mrs.') See I.i.83n.

127 I am served right Possibly aside, especially if a comic effect is sought.

129–37 fight . . . advance The stage picture is now reversed, with Bonvile *en garde* and demanding that an unwilling Lessingham **advance** his sword (cf. 109–12).

135 faind'st 'feigned, invented'.

140–1 disarmed . . . resistance To retain the metaphorical strength of the words, the actor must resist the temptation to sheathe his sword as he speaks these words.

148–9 dangerous . . . body Cf. *Per.* III.i.47–9: 'The sea works high, the wind is loud, and will not lie till the ship be clear'd of the dead' (cited, with other examples, by Iona Opie and Moira Tatem, *A Dictionary of Superstitions* [Oxford, 1989], p. 97).

152 *Exeunt* Given Bonvile's refusal to travel with Lessingham, they probably leave by opposite doors.

ACT III, Scene ii

0.1 SD Although they may all enter together, the essence of this sequence, which must be established in stage space, is a confrontation between the Nurse defending the child within her 'Cottage' (10), and Compass and his wife arguing to get in.

4 Command! The vehemence of Compass's speech is indicated throughout the scene: 'be patient' (13), 'Storm' (36), 'rough' (47), 'mad' (61).

7 Civil Law . . . otherwise Although there is no likelihood that any court has made a determination against Compass (**found it otherwise**), the Nurse is plausibly saying that a question of pregnancy out of wedlock, and the paternity of an illegitimate child, would be matters for the **Civil Law** (i.e. the church or equity courts, not the common law; but cf. IV.i.74n). The statement is probably designed principally to allow Compass's punning response about 'Uncivil Law' (8).

9 dreadful as a *Shrove-tuesday* By threatening to 'tear thy Cottage' (10–11) Compass alludes to the London apprentices who habitually wrecked brothels in their pre-Lenten rampages, and sometimes theatres; see John Earle's character 'A Player' (*Microcosmographie*, E7ᵛ–E8ʳ): 'Shroue-tuesday hee feares as much as the Baudes, and Lent is more damage to him then the Butcher.' Lucas cites Middleton's *Inner-Temple Masque* (1619) (B3ᵛ): 'Stand forth *Shrouetuesday* . . . Tis in your charge to pull downe

Bawdyhouses . . . cause spoyle in *Shorditch* . . . deface Turnbul, | And tickle Codpiece Rowe.' Cf. *NHo* IV.iii.76–7 and n, and Henke 1988, pp. 231–2. And if the Nurse's 'Cottage' is a bawdyhouse, then she is a bawd; as Weis notes, 'wet nurses and mid-wives had a reputation for loose morals, and were not uncommonly associated with prostitution'.

11–12 lay Burglary . . . charge 'charge you with burglary' (see *OED* lay 27b). Dogberry (*Ado* IV.ii.50) uses the same malapropism.

16 to his use 'for his purpose' (*OED* use *n.* 2), but possibly also with legal sense of using for 'profit, or other benefit' (*OED* 4).

17 white 'fair-seeming, specious' (*OED* 10); cf. 'white devil' (*WD* Title-page 1–2n).

20 by the wifes Coppy-hold 'W is here using "Coppy-hold" in a double sense . . . The child is admittedly Compass's wife's but not his; so he refers to it as her *likeness*, hence her Coppy-hold. At the same time, he likens the child to land held by his wife by copy of court roll and means to imply that, since his wife has an interest therein, he, as her husband, has the right of possession, management, and use. For, as every man of that day probably knew, the husband acquired such rights in lands of his wife for their joint lives at least; and copyholds, as limited by the customs of the manor, were no exception' (Paul S. Clarkson and Clyde T. Warren, *The Law of Property in Shakespeare and the Elizabethan Drama* [New York, 1968], pp. 43–4).

21 try 'examine and determine'.

22 Father in Law 'stepfather' (*OED* 2), with of course a pun on 'Law' (21, 22).

23 betwixt . . . *Tuttle-street* Effectively, all of London, from *Black-wall* in the east to *Tuttle-street* in Westminster, including the courts of **Law** both there and at Guildhall (cf. IV.i.1–2n).

24 does use to 'is accustomed to' (*OED* use *v.* 21); cf. *WD* I.ii.162.

31 So thou shalt In an instant riposte to the Nurse's angry refusal of his indecent prop-osition, Compass says he would rather be hanged than have sex with her.

31.1 *Enter* Logically, Franckford and Luce enter from the door opposite the one the Nurse will appear to be defending (cf. 0.1n).

34 Morrow . . . your wife Franckford's civil inclusion of Urse (**you both**) in his greet-ing provokes Compass to the very particular inclusion of Luce (**your wife**), perhaps with innuendo or business appropriate to his comic 'Storm' (36).

36 belongs to 'is appropriate to' (*OED* 1a).

36 Calm and a Storm Taking up Franckford's 'calmly' (35), Compass justifies the anger he has been venting from the beginning of the scene. There may possibly be a glance here at Donne's verse epistles, 'The Storme' and 'The Calme', in his lifetime amongst his best-known and most admired works.

37 tyed . . . ground i.e. 'tethered your horse in my pasture'.

38 Nag A small horse, evidently, in Franckford's use here, thought of as generically male in contrast to the 'Mare' of 37. There may be additional connotations; cf. Marston, *The Scourge of Villainie*, 'In Lectores prorsus indignos', 43–5 (*Poems*, p. 97): 'hence lewd nags, away . . . Then to *Priapus* gardens'. A pun is also possible on 'nag' = 'annoy'. Wiggins's assertion of a pun on 'knag' ('a short spur or stiff projection from the trunk or branch of a tree' [*OED*]) seems over-confident, but the more general idea of a small lecherous animal representing the penis is not impossible.

39–40 make Hair-buttons i.e. buttons made of horse hair, but with a play, as Lucas notes, on **buttons** = 'excreta' (Partridge 1984, p. 167). Compass's point is that he will make Franckford shit himself with fright.

41 Main Franckford wishes to return to the 'main point', but Compass outwits him by punning on 'mane' ('main', 42).

42 crop his ears i.e. 'cut his ears shorter (or off)', a common way of marking horses, and, for people, a punishment for some felonies (see *OED* crop-ear).

43 back-gaul . . . spur-gaul Although **spur-gaul** is common (= 'gall with spurs'; cf. II.iv.115n), **back-gaul** is not. It may refer to what Markham (*Cavalrice*, 14ᵛ) describes as 'a foule bruse taken by the sitting down of the hinder part of the saddle vpon the horses back, and it is called Nauell-gall, because the crush is upon the signe iust oppost against the horses nauell'. Alternatively, Compass may simply be setting up the repetition, and mean no more than to gall his back, e.g., by beating him.

44 slit his Nose Markham does not note this as an operation on horses. It was occasionally part of punishment for humans (cf. 'crop his ears' [42 and n]), but it is probably introduced here for the sake of **smell**.

44 smell 'detect, have an inkling of' (*OED* 2a); cf. *TN* II.iii.162: 'I smell a device.'

44 Unbritch his Barrel i.e. 'castrate him'. The primary metaphor is from gunnery: the **Barrel** of the cannon will have its breech ('the hindermost part of a piece of ordnance' [*OED* 5]) removed or destroyed (see *OED* unbreech 1). The obvious implications are reinforced by both 'breech' and 'barrel' referring also to the loins of a horse, and by **Unbritch** as 'to strip (a person) of breeches' (*OED* unbreech 2).

44–5 discharge his Bullets Continuing the gunnery imagery, the primary sense seems to be that his semen will be fired off (see *OED* discharge 1b) for the last time, but with a secondary sense that he will be deprived of (*OED* discharge 1e) his testicles. See Partridge 1985, 'bullets', p. 81.

45 gird . . . stinks 'tighten his girth until he farts' (see *OED* gird $v.^1$ 1d). Cf. Dekker, *The Honest Whore, Part II*, I.i.183–5: 'when I came to gird his belly, his scuruy guts rumbled, di Horse farted in my face'. Weis reads 'beat him until he farts' (*OED* gird $v.^2$ 1), but this sense, though appropriate to Compass's threats, has no reference to horses or **stinks**.

45 smell 'detect' as at 44, but now with an intended pun on 'stink' (see 45n).

47–50 maintain— . . . maintain— Frankford is presumably about to say something like 'to **maintain** (your argument with such vehemence)', meaning either 'carry on, keep up' (*OED* maintain 2b), or perhaps 'support or uphold in argument' (*OED* 14a). Compass, however, interrupts to take **Maintain** (48) in the sense of 'bear the expenses of (a person) for living, education, etc.' (*OED* 9a). Then Franckford is interrupted again. Q's full stop after 'maintain' (47) is unlikely, since the verb is left without an object, but could possibly be retained if Franckford is taken to mean 'carry on, keep up' (*OED* 2b), or perhaps 'support or uphold in argument' (*OED* 14a), i.e. 'you are too rough in your arguing'.

48–9 bestow her labor i.e. 'expend (*OED* 5b) her effort', but with the pun on the **labor** of childbirth.

53–4 purse . . . purse i.e. Urse's vagina, and perhaps, given 'Coin' (54), Franckford's scrotum (see Partridge 1984, p. 936).

54 Coin Though it is nowhere else recorded, there seems a clear double entendre here, given 'purse' (53), on **Coin** as 'semen'.

56 treat colder i.e. 'discuss, negotiate' (*OED* treat 1a) more coolly.

62 horn-mad 'passionately mad at being cuckolded' (Partridge 1955, p. 129).

63–5 you . . . Coxcomb At Wellington 1997 Franckford hesitated and stuttered on the 'c' of the word 'cuckold' which Compass was expecting to hear (cf. 63 and 66); **Coxcomb** = 'fool' (*OED* 3), a milder insult.

66 I knew . . . C. Compass presumably shares with the audience his enjoyment at pre-empting Franckford's intention of calling him a cuckold. Cf. 63–5n.

68 past . . . shame Cf. Tilley S271: 'Past shame past amendment.'

69 acknowledge it Q lacks the pronoun, which improves the metre and the rhetorical balance of the line (**acknowledge it . . . enjoy it**). Franckford's speech is printed as prose in Q, and the postulated omission of **it** was from a tight line into which it could not have fitted; moreover, even in Q Franckford's brief statement contains three instances of **it** and one of **'tis**, repetition that might have induced inadvertence in a compositor or scribe seemingly prone to omitting this pronoun (cf. II.iv.12 and V.ii.138). Presenting Franckford's three lines as verse increases the air of formal declaration, and the fact that 'As' (68), though falling within a line set as prose in Q, has an anomalous capital, implies a verse line in manuscript.

71 off i.e. 'distant or remote in fact' (*OED* 2c) from being.

73 Merchants 'fellows' (see *OED* 3, and *DLC* III.ii.124n). The standard sense, which carries connotations of cheating in such phrases as 'play the merchant' (*OED* 1c), is also, of course, applicable to Franckford.

74, 78 Urse, Luce Like the duel proposed by Lessingham at I.ii.75–9, the seconds (the wives, silent bystanders until this point) also take part in this altercation (quite physically at Wellington 1997).

75 knew i.e. 'had carnal knowledge of (= had sex with)'.

79 allow my sufferance 'accord [*OED* allow 11] my acquiescence [*OED* sufferance 6]'.

80 In lieu i.e. 'in substitution' (*OED* lieu, instead 1) for the fact that.

82–6 Let him . . . agen This entire attack is directed at Luce, which may be decisive in leading Franckford to abandon what has been a total failure as attempted reconciliation.

82 dung . . . ground Clearly with a sexual innuendo, involving play on **dung** = 'fertilize', and hence 'impregnate' (cf. Henke 1988, pp. 157 and 240–1).

83 plant . . . garden Again with clear sexual implications, where **Reddish** (i.e. radish) = 'penis'.

84 Mutton A slang term for a loose woman, or prostitute: cf. *WD* I.ii.89 and n.

85–6 distaff . . . spindle The **distaff** (in hand-spinning, a long staff, usually held under the left arm, on which the unspun wool or flax is supported) and the **spindle** (a smaller tapered rod which is spun to impart twist, and onto which the **yarn** is wound) are both traditional emblems of women's work. Here the **spindle**, because of its shape, refers to Franckford's penis (see Partridge 1955, p. 191); **distaff**, given that it usually has a cleft end (to hold the wool in place), may imply Urse's genitals. The **head** is presumably the spun **yarn** removed from the **spindle** (figuratively, the child), though *OED* does not record this sense (but cf. *OED* head 11a, referring to bundles of flax). For spinning as coition (Rubinstein, p. 249), based on the **distaff** held upright between the legs rather than under the left arm, cf. *TN* I.iii.93–104, where Sir Andrew's hair is described as hanging like 'flax on a distaff', and Sir Toby hopes 'to see a huswife take [him] between her legs and spin it off'. Cf. *WD* I.ii.163 and *DLC* IV.ii.207–8 and n.

87 words, then; let ('words, then let' Q) Emendation seems necessary, since 'then' meaning 'next' is found only in Woodroff's narrative of the naval battle (several instances starting at III.iii.79), whereas an appended 'then' meaning 'in that case' occurs frequently. Cf. 82, where punctuation is similarly emended.

92–3 two hands . . . used The stage picture (**this**) will precisely illustrate what the Nurse says: that **the law** will have **hands** extended on each side to take money from them both, probably to little purpose. Cf. similar symmetrical staging at *WD* I.i.29–30 (see n), *DM* I.i.279–316, and *DLC* I.ii.105–7. **used** = 'employed to advantage' (see *OED* use 10a).

94–8 Gender . . . case Franckford puns on **Gender** as both a grammatical term and as 'genderer', i.e. 'begetter' (see *OED* gender *v.* 4), to make the point that in **law**, as in grammar, the **case** is so obvious that a **School-boy** can determine it. Compass then counters with an elaboration of the grammatical pun, with **declines** (with a second meaning of 'turn aside' [*OED* 11b]), *Genetive* (i.e. in grammar, but also 'pertaining to generation' [*OED* 2], and linked to **case** = vagina [cf. *DLC* IV.ii.236n], with a pun on genitals [Partridge 1955, p. 119]), and *Hujus* (Latin, genitive case of 'hic, haec, hoc', = 'of this woman'), where seventeenth-century pronunciation provides a pun on 'hugeous', i.e. enormous (see Dale F. Coye, *Pronouncing Shakespeare's Words* [Westport, Conn., 1998], p. 14).

101–5 Although Compass calls after the departing Franckford and Luce at 101–2, it seems likely that the rest of this speech is triumphantly to the audience.

105 by-betting An obscure phrase, which the only *OED* entry fails to explain (by-bet *n.*, citing Middleton and Rowley, *The Changeling*, IV.i.87–8: 'the gold | Is but a by-bet to wedge in the honour'; Bawcutt's note to IV.i.88 partly explains the phrase). Given **win by play**, the reference seems almost certainly to betting on the **by**, or 'chance', at the game of hazard, rather than betting on the 'main' (see *OED* main *n.*³, which explains the game, and gives a 1598 quotation apposite to Compass's situation: 'Diceplayers, that gaine more by the bye then by the maine'). The point is that Compass has not successfully thrown a 'main' (the winning number called at the start), but may still win by throwing a **by** (a repeat of his actual first throw). This is more likely than Lucas's speculation 'betting on another's performance'.

105 *Exeunt* The Nurse may have left already, either at 93 or, more likely, when Franckford and Luce exit after 100.

ACT III, Scene iii

4 this Bonvile's will, a separate document from the 'Letter' (1).

5 estated 'endowed' (see *OED* estate 1).

8 I am lost A phrase of which W seems particularly fond: it not only recurs in *CC* (IV.ii.27 and 107), but is used also in *WD* (I.ii.3) and *DLC* (II.ii.28 and II.iii.172).

9–16 Oh fool . . . lost Though Clare reveals that Lessingham has **mistook my injunction utterly**, what she meant remains obscure until IV.ii, when, in stages (15–17, 43–66, 130–2), the truth behind her equivocation is revealed.

13 too i.e. 'to'; cf. I.ii.38n.

14 cry . . . mercy 'apologize [*OED* cry 1b] to my heart'.

22 Let me go This may indicate that Raymond is obstructing Clare's attempt to leave (cf. 30n), or possibly that he is attempting to embrace her. The entire episode with Raymond suggests not just Clare's power of attraction, but more importantly her lack of interest in alternative suitors; see p. 273.

25 spight Clare puns on Raymond's 'in spight of your heart' (23).

30 no further Clare does not speak again, and Raymond's comment at 30–1 would be more appropriate as a comment on her exiting than spoken as Woodroff and the others enter; but there is no SD in Q, and her comment that she can command her ears (29) may imply that she remains.

30–1 On . . . strangely Certainly spoken aside, but whether to the Gallants or to the audience is unclear.

31 off o'th hindges i.e. 'unhinged, deranged'. Cf. 30n.

31.1 *Saylor* The Sailor from II.iv.

37 Allyance 'kindred' (*OED* 4).

42 purchas'd 'acquired by effort' (*OED* 1).

43–4 high providence . . . creatress Rochfield builds his compliment around play on **high providence** (God, the sole creator) and Annabel as **sole creatress**.

55 three Spanish men of War Probably a topical reference to skirmishes with ships from the Spanish Netherlands in the autumn of 1624; see p. 263.

56 English Cross 'the cross of St George on the English flag' (Weis).

57 Salute . . . strike i.e. 'greet us with a cannon to force us to lower our flag in surrender' (cf. 71, and *OED* salute 2c (b), piece 11a, strike 17c).

58 Ours i.e. 'our sailors'.

63 Event 'outcome' (*OED* 3).

64 Sea room 'space at sea for manoeuvring' (see *OED*).

67 Master 'The Maister is to see to the cunning [i.e. conning, steering] the Ship, and trimming the sailes' (*OED n.*[1] 2b, citing Capt. Smith, 1626). Here the **Master** is clearly the second in command of a small ship with no other officers.

70 manage 'handle, work (a ship)' (*OED* 2c), with possibly also a sense of 'conduct or carry on (a war, an undertaking)' (*OED* 3a).

71 goods A privateer normally intended to capture **goods** rather than to carry cargo of its own, but possibly Woodroff was combining trade with the opportunity for plunder; cf. 'fraughted', II.iv.137 and n.

72 mediate for 'sue, ask for' (see *OED* mediate 4a). Cf. *AV* II.i.40n.

72 Nay Cous, proceed This seems to indicate a pause by Rochfield, presumably from modesty (cf. 78), emotion, or exhaustion.

78 unite i.e. 'united' (*OED ppl. a.* 1b); cf. V.i.30.

81 Lin-stocks short staffs with a fork or grip for holding the lighted slow match used to fire a gun (see *OED*). Cf. Marston, *Antonio and Mellida*, II.i.17–20: 'The match of furie is lighted, fastned to the linstock of rage, and will presently set fire to the touchstone of intemperance, discharging the double culverin of my incensement.'

87 third (Dyce; Q 'three') Q's error presumably arose from manuscript use of an Arabic or Roman numeral, perhaps followed by an easily-overlooked superscript 'rd' ('3rd').

87 lyes on the Lee Probably 'with sails aback' (*OED* lee $n.^1$ 2b); i.e. the ship is brought up into the wind, either to prevent it heeling so far over that water enters through damaged timbers, or to stop sailing so that the sailors will be free to repair 'her leakes' (88). Weis glosses 'heels over to leeward', which is possible if he means that the ship deliberately allows itself to be taken aback so as to expose damage below the waterline, but this sense, though logical, is not supported by *OED*.

97 venturer i.e. 'a merchant-venturer; one who undertakes or shares in a trading venture' (*OED* venturer 2). Cf. *DLC* I.i.48n.

103 of small venturers 'from being small venturers' (Weis; see *OED* of 1a).

ACT IV, Scene i

0.1–.2 SD Since at 22.1 '*They sit down*', and at 22.2–.3 Franckford's group enter '*to another Table*', we must assume that stage attendants place two tables and ensure a sufficient number of stools or benches, at the start of the scene. The **Boy** seems to be Jack (see II.iii.0.1n), to judge by 6–7 (cf. 4n). He may lead them in, or may enter by another door so as to welcome them. The presence of **LYONEL** is unexplained, except insofar as Compass is Woodroff's neighbour as well as Franckford's (see 196, V.ii.90, III.ii.33). Splitting the group of Gallants between the two antagonists (see 22.1–.3n) may foreshadow the reconciliation to come as well as creating a crowded tavern and, in effect, trial scene. **PETTIFOG** will no doubt be identifiable as an *Attorney* not only by his gown, but also by inkhorn, penholder, and, to judge by earlier plays by W, a vast buckram bag stuffed with his papers (see 22.1 SD, and cf. *WD* III.ii.46–7n; *DLC* IV.ii.35, and Fig. 5).

1–2 Three Tuns . . . Guild-hall Sugden (p. 515) notes that **Three Tuns** were depicted on the arms of the Vintners' Company, making it a favourite sign for taverns, the most famous of them being that in **Guild-hall** Yard. He also cites Herrick, 'An Ode for him [Ben Jonson]': 'Ah *Ben*! | Say how, or when | Shall we thy Guests | Meet at those *Lyrick* Feasts, | Made at the *Sun*, | The *Dog*, the triple *Tunne*?' (*Works*, p. 289). Equally important, **Guild-hall** was the site of a number of courts (Sugden, p. 238); cf. 77–8n.

2 Mr. Abbreviation of 'Master' (pronounced 'Mister' or 'Master'; cf. I.i.136n).

2 **Show a room** Both Compass's group and Franckford's group ask for a 'private room' (23), as was frequent in taverns at the time. The two parties do not take notice of each other's presence until Woodroff's entry at 133.1, so possibly we are meant to think of them in separate rooms until that point.

4 *Hodge* Actually Jack (cf. 6–7, and II.iii.0.1n). *Hodge*, a familiar form of the name Roger, was often used 'as a typical name for a rustic' (*OED* 1).

6 *Crack-roap* i.e. 'a gaol-bird, born to be hanged' (Partridge 1984, p. 263). Cf. 'Crack-hemp' (*Shr.* V.i.46).

7 **bound Prentice** Apprentices were usually bound in their late teens for a minimum of seven years.

9 **jumble Bastard** (1) 'stir up, mix the ingredients' (*OED* jumble 3) of 'sweetened wine' (*OED* bastard 4), and (2) 'have intercourse' (*OED* jumble 6) and engender 'an illegitimate child' (*OED* bastard 1). The reference to the 'pleasure of thy Mistriss' (10) reinforces the similar innuendo at II.iii.27 about apprentices.

14 **Ellegant** i.e. 'Alicant', a red wine made at Alicante, in Spain. Lucas notes 'the converse pun' in *Wiv.* II.ii.68, where Mistress Quickly talks of wine, and letters written in 'alligant terms'.

15 **con her thank** 'thank her' (see *OED* thank 4a).

15 **of her side** i.e. 'of her opinion', which Compass (16–17) jokingly intensifies to 'of our party in the dispute'.

18 **neat** 'undiluted'.

21 **Metheglin** 'Welsh spiced mead'; cf. 'Welch' (19) and 'Britain' (22 and n). Adulteration of wine was a perennial problem for the Vintners' Company, which in 1628 ordered 'that no retailer of wine in the city or within a three mile radius was to keep in the cellar of any house where wine was retailed any cider, perry or metheglin . . . on pain of a £3 fine for each offence' (Anne Crawford, *A History of the Vintners' Company* [London, 1977], p. 88).

22 **true Britain** i.e. Welsh, 'a true Briton' (see *OED* Britain *n.*² 1, and Briton 1b). Cf. Heywood's *The Rape of Lucrece* (1630), III.v (F4ᵛ), 'The Brittaine, he metheglen quaffes.' Jack swears as a **true Britain**; but since he is a false Welshman (i.e. not Welsh), he can, paradoxically, be true to the stereotype of a false Welshman (i.e. duplicitous) by adding 'Metheglin' (21; and see n). Cf. *1H4* II.i.91–4: 'Gads.: Thou shalt have a share in our purchase, as I am a true man. Cham.: Nay, rather let me have it as you are a false thief.'

22.1–.3 **SD** The *Drawer* is referred to as 'boy' at 24, so it is possibly Jack again as at 0.1, but we have allowed Q to stand (cf. 53.1n). **MR. DODGE** presumably duplicates Pettifog (see 0.1–.2n). **RAYMOND** is included here (so Lucas) because he has lines to speak from 193, and Q provides him no entry. He could come in with Compass at 0.1, but it may be more appropriate for the wealthy Franckford to have a larger following than Compass. Alternatively, since **EUSTACE** speaks only one line, at 25, it is possible the playwrights intended only one Gallant to each party, and were careless in identifying which one they attached to Franckford.

23 **private room** See 2n.

27 **brabling** 'litigious, (noisily) quarrelsome' (see *OED* brabbling *ppl. a.* a). Cf. 109.

29 Canary A sweet wine from the Canary Islands.

35–6 Affidavit . . . Answer . . . Declaration Like Pettifog, Dodge also '*pulls out papers*' (22.1). These various preliminary legal documents in a suit between parties may imply a procedure in church or equity courts; cf. 74n.

37–8 at charge . . . Charge Franckford puns on **at charge** = 'bearing the expense or cost' (*OED* charge 10e) and **Charge** = 'pecuniary burden, expense' (*OED* 10a), and possibly 'accusation' (*OED* 16a), since claiming the child entails an acknowledgement of the crime of adultery.

45 Abilities 'faculties' (*OED* ability 6); cf. *Tro.* I.iii.179: 'All our abilities, gifts, natures, shapes'.

50 sues 'makes legal claim, brings a suit' (see *OED* 21b).

51 Swabber 'low fellow' (because behaving 'like a sailor of low rank' whose job was 'to swab the decks'; see *OED* 2, 1).

53.1 *Drawer* In performance, Jack, who is given an entry direction at 55.1, could be the *Drawer* for both groups (cf. 22.1–.3n).

56 Score . . . *Woodcock* i.e. 'chalk up the cost for the wine I am serving in the Woodcock Room'. For named inn rooms, see, e.g., *1H4* II.iv.27–8, 37–8. Since woodcocks were proverbially foolish (cf. Tilley W746), the choice of name is probably also a glance at Compass, who ordered the **Allegant**.

56.1 *like a Musician* Given 'scrape' (63), it seems that Rafe (see 62, and 22.1–.3n) is playing a stringed instrument, probably a fiddle. His appearance will transfer audience attention back to the Compass group.

59–60 Cuckoes . . . Nightingale Harbingers of spring, the cuckoo and the nightingale were both ***April*** arrivals. To hear the cuckoo before the nightingale was seen as a bad omen for lovers. As Weis notes, 'Rafe and Jack are **Cuckoes** because they alerted Compass to the fact that he was a cuckold, whereas Urse is the mournful **Nightingale** whose child has been taken from her. Her situation recalls Virgil's mourning nightingale from *Georgics*, IV.511–13.' Cf. V.ii.136–7 and n.

61 Taylor . . . leering eye i.e. 'your sly sideways glances [see *OED* leer *n.*²] show you are as dishonest as a tailor [see Tilley T22, 25]'. Cf. *DLC* II.i.62–3.

62–3 make a leg . . . company i.e. 'bow yourself out of our company'. The instruction to **make a leg** ('bow' [*OED* leg 4]) is for the sake of puns on **scrape** = (1) 'bow' (from the drawing, or scraping back of the foot; see *OED* 8), (2) 'play a fiddle, scrape catgut' (*OED* 6; cf. *WHo* V.i.9–10: 'They are but rozining, sir, and theile scrape themselves into your company presently'), and (3) a play on the idiomatic 'scrape acquaintance' (see preceding example, and *OED* 5b).

65–6 Defendant . . . Trespass It is not clear if the audience is meant initially to think the **Defendant** is Franckford, and that he has been **arrested**, although this is clearly not the case in respect of Compass's claim for the child. The comedy lies, first, in the typical lawyerly jargon about which legal form has been, or should be used in a particular instance; second, in the introduction of common-law terminology (***Latitat*** and **Action of Trespass**) into a subject that would never normally be a matter for the common law; and, third, in the concept of **Trespass** (with its many legal meanings) to describe seduction. It also sets up the further legal debate and obscene quibbles with

'Action of the Case' (67–8 and n). *Latitat*, the Bill of Middlesex, is a summons before the Court of King's Bench on the legal fiction that the defendant 'lies hid' (Latin) elsewhere in the country; see Jowitt, pp. 218, 1067, and Lucas.

67.8 Action of the Case Comedy is here based partly on the typical legal argument over writs and jurisdictions (an **Action of** [technically, 'on'] **the Case** being, by this period, an alternative procedure to the 'Action of Trespass' [66] from which it developed; cf. 65–6n); and partly on **Case** = 'vagina' (cf. II.iii.25 and III.ii.94–8 and n), which then colours the sense of **Action**, as well as 'point' (70), 'ticklish' (70) and possibly 'skill' (69) and 'overthrow' (71). For detail of the writ, see Lucas, and Jowitt, pp. 41, 1084).

70 point (1) 'instance', (2) 'penis' (Partridge 1955, p. 169).

70 ticklish (1) 'delicate or difficult', (2) 'susceptible to sexual tickling', referring to both 'Case' (68) and 'point' (see Partridge 1955, p. 205).

71 overthrow (1) 'defeat', (2) 'tumble, throw sexually' (see Partridge 1955, 'throw down', p. 204).

72 Sans 'without'.

73–4 Ward ... stronger Ward Pettifog puns on **Ward** as (1) 'a minor under the control of a guardian or a court', and (2) 'a defensive posture or movement' in fencing (*OED n.*[2] 8a; cf. *1H4* II.iv.194–5: 'Thou knowest my old ward: here I lay, and thus I bore my point'). The legal dispute over the child is similar to those heard by the Court of Wards.

74 partus sequitur ventrem 'the offspring follows the womb' (legal Latin). Pettifog adds to the comic legal confusion by correctly quoting this maxim of **Civil Law** (see 75n), but doing so in England where it did not apply: 'the rule of law in England is that the offspring shall always follow the condition of the father; never that of the mother' (Sir Edward Coke, quoted by Jowitt, p. 1087). Cf. 171–2 and n.

75 Civil Law (1) 'Roman law', (2) 'law regulating private rights and duties' (*OED*). Confusion and, here, comedy are based on the Roman code in England, and its procedures in non-common-law jurisdictions, being familiar to lawyers (especially the few who attended university), but its maxims rarely applying in English courts. Cf. 'common Law' (75–6 and n), and 171–2n.

75–6 within ... common Law In direct contradiction of his citation of European 'Civil Law' (75 and n), Pettifog's reference to **the four Seas** (the seas bounding Britain; see *OED* sea 2b) invokes English **common Law**. Confusion is compounded by the fact that the case of the child is not in common-law jurisdiction.

77–8 Guild-hall A number of courts sat at *Guild-hall* (cf. 1–2n, and Sugden, p. 238); cf. Jonson, *Every Man in His Humour* I.ii.88–9: '*draw your bill of charges, as vnconscionable, as any Guild-hall verdict will giue it you*'. Given the mediation which takes place (see 133.1n), there may be reference here to the courts of assistants at Guildhall, where officials of the livery companies tried to resolve disputes before they came to a formal hearing; or perhaps to some aspect of the custom of London. The comic point seems to be the legal complexities and overlapping jurisdictions. Cf. also 79n, 105, and 114.

79 You ... Jury i.e. 'Atorneys in *Guild-hall*' (77–8) are; a frequent complaint by common-law lawyers about jurisdictions following civil-law procedures (cf. 75n).

80–1 you will . . . Cause The jibe involves a sense of lawyers both despising their clients and manufacturing profitable causes.

82 Barber . . . away The point being that the **Barber**, eager to be away, is perfunctory in his hair- or beard-trimming.

83 ordinary (1) 'unexceptional', (2) 'within the jurisdiction of a civil law judge having authority "in his own right"' (Jowitt, p. 1291), and possibly (3) 'appropriate to a cheap daily eating house' (see *OED* 14b).

83 *Nisi Prius* An 'ordinary' (83) and quick legal formality (cf. 81–2) determining that an action might not be heard at Westminster 'unless beforehand' (legal Latin) it had been tried at the court of assizes in the county where the cause originated (see Jowitt, pp. 1239–40).

93 *Sound of Denmark* The **Sound**, between Sweden and **Denmark**, links the Kattegat to the Baltic; the Danes exacted a toll (**Custom**) at Elsinore from this busy shipping lane. Weis notes that 'the Danes were thought to be great drinkers, so that 1 Client's tribute would be especially welcome'.

95 Declaration Cf. 35–6 and n.

96 pottle This half-gallon measure (somewhat over two litres) doubles the 'quart' (89) of 1 Client.

100 Mr. Abbreviation of 'Master' (pronounced either 'Master' or 'Mister'; see I.i.136n).

105 Councellors Fee i.e. 'fee paid to a lawyer' (see *OED* counsellor 3).

107 young Clerks . . . Clients Cf. *DLC* IV.i.101–2.

108 Cucking-stool See *DLC* V.iv.37n. Compass is right that this summary punishment at parish level would apply to the sort of disorderly behaviour that might otherwise bring people before the courts at '*Guild-hall*' (106) or elsewhere (and thereby generate fees for lawyers).

109 brables i.e. 'brabbles', noisy quarrels or paltry actions at law (cf. 27, and *OED* 3, 2).

111–14 defamatory . . . *Guild-hall* Charges of slander could be brought before the London courts. Compass may react sharply to *Cuckolds curr* (so Wellington 1997).

116 the Ballad of *Flood* No **Ballad** relating to *Flood* seems to have survived, but Lucas discovered a pamphlet which tells us a good deal about 'Griffin Flood, Informer, whose cunning courses, churlish manners, and troublesome Informations molested a number of plaine-dealing people in this City of *London*'. Refusing to plead on a murder charge, he was **prest** (i.e. pressed to death; cf. *WD* III.iii.25 and n) at Newgate on 18 January 1624 (see p. 263). Lucas notes that 118–28 seems to be related to an incident in the pamphlet. 'There it is said that he had successfully blackmailed an ale-wife for employing a tailor not free of the city; encouraged by this he visited her ale-house with a view to further triumphs and there "espied the good wife run down into the Cellar with a blacke Pot or two, measures contrary to the Cities custom". So he pursued her and demanded hush-money; but the ale-wife caught up a quart-pot of pewter and broke his head, crying "Oh help, murther, murther". To her neighbours rushing in she explained that Flood had tried to ravish her; the denials of such a man were unconvincing; and Flood had to sit in prison until he had paid her damages.'

119 Turnball-street i.e. Turnbull Street, 'the most disreputable street in London', notorious for its brothels (Sugden, p. 533); cf. Jonson, *Bartholomew Fair*, IV.v.61: 'Yonder is your *Punque* of Turnbull, Ramping Ales [Alice].'

121 Tweak ... Play A *Tweak* is a 'harlot' (*OED* n.²), but Compass mistakes **Bronstrops** ('bawd' [*OED* bawdstrot]) for a synonym. The **Play** he has seen, Middleton and Rowley's *A Fair Quarrel*, refers at IV.iv.171–2 (1622 additions) to two women, one a whore, the other a bawd: 'mayst thou first serve out thy time as a tweak, and then become a bronstrops, as she is!'

122 dealings 'sexual intercourse'; cf. *DLC* IV.ii.358–9n.

123 Goose 'venereal disease', usually referring to a swelling in the groin (from 'Winchester goose', a prostitute; see *OED* goose 3). Cf. '*Winchester*' (128 and n).

124 two i.e. a double dose.

124 away with 'put up with, tolerate' (*OED* 16a). Cf. *DLC* IV.ii.544.

126–8 Cannes ... Winchester measure The informer reported her for illegal **Cannes** ('drinking vessels' [*OED* can n.¹ 1]), but she testified (see *OED* depose 5) in **Court** that she gave him **true *Winchester* measure** = (1) as much drink as legally defined by the official 'Winchester measure' standard for quarts, gallons, etc. (see *OED* Winchester 1), and (2) appropriate revenge from a 'Winchester goose' (a whore from the brothels in Southwark owned by the Bishops of Winchester; cf. 123n).

130 Mr. Abbreviation of 'Master' (pronounced either 'Master' or 'Mister'; see I.i.136n).

132 Compremiser 'arbitrator' (see *OED* compromiser 1); cf. 133.1n. Although Q's spelling is not listed in *OED*, 'e' for 'o' is common in 'compromise'.

133.1 Enter ... WOODROFF Their entrance is acknowledged by both parties, who now clearly occupy the same fictional space (cf. 2n). The **Councellor**, and Woodroff, as a 'Justice' (130) of the Peace, have evidently been agreed on as the legal arbitrators (see 'Compremiser' [132]) for the dispute, a common procedure in equity courts.

134–5 your ... your Woodroff is probably in both cases addressing both Franckford and Compass.

136–7 as we ... end i.e. 'so far as we can establish, the law will render a verdict'.

137 sought the Cases 'gone through the precedents' (Weis).

139 conditions ... head-long Compass will accept any arbitrated settlement which gives him the child, but will otherwise continue the legal process.

140 Foot-man Given **run by**, the reference here is either to (1) 'a runner in attendance upon a rider of rank' (*OED* 3), or (2) 'one who competes in a foot-race' (*OED* 1b, citing *AV* I.i.48). Footmen also carried messages (a sense not recorded in *OED*; but see Dorothy Marshall, *The English Domestic Servant in History* [London, 1949], p. 6).

146 Censure 'judgement; opinion' (*OED* 3).

147 yield ... Childe i.e. 'I will consent to no outcome but the return of my child.'

148 as vain 'pointless'.

148 seek your peace i.e. 'seek to establish concord, amity' (*OED* peace 4a).

153 charge ... Parish Poor Laws laid on the **Parish** the unwelcome financial responsibility for orphans and others unable to support themselves.

157–8 reason . . . grounded The word **reason** may signal a move to arguments of Common **Law**, having previously dealt with illegitimacy (151) and the Parish (153), realms of ecclesiastical law. Cf. 171–2n.

164 lops 'loppings, faggot-wood' (*OED* lop *n.*³ 1).

168 earth our Mother Compass neatly makes explicit the Councellor's identification of the earth as mother (167–76), and seizes on Pettifog's maxim '*partus sequitur ventrem*' (75 and n) to insist that civil law is therefore on his side. Cf. 171–2n.

168–70 earth . . . best children Continuing the image of **earth** as mother (see 168n), Compass adds another common trope (all her **children** returning to mother earth in death), and adds a double jest about even **Lawyers** being included despite (1) any **Law** they might use to try to evade their fate, and (2) their being undesirable, even to their mother (**none of her best children**).

171–2 Civil-law . . . Common-law The comedy of legalisms reaches its climax in this speech as Compass sums up a supposed **Civil-law** argument (in a country where it is well understood by lawyers but does not apply; see 75n and 168n), before triumphantly extending the Councellor's argument (157–66) at **Common-law** (which has no jurisdiction; see 75–6n) with his barnyard analogy.

172–3 ground . . . adversary Compass is presumably on his feet by now (and probably has been since the entry of Woodroff), and his assignment of both territory and roles to Franckford, himself, and his **wife** gives his animal husbandry argument visual (and comic) force. Tischner (*Die Verfasserschaft der Webster–Rowley-Dramen*, unpublished University of Marburg dissertation, 1907) compares Rowley's *A Search for Money* (1609) (D2ʳ) describing a law-suit in Westminster Hall: 'here two neighbours together by the purses the good man Nebuloes goose had laid an eg in good man Corridons barne and he pleaded possession and the trespasse of the goose that had committed burglary to come in the wrong way'. Cf. III.ii.7n.

174 foaming 'covered with the sweat of lust' (Weis).

174 jumbles 'copulates' (see *OED* 6); cf. 9n.

175 wallowes in her mire With a clear sexual innuendo.

184 found it in my self i.e. 'I came to that conclusion myself.'

188 Forgive my charges i.e. 'free you from any obligation in respect of costs I have borne' (for the support of the child). Franckford may also include reference to legal costs.

191–4 Capon . . . sawce Compass initiates this series of double entendres by offering Franckford a **Capon** (a castrated cock) rather than **Mutton** (sexually available female flesh; cf. III.ii.84n), and cheerfully continues it by rejecting Raymond's lewd suggestion of **legs opened** (punning on 'carved'; see *OED* open *v.* 4a) and **Venison sawce** (suggesting 'venery' as both hunting and sexual gratification, and **sawce** = 'desire' [Partridge 1955, 'saucy', p. 183]).

196 brother, and neighbor i.e. Franckford (his brother-in-law) and Compass.

199–200 Councel . . . Lawyer Cf. *WD* I.ii.81.

200 Physick 'medicine'.

201 spightful brand 'shameful [*OED* 1b] stigma [*OED* 4b]'.

202–3 Onion . . . scar Ambroise Paré, in *The Method of Curing Wounds*, tr. Walter Hamond (1617), p. 7, recounts his experience of this traditional remedy: 'one of the Guard . . . hauing drunke hard, by indiscretion set his Flaske afire, which caused a great disaster both to his hands and face; and being called to dresse him, I applyed of the saide Onions on the one halfe of his face; and on the other side, of other common remedies. At the second dressing, I founde that part where I had applyed the Onions to be altogether without blisters or any excoriation, and the other altogether blistred.' A **green** wound is 'unhealed, raw' (*OED* 10a). The reference to **left hand** is obscure, unless it is simply comic circumstantiality.

204 receipt Probably 'drug' (*OED* 2), given 'Physick' (200) and 'medicine' (208), but 'prescription, recipe' (*OED* 1a) and 'remedy' (*OED* 1b) are also possible.

204 content you 'compensate, remunerate you' (see *OED* 4).

207 blotted i.e. 'blotted out'.

212 Bishops-Hall Probably Bishop Bonner's house, just on the Blackwall side of Bethnal Green (see Sugden, p. 62). Weis suggests a pun on **Pease** and 'peace' (i.e. reconciliation).

212–13 Swads and the Cods Comically tautologous, since **Swads** and **Cods** are the same: the seed pods of (here) peas (see 'Pease-field' 212). As Weis notes, 'peascods were a popular love-token used to divine whether a wooing would be successful'.

223–4 dagger . . . Weapon Raymond's offer presumably relates to the wearing of a (short) **dagger** as ornament; Compass puns on **long Weapon** as (1) 'sword', and (2) 'penis' (Partridge 1955, p. 219).

ACT IV, Scene ii

0.1 Enter Lessingham's recent return is likely to be signalled by his still being booted and perhaps wearing his cloak (cf. III.i.0.1n), and entering by a different door from Clare.

8 condition 'stipulation, prerequisite to the granting of something else' (*OED* 1a).

27 I am lost for ever Cf. 107, III.iii.8, and *WD* I.ii.3.

28 recovered This is the first of several 'strange changes' (38) in which characters suffer sudden and arbitrary swings of intention and emotion.

30 Rue . . . Violets '"rue" is a common symbol of repentance and puns on "to rue", i.e. to regret, while "violets" symbolize modesty and requited love' (Weis).

31 strewings Given 'grave' (39), the reference here is probably to flowers strewn on the marriage bed (rather than 'strewn in the bride's path to church', as Weis suggests). Cf. *Ham.* V.i.245–6: 'I thought thy bride-bed to have deck'd, sweet maid, | And not have strew'd thy grave.'

43 ta'ne . . . heart Cf. *DM* III.ii.113–15.

44 despair Given also 'I fell into despair' (60), Clare's admission may be felt to have more than casual significance. On **despair** as a state of spiritual hopelessness in which the sufferer is convinced of his or her impending damnation see *WD* V.iv.136n; also *DM* IV.i.73–4 and n.

46–8 Downs ... Harbor Probably referring to the North **Downs**, from which the most likely **Harbor** to view would be Dover; but possibly, by association with the famous roadstead off the east coast of Kent called the Downs, meaning Deal or Sandwich (see V.i.48n).

54–6 love . . . beyond reason Cf. Lodovico's very similar admission (*WD* IV.iii.114–16).

57 neare i.e. 'ne'er' (Q 'near'). Lucas, who nevertheless regularizes to 'ne'er', calls Q's 'an old variant-form'; but it never occurs within texts associated with W, whereas the much more common spelling **neare** is found in *MonH* (Lucas) (47, 58, 67), *NHo* (III.ii.127), and *WHo* (I.ii.54, 209).

66 amazement 'bewilderment, perplexity, distraction' (*OED* 2).

75–6 Trust . . . henceforward Cf. *WD* V.vi.157.

77 Lapland Witches 'for their notorious sorcery, especially with winds, cf. *Err.* IV.iii.11; Milton *Par. Lost*, II.665; Burton, *Anat. of Mel.* I.2.I.2: Elizabethan dramatists *passim*; the narratives of Regnard and Leems in Pinkerton's *Voyages* (1808), vol. 1; and Frazer, *Golden Bough*, I.326, whence it appears that the Lapp idea of tying the wind up in knots (three was their usual number; the untying of each increased the fury of the gale) has been world-wide from the days of Aeolus and Odysseus down to the old wind-selling witch whom Sir Walter Scott visited in the Orkneys' (Lucas).

80 paint 'apply cosmetics' (see *OED* 4a).

80 Cloth of Tissue Rich cloth interwoven with gold or silver thread; see *WD* II.i.55n.

91 Dog-days The hottest (and most unhealthy) days of the summer; see *WD* III.ii.202n.

95 talk to your self This self-consciously theatrical reference to Lessingham speaking aside to the audience may point to a level of grotesque humour in the scene.

97–100 do somewhat . . . devil Just as the irrationality of love and the demands of a tragicomic plot have induced Clare's 'strange changes' (38), so Lessingham now produces one of his own. Cf. *DLC* III.iii.369–71.

101 leave me Clare's line implies that Lessingham has started to exit.

103 impostumed 'abscessed'; cf. *WD* IV.ii.145.

104–6 Womans cruelty . . . undone Almost certainly direct address to the audience.

105 black and fatal thread i.e. the thread of destiny and life spun by the Fates.

108 unvalued Jewels This belated recognition of Lessingham's worth starts to prepare for the final reconciliation.

112 Cross and Pile i.e. 'gambling (cf. "plays" [111]) by tossing coins to see if they land **Cross** ("head") or **Pile** ("tail")'; see *OED* cross 21c, and Overbury, *Characters* (1614), 'Countrey Newes' (G1ᵛ): 'good and ill is the crosse and pile in the game of life'. The entry of Bonvile at the end of this line seems to illustrate Clare's point.

112.1 SD Bonvile's entrance is indeed an unexpected throw by 'Fortune' (111) for Clare, who a moment before believed him to be dead in Calais. Like Lessingham, Bonvile is presumably still wearing boots and his cloak (see 0.1n).

113 Bonvile After Clare's speech ending at 135, Q prints, as a single line, '*Enter Bonvile. Friend?*', following this, on the next line, with '*Clare.* Oh you are . . .'. The question, therefore, is whether **Friend** is a greeting by Bonvile, or the first word of Clare's next speech. The former seems more likely, Bonvile's entry direction also serving as a speech prefix. (Q's *'Enter boy'* on E4ᵛ [IV.i.55] is similarly inset in the manner of a speech prefix, and immediately followed by a one-line speech.) Clare has finished her self-recriminations with a rhyming couplet at 111–12, and a minimal salutation from Bonvile, drawing attention to his sudden arrival, would lead naturally into a new speech by Clare. Alternatively her line 113 speech prefix is redundant, **Friend** reflecting Clare's astonishment at seeing the supposedly dead Bonvile, rather than his greeting to the woman he believes plotted to kill him (so Weis). In *DLC* there are two redundant speech prefixes, the first falling immediately after an entry direction (III.iii.365, IV.ii.32).

118–19 Sea-sick . . . Physick i.e. 'sea-sickness acts like a purgative medically prescribed' (see *OED* physic 3c). Cf. II.iv.135.

129 that Letter The letter Clare sent to Lessingham in I.i, and which he gave to Bonvile at III.i.60.

135 violence on your friend i.e. 'doing Lessingham deep wrong (by intending him, without his knowledge, as the agent of your death)'. The third use of **violence** in three lines means that Bonvile is in effect quoting the word, which helps an understanding that it does not here mean physical force, and that **your friend** must refer to Lessingham. Lines 136–7 are an explanatory appositional clause. Brooke, Lucas, and Forker regard this as the major textual crux of the play. Lucas, following Brooke, emended and repunctuated to read 'violence: and your friend,' but no emendation is needed if plot and character are considered carefully (see pp. 273–4). For full discussion, see Carnegie and Jackson.

139 extremity 'extreme need or suffering' (*OED* 7).

141–6 No . . . If Clare's willingness to restrain the love she still feels (cf. 138–40) marks the end of her 'madness' (75) and the beginning of 'reason' (153); cf. 203n.

143 knit the brow Cf. *WD* II.i.199.

155 observance 'dutiful service' (*OED* 3).

160 too i.e. 'to'; cf. I.ii.38n.

160–1 observant . . . request i.e. 'how attentive, assiduous [see *OED* 2] he will prove in response to nobler requests on your part'.

165–6 steerage . . . Compass As Weis notes, 'the nautical metaphor picks up the thread of the subplot'; **steerage** is 'a course held or steered, esp. a course of conduct' (*OED* 2c).

169 deliver of him 'report concerning him' (see *OED* deliver 11c).

175–8 worse . . . Whore? Cf. *WD* IV.ii.56–7. Bonvile is deliberately dispraising Lessingham and Clare in order, it seems, to cure her. See 203n.

179 Is . . . beloved? Cf. *DM* II.i.41–2.

182 strange alteration Unlike earlier 'strange changes' (38), this one turns out to be a further step, though not immediately evident as such, in the direction of stability.

197 convert 'turn, direct' (*OED* 2a).

202–3 And on that turn ... end From Daniel, *The Queenes Arcadia* (1606), IV.iv (H4ʳ): 'And on that turne of Fortunes Scene depend, | When all extremities must mend, or end' (Sykes). Cf. V.i.282–3.

203 *Exeunt* Clare's next appearance is with Bonvile (V.i.186.1), and everything she does from this point is directed towards reconciliation. It is possible, therefore, that a silent indication of her acquiescence is intended, and perhaps a joint exit. (At Wellington 1997 she did not go so far, but watched his exit thoughtfully.)

ACT IV, SCENE iii

0.1 COMPASS His last instruction to Urse was 'change your Clothes' (IV.i.215–16), so he himself may now be dressed as 'Master Bridegroom' (129); or possibly in the black of mourning.

2 evidence 'witnesses' (*OED* 7); cf. *Lr.* III.vi.35: 'I'll see their trial first, bring in their evidence'.

5 come off 'emerge'.

5 smooth a forehead i.e. without a cuckold's horns.

6 sometimes 'the joke consists in the unexpected insertion of this word' (Lucas).

7 teeming 'breeding, child-bearing' (*OED* 1).

9 and let it be i.e. 'even if it were'.

10 do but note This conclusion may be motivated by his seeing Urse entering before the Gallants do.

11.1 *Wife* Presumably she will have obeyed Compass's injunction to 'change your Clothes' (IV.i.215–16), and will now be dressed in her best; and possibly in white and with her hair down like a virgin bride (cf. *WD* V.i.0.1–.3n), or in black like a 'widdow' (19; so Wellington 1997).

24 quoth a Literally 'said he', but generally used, as here, as an intensifier, meaning 'indeed, forsooth' (*OED*). Q has, impossibly, 'quotha, a'. The two forms of the collo-quialism current in W's time were **quoth a** and 'quotha', and Q's anomalous comma is more likely to have intruded into the first of these than into the single word.

25 By my feck 'By my faith' (*OED* fegs).

26–8 If ... new 'nor even in a **whole parish**, one might often truly say, for fishmon-gers can call "fresh fish" even though the **Mackarel** is **stincking**'. This may well be to the audience, especially given Raymond's comment following, which may itself be to the audience.

30 silence ... enjoyned i.e. 'silence was one of the terms agreed to'. Comic byplay here and at 40 is possible as Eustace tries to keep Raymond quiet (so Wellington 1997).

37–8 such ... so Compass is indicating himself, perhaps to the audience as much as to Urse.

37 proportion 'form, shape' (*OED* 7).

39 taught Raymond's point is not entirely clear. He may be using **taught** ('learned, instructed' [*OED ppl. a.* 1]) ironically: Weis glosses thus as 'so little educated, i.e. such a fool'.

40 the Law of 'silence and observation' (13); cf. 30.

47 one i.e. 'own' (a seventeenth-century spelling listed in *OED*).

48 chopping 'big and vigorous, strapping', but setting up the pun at 50–1.

54 faculty 'occupation, trade' (*OED* 8).

60–70 one thing . . . alas Up to this point Compass must be delighted with Urse's/his Wife's complaisant acting, but she now takes the initiative, introducing her own concerns into the scenario. Possibly she also puns on how **burdensome** is the responsibility to control her **thing** (= 'vagina').

62 distaste 'dislike' (*OED* 2).

64 slip 'error in conduct, transgression' (*OED* 10), punning, as Weis notes, on a counterfeit coin (i.e. 'the bastard in the woman's womb'). See Partridge 1984, p. 1088.

65–7 As . . . coin 'Just as **Lawyers** suffer a loss of income during **long** (i.e. summer) **vacations**, so too **Tradesmen** drop their prices even more than they would ordinarily for **ready coin** (i.e. immediate cash payment).'

70 can we do withal? i.e. 'can we help it?' (see *OED* do 54, which cites Chapman, *May-Day*, I.i.120: 'It is my infirmity, and I cannot doe withall').

73 bear Perhaps 'conduct himself' (*OED* 4). Other possible readings include: 'endure (the pain)' (*OED* 15b), 'bear with, make allowance for (Urse's conduct)' (*OED* 17), a reversal of the common 'bear hard' (*OED* 16), or 'uphold [a] course of action' (Weis).

76–7 Hen . . . afterwards 'having been mounted [see *OED* taste 3b] by **the Cock**, a hen lays **Eggs** even after he has been slaughtered'.

81 discretion 'discernment, sound judgement' (*OED* 6).

84–5 In the old world 'in ancient (mythical) times'.

89 Sou-Wests i.e. 'Sou-West's'. Q's 'Sou-West' ends a full prose line. Lucas emended to indicate the possessive, but although ''s' is used well over a hundred times in Q as a contraction of 'is' or 'has' (the phrase 'the childe 's your wifes' at IV.i.185 being typical), the apostrophe is almost invariably absent from the possessive, the sole exception being in 'own tongue's confession' (V.ii.29). The double modifier in Q's 'Sou-East and Sou-West daughters' makes the unemended reading just possible, but it seems more probable that a final 's' has been squeezed out of the line.

91–3 baudy . . . street Compass whimsically compares the **baudy** winds with itinerant **Bellows-menders** who attempt (*OED* offer 5b) to lift (*OED* take 93a) women's skirts or petticoats (*OED* coat 2a) **in the street**.

96 do our commendations 'deliver [*OED* do 7c] our respects, compliments [*OED* commendation 4]'.

102–3 Here's . . . friends Compass presumably signals the Gallants forward, where they admit to Urse, who has evidently not seen them till now, that they 'heard all the rest' (105).

105 niceness 'fastidiousness' (*OED* 6) or perhaps 'over-refinement' (*OED* 5a).

106 sinks the deepest The image is of the **stroke** of a sword that penetrates to the heart. Cf. Tilley L478: 'The first love is fastest.' Q's 'thee', here emended to **the**, is probably the product of misunderstanding, rather than Q's only instance of a variant spelling of the definite article. The compositor presumably took **the** as 'thee', and the object of **sinks**; but Urse could scarcely be immersed, like a sunken vessel, by a **stroke**.

114 fetch it off fair   i.e. 'bring it off well' (see *OED* fetch 16a). This is primarily to Raymond and the Gallants, but could also include the audience.

117–18 *Petty Lassery* **. . . general pardon**   Compass, in his efforts to say that anyone calling him a cuckold (115) will be guilty of worse than 'slander' (116), makes two comic errors. He seems to think petty larceny (*Petty Lassery*) an appropriate and very serious charge, though in fact it dealt with theft, and then only of 'goods to the value of a shilling or under' (Jowitt, p. 1357). Possibly Compass intends 'grand larceny', equally inappropriate, but more serious. He also thinks the charges so serious they will be 'beyond the scope' (**without compass**, also punning on his name) of **the general pardon**; but although the general pardon of 1624 had five pages of exclusions— including adultery—Compass's imagined charges were not excluded.

118–19 foul sheet . . . clean   The meaning is not entirely clear, but is based on the physical, legal, and moral opposition between **foul** and **clean**. If nautical, the metaphor is either of a **sheet** (a rope for controlling a sail) becoming fouled (tangled), or of a sail (*OED* sheet 4; but cf. II.iii.146–7n) with unfavourable wind (*OED* foul 15, 16), and with a further pun on bed sheets as at II.iii.146. Compass may be punning on **clean** in relation to the 'general pardon' (118), which gave certain categories of criminal a 'clean sheet', and on the legal meaning of **foul sheet** as a sheet containing charges of a **foul** nature ('disgraceful, shameful': *OED* 13a), relating particularly to slanderous charges of cuckoldry (118–19). There may also be a dig at Franckford as a fornicator, and the white sheet of penitence (*OED* 1b); cf. Lording Barry, *The Family of Love* (1607), IV.iv (G1ᵛ): 'I can describe how often a man may lye with another mans wife, before a come to the white sheete.'

123 some   Compass jocularly avoids any absolute claim for the number of virtuous women, and in effect makes no claim at all for Urse.

126 come . . . agen   i.e. 'they will meet in a frown again'; or perhaps Eustace is hinting that once he is married the cuckold's horns will grow again.

130 Ebb and Tide   'ebb and flow' (*OED* tide 2); i.e. before six hours has elapsed.

ACT V, Scene i

11 Complement   'politeness, courtesy' (*OED* 8b).

13 asperst on   'imputed to'. *OED* (asperse 6) records this usage as obsolete and rare, citing instances only in 1630 and 1635, and giving the definition 'cast (a damaging imputation or false charge) *upon*'. In the closely related senses, to traduce a person (5a) or a character, reputation, or honour (5b), the verb is a Heywood speciality, as in 'Asperse the honour of a noble friend' in *The English Traveller* (1633), III.i (F1ʳ).

14 Apology   'apologize'. *OED* notes that this use of **Apology** as a verb is obsolete and rare, citing only this instance and one from Heywood's *The English Traveller*, III.i (F4ʳ), which falls within the same act as 'asperse' (see 13n).

17 endeer'd   'bound by obligations of gratitude' (*OED* endear 6b).

18.1 *Enter* Lessingham seems not to notice Rochfield and Annabel in 'private Conference' (32) until 25.

20 Lets 'impediments, obstructions'.

22 project 'plan, scheme' (*OED* 5a).

23–4 without A speedy birth 'i.e. unless it finds speedy deliverance and execution' (Lucas).

24 throwes 'throes'.

25 Occasion The personification of opportunity, who usually needs to be seized by the forelock (see *OED* 1b). Evidently Lessingham has just seen Annabel and Rochfield in 'private Conference' (32). Cf. 18.1n.

28 ingrafted 'incorporated into' (*OED* engraft 2a).

29 Houses Minion i.e 'favourite [*OED* minion 1b] of the family'.

30 unite 'united' (*OED*).

31 Speak . . . largely 'describe [*OED* speak 30c] him so generously [*OED* largely 1]'.

38 I kiss your hand Lessingham's observation of this evidence of familiarity between Rochfield and Annabel will strengthen his sense of this being 'fit ground to work upon' (26), the more so as he may be at a distance and regarded as not hearing what they say.

48 *Dover, Sandwich* Two of the original Cinque Ports on the east coast of Kent; Sandwich is between 'Marget' (49; i.e. Margate, also associated with the Cinque Ports) and Dover. Cf. II.iv.135n and IV.ii.46–8n. The prestige of the Cinque Ports reflects honour on Rochfield here.

49 *Marget* The previous association with '*Lee*' (see II.iv.135 and n) confirms that Margate is intended, not St Margaret at Cliffe.

52 expressions 'utterance' (*OED* 2a).

64 well parted 'talented, accomplished' (*OED* parted 5).

67–8 grow . . . particulars i.e. 'get to the point' (see *OED* grow 11c, and particular *n.* 2b).

74 Bridal-day Although Q's 'Bride-day' is just possible from the point of view of sense (see *OED* bride *n.*[1] 5a for such combinations), it leaves the line metrically defective, and is otherwise unknown to English drama. **Bridal-day** is, in contrast, common; and cf. 'Bridal-bed' at III.i.45.

78 Aswell = As well (*OED*).

81–2 do . . . challengeth i.e. 'perform [*OED* do 6a] those neglected duties or services [*OED* office 2b] which her youth and beauty claim [*OED* challenge 5]'. The **neglected offices** are the 'Nuptial sweets | That night expected' (75–6).

88 Yet Q's speech prefix '*Less.*' in the middle of Rochfield's speech is clearly wrong. Expanded and incorporated into the dialogue, the speech prefix would neatly fill the metrical gap in line 87, yielding 'So fair and sweet occasion, *Lessingham?*' But for Rochfield to address Lessingham by his bare surname would be uncharacteristic, elaborate politesse being the norm, while the shortness of line 87 creates a not inappropriate pause after Rochfield's rhetorical, or unanswered, question.

99 inward 'intimate, familiar' (*OED* 3).

112 co-parts 'shares' (*OED* 1).

114–15 old ... Springes Cf. Tilley F647: 'An old Fox cannot be taken by a snare.'

118 Oh sir! Presumably Lessingham pretends great emotional turmoil.

123 go over i.e. cross the English Channel.

128 gives him dead 'reports [*OED* give 25] him to be dead'.

138–9 I do ... Aches Woodroff is sweating **already** out of anxiety, and wishes to be told the rest so that he can **sweat more**, quibbling on the idea, then current medically, that sweating helps **to cure Aches**. There may perhaps be a glance here at the use of the sweating tub in the treatment of venereal disease.

145 *Callis-sands* Cf. I.ii.90n.

146 Sword and Ponyards length i.e. in a duel; cf. I.ii.96–9n.

153 Rowl 'roll, list'.

157–8 departed ... With 'parted with, given away' (see *OED* depart 12b).

164 he i.e. Rochfield. Q's erroneous 'she' was presumably provoked by the proximity of **should** ('she should').

167 practise 'trickery, artifice' (*OED* practice 6a).

168–9 another Key ... husbands With a double entendre on **Key** = 'penis' (Partridge 1984, p. 641).

171–2 Twelve pence ... for Swearing 'An allusion to 21 Jac. I, c. 20 (1623–4), where this penalty is enacted'; so Lucas, who notes a similar reference in Jonson's *The Masque of Owls* (1624) to a knight 'Who, since the Act against swearing . . . Hath at twelve pence an oath . . . Sworn himself out of his estate'.

173 Lie ... Honor To give ... The Lie was to offer a challenge that could only be answered by a duel; cf. Bryskett, *A Discourse of Civill Life* (1606): 'he that receiveth [the accusation of being a liar] standeth so charged in his honour and reputation, that he cannot disburden himself of that imputation, but by striking of him that hath so given it, or by chalenging him the combat' (quoted in *Shakespeare's England*, II, 402). The **Court of Honor**, as it is also called at *DLC* V.vi.33, is an alternative name for the High Court of Chivalry, where judicial combat took place under the jurisdiction of the Earl Marshal (see *DLC* IV.ii.626–7n, and pp. 51–2). Woodroff thus intensifies his assertion that his honour has been so impugned that a duel must follow, whether formal or 'on *Callis-sands*' (145).

181 Intelligencer 'paid informant, spy'.

182 take order 'take measures or steps' (*OED* order 14).

185–6 give ground ... stand on Lessingham says he does not **give ground** = (1) 'retire, yield' (*OED* give 45), (2) 'bestow land', and further quibbles that he cannot, since **'tis your own** (i.e. Woodroff's) **you stand on** = (1) 'you stand your ground, maintain your position against attack', (2) 'you literally stand on your own property'.

186.1 SD The manner of entry will make it clear to the audience that Clare is reconciled to Bonvile (cf. IV.ii.203n); they, seeing Woodroff's sword drawn and Lessingham departing, will realize that the two men are incensed.

201 favors 'tokens of affection' (*OED* favour 7a).

203 Woodroff Q omits this prefix for Woodroff's speech in response to Bonvile's cue. The accidental omission comes at the top of a new page (H1ᵛ) and forme, and is foreshadowed by the H1ʳ catchword 'Love-', which may have been added after H1ᵛ had been set.

204 Lures . . . stoop The metaphor is from falconry, **Lures** being 'apparatus used by falconers to recall their hawks' (*OED n.*² 1), and **stoop** the swoop of a hawk on its prey or to a lure (see *OED v.*¹ 6a). Cf. *WD* IV.i.132.

208–9 Ha! . . . change colour Bonvile probably moves, as an acting equivalent to the emotion implied by the line; cf. *WD* I.ii.181 and n and *DM* II.i.124n.

211 Guess 'guest' (*OED*).

212 deliver'd me 'told me' (see *OED* deliver 10a).

215 Italian Plague . . . Jealousie Cf. *WD* II.i.163–4.

216–19 Suppose . . . Crotchet i.e. 'it would be a strange business [see *OED* crotchet 9a] if Lessingham, in love with Annabel, had arranged the duel so as to **divide you** from her, just as your **Jealousie** is now doing in a **stronger way**'.

220 stagger 'doubt, hesitate' (*OED* 2a).

222 she comes Annabel's appearance with Rochfield will do nothing to calm Bonvile's jealousy. Evidently Lessingham's decision that his false report about Bonvile and Clare 'goes to *Annabel*' (188) has been carried out; this explains the anger and jealousy with which she enters.

223 brought you . . . self For this exchange to make sense, Clare must be standing with Bonvile, offering him as the **Jewel**, so that their proximity will reinforce Annabel's jealousy, provoked offstage by Lessingham's false report.

224 Fetters Cf. I.ii.184–6, when Annabel's similar reference to her bracelets and necklace was a loving conceit between the two of them.

228 off o'th hinges Cf. III.iii.31.

229–30 Jewel . . . yonder A gesture or look is required to indicate Rochfield.

231 Happily i.e. 'haply, perhaps'.

232 coming over i.e. from France. Lucas suggests a possible double entendre, with **coming over** = 'mounting sexually' (Partridge 1955, p. 90); cf. *AV* III.i. 5–6.

232 Dover? Bonvile seems to be seeking confirmation from Annabel, since of course he knows he sent the will. It may be that Q's query should be read as an exclamation mark.

237 speak with you Bonvile apparently draws Rochfield aside, inciting Woodroff's suspicion at 241. Whispered at Wellington 1997, the line may in effect be an aside to Rochfield.

240 growes upon 'draws to' (*OED* grow 11c); i.e. 'is approaching'.

242–3 Pattent . . . to me The **Pattent** ('a document conferring some privilege, right, etc.' [*OED* patent 1]) is **deadly** because it is a will, and hence comes into effect only after Bonvile's death. **Affection** presumably carries the sense of 'goodwill, love' (*OED* 6a), though it may possibly have the more general sense of 'disposition towards' (*OED* 5). By **deadly** Annabel also conveys, however, the sense of the death of Bonvile's affection for her; otherwise he would not have deserted her on their wedding day, and taken up with Clare.

244 gave . . . dead i.e. 'accounted myself as dead' (see *OED* give 31b).

247–8 man . . . Constancy 'the moon is proverbially changeable, waxing and waning, so that no garment can be made to its measure' (Weis). Cf. also *DM* IV.ii.50–1 and n, with its reference to the man in the moon as an English tailor.

248 Rather then fit i.e. 'sooner than [*OED* rather *adv.* 2b] make one to fit [*OED* fit 5a]'.

252 estated 'endowed' (*OED* 1); cf. III.iii.5.

254 Executor The **Executor** of a will was often also the chief beneficiary; cf. 252–3.

257–8 Executors . . . Legacies Cf. *DLC* IV.i.28.

260 ridest poste 'ride at speed'.

261 Stay Presumably Woodroff starts to exit also, before being prevented by Rochfield.

262 put . . . him i.e. 'pick a quarrel with him'.

264 wisht 'desired, longed-for' (*OED* wished 1).

265–7 French . . . Embraces The French were notorious for the punctilio of quarrels leading to duelling (see Kiernan, pp. 72–9).

267 Cringes Here in the sense of 'bow', but with negative implications of (mock) servility or deference (*OED* cringe 1).

272 sowder 'unite' (*OED* solder 3).

272–4 I heard . . . division A complex statement, which takes up the implications of 'sowder' (272) but involves a music metaphor, linking birdsong (as harmonious) with a pun on **division** as (1) 'dissension, discord' (*OED* 4) and (2) 'a florid phrase or piece of melody, a run' (*OED* 7). Annabel's point is that she seeks harmony, and that Clare is the one who is causing (*OED* work 10) or inciting (*OED* 14b) discord.

274–5 Who? . . . *Lessingham* Clare means 'I **long** to know **Who** the **bird** was who stirred up jealousy in you'; the parenthetical reference to her being a **Maid** is for the sake of the standard sexual joke on their supposed longings.

279 come This seems to imply an initial reluctance by Annabel to 'walk in' (278) with Clare (so Wellington 1997).

279 clew Literally, 'a ball of thread' as used, e.g., by Theseus as a means of 'threading' a way through the Labyrinth; hence, figuratively, 'that which guides through a maze, perplexity, etc.' (*OED* 3). Cf. *DM* I.i.346.

280 toyl 'net, snare'.

282–3 Cankers . . . complexion From Daniel, *The Queenes Arcadia* (1606), II.4 (E2ʳ): 'And note but how these cankers alwayes seaze | The choysest fruites with their infections, | How they are still ordained to disease | The natures of the best complections' (Sykes). Cf. Tilley C56: 'The canker soonest eats the fairest rose (flowers).'

283 *Exeunt* They presumably leave together, thereby signalling Annabel's willingness to be persuaded of the truth of what Clare says (cf. 279n).

ACT V, Scene ii

V.ii A new scene must start here because the stage has been cleared. Time may be thought to have passed. Neither Lucas nor Weis marks a new scene.

12–13 forswear . . . valour i.e. 'you would sooner break your oath than reveal any arrangements made under the code of duelling'.

18–21 Second . . . fierk him It seems surprising, and out of character, that Woodroff adopts the same unusual duelling practice that Lessingham introduced at I.ii.74–9. Nor is it clear whether Rochfield is to **fetch up** ('overthrow', trip up [*OED* fetch 21e]) and **fierk** ('trounce, drub' [*OED* firk 4]) Lessingham's second (**him**), or Lessingham himself ('Hee'l let blood your Calumny' [24]).

22 tools 'weapons' (here swords) (*OED* 1b).

24 let blood i.e. 'bleed' in the dual senses of shedding blood (perhaps fatally) and bleeding for medicinal purposes (see *OED* blood *v.* 1d).

25 *Peccavi* 'I have sinned' (Latin); 'hence an acknowledgement or confession of guilt' (*OED*).

31 belie . . . pleasure i.e. 'he will misrepresent (himself) to gratify you'. Since *OED* states that **belie** in the appropriate sense (*v.*²) is always transitive, and *LION: Drama* affords no intransitive uses, 'himself' must be understood proleptically from 32.

36 friendly posture The manner of their entry will signal to the audience, as to Woodroff, that Bonvile and Annabel have been reconciled by Clare; cf. V.i.186.1n and V.i.222n.

46 So Woodroff's interjections here and following may be primarily to the audience for comic effect, though at 57 he addresses Rochfield.

52 no thought on Q's syntax is obscure. Rochfield may be interrupted as he is about to say **I had no thought on** (any such action); or perhaps we are to understand **no thought on** (it = 'any attempt against her honor' [51]). Lucas emends to 'on't'.

62–3 Jade . . . Necessities i.e. 'my needs [*OED* necessity 11] rode and spurred me on as if I were a worn-out hack [*OED* jade 1a and c]'.

64–5 for that Discourse was our familiarity 'our intimacy [*OED* familiarity 4a] consisted only of this conversation [*OED* discourse 3]'.

69 Censure 'judgement, opinion' (*OED* 3).

72 *Soft Musick* i.e. a string consort (either viols or violins, the playing of which will, of course, be quieter than would be a 'loud', or wind, consort). Violins may be more likely for accompanying dancing (cf. II.iv.59).

74 *to Lessingham* Bonvile evidently indicates Clare.

74 an *Io pæan* 'a Greek and Latin exclamation or song of joy' (see *OED* Io¹), often for a **Wedding**. Cf. 'Hymen' (102), with which **Io** is often combined, as in Thomas Campion's *Somerset Masque*: '*Io, Io Hymen*' (*Works*, p. 274, 281). Cf. also Lyly, *Midas*, V.iii.135: '*Iô* pæans let vs sing.' Q has 'a *Jopæan*'. It appears the compositor mistook the classical phrase for an unfamiliar Latin word in which the '*I*' or '*J*' would have been pronounced as modern 'j' (cf. 'Hujus'; see III.ii.94–8n); hence the 'a' in place of 'an'.

76   *to Clare* Although logic might suggest Bonvile is most owed an apology by Lessingham, the previous line directs attention to the required reconciliation between Clare and Lessingham, and for them now to exchange apologies (so Wellington 1997) is dramatically effective. Cf. IV.ii.196–201. A decision that these lines are spoken to Bonvile, however, might be supported by Clare's 'though you forgive me not' (83).

77   condition 'character, moral nature, disposition' (*OED* 11a).

82   Have ... original i.e. 'have their source, cause [*OED* original *n*. 2a] in my perverse, capricious [*OED* peevish 4] will'.

85   Which . . . to it Probably 'that would otherwise be required because of your "peevish will" (82)'. An alternative reading, based on the lack of Q punctuation after 'then' (84), would take 'then' as 'than', meaning that Clare has no need for repentance beyond what is intrinsic to whatever fault she may impute to herself; i.e. there's nothing to be repented on Lessingham's behalf. It seems unlikely, however, that a line would end with 'than' in this comparative sense. Lucas glosses 84–6 as 'the very fact of your repenting makes repentance needless (Which = "a fact which")'.

86.2   [URSE *as a*] Bride For her possible appearance as a ***Bride***, cf. I.i.111.1–.2n.

86.3   *Childe* Presumably a babe in arms held by the ***Nurse***; cf. *DM* III.iv.6.4n.

87   Musick Even if the consort is playing violins (cf. 72n), it is likely to include a bass instrument as well, usually held between the knees; the musicians, therefore, probably remain seated in the music room rather than entering with the wedding party.

105   *Shedding of Horns* i.e. a cure for a cuckold.

109   old trick i.e. cuckoldry and the cuckold's horns.

112–13   I am . . . brother Since Franckford is to act as father of the bride (111), Compass casts himself as **his son**, but while emphasizing that he is **all the sons** Franckford has, and that the infant is the latter's **Grand-childe**, Compass cannot resist adding that the infant is also **my elder brother**.

114–15   he begat . . . Before me Compass puns, turning Woodroff's **before** (i.e. 'earlier, sooner': *OED adv.* 5a) into a lewd 'in sight, presence, of' (*OED prep.* 3a).

119–27   hold . . . own A series of puns begins with Compass turning Woodroff's **hold** = 'last, endure' (*OED* 23a) to 'sustain, bear' (*OED* 4), and then Woodroff taking Compass's **two knots** in the sense of 'two nots', setting up play on the idea that two negatives make a positive. Eustace joins in with the observation that **though it hold on the contrary** (i.e. 'though two negatives make an affirmative'), **two *Affirmatives*** do not make a ***Negative***, and Compass completes the play with a gesture to the child as **this little *Negative***, which he can ***Affirm*** (i.e. state in the affirmative) **to be mine own**.

128   proves ... substantial 'proves the previous [*OED* before D. 1] marriage real [*OED* substantial 15]', with perhaps a play on **substantial** = 'corporeal', given the physical presence of the infant.

135   foul . . . Monologist Lyonel's pun on **foul word** as (1) the offensive 'word of Scandal', and (2) the '*Cuckow*' (136) uttered by the bird (fowl) establishes the sense of **fatal Monologist**. Although **Monologist** is not cited in *OED* until 1711, the definition 'one who talks in monologue' (which perplexes Lucas and Weis) is apposite in terms of early seventeenth-century understanding of 'monologue' as a person who 'talkes very much about very little' (*OED*, citing Cotgrave). Chapman makes explicit the applicability of this term to the cuckoo in *The Conspiracy of Charles Duke of Byron*, III.ii.60–1: 'Which the Welch Herrald of their praise, the Cucko, | Would scarce haue put, in his monology'. The point is, as an *OED* citation of 1616 makes clear, that 'monology' is 'speaking still of one thing, a long tale of one matter', a description which perfectly fits the repeated summer call of the **fatal** ('ominous' [*OED* 4c] or perhaps 'prophetic' [4b]) cuckoo. Cf. 136–7n.

136–7 *Cuckow* **. . . Nightingale** Both the italic *Cuckow* and the context suggest that Woodroff imitates a cuckoo's call rather than saying the word, and that Compass cheerfully pretends to misidentify the bird call. The *Cuckow* was proverbially associated with cuckolds, both from its call and from its practice of laying its eggs in the nests of other birds. Cf. 135n.

138 **much . . . you** The absent pronoun 'it' is understood ('may it do'). Dyce supplied it in 1830 but reverted to Q in 1857, claiming that the elliptical expression is idiomatic in colloquial English of W's time. *LION: Drama* supports this view, with three instances of **much good may do** in Fletcher plays and one in Middleton's *Women Beware Women*. Although 'much good may it (may't) do you (ye, thee)' greatly predominates in the period 1576–1642 (with *LION: Drama* affording sixteen instances, including three in collaborations involving Rowley, who wrote this section of *CC*), and Q accidentally omitted 'it' at II.iv.12 and III.ii.69, the version without the pronoun was evidently current when *CC* was composed; in the later seventeenth century it became the more common form.

144 **take us with you** i.e. 'let us accompany you to church' (Lucas; not, as Dyce thought, 'enable us to understand' [*OED* take 59b]). The line implies that Compass and his party may be starting to leave until stayed by Woodroff.

146 **imperfect** Woodroff presumably considers Bonvile and Annabel's wedding **imperfect** because it has not yet been consummated. Legally, however, this was not the position. Cf. H. Swinburne, *A Treatise of Spousals, or Matrimonial Contracts* (written *c.* 1600; pub. 1686), p. 14: 'A present and perfect consent alone maketh matrimony, without either public solemnization or carnal copulation, for neither is the one or the other the essence of matrimony, but consent only.' See *DM* I.i.462n. It may well be, also, that **imperfect** has sexual connotations, deriving from Aristotelian theories of conception and generation, whereby the role of the male is that of imparting quality to, or 'perfecting', an embryo whose quantity is determined by the female. See Jay L. Halio, 'Perfection and Elizabethan Ideas of Conception', *ELN* 1 (March 1964), pp. 179–82; also D. C. Gunby, '"In her effected": a Websterian Crux resolved?', *ELN* x (December 1972), pp. 107–10, and *WD* III.ii.59n.

149–50 **And so . . . shed** Almost certainly to the audience.

150–1 *FINIS* Q follows this with a horizontal rule (made up of ten short rules) and the publisher's advertisement: '*If any Gentlemen please to repair to my House aforesaid, they may be furnished with all manner of English, or French Histories, Romances, or Poetry; which are to be sold, or read for reasonable Considerations.*' Evidently Kirkman not only sold books but also ran a lending library for fee-paying customers.

Sources

Discussions of the source of the tragicomic romance plot of *A Cure for a Cuckold* have traditionally focused on its undeniably close relationship with the Leonora–Cleremond plot of Massinger's *The Parliament of Love*. The priority of *A Cure for a Cuckold* having now been established—Massinger's play was licensed by Sir Henry Herbert as 'For the Cockp: comp: A new P.' on 3 November 1624[1]—attention can be directed to Marston's *The Dutch Courtesan* (1603–4), which is accepted as having been a source for both, directly or indirectly, and to Marston's source, Nicolas de Montreux's romance, *Les Bergeries de Juliette* (1585).

That *Les Bergeries de Juliette* was the source of the main plot of *The Dutch Courtesan* was first noted by John J. O'Connor,[2] who pointed out the close resemblance of the Freevill–Malheureux–Franceschina plot to the story, in the first book of Montreux's romance, concerning the friendship of two young men, a Venetian named Dellio and a Frenchman, the Sieur de la Selve, and their love for a courtesan, Cinthye. In Montreux Dellio relinquishes Cinthye because he sets friendship above the love of a woman. Cinthye, enraged at Dellio's rejection of her, and subsequent betrothal to Angelicque, agrees to take de la Selve as a lover on condition that he kill Dellio, but he reveals this to his friend and they devise a plan whereby Cinthye will think Dellio has been killed, though in fact he has gone into hiding in the country. Cinthye then tells Dellio's parents that de la Selve has killed their son, and he is arrested and condemned to death. She also attempts to harm Angelicque by telling her that Dellio had agreed to marry her only to please his parents. Tragedy is avoided when Dellio returns from the country in time to prevent de la Selve's execution and to convince a desperately ill Angelicque that he loves her. Cinthye, foiled, leaves Venice, Dellio and Angelicque are married, and de la Selve returns to France.

In *The Dutch Courtesan*, as O'Connor notes, Marston makes little alteration to the story, but considerably alters its focus and implications. For where in Montreux the emphasis is on the young men's friendship, with Marston the focus is much more, as the play's title indicates, on Franceschina and her revenge, while the bonds of friendship between Freevil and Malheureux are more fragile and problematic. Thus Freevil does not give up Franceschina out of love for his friend. She has already been cast off in favour of Beatrice, and her viciousness derives from this. Equally, Malheureux consents to murder Freevil not simply to placate the Dutch courtesan, but because lust is stronger than love. Marston's world is thus a much darker one than Montreux's. As O'Connor comments: 'Marston is very much concerned with morality, and *The Dutch Courtesan* is fervid with his sense of sin.'[3]

In *A Cure for a Cuckold* Webster, Rowley, and Heywood modify and considerably complicate what they derive from Marston. For Bonvile (Dellio and Freevil) has never been Clare's lover, and she does not seek his death, though she is mutely and despairingly in love with him. Rather, by the gnomic injunction which she lays on Lessingham (de la Selve and Malheureux) to '*Kill for my sake that Friend that loves thee dearest*' (I.i.98) she intends herself, hoping that Lessingham will thus put her out of her misery. Hence when Lessingham returns from Calais, declaring that Bonvile is dead, Clare is horrified. In other respects, however, *A Cure for a Cuckold* quite closely follows *The Dutch Courtesan*. Thus Lessingham and Bonvile do not fight (albeit for a different reason: Bonvile declares that their friendship is dead, and so he is dead to Lessingham, and can be declared so), and Lessingham returns to claim Clare. Her declaration that she had loved Bonvile passionately but now, freed of that passion by his death, will give herself to Lessingham provokes uncontrollable jealousy in the latter, and (assuming somewhat the role of Franceschina and Cinthye) he attempts to poison Bonvile's marriage to Annabel (Marston's Beatrice) by suggesting that she has betrayed him with Rochfield. In resolving the situation, likewise, Webster reverses a role, since it is Clare who acts as the force for good, effecting reconciliation between Annabel and the briefly jealous Bonvile, and aiding Lessingham's return to emotional and moral stability. Thus all ends more happily than in *The Dutch Courtesan*, since Bonvile (Freevil) and Annabel (Beatrice) are joined in felicity by Clare (Franceschina) and Lessingham (Malheureux).

Although Rochfield is briefly implicated in the main action (albeit only by Lessingham's lies) he is active only in the distinct and subordinate sub-plot involving him and Annabel. For this no source is known, and one seems unlikely, given the routine nature of the plot situation, involving the reclaiming of a scapegrace younger son.

The Compass plot likewise has no known source but it may well be, as Lucas notes,[4] that it derives either from some custom in London riverside suburbs or from a particular incident. Two pieces of evidence point to this. One is Francis Kirkman's comment, in his preface to the play: '*The Expedient of Curing a cuckold (after the maner set down in this* Play) *hath bin tried to my knowledge, and therefore I may say* Probatum est' (22–4). The other, which perhaps points more to custom than an isolated incident, is found in *Anything for a Quiet Life* (c. 1621), where Knavesbee, urging his wife to prostitute herself to Lord Beaufort, adds: 'when 'tis done, we will be married again wife, which some say is the onely *Supersedeas* about *Limehouse*, to remove Cuckoldry' ([Lucas] II.i.120–2).[5]

1. Bawcutt, p. 157.
2. John J. O'Connor, 'The Chief Source of Marston's *Dutch Courtezan*', *Studies in Philology* LIV (1957), pp. 509–15. O'Connor's discovery laid to rest the earlier belief that Webster and Heywood drew the main plot of *A Cure for a Cuckold* from Bandello's account of the scandalous life and death of Bianca, Countess of Celant, as mediated through Painter's *The Palace of Pleasure*, albeit indirectly, via *The Dutch Courtesan* (see Lucas, III, 5–6).
3. O'Connor, 'The Chief Source of Marston's *Dutch Courtezan*', p. 512.
4. Lucas, II, 9.
5. The scene is one attributed to Webster: see Lucas, IV, 66–7.

APPIUS AND VIRGINIA

Date

No evidence has been found by which *Appius and Virginia* might be precisely dated. The play was not printed until 1654, and the only earlier reference to it, in a list dated 10 August 1639 of forty-five plays appropriated to 'the kinges and Queenes young Company of Players at the Cockpitt in Drury Lane',[1] is of no help, since Webster was almost certainly then dead. Equally, any attempt to date the play by reference to the company which owned it fails because, as Bentley observes, 'Other plays in this list had once been the property of Prince Charles's (I) company, Lady Elizabeth's company, Queen Anne's company, or Queen Henrietta's company, so that nothing of the play's date or original company can be deduced from this list.'[2] That *Appius and Virginia* was written for one of Beeston's companies is, nonetheless, likely (see p. 488).

Concerning attempts at dating *Appius and Virginia* Bentley is equally uncompromising, describing them as 'chaotic' and adding, acerbically, that 'In each case the evidence presented seems to me at best inadequate, often absurd, and frequently tied to arguments for hypothetical collaborators.'[3] In bracketing Lucas's attempt to date the play with such speculative determinations as those of Fleay (*c.* 1609) and Brooke (*c.* 1608), however, Bentley is over-severe. For while Lucas's use of metrical tests in establishing a final sequence of Webster's plays may be questioned, his evaluation of possible topical references deserves respect, and his tentative conclusion, that *Appius and Virginia* should be dated 1625–7, has much to commend it.

A key piece of evidence in arguing for such a date is to be found in the fact that, as Lucas observes, 'the plot of *Appius* . . . follows Roman history with unusual closeness, except in one respect—the famine in the camp. For this there is no historical basis at all.'[4] Yet the sufferings of the troops are dwelt upon in considerable detail in three scenes, stress being laid upon their arrears of pay, their hunger, and their conviction—accurate enough—that Appius is indifferent to the fate of their army in the field.

As Lucas notes,[5] just such views were being widely expressed in England in the years 1624–6, particularly in relation to the disaster which befell an English expeditionary force pressed to serve under a mercenary, Count Mansfeld, on behalf of King James's son-in-law, Frederick, the

Elector Palatine, who had been evicted by the Hapsburg Emperor and his allies from the Palatinate. Recruited in October and November 1624, the twelve thousand-strong force was from the first scandalously neglected, the troops left without pay or provisions at their Dover rendezvous, and resorting to theft and pillage to survive. Transported to Flushing in February 1625, and thence to Gertruidenberg, they suffered even greater hardship, and, ravaged by starvation and disease, the force was reduced by June to a mere three thousand.[6] Governmental and local incompetence played some part in the disaster, but the callousness and greed of Mansfeld were commonly held to be a primary cause. Lord Cromwell, whose regiment had been reduced by disease and starvation to just two hundred and twenty men, wrote to Dudley Carleton on 7 June 1625: 'Our General studies his profit, and how to ruin us, I think.'[7]

But though the fate of the force sent to the Palatinate was the worst example of governmental incompetence during the mid-1620s, it was by no means the only one, and Lucas notes that throughout 1626 there were similar and repeated examples of both soldiers and sailors petitioning the Duke of Buckingham, the King's favourite, Chief Commissioner of War, and Lord High Admiral, for pay and provisions (Lucas, for instance, cites a case in August 1626 when two hundred unpaid sailors from Portsmouth waylaid the Duke of Buckingham, who promised them a hearing that afternoon, but gave them the slip).[8]

The emphasis laid in *Appius and Virginia* on the suffering of the army and the indifference of those in power strongly suggests that topical references are being made, and if this is so, then there is sufficient reason to argue, as Lucas does, that the play dates from the years 1625–7. Closer dating than that is highly speculative, but what appear to be coded references to Buckingham (see pp. 470–2) would have been particularly apt in the first half of 1626, when attacks on him in Parliament were particularly virulent and outspoken,[9] while the series of derogatory references to the French by the Lictors and Corbulo early in II.ii may perhaps relate to the anti-French feeling which in March 1626 followed the revelation that the French had the previous month signed a secret treaty with Spain, or perhaps to the expulsion of the French household of Queen Henrietta Maria, threatened in July 1626 and carried out in August.[10]

One further point relating to the dating of *Appius and Virginia* might be made: namely that the theatres were closed for most of 1625, first following the death of King James on 27 March, and then because of the plague, not opening again until late November or early December.[11] Even if, therefore, *Appius and Virginia* was completed in 1625, it might not have received its first performance until the following year, when allusions to Buckingham and to French perfidy could easily have been incorporated.

A firm date for the writing and performance of *Appius and Virginia* remains elusive, then. But such indicators as there are suggest that 1625 or 1626, with perhaps a leaning towards the latter, is the most likely period of composition and first performance.[12]

1. Bentley, I, 330.
2. Ibid., V, 1247–8.
3. Ibid., V, 1246.
4. Lucas, III, 125.
5. Ibid.
6. Ibid.
7. Gardiner, V, 336.
8. Lucas, III, 126, quoting T. Birch, *Court and Times of Charles I* (London, 1848) I, 141.
9. Lockyer, pp. 312–13, 319–25.
10. Ibid., pp. 300, 334–5. Similarly derogatory references to France and the French in J. W.'s *The Valiant Scot* are part of an argument for dating the play 1626, an argument which also includes the likely identification of the unadmirable Grimsby with Buckingham, and Queen Elinor with Charles I's wife, Henrietta Maria. See J. W., *The Valiant Scot*, pp. 57–64.
11. Bentley, II, 657.
12. David Gunby and Hester Lees-Jeffries, 'George Villiers, Duke of Buckingham, and the Dating of Webster and Heywood's *Appius and Virginia*', *N&Q* n.s. XLIX (September 2002), pp. 324–7.

Critical introduction

DAVID GUNBY

Appius and Virginia has not engendered as positive a critical response as it deserves. Apart from William Archer, who declared it 'vastly superior'[1] to *The White Devil* and *The Duchess of Malfi*, no doubt because in structure it came much closer to late nineteenth-century ideas about the well-made play, those who have written about *Appius and Virginia* have tended to be at best tepid in their praise. Hazlitt set the tone early when he described it as 'a good, sensible, solid tragedy' in which there was 'little to blame or praise',[2] and a century later Lucas commented on its 'adequate handling of a not very brilliant theme'.[3] In between, Stoll wrote of its 'frigidity and academic character',[4] and Brooke (convinced that it was written in its entirety by Heywood) of its 'forthright and unthinking simplicity'.[5] Yet *Appius and Virginia* has merits which deserve attention. It may not meet the usual critical expectations of Jacobean or Caroline tragedy, or bear comparison with *The White Devil* and *The Duchess of Malfi*, but in its carefully crafted austerity it achieves other ends, most notably, it seems, political.

Brooke's conviction of Heywood's sole authorship of *Appius and Virginia* has not been shared by others, the consensus now being essentially as established by Lucas, following Gray: joint authorship by Webster and Heywood, with the former the senior partner (see pp. 498–9).[6] Nor has support for an early date for *Appius and Virginia* been forthcoming, consensus here being that it is the last of Webster's dramatic works, probably written 1625–6 (see pp. 443–5). But if these problematic areas relating to the play have been more or less dealt with, there remain others which continue to arouse critical debate, not least relating to structure, to dramatic options taken by Webster and Heywood, and ultimately to its quality.

Webster's earlier tragedies, *The White Devil* and *The Duchess of Malfi*, are structurally complex, *The White Devil* particularly so. *Appius and Virginia*, by contrast, could in this respect scarcely be simpler. Lucas praises its 'almost classical simplicity of construction',[7] and indeed its single action, involving conflict between the decemvir, Appius, and the general, Virginius, in both the public and private spheres, is akin in its directness to those of Shakespeare's *Antony and Cleopatra* and *Coriolanus*, as described by Derek Traversi:

> we are conscious of the smooth progress of a single narrative current, unimpeded from the beginning of the action to its logical conclusion. Events follow one another easily and without turning back upon themselves: the tragic sequence has a single trajectory, and the dominating purpose is written into the action for all to see and participate in its impact.[8]

Akin, that is, in all save the final respect, for 'the dominating purpose' of *Appius and Virginia* is far from agreed, and Peter B. Murray, for one, can find no thematic core to the play at all.[9]

About the simplicity of the structure and the directness of the narrative, however, there is no disagreement. Act I sets out the terms of reference for what is to follow, with Appius assuming power, and initiating his plan to seduce Virginia by denying Virginius pay and provisions for his troops and plotting with Marcus Clodius to seize her. Act II enlarges on this, while in Act III the various conflicts are brought to crisis point, with Virginia arrested, and Virginius hurrying to Rome. Act IV provides the climax, with the trial, Virginia stabbed, and her father's return to the camp, while Act V deals with the aftermath, both political and personal, with the reconciliation between Virginius and Icilius, the punishment of Appius and his accomplice Clodius, and the political liberation of Rome.

The material which Webster and Heywood found to hand in Dionysius and Livy (see pp. 640–2) lent itself to straightforward handling in all save one respect. Historically, Appius had Siccius, a military hero, murdered, but as Murray observes,[10] *Appius and Virginia* would 'break in two' if the Siccius story were developed. Therefore the dramatists made Virginius the object of Appius's machinations, as part of the plot to seize Virginia. The result is a tightening and unifying of the story line, but also a reduction in what Webster and Heywood have to work with. And this is not a great deal, for the story of Appius and Virginia has but two great dramatic episodes, the confrontation in the Forum, culminating in the death of Virginia, and the meeting between Virginius and Icilius in V.i. While eschewing a Siccius sub-plot, therefore, the dramatists had to add bulk to the main action. And one way of doing this was to make Virginius the anguished general of a starving and mutinous army, providing thereby two considerable camp scenes as well as material for a good deal of dramatic debate in Rome.

These camp scenes, highly effective dramatically, certainly bulk out

Appius and Virginia. They also enhance a comparison, found elsewhere in the play, between Appius and Virginius. Murray notes, for instance, how in II.ii, the first camp scene, Virginius's actions echo those of Appius in I.iv:

> Each of them has used pretence and put down supplicants who threatened their authority, but whereas Appius did so to further his lust, Virginius has done so to serve the public interest, hiding his own humiliation and even upholding the reputation of the man who humiliated him.[11]

But the usefulness of the camp scenes goes much further than this. For in lieu of a contrasting sub-plot Webster and Heywood develop a system of generally alternating scenes, for the most part contrasting the public and political world of Rome (scenes involving Appius, Senators, and Marcus Clodius) with the private, familial worlds of Numitorius and Virginius. This is evident from the outset, as I.i, a public scene in which Appius is 'forced' to accept appointment as a decemvir, is followed by I.ii, set in Virginius's home and focussing upon the betrothal of Virginia and Icilius; likewise I.iii, in which Appius and Clodius plot, is succeeded by I.iv, in which a first half involving public life, where Virginius pleads for supplies for his army, is followed by a second half which is private and familial, with Virginius approving the marriage contract entered into in I.ii.[12]

Given the nature of the story, however, at least as Webster and Heywood choose to tell it, there is not sufficient material in the private world for them to continue to alternate exclusively in this fashion. And here the camp scenes serve a similar purpose. Thus in Act II the first camp scene (II.ii) is placed between two in which the public and private worlds collide. In the first of these (II.i), at Virginius's house, Clodius intrudes as the unwelcome bringer of Appius's message of love, while in II.iii, in Appius's house, an angry Icilius confronts the decemvir over his advances to Virginia. In Act IV, likewise, the camp scene has a valuable structural role, for following the climactic scene in the Forum in which Virginia is killed, we move to the camp, where Virginius wins over the army to support him against Appius, before moving back to Rome, in Act V, to find Appius and Clodius already in custody, the play concluding with the uniting of the camp and Rome, the military and civil.

The camp scenes are not the only means Webster and Heywood use to enlarge their dramatic material, and provide contrast. The Corbulo material serves somewhat the same purpose, most notably in III.v, where an entire scene is given over to the Clown's melancholy encounter with two Serving-men. The scene demonstrates Corbulo's devotion to his mistress, and his forebodings about the outcome of the trial, but its structural value lies in its interposition between III.iv, in which Appius and Clodius continue their plotting against Virginius, seeking to prevent his attendance at the trial, and the trial scene itself.

This process of interposition, separating two powerful scenes by one not only markedly different but also low-key in its demands, thereby enabling the audience to draw breath and recover its emotional equilibrium, is as evident in the other, briefer appearances of Corbulo as it is in III.v. In III.i, for instance, the first fourteen lines are given over to the Nurse and Corbulo, in an exchange which no doubt Murray had in mind when he referred to 'Heywood's relatively inane banter'.[13] But the sexual innuendo and domestic trivia serve most importantly to provide a brief intermission between the end of II.iii, where Appius and Clodius are plotting, and the conference between Numitorius, Icilius and their friends which is a response to the threat which Appius's plotting poses. Likewise, the brief exchange between Corbulo and Virginia at the beginning of II.i serves to separate the family discussion, sealing the betrothal of Virginia and Icilius, and the advances made to Virginia on Appius's behalf by Clodius from II.i.26 onwards—advances which have threatened throughout the banter between Corbulo and his mistress, as Clodius lurks in the background, '*with presents*' (II.i.0.1).

That 'the plot gives him nothing whatever to do' as Charles Forker puts it, is true enough, but 'amusing badinage' is not Corbulo's 'sole excuse for being'.[14] Nor is he as usefully compared (as again by Forker) with Mercutio and the Nurse in *Romeo and Juliet* as with Peter and Musicians, who appear at the beginning and end of IV.iv. For just as they serve to cordon off with domestic trivia and chop-logic the emotionally difficult (for an audience) mock death of Juliet, so Corbulo, and (to a lesser extent) the Nurse, serve the same crucial separating function in *Appius and Virginia*.

It is worth returning, at this point, to the camp scenes, and particularly to the mutiny, to consider further their place in *Appius and Virginia*. Critics since Stoll have been severe on Webster (and Heywood) for including these, some, like Stoll himself, feeling that the populace is being blackguarded unjustifiably.[15] But Melvin Seiden, while agreeing with Stoll that 'there is no political justification for portraying the soldiers in the spirit of "the stinking, filthy, brutal mobs in *Julius Caesar* and *Coriolanus*"',[16] finds in this a dramatic strategy showing Virginius suffering injustice as much at the hands of friends as, in I.iv, of enemies. 'The irony of being misunderstood and misjudged by one's own friends is compounded', Seiden argues, 'by the fact that the mistake which causes them to be unjust is the direct result of the machinations of the man who is the enemy of both the soldiers and Virginius. Thus the behaviour of the soldiers unwittingly furthers Appius' evil ends.'[17]

But Seiden, having perceived a dramatic strategy behind the mutiny, concludes that it is mishandled because the revolt is displayed as 'despicable' yet 'nowhere is it denied that the soldiers' grievances are just', and because Virginius's response is 'angry and violent'. 'It is impossible to pity Virginius as he plays the martinet in cowing the mutineers', Seiden comments, 'Virginius has become Coriolanus.'[18] 'The effect of the scenes as a whole', Seiden therefore concludes,

> is divisive and emotionally incoherent. The mutiny scene is 'good theatre' only insofar as it is considered as an isolated incident, a set piece; and that is because the dramatist's temptation to sacrifice the cumulative effect of the whole to the palpable appeal of the part is as potent a motive as his need to fill out five acts of drama.[19]

Seiden's indictment of Webster and Heywood's dramaturgical skills and judgement is, however, considerably astray; astray, in the first instance, because he, like Stoll, sees the soldiers negatively portrayed in the two camp scenes. Yet an examination of II.ii up to the entry of Virginius shows us nothing like Stoll's 'stinking, filthy, brutal mobs in *Julius Caesar* and *Coriolanus*'.[20] On the contrary, the soldiers, though at times foolish and gullible, display considerable dignity in deciding to mutiny ('a motion | Which nature and necessity commands' as 1 Soldier puts it at II.ii.8–9), and their spokesman considerable rhetorical skill in putting their 'just complaint' (20) at 23–32. 1 Soldier is no mob leader, but an articulate spokesman for rightly desperate men, and in what follows he strengthens his case, declaring Rome to be 'growne a most unnaturall mother' (39), and claiming that the generals (as representing Rome) 'account the expence of Ingines, and of swords, | Of horses and of armor dearer far, | Then souldiers lives' (66–8). This last comment, it should be noted, is made in relation to the fact that the army is not actively engaging 'the affrighted enemy' (62), a shame which 1 Soldier links to the age-old complaint of the rank and file: that the credit for victories (and the accompanying spoil) goes to 'the Generall and Commanders' (57), while 'in our overthrowes, where lies the blame? | The common souldiers fault, ours is the shame' (59–60).

The only point at which, indeed, the mutinous troops grow violent—and then only verbally—is when their spokesman threatens, if Virginius returns, to

> drag him to the slaughter by his locks,
> Turned white with riot and incontinence,
> And leave a president to all the world,
> How Captaines use their souldiers. (II.ii.80–3)

It is, of course, at this moment that Virginius returns, and his immediate ascendancy over the soldiers serves more, surely, to demonstrate his qualities as a leader of men than to portray them as comically foolish. He uses anger as part of his means of bringing them to order. Minutius then effects the reconciliation and justly assesses the mutineers in pardoning them (174–83).

If the behaviour of the soldiers in II.ii is scarcely akin to that of the populace in *Julius Caesar* or *Coriolanus*, their behaviour in IV.ii rules out kinship entirely. For the soldiers' dialogue which opens the scene—yet another example of the use of minor characters interpositionally—shows them bearing their hardships with a sardonic humour and abstaining from blaming their commanders. And later, again responding quickly to Virginius, they play a significant part in the about-face which leads to his being given command of the army rather than arrested, for when Minutius hesitates, the soldiers (and the anonymous Roman appointed to succeed Virginius) declare for him, and Minutius concurs with 'It shall be so' (IV.ii.157). Significantly, too, at the end of the scene, as Virginius hesitates, it is 1 and 2 Soldiers who encourage him and trigger his acceptance:

> *1 Souldier.* We will by you our noble General.
> *2 Souldier.* He that was destin'd to preserve great *Rome*.
> *Virginius.* I accept your choice. (IV.ii.180–2)

Stoll and Seiden's judgements, then, are considerably astray. Fickle the mutinous soldiers of II.ii may be, but no brutal mob, while in IV.ii they are exemplary in their endurance of hardship and take the lead in the endorsement of Virginius as leader.

That Webster and Heywood needed to expand on the material which lay to hand in their sources is generally agreed. The camp scenes and those involving Corbulo and the Nurse are part of that expansion. It remains puzzling, however, why the dramatists did not adopt what seems an obvious means of expanding and enriching the dramatic action: development of the Icilius–Virginia relationship. Lucas, discussing the 'inherent difficulties' in the source material, links this unadopted possibility with what he sees as a general problem in *Appius and Virginia*, 'that its conflicts are all external'.[21] Critics generally agree, Margaret Loftus

Ranald commenting, for instance, on 'a cardinal difficulty with *Appius and Virginia*': namely, that 'the characters are drawn from the outside so that their motivations are not fully developed . . . Without revelatory soliloquies as a guide, one cannot know what lies beneath the appearance and must regard the play with detachment.'[22]

Analysis of the major characters demonstrates the general truth of this assessment, for few are presented in more than typical terms, or individuated to any degree. Thus Minutius is the archetypal general, loyally obeying the powers-that-be until at the last convinced that he should join Virginius in opposing Appius, while Numitorius is a family man, brother and uncle, cautious and for a time gullible, and in III.i (this the only individuating feature), a distinctly anxious and uneasy conspirator. Icilius, the impetuous young lover, is given a little more individuality, particularly in II.iii, where he first pleads that Virginius be compensated for the money he has spent supplying his troops, and then confronts Appius with evidence of his lustful intentions concerning Virginia. Here the impetuous young man—Appius refers contemptuously to him as 'boy' (86) and talks of 'the rashnesse | And blind misprision of distempred youth!' (122–3)—not only manages to dissemble by apologizing to Appius (this made clear in III.i), but also declares his love for Virginia (II.iii.99–103).

Yet curiously, Webster and Heywood, allowing Icilius to declare that 'Shee's mine, my soul is crownd in her desire, | To her I'ld travell through a land of fire' (II.iii.112–13), deny him the opportunity to proclaim or display his love for Virginia directly, eschewing a wooing scene, and cutting short the betrothal which might, even in the presence of family, compensate for it. For no sooner has Icilius declared his feelings and Virginia briefly replied than a servant enters with news that Virginius has arrived in Rome, and forebodings of ill-tidings take over. Moreover the declaration which Icilius does make is cast in austere and abstract terms:

> here I hold
> My honorable patterne, one whose minde
> Appeares more like a ceremonious chappell
> Full of sweet musick, then a thronging presence.
> I am confirm'd, the court doth make some shew
> Fairer then else they would doe; but her port
> Being simple vertue, beautifies the court.   (I.ii.11–17)

Thereafter, save in anger to Appius, Icilius is given no opportunity to speak of his love, while following the stabbing he is silent. In the encounter with Virginius in V.i, where again there would be opportunities to express his anguish at the loss of Virginia, he does not even mention her by name, and his questioning of Virginius is cast in general, even symbolic, terms (V.ii.37–44). Again, it seems Webster and Heywood deliberately avoid giving Icilius opportunity to express his personal loss. Nor, in V.iii, does his entry with the body of Virginia much alter the situation, for his speech is about revenge, and designed to strengthen Virginius's resolve to punish Appius (V.iii.88–96).

The limits which Webster and Heywood place on Icilius they impose also on Virginia. Her first speech, a response to Icilius's praise, is lovingly teasing:

> It is a flattery (my Lord)
> You breath upon me, and it shewes much like
> The borrowed painting which some Ladies use,
> It is not to continue many dayes;
> My wedding garments will outweare this praise.   (I.ii.18–22)

This, however, is all she is allowed, while in II.i, where she is given more opportunity to speak, what she says is contained by circumstance. For Virginia thinks it is at Icilius's bidding that Clodius comes, and responds to his Petrarchan commonplaces with witty assurance (II.i.57–62). But when Clodius reveals that he comes on behalf of Appius, and derides Icilius as 'a man so much beneath | The merit of your beauty' (67–8), she reacts strongly, with

> Let thy Lord know, thou Advocate of lust,
> All the intentions of that youth are honourable,
> Whil'st his are fill'd with sensuality.
> And for a finall resolution know,
> Our hearts in love like twins alike shall grow.   (II.i.77–81)

Spoken to Icilius, the final line would have emotional power: here it is the clinching line in a cool rejection of Appius, of a piece with her only speech in III.i, where she explains (62–71) to those met at her uncle's house how she handled Appius's constant importunings.

Virginia's remaining utterances are in similar vein. After a minor part in the exchange between Corbulo and the Nurse early in III.iii, her role is to reject with fierce pride Clodius's allegation that she is slave-born (75–7), and to remain strong and resourceful, as with her firm but respectful request for a delay until her father comes (247–9). The end of the scene is curious, however, and instructive, for the exchange between Icilius and Virginia (305–21), which might have been a moment of mutual tenderness, is given over entirely to philosophizing, which it is hard to see as other than a most rigorously applied exclusion of the lovers' emotions, a refusal to allow rein to this dimension in *Appius and Virginia*. It is equally carefully excluded in IV.i, where the emotional dimension is restricted to Virginia and her father as she pleads with him to kill her rather than allow her to be enslaved (IV.i.30–4). And here again Virginia concludes with a philosophical generalization, which limits emotional engagement on our part:

> Happy the Wretch
> Who born in bondage lives and dies a slave,
> And sees no lustful projects bent upon her,
> And neither knowes the life nor death of honor. (IV.i.34–7)

During the hearing itself, Virginia is restricted to acid comments on proceedings and to a fierce denunciation of Appius (IV.i.225–9). This is her final speech, for Webster and Heywood allow her no response to Virginius's lengthy farewell (280–95). Again, her role, and the emotional energy which might accrue round her, have been circumscribed, one can only assume deliberately.

Unlike the lovers, Virginius is from the beginning given ample utterance. At his first appearance, in I.iv, he pleads at length and passionately for pay and supplies for the army. Lucas feels that 'Virginius does ill justice to his cause by the truculence with which he pleads it, seeing this as Virginius's "tragic error"'.[23] But as Seiden points out, Appius has set a trap, and there is no possibility of funds being provided, however tactful Virginius might be. 'What Lucas calls truculence', Seiden comments, 'is sincerity and depth of feeling. There is no suggestion that Virginius has overstated his case or stated it too bluntly.'[24] An examination of Virginius's address to the decemvirs bears this out. Virginius may challenge his hearers with 'Prove not to us | (Being our friends) worse foes then we fight with: | Let's not be starv'd in kindnesse' (I.iii.79–81), but he also pleads with dignity for 'Food to maintain life in the Camp' (89), and responds eloquently to Appius's calculated arrogance:

> if you have charity,
> If you be humane, and not quite giv'n ore
> To Furs and Metall, if you be Romans,
> If you have any souldiers bloud at all
> Flow in your veins, help with your able arms
> To prop a sinking camp. (I.iii.111–16)

Appius's 'perhaps at further leasure | We'l help you' (120–1) angers Virginius (as it is meant to), but even so he manages to restrict himself to

'I will not curse thee, *Appius*, but I wish | Thou wert i'th' camp amongst the Mutineers | To tell my answers, not to trouble me' (122–4). His passionate concern is not only his troops, but also Rome, and it is to this that he devotes most of his final plea, fearing that 'The rottenness of this misgovern'd State | Must grow to some Disease, incurable | Save with a sack or slaughter' (138–40).

Virginius's speeches thus bear out Seiden's judgement: they are not intemperate, given the carefully judged provocation. Indeed, his standing is enhanced by his measured and principled response, and his overriding concern for the public good (I.iii.166–9). So, too, is it by the brief glimpse we have of him as a father, approving his daughter's betrothal to Icilius (186–9), though it is with Rome's interest at heart that Virginius ends the scene: 'short farwels now must serve, | The universal businesse calls me hence, | That toucheth a whole people' (204–6).

As Virginius is in I.iii so is he in the rest of the play. In II.ii, quelling the mutiny, he displays courage, while in concealing from the army the treatment he received at the hands of Appius he puts the interests of the state ahead of his own (II.ii.125–6). Thereafter, we do not see him again until he enters dressed *'like a slave'* in IV.i. The opening of this scene, prior to the entry of Appius, is interesting both for what Virginius says, and for what he does not. Virginia asks him to take her life rather than see her handed over to Appius. It is a powerful statement, yet Virginius makes no direct response to it. Indeed, Webster and Heywood first have Icilius speak, pessimistically foretelling the outcome of the hearing, and then let Virginius respond only to Icilius, and without mentioning Virginia (IV.i.42–8). Again, it seems clear that the dramatists avoid developing the personal relationship between father and daughter, so far, at least, as it affects the characterization of Virginia.

With the entry of Appius and his entourage, the public scene begins, and the focus becomes—and remains—Virginius's struggle to refute the allegations of Clodius. The Orator (in lineal descent from Contilupo, in *The Devil's Law-Case*) is devious and eloquent, and Virginius is no match for him, particularly with Appius brilliantly managing the whole business. Hence, though making an occasional telling point, as when he asks why, if his wife deceived him into thinking a slave's child was his, she did not provide 'an Issue male to chear the father?' (IV.i.218), Virginius is limited largely to protests and only after Appius is about to give his judgement in favour of Clodius vents his anger (263–6).

Earlier, Virginia had appealed to her father to sacrifice her life, rather than let her be enslaved, but he made no direct response. Now he does address his daughter, but the dramatists allow her no response. It seems that the focus is to be on Virginius alone, and on his feelings, rather than on their relationship. Curiously, too, though he opens his speech with regret that 'never, never | Shall I taste fruit of the most blessed hope | I had in thee' (IV.i.280–2), his memories are entirely of Virginia's 'most pretty infancy' (283),

> when my Girl
> Would kiss her father in his burganet
> Of glittering steel hung 'bout his armed neck;
> And viewing the bright mettal, smile to see
> Another fair *Virginia* smile on thee. (IV.i.285–9)

And though, in concluding, he once more directly addresses his daughter, it is with a philosophical commonplace: 'O my *Virginia*, | When we begun to be, begun our woes, | Increasing still, as dying life still growes' (293–5).

The effect of this farewell speech is to limit drastically our sense of the present Virginia and equally drastically, by drawing attention only to the past and the forfeited future, her relationship with Virginius. And thus, more or less erased, she dies silently, the focus remaining on her father:

> *Virginius.* Hold, without Sentence I'l resign her freely,
> Since you will prove her to be none of mine.
> *Appius.* See, see, how evidently Truth appears.
> Receive her *Clodius.*
> *Virginius.* Thus I surrender her into the Court
> Of all the Gods. *Kills her [with a knife].*
> And see proud *Appius* see,
> Although not justly, I have made her free.
> And if thy Lust with this Act be not fed,
> Bury her in thy bowels, now shee's dead. (IV.i.298–306)

Virginius is condemned by all for a 'horrid act!' (307), but the deed has been prepared for since Virginia's plea for death before dishonour at lines 30–7. He is doing what he feels he must, but also what Virginia wishes. Yet where Webster and Heywood allow the father to express his feelings, they deny the daughter expression of hers.

In the following scene we are warned by 1 Soldier to expect '*Virginius* in a strange shape of distraction' (IV.ii.60), and his entry '*with his knife, that and his arms stript up to the elbowes all bloudy*' (74.1–.2) reinforces that expectation. But despite his opening plea for death, and his ready acceptance of arrest, he speaks cogently enough, admitting that he has killed his daughter, 'Willingly, with advice, premeditation, | And settled purpose'

(110–11). Not intended as a political speech, his explanation (124–36) nonetheless serves that purpose, leading to the offer of command. Virginius, 'Weary of life, and covetous of a grave' (163) initially refuses, but is swayed by Minutius's question: 'Who, if you dye, will take your cause in hand, | And proscribe *Appius*, should you perish thus?' (169–70). His response is apropos: out of self-concern alone, 'Thou oughtest *Minutius*. Soldiers, so ought you' (171–2). But when pressed, he accepts, 'in hope to guard you all | From my inhumane sufferings' (182–3), ending the scene with a transmutation of Virginia's death from a personal tragedy to a public sacrifice: 'Be't my pride | That I have bred a daughter whose chast blood | Was spilt for you, and for *Romes* lasting good' (183–5).

Given that Virginius is appointed to command so that Appius may be overthrown, it is a surprise to discover in the next scene that the latter is already in custody. Our dramatic expectations are thus foiled, and following the interpositional chatter involving Oppius and the time-serving Orator we witness an encounter not between Virginius and Appius, but Virginius and Icilius. Since the latter had said nothing when Virginia was slain, it is not clear what the precise nature of this encounter will be, but Virginius's precarious physical and psychological state and Icilius's reaction to it—''Tis the gods | Have powred their Justice on him' (V.ii.32–3)—make clear what is to follow: a passionate debate over the rightness or otherwise of Virginius's slaying of his daughter, and over the competing claims of public and private duties.

Icilius makes his point succinctly: 'Old man, thou hast shewed thy self a noble *Roman*, | But an unnatural Father' (V.ii.37–8). Virginius endorses this 'true description' (45) but claims that 'posterity, which truely renders | To each man his desert, shal praise me for't' (49–50). His justification relies on traditional Roman virtues, recalling that Icilius, as a knight, swore an oath 'Rather to die with honour, then to live | In servitude' (56–7), and he makes the point that if Virginia had been ravished, and Virginius tolerated it, Icilius's 'love and pity quickly had ta'ne end' (59). Virginius also challenges Icilius to make plain what he means to do, pointing out that conflict between them would damage the interests of the state. Since Icilius shares his senior's concern for Rome the two are reconciled to such a degree that Icilius can 'hope yet you may live, | To outwear this sorrow' (99–100). Virginius's response is emphatic—'O impossible. | A minutes joy to me, would quite crosse nature' (100–1)— but the scene ends with the public not the private, as Icilius gives the order to 'March on, and let proud *Appius* in our view | Like a tree rotted, fall that way he grew' (111–12).

The final scene continues the Icilius–Virginius contrasts in their responses to Appius's plea for clemency. Virginius is moved to pity and Icilius, noting what he regards as 'too relenting age' (V.iii.61), leaves to 'fetch that shall anatomize his [Appius's] sin' (69). While he is gone, Numitorius and Minutius both impress on Virginius the need to execute justice, the former urging him to 'fashion now | Your actions to your place, not to your passion' (71–2) since 'Severity to such acts is as necessary | As pity to the tears of innocence' (73–4). The issue is clear, and the appearance of Icilius with the body of Virginia hardens her father's resolve once more, though without extinguishing the feelings (98–102). Yet ironically it is Appius who responds to Virginius, with 'Leave this passion, | Proceed to your just sentence' (102–3), which Virginius does in giving Appius and Clodius the opportunity to commit suicide (105–6). Having approved Appius's death in the manner of 'every true bred Roman' (135), Virginius then says little until his (and the play's) final speech. Icilius and Minutius pronounce the ancient liberties restored, and Virginius and Icilius are declared consuls.

To turn from Virginius to Appius and his instrument, Clodius, is to move from antique Roman virtues to Machiavellian intrigue. With admirable economy the opening scene makes this clear, setting the apparent unwillingness of Appius to accept appointment as a decemvir against the eagerness he reveals when alone with Marcus Clodius (I.i.45–7). The intensity of his desire for office is revealed in the statement he makes just prior to the re-entry of Oppius and Minutius to hear his decision:

> Had I as many hands
> As had *Briarius*, I'de extend them all
> To catch this office; 'twas my sleeps disturber,
> My dyets ill digestion, my melancholy
> Past physicks cure. (I.i.59–63)

The metaphor of illness chosen to display this desire echoes the statement made earlier by Clodius, who 'was be-agued, fearing lest the Senate | Should have accepted at your fain'd refusall' (36–7). From the outset the two are in concert.

The first scene sketches Appius's villainy effectively but economically. The third, in which he enters '*melancholly*' (I.iii.0.1), adds a further dimension when he admits to Clodius that he is in love. Clodius responds with encouragement, offers to act as Appius's agent (32–5), and within seconds of learning that the object of Appius's affections is Virginia becomes his 'comforter' (40), having 'already found | An easie path which you may safely tread, | Yet no man trace you' (38–40).

The 'easie path' which Clodius proposes (I.iii.41–51) neatly encapsulates his debased view of human nature: his conviction that Virginia can be tempted with 'gifts and rewards', that Virginius himself may be brought to plead with his daughter if financially embarrassed, and that 'feare and power' can be brought to bear as a last resort. But above all, his plan is significant for its complete disregard of the public good, a disregard shared by Appius, who falls in immediately with Clodius's scheme, even though in I.i, in his first act as decemvir, he had instructed Minutius to take reinforcements and provisions to the army.

By the end of I.iii.54 the villainy of Appius and Clodius is fully established. From 55 we see it in operation, as Appius consummately outmanoeuvres Virginius. Speaking on behalf of the decemvirs, he dresses him down for presuming to lecture them and asserts their prerogative right to act as they choose (98–107). The speech is masterly in its combination of personal humiliation ('any petty fellow wag'd by us') and deliberate vagueness as to what help may be given and when. Never outright refusing to help, Appius nonetheless succeeds in doing exactly what Clodius suggested, as we see when Virginius declares his intention of spending his own 'smal possessions' (167) on provisions.

In II.i we see Clodius alone for the first time, playing the tempter and praising himself for an 'opportunity . . . subtilly waited' (26) as, musicians playing, he approaches Virginia. The encounter is neatly ironic, with Clodius using the language of courtly love, replete with out-of-date Petrarchan terminology (50–1) and flattery, but when he makes it clear that he is pleading on behalf of Appius, a complete failure.

In II.iii Clodius is once more Appius's secretary. The entry of Icilius 'troubled' disturbs him, as his aside, '*Icilius*! I pray heaven she have not blab'd' (22) reveals. That Icilius does know of his advances to Virginia becomes clear when he threatens Appius with violence. Despite apparently placating Icilius (117–34), Appius decides that he must be got rid of: 'Go to thy death, thy life is doom'd and cast. | *Appius* be circumspect, and be not rash | In blood as th'art in lust' (142–4). This coolness is shown, when Clodius enters, to be masking both anger—at Clodius for admitting Icilius—and humiliation, yet even so Appius checks Clodius's 'I'l after him, and kill him' (163) with the cunning of the born Machiavel (163–72). Clodius then reverts to his customary role as schemer, producing, again at a moment's notice, his plan to trap Virginia by 'proving' that she is 'the daughter of a bond woman. | And slave to me' (178–9). Then, he tells Appius, 'You may pronounce the sentence on my side, | And she become your Strumpet not your Bride' (184–5). As Appius observes, Clodius has 'a copius brain' (186), and the speed with which his mind works is demonstrated in the scenario he lays before Appius (190–9).

Left thus to Clodius's 'manage', events move fast. In III.ii, he sets his trap, and in III.iii Virginia is seized. She at once realizes what is afoot, and when Icilius and Numitorius arrive only the timely—and presumably pre-arranged—appearance of Appius prevents her forcible rescue. What follows is masterly, as Appius plays the upright judge, seemingly antipathetic towards Clodius. The dramaturgy is masterly, too, as Icilius becomes the catalyst which ensures that a preliminary hearing of the case takes place immediately—a situation far more dramatic than merely haling Virginia off to prison would be, and one which gives Appius and Clodius full opportunity to display their villainous brilliance. Appius's part here is to come down hard on Clodius, making it appear that he will decide in Virginia's favour. To that end he describes Clodius's past in the most unflattering of terms—whether truly or not is never clear, though Clodius protests that it is falsehood, spread (as ironically he claims) by 'some soothing sicophant, | Some base detracting Rascal' (III.iii.210–11)—and then deals with the troublesome matter of the letters he has sent Virginia by accusing Clodius of forging them: which the latter conveniently admits (212–29). In the short scene which follows, Appius and Clodius are mutually appreciative, as well they might be, since their masterly double act, climaxing in Appius's dismissal and imprisonment of Clodius (285–95), has set up the trial scene (IV.i), and ensured its outcome.

The dynamics of the trial differ considerably from those of the preliminary hearing, not least because Clodius is now represented by an advocate. This radically reduces his role, since he is called upon to do little more than provide occasional corroboration of a point made by the Orator. The brilliant double act of III.iii thus gives way to a solo performance by Appius, who displays consummate skill in shifting his ground from apparent sympathy for Virginius and scepticism about Clodius's case, through evenhandedness to scepticism about, and eventual dismissal of, Virginius's case. Icilius sees in the interplay between Appius and the Orator 'a practis'd Dialogue', adding 'Comes it not rarely off?' (IV.i.128–9). It does indeed, and enables Appius to wait until late in proceedings before showing his hand, overruling the cogent objections of Numitorius and Virginius (214–21). This done, he can dismiss Virginius's protest as 'scandal' (230) and Icilius's attempt to produce Appius's letters to Virginia as 'dilatory shifts' (235) before arresting Icilius for what in English terms would be contempt of court. Yet even so, in his dealings with Virginius he maintains a facade of good will, responding to the latter's disparagement of his ancestry with 'Your madness wrongs you, by my soul I love you' (261), before greeting Virginius's request that he be allowed to bid Virginia farewell with the effrontery of 'Now my Lords, | We shall have fair confession of the truth. | [*to Virginius*] Pray take your course' (278–9).

Virginia's death leaves Appius unaffected, his only utterances following her murder relating to the apprehension of Virginius, and this—and the absence of a scene early in the play in which Appius might see, and express his desire for, Virginia, and indeed of any direct encounter between them—makes it plain that, dramatically, 'Appius's lust for Virginia . . . never becomes more than simply the motive for his plotting.'[25] V.iii reinforces that judgement, for in discussion with Clodius the emphasis is on the fickleness of 'the Hydra headed multitude' (V.iii.2) and the suddenness of their fall, while in response to Icilius's accusations Appius, confessing himself guilty of what Icilius describes as 'Lust and blood' (44), makes no mention of Virginia, but in the vein of *A Mirror for Magistrates* describes his fall from power in *de casibus* terms: '*Virginius*, thou dost but supply my place, | I thine. Fortune hath lift thee to my Chair, | And thrown me headlong to thy pleading bar' (46–8).

The plea for clemency which accompanies this (for the 1620s) remarkably old-fashioned view of a tragic villain's downfall shows that Appius's effrontery is not a whit diminished, while his indifference to Virginia's corpse, and his dismissal of Virginius's grief with 'Leave this passion, | Proceed to your just sentence' (102–3) further demonstrate how little she meant to him. His final speech is impressive in its acknowledgement of guilt and willingness to face death, yet curiously abstract, appropriate, perhaps, where a contrast is being set up between Appius's courage and Clodius's cowardice, but falling short of what we expect in a tragic villain.

Appius offers Clodius an example 'bravely how to dy' (129) but the latter shows himself incapable of following it. Heywood departs from his sources here, since historically Marcus Clodius was banished, and it is clear that he does so in order to make a point essentially social and hierarchical: that '*Appius* dy'd like a Roman Gentleman' (159) whereas Clodius, 'one bred from the rabble', as Icilius puts it (157), cannot bring himself to commit suicide, and so must be condemned to hang. This ending lets down both the play and Marcus Clodius, who in his earlier vigour, inventiveness, and intelligence, however malignly applied, is greater than this. His dramatic antecedents, whether comic (as for instance Mosca) or tragic (like Flamineo) point to a better end than Heywood, seemingly intent, as Seiden puts it, on 'underlining social principles',[26] will allow him.

The villainous interplay of Appius and Clodius constitutes one of the high points of *Appius and Virginia*, yet the dramatists' handling of the two has not gone uncriticized. Seiden, in particular, sees problems. In his view, Clodius is not actually needed, since 'having secured a high position both politically and judicially, Appius can plot against Virginius and Virginia with perfect impunity'. Nor, Seiden feels, is Clodius 'needed either to increase the efficacy of Appius's deeds or to render Appius impregnable once these deeds have been done'. 'In these respects', Seiden concludes, 'Clodius is superfluous.'[27]

But if Clodius is 'superfluous', he is also dramatically fascinating, and for Seiden this constitutes a further problem, in that 'one feels that Clodius does for Appius not only what he alone *could* do but also that without Clodius' ingenuity there would be no machinations at all'.[28] The outcome, for Seiden, is a diminution of Appius, since 'Clodius not only possesses the genius which makes possible the realization of Appius's evil desires; he is also so much the villain's protector that he deflates whatever awe Appius has been able to inspire in us by his evil.'[29]

Seiden's critique is interesting but in essential respects awry. For while it is true that Appius early establishes his political and judicial ascendancy, it is not clear that he at that point possesses the absolute authority which would allow him openly to seize Virginia, nor, indeed, would acting in that way accord with his character. For Appius prefers to maintain a facade of legality, of respectability. He has the Machiavel's ability to dissemble, and enjoys doing so. His use of Clodius feeds this aspect of his personality and enables him to maintain a patrician aloofness from the machinations designed to put Virginia in his power.

Equally astray is Seiden's assertion that without Clodius there would be no machinations, that Appius lacks the motivation or energy to put his desires into action. For Webster and Heywood have no need to show Appius engaging in machinations when from the outset he has an eager sycophant working on his behalf. Nor, busy though he is, and successful, does Clodius overshadow Appius, as Seiden asserts. Indeed, care is taken to ensure that that does not happen by allowing only one spectacularly successful double act (III.iii) and in the trial scene which is its successor marginalizing an almost mute Clodius. The result, dramatically, is a clear focus on Appius, demonstrating by his agent's unimportance that it is he, and not Clodius, who is the driving force in the conspiracy.

Only three characters in *Appius and Virginia* are developed to any significant degree: Appius, Clodius, and Virginius. And of these it is Clodius, the least significant in plot terms, who is perhaps the most satisfyingly represented. In *The White Devil* and *The Duchess of Malfi* Webster develops the equivalent figures, Flamineo and Bosola, far more deeply, Bosola particularly, but in the constrained terms of *Appius and Virginia* Clodius is developed as fully as he needs to be. We know from Appius of his humble origins and his dubious past, and we know from Clodius himself of his sycophantic attachment to Appius and his delight in scheming. More is not required. With his master, however, there is a gap between what we know and what we would like to know. For as Forker puts it, 'even Appius, the most complex character in the cast, is psychologically transparent by mature Websterian standards, being a relatively simple compound of lechery . . . and deceit—in other words of "a divel" (II.iii.90) and a "Fox" (III.iii.120)'.[30] We know, and experience, Appius's lust for power, and we observe, and in a sense admire, his capacity for dissembling, but we are never sufficiently privy to the inner man to feel the force of his lust for Virginia: it is stated but not demonstrated.

Virginius presents the same difficulty. As Ranald puts it, speaking of the killing of Virginia: 'Virginius's murderous reaction is unexplained, because nothing is revealed about his inner emotional life. The trial scene allows him his expression of love, yet it lacks credibility because it comes from a poetically undeveloped character.'[31] About Virginius's other passion, his concern for the well-being of the state, we are told (and shown) more, but even here there is less in the way of character revelation than we are accustomed to in Webster, or than we find, for instance, in Heywood's finest tragedy, *A Woman Killed with Kindness*. The impression which is given is well described by Forker as 'more akin to line drawings than to the florid and disturbing canvasses that we think of as typically Websterian'.[32]

That these line-drawn characters are the result of slipshod or incompetent dramaturgy seems unlikely. So much else in *Appius and Virginia* demonstrates the skills of the veteran dramatists—the elaboration of the thin plot line, the neatness of the exposition and the sure handling of key scenes, the cleverness with which minor characters such as Corbulo, the soldiers, and the Orator are used interpositionally—that incompetence in other respects seems out of the question. Rather, we must seek for

reasons why Webster and Heywood chose to eschew character development in the way we expect in tragedy at this period, and why, equally,
they avoid dramatic situations—such as a love scene between Virginia
and Icilius or an encounter between Appius and Virginia which triggers
his ungovernable lust—which would readily enrich the play.

The principal reason for the self-denying ordinance which Webster
and Heywood imposed upon themselves in fashioning *Appius and
Virginia* seems to be that 'the focus of interest . . . appears not to be character but the configuration of the ideas'.[33] For the handling of the story
line, with the reduction of Virginia to little more than a symbolic presence, the relationships with her father and Icilius strictly circumscribed,
and the absence of any evidence, beyond assertion, of Appius's over-
whelming lust for Virginia, points to Virginius as the central figure, and
his struggle with Appius as crucial. And the ideas with which their struggle seems constantly to deal are public, not private: the concept of service
to the state, and the place of the personal when it comes into conflict
with the public. 'For Shakespeare', writes R. B. Parker, 'Rome is always
intensely patriarchal, with a strict, military code of personal "honour"
and duty to the state to which all other values must be subordinated.'[34]
So, too, it is for Webster and Heywood in *Appius and Virginia*.

In the opening moments of the play, Appius makes a high-flown statement about the personal qualities required in one who 'must steer at th'
head of an Empire' (I.i.13): such a one, he says, 'ought to be the Mirrour
of the times for Wisdome and for Policie' (14). Such he is not, but
Virginius comes across in his appeal to the decemvirs as absolute in his
commitment to the public good. He lacks 'Policie'—he is in this a
stereotypical blunt soldier—but in other respects he is a 'Mirrour of the
times', willing to beggar himself to provide for those serving under him
(I.iii.166–9) and shielding Appius and the authorities in Rome from the
opprobrium which rightly attaches to them because, as he says in an
aside, 'men must slight their wrongs, or else conceal them, | When
generall safety wills us not reveale them' (II.ii.214–15).

A distinction, then, is clearly drawn between Appius, who insou-
ciantly risks the safety of the state in order to seize Virginia, and
Virginius, who suffers personal loss and humiliation in the public interest. The contrast is pointed up in II.iii when Icilius urges Appius to 'be
kind unto the Camp' (43), explaining what it has cost Virginius 'To wage
his souldiers, and supply the Camp' (48), to be met by the smooth lie of
'The Camps supplies doth not consist in us, | But those that keep the
common Treasury' (52–3). When Appius then offers Icilius a dowry

treble that which came with Virginia to marry elsewhere, Icilius reacts sharply with a statement which represents at its most acute the priority which Appius gives to his own interests: 'Will you from your own coffers | Grant me a treble Dowry, yet interpose me | A poor third from the common Treasury?' (70–2). What follows is personal, as the enraged Icilius confronts Appius with his attempts to seduce Virginia, but the context is public.

In IV.ii, we find duty to the fore as Minutius puzzles over the letter from Appius requiring Virginius's arrest, concluding either that '*Virginius* is degenerate | From the ancient vertues he was wont to boast, | Or in some strange displeasure with the Senate' (37–9). Yet puzzled or not, Minutius complies with Appius's order, since he is 'of faction | Oppos'd in all things to the least misdeed' (46–7). He thus cashiers Virginius and bestows his command on a 'worthy Roman' (55) who remains nameless, but demonstrates his fitness for command with a speech which is the essence of *romanitas* (56–9).

Together with the scene's opening dialogue between the two soldiers, stoically and with wry humour accepting their deprivation, this incident establishes the admirable virtues to be found throughout the camp. This is Romanness such as Rome ought to display, but does not, and it is important that it be established at the outset, since it intensifies the significance of, and validates, what follows, as Virginius convinces first the rank and file, then the unnamed 'Roman', and finally Minutius, that they must take up arms against Appius and the decemvirs. 'It is a common cause', comments the Roman (153), while 2 Soldier proclaims Virginius 'He that was destin'd to preserve great *Rome*' (181). In their handling of this scene, Webster and Heywood avoid the least taint of disloyalty or mutiny attaching to the army. It is obeying the call of duty in taking action.

The encounter between Virginius and Icilius in V.ii continues this theme. He may condemn Virginius for being 'an unnatural Father', but Icilius nonetheless accepts that 'thou hast shewed thy self a noble *Roman*' (37). What he means by this is presumably shown in the speech in which Virginius explains his action, calling on Icilius to acknowledge that as 'a *Roman* Knight' (53) he took an oath which included, *inter alia*, 'Rather to die with honour, then to live | In servitude' (56–7). By this code, we are meant to realize, Virginia chose to die, and Virginius honoured her choice. In what was an intensely personal dilemma, father and daughter chose the Roman way out, and implicitly Icilius accepts this, since the issue is not mentioned again. What follows is, rather, devoted to public issues, to Icilius's action in apprehending Appius, and now appearing in opposition to Virginius. 'My faction', Virginius declares, 'shal not give the least advantage | To murtherers, to banquerouts, or theeves, | To fleece the common Wealth' (68–70), while Icilius also calls on the common good in urging Virginius to avoid raising 'the least uproare' (86) lest the populace, evidently in upheaval, may do serious damage to the city. The joining of forces and personal reconciliation which ensue are thus appropriate: both men place the good of the state above personal considerations, and are agreed on what that requires.

Of the death of Virginia Dena Goldberg comments:

> Virginius' sacrifice of his daughter's life is not an isolated act, but rather an extreme expression of his general code of behaviour. If Virginius is able to resist the natural impulse to keep Virginia alive, no matter what, it is because throughout his life he has subordinated such natural impulses to his ethics. Virginius' ability to act in contradiction to his feelings may remain repelling to the audience as it does to Icilius, but it is clearly demonstrated that the same ability is what makes Virginius a capable, trustworthy leader of society.[35]

It would be helpful to be able to interpret Virginius's inclination to pardon Appius in like terms: to see him setting aside personal inclinations or weakness for the public good. That it might be so read seems to be suggested by the exchange which takes place between Virginius and Icilius. The latter asks if Virginius thinks that Appius, pardoned, and restored to 'the Ivory Chair', 'would be wary to avoid the like, | Become a new man, a more upright Judge, | And deserve better of the Common Weal?' (V.iii.65–7). Virginius's ''Tis like he would' (68) draws reproofs from Numitorius and Minutius, and sends Icilius off to 'fetch that shall anatomize his [Appius's] sin' (69). His reappearance with Virginia's body stiffens Virginius's resolve, and Appius and Clodius are condemned to death. Goldberg is critical of this outcome, commenting that in judging Appius Virginius 'is acting as much from personal passion as Appius ever did when he sat on the bench'. 'After all the emphasis on discipline, duty, justice, and dispassion,' Goldberg adds, 'the play ends on a confession of the fragility of these values. When justice is achieved, it is the passionate justice of rebellion and revenge.'[36]

It seems unlikely that this is what the dramatists (and here specifically, Heywood) intended. Yet it cannot be denied that Goldberg's reading of the last scene is readily arrived at. Like the socially distinguished attitudes to death of Appius and Clodius, Virginius's urge to pardon, which provides the opportunity for the production of the body of Virginia, tends to confuse matters rather than to clarify them.

Appius and Virginia ends in proclamatory mode, with Icilius and Minutius declaring Rome 'Restored unto thine ancient liberty . . . Of Consuls' (V.iii.169–70) and Minutius announcing that Virginius and Icilius are appointed to that office 'by the peoples suffrage' (173). Then, combining the public and the personal, Virginius makes the play's final statement:

> We martial then our souldiers in that name
> Of Consuls, honoured with these golden bayes.
> Two Ladies fair, but most infortunate,
> Have in their ruins rais'd declining *Rome*,
> *Lucretia* and *Virginia*, both renown'd
> For chastity. Souldiers and noble Romans
> To grace her death, whose life hath freed great *Rome*,
> March with her Corse to her sad Funeral Tomb. (V.ii.174–81)

Given the emphasis on Rome and the public good, a linking here of Virginia with Lucrece, whose rape and suicide triggered the expulsion of the Tarquins, is not surprising. Nor, again, are the final two-and-a-half lines, a concluding statement typical of tragedy. What is surprising is to find Virginius saying these things, particularly since Heywood here departs from his sources. And though we might read in this Virginius's willingness again to set aside his personal wishes in the public interest, for us to accept that this is what he is doing requires reiteration, or at least acknowledgement, of the world-weariness and desolation he expressed in IV.ii. As it is, that seems forgotten, and what we are left with is a situation as disconcerting and unsatisfactory as that which would obtain in *King Lear* if Lear himself, or Kent, not only survived but proved willing to take charge of a resurgent Britain.

To make this comparison is, however, to point up precisely the difference between *Appius and Virginia* and more orthodox tragedies. 'Shakespeare', writes E. K. Chambers of *Julius Caesar*, 'is deliberately experimenting in a classical manner, with an extreme simplicity both of vocabulary and of phrasing.'[37] Somewhat the same may be said of *Appius and Virginia*, but with this crucial addition: that Webster and Heywood seem intent also on an 'extreme simplicity' of characterization (the 'line drawings' of which Forker writes) and of plot. By comparison with *The White Devil* and *The Duchess of Malfi* there is also a marked austerity of metaphor.[38] The result is a play displaying considerable skill in handling a rather meagre plot line, and creating some memorable scenes, but lacking 'the sense of ambiguity attendant upon a tragic perception of man and the universe'.[39] That the dramatists chose to eschew such ambiguity cannot be doubted, as the catalogue of situations avoided makes abundantly clear. 'Shakespeare', writes Paul A. Cantor, sees 'austerity as distinctively Roman.'[40] So, it seems, do Webster and Heywood. And in *Appius and Virginia* they have produced a tragedy which is a veritable embodiment, dramaturgically, of austerity. It is not entirely successful, both because of the confusion engendered in the final scene by Heywood and, more generally, because it fails to provide us with what we expect in terms of tragic experience, even in a Roman play. *Appius and Virginia*, Ranald concludes, 'is somewhat chilly. If admirable in its use of rhetoric, careful in its linear construction, classical in its discipline, noble in its assertion of ideals, yet it still lacks "heart".'[41] Murray puts this failure down to collaboration,[42] but though the problems associated with the last scene may perhaps be put down to differences in approach by the two dramatists, the other distinctive features of *Appius and Virginia* seem to represent rather a conscious decision on their parts to limit the range of the play, and thereby to focus attention on its Roman theme: the primacy of duty over private claims and concerns.

Much has already been adduced to show the strength and (save by Appius and Clodius) the ubiquity of the sense of duty felt by the main characters. It is this which drives Virginius to plead so forcefully in I.iii, Minutius to obey Appius and remove Virginius from command, Icilius to seize Appius, and Virginius and Icilius, initially, to oppose each other in V.ii. It is this also which motivates the nameless Roman who replaces Virginius, and which is present in the complaints of the soldiers. Set against this powerful sense of obligation, however, we have the selfishness of Appius and the amorality of his parasite, Clodius. This stark contrast, between political indifference and irresponsibility and the dedication of the army, suggests strongly that Webster and Heywood were intent on making a political point, and that issues topical at the time were being addressed, albeit (and necessarily) obliquely.

What those issues might be Lucas first suggested in his discussion of the dating of *Appius and Virginia*,[43] noting that the famine in the camp occurs nowhere in the sources, and that by the neglect and incompetence of the government just such a disaster befell the English troops under Count Mansfeld, who in October and November 1624 were pressed to fight on the continent in support of King James's son-in-law, Frederick, the Elector Palatine (see pp. 443–4). Widespread public anger at the failure of the government to provide adequately for its forces engaged in the Protestant cause makes it quite possible that *Appius and Virginia* is a vehicle for oblique but recognizable criticism of the failure of the government, and particularly of the Duke of Buckingham, Charles I's hated but all-powerful favourite. [44]

About the use of the theatre as a medium for Protestant propaganda Hans Werner has written persuasively, demonstrating how two plays— Dekker and Massinger's *The Virgin Martyr* (1620) and John Drue's *The Duchess of Suffolk* (1624)—both of which, Werner notes, 'were subject to extraordinary intervention by the Master of the Revels', who 'took the unprecedented step of insisting on seeing the two production scripts both before and *after* he had given his directions for excisions', form part of a Protestant propaganda drive to cast Princess Elizabeth, ousted with her husband from the Palatinate, as a saint and martyr.[45] There would be nothing surprising, on the evidence Werner advances, in discovering in *Appius and Virginia* yet another coded commentary on the role England was, or rather was not, playing in the Thirty Years' War.

That in Virginia Webster and Heywood figure Princess Elizabeth is possible, particularly since Virginia is explicitly compared, at the end of the play, to Lucrece, so significant in Renaissance iconography as the virtuous but defenceless victim, the martyr who inspires an uprising to overthrow corrupt rulers and restore ancient liberties, and an exemplar of traditional virtues.[46] Virginia is likewise iconic. Passive rather than active, she is the martyr who inspires those who act against tyranny, her body, produced at the end of the play, symbolizing both her suffering and the reasons why Virginius and Icilius took up arms against authority (see Fig. 10).

As Martin Butler argues,[47] a series of tragedies, beginning with Jonson's *Sejanus* (1606) and ending with Nathaniel Richards's *Tragedy of Messallina* (1634–6), but most notably Massinger's *The Roman Actor* (1626) and Thomas May's *Julia Agrippina, Empress of Rome* (1628), offer coded critiques of Stuart absolutism, and in particular of the government of Charles I and Buckingham. But where Massinger and the others follow Jonson in going to Tacitus or Suetonius for their subjects, Webster and Heywood return to an earlier favourite source, Livy, for theirs, and to the early days of republican Rome.

In employing a narrative set in republican Rome, however, to convey an implicit critique of the handling of a current crisis, the two dramatists are not breaking entirely new ground, as *Coriolanus* demonstrates. For there, as Parker notes, 'one of Shakespeare's main changes from Plutarch is to focus particularly on famine as the chief cause of the plebeians' revolt', this re-emphasis deriving strength and pertinence from the serious social unrest in the Midlands during 1607–8, when peasant rioting over enclosures mutated 'into protests about the shortage of grain—partly the result of the severe winter of 1607–8 . . . and its attendant evils of hoarding and price-rigging'.[48]

If *Appius and Virginia* is a coded critique of government mismanagement and indifference, how far can we go in seeing particular individuals aimed at? Lucas comments that 'it does not seem to me impossible that Buckingham is aimed at in Appius', and notes that there is an attack on Buckingham's 'creature', the astrologer, Dr Lamb, as Doctor Lambestones in V.ii of *The Fair Maid of the Inn*, a scene attributed to Webster.[49] It would certainly not be far-fetched to find Buckingham and Lamb in Appius and his creature Clodius, particularly since Lamb was popularly believed to be Buckingham's procurer, as Clodius is Appius's. As Martin Butler points out, Lamia's protest at Parthenius's commandeering of Lamia's wife Domitia for Domitian (*The Roman Actor*, I.ii.65–9) is expressed in terms of a 'shocking violation of his security of property' and a fundamental infringement of personal liberties. Clodius's seizure of Virginia for Appius likewise threatens the fundamental rights of Roman citizens, manipulating legal process to enslave the free-born Virginia, who protests, as Butler notes, in similar terms (III.iii.75–7).[50] In the England of the mid-1620s, when Buckingham wielded enormous power, parallels would readily have been drawn.

In certain respects, of course, *Appius and Virginia* seems to refuse such identifications. The play is, after all, set in Livy's republican Rome, rather than the imperial Rome of Tacitus and Suetonius, and there is thus no king or emperor on whose behalf Appius governs, and who might be read, covertly, as Charles I. But the situation is not as clear-cut as it at first appears. For one thing, Appius, though one of the decemvirs, is never shown with them, or even talked of as *primus inter pares*, but always appears governing alone, while the terms in which he does so are rendered ambiguous by the semantic slippage in his use of the terms 'we' and 'our'. In his speech of acceptance, for instance, Appius refers to himself as 'I' (I.i.78–84), but shortly refers to 'our person' (93) before reverting to 'I' in the rest of his speech to his kinsmen. Then, in the final speech, in which he orders Minutius to arrange provisions for the army, Appius employs the pronouns 'our' and 'we'. The terms in which he does so are perhaps ambiguous. 'Now to our present businesse at the camp: | The army that doth winter 'fore *Algidon*, | Is much distrest we heare' (122–4) can be taken to be a statement on behalf of the decemvirs (though none seem to be present) or on behalf of himself and Oppius, representing the

Senate. In I.iii this role as spokesman is made clear when Appius asks, and is given, permission to reply to Virginius as 'the Cities voyce' (I.iii.94), the recurrence of 'we' and 'our' thereafter appropriate to that role, but earlier there are clear examples of Appius's use of 'we' and 'our' which cannot be taken as anything other than royal in pretension. For not only does Appius privately instruct Clodius to 'Arme thee with all our bounty, oratory, | Variety of promise' (53–4), but when Valerius enters to convey the decemvirate's entreaty that he attend 'this dayes Senate' (56) replies with 'We will attend the Senate' (58). Webster and Heywood may be confusing the political situation vis-à-vis the decemvirs and the Senate (who historically gave up their powers to the former for two years) by not distinguishing between the two, but they make very plain Appius's sense of himself as exercising royal powers. Given the widespread feeling in England that Buckingham acted, with Charles's approval, in a quasi-royal fashion, this use by Appius of the royal 'we' seems significant, not least because this was a major element in the celebrated attack on Buckingham made on 10 May 1626 by Sir John Eliot during the impeachment debate in the House of Commons. Noting that in Tacitus's account of Tiberius's favourite, Sejanus, the latter 'would so mix his business with the prince's, seeming to confound their actions, that he was often styled *labrum imperatoris socius* [the companion of the emperor's labours]', Eliot continues:

> And does not this man do the like? Is it not in his whole practice? How often, how lately have we heard it? Did he not, in this same place, in this very Parliament, under colour of an explanation for the King, before the committees of both houses, do the same? Have not your lordships heard him also ever mixing and confusing the King and the State, not leaving a distinction between them? It is too, too manifest.[51]

There are other points in *Appius and Virginia* where Buckingham may also be alluded to in a fashion readily comprehended by Webster and Heywood's first audience. Two of the most likely occur in the first scene of the play, during the exchange between Appius and his kinsmen. Reproaching him for his apparent reluctance to accept appointment as a decemvir, they make it plain that they expect his appointment to 'So Eminent a place' to be 'a meanes | To raise your kindred' (I.i.30–1). Appius responds to their conviction, at his acceptance of office, that 'We are made for ever' (86), with a lengthy rebuke, which would seem to set him in contradistinction to Buckingham, whose nepotism was notorious and much resented, but Appius's high-flown assertion of impartiality is exposed by the aside of Marcus Clodius, who perceives its hypocritical nature (115–17), while the odd statement with which Appius concludes, with its reference to 'a masse of Pearle | Or Diamonds' (113–14) rather than the expected 'Gold' tipping the balance in the scales of justice, may involve an oblique reference to Buckingham's extreme ostentation of dress, and to his penchant for suits adorned with pearls and diamonds.[52]

Such coded allusions to Buckingham, established in the opening scene, would make others, later in the play, easily recognized. In I.iii, for example, Virginius, having pleaded passionately for the wages due to his troops but been put off with 'Hereafter' (rather as unpaid sailors were by Buckingham), rails against those who 'ne'er saw danger', who 'will not spare a *Drachma*' for 'us that stand betwixt them and disaster' (158, 165–6). One of the criticisms of Buckingham in Parliament (10 February and 11 March 1626) was that he had not led the disastrous Cadiz expedition in person, when it was his project.[53] Here, and at II.ii.51–3, where 1 Soldier unjustly rails against Virginius, speculating that 'belike hee'l turne | An usurer, and in the City aire | Cut poore mens throats at home sitting in's chaire', jibes at armchair generals would readily have been applied to Buckingham.

One further point should be noted. In the imperial tragedies, deriving from Tacitus, the deaths of the depraved tyrants cannot ensure a return to good government. Corruption, national and personal, is too endemic for that. In *Appius and Virginia*, on the other hand, as in Heywood's earlier *The Rape of Lucrece*, also taken from Livy, there is no such sense of widespread corruption. With wicked tyrants purged, these plays end optimistically, good government restored. The difference is fundamental, and sets *Appius and Virginia* apart from other Roman plays carrying more obviously coded messages for the England of the mid-1620s, such as *Nero*, *The Roman Actor* and *Julia Agrippina*.[54] Yet the differences should not obscure the similarities. Like these plays, *Appius and Virginia* is easily read as a commentary on the times, a commentary rendered all the more evident by the refusal of Webster and Heywood to distract themselves from the primary task of setting up an opposition between duty and self-indulgence, between those who serve the national interest and those who serve their own. The many curious features of the dramaturgy of *Appius and Virginia*, amounting, so it seems, to a deliberate avoidance of what might be expected in a play on this subject, such as emphasis on the love of Virginia and Icilius and greater development of the father–daughter relationship, seem to reinforce the sense that in this, the last of Webster's plays, there is, more than in any of his other plays, a political agenda.

1. William Archer, 'Webster, Lamb, and Swinburne', *New Review* 8 (1893), p. 105.
2. William Hazlitt, *Lectures on the Dramatic Literature of the Age of Elizabeth* (London, 1821), p. 114.
3. Lucas, III, 147.
4. Stoll, *Periods*, p. 40.
5. Brooke, p. 169.
6. Lucas, III, 134–45; H. D. Gray, '*Appius and Virginia*: by Webster and Heywood', *SP* XXIV (1927), pp. 275–89. MacD. P. Jackson has more recently confirmed and refined these conclusions: see pp. 498–9.
7. Lucas, III, 146.
8. Derek Traversi, *Shakespeare: The Roman Plays* (London, 1963), p. 10.
9. Murray, p. 252.
10. Ibid., p. 241.
11. Ibid., p. 242.
12. There is, however, a marked permeability between the public and private scenes, akin to that in *Julius Caesar*, where 'the public scenes tend to develop private concerns as well as public ones, and . . . the private scenes are simultaneously public ones in intent and result' (Marvin Spevack, ed., *Julius Caesar* [Cambridge, 1988], p. 17).
13. Murray, p. 245.
14. Forker, p. 210. It might be noted, *inter alia*, that in character terms Corbulo relieves Virginia, through his sexual innuendo, of any accusation of priggishness.
15. 'Some excuse there was for painting the People black, with a high-flying patrician of Coriolanus's stamp on one's hand for a hero: but with the tyrant Appius for villain there could be none' (Stoll, *Periods*, p. 194).
16. Seiden, p. 123.
17. Ibid., pp. 125–6.
18. Ibid., p. 126.
19. Ibid., p. 127.
20. Stoll, *Periods*, p. 194. Nor, indeed, are the plebeians in *Coriolanus* stinking, filthy, and brutal. See Anne Barton, 'Livy, Machiavelli and Shakespeare's *Coriolanus*', *Shakespeare Survey* XXXVIII (1985), pp. 115–29.
21. Lucas, III, 147.
22. Ranald, pp. 108–9.
23. Lucas, III, 228.
24. Seiden, p. 125.
25. Robert P. Griffin, *John Webster: Politics and Tragedy* (Salzburg, 1972), p. 47.
26. Seiden, p. 137.
27. Ibid., p. 134.
28. Ibid., pp. 134–5.
29. Ibid., p. 135.
30. Forker, p. 212.
31. Ranald, p. 108.
32. Forker, p. 211. The almost complete absence of soliloquies invites comparison with *Coriolanus*, where 'there is very little soliloquy in the play—only thirty-six lines in all—and what exists is significantly non-introspective, with a "strangely hobbled quality" that suggests discomfort with thought' (Parker, p. 71, quoting Carol M. Sicherman, '*Coriolanus*: the Failure of Words', *ELH* XXXIX [1972], p. 201).

33. Griffin, p. 141.

34. Parker, *Coriolanus*, p. 12.

35. Goldberg, p. 136

36. Ibid., p. 138.

37. E. K. Chambers, *William Shakespeare: A Study of Facts and Problems* (Oxford, 1930), I, 399.

38. Inga-Stina Ekeblad, 'Storm Imagery in *Appius and Virginia*', *N&Q* n.s. III (January 1956), pp. 5–7.

39. Griffin, p. 141.

40. Paul A. Cantor, *Shakespeare's Rome: Republic and Empire* (Ithaca, 1976), p. 30.

41. Ranald, p. 109.

42. Murray, p. 252.

43. Lucas, III, 125.

44. For a detailed account of Buckingham's unpopularity and its causes, see Lockyer, Chap. 8. Two passages in *Appius and Virginia* seem most particularly to suggest coded reference to current or recent events: 1 Soldier's reference (II.ii.37–8) to 'our pay detained | By those that are our Leaders' (precisely applicable to the notorious embezzlement of funds allocated to Mansfeld for the provisioning of his troops, but in no way to the Roman army's leadership), and his comment at IV.ii.38–9 that in their hunger the soldiers 'dine to day | As Dutch men feed their souldiers'. Of the latter Clifford Ronan comments: 'a well-placed anachronism lets a drama bear on pressing contemporary issues' (p. 23). Blair Worden, surveying the portrayal of 'Favourites on the English Stage', concludes that Buckingham was 'a theatrical target, most vividly and daringly perhaps' in Massinger's *The Maid of Honour* (1621–2), in which King James's favourite is 'unmistakably figured by the "state cata-mite" Fulgentio, the upstart and effeminate monopolist of favour and profit, under whose regime the nation has settled for a slothful peace abroad while the navy has fallen into neglect' (in *The World of the Favourite*, ed. J. H. Elliott and L. W. B. Brockliss [New Haven, 1999], p. 172).

45. Hans Werner, '*The Hector of Germanie, or The Palsgrave, Prime Elector* and Anglo-German relations of Early Stuart England: the View from the Popular Stage', in *The Stuart Court and Europe*, ed. R. Malcolm Smuts (Cambridge, 1996), p. 115 and n. 9.

46. See Ian Donaldson, *The Rapes of Lucretia: A Myth and its Transformation* (Oxford, 1982).

47. Martin Butler, 'Romans in Britain: *The Roman Actor* and the Early Stuart Classical Play', in *Philip Massinger: A Critical Reassessment*, ed. Douglas Howard (Cambridge, 1985), pp. 139–70.

48. Parker, *Coriolanus*, p. 6.

49. Lucas, III, 126, n. 1. On the authorship of *The Fair Maid of the Inn* see Cyrus Hoy, 'The Shares of Fletcher and His Collaborators in the Beaumont and Fletcher Canon (V)', *SB* XIII (1960), p. 102.

50. Butler, p. 165.

51. Gardiner, VI, 105–6.

52. See I.i.114–15n.

53. See Lockyer, p. 313 and I.iii.157–8n.

54. A clue to the greater caution of Webster and Heywood in coding their attack on Buckingham may be suggested by Heywood's insistence, in his *Apology for Actors*, on

the role of the playwright in maintaining social order. Plays, he wrote, were 'writ with this ayme, and carryed with this methode, to teach the subiects true obedience to their King, to shew the people the vntimely ends of such as haue moued tumults, commotions and insurrections, to present them with the flourishing estate of such as liue in obedience, exhorting them to allegeance, dehorting them from all trayterous and fellonious stratagems' (F3ᵛ). Equally, though, a clue to such an attack may be found in the fact that Heywood shared with Webster a fervent admiration of Prince Henry, Charles I's elder brother, who had died of typhoid in 1612, and on whom hopes of a militant Protestant policy had centred. That Buckingham himself favoured an aggressive anti-Catholic policy, through alliance with France against the Hapsburgs, counted for little when the French made their secret treaty with Spain and Buckingham's military expeditions ended in humiliation. See Kathleen McLuskie, 'Politics and Dramatic Form in Early Modern Drama', in J. R. Mulryne and Margaret Shewring, eds., *Theatre and Government under the Early Stuarts* (Cambridge, 1993), pp. 221–5.

Theatrical introduction

DAVID CARNEGIE

THE PATTERN OF THE PLAY

THE SCRIPT

Appius and Virginia, at approximately 2,100 lines, is short enough to be performed uncut.[1] Apart from a few confusions over minor characters which would have needed resolution in rehearsal (e.g., whether Sertorius or Valerius is sent for by Icilius in III.iii), the text is immediately playable.

Language and syntax are much less elaborately wrought than in Webster's earlier plays, and the major set speeches, such as Virginius's plea on behalf of his soldiers in I.iii, or the judgement and death speeches of V.ii, may be deliberately austere in keeping with the *romanitas* of the play. The Roman context is reinforced by references to senators, lictors, plebeians, and the use of Roman names, places, and gods. On the other hand, both Appius's intriguing with Marcus Clodius and the comedy of soldiers, lictors, and Corbulo the Clown are in the familiar idiom of Jacobean London. This is a world of kings, courtiers, chapels, Parliament, tilting staffs and heralds, as well as footmen, Frenchmen, Dutchmen, local London prisons, City usurers, and under-yeomen-fewterers.

PRODUCTION

Costuming on the Jacobean stage was a major visual feature of any play, but in *Appius and Virginia* the degree of Romanism is crucial. The three main possibilities appear to be that costume was contemporary, that it was a Renaissance version of Roman, or that it was a mixture of the two.

In the most detailed study to date of the dramaturgy of costume in the period, Jean MacIntyre cites the often-noted apparent anachronisms in *Julius Caesar*: 'A reference to Caesar's doublet in Act I implies that its characters wore Elizabethan dress.'[2] She goes on to enumerate the examples of costume reference implying contemporary rather than Roman garments, such as hats, cloaks, and gowns, and notes a similar reference to 'Renaissance accessories: silk stockings, ladies' masks and cork-soled shoes, rebatoes, billements (spangled headtires) and similar finery' in Heywood's *The Rape of Lucrece*.[3] The dress of the Senators becomes particularly significant in this context. Virginius prophesies that sword and slaughter will 'Chase the gown'd Senate through the streets of Rome, | To double dye their robes in Scarlet' (I.iii.131–2). Many other references from plays of the period seem to confirm that senators on stage normally wore scarlet gowns.[4] If so, and if the costuming was Jacobean, then the stage image of the Senate would be of an assembly of judges.[5] Such a grouping, insofar as it suggests corporate authority, may well seem a reasonable analogue to a Roman senate in a stage picture in which other men were wearing doublet and hose (sometimes with the addition of armour or military variation to their costume such as gorgets, scarves, and boots, or 'sogers cottes' for the ordinary soldiers, and the women conventional Jacobean garb).[6]

The robe in which Appius is attired to indicate his ascension to the decemvirate (as, in effect, the pre-eminent judge) may have had slightly different connotations. 'A robe was a ceremonial garment, worn with a crown for coronation', says MacIntyre, citing the royal implications of both Cleopatra and Caesar.[7] The implication is that Appius's ceremonial garment, especially when he is seated in state on the 'Judgment seat' (I.iii.108), would make him look, to a London audience, like a king surrounded by his judges or nobility.

Other scholars have put forward a contrary view: that plays may have been costumed in a fairly thoroughgoing Roman manner (or at least, Roman as the Renaissance understood its costuming). Arthur Humphreys, for instance, in his Oxford edition of *Julius Caesar*, draws together a number of studies to point out implications of the Henslowe inventory of a senator's gown and senators' capes, of 'Antique fashions' for plays at Oxford in 1655, for masque designs for Roman shaped breastplates, military skirts, and plumed helmets (see *Webster*, I, Fig. 3), and of the fact that doublets, cloaks, and hats may possibly refer to Roman articles of clothing.[8] MacIntyre notes that 'gown' was the word 'used in sixteenth-century dictionaries to translate Latin *toga*'.[9] And Clifford Ronan cites, in support of his contention that stage senators were dressed in a distinctively Roman style, a costume for a Garter investiture with sleeves 'wrought after the manner of a long pretext or senator's robe'. He adds that although historically senators had only a band of 'purpura' bordering

7. Renaissance Roman costume (drawing based on Shakespeare's *Titus Andronicus*, attributed to Henry Peacham).

their white togas, Renaissance authorities seem to have understood the 'Scarlet Gowne' of the Senate to have been entirely the colour of 'purple blood'.[10]

The Peacham drawing of *Titus Andronicus* (see Fig. 7) is usually interpreted as implying a 'mixed style' in which, as Anthony Miller expresses it, 'the leading male characters wore ancient costume (as it was visualised in the Renaissance), but that lesser characters, and all the female characters, "were simply costumed from the theatrical stock as well as could be managed"'.[11] Miller also acknowledges that the style may have been 'mixed' in terms of the costuming of individual leading male characters themselves, given what he takes to be the anachronistic references in *Julius Caesar* to doublets, hats, and cloaks.[12]

In either a purely Roman or a Peacham 'mixed style', the scarlet togas of the Senators are likely to be in more striking contrast both to Appius and to the military costumes of the soldiers than in a Jacobean costuming. This would have the effect of emphasizing the extraordinary pre-eminence of Appius, and of rendering even more striking the final scenes in which the civilian city and the camp (the army) combine forces to bring down the decemvirs. The playwrights' conception of soldiers who 'dine to day | As Dutch men feed their souldiers' (IV.ii.30–1) might

8. Officers with halberds, and musicians (1628 title-page woodcut from
The Counter-Ratt by R[obert] S[peed]).

well, however, include an expectation of their costuming and weaponry
matching their vocabulary.

The costume of the Lictors presents a special problem, since they seem
to have two distinct roles. Historically, lictors had the ceremonial function of entering in advance of magistrates, bearing the *fasces* as symbols of
authority, and stage directions in *Appius and Virginia* typically specify, e.g.,
'*Enter Appius, Oppius, Clodius, six Senators, Lictors*' (IV.i.48, Q SD). They
have a much more Jacobean London feel, however, in III.ii and III.iii
when they enter like sergeants or bailiffs to arrest Virginia with, presumably, halberds rather than fasces in their hands. Even in a partly classicized
'mixed style' such as the Peacham drawing, they are likely, perhaps, to
have looked like the officers depicted in *The Counter-Ratt* (see Fig. 8).

Linked also to the Jacobean world of prisons and law-courts is the
Orator (or, as he is identified in V.i in Q, the Advocate). His lawyer's
gown and English coif, like his mass of papers and his overblown rhetoric, associate him with Webster's equally contemporary lawyers in *The
White Devil* and *The Devil's Law-Case* in particular. It is hard to believe
that the picture was not completed with a lawyer's buckram bag.

Another costume that seems more likely than most to be Jacobean

9. A stage fool's costume, with long coat ('guarded' with horizontal bands of cloth)
and hat with coxcomb (1634 title-page woodcut from *A Maidenhead Well Lost*
by Thomas Heywood).

rather than Roman is that of the Clown playing the licensed fool
Corbulo. David Wiles has surveyed the limited evidence, and his findings
support the conclusion that from the early seventeenth century stage fools
would generally be identifiable by either a motley coat or a 'guarded' (i.e.,
with horizontal bands of cloth, usually indicating livery) version of the
idiot's plain long side-coat; either might be surmounted by a traditional
fool's cap (sometimes with a coxcomb), and perhaps elaborated with bells
at the elbows or with other conventional attributes (Fig. 9).[13] In a sense
his fool's costume will associate him neither with Rome nor with
Jacobean London, but with his anticipated dramaturgical role on stage.

One final costuming specification demands comment: the 'habit,
bond-slave like' (IV.i.207) which both Virginia and her father wear to the
trial. The wearing of *sordidatus* ('soiled and simple array') is drawn from
Livy (*Romane Historie*, p. 119), and the playwrights emphasize the visual
contrast they expected between the old worn clothes and the richer attire
the audience will have seen earlier. At the Victoria University production
in Wellington in 1999, the contrast was reinforced by having Virginia's
usual rich apparel include a lot of 'Jewels that she wore, | More worth
then all her Tribe' (IV.i.203–4).

The same Wellington production kept Virginius in his slave rags for the rest of the play, so that when the body of Virginia was brought on in V.iii (still in her ragged habit), the two were still visually associated. Alternatives to these choices would be possible, and might include the hasty provision of a toga or cloak and garland for Virginius as he is named consul at the end of the play, thus reversing the ceremonial ironies of the robing of Appius at the start.

The other major visual link between Virginius and Virginia is the blood shed at her death, blood which is still in evidence in IV.ii: '*Enter* VIRGINIUS *with his knife, that and his arms stript up to the elbowes all bloudy*' (IV.ii.74.1–.2). The phrase '*his arms stript*' indicates that his lower arms are bare, any sleeves 'stripped' (i.e., rolled up or removed). In the Wellington 1999 production his hand and arm were still bloody in V.ii, and therefore Icilius's reconciliation with him was visually difficult: 'I love your friendship; yes in sooth I do, | But wil not seale it with that bloody hand' (V.ii.95–6). Icilius visibly recoiled from the bloody proffered hand, and eventually put his own hand gently on the old soldier's shoulder instead. As in other plays by Webster and others (cf. *Webster*, I, 86–7), stage blood is a powerful element of the dramaturgy. In a Roman play it has added importance, as Clifford Ronan demonstrates in his extensive catalogue of both verbal and physical references: 'in the Early Modern view, Romans had an almost physical appetite for human gore—an insatiable urge that variously demonizes them, wraps them in pathos, or makes caricatures of them'.[14] The blood on Virginius's knife and arms will inevitably recall the bloodstained conspirators of *Julius Caesar* who 'bathe [their] hands in Caesar's blood, | Up to the elbows, and besmear [their] swords' (III.i.106–7). Virginia herself was already an icon of innocent bloodshed in art (see Fig. 10), and related to the even better-known imagery of the suicide of Lucrece. Virginia's martyrdom is further emphasized in V.iii by the blood flowing in the presence of the guilty party (cf. *Richard III*, I.ii.55–8).

Costume aside, most of the staging requirements are simple. Two doors would be sufficient to achieve the highly charged confrontation in V.ii between the Roman defenders (largely civilian) and the 'Camp' (in effect, an ahistorical Roman standing army in the early republic); but the absence of actual battles makes it easy to envisage production in a small playhouse such as the Phoenix (the Cockpit in Drury Lane). There is no call for the upper level, nor for a trap. A discovery space could be used to reveal Appius and Marcus Clodius as prisoners in V.iii, as Lucas imagined, but there is absolutely no necessity for such elaboration.

10. 'Virginius Killing his Daughter' (engraving by Georg Pencz, *c.* 1546).

The only major large property is the 'Judgment seat' (I.iii.108) which is, by implication, the *sella curulis*, the 'Ivory Chair' (V.iii.64) of kingship retained as a symbol of authority in early republican Rome. It may well, on the Jacobean stage, have been a state, a raised throne on a dais. Whether it would have been thrust forth only for the scenes for which it was required, or remained on stage throughout the play as a symbol of justice (as at Wellington 1999) is uncertain.

One or more than one dais may also have been used in the Senate scenes. Senators in plays of the period do normally sit; see, e.g., the business in Jonson's *Catiline* when Cato refuses to sit by Catiline (IV.142–68). The seats themselves may be cushions, as in *Coriolanus*, where two Officers enter '*to lay cushions, as it were in the Capitol*' (II.ii.0.1–.2); further references to cushions at III.i.103 and IV.vii.43 are clearly metaphors for the Senate, as Parker points out in his Oxford edition (not, as *OED* would have it, simply indicating luxury). Philip Brockbank suggests the cushions may have been of seat size, like the woolsack in Parliament.[15] The possible use of a dais is suggested by Chapman's *Caesar and Pompey*, where the 'Bench' (i.e., the place where the Consuls and Senators preside) seems to be up several steps ('degrees'):

> And where the Senate sit, are Ruffians pointed
> To keepe from entring the degrees that goe
> Vp to the Bench all others but the Consuls,
> *Caesar* and *Pompey*, and the Senators   (I.i.51–4)

The next scene is the Senate scene, and '*The Consuls enter the Degrees*' (I.ii.0.3–.4), and a few lines later other Senators '*Enter the Lists, ascend and sit*'. 'Lists' normally means 'the palisades or other barriers enclosing a space set apart for tilting' (*OED n.*[3] 9a), but here suggests a barrier with narrow entrances (where the appointed 'Ruffians' can monitor entry), and 'degrees': either tiered seating, or, more likely, steps like those of a dais up to the seats. In other words, Senators may have had stools, benches, chairs, or large cushions on one or more daises similar to that used for a state (or, in this play, for the 'Judgment seat' of Appius). This might imply a stage arrangement either like a bench of judges, or possibly two tiers facing each other, like the English Parliament. Chapman, however, was probably writing about twenty years earlier than *Appius and Virginia*, and for a boys' company with different conditions of performance; furthermore, it is unknown if his play was ever performed. We can draw no firm conclusions about whether such elaboration was common in Roman plays on stage.

11. 'Advance your Pike'; pike drill in three 'Motions' (engravings from
The Military Art of Trayning [1622]).

Other properties, apart from a table and a few chairs, are small. Some
are almost costume accoutrements, such as poniards, knives, and swords.
Prisoners are fettered. The soldiers have pikes (see Fig. 11) and possibly
Roman standards or flags (see IV.ii.51n), and probably wear military
gorgets and scarves.[16] They also need a knapsack, old bread, and maggoty
cheese. The officers, by contrast, have wine available at their parley in
V.ii, as is indicated in an unusual marginal note in Q opposite line 1
which may signal manuscript attention to stage requirements (cf. pp.
497–8). The purpose of the wine seems to be to demonstrate physically
and visually Virginius's feverish shaking, and Numitorius's sympathetic
care to assist him. Similar attention to the stage picture may lie behind the
entry direction for II.i that Marcus Clodius should enter *with presents*.
The presents are nowhere mentioned in the dialogue; the likelihood,
therefore, is that Marcus Clodius is still ruefully holding the presents
(perhaps elaborately wrapped, as at Wellington 1999) at the end of the
scene.

Petitions, depositions, and other legal papers constitute another entire
category of small props, and deadly they prove for Virginia and her
family. They may also have been comic, associated as they so often are in
Webster with an ignorant pompous lawyer (see Fig. 5).

Modern productions may choose to employ stage lighting effects to emphasize a number of polarities in the play: private and public spaces, indoor and outdoor, Rome and the camp, Appius with his confederates and Virginius with his family and allies. Lights are actually called for in III.i, in order to signal the night-time secrecy and danger of the meeting. They could be used in V.iii as well, to suggest the darkness of the 'deep dungeon' (V.iii.35).

Music is another area that supports the emotion of the play, most notably in trumpet flourishes for Senators and the armies, and in the very different music brought by Marcus Clodius to serenade Virginia in II.i (see Fig. 8 for a typical consort of the period). There would presumably have been entr'acte music also between each of the five acts into which the play's performance is divided.[17]

ACTING

Appius is the principal villain of the play, but the role is one of some complexity. And characterization apart, he is the motor which drives the plot until well into Act IV. Smooth hypocrisy in masking his early ambition is needed, and to cover his barefaced lying in the lead-up to the carefully fabricated trial. Surprisingly, however, the attitude of the Petitioners in II.iii implies that Appius is usually just to the oppressed; nor, apart from a sour denunciation by Marcus Clodius, when they are both in prison, of 'a thousand sentences | Wrongly denounc'd' (V.iii.29–30), is there evidence of bribery or other corruption. Lust, therefore, becomes a new and crucial impulse to power for Appius after the play has started. Significantly, his death is suicide in the Roman manner; he acknowledges his faults and in part redeems himself in the eyes of the Romans by the nobility of his death.

In deliberate contrast is the death of his tool Marcus Clodius. He does not accept his own guilt, grovels for mercy, and lacks the nobility to accept the offered suicide. He is never portrayed as other than a devious and amoral servant (who, he says, would prostitute his own wife or daughter to Appius), but he provides the intellect for the elaborate plotting. He is also, like Appius, an accomplished actor in public, and in I.i shares with the audience his pleasure in watching consummate deception.

In complete contrast, the bluff old campaigner Virginius is a sympathetic figure, endued with classical Roman virtues of simplicity, patriotism, bravery, and unshakeable principles. Unlike Appius and Marcus Clodius, whose speeches tend to be dialogue with others, Virginius has long speeches only occasionally interrupted, which suggests a more formal, almost archaic mode of utterance in keeping with his *gravitas* and *romanitas*. His typical position is surrounded by enemies: the Senate, rebellious soldiers, lawyers and judges. As was evident in the Wellington production in 1999, however, there is also great potential for tenderness with Virginia, and for extraordinary pathos with the soldiers and, subsequently, with Icilius late in the play. His portrayal can sustain in performance the sense of 'world weariness and desolation' that has arguably disappeared from the writing in the final moments of the play (see p. 467). Albeit Virginia is the eponymous heroine opposite Appius, Virginius has almost as many lines as Appius, and is the survivor at the end of the play.

Icilius, Virginius's son-in-law, and Minutius, his erstwhile commander, though different from each other in character, are equivalent in their supporting roles. Icilius is young, noble, but somewhat rash in confronting Appius. His support for Virginia is inadequate, therefore, since he cannot persuade Numitorius to protect her sufficiently. Icilius's suffering is parallel with, but has to be subordinated to, that of Virginius, on whom the dramatists place the primary tragic weight. Minutius, though not directly affected by the death of Virginia as Icilius is, plays a similar role. He is shown as not quite the soldier Virginius is (he cannot quell the mutiny), but of sufficient stature to recognize and support the virtues of Virginius, and ultimately to hand over his command so that Virginius and Icilius can combine the forces of camp and city against Appius.

Valerius is of much the same youth and rank as his kinsman Icilius (as may be Horatio, who by Act V is sharing a subordinate command with Valerius). His presence, therefore, lends pre-eminence to Icilius. The older generation is led by the cautious Numitorius. Just as his dignified belief in Roman virtue is a silent touchstone against which to measure Appius, so his deference and deep concern for his brother lend Virginius authority and humanity.

Among the antagonists to Virginius, the Orator has a bravura part in IV.i, and much of it is comic pomposity and verbosity in the same mode as Contilupo in *The Devil's Law-Case*. More than any other character in the scene, he can play to the audience. His role in V.i is somewhat different, much more concerned with verbal quips and performing as a butt for anti-lawyer satire.

Verbal comedy is also the strength of the Clown, Corbulo, and the same actor may possibly have played both. Corbulo is kept almost entirely external to the plot, however, and is given joking that is almost totally Jacobean rather than Roman. What is not evident in the text is the extent to which this may have been an opportunity for elaborate physical business as well. The Clown in the 1999 Wellington production not only darted about the stage with much gestural amplification of meaning and innuendo, but also played direct to the audience whenever possible. The Nurse often serves as Corbulo's foil, and can therefore earn a number of laughs as well, especially in resentment of Corbulo's bawdy.

Further comedy, both verbal and physical, comes from 1 and 2 Soldiers, 1 and 2 Lictors, and 1 and 2 Serving-men (probably all played by the same actors). Great play, for instance, can be made with the hard bread and maggoty cheese. There is a danger, however, if the soldiers who mutiny in II.ii are allowed so much comedy as to weaken the significance of Virginius facing them down single-handed.

Among the female characters, only Virginia is of any significance to the plot and theme, and she has few lines with which to assert herself. With neither Icilius nor Virginius does she reveal an interiority that makes her live on the page (cf. pp. 453–4). Nevertheless, in performance her symbolic importance as an icon of innocence and virtue is humanized, and she can be powerful in her silent awareness and resistance. At Wellington in 1999 her affection for her father was particularly marked by long holding of his hands and gazing into his eyes (and in that production, indeed, she took the initiative, based on the line 'take the life you gave me' [IV.i.32], in urging a reluctant Virginius to kill her). In addition, her body on stage in the final scene, with her wounds bleeding afresh, emphasizes her thematic centrality as the martyr whose death brought about the political cleansing of Rome.

Of the extras who create a wider sense of Rome, it is perhaps worth mentioning the Senators. They seem in the play to be conflated with the decemvirs, and the ambiguity of their position is increased by the absence of any reference to the nine members of the decemvirate additional to Appius. In performance, therefore, they may appear to be the aristocracy of Rome, naturally siding with the arrogant authority assumed by Appius, or they may, rather, appear weak yes-men with no will other than to flatter their overlord. Either way, they are live actors in performance, and their demeanour will have a bearing on how the play is perceived by the audience.

STAGE HISTORY

THE ORIGINAL PRODUCTIONS

The dating of *Appius and Virginia* is uncertain, and nothing is known of the play's first performance. By 1639 *Appius and Virginia* was in the possession of William Beeston and the King and Queen's Young Company ('Beeston's Boys' at the Cockpit in Drury Lane), as we know from the Lord Chamberlain's edict of 10 August that year forbidding any other company to perform the play.[18] Although there is no direct evidence that William Beeston's father Christopher, who died in 1638, had *Appius and Virginia* in the repertory of Queen Henrietta's Men, it may be worth noting that *A Cure for a Cuckold* went to one of Beeston's companies (see pp. 290–1), and that by 1631 Christopher Beeston had *The White Devil* at the Cockpit (or Phoenix),[19] and *The Devil's Law-Case* was in the repertoire of Beeston's Queen Anne's Men.[20] If the dating of *Appius and Virginia* to the mid-1620s is correct, therefore, it is not unlikely that the play was written for one of Christopher Beeston's companies.[21]

Whichever company first presented the play may have found its acting resources strained. Using the assumptions about casting and doubling elaborated in *Webster*, I (98–100, 426–7), it is apparent that most of *Appius and Virginia* would be easily accommodated by ten principal actors, six hired men, and four boys. The trial scene (IV.i), however, in combination with IV.ii which follows it, has heavier demands, and is what David Bradley calls a 'limiting scene'. Bradley himself calculates a minimum required adult cast of twenty-one.[22] But such a much higher number of adult actors than the approximately sixteen which is so often the norm for other plays, and is sufficient for most of the rest of this play, justifies close scrutiny of how doubling might be managed.

Bradley's cast of twenty-one adults is presumably based on IV.i requirements of all the principal roles except Minutius and Corbulo being on stage until the end (i.e., Oppius, Appius, Marcus Clodius, Numitorius, Icilius, Valerius, Virginius, and Horatio); and in addition '*six Senators*' and the Orator entering with at least two '*Lictors*' (IV.i.48 SD), for a total of seventeen. To this total must then be added 1 Soldier and 2 Soldier, who, since they enter at the start of IV.ii, cannot be on stage to the end of IV.i; Minutius, who enters soon after in IV.ii; and Corbulo, whose Clown part in the play appears to be over; for a total of twenty-one. The musicians in II.i are not included in this count of actors. Nor is the ghost character '*Spurius*', whose name precedes '*Opius*' in the I.iii.59.1 entry direction (Q

SD), since this seems to be a misreading, as two characters, of Livy's 'Sp. Oppius' (*Romane Historie*, pp. 116, 120, 128).

The total can easily be reduced to nineteen by having Minutius play a Senator, and by doubling Corbulo and the Orator. For a supporting principal role to be doubled with a mute Senator would be even easier than, e.g., Delio doubling a Madman in *The Duchess of Malfi* (cf. *Webster*, I, 426). However, to suggest having the company clown doubling the Orator in IV.i and V.i raises the question of whether clowns ever doubled. David Wiles finds 'no evidence that Kemp ever doubled (in the sense of changing character and role-name)'.[23] King, however, assumes that the clown role was doubled with a different named character in plays later than Kemp such as *Othello*, *Hamlet*, and *Macbeth*.[24] Certainly the end of Corbulo's role in III.v corresponds neatly (given the act break) with the appearance of the comic Orator in IV.i. It is even possible that Corbulo's elaborate joking in his final speech about 'a new Role' (III.v.61–2) refers to the Clown's imminent assumption of a new character.

A further reduction to seventeen is not impossible, though it would have required some very rapid doubling of the sort that playwrights and plotters seem usually to have been at pains to avoid. The particular problem here would be that every adult actor in the company would be on stage until the end of IV.i (Minutius as a Senator, the Clown now the Orator, plus hired men playing five Senators and two Lictors). Then two hired men would have to get offstage and doff senatorial or lictorial costume or props quickly enough, under cover of the dramatic confusion of Virginius's flight and the time taken for a general exeunt, to appear as the pair of comic Soldiers at the start of IV.ii.

This possible cast of seventeen allows the rest of the play to operate smoothly with a little doubling for the actors of Valerius and Horatio, and a satisfactory pattern for the hired men. Valerius and Horatio could double both Cousins in I.i and both Petitioners in II.iii, and Horatio would be available to be one of the '&c.' (presumably a Senator) called for at I.iii.59.1 (Q SD), if needed. The two hired men who play 1 Soldier and 2 Soldier in II.ii and IV.ii and in Act V could retain their comic pairing for 1 and 2 Lictor in III.ii and III.iii, and the two Serving-men in III.v, as well as being available as Senators when needed. Of the other five hired men, one is needed as the Lieutenant in I.i and II.ii, possibly as the 'Roman' in IV.ii, and as the speaking Senator in V.i, while the other four make up Soldiers 3 to 6 in II.ii and IV.ii, as well as providing two Lictors and two Senators in IV.i and other scenes. Four Lictors are present throughout III.ii and III.iii; one of the other hired men, who may play the Servant in I.ii, can be Sertorius in III.iii, and another can be Appius's Secretary in III.iii and his Servant in III.iv.

It is surprising that the '*six Senators*' of IV.i appear not to be all the same hired men who play the '*six Souldiers*' at the start of II.ii (since two of the Soldiers must be Lictors in IV.i). Since this might indicate either a careless recollection by the playwrights of how they had plotted their resources at that stage (and hence is a problem that would have been solved by the plotter or in rehearsal by, for instance, reducing the number of Senators in IV.i), or, since it is the only scene with so many actors, a deliberate decision may have been made to bring in extra mute actors (e.g., gatherers, tire-men, boys) for this scene alone.[25] If so, we should examine whether the rest of the play could be acted, as so many were, with a cast of only sixteen adult actors.

The answer is yes, but only with a number of provisos. Valerius (or Horatio) would have to double the Lieutenant in I.i and II.ii. The speech prefix '*Val.*' in Q at II.ii.94 raises the possibility that this is what happened. In that case he could not pair with Horatio for minor roles, and one of the hired men would have to become 2 Cousin and 2 Petitioner. This is made possible by the exit of the Soldiers and Lieutenant before the end of II.ii, allowing them time to change costume. (This early exit was probably needed anyway, in order to assist two other Soldiers to switch to Lictors for II.iii.) The 'Roman' of IV.ii would have to be one of the six Soldiers raised from the ranks, although promoting the Lieutenant would seem dramatically preferable, and the number of Soldiers in V.ii would have to be reduced by one in order to provide the Senator in V.i and the Attendant with wine in V.ii. And, of course, extra mute actors would need to be brought in as Senators in IV.ii.

The women's roles, two speaking and two mute, require four boy actors, since all four are on stage for IV.ii.

Whatever the size of the original cast, the likely prominence of the two men who probably played 1 and 2 Soldiers, 1 and 2 Lictors, and 1 and 2 Serving-men is notable. (It seems unlikely they played the Cousins in I.i or the Petitioners in II.iii, since those roles do not appear to be written for comedy.) The audience would obviously see a pair of comic actors switching about between rather similar roles, and the personalities of the actors would presumably become more significant than the characters impersonated. The principal roles, however, with very little doubling (apart from the likely Corbulo/Orator switch), do not draw self-conscious theatrical attention to themselves in the same way.

The staging requirements of *Appius and Virginia* are very simple. There is no call for an upper level, nor for the trap; a discovery may be intended to reveal Appius and Marcus Clodius as prisoners at the start of V.iii, but it is not essential. In fact only two doors are needed to serve the requirements of the play (unless a larger central space was needed from which to thrust forth the ivory chair on a raised dais which is frequently implied as an essential property for Appius). Where the Senators sit when they are on stage is, as has been discussed above, uncertain.

RESTORATION PRODUCTIONS

Pepys seems to have seen *Appius and Virginia* on 12 May 1669: 'After dinner my wife and I to the Duke of York's playhouse, and there, in the side balcony, over against the musick, did hear, but not see, a new play, the first day acted, "The Roman Virgin", an old play, and but ordinary, I thought.' That this 'new play' *The Roman Virgin* was the 'old play' *Appius and Virginia* seems confirmed by a new issue of the 1654 Quarto in 1679 with a new title-page. It reads 'Appius and Virginia, Acted at the Dukes Theater under the name of The Roman Virgin Or Unjust Judge, A Tragedy'. John Downes, however, ascribes the play to Thomas Betterton:

> The Unjust Judge, or *Appius Virginia*, done by the same Author. *Virginius Acted* by *Mr. Betterton*, Appius, the Unjust Judge, by *Mr. Harris*: Virginia, by *Mrs. Betterton*. And all the other Parts *Exactly* perform'd, it lasted Successively 8 Days, and very frequently *Acted* afterwards.[26]

Bentley believes that Betterton is more likely to have revised Webster and Heywood's play than to have written a new one, but suggests that the 1679 reissue of *Appius and Virginia* was an attempt to capitalize on the popularity of Betterton's adaptation. Bentley also believes that Betterton's version may have been independently published, citing Gerald Langbaine:

> *And* Appius and Virginia, *written by* Webster, *is afterwards ascribed to T.B. though as the deceased Comedian Mr.* Cartwright, *a Bookseller by Profession, told me, 'twas onely the old Play Reprinted, and Corrected by the above-mentioned* Mr. Batterton; *with several others.*[27]

Equally likely, however, is that Betterton never did more than adapt *Appius and Virginia* for stage presentation, and that Cartwright was simply explaining to Langbaine that the 1679 reissue was essentially Webster's play (which may well have come to be associated with Betterton through playbills and performance rather than a printed text).[28]

At all events, *Appius and Virginia* apparently suited a Restoration taste for neo-classical tragedy. With the leading actor of the period taking the role of Virginius, and his talented wife playing Virginia, we may assume that the pathos of her death, and the anguish of the parricide, were powerfully performed.

SUBSEQUENT PRODUCTIONS

No professional productions since the Restoration are known. A student production at Victoria University of Wellington in 1999 made a raised *sella curulis*, the ivory chair of justice of early Rome (cf. p. 483), the central set element within arena staging which had the tiered audience looking down into an acting pit as if for Colosseum blood sports. Romanized costume, brass fanfares, and programme material about the rape of Lucrece, ensured a historical and critical distance.

The portrayal of Virginia was of particular importance, as the director focused attention on the question of her limited control over her own destiny. A highly developed set of extra-textual (and even counter-textual) actions made clear that Virginia felt betrayed and isolated by Icilius and Numitorius; and she herself carried the hidden knife for her death in IV.i, and in silent action persuaded the deeply emotional Virginius, despite his initial refusal, to use it on her. Her characterization, therefore, became utterly central to the production, and foregrounded questions about the use of female chastity as a political counter, whether in Rome, Jacobean England, or now.

The production was in other respects a straightforward reading of the play, and demonstrated, for instance, the authority given Appius by his robing and elevation to the *sella curulis*, the helplessness felt by senators and honest men such as Numitorius at the growing centralization of power, and the typically Websterian development of the striking trial scene in IV.i. The confrontation of the two armies and their hostages and spokesmen in Act V was also powerful, and made deeply moving the plight of the man who had killed his daughter for the good of Rome.[29] The play proved its stageworthiness.

1. See Andrew Gurr, 'Maximal and Minimal Texts of Shakespeare', *Shakespeare's Globe Research Bulletin* 4 (April 1998).
2. MacIntyre, p. 178.
3. Ibid., pp. 258-9.
4. Ronan, p. 78.
5. For the dress of an English judge see *DLC* IV.i.51.1n. Heywood's *The Silver Age* refers to 'hels Iudges in their scarlet robes' (III.i [H2ʳ]), and Dekker's *The Virgin Martyr*, in reference to a Roman judge, 'The scarlet robe of bold authority' (I.i.173). Lucas's

supposition 'that Webster would think of the Alderman's red of the London City Fathers' (Lucas, I.iv.75n) also seems at odds with their usual dress of calaber [fur] cloaks (cf. I.iv.55n).

6. See MacIntyre, pp. 166, 294, and Henslowe, *Diary*, p. 317.
7. MacIntyre, p. 179.
8. Arthur Humphreys, ed., *Julius Caesar* (Oxford, 1984), Introduction, pp. 50–1. He notes an occurrence of 'doublet' in North's Plutarch.
9. MacIntyre, p. 302.
10. Ronan, pp. 76–9.
11. Anthony Miller, ed., *Julius Caesar* (Marrickville, N.S.W., 1996), Introduction, p. 6, quoting John Astington.
12. Ibid., p. 6.
13. David Wiles, *Shakespeare's Clown: Actor and Text in the Elizabethan Playhouse* (Cambridge, 1987), pp. 182–91.
14. Ronan, p. 134.
15. Philip Brockbank, ed., *Coriolanus*, Arden Shakespeare (London, 1976), note to II.ii.0.1 SD.
16. MacIntyre, p. 166, notes that the gorget was on occasion 'symbolic of full armor'.
17. See Taylor.
18. Bentley, I, 330–1 and V, 1246.
19. See *Webster*, I, 108.
20. See pp. 45–6.
21. See Gurr 1996, pp. 404–5, 419; for the relationship between Heywood and Beeston, see Bentley, IV, 556.
22. Bradley, pp. 21, 243.
23. Wiles, *Shakespeare's Clown*, p. 90.
24. King 1992, pp. 206, 208, 210, 220, 222, 227.
25. See Bradley, p. 42.
26. John Downes, *Roscius Anglicanus* (1708), p. 30.
27. *Momus Triumphans* (1688), Preface, A2ᵛ; cited in Bentley, V, 1248.
28. A similar conclusion is reached by Judith Milhous in 'Thomas Betterton's Playwriting', *Bulletin of the New York Public Library* LXXVII, 4 (Summer 1974), pp. 375–85, esp. pp. 383–4.
29. A fuller description of this production may be found in *Research Opportunities in Renaissance Drama* (XL (2001), pp. 104–6).

Textual introduction

MacDonald P. Jackson

FIRST PUBLICATION

The sole Quarto of *Appius and Virginia* was printed for Richard Marriot, to whom it was entered in the Stationers' Register on 13 May 1654. It survives in no fewer than five issues, with successive cancels replacing the original title leaf.[1] The first and second issues are dated 1654; the third—extant in only two copies—is dated 1655; the fourth is dated 1659 and names as publisher Humphrey Moseley, to whom the rights had been transferred on 11 June 1659; and the fifth, proclaiming that the tragedy had been acted at the Duke's Theatre under the name of *The Roman Virgin or Unjust Judge*, is as late as 1679. Thomas Betterton had adapted and retitled the play for a revival in 1669, but the text of 1679 remains that of the sole seventeenth-century edition.[2] The collation is A1 B–H⁴ I⁴ (–I4), the dialogue beginning on B1ʳ and ending on I3ʳ. The printer, not named on the title-page, has been identified as Thomas Maxey, who is known to have printed several of Marriot's publications during the period 1651–5.[3]

Jackson subjected the Quarto to detailed bibliographical analysis.[4] He showed that a single skeleton was used for the printing of sheets B–E, inner and outer formes alike; that this skeleton also machined both formes of G and the outer formes of H and I; but that a second skeleton was introduced to machine both formes of F and the inner formes of H and I. The introduction of a second skeleton coincided with a change in the compositorial pattern, since two men shared the typesetting of sheets B–E, while all, or almost all, of the pages in sheets F–I were set by only one of these men. Compositor A preferred 'do', 'go', 'I'l', '-ness', '-l' in words of more than one syllable, and spellings without final '-e' in various other common words and phonetic combinations; he always set '*Clod.*' as the speech prefix for Marcus Clodius, except for one instance of '*Clo.*' in a full line; and he frequently employed insufficient spacing between a speech prefix and the dialogue that followed. Compositor B preferred

494

'doe', 'goe', 'I'le' or 'Ile', '-nesse', '-ll' in words of more than one syllable, and spellings with final '-e' in those further words and phonetic combinations from which Compositor A regularly omitted '-e'; he always set some form other than '*Clod.*' in speech prefixes for Marcus Clodius; and he was more careful than Compositor A about providing desirable spacing. Compositor A's avoidance of final '-e' makes the spelling in his stints seem more 'modern'. The division of labour appears to have been as follows:

Compositor A: C1^r–C2^r, C4^v, D2^v–D3^r, D4^r–E1^v, F1^v–G4^v, H1^v–I3^r
Compositor B: B1^v–B4^r, C2^v–C4^r, D1^r–D2^r, E2^v–E4^v
Doubtful: B1^r, B4^v, D3^v, E2^r, F1^r, H1^r

It is conceivable that the doubtful D3^v and H1^r, which each fall within a long series of pages attributable to Compositor A, were set by a third workman. It is unsurprising that B1^r, the opening page of text, is anomalous: Compositor B probably set it, without at first imposing his own preferences. The other doubtful pages intervene between a group of pages clearly assignable to Compositor A and a group of pages clearly assignable to Compositor B. Perhaps each of these three doubtful pages (B4^v, E2^r, and F1^r) was set by the man who set the immediately following pages, and he again took a while to reassert his preferences as he began a new stint; or the setting of some pages may have been shared; or in these pages also a third compositor may have been involved. The significant point is that, with the exception of only half a dozen pages, the stints of two compositors can confidently be disentangled, so that linguistic and bibliographical minutiae bearing no relation to the compositorial pattern must derive from their manuscript copy, and may well serve to identify the shares of collaborating authors.

Collation of all available copies of the Quarto reveals a handful of trivial press variants in outer G and in a single page (B4^r) of inner B. The uncorrected readings of inner B are found only in the Library of Congress copy, which, with the New York Public Library copy, is one of only two with outer G in the uncorrected state.

PRINTER'S COPY

Not surprisingly, given its date, the Quarto lacks any motto, dedication, preliminary address, or list of dramatis personae. It is, however, divided into acts (though not scenes), with the headings '*Actus Primus Scena Prima*', and so on, and each act but the last (followed by '*FINIS*') ends with the '*Explicit Actus* . . .' formula, which is a likely pointer to Thomas Heywood's part-authorship of the tragedy.[5] The Quarto requires little substantive emendation, and, although lines of verse are not capitalized, most are set out correctly, mislineation being confined to the printing of a few short patches of prose as verse and to occasional instances of the kind of local disruption seen in the play's second speech, where the first four words of the Lictor's 'He is, my Lord, and will attend | your Lordships presently' (B1ʳ) should complete Minutius's 'with the decree o'th' Senate', with the Lictor's remaining words forming a regular iambic pentameter. Like *A Cure for a Cuckold*, *Appius and Virginia* distinguishes i/j and u/v phonetically, in the modern manner.

Nearly all essential entries and exits are provided—or, in the case of exits, are sufficiently implicit in the dialogue for the actor to get himself offstage—and nearly all speeches are accurately assigned, but there are some errors and ambiguities. Corbulo the Clown is variably '*Corbulo*' (or '*Corb.*') and '*Clown*' (or '*Clowne*' or '*Clo.*') in stage directions and speech prefixes. The Quarto's one '*Cl.*' and seven '*Clo.*' speech prefixes for Marcus Clodius could cause confusion with the Clown, but the abbreviated forms may have been introduced by Compositor B. There is potential ambiguity in the frequent abbreviations for Virginius and Virginia, both usually '*Virg.*', even when present in the same scene, but the compositors, presumably following their manuscript copy, printed the full forms at those points where a reader might be in genuine doubt whether father or daughter should speak.[6] On C1ᵛ the stage direction has Virginius enter where Virginia is required, but the error may well have been the compositor's. Lucas argued strongly for the reassignment to Appius of five words attributed by the Quarto to Numitorius at IV.i.56 (F4ᵛ), but in assessing the evidence in our commentary we conclude that emendation is unwarranted. On F1ᵛ '*Enter Valerius*' is wrong, since it is Sertorius who has been called for on E4ᵛ and is dismissed on F2ᵛ. Also, Minutius evidently has a Lieutenant, who is not Valerius and who is omitted from entry directions. An Orator in IV.i (G1ʳ–G3ʳ), where he is given no entry, becomes, somewhat anachronistically, an Advocate in V.i (H2ᵛ–H3ʳ).

Minor characters are often designated by a number: '1', '2', and so on, followed by a generic title, such as '*Cozen*', '*Petitioner*', or '*Serving.*' (for Serving-man). In three scenes numbers alone are used: in II.ii '*six Souldiers*' are given numerals in speech prefixes; in III.ii two of '*foure Lictors*' speak alternately as '1' and '2'; and in IV.ii '*two Souldiers*' are indicated in the same way. The total number of Soldiers who speak and the correct assignment of speeches among them are far from obvious, and our solution necessitates adjustment to an exit direction in IV.ii.[7]

The imperfections mentioned so far are of a kind traditionally associated with a playwright's 'foul papers', rather than with scripts prepared for performance, but they might not be considered intolerable in a seventeenth-century theatrical 'book' of the play. But certain descriptive directions seem clearly authorial, notably: '*Enter Virginius with his knife, that and his arms stript up to the elbowes all bloudy; coming into the midst of the souldiers, he makes a stand*' (H1^r). Appius enters '*melancholly*' on B3^r, as does Corbulo on F3^r. Icilius enters '*troubled*' on D2^r. Corbulo enters '*whispering Virginia, after her M. Clodius with presents*' on C2^r: Marcus Clodius's entry here is inconsistent with the direction some twenty-five lines later, '*Enter Clodius and Musicians*'; we have assumed that Marcus Clodius and the Musicians lurk in the background and come forward at the later point. On F4^r both Virginius and Virginia enter '*like a slave*', and on H1^r '*the first mutinous Souldier*' enters '*in haste*'. On I1^r '*Enter Appius, and Marcus Clodius, fettered and gyved.*' In an entry direction on B4^r various Senators and Lictors are indicated by a vague '*&c*', as are extras by '*others*' on H3^v. The number of Lictors entering is indefinite on B1^r, B2^r, D2^v, and F4^v, though four are specified on E2^v and E3^r (see also pp. 488–90). On B2^v '*Enter a Servant, whispers Icilius in the eare*', spread over three lines against the right-hand margin, begins a line too late.

One feature of the Quarto that may tell against a theatrical origin for the printer's copy is the tendency in some scenes for very short speeches that continue a line of verse to occupy the same line as the preceding speech ending. As Greg explained, 'In all manuscripts intended for stage use every speech begins a fresh line of writing, irrespective of metrical divisions', prefixes being placed in the left margin and speeches being separated by short horizontal rules.[8] The untheatrical setting out of some speeches so as to share a line occurs in the stints of both compositors and in various positions on the pages, which are seldom unduly crowded. It may, nevertheless, have been a printing-house strategy for, as it were, 'justifying' a page, so as to fit a predetermined amount of copy within a given number of type lines. Yet the practice is characteristic of Webster in all three of his unaided plays, and—to anticipate the question of authorship—in *Appius and Virginia* it is confined to scenes in which there are other strong indications of Webster's hand.

There are, however, a few marginal directions suggestive of a book-keeper's annotations. On H3^v '*Wine*', against the right-hand margin, comes ten short speeches before Virginius actually calls 'Wilt a, wilt a give me some Wine?' The marginal '*Song*', twice on C2^{v}, and '*A Shout*' on D1^{r} and I2^{r} may have had a similar provenance.

Evidence for the nature of the printer's copy is inconclusive, but consistent with authorial papers, which may have received some attention from the book-keeper (or 'prompter'), whether or not they served as the actual playbook.

AUTHORSHIP

In referring to 'authorial papers' we have avoided the question of how many authors were involved. The Quarto title-page ascribes the tragedy to John Webster alone, but since 1913, when Rupert Brooke argued that Webster had done no more than revise two scenes (I.i and IV.i) of a play written by Thomas Heywood, most scholars have regarded it as a work of collaboration between the two dramatists.[9] Brooke certainly exaggerated the extent of Heywood's responsibility. Lucas found traces of Webster in almost every scene, but accepted that Heywood had contributed substantially to the finished product.[10] His case for Heywood's participation rested mainly on the citation of verbal parallels.

Jackson reviewed the findings of later commentators and sought to reinforce and refine them with bibliographical data.[11] He searched all Webster's and Heywood's unaided plays for linguistic discriminators between the two dramatists—their preferences in the use of contractions, expletives, and connectives. While Heywood favoured very few forms that were not also used by Webster, Webster was partial to several that Heywood used sparingly or avoided altogether. In *Appius and Virginia* the highest concentration of Webster forms was found within I.ii, II.ii, Lucas's III.ii (our III.ii and III.iii), Lucas's III.iii (our III.iv), IV.i, IV.ii, and Lucas's V.i (our V.i and V.ii). The infrequency of Webster's favourites in certain scenes assigned by Lucas and others to Heywood, together with the presence of 'betwixt', 'whilst', and 'tush'—more characteristic of Heywood than of Webster—confirms the play's dual authorship. Lucas listed twenty-two words in *Appius and Virginia* that he considered typical of Heywood's latinate diction.[12] Only four of these occur within the scenes listed above as showing most linguistic evidence of Webster, although these constitute some 58 per cent of the play; and three of the Heywoodian words are confined to a short passage in the middle of IV.ii (68–90), whereas linguistic pointers to Webster's hand in this scene accumulate within the first and last forty lines. It cannot be coincidental that Heywood's diction clusters in portions of the text free from Webster's linguistic traces.

Corbulo the amiable punster seems to have been Heywood's creation. He is always named (either in full or in abbreviated form) in speech prefixes in II.i, III.i, and III.v, and although in II.i and III.i he enters as '*Clown*' (C2^r and D4^v), he exits II.i as '*Corbulo*' (C2^v), and in III.v he enters as 'Corbulo *the Clowne*' (F3^r). The linguistic evidence supports the generally held view that II.i, III.i, and III.v are predominantly Heywood's scenes. In III.iii, in contrast, Corbulo not only enters as '*Clowne*' but is designated '*Clown*' (or '*Clow.*' or '*Clo.*') in speech prefixes, and in this scene, which, along with the short III.ii, exhibits a wealth of diverse linguistic indicators of Webster's presence, the unnamed character adopts a markedly more satirical, Websterian vein.

The writers of the two largest, most comprehensive studies of Webster are in substantial agreement about Webster's and Heywood's shares in the collaboration. Fernand Lagarde attributed to Webster, 'sans réserve', I.i, I.ii, II.ii, III.ii, III.iii, III.iv, IV.i, V.i, and V.ii (as they are in our edition), and thought that he had taken some part in other scenes as well.[13] Charles R. Forker endorses an emerging consensus: 'This gives Webster credit for planning the play and for most of the writing, but it allows Heywood a minor share, most noticeably in I.iii–iv, II.i, III.i, IV.ii, and V.ii'—this last scene being our V.iii.[14] The linguistic data presented by Jackson support these conclusions, except in I.i, which, though markedly Websterian in style, exhibits few linguistic or bibliographical signs of his hand, while using Heywood's connectives 'betwixt' and 'whilst'. Jackson tentatively suggested that Heywood began copying out the play, the first five scenes of the printer's manuscript copy being in his handwriting, but that thereafter the handwriting of the authorial papers alternated with dominant authorship. But there are insufficient grounds for discounting the possibility that the whole manuscript was a transcript of the joint papers, made either by Heywood or by a scribe. This would account for the rarity of Webster's 'o'th'' and 'a'th'' in the Quarto, but their absence might equally well be due to normalization in the mid-seventeenth-century printing-house. As 'o'th'' occurs in the second line of the play, and 'at th'' in the fourteenth, it seems likely that Compositor B, after showing initial tolerance of 'o'th'' and partial tolerance of 'a'th'', normalized to 'of the', and that Compositor A normalized throughout his stints.

SUBSEQUENT EDITIONS

The five issues of the original Quarto (1654–79) were not followed by later seventeenth-century editions. Dilke edited it in the sixth volume

(1815) of his selection of *Old English Plays*, making most of the necessary emendations to the dialogue and being, for a nineteenth-century editor, unusually generous in supplementing the Quarto's stage directions. Dilke and Dyce (1830, 1857) between them made almost all desirable changes to the Quarto lineation. Hazlitt (1857), and Lucas (1927) included the tragedy in their collections of Webster's works, Lucas displaying his customary accuracy and astuteness. Lucas failed to collate Dilke's edition and ignored Thorndike's (1912), which had added nothing of editorial value. *Appius and Virginia* is in Dyce's volume II, Hazlitt's III, and Lucas's III. The main contribution of the present text lies in its clarification of the characters' comings and goings and their interactions on stage.

1. Greg, *Bibliography*, II, 733, recorded five issues. The revised Wing *Short-Title Catalogue* distinguishes between the Princeton and Library of Congress copies of the 1655 issue, numbering them as W1217 and W1217A, but their title-pages are in fact identical. The Library of Congress copy does have two formes in an earlier state of press correction than other surviving copies. Wing uses the formula 'Anr. ed.' to refer to what, in strict bibliographical terms, is simply a separate issue. Wing's second issue is Greg's first, and vice versa. There appears to be no decisive evidence to determine the correct sequence, but more of the third issue's typographical features are shared with Wing's second issue than with its first.
2. See p. 491.
3. Jackson 1985.
4. Ibid. and Jackson 1998, which offers further spelling evidence for determining the stints of two compositors.
5. Jackson 1999.
6. See IV.i.56–62n.
7. See IV.ii.32.1n and IV.ii.35n.
8. Greg, *Documents*, II, 207.
9. Rupert Brooke, 'The Authorship of the Later *Appius and Virginia*', *MLR* VIII (1913), pp. 433–53; expanded as an appendix to his book (1916).
10. Lucas, III, 134–5.
11. Jackson 1985.
12. Lucas, III, 137.
13. Fernand Lagarde, *John Webster* (Toulouse, 1968), I, 299.
14. Forker, p. 202.

APPIUS

AND

VIRGINIA.

A

TRAGEDY.

BY
J O H N   W E B S T E R,

LONDON,
Printed for *Rich. Marriot,* in S. *Dunſtans*
Church-Yard *Fleet-ſtreet,* 1654.

12. Title-page of *Appius and Virginia* (1654).

[Dramatis personae
(in order of appearance)

Minutius (a General)
Oppius (a Senator)
Appius (appointed one of the Decemviri)
Two Cousins of Appius
Marcus Clodius (secretary to Appius)
Numitorius (brother to Virginius)
Icilius (betrothed to Virginia)
Virginia (daughter of Virginius)   10
Valerius (friend of Icilius)
Virginius (a Captain, father of Virginia)
Corbulo, a Clown
Nurse
Horatio
Sertorius
Two Serving-men
Julia
Calphurnia
Orator   20
A Roman
Lieutenant, Lictors, Servants, Senators, Musicians, Soldiers, Petitioners,
Secretary, Attendant.]

APPIUS
AND
VIRGINIA.

Actus Primus Scena Prima. [I.i]

     Enter Minutius, [*his Lieutenant,*] Oppius, *and Lictors.*

Minutius.   Is *Appius* sent for, that we may acquaint him
    With the decree o'th' Senate?

Lictor.   He is, my Lord,
    And will attend your Lordships presently.

Oppius.   Lictor, did you tell him that our businesse
    Was from the Senate?

Lictor.   I did, my Lord, and here he is at hand.

     Enter Appius, *his two Cozens, and* Marcus Clodius.

Appius.   My Lords, your pleasure?

Minutius.   *Appius*, the Senate greet you well, and by us do signifie unto
    you that they have chosen you one of the Decemviri.

Appius.   My Lords, far be it from the thoughts of so poor a Plebeian, as   10
    your unworthy servant *Appius*, to soar so high: the dignity of so
    eminent a place would require a person of the best parts and blood in
    Rome. My Lords, he that must steer at th' head of an Empire, ought to
    be the Mirrour of the times for Wisdome and for Policie, and therefore
    I would beseech the Senate to elect one worthy of the place, and not
    to think of one so unfit as *Appius*.

Minutius.   My Lord, my Lord, you dally with your wits.   [B1^v]
    I have seen children oft eat sweet meats thus,
    As fearfull to devoure them:
    You are wise, and play the modest courtier right,   20
    To make so many bits of your delight.

Oppius.   But you must know, what we have once concluded
    Cannot for any private mans affection
    Be slighted: take your choice then with best judgement

0.1 *his Lieutenant,*] This ed.; *not in* Q

Of these two proffers, either to accept
The place propos'd you, or be banished Rome
Immediately: *Lictors* make way: we expect
Your speedy resolution.

        Exeunt Oppius, Minutius, [his Lieutenant, Lictors].

1 Cozen.   Noble cozen,
 You wrong your selfe extremely to refuse
 So Eminent a place.
2 Cozen.   It is a meanes   30
 To raise your kindred. Who shall dare t'oppose
 Himselfe against our Family, when yonder
 Shall sit your power, and frowne?
Appius.   Or banisht Rome!
 I pray forbear a little. *Marcus.*   [*Cousins stand apart.*]
Marcus Clodius.   Sir.
Appius. How dost thou like my cunning?
Marcus Clodius.   I protest
 I was be-agued, fearing lest the Senate
 Should have accepted at your fain'd refusall.
 See how your kindred and your friends are muster'd
 To warme them at your sun-shine. Were you now
 In prison, or arraign'd before the Senate   40
 For some suspect of treason, all these swallowes
 Would flie your stormy winter, not one sing:
 Their Musick is the Summer and the Spring.
Appius. Thou observest shrewdly: well, Ile fit them for't.
 I must be one of the *Decemviri*,
 Or banish't Rome. Banisht! Laugh, my trusty *Marcus*,
 I am inforc't to my ambition.
 I have heard of cunning footmen that have worne
 Shooes made of lead some ten dayes 'fore a race
 To give them nimble and more active feet: 50
 So great men should, that aspire eminent place,
 Load themselves with excuse and faint denyall,
 That they with more speed may performe the trial:
 Marke his humility, saies one; how far
 His dreames are from ambition, saies another;

---

28 SD] *his Lieutenant, Lictors*] This ed.; *not in* **43** Musick is] Q; music's in Dilke
 Q; *and Lictors* Dilke   **54** humility,] ~ˎ Q
34 SD] *after* Lucas; *not in* Q

He would not shew his Eloquence, lest that   [B2ʳ]
Should draw him into office: and a third
Is meditating on some thrifty suite
To beg 'fore dinner. Had I as many hands
As had *Briarius*, I'de extend them all   60
To catch this office; 'twas my sleeps disturber,
My dyets ill digestion, my melancholy
Past physicks cure.

    Enter OPPIUS, MINUTIUS, [*his Lieutenant,*] *Lictors* [*with robes*].

Marcus Clodius.   The Senators returne.
Minutius.   My Lord, your answer?
Appius.   To obey, my Lord, and to know how to rule
Doe differ much: to obey by nature comes,
But to command by long experience.
Never were great men in so eminent place
Without their shadowes. Envy will attend
On greatnesse till this generall frame takes end.   70
'Twixt these extreames of state and banishment,
My minde hath held long conflict, and at last
I thus returne my answer: [*to Cousins and Marcus Clodius*] noble
   friends,
We now must part, necessity of State
Compells it so.
I must inhabit now a place unknowne,
You see't compels me leave you. Fare you well.
1 Cozen.   To banishment, my Lord?
Appius.   I am given up
To a long travell full of fear and danger,
To waste the day in sweat, and the cold night   80
In a most desolate contemplation,
Banisht from all my kindred and my friends,
Yea banisht from my selfe; for I accept
This honourable calling.
Minutius.   Worthy *Appius*,
The gods conduct you hither: *Lictors*, his robes.

---

63 SD] *placed as* Dilke; *To right of 62 and 63a in*
  Q *his Lieutenant,*] This ed.; *not in* Q
  with robes] This ed.; *not in* Q
64 answer?] ~. Q
65 obey,] ~ₐ Q

73 answer:] ~, Q SD] This ed.; *not in* Q; *to*
  his Cousins Dilke
76 inhabitₐ] ~, Q
85 his] His Q

2 *Cozen* [*aside*].   We are made for ever; [*to Appius*] noble kinsman,
  'Twas but to fright us.
Appius.   But my loving kinsmen,
  Mistake me not, for what I spake was true,
  Bear witnesse all the gods: I told you first,
  I was to inhabit in a place unknown;   90
  'Tis very certaine, for this reverend seat
  Receives me as a pupill, rather gives
  Ornament to the person, then our person
  The least of grace to it. I shewed you next
  I am to travell; 'tis a certaine truth:
  Look by how much the labour of the minde   [B2ᵛ]
  Exceeds the bodies, so far am I bound
  With paine and industry, beyond the toyle
  Of those that sweat in warre, beyond the toyle
  Of any Artisan; pale cheeks, and sunk eyes,   100
  A head with watching dizied, and a haire
  Turn'd white in youth, all these at a dear rate
  We purchase speedily that tend a State.
  I told you I must leave you, 'tis most true.
  Henceforth the face of a Barbarian
  And yours shall be all one, henceforth Ile know you
  But only by your vertue: brother or father
  In a dishonest suite shall be to me
  As is the branded slave. Justice should have
  No kindred, friends, nor foes, nor hate, nor love,   110
  As free from passion as the gods above.
  I was your friend and kinsman, now your Judge,
  And whilst I hold the scales, a downy feather
  Shall as soone turne them as a masse of Pearle
  Or Diamonds.
Marcus Clodius [*aside*].   Excellent, excellent Lapwing;
  There's other stuffe closed in that subtle brest.
  He sings and beats his wings far from his nest.
Appius.   So Gentlemen, I take it, here takes end
  Your businesse, my acquaintance; fare you well.

---

86 *aside*] This ed.; *not in* Q ever;] ~, Q *to*   **108** a] Dyce 2; *not in* Q
 Appius] This ed.; *not in* Q   **115** SD] *as* Dilke Lapwing;] ~, Q
100 Artisan;] ~, Q   **119** businesse,] ~; Q acquaintance;] ~, Q

1 Cozen.   Heres a quick change, who did expect this cloud?   120
    Thus men when they grow great doe strait grow proud.

                                        [*Exeunt Cousins.*]

Appius.   Now to our present businesse at the camp:
    The army that doth winter 'fore *Algidon,*
    Is much distrest we heare: *Minutius,*
    You with the levies and the little corne
    This present dearth will yield, are speedily
    To hasten thither, so to appease the minde
    Of the intemperate souldier.

Minutius.   I am ready,
    The levies doe attend me; our Lieutenant,
    Send on our Troopes.

Appius.   Farewell *Minutius.*   130
    The gods goe with you, and be still at hand
    To adde a triumph to your bold command.   *Exeunt.*

                            [I.ii]

            Enter NUMITORIUS, ICILIUS, VIRGINIA.

Numitorius.   Noble *Icilius* welcome, teach your selfe
    A bolder freedome here, for, by our love,
    Your suite to my faire Neece doth parallell   [B3ʳ]
    Her kindreds wishes. There's not in all Rome
    A man that is by honour more approv'd
    Nor worthier, were you poore, to be belov'd.

Icilius.   You give me (noble Lord) that character
    Which I cood never yet read in my selfe:
    But from your censure shall I take much care
    To adorne it with the fairest ornaments   10
    Of unambitious vertue: [*taking Virginia's hand*] here I hold
    My honorable patterne, one whose minde
    Appeares more like a ceremonious chappell
    Full of sweet musick, then a thronging presence.
    I am confirm'd, the court doth make some shew

---

121 SD] Dyce 1   I.ii] *as Dyce* 1; *not in* Q
123 *Algidon*] Lucas; *Agidon* Q   2 for,] ~ꞈ Q   love,] ~ꞈ Q
128 ready,] ~ꞈ Q   11 SD] *after* Lucas; *not in* Q
129 me;] ~, Q   Lieutenant,] ~ꞈ Q

Fairer then else they would doe; but her port
Being simple vertue, beautifies the court.

Virginia.   It is a flattery (my Lord)
You breath upon me, and it shewes much like
The borrowed painting which some Ladies use,   20
It is not to continue many dayes;
My wedding garments will outweare this praise.

Numitorius.   Thus Ladies still foretell the funerall
Of their Lords kindnesse.

      Enter a Servant, whispers Icilius in the eare.
        But my Lord, what newes?

Icilius.   *Virginius,* my Lord, your noble brother
Disguis'd in dust and sweat, is new arriv'd
Within the City: troopes of artisans
Follow his panting horse, and with a strange
Confused noyse, partly with joy to see him,
Partly with fear for what his hast portends,   30
They shew as if a sudden mutiny
Orespread the City.

Numitorius.   Cozen take your chamber. *[Exit Virginia.]*
What businesse from the camp?

Icilius.   Sure Sir it beares
The forme of some great danger, for his horse
Bloody with spurring, shewes as if he came
From forth a battel: never did you see
'Mongst quailes or cocks in fight a bloodier Heele,
Then that your brother strikes with. In this forme
Of orespent horseman, having as it seemes,
With the distracting of his newes, forgot   40
House, friends, or change of raiment, he is gone
To th'Senate house.

Numitorius.   Now the gods bring us safety!
The face of this is cloudy, let us haste   [B3ᵛ]
To'th Senate house, and there enquire how neare
The body moves of this our threatned fear. *Exeunt.*

---

17 court.] ~, Q   **32** SD] *as* Dilke; *not in* Q
24 SD] *placed as* Lucas; *to right of lines 24–6* Q **42** safety!] ~, Q

[I.iii]

Enter APPIUS *melancholly; after,* MARCUS CLODIUS.

Marcus Clodius.　　My Lord.

Appius.　　Thou troublest me.

Marcus Clodius.　　My hand's as ready arm'd to work your peace
　　As my tongue bold to inquire your discontents.
　　Good my Lord hear me.

Appius.　　　　　　　　　　I am at much variance
　　Within my selfe, there's discord in my blood,
　　My powers are all in combat, I have nothing
　　Left but sedition in me.

Marcus Clodius.　　　　　　　　Trust my bosom
　　To be the closet of your private griefs.
　　Beleeve me, I am uncranied.

Appius.　　　　　　　　　　May I trust thee?　　　　　　　　　　　　10

Marcus Clodius.　　As the firme centre to indure the burden
　　Of your light foot, as you would trust the poles
　　To bear on them this airy cannopy,
　　And not to fear their shrinking. I am strong,
　　Fixt and unshaking.

Appius.　　　　　　　　Art thou? Then thine ear:
　　I love.

Marcus Clodius.　　Ha ha he!

Appius.　　Can this my ponderous secresie
　　Be in thine ear so light? Seemes my disturbance
　　Worthy such scorne that thou deridest my griefs?
　　Beleeve me, *Clodius*, I am not a twig
　　That every gust can shake, but 'tis a tempest　　　　　　　　　20
　　That must be able to use violence
　　On my grown branches. Wherefore laugh'st thou then?

Marcus Clodius.　　Not that y'are mov'd, it makes me smile in scorne
　　That wise men cannot understand themselves,
　　Nor know their own prov'd greatnesse. *Clodius* laughes not
　　To think you love, but that you are so hopelesse
　　Not to presume to injoy whom you affect.
　　What's she in Rome your greatnesse cannot awe

I.iii] *as* Dyce 1; *not in* Q　　　　　　　　**15** ear] Dyce 1; ever Q
0.1 *melancholly; after,*] ~∧ ~∧ Q　　　　　**16** he!] ~. Q

Or your rich purse purchase? Promises and threats
Are statesmens Lictors to arrest such pleasures   30
As they would bring within their strict commands;
Why should my Lord droop, or deject his eye?
Can you command Rome, and not countermand
A womans weaknesse? Let your Grace bestow
Your purse and power on me, I'le prostrate you.   [B4ʳ]

Appius.   Ask both and lavish them to purchase me
    The rich fee-simple of *Virginia's* heart.

Marcus Clodius.   *Virginia's!*

Appius.   Hers.

Marcus Clodius.   I have already found
    An easie path which you may safely tread,
    Yet no man trace you.

Appius.   Thou art my comforter.   40

Marcus Clodius.   Her father's busied in our forreign wars,
    And there hath chief imployment; all their pay
    Must your discretion scantle: keep it back,
    Restraine it in the common Treasury.
    Thus may a states-man 'gainst a souldier stand,
    To keep his purse weak, whil'st you arme his hand.
    Her father thus kept low, gifts and rewards
    Will tempt the maide the sooner; nay haply draw
    The father in to plead in your behalfe.
    But should these faile, then siege her Virgin Tower   50
    With two prevailing engines, feare and power.

Appius.   Go then and prove a speeding advocate;
    Arme thee with all our bounty, oratory,
    Variety of promise.

                  Enter VALERIUS.

Valerius.   Lord *Appius*, the *Decemvirate* intreat
    Your voice in this dayes Senate. Old *Virginius*
    Craves audience from the camp with earnest suite
    For quick dispatch.

Appius.   We will attend the Senate.   [*Exit Valerius.*]
    Clodius, be gone.   [*Exit Marcus Clodius.*]

---

30 statesmens] *as* Hazlitt (*statesmen's*);
    statemens Q
35 me,] ~. Q
51 two] Dyce 2; *conj.* Dyce 1; too Q

55 *Lord*] L. Q
58, 59 SDs] This ed.; *not in* Q; *Exeunt Valerius*
    and Marcus Claudius. to right of line 59 Dyce 1
59 be] Be Q

Enter OPPIUS, VALERIUS, NUMITORIUS, [*Senators, and Lictors*].

Oppius.   We sent to you to assist us in this counsell   60
    Touching the expeditions of our war.
Appius.   Ours is a willing presence to the trouble
    Of all State cares. Admit him from the camp.

                 Enter VIRGINIUS.

Oppius.   Speak the camps will.
Virginius.   The camp wants money, we have store of knocks,
    And wounds Gods plenty, but we have no pay,
    This three moneths did we never house our heads,
    But in yon great star-chamber; never bedded
    But in the cold field-beds, our vittaile failes us,
    Yet meet with no supply; we're fairly promis'd,   70
    But souldiers cannot feed on promises;
    All our provant apparell's torne to rags,
    And our Munition fails us: Will you send us   [B4ᵛ]
    To fight for *Rome* like beggars? Noble Gentlemen,
    Are you the high State of *Decemviri*,
    That have those things in mannage? Pity us,
    For we have need on't. Let not your delays
    Be cold to us, whose bloods have oft been heated
    To gaine you fame and riches. Prove not to us
    (Being our friends) worse foes then we fight with: 80
    Let's not be starv'd in kindnesse. Sleep you now
    Upon the bench, when your deaf ears should listen
    Unto the wretchlesse clamours of the poor?
    Then would I had my Drums here, they might rattle,
    And rowse you to attendance. Most grave Fathers,
    Shew your selves worthy stewards to our Mother
    Fair *Rome*, to whom we are no bastard sons,
    Though we be souldiers. She hath in her store
    Food to maintain life in the Camp, as wel
    As surfet for the City. Do not save   90
    The foe a labour; send us some supply,
    Lest ere they kill us, we by famine die.
Appius.   Shall I (my Lords) give answer to this souldier?

59.1 OPPIUS,] This ed.; *Spurius, Opius,* Q   **72** provant‸] ~, Q
Senators, and Lictors] This ed.; *&c.* Q; *Enter*
OPPIUS *and* SENATORS (*as complete* SD) Dyce
I

Oppius.   Be you the Cities voyce.
Appius.   *Virginius,* we would have you thus possess'd,
      We sit not here to be prescrib'd and taught,
      Nor to have any suter give us limit,
      Whose power admits no curb. Next know, *Virginius,*
      The Camp's our servant, and must be dispos'd,
      Controul'd and us'd by us, that have the strength   100
      To knit it or dissolve it. When we please
      Out of our Princely grace and clemency
      To look upon your wants, it may be then
      We shall redress them: But till then, it fits not
      That any petty fellow wag'd by us
      Should have a tongue sound here before a Bench
      Of such grave Auditours. Further,—
Virginius.   Pray give me leave,
      Not here? Pray *Appius,* is not this the Judgment seat?
      Where should a poor mans cause be heard but here?
      To you, the Statists of long flourishing Rome,   110
      To you I call, if you have charity,
      If you be humane, and not quite giv'n ore
      To Furs and Metall, if you be Romans,
      If you have any souldiers bloud at all
      Flow in your veins, help with your able arms
      To prop a sinking camp, an infinite   [C1ᵛ]
      Of fair Rome's sons, cold, weak, hungry, and clothless,
      Would feed upon your surfet. Will you save them,
      Or shall they perish?
Appius.   What we will, we will,
      Be that your answer: perhaps at further leasure   120
      We'l help you; not your merit but our pleasure.
Virginius.   I will not curse thee, *Appius,* but I wish
      Thou wert i'th' camp amongst the Mutineers
      To tell my answers, not to trouble me.
      Make you us dogs, yet not allow us bones?
      Oh what are souldiers come too! Shall your camp,
      The strength of all your peace, and the iron wall
      That rings this Pomp in from invasive steel,

96 prescrib'd] Dilke; prescib'd Q   121 you;] ~, Q
110 you,] ~ˌ Q   128 steel,] ~; Q
111 if] If Q

Shall that decay? Then let the forrain fires
Climb o're these buildings; let the sword and slaughter   130
Chase the gown'd Senate through the streets of Rome,
To double dye their robes in Scarlet; let
The enemies stript arm have his crimson'd brawns
Up to the elbowes in your traiterous bloud;
Let *Janus* Temple be devolv'd, your Treasures
Ript up to pay the common adversaryes
With our due wages. Do you look for lesse?
The rottenness of this misgovern'd State
Must grow to some Disease, incurable
Save with a sack or slaughter.
Appius.   Y'are too bold.   140
Virginius.   Know you our extremities?
Appius.   We do.
Virginius.   And will not help them?
Appius.   Yes.
Virginius.   When?
Appius.   Hereafter.
Virginius.   Hereafter? When so many gallant spirits
    That yet may stand betwixt you and destruction,
    Are sunk in death? Hereafter? When disorder
    Hath swallowed all our Forces?
Appius.   We'l hear no more.
Oppius.   Peace, fellow, peace, know the *Decemviri*,
    And their Authority; we shall commit you else.
Virginius.   Do so, and I shall thank you; be relieved
    And have a strong house o're me, fear no Alarmes   150
    Given in the night by any quick perdue.
    Your Guilty in the City feeds more dainty
    Then doth your Generall. 'Tis a better Office   [C1ᵛ]
    To be an under Keeper then a Captain;
    The gods of Rome amend it.
Appius.   Break up the Senate.
Virginius.   And shall I have no answer?
Appius.   So farewel.
                                   [*Exeunt, except Virginius.*]
Virginius.   What Slave would be a soldier to be censured

147 fellow,] ~ₐ Q   **156.1** SD] Lucas; *not in* Q

By such as ne'er saw danger? To have our pay,
Our worths and merits ballanc'd in the scale
Of base moth-eaten peace? I have had wounds   160
Would have made all this Bench faint and look pale
But to behold them searcht. They lay their heads
On their soft pillowes, pore upon their bags,
Grow fat with laziness and resty ease.
And us that stand betwixt them and disaster
They will not spare a *Drachma*. O my souldiers,
Before you want, I'l sell my smal possessions
Even to my skin, to help you, Plate and Jewels
All shall be yours. Men that are men indeed,
The earth shal find, the Sun and air must feed.   170
          Enter NUMITORIUS, ICILIUS, VALERIUS, VIRGINIA.
Numitorius.   Your daughter, noble brother, hearing late
      Of your arrival from the Camp, most humbly
      Prostrates her filial Duty.   [*Virginia kneels.*]
Virginius.   Daughter rise.
      And, brother, I am only rich in her,
      And in your love, link't with the honour'd friendship
      Of these fair Romane Lords. For you *Icilius*,
      I hear I must adopt you with the title
      Of a new son; you are *Virginia's* chief,
      And I am proud she hath built her fair election
      Upon such store of vertues. May you grow,   180
      Although a Cities child, to know a souldier
      And rate him to his merit.
Icilius.   Noble father,
      (For henceforth I shal onely use that name)
      Our meeting was to urge you to the processe
      Of our fair contract.
Virginius.   Witnesse Gentlemen,
      Here I give up a fathers interest,
      But not a fathers love, that I wil ever
      Wear next my heart, for it was born with her

160 peace?] ~. Q
168 skin,] ~∧ Q
170.1 VIRGINIA] Dilke; *Virginius* Q
172 arrival] Dilke; arrvial Q

173 SD] Lucas, *after* Dilke; *not in* Q
174 And, brother,] ~∧ ~∧ Q
176 these] Lucas; those Q

And growes still with my age.

Numitorius.   *Icilius,*
    Receive her: witnesse noble Gentlemen.   190

Valerius.   With all my heart. I would *Icilius*
    Could do as much for me; but Rome affords not
    Such another *Virginia.*

Virginia.   I am my fathers daughter, and by him
    I must be swaid in all things.

Numitorius.   Brother, this happy Contract asks a Feast,
    As a thing due to such solemnities.
    It shall be at my house, where we this night
    Will sport away some hours.

Virginius.   I must to horse.

Numitorius.   What, ride to night?

Virginius.   Must see the Camp to night.   200
    'Tis full of trouble and destracted fears,
    And may grow mutinous. I am bent to ride.

Valerius.   To night?

Virginius.   I am ingag'd: short farwels now must serve,
    The universal businesse calls me hence,
    That toucheth a whole people. *Rome,* I fear,
    Thou wilt pay use for what thou dost forbear.   *[Exeunt.]*
                    Explicit Actus I.

        Actus Secundus Scena Prima. [II.i]

Enter Clown [CORBULO] *whispering* VIRGINIA, *after her* MARCUS CLODIUS
        with presents [*and Musicians*].

Virginia.   Sirrah, go tell *Calphurnia,* I am walking
    To take the air: intreat her company.
    Say I attend her coming.

Corbulo.   Madam, I shall: but if you could walk abroad, and get an Heir,
   it were better, for your father hath a fair revenue, and never a son to
   inherit.

Virginia.   You are, sirrah—

---

207 SD] Dilke; *not in* Q   0.2 *and Musicians*] This ed.; *not in* Q
0.1 *Clown* [CORBULO]] *Clown* Q; CORBULO   1 *Calphurnia*] *as* Dilke; *Calpharina* Q
Dilke

Corbulo.   Yes I am sirrah: but not the party that is born to do that;
 though I have no Lordships, yet I have so much manners to give my
 betters place.   10
Virginia.   Whom mean you by your betters?
Corbulo.   I hope I have learnt to know the three degrees of comparison:
 for though I be *bonus*, and you *melior* as well as *mulier*, yet my Lord
 Icilius is *optimus*.
Virginia.   I see there's nothing in such private done,
     But you must inquire after.
Corbulo.   And can you blame us (Madam) to long for the merry day, as
 you do for the merry night?
Virginia.   Will you be gone sir?   [C2ᵛ]
Corbulo.   Oh yes, to my Lady *Calphurnias.* I remember my errand.   20
                                                       Exit Corbulo.

Virginia.   My father's wondrous pensive, and withall
     With a supprest rage left his house displeas'd,
     And so in post is hurried to the camp:
     It sads me much; to expell which melancholy,
     I have sent for company.
         Marcus Clodius [comes forward, with] Musicians.
Marcus Clodius [aside].   This opportunity was subtilly waited,
     It is the best part of a polititian
     When he would compasse ought to fame his industry
     Wisely to waite the advantage of the houres;
     His happie minutes are not alwayes present.   30
     [*to Musicians*] Expresse your greatest art, *Virginia* hears you.   *Song.*
Virginia [aside].   Oh I conceive the occasion of this harmony.
     Icilius sent it, I must thank his kindnesse.
Marcus Clodius.   Let not *Virginia* rate her contemplation
     So high, to call this visit an intrusion;
     For when she understands I tooke my message
     From one that did compose it with affection,
     I know she will not only extend pardon,
     But grace it with her favour.

9 Lordships] *as* Dilke; Lorships Q
13 *mulier,*] ~; Q
20 Corbulo.] *as* Lucas; Corbula Q
20 *Calphurnias*] *as* Dilke (Calphurnia's);
   Calpharniaes Q
20.1 SD] *to right of line 21* Q

25.1 SD] *as* Lucas; *Enter Clodius and
   Musicians.* Q
26 SD] Lucas; *not in* Q
31 SD] *after* Dilke; *not in* Q
32 SD] This ed.; *not in* Q
34 rate] Dilke; wate Q

Virginia.   You mediate excuse for courtesies,   40
    As if I were so barren of civility,
    Not to esteeme it worthy of my thanks;
    Assure your selfe I could be longer patient
    To hear my eares so feasted.
Marcus Clodius [to Musicians].   Joyne all your voyces till you make the aire
    Proud to usurpe your notes, and to please her
    With a sweet eccho; serve *Virginias* pleasure.   *Song.*
    [*to Virginia*] As you have been so full of gentlenesse
    To heare with patience what was brought to serve you,
    So hearken with your usuall clemency   50
    To the relation of a lovers sufferings:
    Your figure still does revell in his dreames,
    He banquets on your memory, yet findes
    Not thoughts enough to satisfie his wishes,
    As if *Virginia* had compos'd his heart,
    And fills it with her beauty.
Virginia.   I see he is a miser in his wishes,
    And thinks he never has enough of that
    Which onely he possesses: but to give
    His wishes satisfaction, let him know   60
    His heart and mine doe dwell so near together,
    That hourely they converse, and guard each other.   [C3ʳ]
Marcus Clodius.   Is faire *Virginia* confident she knowes
    Her favour dwels with the same man I plead for?
Virginia.   —Unto *Icilius.*
Marcus Clodius.   Worthy faire one,
    I would not wrong your worth so to employ
    My language for a man so much beneath
    The merit of your beauty: he I plead for
    Has power to make your beauty populous,
    Your frowne shall awe the world, and in your smile   70
    Great Rome shall build her happinesse;
    Honour and wealth shall not be stil'd companions,
    But servants to your pleasure.
    Then shall *Icilius* (but a refin'd Citizen)
    Boast your affection, when Lord *Appius* loves you?

45 SD] *after* Dilke; *not in* Q   56 fills] Q; fill'd Hazlitt
48 SD] This ed.; *not in* Q   75 you?] ~. Q

Virginia.   Blesse his great Lordship, I was much mistaken,
        Let thy Lord know, thou Advocate of lust,
        All the intentions of that youth are honourable,
        Whil'st his are fill'd with sensuality.
        And for a finall resolution know,   80
        Our hearts in love like twins alike shall grow.   *Exit.*
Marcus Clodius.   Had I a wife, or daughter that could please him
        I would devote her to him, but I must
        Shadow this scorne, and sooth him still in lust.
                            Exeunt [Marcus Clodius and Musicians].

                            [II.ii]

                        Enter six Souldiers.
1 Souldier.   What newes yet of *Virginius* returne?
2 Souldier.   Not any.
1 Souldier.   O the misery of Souldiers!
        They doubly starve us with faire promises.
        We spread the earth like haile, or new reapt corne
        In this fierce famine; and yet patiently
        Make our obedience the confined Jaile
        That starves us.
3 Souldier.   Souldiers, let us draw our swords
        While we have strength to use them.
1 Souldier.   'Tis a motion
        Which nature and necessity commands.
                        Enter MINUTIUS *[and his Lieutenant].*
Minutius.   Y'are of *Virginius* Regiment?
Omnes.   We are.   10
Minutius.   Why doe you swarme in troopes thus? To your quarter!
        Is our command growne idle? To your trench!
        Come I'le divide you, this your conference
        Is not without suspect of mutiny.

84.1 SD] This ed.; *Exit.* Q
II.ii] *as* Dyce 1; *not in* Q
1 *1 Souldier.*] *as* Dilke; 1. Q (*so to end of scene*)
2 *2 Souldier.*] *as* Dilke; 2. Q
7 us.] ~: Q

7, 97 *3 Souldier.*] *as* Dilke; 3. Q
9.1 *and his Lieutenant*] This ed.; *not in* Q
10 Regiment?] ~. Q
11 quarter!] ~. Q
12 trench!] ~. Q

1 Souldier.   Souldiers, shall I relate the grievances
    Of the whole Regiment?
Omnes.   Boldly.
1 Souldier.   Then thus my Lord.
Minutius.   Come, I will not hear thee—
1 Souldier.   Sir you shall:
    Sound all the Drums and Trumpets in the camp,
    To drowne my utterance, yet above them all
    I'le rear our just complaint. Stir not my Lord,   20
    I vow you are not safe if you but move
    A sinew till you heare us.
Minutius.   Well sir, command us:
    You are the Generall.
1 Souldier.   No my Lord, not I,
    I am almost starved; I wake in the wet trench,
    Loaded with more cold iron then a Jaile
    Would give a murderer, while the Generall
    Sleeps in a field bed, and to mock our hunger
    Feeds us with scent of the most curious fare
    That makes his tables crack, our pay detained
    By those that are our Leaders: and at once   30
    We in this sad, and unprepared plight,
    With the Enemy, and Famine daily fight.
Minutius.   Doe you threaten us?
Omnes.   Sir you shall hear him out.
1 Souldier.   You send us whips, and iron manackles,
    And shackles plenty, but the devill a coine.
    Would you teach us that caniball trick, my Lord,
    Which some rich men i'th' City oft doe use:
    Shall's one devoure another?
Minutius.   Will you hear me?
1 Souldier.   O Rome th'art growne a most unnaturall mother,
    To those have held thee by the golden locks   40
    From sinking into ruine; *Romulus*
    Was fed by a she wolfe, but now our wolves
    Instead of feeding us devoure our flesh,

16 Regiment?] ~. Q   **36** you] Dilke; you would Q
17 thee—] ~, Q   **37** i'th'] 'ith' Q

Carouse our blood, yet are not drunk with it,
For three parts of 't is water.
Minutius.   Your Captaine,
   Noble *Virginius* is sent to Rome,
   For ease of all your grievances.
1 Souldier.   'Tis false.
Omnes.   I, 'tis false.
1 Souldier.   Hee's stolne away from's, never to returne,
   And now his age will suffer him no more   50
   Deale on the Enemy; belike hee'l turne
   An usurer, and in the City aire
   Cut poore mens throats at home sitting in's chaire.   [C4ᵛ]
Minutius.   You wrong one of the honorablest Commanders.
Omnes.   Honorable Commander?
1 Souldier.   Commander? I my Lord, there goes the thrift:
   In victories, the Generall and Commanders
   Share all the honour as they share the spoile;
   But in our overthrowes, where lies the blame?
   The common souldiers fault, ours is the shame.   60
   What is the reason that being so far distant
   From the affrighted enemy, wee lie
   I'th' open field, subject to the sick humors
   Of heaven and earth: unlesse you cood bestow
   Two summers of us? Shall I tell you truth?
   You account the expence of Ingines, and of swords,
   Of horses and of armor dearer far,
   Then souldiers lives.
Omnes.   Now by the gods you doe.
1 Souldier.   Observe you not the ravens and the crowes
   Have left the City surfet, and with us   70
   They make full banquets? Come you birds of death,
   And fill your greedy croppes with humane flesh;
   Then to the City flie, disgorge it there
   Before the Senate, and from thence arise
   A plague to choake all Rome!
Omnes.   And all the Suburbs!

46 to] Dilke; *not in* Q   62 enemy,] ~? Q
48 'tis] 'Tis Q   65 truth?] ~, Q
51 Enemy;] ~, Q   71 banquets?] ~. Q
56 thrift:] ~ₐ Q   75 Rome!] ~. Q   Suburbs!] ~. Q

Minutius.   Upon a souldiers word, bold Gentlemen,
  I expect every houre *Virginius*
  To bring fresh comfort.
Omnes.   Whom? *Virginius*?
1 Souldier.   Now by the gods, if ever he returne,
  Wee'le drag him to the slaughter by his locks,   80
  Turned white with riot and incontinence,
  And leave a president to all the world,
  How Captaines use their souldiers.
         Enter VIRGINIUS.
Minutius.   See, hee's returned.
  Virginius, you are not safe, retire,
  Your troopes are mutinous, we are begirt
  With Enemies more daring, and more fierce,
  Then is the common foe.
Virginius.   My Troopes, my Lord?
Minutius.   Your life is threatned by these desperate men,
  Betake you to your horse.
Virginius.   My noble Lord,
  I never yet profest to teach the art   90
  Of flying. Ha, our troopes grown mutinous?
  He dares not look on me with half a face   [C4ᵛ]
  That spread this wildfire. Where is our Lieutenant?
Lieutenant.   My Lord.
Virginius.   Sirrah, order our companies. *[Exit Lieutenant.]*
Minutius.   What do you mean, my Lord?
Virginius.   Take air a little, they have heated me.
  [to 3 Souldier] Sirrah, i'st you will mutiny?
3 Souldier.   Not I Sir.
Virginius.   Is your gall burst, you Traitor?
4 Souldier.   The gods defend Sir.
Virginius.   Or is your stomack sea-sick, doth it rise?
  I'l make a passage for it.
5 Souldier.   Noble Captain,   100
  I'l dye beneath your foot.
Virginius.   You rough porcupine, ha,
  Do you bristle, do you shoot your quils you rogue?

---

94 *Lieutenant.] Val.* Q SD] This ed.; *not in*
Q
97 SD] This ed.; *not in* Q

98 *4 Souldier.] as* Dilke; 4. Q
100 *5 Souldier.] as* Dilke; 5. Q

1 Souldier.   They have no points to hurt you, noble Captain.

Virginius.   Wast you (my nimble shaver) that would whet
    Your sword 'gainst your Commanders throat, you sirrah?

6 Souldier.   My Lord I never dream't on't.

Virginius.   Slaves and cowards,
    What, are you cholerick now? By the gods
    The way to purge it were to let you blood.
    I am i'th' center of you, and I'l make
    The proudest of you teach the Aspen leaf   110
    To tremble, when I breath.

Minutius.   A strange Conversion.

Virginius.   Advance your pikes. The word!

Omnes.   Advance your pikes.

Virginius.   See noble Lord, these are no Mutineers,
    These are obedient souldiers, civil men:
    You shal command these, if your Lordship please,
    To fil a ditch up with their slaughtered bodies,
    That with more ease you may assault some Town.
    [*to Souldiers*] So now lay down your Arms. Villains and Traitors,
    I here cashier you. Hence from me, my poison,
    Not worthy of our Discipline: Go beg,   120
    Go beg, you mutinous rogues, brag of the service
    You ne'er durst look on; it were charity
    To hang you, for my mind gives, y'are reserv'd
    To rob poor market women.

Minutius.   O *Virginius!*

Virginius.   I do beseech you to confirm my sentence,
    As you respect me. I will stand my self
    For the whole Regiment, and safer far
    In mine owne single valour, then begirt
    With cowards and with traitors.   [D1ʳ]

Minutius.   O my Lord,
    You are too severe.

Virginius.   Now by the gods, my Lord,   130
    You know no discipline, to pitie them.
    Pretious divells! No sooner my back turn'd,
    But presently to mutinie!

---

106 *6 Souldier.*] *as* Dilke; 6. Q
107 What,] ~∧ Q
112 word!] ~, Q

118 SD] This ed.; *not in* Q
119 me,] ~∧ Q
124 *Virginius!*] Dilke; *Viginius.* Q

Omnes.   Dear Captaine.

Virginius.   Refuse me if such traiterous rogues
    Would not confound an Army. When doe you march?
    When doe you march, gentlemen?

1 Souldier.   My Lord, wee'l starve first,
    Wee'le hang first, by the gods, doe any thing
    Ere wee'le forsake you.

Minutius.   Good *Virginius,*
    Limit your passion.

Virginius.   Sir, you may take my place,   140
    Not my just anger from me: these are they
    Have bred a dearth i'th' campe: I'le wish our foes
    No greater plague then to have their company:
    Show but among them all so many scars
    As stick upon this flesh, I'le pardon them.

Minutius.   How now, my Lord, breathlesse?

Virginius.   By your favour. I ha said.
    Mischiefs confound me if I could not wish
    My youth renewed againe, with all her follies,
    Onely to 'ave breath enough to raile against
    These—'Tis too short.   150

Minutius.   See Gentlemen, what strange distraction
    Your falling off from duty hath begot
    In this most noble souldier: You may live,
    The meanest of you, to command a Troope,
    And then in others youle correct those faults,
    Which in your selves you cherisht; every Captain
    Beares in his private government that forme,
    Which Kings should ore their Subjects, and to them
    Should be the like obedience. We confesse
    You have been distrest: but can you justly challenge   160
    Any commander that hath surfeted,
    While that your food was limited? You cannot.

Virginius.   My Lord, I have shared with them an equall fortune,
    Hunger, and cold, marcht thorough watery fens,
    Borne as great burdens as the pioneer,
    When scarce the ground would bear me.

---

153 live,] ~ₐ Q   **156** cherisht;] ~, Q
154 you,] ~ₐ Q   **159** obedience] Dilke; obedient Q

Minutius.   Good my Lord, give us leave to proceed;
    [*to Souldiers*] The punishment your Captaine hath inflicted
    Is not sufficient; for it cannot bring   [D1ᵛ]
    Any example to succeeding times   170
    Of pennance worth your faulting: happily
    It may in you beget a certaine shame;
    But it will breed in others a strong hope
    Of the like lenity. Yet gentlemen,
    You have in one thing given me such a taste
    Of your obedience; when the fire was raised
    Of fierce sedition, and the cheeke was swolne
    To sound the fatall Trumpet, then the sight
    Of this your worthy Captaine did disperse
    All those unfruitfull humours, and even then   180
    Convert you from feirce Tigers to stayed men:
    We therefore pardon you, and doe restore
    Your Captaine to you, you unto your Captaine.
Omnes.   The gods requite you, noble Generall!
Minutius.   My Lord, my Lord.
Omnes.   Your pardon noble Captaine.
Virginius.   Well, you are the Generall, and the fault is quit,
    A souldiers teares, an elder brothers wit
    Have little salt in them, nor doe they season
    Things worth observing, for their want of reason.
    [*to Souldiers*] Take up your armes and use them, doe, I pray,   190
    Ere long youle take your legs to run away.   [*Exeunt Souldiers.*]
Minutius.   And what supply from *Rome*?
Virginius.   Good store of corne.
Minutius.   What entertainment there?
Virginius.   Most honourable,
    Especially by the Lord *Appius.*
    There is great hope that *Appius* will grow
    The souldiers patron: with what vehemency
    He urg'd our wants, and with what expedition
    He hasted the supplies, it is almost
    Incredible. There's promis'd to the souldier
    Besides their corne a bounteous donative;   (*A shout.* 200
    But 'tis not certaine yet when't shall be paid.

168 SD] This ed.; *not in* Q
173 breed] Dyce 2; *not in* Q
184 Generall!] ~. Q

190 SD] This ed.; *not in* Q   doe,] ~ₐ Q
191 SD] This ed; *not in* Q

Minutius.   How for your owne particular?
Virginius.   My Lord,
    I was not enter'd fully two pikes length
    Into the Senate, but they all stood bare,
    And each man offer'd me his seat: The businesse
    For which I went dispatcht, what guifts, what favours
    Were done me, your good Lordship shall not hear,
    For you would wonder at them; onely this,
    'Twould make a man fight up to'th' neck in blood,   [D2ʳ]
    To think how nobly he shall be received   210
    When he returnes to'th' City.
Minutius.   'Tis well,
    Give order the provision be divided
    And sent to every quarter.
Virginius.   Sir, it shall.
    [*aside*] Thus men must slight their wrongs, or else conceal them,
    When generall safety wills us not reveale them.   *Exeunt.*

[II.iii]

Enter two Petitioners [*with papers*] *at one doore, at the*
other MARCUS CLODIUS.

1 Petitioner.   Pray is your Lord at leasure?
Marcus Clodius.   What is your suite?
1 Petitioner.   To accept this poore Petition which makes knowne
    My many wrongs in which I crave his Justice,
    And upright sentence to support my cause,
    Which else is trod downe by oppression.
Marcus Clodius [*taking petition*].   My Lords hand is the prop of Innocence,
    And if your cause be worthy his supportance
    It cannot fall.
1 Petitioner.   The gods of *Rome* protect him!
Marcus Clodius.   What, is your paper too petitionary?
2 Petitioner.   It leanes upon the Justice of the Judge,   10
    Your noble Lord, the very stay of *Rome.*

---

205 businesse] Dilke; bnsinesse Q (*turned* u)   **0.1** *with papers*] This ed.; *not in* Q
208 them;] ~, Q   **2** knowne∧] ~, Q
214 SD] *as* Dyce 2; *not in* Q   **6** SD] This ed.; *not in* Q
II.iii] *as* Dyce 1; *not in* Q   **8** him!] ~. Q

Marcus Clodius [*taking petition*].   And surer basis, for a poore mans cause,
    She cannot yeeld. Your papers I'le deliver,
    And when my Lord ascends the Judgement seate,
    You shall find gracious comfort.
Enter ICILIUS troubled.

Icilius.   Where's your Lord?
Marcus Clodius [*aside*].   *Icilius!* Faire *Virginia's* late betroth'd!
Icilius.   Your eares, I hope, you have not forfeited,
    That you returne no answer. Where's your Lord?
Marcus Clodius.   At's studie.
Icilius.   I desire admittance to him.   20
Marcus Clodius.   Please you attend, I'le know his Lordships pleasure.
    [*aside*] *Icilius!* I pray heaven she have not blab'd.   [*Exit.*]
Icilius.   Attend! A petty Lawyer t'other day,
    Glad of a fee, but cal'd to eminent place,
    Even to his betters, now the word's, Attend.
    This gowned office, what a breadth it bears!
    How many tempests waite upon his frowne!
Enter MARCUS CLODIUS.

Marcus Clodius.   All the petitioners withdraw. Lord *Appius*
    Must have this place more private, as a favour   [D2ᵛ]
    Reserv'd for you, *Icilius.*
Enter APPIUS with Lictors afore him. [Exeunt Petitioners.]
Here's my Lord.   30

Appius.   Be gone, this place is only spar'd for us,
    And you *Icilius.*   [*Exeunt Marcus Clodius and Lictors.*]
Now your business.

Icilius.   May I speak it freely?
Appius.   We have suffering ears,
    A heart the softest downe may penetrate.
    Proceed.
Icilius.   My Lord.
Appius.   We are private, pray your courtesie.
Icilius.   My duty.

---

12 SD] This ed.; *not in* Q
17 SD] *as* Dilke; *not in* Q
22 *aside*] *as* Dilke; *not in* Q   Exit.] Dilke; *not in* Q
28 Lord] L. Q

30 *Enter . . . him.*] *after line 30* Q   *Exeunt Petitioners.*] *after* Dilke (*to right of* withdraw. *in line 28*); *not in* Q
32 SD] *as* Lucas (*to right of line 32*); *Exeunt Lictors* Dyce 2
35 pray] Pray Q

Appius.　　　　　Leave that to th' publick eye
　　　Of *Rome*, and of *Romes* people. *Clodius* there!
　　　　　　　[*Enter* MARCUS CLODIUS.]
Marcus Clodius.　My Lord.
Appius.　　　　　Place me a second Chaire; that done,
　　　Remove your self.　　　　　　[*Marcus Clodius places a chair.*]
　　　　　　　So now, your absence *Clodius.*
　　　　　　　　　　　[*Exit Marcus Clodius.*]
　　　Icilius sit, this grace we make not common　　　　　　40
　　　Unto the noblest Romane, but to you
　　　Our love affords it freely. Now your suit?
Icilius.　It is, you would be kind unto the Camp.
Appius.　Wherein, *Icilius*, doth the Camp touch thee?
Icilius.　Thus: Old *Virginius*, now my father in Law,
　　　Kept from the publick pay, consumes himself,
　　　Sels his Revenues, turnes his plate to coyn,
　　　To wage his souldiers, and supply the Camp,
　　　Wasting that useful substance which indeed
　　　Should rise to me, as my *Virginia*'s Dowry.　　　　　　50
Appius.　We meet that opposition thus *Icilius*.
　　　The Camps supplies doth not consist in us,
　　　But those that keep the common Treasury;
　　　Speak or intreat we may, but not command.
　　　But Sir, I wonder you, so brave a Youth,
　　　Son to a thrifty Romane, should ally you,
　　　And knit your strong armes to such falling branches;
　　　Which rather in their ruine will bear down
　　　Your strength, then you support their rottenness.
　　　Be swayed by me, fly from that ruinous house　　　　　　60
　　　Whose fall may crush you; and contract with mine,
　　　Whose bases are of Marble, deeply fixt
　　　To mauger all gusts and impending stormes.
　　　Cast off that beggars daughter, poor *Virginia*,
　　　Whose dowry and beauty I'l see trebled both,
　　　In one ally'd to me. Smile you *Icilius*?　　　　　　[D3ʳ]
Icilius.　My Lord, my Lord, think you I can imagine

---

37 there!] ~. Q
37.1 SD] *after* Lucas; *not in* Q
39 *Marcus . . . chair.*] *after* Dilke (*Claudius places a chair and then retires. to right of line 39*)
39.1 *Exit Marcus Clodius.*] *as* Dyce 2
55 wonder∧ you,] ~, ~∧ Q
65 beauty∧] ~, Q
67 you∧] ~, Q

Your close and sparing hand can be profuse
To give that man a Palace, whom you late
Deny'd a cottage? Will you from your own coffers   70
Grant me a treble Dowry, yet interpose me
A poor third from the common Treasury?
You must move me by possibilities,
For I have brains; give first your hand and Seal,
That old *Virginius* shall receive his pay
Both for himself and souldiers, and that done,
I shall perhaps be soon induc'd to think,
That you who with such willingness did that—

Appius.   Is my Love mispriz'd?

Icilius.   Not to *Virginia.*

Appius.   *Virginia?*

Icilius.   Yes *Virginia*, Lustful Lord.   80
I did but trace your cunning all this while.
You would bestow me on some Appian Trull,
And for that dross to cheat me of my Gold;
For this the Camp pines, and the City smarts.
All *Rome* fares worse for thy incontinence.

Appius.   Mine, boy?

Icilius.   Thine, Judg. This hand hath intercepted
Thy Letters, and perus'd thy tempting guifts,
These ears have heard thy amorous passions, wretch,
These eyes beheld thy treacherous name subscrib'd.
A Judg? A Divel!

Appius [*rising*].   Come I'l hear no more.   90

Icilius [*drawing his poniard*].   Sit still, or by the powerful Gods of *Rome*
I'l nail thee to the Chair. But suffer me,
I'l offend nothing but thine ears.

Appius [*calling*].   Our Secretary!

Icilius.   Tempt not a Lovers fury, if thou dost,
Now by my vow, insculpt in heaven, I'l send thee—

Appius.   You see I am patient.

Icilius.   But withal revengeless.

86 Mine,] ~ᴧ Q   Thine,] ~ᴧ Q   93 SD] *after* Dilke; *not in* Q   Secretary!] ~.
87 guifts] *as* Dyce 1 (gifts); guests Q   Q
90 Judg?] ~, Q   Divel!] ~. Q   SD] This ed.;   94 dost,] ~ᴧ Q
   not in Q   95 thee—] ~.— Q
91 SD] This ed.; *not in* Q

Appius.   So, say on.
Icilius.   Hope not of any grace, or the least favour,
          I am so covetous of *Virginia's* love,
          I cannot spare thee the least look, glance, touch,   100
          Divide one bare imaginary thought
          Into a thousand, thousand parts, and that
          I'l not afford thee.
Appius.   Thou shalt not.   [D3ᵛ]
Icilius.   Nay, I will not.
          Hadst thou a Judges place above those Judges
          That judg all souls, having power to sentence me,
          I would not bribe thee, no not with one hair
          From her fair temples.
Appius.   Thou shouldst not.
Icilius.   Nay, I would not.
          Think not her Beauty shall have leave to crown
          Thy lustfull hopes with the least spark of blisse,
          Or have thine ears charm'd with the ravishing sound   110
          Even of her harshest phrase.
Appius.   I will not.
Icilius.   Nay, thou shalt not.
          Shee's mine, my soul is crownd in her desire,
          To her I'ld travell through a land of fire.
Appius.   Now have you done?
Icilius.   I have spoke my thoughts.
Appius.   Then will thy fury give me leave to speak?
Icilius.   I pray say on.
Appius.   *Icilius,* I must chide you, and withall
          Tell you, your rashnesse hath made forfeiture
          Even of your precious life, which wee esteeme
          Too deer to call in question. If I wisht you   120
          Of my allyance, graft into my blood,
          Condemn you me for that? Oh see the rashnesse
          And blind misprision of distempred youth!
          As for the Maid *Virginia,* wee are far
          Even in least thought from her; and for those Letters,
          Tokens and Presents, wee acknowledg none.
          Alas, though great in place, wee are not gods.
          If any false impostor hath usurpt
          Our hand or greatnesse in his own behoof,

Can wee help that? *Icilius*, there's our hand,   130
Your rashnesse we remit; let's have hereafter
Your love and best opinion. For your suit,
Repair to us at both our better leisures,
Wee'l breathe in it new life.
Icilius.   I crave your pardon.
Appius.   Granted ere crav'd, my good *Icilius*.
Icilius.   —Morrow.
Appius.   It is no more indeed. Morrow *Icilius*.
If any of our servants wait without,
Command them in.
Icilius.   I shall.
Appius.   Our Secretary,   [D4ᵛ]
We have use for him. *Icilius*, send him hither.   140
Again good morrow.   *Exit Icilius.*
Go to thy death, thy life is doom'd and cast.
Appius be circumspect, and be not rash
In blood as th'art in lust: Be murderous stil,
But when thou strik'st, with unseen weapons kill.
                        Enter MARCUS CLODIUS.
Marcus Clodius.   My Honourable Lord.
Appius.   Deride me, dog?
Marcus Clodius.   Who hath stirr'd up this tempest in your brow?
Appius.   Not you? Fie, you!
Marcus Clodius.   All you Panthean Gods,
Confound me, if my soul be accessary
To your distractions.
Appius.   To send a ruffian hither,   150
Even to my closet, first, to brave my Greatness,
Play with my beard, revile me, taunt me, hisse me;
Nay after all these deep disparagements,
Threat me with steel, and menace me unarm'd,
To nail me to my seat, if I but mov'd:
All these are slight, slight toyes.
Marcus Clodius.   *Icilius* do this?
Appius.   Ruffian *Icilius*, he that in the front
Of a smooth Citizen, bears the rugged soul
Of a most base Bandetto.
Marcus Clodius.   He shall die for't.

Appius.   Be not too rash.   160
Marcus Clodius.   Were there no more men to support great *Rome*,
    Even falling *Rome* should perish, ere he stand:
    I'l after him, and kill him.
Appius.   Stay, I charge thee.
    Lend me a patient ear; To right our wrongs,
    We must not menace with a publick hand;
    We stand in the worlds eye, and shall be taxt
    Of the least violence, where we revenge:
    We should smile smoothest where our hate's most deep,
    And when our spleen's broad waking, seem to sleep.
    Let the young man play still upon the bit,   170
    Till we have brought and train'd him to our lure;
    Great men should strike but once, and then strike sure.
Marcus Clodius.   Love you *Virginia* still?
Appius.   Do I still live?
Marcus Clodius.   Then she's your own. *Virginius* is, you say,   [D4ᵛ]
    Still in the Camp?
Appius.   True.
Marcus Clodius.   Now in his absence will I claim *Virginia*
    To be the daughter of a bond woman,
    And slave to me; to prove which, I'l produce
    Firme proofs, notes probable, sound Witnesses;   180
    Then having with your Lictors summond her,
    I'l bring the cause before your Judgement Seat,
    Where, upon my infallid evidence,
    You may pronounce the sentence on my side,
    And she become your Strumpet not your Bride.
Appius.   Thou hast a copius brain, but how in this
    Shall we dispose *Icilius*?
Marcus Clodius.   If he spurne
    Clap him up close, there's wayes to charm his spleen.
    By this no scandal can redound to you;
    The Cause is mine; you but the Sentencer   190
    Upon that evidence which I shall bring.
    The business is to 'ave Warrants by Arrest,
    To answer such things at the Judgment Bar

175 Camp?] ~. Q

531

As can be laid against her; Ere her friends
Can be assembled, ere her self can study
Her answer or scarce know her cause of summons
To descant on the matter, *Appius* may
Examine, try, and doom *Virginia*.
But all this must be sudden.
Appius.   Thou art born
To mount me high above *Icilius* scorn.   200
I'l leave it to thy manage.   *Exeunt.*
                    Explicit Actus secundus.

Actus Tertius Scena Prima. [III.i]

Enter Nurse and the Clown [CORBULO].
Corbulo.   What was that you said, Nurse?
Nurse.   Why, I did say thou must bestir thy selfe.
Corbulo.   I warrant you I can bestir my stumps as soon as another, if fit occasion be offered; but why do you come upon me in such haste? Is it because (Nurse) I should come over you at leisure?
Nurse.   Come over me, thou knave? What dost thou mean by that?   [E1ʳ]
Corbulo.   Only this, if you will come off, I will come on.
Nurse.   My Lord hath strangers to night: you must make ready the Parlour, a table and lights; nay when, I say?
Corbulo.   Me thinks you should rather wish for a bed then for a board,   10
for darkness then for lights; yet I must confess you have been a light woman in your time: but now—
Nurse.   But now? What now, you knave?
Corbulo.   But now I'l go fetch the table and some lights presently. [*Exit.*]
          Enter NUMITORIUS, HORATIO, VALERIUS, ICILIUS.
          [CORBULO *follows with Attendants who set table and lights.*]
Numitorius.   Some lights to usher in these Gentlemen,
          Clear all the roomes without there.
          [*to Horatio, Valerius, Icilius*] Sit, pray sit.
          [*to the rest*] None interrupt our conference.

0.1 CORBULO.] *as* Dilke (*replacing* Q *the Clown.*); *not in* Q
12 now—] ~. Q
14 SD] This ed.; *not in* Q
14.2 SD] This ed.; *not in* Q
16 SD] This ed.; *not in* Q
17 SD] This ed.; *not in* Q

532

Enter VIRGINIA.

Ha, whose that?

Nurse.   My masters child, if it please you.

Numitorius.   Fair *Virginia*, you are welcome.

   The rest forbear us till we call.

                              [*Exeunt Nurse, Corbulo, and Attendants.*]

                              Sweet cozen,   20

   Our business, and the cause of our discourse

   Admits you to this Councel. Take your place.

   Icilius we are private, now proceed.

Icilius.   Then thus; Lord *Appius* doth intend me wrong,

   And under his smooth calmnesse cloaks a tempest,

   That will ere long break out in violence

   On me and on my fortunes.

Numitorius.   My good cozen,

   You are young, and youth breeds rashness. Can I think

   Lord *Appius* will do wrong, who is all Justice,

   The most austere and upright Censurer   30

   That ever sate upon the awful Bench?

Valerius.   *Icilius*, you are neer to me in blood,

   And I esteem your safety as mine owne.

   If you will needs wage eminence and state,

   Chuse out a weaker opposite, not one

   That in his arm bears all the strength of *Rome*.

Numitorius.   Besides *Icilius*,

   Know you the danger, what it is to scandal

   One of his place and sway?

Icilius.   I know it kinsmen, yet this popular Greatness   40

   Can be no bug-bear to affright mine innocence.

   No, his smooth crest hath cast a palped film

   Over *Romes* eyes. He juggles, a plain Juggler.

   Lord *Appius* is no lesse.

Numitorius [*rising*].   Nay then, Cozen,   [E1ᵛ]

   You are too harsh, and I must hear no more.

___

18 masters] *as* Lucas (master's); most— Q;
   most sweet Dilke; most dear Dyce 2;
   foster- Thorndike, *conj.* Dyce
20 SD] This ed.; *not in* Q; *Exit Nurse and
   Corb.* Dilke
38 danger,] ~ₐ Q
42 No,] ~ₐ Q
44 SD] *after* Lucas (*to right of* presence *in line
   48*); *not in* Q   Nayₐ then,] ~, ~ₐ Q

It ill becomes my place and gravity,
To lend a face to such reproachful terms
'Gainst one of his high presence.
Icilius.   Sit, pray sit,
To see me draw his picture 'fore your eyes,
To make this man seem monstrous, and this god   50
Rome so adores, a divel, a plain divel.
This Lord, this Judg, this *Appius*, that professeth
To all the world a vestal chastity,
Is an incontinent, loose Leacher growne.
Numitorius.   Fy cozen!
Icilius.   Nay 'tis true. Daily and hourely
He tempts this blushing Virgin with large promises,
With melting words and Presents of high rate,
To be the stale to his unchaste desires.
Omnes.   Is't possible?
Icilius.   Possible!   60
'Tis actual Truth, I pray but ask your Neece.
Virginia.   Most true, I am extremely tyr'd and wearied
With messages and tokens of his love;
No answer, no repulse will satisfie
The tediousness of his importunate suit.
And whilst I could with modesty and honour,
Without the danger of reproach and shame,
I kept it secret from *Icilius*;
But when I saw their boldness found no limit,
And they from fair intreaty grew to threats,   70
I told him all.
Icilius.   True: understanding which
To him I went.
Valerius.   To *Appius*?
Icilius.   To that Gyant,
The high Colossus that bestrides us all;
I went to him.
Horatio.   How did you bear your self?
Icilius.   Like *Appius*, at the first, dissemblingly,
But when I saw the coast clear, all withdrawn,

55 cozen!] ~. Q

534

And none but we two in the Lobby, then
I drew my Poinyard, took him by the throat,
And when he would have clamor'd, threatned death,
Unlesse he would with patience hear me out.　　　　　　　80
Numitorius.　　Did he, *Icilius?*
Icilius.　　　　　　　I made him that he durst not squeake,　　　[E2ʳ]
Not move an eye, not draw a breath too loud,
Nor stir a fingar.
Horatio.　　　　　　What succeeded then?
Numitorius [*calling*].　　Keep fast the door there: [*to Icilius*] Sweet Couz not
　　　too loud.
What then succeeded?
Icilius.　　　　　　　Why, I told him all,
Gave him his due, call'd him lascivious Judge,
(A thousand things which I have now forgot)
Shewd him his hand a witnesse 'gainst himself,
And every thing with such known circumstance,
That he might well excuse, but not deny.　　　　　　　90
Numitorius.　　How parted you?
Icilius.　　　　　　　Why Friends, in outward shew.
But I perceiv'd his heart: that Hypocrite
Was born to gull *Rome*, and deceive us all.
He swore to me quite to abjure her love;
Yet ere my self could reach *Virginia*'s chamber,
One was before me with regreets from him,
I know his hand. Th' intent of this our meeting
Was to intreat your counsell and advice:
The good old man her Father is from home,
I think it good that she now in his absence　　　　　　100
Should lodg in secret with some private friend,
Where *Appius* nor his Lictors, those blood-hounds,
Can hunt her out. You are her unkle Sir,
I pray counsell the best.
Numitorius.　　　　　To oppose our selves
Now in this heat against so great a man,
Might in my judgment to our selves bring danger,

And to my Neece no safety. If we fall
She cannot stand; lets then preserve our selves
Until her father be discharg'd the Camp.

Valerius.   And good *Icilius*, for your private ends,   110
And the dear safety of your friends and kindred,
Against that Statist, spare to use your spleen.

Icilius.   I will be sway'd by you. My Lords, 'tis late,
And time to break up conference. Noble Uncle
I am your growing Debtor.

Numitorius [*calling*].   Lights without there.

Icilius.   I will conduct *Virginia* to her lodging.
Good night to all at once.

Numitorius.   The Gods of *Rome* protect you all, and then
We need not fear the envious rage of men.   *Exeunt.*

[III.ii]

Enter MARCUS CLODIUS, *with foure Lictors.*   [E2ᵛ]

Marcus Clodius.   *Lictors* bestow your selves in some close shops,
About the *forum*, till you have the sight
Of faire *Virginia*, for I understand
This present morning shee'l come forth to buy
Some necessaries at the Sempsters shops:
How ere accompanied be it your care
To sease her at our action. Good my friends,
Disperse your selves, and keep a carefull watch.   [*Exit.*]

1 Lictor.   'Tis strange that Ladies will not pay their debts.

2 Lictor.   'T were strange indeed, if that our Romane Knights   10
Would give them good example and pay theirs.

1 Lictor.   The Calender that we *Lictors* goe by, is all dog dayes.

2 Lictor.   Right, our common hunt is still to dog unthrifts.

1 Lictor.   And whats your book of common-prayer?

2 Lictor.   Faith onely for the increase of riotous young Gentlemen i'th'
countrey, and banquerouts i'th' City.

1 Lictor.   I know no man more valiant then we are, for wee back Knights
and Gentlemen daily.

---

115 SD] This ed.; *not in* Q   9 *1 Lictor.*] *as* Dilke; 1. Q (*so to end of scene*)
III.ii] *as* Dyce 1; *not in* Q   10 *2 Lictor.*] *as* Dilke; 2. Q (*so to end of scene*)
8 SD] Dyce 1; *not in* Q   'T] 'It Q

2 *Lictor.*   Right, we have them by the back hourely: your French flye
     applied to the nape of the neck for the French Rheume, is not so sore a   20
     drawer as a *Lictor.*

1 *Lictor.*   Some say that if a little timbred fellow would justle a great
     logerhead, let him be sure to lay him i'th' kennell; but when we shoul-
     der a Knight, or a Knights fellow, we make him more sure, for we
     kennell him i'th' counter.

2 *Lictor.*   Come, lets about our businesse.   *Exeunt.*

                              [III.iii]

              Enter VIRGINIA, *Nurse, and Clowne* [CORBULO].

Virginia.   You are growne wondrous amorous of late,
        Why doe you looke back so often?

Corbulo.   Madam, I goe as a Frenchman rides, all upon one buttock.

Virginia.   And what's the reason?

Corbulo.   Your Ladiship never saw a Monky in all your life time have a
     clog at's taile, but hee's still looking back to see what the devil 'tis that
     followes him.

Nurse.   Very good, we are your clogs then.

Virginia.   Your crest is growne regardant; [*pointing to Nurse*] here's the
        beauty
        That makes your eyes forgetfull of their way.   10

Corbulo.   Beauty? O the gods! Madam I cannot indure her complexion.

Nurse.   Why sir, what's my complexion?

Corbulo.   Thy complexion is just between a moore and a french woman.

Virginia.   But she hath a matchlesse eye sir.

Corbulo.   True, her eyes are not right matches, besides she is a widow.

Nurse.   What then, I pray you?

Corbulo.   Of all waters I would not have my beefe powder'd with a   [E3ʳ]
        widowes teares.

Virginia.   Why, I beseech you?

Corbulo.   O they are too fresh Madam, assure your selfe they will not last   20
        for the death of fourteen husbands above a day and a quarter; besides,

III.iii]   This ed.; *not in* Q

0.1 CORBULO] Dilke (*replacing* Q *Clowne*); *not
   in* Q

3 *Corbulo.*] *as* Dilke; *Clown.* Q (*so to end of
   scene as* Clown. *or* Clow.)

9 SD] Lucas (*to right of line 10*), *after* Dilke; *not
   in* Q

13 and] & Q

14 sir.] ~, Q

if a man come a wooing to a widow, and invite her to a banquet, contrary to the old rule she will sooner fill her eye then her belly. Besides
that, if he looke into her estate, first, look you, here are foure fingers,
first the charge of her husbands funerall, next debts, and legacies, and
lastly the reversion; now take away debts and legacies, and what
remaines for her second husband?

Nurse.   I would some of the Tribe heard you.

Corbulo.   There's a certaine fish, that as the learned divulge, is call'd a
sharke. Now this fish can never feede while he swims upon's belly,   30
marry when he lies upon his back, oh he takes it at pleasure.

Virginia.   Well sir, about your businesse, make provision
    Of those things I directed.

Corbulo.   Sweet Lady, these eyes shall be the clarks of the kitchin for
your belly; but I can assure you Woodcocks will be hard to be spoke
with, for there's a great feast towards.

Virginia.   You are very pleasant.

Corbulo.   And fresh cod is taken down thick and threefold, women
without great bellies goe together by the ears for't, and such a number
of sweet tooth'd caters in the market, not a calves head to be got for   40
love or money; Muttons mutton now.

Virginia.   Why, was it not so ever?

Corbulo.   No Madam, the sinners i'th' Suburbs had almost tane the name
quite away from't, 'twas so cheap and common: but now 'tis at a sweet
reckoning, the Terme time is the muttonmonger in the whole calender.

Nurse.   Doe your Lawyers eat any sallets with their mutton?

Corbulo.   Yes, the younger revellers use capers to their mutton, so long
till with their shuffling and cutting some of them be out at heeles
againe. A bountifull minde and a full purse ever attend your Ladiship.   50

Virginia.   O I thank you.

    Enter [behind] MARCUS CLODIUS, *and foure Lictors.*

Marcus Clodius.   See, yon's the Lady.

Corbulo.   I will buy up for your Ladiship all the young cuckoes in the
market.

Virginia.   What to doe?

---

22 banquet,] ~∧ Q   47 mutton?] ~. Q
23 rule∧] ~, Q   51.1 *behind*] This ed.; *not in* Q
24 here] Here Q   52 *Marcus Clodius.*] Clo. Q

Corbulo.   O 'tis the most delicatest dish Ile assure you, and newest in
   fashion: not a great feast in all *Rome* without a cuckoe.
Marcus Clodius [*advancing*].   *Virginia.*
Virginia.   Sir.
Marcus Clodius.   Mistris you doe not know me,   60
         Yet we must be acquainted: follow me.
Virginia.   You doe salute me strangely. Follow you?   [E3ᵛ]
Corbulo.   Doe you hear sir? Me thinks you have followers enough.
   Many Gentlemen that I know, would not have so many tall followers
   as you have for the price of ten hunting geldings, I'le assure you.
Marcus Clodius.   Come, will you goe?
Virginia.   Whither? By what command?
Marcus Clodius.   By warrant of these men, and priviledge
         I hold even on thy life. Come ye proud dame,
         You are not what you seeme.   [*Seizes her.*]
Virginia.   Uncivill sir,
         What makes you thus familiar and thus bold?   70
         Unhand me villaine.
Marcus Clodius.   What, Mistris, to your Lord?
         He that can set the rasor to your throate,
         And punish you as freely as the gods,
         No man to aske the cause? Thou art my slave,
         And here I sease what's mine.
Virginia.   Ignoble villaine,
         I am as free as the best King or Consull
         Since *Romulus.* What dost thou meane? Unhand me.
         [*to Corbulo*] Give notice to my uncle and *Icilius,*
         What violence is offer'd me.
Marcus Clodius.   Doe, doe.
Corbulo.   Doe you presse women for souldiers, or do you beg women,   80
   instead of other commodities, to keep your hands in ure? By this light
   if thou hast any eares on thy head, as it is a question, I'le make my Lord
   pull you out by th' eares, though you take a Castle.   *Exit.*
Marcus Clodius.   Come, will you goe along?

---

58 SD] This ed.; *not in* Q   69 SD] This ed.; *not in* Q; *Takes hold on her.*
62 you?] ~. Q   Dilke (*to right of line 68*)
63 sir?] ~, Q   71 What,] ~ₐ Q
                                            78 SD] *as* Dilke; *not in* Q

Nurse. Whither should she goe sir? Here's pulling and haling a poore
    Gentlewoman.

Marcus Clodius. Hold you your prating, reverence the whip
    Shall cease on you for your smooth cozenage.

Virginia. Are not you servant to Lord *Appius*?

Marcus Clodius. How ere, I am your Lord, and will approve it   90
    'Fore all the Senate.

Virginia.   Thou wilt prove thy selfe
    The cursed pander for anothers lust,
    And this your plot shall burst about your Ears
    Like thunderbolts.

Marcus Clodius.   Hold you that confidence?
    First I will sease you by the course of law,
    And then I'le talke with you.

                  Enter ICILIUS, *and* NUMITORIUS.

Numitorius. How now, faire cozen?

Icilius.   How now, Gentlemen?
    What's the offence of faire *Virginia*,   [E4^r]
    You bend your weapons on us?

Lictor.   Sir stand back,
    We fear a rescue.

Icilius.   There's no need of feare,   100
    Where there's no cause of rescue: what's the matter?

Virginia. O my *Icilius*! Your incredulity
    Hath quite undone me, I am now no more
    Virginius daughter, so this villaine urges;
    But publish't for his bondwoman.

Numitorius.   How's this?

Marcus Clodius. 'Tis true my Lord, and I will take my right
    By course of Law.

Icilius.   Villaines set her free,
    Or by the power of all our Romane gods,
    I'le give that just revenge unto my rage
    Which should be given to Justice. Bondwoman!   110

Marcus Clodius. Sir, we doe not come to fight, wee'le deale
    By course of Law.

---

87 prating, reverence₍ₐ₎] ~₍ₐ₎ ~, Q   **90** ere,] ~₍ₐ₎ Q
89 *Appius*?] ~. Q   **94** confidence?] ~, Q

Enter APPIUS [*and a Secretary*].
My Lord we fear a rescue.

Appius.   A rescue? Never fear't, here's none in presence
But civill men. [*to Numitorius*] My Lord, I am glad to see you.
Noble *Icilius*, we shall ever love you.
Now Gentlemen reach your Petitions.

Icilius.   My Lord, my Lord.

Appius.				Worthy *Icilius*,
If you have any businesse defer't
Untill to morrow, or the afternoone,
I shall be proud to pleasure you.

Icilius [*aside to Numitorius*]			The Fox				120
Is earth't, my Lord, you cannot winde him yet.

Appius.   Stooles for my noble friends.—I pray you sit.

Marcus Clodius.   May it please your Lordship—

Appius.				Why, uncivill sir!
Have I not beg'd forbearance of my best
And dearest friends, and must you trouble me?

Marcus Clodius.   My Lord, I must be heard, and will be heard,
Were all the gods in Parliament, I'de burst
Their silence with my importunity,
But they should heare me.

Appius.				The fellow's mad;
We have no leasure now to heare you sir.				130

Marcus Clodius.   Hast now no leasure to heare just complaints?
Resigne thy place O *Appius*, that some other
May doe me Justice then.

Appius.				Wee'l hear't to morrow.

Marcus Clodius.   O my Lord,
Deny me Justice absolutely, rather
Then feed me with delayes.				[E4ᵛ]

Icilius.				Good my Lord hear him,
And wonder when you heare him, that a case
So full of vile Imposture, should desire
To be unfoulded.

Marcus Clodius.		I my Lord, 'tis true,
The Imposture is on their parts.

112 *Enter* APPIUS] *to right of line 111* Q   *and a*
	Secretary] *This ed.; not in* Q
114 SD] *This ed.; not in* Q
120 SD] *after* Thorndike; *not in* Q

121 Lord,] ~ₐ Q
123 Lordship—] ~. Q   Why,] ~ₐ Q
136 Then] *as* Dilke (Than); them Q; then *as*
	c.w. Q

Appius.   Hold your prating,   140
    Away with him to prison, clamorous fellow.
    Suspect you our uprightnesse?
Marcus Clodius.   No my Lord:
    But I have mighty Enemies, my Lord,
    Will overflow my cause. See, here I hold
    My bondwoman that brags her selfe to be
    Descended of a noble family.
    My purse is too scant to wage Law with them,
    I am inforc't be mine own advocate,
    Not one will pleade for me. Now if your Lordship
    Will doe me justice so, if not then know   150
    High hills are safe, when seas poore dales or'eflow.
Appius.   Sirra, I think it fit to let you know,
    E're you proceed in this your subtle suite,
    What penalty and danger you acrue,
    If you be found to double. Here's a virgin
    Famous by birth, by education noble,
    And she forsooth, haply but to draw
    Some piece of money from her worthy father,
    Must needs be challeng'd for a bondwoman.
    Sirra take heed, and well bethink your selfe,   160
    I'le make you a president to all the world,
    If I but finde you tripping.
Marcus Clodius.   Doe it freely.
    And view on that condition these just proofes.   [*Proffers papers.*]
Appius.   Is that the Virgins nurse?
Nurse.   Her milch Nurse my Lord, I had a sore hand with her for a year
    and a quarter, I have had somewhat to doe with her since too, for the
    poore Gentlewoman hath been so troubled with the green sicknesse.
Icilius.   I pray thee Nurse intreat *Sertorius*
    To come and speak with me.   [*Exit Nurse.*]
Appius.   Here is strange circumstance, view it my Lord,   170
    If he should prove this, it would make *Virginius*
    Think he were wronged.
Icilius.   There is a devilish cunning
    Exprest in this black forgerie.   [F1ʳ]

163 SD] *after* Dilke; *not in* Q   169 SD] Dilke; *not in* Q
164 nurse?] ~. Q

Appius.   *Icilius* and *Virginia*, pray come near,
         Compound with this base fellow. You were better
         Disburse some trifle then to undergo
         The question of her freedome.
Icilius.   O my Lord!
         She were not worth a handfull of a bribe,
         If she did need a bribe.
Appius.   Nay, take your course,
         I onely give you my opinion,   180
         I aske no fee for't. Do you know this fellow?
Virginia.   Yes my Lord, he's your servant.
Appius.   Y'are i'th' right:
         But will you truly know his character?
         He was at first a pettie Notary,
         A fellow that being trusted with large summes
         Of honest Citizens, to be imploy'd
         I'th' trade of usury, this Gentleman,
         Couching his credit like a tilting staffe
         Most cunningly, it brake, and at one course
         He ran away with thirty thousand pound;   190
         Returning to the City seven year after,
         Having compounded with his creditors
         For the third moity, he buyes an office
         Belonging to our place, depends on us,
         In which the oppression and vile injuries
         He hath done poore suters, they have cause to rue,
         And I to pity: he hath sold his smiles
         For silver, but his promises for gold,
         His delayes have undone men.
         The plague that in some foulded cloud remaines,   200
         The bright Sun soone disperseth; but observe,
         When black infection in some dunghill lies,
         There's worke for bells and graves, if it doe rise.
Numitorius.   He was an ill prop to your house, my Lord.
Appius.   'Tis true my Lord, but we that have such servants,
         Are like to Cuccolds that have riotous wives,
         We are the last that know it: this is it

187 usury,] ~; Q   190 pound;] ~, Q
189 cunningly,] ~‸ Q

Makes noblemen suspected to have done ill,
When the oppression lies in their proud followers.
Marcus Clodius.   My Lord, it was some soothing sicophant,   210
Some base detracting Rascal that hath spread
This falsehood in your ears.
Appius.   Peace Impudence!
Did I not yester day, no longer since,
Surprize thee in thy Study counterfeiting   [F1ᵛ]
Our hand?
Marcus Clodius. 'Tis true, my Lord.
Appius.   Being subscribed
Unto a Letter fill'd with amorous stuff
Unto this Lady?
Marcus Clodius.   I have askt your pardon,
And gave you reason why I was so bold
To use that forgery.
Appius [to Virginia].   Did you receive it?
Virginia.   I did my Lord, and I can shew your Lordship   220
A packet of such Letters.
Appius [to Marcus Clodius].   Now by the Gods,
I'l make you rue it. I beseech you Sir,
Show them the reason mov'd you counterfeit
Our Letter.
                        Enter SERTORIUS.
Marcus Clodius. Sir, I had no other colour
To come to speak with her.
Appius.   A goodly reason!
Did you until this hour acquaint the Lady
With your intended suit?
Marcus Clodius.   At several times,
And would have drawn her by some private course
To have compounded for her liberty.
Virginia.   Now by a Virgins honour and true birth,   230
'Tis false, my Lord, I never had a dream
So terrible as is this monstrous divel.
Appius.   Well Sir, referring my particular wrong

---

212 Impudence!] ~, Q   **221** SD] This ed.; *not in* Q
213 since,] ~ₐ Q   **224** SERTORIUS.] Dilke; *Valerius.* Q
219 SD] This ed.; *not in* Q

　　To a particular censure, I would know
　　What is your suit?
Marcus Clodius.　　　　My Lord, a speedy tryal.
Appius.　You shall obtain't with all severity,
　　I will not give you longer time to dream
　　Upon new slights to cloak your forgery.
　　Observe you this Camelion, my Lords,
　　Ile make him change his colour presently.　　　　　240
Numitorius.　My Lord, although th' uprightness of our cause
　　Needs no delayes, yet for the satisfaction
　　Of old *Virginius*, let him be present
　　When we shall crave a tryal.
Appius.　　　　　　　　Sir it needs not:
　　Who stands for father of the Innocent,
　　If not the Judg? Ile save the poor old man
　　That needless travel.
Virginia.　　　　　　With your favour Sir,
　　We must intreat some respit in a business
　　So needful of his presence.　　　　　　　　[F2ʳ]
Appius.　　　　　　　I do protest,
　　You wrong your selves thus to importune it.　　250
　　Well, let it be to morrow, I'l not sleep
　　Till I have made this thicket a smooth plain,
　　And giv'n you your true honor back again.
Icilius.　My Lord, the distance 'twixt the Camp and us
　　Cannot be measured in so short a time.
　　Let us have four dayes respit.
Appius.　　　　　　　You are unwise;
　　Rumor by that time will have fully spred
　　The scandal, which being ended in one hour
　　Will turn to air: To morrow is the Tryal,
　　In the mean time, let all contented thoughts　　260
　　Attend you.
Marcus Clodius.　My Lord, you deal unjustly
　　Thus to dismiss her; this is that they seek for,
　　Before to morrow they'l convey her hence
　　Where my claim shall not seise her.
Appius.　　　　　　　　Cunning knave,
　　You would have bond for her appearance? Say.

Marcus Clodius.   I think the motion's honest.

Appius.   Very good.
  Icilius shall engage his honoured word
  For her appearance.

Marcus Clodius.   As you please, my Lord,
  But it were fitting her old Uncle there
  Were jointly bound with him.

Appius.   Well Sir, your pleasure   270
  Shall have satiety. You'l take our word
  For her appearance; will you not Sir, I pray?

Marcus Clodius.   Most willingly my Lord.

Appius.   Then Sir you have it,
  And i'th' mean time I'l take the honoured Lady
  Into my guardianship, and by my life,
  I'l use her in all kindness as my wife.

Icilius.   Now by the Gods you shall not.

Appius.   Shall not what?

Icilius.   Not use her as your wife Sir.

Appius.   O my Lord,
  I spake it from my heart.

Icilius.   I, very likely.
  She is a Virgin Sir, and must not lye   280
  Under a mans forth coming; do you mark?
  [*aside*] Not under your forth coming, leacherous *Appius.*

Appius.   Mistake me not, my Lord. Our Secretary,   [F2ᵛ]
  Take bonds for the appearance of this Lady.
  [*to Marcus Clodius*] And now to you sir, you that were my servant,
  I here casheire you; never shalt thou shrowde
  Thy villanies under our noble roofe,
  Nor scape the whip, or the fell hangmans hook
  By warrant of our favour.

Marcus Clodius.   So, my Lord;
  I am more free to serve the Gods, I hope,   290
  Now I have lost your service.

Appius.   Harke you sirra,

266 motion's] motions Q   282 SD] *as* Dilke; *not in* Q
277 not∧] ~, Q   285 SD] This ed.; *not in* Q
279 I,] ~∧ Q   289 So,] ~∧ Q   Lord;] ~, Q

546

Who shall give bonds for your appearance, ha?
    To justifie your claim?
Marcus Clodius.   I have none, my Lord.
Appius.   Away, commit him prisoner to his chamber:
    I'le keep you safe from starting.
Marcus Clodius.   Why my Lord?
Appius.   Away, I wil not hear you.   [*Exeunt Lictors with Marcus Clodius.*]
    A Judges heart here in the midst must stand,
    And move not a haires bredth to either hand.   *Exit.*
Numitorius.   O were thy heart but of the self same piece
    Thy tongue is, *Appius*; how blest were *Rome*!   300
Icilius.   Post to the campe *Sertorius*, thou hast heard
    Th'effect of all, relate it to *Virginius*.
    I pray thee use thy ablest horsemanship,
    For it concerns us near.
Sertorius.   I goe my Lord.   *Exit.*
Icilius.   Sure all this is damn'd cunning.
Virginia.   O my Lord,
    Seamen in tempests shun the flattering shore,
    To bear full sails upon't were danger more.
    So men o're born with greatness stil hold dread
    False, seeming friends that on their bosomes spread:
    For this is a safe truth which never varies,   310
    He that strikes all his sailes seldome miscarries.
Icilius.   Must we be slaves both to a tyrants will,
    And to confounding ignorance at once?
    Where are we, in a mist, or is this hell?
    I have seen as great as the proud Judge have fell:
    The bending Willow yeilding to each wind,
    Shall keep his rooting firme, when the proud Oak
    Braving the storme, presuming on his root,
    Shall have his body rent from head to foote;
    Let us expect the worst that may befal,   320
    And with a noble confidence beare all.   *Exeunt.*

---

296 SD] This ed.; *not in* Q; *Exeunt Appius*   308 dread∧] ~, Q
    Claudius, Marcus Claudius, and Lictors. after   309 False,] ~∧ Q
    line 298 Dyce 1   313 to] Dyce 2; *not in* Q

[III.iv]

Enter APPIUS [*with letters*], MARCUS CLODIUS, *and a Servant.* [F3ʳ]
Appius [*to Servant*].　Here, bear this packet to *Minutius*,
　　And privately deliver't, make as much speed
　　As if thy father were deceas'd i'th' Camp,
　　And that thou went'st to take th'Administration
　　Of what he left thee. Fly.
Servant.　　　　　　　I go my Lord.　　　　　*Exit.*
Appius.　O my trusty *Clodius.*
Marcus Clodius.　　　　　My dear Lord,
　　Let me adore your divine policy.
　　You have poison'd them with sweet meats, you have my Lord.
　　But what contain those Letters?
Appius.　　　　　　　Much importance.
　　Minutius is commanded by that packet　　　　　　　　10
　　To hold *Virginius* prisoner in the Camp
　　On some suspect of Treason.
Marcus Clodius.　　　　　But my Lord,
　　How will you answer this?
Appius.　　　　　　Tush, any fault
　　Or shadow of a Crime will be sufficient
　　For his committing: thus when he is absent
　　We shall in a more calm and friendly sea
　　Sail to our purpose.
Marcus Clodius.　　　Mercury himself
　　Could not direct more safely.
Appius.　　　　　　　O my *Clodius,*
　　Observe this rule, one ill must cure another;
　　As *Aconitum*, a strong poison, brings　　　　　　　　20
　　A present cure against all Serpents stings.
　　In high attempts, the soul hath infinite eyes,
　　And 'tis necessity makes men most wise.
　　Should I miscarry in this desperate plot,
　　This of my fate in after times be spoken,
　　I'l break that with my weight on which I am broken.　　*Exeunt.*

III.iv]　This ed.; *not in* Q; SCENE III. Dyce 1　　　1 SD]　This ed.; *not in* Q
0.1 *with letters*]　This ed.; *not in* Q　*Servant*]　　20 *Aconitum,*]　~∧ Q
　servant Q

[III.v]

Enter Two Serving men at one door, at the other CORBULO *the Clowne*
melancholy.

1 Serving man.   Why how now *Corbulo*? Thou wast not wont to be of
this sad temper. What's the matter now?

Corbulo.   Times change, and seasons alter,
    Some men are born to the Bench, and some to the halter.
    What do you think now that I am?

1 Serving man.   I think thee to be *Virginia's* man, and *Corbulo*.

Corbulo.   No, no such matter: ghess again, tell me but what I am, or
what manner of fellow you imagine me to be?

1 Serving man.   I take thee to be an honest good fellow.

Corbulo.   Wide of the bow hand stil: *Corbulo* is no such man.   [F3ᵛ]

2 Serving man.   What art thou then?   11

Corbulo.   Listen, and I'l describe my self to you: I am something better
then a Knave, and yet come short of being an honest man; and though
I can sing a treble, yet am accounted but as one of the base, being
indeed, and as the case stands with me at this present, inferiour to a
rogue, and three degrees worse then a Rascal.

1 Serving man.   How comes this to passe?

Corbulo.   Only by my services successe. Take heed whom you serve, Oh
you serving Creatures; for this is all I have got by serving my Lady
Virginia.   20

2 Serving man.   Why, what of her?

Corbulo.   She is not the woman you take her to be; for though she have
borrowed no money, yet she is entered into bonds; and though you
may think her a woman not sufficient, yet 'tis very like her bond will
be taken. The truth is, she is challenged to be a bond woman; now if
she be a bondwoman and a slave, and I her servant and Vassal, what did
you take me to be? I am an Ant, a Gnat, a worm, a Woodcock amongst
birds, a Hodmondod amongst flies, amongst Curs a trindle tale, and
amongst fishes a poor Jhon; but amongst Serving men worse, worse
then the mans man to the under Yeoman Fewterer.   30

1 Serving man.   But is it possible, thy Lady is challenged to be a slave?
What witness have they?

III.v] This ed.; *not in* Q; SCENE IV. Dyce 1   **29** Jhon] *as* Lucas; Iper Q
19 you] Dilke; yon Q   **30** Yeoman] *as* Dyce 2; Yeomen Q
26 did] Q; do Dyce 2

Corbulo [*weeping*]. Witness these Fountains, these Flood-gates, these
   Well-springs: the poor Gentlewoman was Arrested in the open
   Market; I offered, I offered to bail her, but (though she was) I could
   not be taken. The grief hath gone so near my heart, that until I be
   made free, I shall never be mine own man. The Lord *Appius* hath committed her to Ward, and it is thought she shall neither lye on the
   Knight side, nor in the Twopenny Ward, for if he may have his will of
   her, he means to put her in the Hole. His Warrant hath been out for   40
   her, but how the case stands with him, or how matters will be taken up
   with her, 'tis yet uncertain.
2 Serving man.   When shall the Tryal be?
Corbulo.   I take it to be as soon as the morning is brought a bed of a new
   son and Heir.
2 Serving man.   And when is that?
Corbulo.   Why to morrow, for every morning you know brings forth a
   new sun, but they are all short liv'd, for every night shee drowns them
   in the Western sea. But to leave these *Ænigmaes*, as too high for your
   dull apprehensions, shall I see you at the Tryal to morrow?   50
1 Serving man.   By *Joves* help I'l be there.
2 Serving man.   And I, if I live.   [F4ʳ]
Corbulo.   And I, if I dye for't: Here's my hand I'l meet you. It is thought
   my old master will be there at the Bar; for though all the timber of his
   house yet stand, yet my Lord *Numitorius* hath sent one of his Posts to
   the Camp to bid him spur cut and come to the sentence. Oh we have a
   house at home as heavy as if it were covered with lead. But you will
   remember to be there?
1 Serving man.   And not to fail.
Corbulo.   If I chance to meet you there, and that the Case go against us, I   60
   will give you a quart, not of Wine, but of Tears; for instead of a new
   Role, I purpose to break my Fast with sops of sorrow.   [*Exeunt.*]
                        Explicit Actus tertius.

---

33 SD] This ed.; *not in* Q
39 Twopenny] *as* Dyce 1, *conj.* Dilke;
    Troping Q
50 apprehensions,] ~. Q
58 there?] ~. Q
62 SD] Dyce 1; *not in* Q

Actus Quartus Scena Prima. [IV.i]

Enter VIRGINIUS *like a slave,* NUMITORIUS, ICILIUS, VALERIUS,
  HORATIO[, *Orator,*] VIRGINIA *like a slave,* JULIA, CALPHURNIA, *Nurse.*
Virginius.   Thanks to my noble friends; it now appears
        That you have rather lov'd me then my fortune,
        For that's near shipwrackt: chance you see still ranges,
        And this short dance of life is full of changes.
        Appius! How hollow that name sounds, how dreadful!
        It is a question, whether the proud Leacher
        Will view us to our merit; for they say,
        His memory to vertue and good men
        Is still carousing *Lethe.* O the Gods,
        Not with more terror do the souls in hell   10
        Appear before the seat of *Rhadamant,*
        Then the poor Clyent yonder.
Numitorius.   O *Virginius,*
        Why do you wear this habit? It ill fits
        Your noble person, or this reverend place.
Virginius.   Thats true, old man, but it well fits the case
        Thats now in question. If with form and shew
        They prove her slaved, all freedome I'le forgoe.
Icilius.   Noble *Virginius,*
        Put out a bold and confident defence:
        Search the Imposture, like a cunning Tryer,   20
        False mettals bear the touch, but brook not fire:
        Their brittleness betrayes them; let your breath   [F4ᵛ]
        Discover as much shame in them, as death
        Did ever draw from Offenders. Let your truth
        Nobly supported, void of fear or art,
        Welcome what ever comes with a great heart.
Virginius.   Now by the Gods, I thank thee noble youth.
        I never fear'd in a besieged Town
        Mines or great Engines like yon Lawyers Gown.
Virginia.   O my dear Lord and father, once you gave me   30
        A noble freedom, do not see it lost

0.2, *Orator,*] This ed.; *not in* Q; *at line 48* SD   **1** friends;] ~, Q   it now] itnow Q
     Lucas   CALPHURNIA] Dilke; *Calphurina* Q   **12** *Virginius,*] ~. Q

Without a forfeit; take the life you gave me
And sacrifice it rather to the gods
Then to a villains Lust. Happy the Wretch
Who born in bondage lives and dies a slave,
And sees no lustful projects bent upon her,
And neither knowes the life nor death of honor.

Icilius. We have neither Justice, no nor violence,
Which should reform corruption, sufficient
To cross their black premeditated doom.   40
Appius will seize her, all the fire in hell
Is leapt into his bosom.

Virginius.   O you Gods,
Extinguish it with your compassionate tears,
Although you make a second deluge spread,
And swell more high then *Tenerife*'s high head.
Have not the Wars heapt snow sufficient
Upon this aged head, but they will stil
Pile winter upon winter?

Enter APPIUS, OPPIUS, MARCUS CLODIUS [*with papers*], *six Senators,*
Lictors.

Appius [*aside to Marcus Clodius*]. Is he come? Say.
Now by my life I'l quit the General.

Numitorius. Your reverence to the Judge, good brother.   50

Virginius. Yes Sir, I have learnt my complement thus;
Blest mean estates who stand in fear of many,
And great are curst for that they fear not any.

Appius. What, is *Virginius* come?

Virginius.   I am here my Lord.

Appius. Where is your daughter?

Numitorius.   Here my reverend Lord.
[*to Virginia*] Your habit shewes you strangely.

Virginia.   O 'tis fit,
It sutes both time and cause. Pray pardon it.

Appius [*to Virginius*]. Where is your Advocate?   [G1ʳ]

Virginius.   I have none my Lord.
Truth needs no Advocate, the unjust Cause
Buyes up the tongues that travel with applause   60

---

39 corruption,] ~ₐ Q
48 *with papers*] This ed.; *not in* Q SD] *after*
  Dilke; *not in* Q
51 thus;] ~, Q

54 What,] ~ₐ Q
56 SD] *as* Dilke; *not in* Q
57 it.] ~, Q
58 SD] This ed.; *not in* Q

In these your thronged Courts. I want not any,
And count him the most wretched that needs many.
Orator.   May it please your reverend Lordships?
Appius.   What are you Sir?
Orator.   Of counsel with my Clyent *Marcus Clodius.*
Virginius.   My Lord, I undertake a desperate combat
    To cope with this most eloquent Lawyer:
    I have no skill i'th' weapon, good my Lord;
    I mean, I am not travell'd in your Lawes.
    My suit is therefore by your special goodness
    They be not wrested against me.   70
Appius.   O *Virginius*, the gods defend they should.
Virginius.   Your humble servant shall ever pray for you.
    Thus shall your glory be above your place,
    Or those high titles which you hold in Court,
    For they dy blest that dy in good report.
    [*to Orator*] Now Sir I stand you.
Orator.   Then have at you Sir.
    May it please your Lordships, here is such a Case
    So full of subtilty, and as it were,
    So far benighted in an ignorant mist,
    That though my reading be sufficient,   80
    My practice more, I never was intangled
    In the like pursenet. Here is one that claimes
    This woman for his daughter. Heres another
    Affirms she is his Bond-slave. Now the Question
    (With favour of the Bench) I shall make plain
    In two words only without circumstance.
Appius.   Fall to your proofs.
Orator.   Where are our papers?
Marcus Clodius.   Here Sir.
Orator.   Where Sir? I vow y'are the most tedious Clyent.
    Now we come to't my Lord. Thus stands the Case,
    The Law is clear on our sides. [*to Marcus Clodius*] Hold your prating!   90
    That honourable Lord *Virginius*,
    Having been married about fifteen year,
    And Issuless, this Virgins politick mother
    Seeing the Land was likely to descend

76 SD] This ed.; *not in* Q   **90** SD] *after* Dilke; *not in* Q   prating!] ~. Q
87 papers?] ~. Q

To *Numitorius*—I pray Sir listen.
You my Lord *Numitorius* attend,
We are on your side—old *Virginius*
Imployed in forraign wars, she sends him word
She was with child; observe it, I beseech you,
And note the trick of a deceitful woman: 100
She in the mean time fains the passions
Of a great bellyed woman, counterfets
Their passions and their qualms, and verily
All *Rome* held this for no imposterous stuff.
What's to be done now? Heres a rumor spread
Of a young Heir, gods bless it, and a belly
Bumbasted with a cushion: but there wants,
(What wants there?) nothing but a pretty babe,
Bought with some piece of mony, where it skils not,
To furnish this supposed lying in.   110
Nurse.   I protest my Lord, the fellow i'th' night cap
    Hath not spoke one true word yet.
Appius.   Hold you your prating woman til you are call'd.
Orator.   'Tis purchast. Where? From this mans bond-woman.
    The mony paid. [*to Marcus Clodius*] What was the sum of mony?
Marcus Clodius.   A thousand Drachmas.
Orator.   Good, a thousand Drachmas.
Appius.   Where is that bond-woman?
Marcus Clodius.   She's dead, my Lord.
Appius.   O dead, that makes your Cause suspicious.
Orator.   But here's her deposition on her death bed,
    With other testimony to confirm   120
    What we have said is true. Wilt please your Lordship
    Take pains to view these writings. [*Proffers papers.*] Here, my Lord,
    We shall not need to hold your Lordships long,
    We'l make short work on't.
Virginius   My Lord.
Appius.   By your favour.
    [*to Marcus Clodius*] If that your claim be just, how happens it

95 *Numitorius*—] ~. Q
97 side—] ~. Q
106 a belly] Dyce 2; belly Q
107 there] Dilke; their Q
114 bond-woman.] ~ₐ Q

115 SD] *after* Dilke; *not in* Q
117 bond-woman?] ~. Q
122 SD] This ed.; *not in* Q
125 SD] This ed.; *not in* Q; *to Orator* Lucas

That you have discontinued it the space
Of fourteen years?
Orator.   I shall resolve your Lordship.
Icilius.   I vow this is a practis'd Dialogue:
Comes it not rarely off?
Virginius.   Peace, give them leave.
Orator.   'Tis very true, this Gentleman at first   130
Thought to conceal this accident, and did so,
Only reveal'd his knowledg to the mother
Of this fair bond-woman, who bought his silence
During her life time with great sums of Coyn.
Appius.   Where are your proofs of that?
Orator.   Here, my good Lord,
With depositions likewise. [*Proffers more papers.*]
Appius.   Well, go on.   [G2ʳ]
Orator.   For your question
Of discontinuance: put case my slave
Run away from me, dwell in some near City
The space of twenty years, and there grow rich,   140
It is in my discretion, by your favor,
To seize him when I please.
Appius.   That's very true.
Virginia.   Cast not your nobler beams, you reverend Judges,
On such a putrified dunghil.
Appius.   By your favour, you shall be heard anon.
Virginius.   My Lords, believe not this spruce Orator.
Had I but fee'd him first, he would have told
As smooth a tale on our side.
Appius.   Give us leave.
Virginius.   He deals in formal glosses, cunning showes,
And cares not greatly which way the Case goes;   150
Examine I beseech you this old woman,
Who is the truest witness of her birth.
Appius.   Soft you, is she your only witness?
Virginius.   She is, my Lord.
Appius.   Why, is it possible
Such a great Lady in her time of child birth,
Should have no other Witness but a Nurse?

136 SD] This ed.; *not in* Q   143 Judges,] ~ₐ Q
138 discontinuance:] ~. Q

Virginius.   For ought I know the rest are dead, my Lord.
Appius.   Dead? No my Lord, belike they were of counsel
    With your deceased Lady, and so sham'd
    Twice to give colour to so vile an act.   160
    Thou Nurse observe me, thy offence already
    Doth merit punishment beyond our censure,
    Pull not more whips upon thee.
Nurse.   I defie your whips, my Lord.
Appius.   Command her silence Lictors.
Virginius.   O injustice!
    You frown away my Witness; is this Law?
    Is this uprightness?
Appius.   Have you viewed the Writings?
    This is a trick to make our slaves our heirs
    Beyond prevention.
Virginius.   *Appius,* wilt thou hear me?
    You have slandred a sweet Lady that now sleeps   170
    In a most noble Monument. Observe me,
    I would have ta'ne her simple word to gage
    Before his soul or thine.
Appius.   That makes thee wretched.
    Old man, I am sorry for thee that thy love
    By custome is growne natural, which by nature
    Should be an absolute loathing. Note the Sparrow,   [G2ᵛ]
    That having hatch'd a Cucko, when it sees
    Her brood a Monster to her proper kind,
    Forsakes it, and with more fear shuns the nest,
    Then she had care i'th' Spring to have it drest.   180
    Cast thy affection then behind thy back,
    And think.
Orator.   Be wise, take counsel of your friends.
    You have many souldiers in their time of service
    Father strange children.
Virginius.   True: and Pleaders too,
    When they are sent to visit Provinces.
    You my most neat and cunning Orator,
    Whose tongue is Quick-silver, pray thee good *Janus*

174 love∧] ~, Q   **187** pray] Pray Q
182 think.] ~.— Q

Look not so many several wayes at once,
But go to th' point.
Orator.   I will, and keep you out
At points end, though I am no souldier.   190
Appius.   First the oath of the deceased bond-woman.
Orator.   A very vertuous Matron.
Appius.   Join'd with the testimony of *Clodius.*
Orator.   A most approved honest Gentleman.
Appius.   Besides six other honest Gentlemen.
Orator.   All Knights, and there's no question but their oaths
Will go for currant.
Appius.   See my reverend Lords,
And wonder at a Case so evident.
Virginius.   My Lord, I knew it.
Orator.   Observe my Lord how their own Policy   200
Confounds them. Had your Lordship yesterday
Proceeded as 'twas fit, to a just sentence,
The Aparrel and the Jewels that she wore,
More worth then all her Tribe, had then been due
Unto our Client: now to cosen him
Of such a forfeit, see they bring the maid
In her most proper habit, bond-slave like,
And they will save by th' hand too. Please your Lordships,
I crave a sentence.
Virginius.   *Appius!*
Virginia.   My Lord!
Icilius.   Lord *Appius!*
Virginius.   Now by the Gods here's juggling.   210
Numitorius.   Who cannot counterfeit a dead mans hand?
Virginius.   Or hire some villains to swear forgeries?
Icilius.   *Clodius* was brought up in your house my Lord,
And that's suspicious.
Numitorius.   How is't probable,   [G3ʳ]
That our wife being present at the child-birth,
Whom this did nearest concern, should nere reveal it?
Virginius.   Or if ours dealt thus cunningly, how haps it
Her policy, as you term it, did not rather
Provide an Issue male to chear the father?

196 All Knights] AllKnights Q   210 *Appius!*] ~. Q
209 *Appius!*] ~. Q   Lord!] ~. Q

Orator.   I'l answer each particular.

Appius [*indicating depositions*].   It needs not,   220

    Heres witness, most sufficient witness.

    [*to Virginius*] Think you, my Lord, our Lawes are writ in snow,

    And that your breath can melt them?

Virginius.   No my Lord,

    We have not such hot livers: Mark you that!

Virginia.   Remember yet the Gods, O *Appius*,

    Who have no part in this. Thy violent Lust

    Shall like the biting of the invenom'd Aspick,

    Steal thee to hell. So subtil are thy evils,

    In life they'l seem good Angels, in death divels.

Appius.   Observe you not this scandal?

Icilius.   Sir, 'tis none.   230

    I'l show thy Letters full of violent Lust

    Sent to this Lady.

Appius.   Wilt thou breath a lye

    'Fore such a reverend Audience?

Icilius.   That place

    Is sanctuary to thee. Lye? See here they are.   [*He displays letters.*]

Appius [*to Senators*].   My Lords, these are but dilatory shifts.

    [*to Icilius*] Sirrah I know you to the very heart,

    And I'l observe you.

Icilius.   Do, but do it with Justice.

    Clear thy self first, O *Appius*, ere thou judg

    Our imperfections rashly, for we wot

    The Office of a Justice is perverted quite   240

    When one thief hangs another.

1 Senator.   You are too bold.

Appius.   Lictors take charge of him.

Icilius.   'Tis very good.

    Will no man view these papers? What not one?

    Jove thou hast found a Rival upon earth,

    His nod strikes all men dumb.

          [*Lictors advance. Icilius kneels to Appius.*]

             My duty to you.

220 SD] This ed.; *not in* Q   236 SD] This ed.; *not in* Q
222 SD] This ed.; *not in* Q   237 Do,] ~ₐ Q
234 SD] This ed.; *not in* Q   240 of a] Q; of Dyce 2
235 SD] This ed.; *not in* Q   245 SD] This ed.; *not in* Q

The Ass that carried *Isis* on his back,
Thought that the superstitious people kneel'd
To give his dulnesse humble reverence.
If thou thinkst so, proud Judg, I let thee see
I bend low to thy Gown, but not to thee.   *[Lictors seize Icilius.]*   250

Virginius.   There's one in hold already. Noble youth,   [G3ᵛ]
Fetters grace one being worn for speaking truth;
I'l lye with thee, I swear, though in a dungeon;
[to Appius] The injuries you do us we shall pardon,
But it is just the wrongs which we forgive,
The gods are charg'd therewith to see revenged.

Appius.   Come, y'are a proud *Plebeian.*

Virginius.   True my Lord.
Proud in the glory of my Ancestors,
Who have continued these eight hundred years:
The Heralds have not knowne you these eight months.   260

Appius.   Your madness wrongs you, by my soul I love you.

Virginius.   Thy soul?
O thy opinion old *Pythagoras!*
Whither, O whither should thy black soul fly,
Into what ravenous bird or beast most vile?
Only into a weeping Crocodile.
Love me?
Thou lov'st me (*Appius*) as the earth loves rain,
Thou fain wouldst swallow me.

Appius.   Know you the place you speak in?

Virginius.   I'l speak freely.   270
Good men too much trusting their innocence
Do not betake them to that just defence
Which Gods and Nature gave them; but even wink
In the black tempest, and so fondly sink.

Appius.   Let us proceed to sentence.

Virginius.   Ere you speak
One parting farwel let me borrow of you
To take of my *Virginia.*

Appius.   Now my Lords,
We shall have fair confession of the truth.
[to Virginius] Pray take your course.

250 SD] *after* Dilke (*after* him. *in line 242*); *not*
in Q
251 youth,] ~ₐ Q

254 SD] *as* Dilke; *not in* Q
263 *Pythagoras!*] ~, Q
279 SD] This ed.; *not in* Q

559

Virginius.   Farewel my sweet *Virginia*, never, never   280
         Shall I taste fruit of the most blessed hope
         I had in thee. Let me forget the thought
         Of thy most pretty infancy, when first
         Returning from the Wars, I took delight
         To rock thee in my Target, when my Girl
         Would kiss her father in his burganet
         Of glittering steel hung 'bout his armed neck;
         And viewing the bright mettal, smile to see
         Another fair *Virginia* smile on thee;
         When I first taught thee how to go, to speak;   290
         And when my wounds have smarted, I have sung
         With an unskilful, yet a willing voice,   [G4ᵛ]
         To bring my Girl asleep. O my *Virginia*,
         When we begun to be, begun our woes,
         Increasing still, as dying life still growes.
Appius.   This tediousness doth much offend the Court.
         Silence: attend her Sentence.
Virginius.   Hold, without Sentence I'l resign her freely,
         Since you will prove her to be none of mine.
Appius.   See, see, how evidently Truth appears.   300
         Receive her *Clodius*.
Virginius.   Thus I surrender her into the Court
         Of all the Gods.   *Kills her* [*with a knife*].
                 And see proud *Appius* see,
         Although not justly, I have made her free.
         And if thy Lust with this Act be not fed,
         Bury her in thy bowels, now shee's dead.
Omnes.   O horrid act!
Appius.   Lay hand upon the Murderer.
Virginius.   Oh for a ring of pikes to circle me.
         What! Have I stood the brunt of thousand enemies,   310
         Here to be slain by hang-men? No. I'l fly
         To safety in the Camp.   [*Exit.*]
Appius.   Some pursue the villain,
         Others take up the body. Madness and rage
         Are still th' Attendants of old doting age.   [*Exeunt.*]

---

289 thee;] ~. Q
290 speak;] ~, Q
303 *Kills her*] *to right of line 302* Q   *with a knife*] This ed.; *not in* Q

310 enemies,] ~ₐ Q
312 SD] Dilke; *not in* Q
314 SD] Dilke; *not in* Q

[IV.ii]

Enter two Souldiers [one with a knapsack].

1 Souldier.   Is our Hut swept clean?

2 Souldier.   As I can make it.

1 Souldier.   'Tis betwixt us two;
But how many think'st thou, bred of Roman blood,
Did lodg with us last night?

2 Souldier.   More I think then the Camp hath enemies,
They are not to be numbred.

1 Souldier.   Comrague, I fear
Appius will doom us to *Acteons* death,
To be worried by the Cattel that we feed.
How goes the day?

2 Souldier.   My stomack has struck twelve.

1 Souldier.   Come see what provant our knapsack yeilds.   10
                    [He takes out a crust and old cheese.]
This is our store, our Garner.

2 Souldier.   A smal pittance.

1 Souldier.   Feeds *Appius* thus, is this a City feast?
This crust doth taste like date stones, and this thing
If I knew what to call it—

2 Souldier.   I can tell you: [G4ᵛ]
Cheese struck in years.

1 Souldier.   I do not think but this same crust was bak'd
And this cheese frighted out of milk and whey
Before we two were souldiers: though it be old
I see 't can crawl; what living things be these
That walk so freely 'tween the rind and pith?   20
For here's no sap left.

2 Souldier.   They call them Gentles.

1 Souldier.   Therefore 'tis thought fit,
That Souldiers by profession Gentlemen
Should thus be fed with Gentles. I am stomack sick,
I must have some strong water.

2 Souldier.   Where will you hav't?

IV.ii] *as* Dyce 1; *not in* Q   **2** *2 Souldier*] *as* Dilke; 2 Q *(so to line 33)*
0.1 *one . . . knapsack*] This ed.; *not in* Q   **10.1** SD] This ed.; *not in* Q
1 *1 Souldier*] *as* Dilke; 1 Q *(so to line 33, except*   **14** it—] ~. Q
    for 1. *at line 6)*

1 Souldier.   In yon green ditch, a place which none can pass
　　　But he must stop his nose, thou know'st it well,
　　　There where the two dead dogs lye.
2 Souldier.　　　　　　　　　　Yes I know't.
1 Souldier.   And see the Cat that lyes a distance off
　　　Be flead for supper. Though we dine to day　　　　　30
　　　As Dutch men feed their souldiers, we will sup
　　　Bravely like *Roman* Leaguerers.
　　　　　Enter MINUTIUS *with his Souldiers, reading a Letter.*
2 Souldier.   Sir, the General.
1 Souldier.　　　　　　　Wee'l give him place,
　　　But tell none of our dainties, lest we have
　　　Too many guests to supper.　　　　　　　　[*Exit.*]
Minutius [*aside*].   Most sure 'tis so, it cannot otherwise be,
　　　Either *Virginius* is degenerate
　　　From the ancient vertues he was wont to boast,
　　　Or in some strange displeasure with the Senate;
　　　Why should these letters else from *Appius*　　　40
　　　Confine him a close prisoner to the Camp?
　　　And which confirmes his guilt, why should he fly?
　　　Needs then must I incur some high displeasure
　　　For negligence to let him thus escape;
　　　Which to excuse, and that it may appear
　　　I have no hand with him, but am of faction
　　　Oppos'd in all things to the least misdeed,
　　　I will casheir him, and his Tribuneship
　　　Bestow upon some noble Gentleman
　　　Belonging to the Camp. [*to the Souldiers*] Souldiers and friends,　50
　　　You that beneath *Virginius* Colours marcht,
　　　By strict command from the *Decemvirat*,
　　　We take you from the charge of him late fled,　　　　[H1ʳ]
　　　And his Authority, Command, and Honour
　　　We give this worthy Roman. Know his Colours,
　　　And prove his faithful Souldiers.
Roman.　　　　　　　Warlike General,
　　　My courage and my forwardnesse in battel,

32.1 SD] *after line 35* Q   *Souldiers,*] souldiers‸   **36** SD] This ed.; *not in* Q
Q   **50** SD] This ed.; *not in* Q
35 SD] This ed.; *not in* Q; *Exeunt.* Dilke

Shal plead how well I can deserve the title,
To bee a Roman Tribune.
        Enter the first mutinous Souldier [*1 Souldier*] *in haste.*
Minutius.   Now, the newes?
1 Souldier.   *Virginius* in a strange shape of distraction,   60
Enters the Campe, and at his heels a legion
Of all estates, growths, ages, and degrees,
With breathlesse paces dog his frighted steps.
It seemes half *Room's* unpeopled with a traine
That either for some mischiefe done, pursue him,
Or to attend some uncouth novelty.
Minutius.   Some wonder our fear promises. Worthy souldiers,
Martial your selves, and entertaine this novel
Within a ring of steele: Wall in this portent
With men and harnesse, be it ne're so dreadful.   [*Shout within.*]   70
Hee's entred, by the clamour of the camp,
That entertaines him with these ecchoing showts.
Affection that in Souldiers hearts is bred,
Survives the wounded, and out lives the dead.
    Enter VIRGINIUS *with his knife, that and his arms stript up to the elbowes all*
        bloudy; coming into the midst of the soldiers, he makes a stand.
Virginius.   Have I in all this populous Assembly
Of souldiers that have prov'd *Virginius* valour,
One friend? Let him come thrill his partisan
Against this brest, that through a large wide wound,
My mighty soule might rush out of this prison
To flie more freely to yon christal pallace,   80
Where honour sits inthronis'd. What, no friend?
Can this great multitude then yeild an enemy
That hates my life? Here let him seise it freely.
What, no man strike? Am I so wel beloved?
Minutius then to thee. If in this camp
There lives one man so just to punish sin,
So charitable to redeem from torments
A wretched souldier, at his worthy hand
I beg a death.   [H1ᵛ]

59 *1 Souldier*] *as Dyce 2 (replacing Q first*   **71** entred,] ~∧ Q
    mutinous Souldier); *not in Q*   **89** I beg] *Dilke;* beg Q; I beg *c.w.*
70 SD] *This ed.; not in Q*

Minutius.   What means *Virginius*?

Virginius.   Or if the Generals heart be so obdure   90
     To an old begging souldier, have I here
     No honest Legionary of mine own Troop
     At whose bold hand and sword, if not entreat,
     I may command a death?

1 Souldier.   Alas good Captain.

Minutius.   *Virginius*, you have no command at all,
     Your Companies are elsewhere now bestowed.
     Besides, we have a Charge to stay you here,
     And make you the Camps prisoner.

Virginius.   General, thanks.
     For thou hast done as much with one harsh word
     As I beg'd from their weapons. Thou hast kill'd me   100
     But with a living death.

Minutius.   Besides, I charge you
     To speak what means this ugly face of blood
     You put on your distractions? Whats the reason
     All *Rome* pursues you, covering those high hils,
     As if they dog'd you for some damned act?
     What have you done?

Virginius.   I have plaid the Parricide,
     Kill'd mine own child.

Minutius.   *Virginia*?

Virginius.   Yes, even she.
     These rude hands ript her, and her innocent blood
     Flow'd above my elbowes.

Minutius.   Kill'd her willingly?

Virginus.   Willingly, with advice, premeditation,   110
     And settled purpose; and see still I wear
     Her crimson colours, and these withered armes
     Are dy'd in her heart blood.

Minutius.   Most wretched villain!

Virginius.   But how? I lov'd her life. Lend me amongst you
     One speaking Organ to discourse her death;
     It is too harsh an imposition
     To lay upon a father. O my *Virginia*!   [*He weeps.*]

Minutius.   How agrees this? Love her, and murder her?

91 have] Have Q   **107** child.] ~, Q
93 entreat,] ~ˌ Q   **117** SD] This ed.; *not in* Q
102 blodˌ] ~, Q

Virginius.   Yes. Give me but a little leave to drayn
 A few red tears, (for souldiers should weep blood)   120
 And I'l agree them well. Attend me all.
 Alas, might I have kept her chaste and free,
 This life so oft ingag'd for ingrateful *Rome*
 Lay in her bosom. But when I saw her pull'd   [H2ʳ]
 By *Appius* Lictors to be claim'd a slave,
 And drag'd unto a publick Sessions house,
 Divorc'd from her fore Spousals with *Icilius*,
 A noble youth, and made a bond-woman,
 Inforc'd by violence from her fathers armes
 To be a Prostitute and Peramour   130
 To the rude twinings of a leacherous Judge;
 Then, then, O loving Souldiers, (I'l not deny it)
 For 'twas mine honor, my paternal pity,
 And the sole act, for which I love my life,
 Then lustful *Appius*, he that swayes the Land,
 Slew poor *Virginia* by this fathers hand.
1 Souldier.   O villain *Appius!*
2 Souldier.   O noble *Virginius!*
Virginius.   To you I appeal, you are my Sentencers:
 Did *Appius* right, or poor *Virginius* wrong?
 Sentence my Fact with a free general tongue.   140
1 Souldier.   *Appius* is the Parricide.
2 Souldier.   *Virginius* guiltless of his daughters death.
Minutius.   If this be true, *Virginius*, as the moan
 Of all the Roman fry that followes you
 Confirmes at large, this cause is to be pityed,
 And should not dy revengelesse.
Virginius.   Noble *Minutius*,
 Thou hast a daughter, thou hast a wife too,
 So most of you have, Souldiers. Why might not this
 Have hapned you? Which of you all, deer freinds,
 But now, even now, may have your wives deflowred,   150
 Your daughters slav'd, and made a Lictors prey?
 Think them not safe in *Rome*, for mine lived there.
Roman.   It is a common cause.

119 Yes.] ~, Q
123 *Rome*ₐ] ~, Q
130 Peramour] Permour Q
134 life,] ~. Q

137 *Appius!*] ~. Q *Virginius!*] ~. Q
142 *Virginius*] Dilke; *Virginins* Q (turned *u*)
143 *Virginius*,] ~ₐ Q
148 have,] ~ₐ Q

1 Souldier.   *Appius* shall dy for't.

2 Souldier.   Let's make *Virginius* General.

Omnes.   A General, a General, lets make *Virginius* General.

Minutius.   It shall be so. *Virginius* take my Charge,
     The wrongs are thine, so violent and so weighty
     That none but he that lost so fair a child,
     Knowes how to punish. By the Gods of *Rome*,   160
     Virginius shall succeed my full command.

Virginius.   What's honor unto me, a weak old man,
     Weary of life, and covetous of a grave?
     I am a dead man now *Virginia* lives not;
     The self same hand that dar'd to save from shame
     A child, dares in the father act the same.   *Offers to kill himself.*   [H2ᵛ]

1 Souldier [*preventing him*].   Stay noble General.

Minutius.   You much forget revenge, *Virginius.*
     Who, if you dye, will take your cause in hand,
     And proscribe *Appius*, should you perish thus?   170

Virginius.   Thou oughtest *Minutius.* Soldiers, so ought you.
     I'm out of fear, my noble wife's expir'd,
     My daughter (of blest memory) the object
     Of *Appius* lust, lives 'mongst the Elysian Vestals,
     My house yeilds none fit for his Lictors spoil.
     You that have wives lodg'd in yon prison *Rome*,
     Have Lands unrifled, houses yet unseis'd,
     Your freeborn daughters yet unstrumpeted,
     Prevent these mischiefs yet while you have time.

1 Souldier.   We will by you our noble General.   180

2 Souldier.   He that was destin'd to preserve great *Rome.*

Virginius.   I accept your choice, in hope to guard you all
     From my inhumane sufferings. Be't my pride
     That I have bred a daughter whose chast blood
     Was spilt for you, and for *Romes* lasting good.   [*Exeunt.*]
                    Explicit Actus Quartus.

164 not;] ~ₐ Q   **182** you] Dilke; yon Q (*turned* u)
167 SD] This ed.; *not in* Q   **185** SD] Dyce 1; *not in* Q

Actus Quintus Scena Prima. [V.i]

Enter OPPIUS, *a Senator, and Orator.*

Oppius.   Is *Appius* then committed?

Senator.   So 'tis rumor'd.

Oppius [*to Orator*].   How will you bear you in this turbulent state?
    You are a Member of that wretched Faction.
    I wonder how you scape imprisonment?

Orator.   Let me alone, I have learnt with the wise Hedghog
    To stop my cave that way the tempest drives.
    Never did Bear-whelp tumbling down a hill
    With more art shrink his head betwixt his clawes
    Then I will work my safety. *Appius*
    Is in the sand already up to th' chin,   10
    And shal I hazard landing on that shelf?
    Hee's a wise friend that first befriends himself.

Oppius.   What is your course of safety?

Orator.   Marry this.
    Virginius with his Troops is entering *Rome*,   [H3ʳ]
    And it is like that in the market place
    My Lord *Icilius* and himself shall meet.
    Now to encounter these, two such great Armies,
    Where lies my Court of Guard?

Senator.   Why in your heels.
    There are strange dogs uncoupled.

Orator.   You are deceiv'd,
    I have studied a most eloquent Oration,   20
    That shall applaud their fortune, and distaste
    The cruelty of *Appius.*

Senator.   Very good, Sir.
    It seems then you will rail upon your Lord,
    Your late good Benefactor.

Orator.   By the way Sir.

Senator.   Protest *Virginia* was no bond-woman,
    And read her noble Pedigree.

0.1 *Orator.*] This ed.; *the Advocate.* Q   16 Lord] L. Q
2 SD] This ed.; *not in* Q   19 *Orator.*] *Adv.* Q (*so till line 39*)
5 *Orator.*] This ed.; *Advocate.* Q   22 good,] ~ₐ Q
13 *Orator.*] *Advoc.* Q

Orator.   By the way Sir.

Oppius.   Could you not by the way too find occasion
    To beg Lord *Appius* Lands?

Orator.   And by the way
    Perchance I will. For I will gull them all
    Most palpably.

Oppius.   Indeed you have the Art   30
    Of flattery.

Orator.   Of Rhetorick you would say.
    And I'l begin my smooth Oration thus:
    Most learned Captains—

Senator.   Fie, fie, thats horrible, most of your Captains
    Are utterly unlearned.

Orator.   Yet I assure you,
    Most of them know Arithmatick so well,
    That in a Muster to preserve dead payes,
    They'l make twelve stand for twenty.

Oppius.   Very good.

Orator.   Then I proceed:
    I do applaud your fortunes, and commend   40
    In this your observation, noble shake-rags.
    The Helmet shall no more harbour the spider,
    But it shall serve to carowse Sack and Sider.
    The rest within I'l study.

Oppius.   Farewel *Proteus*,
    And I shall wish thy eloquent bravado
    May sheild thee from the whip and Bastinado.
    [*to Senator*] Now in this furious tempest let us glide,   [H3ᵛ]
    With foulded sails at pleasure of the Tyde.   [*Exeunt.*]

30 palpably] Dilke; palbably Q   39 proceed:] ~, Q
32 thus:] ~, Q   47 SD] This ed.; *not in* Q
33 Captains—] ~. Q   48 SD] Dyce 1; *not in* Q

[V.ii]

Enter ICILIUS, HORATIO, VALERIUS, NUMITORIUS (*at one door*) *with*
Souldiers [and Attendant with] Wine; VIRGINIUS, MINUTIUS, *and others at*
the other doore.

Icilius.   Stand.

Virginius.   Make a stand.

Icilius.   A parly with *Virginius.*

Minutius.   We wil not trust our General 'twixt the Armies,
      But upon terms of hostage.

Numitorius.   Well advised!
      Nor we our General: who for the leaguer?

Minutius.   Our selfe.

Virginius.   Who for the City?

Icilius.   Numitorius.

      Minutius and Numitorius meet, embrace, salute the Generals.

Numitorius.   How is it with your sorrow noble brother?

Virginius.   I am forsaken of the gods, old man.

Numitorius.   Preach not that wretched doctrine to your self,
      It wil beget despaire.

Virginius.   What doe you call
      A burning Feaver? Is not that a divel?   10
      It shakes me like an earthquake. Wilt a, wilt a
      Give me some Wine?

Numitorius.   O it is hurtful for you!

Virginius.   Why so? Are all things that the appetite
      Of man doth covet in his perfect'st health,
      What ever Art or Nature have invented,
      To make the boundlesse wish of man contented,
      Are all his poison? Give me the Wine there.—When?
      Do you grudge me a poor cup of drink? Say, Say.
      Now by the gods, I'll leave enough behind me
      To pay my debts, and for the rest, no matter   20
      Who scrambles for't.

Numitorius.   Here, my noble brother!   [*Offers wine.*]
      Alas, your hand shakes. I will guide it to you.

V.ii] *as* Dyce 1; *not in* Q   **5.1** SD] *to right of line 5 (three lines)* Q
0.2 *and . . . Wine*] This ed; *Wine* Q (*to right of*   *meet,*] ~∧ Q
      stand in line 1)   **21** SD] This ed.; *not in* Q

Virginius. 'Tis true, it trembles. Welcome thou just palsie,
    'Twere pity this should doe me longer service,
    Now it hath slain my daughter. So, I thank you;
    Now I have lost all comforts in the world,
    It seems I must a little longer live,
    Bee't but to serve my belly.
Minutius [*to Icilius*].   O my Lord,   [H4ʳ]
    This violent Feaver took him late last night,
    Since when, the cruelty of the disease   30
    Hath drawn him into sundry passions
    Beyond his wonted temper.
Icilius.   'Tis the gods
    Have powred their Justice on him.
Virginius.   You are sadly met my Lord.
Icilius.   Would we had met
    In a cold grave together two months since,
    I should not then have curst you.
Virginius.   Ha! Whats that?
Icilius.   Old man, thou hast shewed thy self a noble *Roman*,
    But an unnatural Father; thou hast turned
    My Bridal to a Funeral. What divel
    Did arme thy fury with the Lions paw,   40
    The Dragons taile, with the Bulls double horne,
    The Cormorants beak, the Cockatrices eyes,
    The Scorpions teeth? And all these by a father
    To be imployed upon his innocent child!
Virginius.   Young man, I love thy true description;
    I am happy now, that one beside my selfe,
    Doth peach me for this act. Yet were I pleased,
    I cou'd approve the deed most Just and noble;
    And sure posterity, which truely renders
    To each man his desert, shal praise me for't.   50
Icilius.   Come, 'twas unnatural and damnable.
Virginius.   You need not interrupt me. Here's a fury
    Wil doe it for you! You are a *Roman* Knight.
    What was your oath when you receiv'd your Knighthood?
    A parcel of it is, as I remember,

25 So,] ~ˌ Q   36 you.] ~. Q (*turned apostrophe*)
28 SD] This ed.; *not in* Q   47 peach] This ed.; teach Q; tax Dyce 2
30 diseaseˌ] ~, Q   54 your Knighthood] yourKnighthood Q

Rather to die with honour, then to live
In servitude. Had my poor girle been ravish'd,
In her dishonour, and in my sad griefe,
Your love and pity quickly had ta'ne end.
Great mens misfortunes thus have ever stood,   60
They touch none neerly, but their neerest blood.
What do you meane to do? It seems, my Lord,
Now you have caught the sword within your hand,
Like a madman you'le draw it to offend
Those that best love you; and perhaps the counsel
Of some loose unthrifts, and vile malecontents
Hearten you to't: goe to, take your course,
My faction shal not give the least advantage
To murtherers, to banquerouts, or theeves,   [H4ᵛ]
To fleece the common Wealth.

Icilius.   Do you term us so?   70
Shal I reprove your rage, or is't your malice?
He that would tame a Lion, doth not use
The goad or wierd whip, but a sweet voice,
A fearful stroaking, and with food in hand
Must ply his wanton hunger.

Virginius.   Want of sleep
Wil do it better then all these, my Lord.
I would not have you wake for others ruine,
Lest you turn mad with watching.

Icilius.   O you gods!
You are now a General; learn to know your place,
And use your noble calling modestly.   80
Better had *Appius* been an upright Judg,
And yet an evil man, then honest man,
And yet a dissolute Judg; for all disgrace
Lights lesse upon the person, then the place.
You are i'th' City now, where if you raise
But the least uproare, even your Fathers house
Shal not be free from ransack. Piteous fires
That chance in Towrs of stone, are not so feared
As those that light in Flax shops; for there's food
For eminent ruin.

66 malecontents] male contents Q

571

Minutius [*to Virginius*]. O my noble Lord!   90
    Let not your passion bring a fatal end
    To such a good beginning. All the world
    Shal honour that good deed in him, which first
    Grew to a reconcilement.
Icilius [*to Virginius*].   Come my Lord,
    I love your friendship; yes in sooth I do,
    But wil not seale it with that bloody hand.
    Joine we our armies. No phantastick copy,
    Or borrowed President wil I assume
    In my revenge. There's hope yet you may live,
    To outwear this sorrow.
Virginius.   O impossible.   100
    A minutes joy to me, would quite crosse nature,
    As those that long have dwelt in noisome rooms,
    Swoun presently if they but scent perfumes.
Icilius.   To th' Senate. Come, no more of this sad tale,
    For such a tel-tale may we term our grief,
    And doth as 'twere so listen to her own words,
    Envious of others sleep, because shee wakes.
    I ever would converse with a griev'd person   [11ʳ]
    In a longe journey to beguile the day,
    Or winter evening to passe time away.   110
    March on, and let proud *Appius* in our view
    Like a tree rotted, fall that way he grew.   [*Exeunt.*]

[V.iii]

    Enter APPIUS *and* MARCUS CLODIUS *in prison, fettered and gyved.*
Appius.   The world is chang'd now. All damnations
    Seize on the Hydra headed multitude,
    That only gape for innovation.
    O who would trust a people?
Marcus Clodius.   Nay, who would not,
    Rather then one rear'd on a popular suffrage,

90 SD] This ed.; *not in* Q
93 good] Lucas, *conj.* Dyce 2; *not in* Q
94 SD] This ed.; *not in* Q
100 impossible] Impossible Q

112 SD] Dyce 1; *not in* Q
V.iii] *as* Dyce 1; *not in* Q
0.1 APPIUS∧] Appius, Q
4 *Marcus Clodius.*] Clod. Q (*so to end of scene*)

Whose station's built on Avees and Applause?
There's no firm structure on these airy Bases.
O fie upon such Greatness!
Appius.   The same hands
  That yesterday to hear me conscionate,
  And Oratorize, rung shril Plaudits forth   10
  In sign of grace, now in contempt and scorn
  Hurry me to this place of darkness.
Marcus Clodius.   Could not their poisons rather spend themselves,
  On th' Judges folly, but must it needs stretch
  To me his servant, and sweep me along?
  Curse on the inconstant rabble!
Appius.   Grieves it thee
  To impart my sad disaster?
Marcus Clodius.   Marry doth it.
Appius.   Thou shared'st a fortune with me in my Greatness,
  I hal'd thee after when I climb'd my State,
  And shrink'st thou at my ruine?
Marcus Clodius.   I loved your Greatness,   20
  And would have trac'd you in the golden path
  Of sweet promotion; but this your decline
  Sowrs all these hoped sweets.
Appius.   'Tis the world right.
  Such gratitude a great man still shall have
  That trusts unto a temporizing slave.
Marcus Clodius.   Slave? Good. Which of us two in our
  Dejection is basest? I am most sure
  Your loathsome dungeon is as dark as mine,
  Your conscience for a thousand sentences
  Wrongly denounc'd, much more opprest then mine.   30
  Then which is the most slave?   [I1ᵛ]
Appius.   O double baseness,
  To hear a drudg thus with his Lord compare!
  Great men disgrac'd, slaves to their servants are.

---

8 Greatness!] ~. Q

9 conscionate,] ~. Q

10 Oratorize] Dilke; Orarorize Q

14 Judges folly] Q; judge fully Dyce 2

16 rabble!] ~. Q

18 my Greatness] myGreatness Q

19 climb'd] Dilke; climb Q; clomb Dyce 2

Enter VIRGINIUS, ICILIUS, MINUTIUS, NUMITORIUS, HORATIO,
VALERIUS, OPPIUS *with Souldiers.*

Virginius.   Souldiers, keep a strong guard whilst we survey
Our sentenc'd prisoners. And from this deep dungeon
Keep off that great concourse, whose violent hands
Would ruine this stone building and drag hence
This impious Judg peice-meal, to tear his limbs
Before the Law convince him.   [*Exeunt Souldiers.*]

Icilius.   See these Monsters,
Whose fronts the fair *Virginias* innocent blood   40
Hath visarded with such black ugliness,
That they are loathsome to all good mens souls.
Speak damned Judg, how canst thou purge thy self
From Lust and blood?

Appius.   I do confess my self
Guilty of both: yet hear me, noble Romans;
Virginius, thou dost but supply my place,
I thine. Fortune hath lift thee to my Chair,
And thrown me headlong to thy pleading bar.
If in mine eminence I was stern to thee,
Shunning my rigor, likewise shun my fall.   50
And being mild where I shewed cruelty,
Establish still thy greatness. Make some use
Of this my bondage. With indifference
Survey me, and compare my yesterday
With this sad hour, my heighth with my decline,
And give them equal ballance.

Virginius.   Uncertain fate, but yesterday his breath
Aw'd *Rome,* and his least torved frown was death:
I cannot chuse but pity and lament,
So high a rise should have such low discent.   60

Icilius [*aside*].   He's ready to forget his injury.
(Oh too relenting age!) [*to Virginius*] Thinks not *Virginius,*
If he should pardon *Appius* this black deed,
And set him once more in the Ivory Chair,
He would be wary to avoid the like,

34.2 *Souldiers*] souldiers Q   49 thee,] ~; Q
39 SD] This ed.; *not in* Q   61 SD] *as* Dilke; *not in* Q
43 damned] Dilke; damn'd Q   62 SD] This ed.; *not in* Q
45 Romans;] ~, Q

Become a new man, a more upright Judge,
And deserve better of the Common Weal?
Virginius.   'Tis like he would.
Icilius.   Nay, if you thus begin,   [I2ʳ]
I'l fetch that shall anatomize his sin.   *Exit.*
Numitorius.   Virginius, you are too remiss to punish   70
Deeds of this nature. You must fashion now
Your actions to your place, not to your passion;
Severity to such acts is as necessary
As pity to the tears of innocence.   *A shout.*
Minutius.   He speaks but Law and Justice.
Make good the streets, with your best men at arms:
Valerius and *Horatio,* know the reason
Of this loud uproar, and confused noise.

                    [*Exeunt Valerius and Horatio.*]

Although my heart be melting at the fall
Of men in place and Office, we'l be just   80
To punish murdrous Acts, and censure Lust.

                    Enter VALERIUS *and* HORATIO.

Valerius.   Icilius, worthy Lord, bears through the street
The body of *Virginia* towards this prison;
Which when it was discovered to the people,
Mov'd such a mournful clamour, that their cryes
Pierc'd heaven, and forc'd tears from their sorrowing eyes.

                    Enter ICILIUS *with the body of* VIRGINIA.

Horatio.   Here comes *Icilius.*
Icilius.   Where was thy pity when thou slewest this maid,
Thou wouldst extend to *Appius?* Pity! See
Her wounds still bleeding at the horrid presence   90
Of yon stern Murderer, till she find revenge;
Nor will these drops stench, or these springs be dry
Till theirs be set a bleeding. Shall her soul
(Whose essence some suppose lives in the blood)
Still labour without rest? Will old *Virginius*
Murder her once again in this delay?
Virginius.   Pause there *Icilius.*
This sight hath stiffned all my operant powers,

---

72 passion;] ~, Q   **78.1** SD] *as* Dilke; *not in* Q
77 *Horatio,*] ~∧ Q   **86.1** SD] *after line 87* Q

Ic'd all my blood, benum'd my motion quite.
I'l powre my soul into my daughters belly, 100
And with a soldiers tears imbalm her wounds. [*He weeps.*]
My only dear *Virginia*!
Appius.   Leave this passion,
Proceed to your just sentence.
Virginius.   We will. Give me two swords. *Appius* grasp this,
You *Clodius* that. You shall be your own hang-men,
Do Justice on your selves. You made *Virginius*
Sluce his own blood lodg'd in his daughters brest,
Which your own hands shall act upon your selves.
If you be Romans, and retain their spirits, [I2ᵛ]
Redeem a base life with a noble death, 110
And through your lust-burnt veins confine your breath.
Appius.   *Virginius* is a noble Justicer,
Had I my crooked paths levell'd by thine,
I had not swayed the ballance. Think not Lords,
But he that had the spirit to oppose the Gods,
Dares likewise suffer what their powers inflict.
I have not dreaded famine, fire, nor strage,
Their common vengeance, poison in my cup,
Nor dagger in my bosom, the revenge
Of private men for private injuries; 120
Nay more then these, not fear'd to commit evil,
And shall I tremble at the punishment?
Now with as much resolved constancy,
As I offended, will I pay the mulct,
And this black stain laid on my family,
Then which a nobler hath not place in *Rome*,
Wash with my blood away. Learn of me *Clodius*,
I'l teach thee what thou never studiest yet,
Thats bravely how to dy. Judges are term'd
The Gods on earth; and such as are corrupt 130
Read me in this my ruine. Those that succeed me
That so offend, thus punish. This the sum of all,
Appius that sin'd, by *Appius* hand shall fall. *Kils himself.*
Virginius.   He dyed as boldly as he basely err'd,
And so should every true bred Roman do.

101 SD] *after* Dilke (*after* Virginia! *in line 102*);   **128** studiest] Q; studied'st Dilke
  not in Q   **133** himself.] ~ₐ Q

And he whose life was odious, thus expiring,
In his death forceth pity. *Clodius* thou
Wast follower of his fortunes in his being,
Therefore in his not being imitate
His fair example.

Marcus Clodius.   Death is terrible   140
Unto a conscience that's opprest with guilt.
They say there is *Elizium* and Hel,
The first I have forfeited, the latter fear.
My skin is not sword proof.

Icilius.   Why dost thou pawse?

Marcus Clodius.   For mercy, mercy I intreat you all.
Is't not sufficient for *Virginia* slain
That *Appius* suffered; one of noble blood,
And eminence in place, for a *Plebian*?
Besides, he was my Lord and might command me:
If I did ought, 'twas by compulsion, Lords,   150
And therefore I crave mercy.   [I3ʳ]

Icilius.   Shall I doom him?

Virginius.   Do, good *Icilius*.

Icilius.   Then I sentence thus:
Thou hadst a mercy, most unmerriting slave,
Of which thy base birth was not capable,
Which we take off by taking thence thy sword.
And note the difference 'twixt a noble strain,
And one bred from the rabble: both alike
Dar'd to transgresse, but see their odds in death:
Appius dy'd like a Roman Gentleman,
And a man both wayes knowing; but this slave   160
Is only sensible of vitious living,
Not apprehensive of a noble death.
Therefore as a base Malefactor (we)
And timerous slave, give him (as he deserves)
Unto the common Hangman.

Clodius.   What, no mercy?

Icilius.   Stop's mouth,
Away with him: [*Souldiers seize Marcus Clodius, gag him, and exeunt.*]
              the life of the *Decemviri*

---

167 SD] This ed.; *not in* Q; MAR. CLAUD. *is*
    removed. Dyce 2

Expires in them. *Rome* thou at length art free,
Restored unto thine ancient liberty.

Minutius.   Of Consuls: which bold *Junius Brutus* first   170
Begun in *Tarquins* fall. *Virginius* you
And young *Icilius* shall his place succeed,
So by the peoples suffrage 'tis decreed.

Virginius.   We martial then our souldiers in that name
Of Consuls, honoured with these golden bayes.
Two Ladies fair, but most infortunate,
Have in their ruins rais'd declining *Rome*,
Lucretia and *Virginia*, both renown'd
For chastity. Souldiers and noble Romans
To grace her death, whose life hath freed great *Rome*,   180
March with her Corse to her sad Funeral Tomb.   *Flourish. Exeunt.*

FINIS.

176 Ladies fair, but] Lucas; fair, but Ladies Q   **181** Corse] *as* Dilke; Course Q   SD] *Exeunt.*
Q (*Flourish. on next line below* Tomb)

Press variants

―――――

Symbols used to identify copies are those of the revised Wing *STC*. The copies collated (all known copies to which we had access) are listed below.

BC   Birmingham Central Reference Library (1659)
CH1   Huntington Library KD 178 (1654)
CH2   Huntington Library 148338 (1659)
CN   Newberry Library (1659)
DT   Trinity College, Dublin (1679)
E   Edinburgh University (1654)
EN1   National Library of Scotland Bute 605 (1654)
EN2   National Library of Scotland H.28.e.2(4) (1654)
IAU   University of Iowa (1679)
L1   British Library 82.c.26(4) (1659)
L2   British Library Ashley 4592 (1659)
L3   British Library 644.f.74 (1654)
L4   British Library 644.f.75 (1659)
LC   Library of Congress Longe Collection (1655)
LG   Guildhall, London (1659)
LT   British Library, Thomason Collection E 234(3) (1654)
LVD   Victoria and Albert Museum Dyce Collection (1679)
MB1   Boston Public Library XG.3977.47 (1654)
MB2   Boston Public Library XG.3977.52 (1659)
MH1   Harvard University Houghton Library 14434.28.75 (1654)
MH2   Harvard University Houghton Library 14434.29 (1659)
NN   New York Public Library (1679)
NP1   Princeton University (1655)
NP2   Princeton University (1679)
O1   Bodleian Library Malone 780 (1654)
O2   Bodleian Library Malone 115(5) (1659)
O3   Bodleian Library Malone 72(4) (1679)
O4   Bodleian Library BB 16(4)Art.Seld. (1659)
OW   Worcester College, Oxford (1654)
PU   University of Pennsylvania (1654)
WF   Folger Shakespeare Library (1654)
Y   Yale University (1654)

Greg distinguished five variations of the title-page. In the revised Wing *Short Title Catalogue* these are numbered W1215–1219, with the 1655 Library of Congress copy being designated W1217A. Its title-page is, however, identical to that of the only other extant copy with the same date. The five title-pages are identified below by their imprints, with an inventory of copies belonging to each issue.

Wing W1215 (Greg, second issue), 'Printed in the Year 1654.': CH1, E, EN2, L3, MB1, MH1, O1, OW, PU, Y

Wing W1216 (Greg, first issue), 'Printed for *Rich. Marriot*, in S. *Dunftans* | Church-Yard *Fleet-ftreet*, 1654.': EN1, LT, WF

Wing W1217–1217A (Greg, third issue), 'Printed in the Year , 1655.': LC, NP1

Wing W1218 (Greg, fourth issue), 'Printed for *Humphrey Mofeley*, and are to be sold | at the *prince's Armes* in St. *Paul's* | Church-yard, 1659.': BC, CH2, CN, L1, L2, L4, LG, MB2, MH2, O2, O4

Wing W1219 (Greg, fifth issue), 'Printed, and are to be fold by moft | Bookfellers. 1679.': DT, IAU, LVD, NN, NP2, O3

INNER B

First state: LC
Second state: all other copies

B4ʳ (4) *Virginiae !*] *Virginia's !*
    (14) ftand.] ~,
    (15) To] to
    (25) *Valer ius*] *Valerius*
    (34) camp,] ~.

OUTER G

First state: LC, NN
Second state: all other copies

G1ʳ (7) *Orator,*] ~.
G2ᵛ (13) Quiclk-fiver] Quick-filver
G3ʳ (5) policy‸] ~,
G4ᵛ (8) Gentels] Gentles
    (11) fick‸] ~,
    (18) off,] ~‸
    (36) efcape,] ~;
    (39) mifdeed.] ~,

A few apparent variants are simply the result of poor inking, type damage, or other anomalies in the printing. The University of Missouri does not hold a copy of the Quarto, as recorded by Wing.

Lineation

For the conventions used here see pp. xiii–xiv.

I.i

2b–3] *as* Dilke; . . . attend | Q

8–9] *as* Dyce 2; *verse* . . . well, | . . . you | Q

10–16] *as* Dilke; *verse* . . . thoughts | . . . servant | . . . of so | . . . person | . . . Rome. | . . . an | . . . times | . . . therefore | . . . elect one | . . . think of | Q

I.iii

15–16 Art . . . love.] *as* Dilke; *one line* Q

58b–9] *as* Dyce 2; *one line* Q

I.iv

191–3] *as* Lucas; *two lines* ... much | Q; *three lines* . . . could | . . . Such | Dyce 2

II.ii

22b–3a] *as* Dyce 2; *one line* Q

100b–1a] *as* Dyce 2; *one line* Q

129b–30a] *as* Dyce 2; *one line* Q

III.iii

99b–100a] *as* Dyce 2; *one line* Q

106–7a] *as* Dyce 2; . . . Lord, | Q

117b–8] *as* Dyce 1; *one line* Q

120b–1] *as* Dyce 1; *one line* Q

212b–13] *as* Dilke; *one line* Q

278b–9a] *as* Dyce 2; *one line* Q

III.iv

12b–13a] *as* Dyce 1; *one line* Q

III.v

3–4] *as* Dilke; *prose* Q

IV.i

135b–6a] *as* Dyce 2; *one line* Q

165b–7a] *as* Dyce 2; *two lines* . . . Witness; | Q

267–8] *as* Dyce 2; *one line* Q

IV.ii

6b–7] *as* Dyce 1; *one line* Q

14b–15] *as* Dyce 2; *one line* Q

V.ii

75b–6] *as* Dilke; *one line* Q

V.iii

26–7] *as* Lucas; . . . Dejection | Q; . . . two | Dilke

Commentary

TITLE-PAGE

6–7 BY JOHN WEBSTER For authorship, see pp. 498–9.

9 Rich. Marriot A bookseller who was active in London during the period 1640–80 and who published plays in the 1650s, including Glapthorne's *Revenge for Honour* in the same year as *Appius and Virginia* (1654). He took over the St Dunstan's Churchyard shop from his father John, who had been based there since 1620.

9–10 S. Dunstans . . . Fleet-Street St Dunstan's in the West ran lengthwise along the north side of Fleet Street between Fetter Lane and Chancery Lane, and at the east and west ends were several booksellers' shops, including, for instance, John Smethwicke's, where his 1611 edition of *Hamlet* was 'to be sold at his shoppe in Saint *Dunstons* Church yeard in Fleetstreet' (Sugden, p. 160).

DRAMATIS PERSONAE

4 Oppius Livy refers to him several times as '*Sp. Oppius*', i.e. Spurius Oppius (Livy, *Romane Historie*, pp. 116, 120, 128). Cf. I.iv.0.1n.

13 Corbulo SDs and speech prefixes sometimes indicate 'Clown', sometimes his name, occasionally both (see II.i.0.1n, and, for the significance for authorship, p. 499). Historically, Corbulo was a great general of the early Roman Empire, famed for his physical strength, so the Clown's name may be a joke if the company clown was a small man (cf. Juvenal, *Satires*, III.251 ff.: 'Corbulo himself could scarce bear the weight of all the big vessels and other gear which that poor little slave is carrying with head erect'). On the considerable resemblances between Corbulo and the Clown in Heywood's *The Rape of Lucrece*, see Stoll, *Periods*, pp. 197–9.

15 Horatio Of the Senators in Livy, only Horatius and Valerius spoke out against Appius. See p. 641.

19 Calphurnia probably derived from *JC*; see p. 642.

ACT I, SCENE i

0.1 MINUTIUS and **OPPIUS** are jointly addressed as 'your Lordships' (3), so that in Jacobean terms they must be recognizable as of high rank. 'Senators' (63) implies that they both wear 'Scarlet' (I.iii.2) gowns, togas, or representations of togas (see pp. 477–9), but **MINUTIUS** is a general (see II.ii.184), so may be in military costume. *Lictors* were low-born officers attending on magistrates (in Jacobean terms, 'a Serieant, a Hangman' [*OED*, citing Cockeram, 1623]; cf. I.iii.30–2, IV.i.312). They enter in advance (cf. 27 and n; historically, in single file, clearing the way), probably bareheaded, and identifiable by their carrying fasces; cf. Chapman's *Caesar and Pompey*, I.ii.0.1, '*Enter some bearing Axes, bundles of rods, bare*', and Jonson's *Sejanus* (III.470), '*Lictors*, resume the *fasces*'. Probably there are two of them, though the company's resources could have extended to four (historically six; see *OCD* 'Lictores', and p. 479). Their presence will reinforce the formality of the summons Minutius announces. Minutius's **Lieutenant** has no entry direction or lines, but, since he is addressed at 129–30 (see n), presumably enters both here and at 63.1.

6.1 APPIUS A key visual element of this scene is that Appius and those who enter with him are not distinguishable by robes of office. Cf. 85n. Although he, as a 'Plebeian' (10), will presumably bow or kneel to the Senate's emissaries, thereby strengthening both the formality and hierarchy of the scene, his clothing and bearing will justify his being addressed as 'my Lord' (17), and will set him apart from his **Cozens** and from Marcus Clodius. It is unclear whether his beard (see II.iii.152) is an indication of age, or if, in Jacobean fashion, all the men have beards. For the duality of Roman and Jacobean social references, see pp. 476–80.

8 signifie While the message may be simply verbal, it is possible a document is presented to Appius, thus providing a visual focus for his decision (cf. *WD* I.i.1n).

9 Decemviri Here, the 'Decemviri legibus scribundis', a commission of ten in favour of whom the Roman constitution was suspended in 451 B.C. while they wrote a codification of the law, particularly as it defined the relations between patricians and plebeians. Appius became their leader, but was later remembered for tyranny; the murder of Virginia was said to have instigated a popular rising in 449 B.C. which overthrew the decemvirs. See Cary, p. 77, esp. n. 12, and *OCD* 'Decemviri', 'Claudius (3), Appius', and 'Verginia'.

10 Plebeian 'the name given to the general body of Roman citizens, as distinct from the privileged *patricii*' (*OCD*). Appius was in fact a patrician, but traditionally remembered for at first championing the plebeian claim for a written law code (see 9n).

13 steer 'govern' (*OED* 7).

13 Empire Although the play is set in early republican Rome, about 450 B.C., the reputation of imperial Rome is frequently invoked, particularly in relation to Appius.

14 Mirrour 'pattern, exemplar' (*OED* 5a). Cf. *DM* I.i.192–3: 'Let all sweet Ladies breake their flattring Glasses, | And dresse themselves in her'; also *DLC* III.iii.13.

18–19 children ... devoure them Cf. *DM* I.i.451–2.

21 bits morsels (*OED* bit 2).

23 private i.e. 'not holding public office' (*OED* 2a).

23 affection 'inclination' (*OED* 5).

24 slighted 'treated with indifference or disdain' (*OED* 1).

27 make way Point may be given to this command if the **Lictors**, preceding Oppius and Minutius, take a route that requires the Cousins and Marcus Clodius to fall back (see 0.1n).

30–1 raise your kindred A possible allusion to Buckingham's notorious favours to his kinsfolk (leading eventually to articles of impeachment presented in Parliament on 10 May 1626; see pp. 471–2, and Lockyer, p. 322).

32 yonder It will be clear in performance whether the gesture indicates offstage in the direction of the departed emissaries from the Senate, or an on-stage 'seat' of power (see 99 and n).

33 Or banisht Rome! Cf. *WD* I.i.1 and *DM* III.v.1.

34 forbear 'leave (me) alone' (*OED* 4c).

35 dost thou Appius's adoption of the singular signals the subordinate status of Marcus Clodius.

36 be-agued 'shaken as with a fever'.

37 accepted The usual sense of 'received as offered', but unusual, as Lucas notes, in being followed by **at**.

39 them 'themselves' (*OED* 4).

41–3 swallowes . . . Spring Cf. *DM* III.v. 5–6: 'But your wiser buntings | Now they are fledg'd, are gon.'

44 fit 'punish appropriately' (see *OED* 12).

48–50 I have heard . . . feet Sykes suggests that the source is Montaigne, *Essayes*, II.ii (p. 200), where the author describes how his father used to employ hollow staves filled with lead to exercise his arms 'and shooes with leaden soles, which he wore to enure himselfe to leape, to vault, and to run'. Lucas notes that 'the Italian fencing master Rocko, who taught in England in the closing years of the sixteenth century, made his pupils "weare leaden soules in their shoes to make them more nimble"'.

48 footmen 'competitors in a foot-race' (see *OED* 1b); cf. *CC* IV.i.140.

52 faint denyall Cf. *DLC* I.ii.125–6, and *JC* I.ii.236–43.

58 thrifty 'prosperous' (*OED* 1) in the sense of 'profitable'.

59–61 Had I . . . office Stoll (*Periods*, p. 205) compares Marlowe's *Dr Faustus* 330–1 [I.iii]: 'Had I as many soules as there be Starres, | I'de give them all for *Mephostophilis*', in support of associating Appius with the Marlovian Machiavel type (so Lucas). *Briarius* (Briareos) was one of the hundred-handed giants who aided Zeus against the Titans.

63.1 Lictors As before, they will precede the Senators.

68–9 great men . . . shadowes 'all glory has a dark side to it' (so Lucas, who suggests that '*shadowes* may have been also associated in W's mind here with the Latin use of *umbra* to denote the hangers-on of the great'). See *OED* shadow 8a and *DLC* 'To the Juditious Reader' 5 and n; there may possibly be an allusion to 'the darker part of a picture' (*OED* 3); cf. *MonH* (Lucas) 11.

70 generall . . . end i.e. 'judgement day', when the **generall** ('whole' [*OED* 1c]) **frame** ('universe' [*OED* 8]) **takes end** (= 'ends'; not recorded in *OED*, but analogous with 'take beginning' [take 52b]).

73 noble friends As 83 makes clear, Appius has turned to address 'my kindred and my friends'.

79 travell With, as Lucas notes, a quibble on (1) 'travel', and (2) 'travail, toil'; cf. 95 and *DLC* I.ii.186–7.

85 hither This implies that Minutius is summoning Appius to another part of the stage, probably to a dais holding a 'seat'; cf. 91n.

85 robes The Lictors presumably robe Appius with formality as he starts his long speech. See 91n and pp. 477–8.

91 this reverend seat Although the reference could be abstract, it seems most likely that the 'Ivory Chair' (V.iii.64) is either introduced on stage now, or has been present from the start (cf. 32n, 85n). The 'sella curulis', the ivory chair of state, was retained by republican Rome's consuls from the period of kingship prior to 500 B.C., and became literally the seat of justice. Historically it was a folding seat without back or arms, but may here be similar to a Jacobean state, a raised throne on a dais (see *OCD* 'Sella curulis', and Cary, p. 73). If Appius stands before it to be robed (see 95), and possibly sits on it before starting to exercise authority (perhaps at 'now your Judge' [112], prior to dismissing his kin, and instructing Minutius), his power will be firmly and emblematically established.

93 Ornament 'a quality or circumstance that confers . . . honour' (*OED* 2b).

95 travell Cf. 79n.

105 Barbarian 'foreigner' (*OED* 1), but more specifically here 'one living outside the pale of the Roman Empire and its civilization, applied especially to the northern nations that overthrew them' (*OED* 2b). Cf. *Cor.* III.i.237–8: 'I would they were barbarians . . . not Romans.'

107 But only 'a not uncommon pleonasm' (so Lucas, who compares *3H6* IV.ii.25: 'For I intend but only to surprise him'). See Abbott, Sect. 130.

108 a Both metre and sense require insertion of the article, which is missing from Q.

109–11 Justice . . . above Cf. Jonson, *Catiline*, V.599: 'Iustice is neuer angrie', and Massinger, *Parliament of Love*, V.i.251–4: 'Wee are resolud, and with an equall hand | Will hold the scale of iustice, pitty shall not | Robb vs of strength and will to draw her sword | Nor passion transport vs', and Hall, *Characters*, pp. 58–9: 'On the bench . . . al priuate respects of blood, alliance, amitie are forgotten; and if his own sonne come vnder triall, hee knowes him not.'

114 turne 'weigh down, preponderate' (see *OED* 58); Appius's point is that 'a masse of Pearle | Or Diamonds' (as a bribe) will no more tip his scales of justice than a 'feather' (113) would.

114–15 masse . . . Diamonds This extravagant image recalls the Duchess of Malfi thinking of death by diamonds or pearls (*DM* IV.ii.203–5), but it may glance at Buckingham's celebrated opulence of dress. Sir Henry Wotton described Buckingham in Paris 'gorgeously clad in a Suit all over-spread with Diamonds' ('A Short View of the Life and Death of *George Villiers*, Duke of Buckingham' [1642], in *The Harleian Miscellany* [London, 1746], VIII, 593). Lockyer notes (p. 367) that 'in February 1627 Buckingham raised £1,500 by having the buttons cut off his pearl suit'. See pp. 471–2.

115–17 excellent Lapwing . . . nest The **Lapwing** lures predators away from its **nest** by fluttering with feigned alarm over a spot distant from the **nest**. Cf. Tilley L68: 'The Lapwing cries most when farthest from the nest', and *Err.* IV.ii.27: 'Far from her nest the lapwing cries away.'

119 Your businesse, my acquaintance; i.e., 'your business with me, and my acquaintance with you' (or 'with it'). The punctuation adopted here is substantially that of

Dyce. Q's 'Your businesse; my acquaintance, fare you well' would seem to require the
unlikely salutation of his 'loving kinsmen' (87) as 'my acquaintance'.

120–1 Heres . . . proud Q supplies no SD, but it makes good sense, theatrically, for the
Cozens to exit here, their departure emphasized by Appius's 'Now to our present businesse at the camp' (122). 1 Cozen's rhyming couplet, a typically Websterian 'sentence',
strongly suggests direct address to the audience.

121 strait 'straightway, immediately' (*OED* straight 2a).

122 present businesse The speed and authority with which Appius adopts the mode of
rule is remarkable, and will be reinforced if he speaks from the 'seat' (91 and n).

122 camp In this Roman context, not merely a temporary accommodation for soldiers,
but an 'intrenched and fortified site, within which an army lodged or defended itself'
(*OED* 1). Cf. the related sense of 'an army on a campaign, a host' (*OED* 2a) at, e.g.,
I.iii.63.

123–4 The army . . . heare For discussion of contemporary **distrest** armies, see
I.iii.65–74 and pp. 443–4.

123 *Algidon* (*Agidon* Q) A Greek form (with stress on the second syllable) of Mt
Algidus, in the 1,000-metre-high Alban Hills about 25 km. southeast of Rome.
Throughout much of the fifth century B.C. Roman forces sought to dislodge the
Aequi from the strategic pass (later the route of the Via Latina) across its col (see
OCD, 'Algidus'). On ***Algidon*** as evidence concerning W and Heywood's source, see
p. 640.

128 intemperate 'unbridled, violent' (*OED* 2), foreshadowing Virginius's report on
the state of the army in I.iii, and the mutiny in II.ii. Cf. I.iii.65–74n.

129 levies i.e. pressed men, such as the English troops serving under Count Mansfeld in
the mid-1620s, as distinct from volunteers, four regiments of whom had been serving
in the Low Countries under Dutch command since 1624; see pp. 443–4.

129–30 Lieutenant, Send Unless **Send** is an error for 'sent' (= 'has already sent'), this
must be a command, and therefore requires a **Lieutenant** on stage to receive it (see
0.1n).

132 *Exeunt* Dramatic logic will be served if Minutius and his Lieutenant exit by one
door, and the Lictors precede Appius, Oppius, and anyone else on stage (cf. 120–1n)
out the door by which they entered. The Lieutenant could exit earlier, at 130.

ACT I, Scene ii

0.1 NUMITORIUS 'old' (III.iii.269), like his brother Virginius. Despite this being a plebeian family (see IV.i.257), the emphasis in the play is principally upon Jacobean terms
denoting honour and high standing: Numitorius may even be a Senator, since he
appears in I.iv. **ICILIUS** is a young man of good birth, described later as a '*Roman*
Knight*' (V.ii.53). **VIRGINIA** will presumably wear rich 'Aparrel' and 'Jewels' (IV.i.203).

7 character With, as Lucas notes, 'a play on the two senses of written character (cf. *read*)
and moral character'.

9 censure 'judgement' (*OED* 3).

10 ornaments Cf. I.i.93.

12 patterne 'an example or model of a particular excellence' (*OED n.* 1). Cf. *H8* V.iv.20–2: 'She shall be . . . A pattern to all princes.'

13 ceremonious 'full of ceremony' (*OED* 2), here with a positive sense of formality and harmony, in contrast with 'a thronging presence' (14).

14 presence i.e. 'presence chamber'; cf. *DM* I.i.78n.

15 confirm'd 'convinced' (see *OED* confirm 9).

15 shew 'appear'.

16 port 'behaviour, conduct' (*OED* 1c).

20 borrowed painting 'counterfeit [*OED* borrowed 2a] use of cosmetics'.

23–4 Thus Ladies . . . kindnesse Numitorius jokingly misinterprets Virginia's modest refusal of flattery as traditional fear that such praise will only last during wooing, but will not survive marriage; cf. *CC* I.i.136–41.

25–42 Virginius . . . Senate house The Servant cannot have had time enough to impart all this information as he '*whispers Icilius in the eare*' (24 SD), but the vivid painting of Virginius's arrival is evidently the prime purpose (even to the extent of Icilius describing the horse and rider as if he were an eyewitness [34–8]).

28 strange 'exceptional, abnormal' (see *OED* 8, 10; but cf. also 9, 'exceptionally great').

31 shew 'appear'; cf. 15.

32 Cozen i.e. 'Neece' (3). This usage is common; cf. *Ado* I.ii.1–2: 'How now, brother, where is my cousin, your son?'

34 forme (1) 'image, likeness' (*OED* 2), and (2) 'character, nature' (*OED* 5).

35 shewes appears; cf. 15n and 31.

37 quailes . . . Heele Shakespeare, in *Ant.* II.iii.37–9, also includes **quailes** as Roman fighting birds; cf. North's Plutarch (1612 ed.), p. 926: 'Oftentimes when they were disposed to see cock-fight, or quails that were taught to fight one with another, *Caesars* cockes or quailes did euer ouercome.' For English cockfights, cf. Gervase Markham, *The Pleasures of Princes* (1635), p. 42: 'that *Cocke* is sayd to be sharpe heeled . . . which every time he riseth hitteth, and draweth blood of his adversary, guilding (as they terme it) his spurres in blood, and threatning at every blow an end of the battell'.

38 forme 'image, likeness' (cf. 34n).

39 orespent 'tired out, exhausted with fatigue' (*OED* overspend 1a).

44–5 how . . . fear Uncertain. Possibilities include 'how close the substance of this threat which makes us fearful is moving', 'how close the Senate is to acting on this threat which makes us fearful', and 'how close the Senate is to considering [see *OED* move 27, though the latest citation is 1509] this threat which makes us fearful'.

ACT I, Scene iii

0.1 melancholly Since this is love melancholy, his clothing may be dishevelled, 'indicating a careless desolation' (*AYLI* III.ii.381). Conventional action probably includes 'Musing and sighing, with [his] arms across' (*JC* II.i.240); cf. *DLC* V.iv.38.1n.

5–8 variance . . . sedition Lucas compares *JC* II.i.66–9: 'The Genius and the mortal instruments | Are then in council; and the state of a man, | Like to a little kingdom, suffers then | The nature of an insurrection.'

7 powers A quibble: (1) 'faculties of mind' (see *OED* 1b), and, anticipating 'combat', (2) 'armies' (see *OED* 8).

10 uncranied i.e. 'uncrannied', with no chink or fissure by which a secret might escape; *OED* cites Drayton, *The Shepheards Sirena*, 69–71: 'that friend, | To whose close uncranied breast | We our secret thoughts may send' (*Works*, III.156).

11–14 firme centre . . . shrinking i.e. 'you may trust me as you would trust the earth, the **centre** of the universe [see *OED* centre 2b], to bear the weight of your foot; or would trust the fixed north and south **poles** to support the celestial sphere, and would not fear them recoiling from the burden (**shrinking**)'. Cf. *WD* V.vi.186–7 and n, and *Troil.* I.iii.85–6: 'The heavens themselves, the planets, and this centre | Observe degree, priority, and place'; and Chapman, *Caesar and Pompey*, V.i.197–200: 'we are now like | The two Poles propping heauen, on which heauen moues; | And they are fixt, and quiet'. On the use of 'to' with the infinitive ('not to fear'), see Abbott, Sect. 349.

15 ear Dyce's emendation of Q's 'ever' is graphically plausible, particularly if a compositor or scribe misread the original as 'e'er' and expanded it. Appius is obviously about to confide in Marcus Clodius.

16 Ha ha he! This is in effect a direction for laughter within Appius's verse line rather than words to be spoken.

16 ponderous 'weighty, serious' (*OED* 3), with a quibble on 'heavy' (*OED* 1) and 'light' (17).

27 affect 'fancy, love' (*OED* 2).

30 statesmens Cf. 'states-man' (45). Q's 'statemens' is found in neither *OED* nor *LION: Drama*.

32 deject 'cast down' (*OED* 1c). Cf. Drayton, *Polyolbion*, XII.229–30: 'One having climb'd some roofe, the concourse to discry, | From thence upon the earth dejects his humble eye' (*Works*, IV.259). Rupert Brooke notes Heywood's use (in a context other than that of lowering the eyes) in *1 If You Know Not Me You Know Nobody* (1605) B4ᵛ: 'deiect your knee' (Brooke, p. 182).

33 countermand Probably used here in the sense of 'control, keep under command' (*OED* 8); cf. Marlowe, *1 Tamburlaine the Great*, III.i.63: 'And all the sea my Gallies countermaund'. Lucas suggests, however, that 'some force can be given to the prefix— in the sense of beating down all opposition and countering it' (see *OED* 7), comparing Daniel, *Complaint of Rosamund*: 'Found well (by proofe) the priuiledge of beutie, | That it had powre to counter-maund all dutie' (*Works of Samuel Daniel* [1609], L5ʳ).

35 I'le prostrate you Perhaps 'I shall submit (your service) reverently (to Virginia)'; see *OED* prostrate 5, and cf. I.iv.173n.

37 fee-simple 'absolute possession' (a term from property law; cf. 'purchase' at 36).

40 trace 'track, follow'.

43 discretion In the sense of 'liberty or power of deciding' (*OED* 4), though there may also be an ironic glance at 'sagacity, sound judgement' (*OED* 6).

43 scantle 'curtail, make scant'.

44 Restraine 'withhold, keep back' (*OED* 4a).

51 two Since W does not elsewhere spell **two** as 'too', Lucas's change is desirable for clarity.

54.1 VALERIUS His clothing and bearing will identify him as a young man of good birth, probably a senator as in Livy (cf. 59.1n); only at III.i.32 do we discover he is also a kinsman of Icilius.

58 We For use of the royal **We**, see pp. 470–1.

58 attend Although this normally means 'wait upon', it seems here also to mean, as at II.i.3, 'await'; see 59.1n.

58 *Exit Valerius* An exit has been provided here because Q gives Valerius another entry direction at 59.1. In performance, however, he may well remain on stage with Appius to await the Senate.

59.1 SD The Senators probably enter in procession, preceded by Lictors, thereby signalling a change of venue, or context, from private to public. As Dyce says, 'instead of Appius going to the Senators, it appears that the Senators come to Appius'. Appius may ascend to the 'Judgment seat' (108; and see 96n). Lucas indicated the beginning of a new scene here, providing an exit direction for Appius, Clodius, and Valerius, and then a new entry direction for Appius, but there is no need for a new scene. The exit and immediate re-entry of Valerius (if it happened; see 58n) is surprising, but an act break rather than a scene break would be needed to entirely smooth out that breach of convention; the additional exit and re-entry for Appius supplied by Lucas is even more unlikely. Elizabethan and Jacobean dramaturgy frequently changed fictive place on the stage without a rigidly realist exit and re-entry of characters; see, e.g., the shift from street to the Capitol in *JC* III.i.

59.1 SD The ***Senators*** probably all wear scarlet gowns or togas, or a representation of togas; see I.i.0.1n, and pp. 477–9. They probably 'sit' (cf. 96n), perhaps on cushions (cf. *Cor.* II.ii.0.1–.2: '*Enter two* OFFICERS *to lay cushions, as it were in the Capitol*'. The Senators may go up steps to their seats; but the nature of Senate seating in Roman plays is uncertain (see p. 483). Q's ghost character '*Spurius*', with no lines or identified function (cf. *WD* II.i.0.2n), appears to be actually spurious, since Livy refers several times to **OPPIUS** as '*Sp. Oppius*' (see Dramatis Personae n). It is just possible, however, that he is simply another Senator. Whether **NUMITORIUS** is a Senator is uncertain (historically, as a plebeian he would not be), but as an old man he would wear a gown, whether or not of senatorial purple.

62–3 Ours . . . cares i.e. 'We willingly involve, associate [see *OED* presence 1a] ourself with the pains, or labour [*OED* trouble 3] of all the anxieties [*OED* care 2] of the state.'

63 camp Both 'army' and 'fortified encampment'; cf. I.i.122 and n.

63.1 VIRGINIUS He will presumably not only be in military costume, but also booted and spurred (as described II.i.33–42), perhaps wearing a cloak, as having just arrived. His age is denoted by his white hair (see IV.i.46–7).

65–74 The camp . . . beggars For contemporary equivalents of ill-supplied, unpaid, and English troops, cf. 72n.

65–6 store . . . plenty Sykes compares Heywood, *The Royal King and the Loyal Subject* (1637), III (E3ʳ): 'wee haue store, of ragges; plenty, of tatters'.

68 star-chamber i.e. 'outside under the sky'. The King's Council sat as a court of law in the **star-chamber**, a room in the palace of Westminster whose ceiling was decorated with stars. The court was so famous that the figurative use is common.

69 field-beds i.e. 'portable beds for use campaigning' (see *OED* 1), but with a clearly ironic reference to beds 'in the open field or upon the ground' (*OED* 2).

70 Yet meet i.e. 'Yet we meet'. On the omission of the nominative in the first person, see Abbott, Sect. 401.

72 provant apparell i.e. clothing 'of or belonging to the **provant** or soldier's allowance; hence, of common or inferior quality' (*OED* provant 3a). Cf. Sir Henry Mervyn to Buckingham: 'The sailors, by reason of want of clothing, are become so loathesome to themselves, and so nastily sick, as to be not only unfit to labour but to live. The "provant clothes" are unserviceable' (*Cal. S. P. Dom.* [Charles I], LXIV, 76 [27 May 1627]).

73 Munition 'ammunition' (*OED* 2a).

74–5 Gentlemen . . . Decemviri No clear distinction is made in the play between decemvirs and Senators, except for the clear pre-eminence of Appius (cf. 102n). Historically, the Senate's powers were temporarily suspended in favour of the decemvirs; see I.i.9n.

76 in mannage i.e. under your 'direction, management' (*OED* manage *n.* 5).

81–2 Sleep . . . bench The decemvirs, or Senate, are a collective magistracy (see 105, 148, and *OED* bench 2a, 3a), paying insufficient attention (cf. *DM* I.i.162–3). Cf. *Tim.* IV.i.5: 'Pluck the grave wrinkled Senate from the bench.'

83 wretchlesse i.e. 'reckless' (see *OED* wretchless 1).

85 Fathers i.e. 'Senators'; see *OED n.* 10b, and, e.g., Jonson, *Catiline*, IV.145–6: 'What face is this, the *Senate* here puts on, | Against me, *Fathers!*'

87–8 no bastard . . . souldiers The point presumably being that illegitimate sons often entered the army.

90 surfet 'superfluity, excessive supply' (*OED* surfeit 1).

91 supply 'provisions' (*OED* 9a), but with the subordinate sense of 'assistance, relief' (*OED* 1).

95 possess'd 'informed' (*OED* possess 10); cf. *MV* I.iii.65: 'Is he yet possess'd | How much ye would?'

96 sit This seems to indicate either that all the decemvirs or Senators are seated (cf. 0.1n); or that Appius is 'Princely' (102) seated alone on the 'Judgment seat' (108) which may have been his since I.i; or both.

96 prescrib'd 'directed, enjoined' (*OED* prescribe 2b).

97 suter i.e. 'suitor'; *OED* recognizes this as an obsolete form.

97 give us limit i.e. 'impose [*OED* give 16a] limits on us'.

102 our Princely Although, as at 96 and elsewhere, Appius is speaking on behalf of the decemvirs and Senate, he manages to make the plural sound like a royal 'we'. This will be reinforced if he is sitting in the 'Judgment seat' (108); cf. 74–5n and 96n.

104 fits not i.e. 'is not seemly, proper' (see *OED* fit 2a).

108 Judgment seat See Rom. 14: 10: 'for we shall all appeare before the iudgement seat of Christ', and *Cor.* III.iii.33–5: 'Th'honor'd gods | Keep Rome in safety, and the chairs of justice | Supplied with worthy men!' Cf. 96n.

110 you, the Statists i.e. 'you statesmen, you with political power' (see *OED* statist 1). Virginius evidently turns to appeal past Appius to the decemvirs and Senators direct.

112 humane i.e. 'human', in the sense of 'characterized by such behaviour towards others as befits a man' (*OED* 1).

113 Furs and Metall Probably 'luxurious clothing and gold' (*OED* metal 1d). Lucas believes that W 'thinks of the Senate as arrayed like City-Fathers of his own day. Fur was worn by prosperous merchants and "Fur-man" is found as seventeenth-century slang for Alderman [Partridge 1984, p. 437]; *Metall* refers to the Alderman's gold chain.' But see 131–2n.

116 an infinite 'a multitude' (see *OED* C. 2c), a substantive usage (not, as Sykes suggests, adverbial, meaning 'an infinite number of'). Cf. Heywood, *The Rape of Lucrece* (1608), V.iii (I1ʳ), 'Before thee infinits gase on thy face, | And menace death', and Chapman, *Caesar and Pompey*, I.ii.109: 'Those infinites of dreadfull enemies'.

124 trouble 'disturb, distress', or 'do harm, oppress' (*OED* 3, 4).

126 too i.e. 'to'; see *CC* II.iv.78n.

128 invasive steel 'invading' (*OED* 2a). Lucas compares Heywood, *The Golden Age*, III.i (F1ᵛ), 'inuasive steele'; also *Jn.* V.i.69: 'arms invasive'.

131–2 gown'd Senate . . . Scarlet Roman plays of the period consistently refer to the scarlet gowns of senators, and gown could mean toga; but if costume was not classicized, the Senators thus described would appear on stage more like an assembly of English judges, who also wore scarlet. Lucas's suggestion of a resemblance to London aldermen is unlikely. Cf. 113n.

133 brawns 'muscles, arms' (see *OED* 1a, 1b).

135 devolv'd 'overthrown' (*OED* devolve 1b). Cf. Heywood, *The Rape of Lucrece*, V.iii (I1ᵛ): 'They behind him will deuolue the bridge.'

135 Treasures 'treasuries, treasure-houses' (see *OED* 3).

150 strong house i.e. the prison to which he would be committed (cf. 148).

151 quick perdue 'alert advanced sentinel' (see *OED* quick 21a, perdue 1b). Cf. Robert Barret, *Theorike and Practike of Modern Warres* (1598), p. 106: 'The proper *forlorne Sentinell* ['sentinel perdue'] is that, which is set either on horsebacke or foote . . . so neare vnto the enemie, that being discryed and seene, he shall with great difficultie retire and escape.'

152 Guilty in the City i.e. those lodged in city prisons; cf. 150.

154 under Keeper Here 'under-gaoler' (see *OED* 2), since, as Lucas notes, 'the dialogue is running on prisons and imprisonment'.

155 gods . . . amend it Lucas compares Heywood, *The Rape of Lucrece*, II.i (B4ᵛ): 'Great *Ioue amend* it.'

155 Break up the Senate On the conflation within the play of the Senate and the decemvirs, see 74–5n.

157–8 soldier . . . danger In February and March 1626 Buckingham was criticized in Parliament for not leading the disastrous Cadiz expedition in person, since it was his project. See p. 472, and Lockyer, p. 313.

159–60 scale Of . . . peace Possibly allegorizing **peace** as holding the **scale** which will balance soldiers fairly.

162 searcht 'probed' (*OED* search 8) by a surgeon.

163 pore upon their bags i.e. 'meditate [*OED* pore 1c] about their money bags [*OED* bag 3]'.

164 resty 'indolent' (*OED a.*¹ 2a). Cf. Jonson, *Epicoene*, I.i.171–2: 'Hee would grow *resty* else in his ease. | His vertue would rust without action.'

166 *Drachma* A small Greek coin worth less than a shilling; cf. *Cor.* I.v.6–7: 'these movers that do prize their hours | At a crack'd drachme!'

170 find 'support, provide for' (*OED* 19a).

173 Prostrates i.e. 'submits reverently' (*OED* 5); cf. I.iii.35n. There is no reason to suppose Virginia herself does more than kneel or offer a deep curtsey.

176 these Q has 'those', but Virginius is addressing present company; 'e/o' confusion is easy in many seventeenth-century hands, and the reverse error occurs in *WD* III.ii.276.

179 election 'choice' (*OED* 2a), but with an added sense of judiciousness (*OED* 2b).

181 Although a Cities child The implication seems to be that those brought up in the city (W and his audience would here be thinking of London) have scant regard for soldiery.

184 processe 'mandate proceeding from a person in authority' (*OED* 11), with a possible glance at legal meanings (cf. *DLC* I.ii.5n and *OED* 7).

188 Wear next my heart Cf. Bosola's comment (*DM* III.ii.301–2).

190 Receive her Evidently Virginia has returned to Numitorius's side while Virginius has been addressing Icilius. Thus flanked by the two older men, the couple's formal betrothal will presumably be reinforced by their clasping each other's hands in handfast in the presence of the **Gentlemen** who **witnesse**.

196 Contract i.e. of betrothal; cf. 190n.

207 pay use . . . forbear i.e. 'pay (heavy) interest [*OED* use 5b] hereafter for what you now withhold [*OED* forbear 7]'.

207 *Exeunt* Virginius's departure for the camp is likely to be signalled by his leaving by the opposite door from the others.

ACT II, Scene i

0.1 *Clown* **[CORBULO]** *whispering* Whatever persona he adopts, the performer will be simultaneously to the audience both the theatre company's *Clown* and the character he portrays (here a fool rather than a clown, named Corbulo, as the Q speech prefix informs the reader). He probably wears an identifying fool's coat and cap; see pp. 479–80. Why or what he should be *whispering* is not explained; it may be to establish for the audience his licensed intimacy with Virginia.

0.1–.2 **MARCUS CLODIUS** *with presents* Q gives Marcus Clodius a double entry, here ('*with presents*') and at 25.1 (with '*Musicians*'). His entry here, remaining in the background, gives added point to his claim to have 'subtilly waited' (26). There is no indication in the text that Clodius gives Virginia the *presents*; their function, therefore, may be to emphasize his rejection when he is left alone still holding them at the end of the scene (so Wellington 1999). Silent business in which he offers them (at, e.g., 'Honour and wealth' [72]) and she rejects them is possible, but unlikely. Marcus Clodius may now be better dressed in order to signal his rise in fortune as a follower of Appius (cf. Bosola: *DM* II.i.0.1n).

0.2 *Musicians* Marcus Clodius presumably has the Musicians with him, despite Q's entry direction being at 25.1 rather than here (see previous note). For an indication of what a contemporary serenading consort might have looked like, see Fig. 8. They are probably the same musicians who have just finished playing during the act break. As Taylor points out, act breaks were standard playhouse practice by the 1620s, and the break here permits what would otherwise be an immediate re-entry for Virginia after the end of the previous scene.

4 **Heir** With, as Lucas noted, a play on 'air' (2).

8 **I am sirrah** Corbulo interrupted Virginia's intended rebuke. He now pretends that her statement was complete, thus allowing him nonsensically to agree with it.

8 **do that** i.e. 'get an Heir' (4).

9 **Lordships . . . manners** Lucas notes the quibble on **manners** and 'manors'.

13 *melior . . . mulier* Corbulo's demonstration of the 'degrees of comparison' (12) as *bonus, melior, optimus* ('good, better, best') allows him to play on the sound of *mulier* (woman), and possibly on Icilius as a noble (see *OED* optimate 1a, where citations include Heywood).

24 **sads** 'saddens' (*OED* 4).

26 **opportunity . . . waited** i.e. 'I subtly deferred action until this opportunity presented itself' (see *OED* wait $v.^1$ 8, 6).

28 **fame** 'render famous' (*OED* 3b).

29 **waite** 'await'; cf. 26n.

31, 47 *Song* Audience pleasure in the two songs will be qualified by the dramatic irony of the absence of 'harmony' (32) in the purpose of their sender. Although the text gives no indication of any particular songs, they are sung by several singers (cf. 45: 'Joyne all your voyces'). At this period such songs might well be madrigals, lighter part songs such as canzonets, or lute songs.

32–3 Oh . . . kindnesse Virginia evidently continues addressing the audience (as at 21–5), presumably turning to Marcus Clodius only when he addresses her.

34 contemplation Marcus Clodius's point is that he is intruding on Virginia when she is alone and apparently lost in meditation.

40 mediate 'procure by intercession' (*OED* 4a) and hence here 'ask for'. Cf. *CC* III.iii.72. As Lucas notes, **mediate** is used a number of times by Heywood; see, e.g., *The English Traveller*, IV.i (I3ᵛ): 'mediate my peace'.

46 usurpe your notes i.e. 'the aire' (45) will borrow (*OED* usurp 4c) and 'eccho' (47) your musical **notes**, as though they were its own.

50–1 hearken . . . sufferings A commonplace of the Petrarchan and courtly love tradition was the suffering and despair experienced by the lover, typically manifested in sighs, tears, and insomnia (as here). Cf. *AYLI* II.vii.147–9: 'And then the lover, | Sighing like furnace, with a woeful ballad | Made to his mistress' eyebrow'.

52 figure 'image, likeness' (*OED* 9).

55 compos'd 'fashioned, put together' (see *OED* compose 1b); cf. *AWW* I.ii.20–1: 'Frank Nature, rather curious than in haste, | Hath well compos'd thee.'

57 miser not miserly with **his wishes**, but in wanting to hoard more 'thoughts' (54) of Virginia which satisfy **his wishes**.

69 populous 'admired by the people, popular' (see *OED* populous 3 and popular 6a).

74 but a refin'd Citizen i.e. 'despite his **refin'd** manners (and hence superior status), he is merely a **Citizen** (as opposed to, in Roman terms, a decemvir or senator, or in English terms, a member of the nobility)'.

75 Boast Probably 'possess as a thing to be proud of' (*OED v.*¹ 7), although *OED* does not record this sense prior to the end of the century. The alternative is 'speak of with pride or ostentation' (*OED* 5b).

81 hearts . . . like twins Cf. Jonson, *The Haddington Masque* (1608), 288–9: 'In GEMINI, that noble power is showne, | That *twins* their *hearts*; and doth, of two, make one.'

82–3 wife . . . to him Cf. *DM* III.ii.231.

84 Shadow 'conceal, keep dark' (*OED* 6a).

ACT II, Scene ii

0.1 Souldiers They evidently carry 'pikes' (see 112 and n), and perhaps 'swords' as well (see 7n).

4 spread i.e. 'are spread over (as corpses)'.

7 draw our swords Since the Soldiers all carry pikes (see 112 and n), this phrase is probably used rhetorically to mean 'take up arms', although it is just possible that one or two of them have stacked their pikes on entry and are now able literally to **draw swords** with which to threaten Minutius (cf. 104–5 and n).

8 motion 'proposal' (*OED* 7a); perhaps, as Lucas suggests, with an allusion to **motion** = 'movement acquired by drill and training (e.g. in fencing)' (*OED* 3c). Cf. *TN* III.iv.275–6: 'he gives me the stuck in with such a mortal motion that it is inevitable'.

9.1 MINUTIUS Presumably booted and spurred, as having just arrived; cf. I.iii.63.1n. He was sent to the camp at the end of I.i.

9.1 his Lieutenant Q gives no entry direction, but he is called for at 93 and replies at 94. His entry here with Minutius is most likely, since he seems to act as 'Lieutenant' to both Minutius (I.i.129–30 and n) and Virginius (83.1), and the entry of Virginius at 93 will be more powerful alone and in contrast to the other two officers ('we are begirt' [86]). Lucas identifies the Lieutenant as Valerius and has him enter with Virginius at 83.1; see 93n.

11 in troopes i.e. 'in such numbers', perhaps suggested by the sense 'a body of soldiers' (see *OED* troop 1d, 1a).

11 quarter 'quarters, assigned station'.

14 suspect 'suspicion' (*OED* 1).

18 Drums and Trumpets There is no suggestion here that Minutius is actually attempting to drown out 1 Soldier's speech as Richard III does the railing queens (*R3* IV.iv.149–54).

20 Stir not By now, if not earlier, the Soldiers are threatening Minutius; cf. 104–5.

22, 33 us Possibly Minutius and his Lieutenant; or Minutius may be adopting the royal plural that is in this play so much the mark of high rank; cf. 86n.

24–8 trench . . . curious fare Cf. Heywood's *The Rape of Lucrece* (1608), III.ii (E3ᵛ), 'thus must poore Souldiers do, | Whilest their commanders are with dainties fed, | They sleep on Downe, the earth must be our bed'.

25 cold iron i.e. his armour and weapons; but perhaps with a glance at the 'manackles, | And shackles' (34–5) which enforce military discipline.

27 field bed i.e. 'portable bed'; cf. I.iii.69n.

28 curious 'exquisitely prepared, delicate' (*OED* 7b).

30 at once i.e. 'simultaneously'.

36 Would you (Dilke; 'Would you would' Q) Dilke comments: 'the soldier intends, I conceive, to ask the question, and not to express it as his wish'.

36–7 caniball . . . City Cf. Marston, *Certaine Satyres*, II.72–6 (*Poems*, p. 74):

> He bit me sore in deepest vsury.
> No Iew, no Turke, would vse a Christian
> So inhumanely as this Puritan.
> *Diomedes* Iades were not so bestiall
> As this same seeming-saint, vile Canniball.

41–2 Romulus . . . wolfe According to myth, **Romulus** and Remus, the founders of Rome, were abandoned as infants and suckled by a **she wolfe**. For the wider implications of wolves in the Jacobean image of Rome, and particularly their parricidal reversal of role to 'devoure our flesh, | Carouse our blood' (43–4), see Ronan, 125–40.

44 Carouse 'drink up, drain', but probably with the implications of 'quaff, swill' (*OED* 2).

47 ease 'relief' (*OED* 10).

51 Deale on 'set to work upon' (*OED* deal 18); cf. *R3* IV.ii.71–3: 'two deep enemies
. . . Are they that I would have thee deal upon'.

52–3 usurer . . . chaire Usurers were typically portrayed sitting down; cf. Massinger,
The Roman Actor (1626), II.i.287.1–.2, where the miser Latinus is '*brought forth a sleepe in
a chayre*'. Their cut-throat behaviour is likewise conventional; cf. Thomas Wilson, *A
Discourse Upon Usury* (1572), ed. R. H. Tawney (London, 1925), p. 358: 'even so the
unmercifull usurer will forbeare for a yere or two, to cut the borrowers throte at laste'.
The usury laws had changed in 1624. For the possibility that this is a cut at
Buckingham as an 'armchair general', see p. 472.

56 thrift 'means of thriving' (*OED* 1a).

59 overthrowes 'defeats' (*OED* 1a).

61–5 What . . . summers of us? Somewhat obscure, because 1 Soldier changes the
syntactic structure within the question. He seems to intend 'Why are we camped in the
open [since we shall die of the winter conditions] unless you can keep it perpetual
summer?' For **of us** = 'on us' see *OED* of prep. 55a, citing Martin Marprelate, *Epitome*
[1589], G1ᵛ: 'ile bestow a whole booke of him'.

61–2 distant . . . enemy The emphasis on privations of soldiers languishing far from
any battlefield reinforces the likelihood of reference to English troops on the south
coast awaiting or returned from European expeditions. See pp. 443–4.

63–4 sick humors . . . earth Cf. Simon Kellwaye, *A Defensative Against the Plague*
(1593), B1ᵛ: 'ouer great and vnnaturall heate and drieth, by great rayne and inundat-
yons of waters, or by great store of rotten and stincking bodies, both of men and
beastes, lying vppon the face of the earth vnburied, as in the time of warres hath bene
seene, which doth so corrupt the ayre, as that thereby our Corne, Fruites, Herbes, and
waters which we dayly vse for our foode and sustenaunce, are infected: also it may
come by some stincking doonghils, filthie and standing pooles of water, and vnsauery
smelles which are neere the places where we dwell'. The belief that diseases such as the
plague were caused by polluted or 'corrupt' air was widespread. Cf. III.iii.200–3 and n.

66–8 You account . . . lives Cf. *WD* V.iii.60–4.

66 Ingines Machines of war, such as ordnance, battering rams, etc. (see *OED* 5a).

69 ravens . . . crowes Traditionally birds of ill-omen; cf. Pliny, *Nat. Historie*,
X.xii.276: '*Of unluckie birds, and namely, the Crow, Raven and Scritch-owle*'.

70 City surfet i.e. 'superfluity, excess (of food) in the **City**'.

75 And all the Suburbs! A theatre joke, since, as Lucas suggests, W's audience was 'very
likely sitting in **the Suburbs** at the moment; and the more disreputable of them would
have had more than a merely dramatic interest in those haunts of evil fame'. Cf. III.iii.43.

81 riot and incontinence The accusation of dissipation and debauchery is counter to
everything we see of Virginius, but is in effect a demand for traditional Roman *gravitas*
in its leaders.

83.1 VIRGINIUS He will still be booted and spurred as at I.iii.63.1; see n. His entry alone
to face down this mutiny is dramatically powerful. The Lieutenant probably entered
with Minutius (see 9.1n), though he could enter here (so Lucas, who identifies him as
Valerius; see 93n).

86 we are begirt The precise sense will depend on the stage picture. Most likely **we** refers only to Minutius and the Lieutenant, who have been **begirt** for some time. They urge Virginius to 'retire' (85) before he is trapped too. Possibly, however, Virginius is included if he has immediately joined the other officers within the ring of mutineers. Minutius is not likely here to be using the lordly 'we' to refer only to himself.

93 our Lieutenant This is probably the **Lieutenant** who serves Minutius in I.i (see I.i.129–30n), who has most likely entered this scene with Minutius (see 9.1n and 83.1n). Cf. 94n.

94 *Lieutenant* Cf. 93n. Q's speech prefix is '*Val.*', but there are both logical and drama-turgical difficulties in identifying Valerius as the Lieutenant. Valerius is always in Rome during other scenes of the play, even when Virginius is at the camp, most noticeably at the family conference in III.i. Even more significantly, in V.i he appears with the Roman party, not with Virginius and Minutius. Textual confusion in III.iii (see 224.1n) about Valerius lends weight to the possibility that the speech prefix for Valerius here is the sort of careless assignment of a part that might have been rectified in performance (by, e.g., giving the role to the 'Roman' who takes over Virginius's command in IV.ii). See pp. 490 and 496.

94 order 'parade' (Lucas), 'marshal' (*OED* 1a). Backstage trumpets or drums could be employed to give evidence that the Lieutenant is carrying out his orders.

95–6 What . . . air Virginius has evidently perplexed Minutius, presumably by briefly walking away from everyone else on stage, which he explains as needing to **Take** (fresh) **air** (see *OED* air 5). He now returns to confront the Soldiers.

98 gall burst For **gall** as 'gall bladder', associated with choler, cf. *Tro.* I.iii.237: 'when they would seem soldiers, they have galls'. Thus a **gall burst** = an overflow of choleric bile.

102 shoot your quils A prevalent misconception about porcupines. Lucas notes Sykes's citation of Dekker, *Satiromastix*, IV.ii.97–8: 'Thou'lt shoote thy quilles at mee, when my terrible backe's turn'd for all this, wilt not Porcupine?' Cf. also Topsell, *Historie*, p. 588: 'When they are hunted the beast stretcheth his skin, and casteth them off, one or two at a time, according to necessity upon the mouths of the Dogs, or legs of the Hunters that follow her, with such violence that many times they stick into trees & wood.'

103 no points . . . Captain Lucas compares *JC* III.i.173: 'To you our swords have leaden points, Mark Antony.'

104–5 shaver . . . throat Given **whet** and **throat**, Virginius clearly intends **shaver** as not only 'fellow' (often used of soldiers and roisterers, but sometimes implying youth; see *OED* 3), but also as 'one who shaves with a razor' (*OED* 1). Possibly the image is literal, if one of the Soldiers had his sword to Minutius's throat when Virginius entered.

107 cholerick Cf. 98n.

108 let you blood 'bleed you' (for medical reasons; see *OED* blood *n.* 1d).

109 i'th' center The image may be literal on stage; cf. 'begirt' (86). If all the soldiers are threatening him with their pikes he will look vulnerable indeed (cf. 112n).

110–11 Aspen . . . tremble Cf. Marlowe, *1 Tamburlaine the Great*, II.iv.4: 'Stand stagger-ing like a quivering Aspen leafe'.

112 Advance your pikes A drill movement in three 'Motions' for a soldier 'to reare his pike vpright against his right shoulder' (see Fig. 11, and Robert Barret, *The Theorike and Practike of Moderne Warres* [1598], p. 34). Cf. *OED v.* 9; and *OED* advanced 4, which cites Clement Edmonds's *Observations upon Caesar's Commentaries* (1604), p. 133: 'it is most fit that all men performe their directions with their pikes aduanced'. As the men bring their pikes up to a vertical position they will not only be all obeying Virginius, but no longer pointing them at him. Cf. *R3* I.ii.40–1: 'Advance thy halberd higher than my breast, | Or by Saint Paul I'll strike thee to my foot.' Later the **pikes** are referred to as partisans, for the terms are partly interchangeable; cf. IV.ii.77n.

112 word 'command' (*OED* 7), but here evidently with the requirement that the sol-diers repeat the **word** of command as they execute the three 'Motions' of the move-ment; see previous note.

115–17 You shal . . . Town Stoll (*Periods*, p. 194) compares this scene with the mutiny in Fletcher, *Bonduca*, especially II.i.110–11: 'Tell the great General, | My companies are no fagots to fill breaches.' Lucas notes that there also 'the soldiers address their com-mander as "Dear, honour'd Captain" [II.i.88], as in 134'.

118 lay down your Arms 'Lay down your pike' was a specific drill movement; cf. 'Advance your pikes' (112 and n). The Soldiers do so (cf. 190), which will change the stage picture entirely, and provide a pregnant pause before Virginius cashiers them. From this point on they are presumably in a single group (unlike the earlier circle) as Virginius alternately addresses them and Minutius.

118–24 Villains . . . market women Lucas suggests the influence of Caesar's 'famous subdual of his mutinous legions in Italy (47 B.C.) by similarly cashiering them and addressing them as "Quirites" ("Citizens") instead of "Soldiers"', and where, 'like Minutius here, Caesar's friends beg the general not to be too harsh'. Cf. Suetonius, *Julius*, 70: 'with one onely word, wherby he named them Quirites, instead of Milites, he did so gently turne and winde, yea and bring them to his bent, that forthwith they made answere, They would be his souldiers still: and so of their owne accord followed him into Africk'.

120 Discipline Cf. Fluellen's obsession with the 'disciplines of war' in *H5*.

123 gives i.e. 'suggests (to me) that' (*OED* 22a).

123 reserv'd 'destined' (see *OED* reserve 6b).

126–7 stand . . . For 'take the place of' (*OED* stand 71h). Cf. Chapman, *Revenge of Bussy D'Ambois*, III.iii.4–5: 'you two onely | Stand for our Armie'.

133 presently 'instantly' (*OED* 3).

135 Refuse me i.e. 'God refuse me!' (= 'May God cast me off'; see *OED* refuse 6b); cf. *WD* I.ii.72.

136 confound 'defeat, bring to nought' their plans (*OED* 1b).

141–2 these . . . campe The mutinous soldiers. Virginius is in effect accusing them of being useless mouths to feed, since they are disloyal.

145 this flesh i.e. Virginius's own body.

146–51 breathlesse . . . distraction Virginius's 'passion' (140), which started at his entry, and increased from 118, leaves him without **breath enough** to continue railing, and finally stalls altogether at 150.

157 private government 'individual, personal exercise of authority' (*OED* private 7a, government 1a).

157 forme 'pattern, example' (*OED* 7).

159 obedience The syntax requires this emendation to Q's 'obedient', since Minutius's claim is that **the like obedience** is due to 'every Captain' (156) as to 'Kings' (158). Minuscule 'c' and 't' are readily confused in Secretary hand, so it is possible that the original spelt the noun 'obedienc', which occurs three times in Hand D of the manuscript play *Sir Thomas More*. But since Q's mistake may have arisen not through misreading, but through a scribe's or compositor's misunderstanding of the form of a sentence in which soldiers and subjects are urged to be 'obedient', emendation to the more common form of the noun seems preferable.

165 pioneer 'footsoldier with spade, pickaxe, etc. to dig trenches, repair roads etc.' (see *OED* 1).

167 give us leave Minutius's plural seems to imply the dignity of his rank; cf. Appius's use of 'we' at I.iii.141.

170 example to succeeding times Cf. *DLC* IV.i.106–8.

171 pennance worth your faulting 'punishment [*OED* penance 5] commensurate with your wrongdoing [*OED* faulting 5a]'.

173 breed The verb, absent from Q but supplied by Dyce, links neatly with 'beget' in the previous line, and, as a monosyllable, fills the metrical gap.

181 stayed i.e. 'restrained, desisting from previous action' (see *OED* stayed *ppl. a.*[1], stay *v.*[1] 2a). Given 'feirce' there may also be a play on 'sedate' (i.e. 'staid'; see *OED* stayed *ppl. a.*[2] 2a).

185 My Lord Virginius's stage position or physical attitude (and perhaps 'teares' [187]) evidently indicate that he needs persuading.

187–9 souldiers teares . . . reason i.e. 'neither a soldier's tears nor an elder brother's wit is to be taken seriously, and hence cannot **season** (= [1] add **salt** to, [2] "imbue with opinions" [*OED* 2b]) serious matters because of their lack of **reason**'. Cf. Tilley B687: 'The younger brother has the more wit', and Overbury, *Characters*, 'An Elder Brother'.

190 Take up Although it does not sound as if Virginius is issuing a direct order, 'Take up your pike' was a drill movement, and the Souldiers must do so before they exit (cf. 112n and 191n).

191 SD Provision of an exit direction for the *Souldiers* (and probably the Lieutenant) is justified by several considerations. First, Virginius's final rhymed couplet to them (190–1) sounds like a dismissal, particularly with its jest about how the Soldiers will use their legs. Second, the rest of the scene is entirely between Virginius and Minutius. Third, doubling arrangements for the Soldiers to become Lictors for the next scene appear to have required an exit here (see pp. 489–90). Elsewhere in the text exits have had to be supplied, notably for 1 Soldier at IV.ii.35. And although the '*shout*' (200) of the Soldiers would require (in modern dramatic logic) that they have remained on stage to hear Virginius's news of the 'bounteous donative', in fact it is clearly offstage, and therefore demands this exit (see 200n).

200 donative 'gift, largess' (*OED* 1); here used in its original sense of a bounty paid by the Roman state to the army.

200 (*A shout* The SD ***shout*** 'almost always signals a sound from within' (Dessen and Thomson, p. 197). For a similar non-naturalistic shout, in which commoners within shout about something that has only just transpired on stage, and which they could not realistically know, see *The Costlie Whore* (1633), E2ᵛ.

201 'tis not . . . paid 'A climax of Virginius' irony; only surpassed by 209–11' (Lucas).

214 slight 'ignore, disregard' (*OED* 3a). Cf. *2H4* V.ii.94: 'See your most dreadful laws so loosely slighted'.

ACT II, Scene iii

7 supportance 'support, backing' (*OED* 1); cf. Heywood, *The Rape of Lucrece*, V (E3ʳ): 'We are of our selfe | Without supportance, we all fate defy | Aidlesse.'

9 too petitionary i.e. 'also a petition' (see *OED* petitionary 1).

11 stay 'prop, buttress'; cf. 'basis' (12).

12 basis (1) 'foundation' (*OED* 1), (2) 'base of a pillar' (*OED* 2); cf. 'stay' (11).

14 Judgement seate It may already be on stage, and a visual point of reference. Cf. I.iii.96n.

15.1 troubled No specific stage action is known that signals all the possible varieties of *troubled* or 'discontented'.

18 eares . . . forfeited 'This is not just a metaphor. The sting lies in the suggestion that Clodius is a felon who has had his ears cropped. Cf. III.iii.82; *IndM* 87' (Lucas). It will be as evident from Icilius's manner as from his words that he is not deferring to Marcus Clodius as the Petitioners did.

23 attend 'wait' (*OED* 16). Sykes cites Gervase Markham and Lewis Machin, *The Dumb Knight* (1608), III.i:

> We must attend, vmph! euen snailes keep state
> When with slow thrust their hornes peep forth the gate.
> We must attend, 'Tis customs fault not mine
> To make men proud, on whom great fauours shine,
> Its somewhat gainst my nature to attend.
> But when we must, we must be patient,
> A man may haue admittance to the king
> As soone as to these long-roabes, and as cheap.   [F1ʳ⁻ᵛ]

26 gowned office Marcus Clodius may have been wearing the long robe appropriate to a secretary or attendant to a noble (cf. 23n) since I.iii, or may here be seen to have risen in rank.

26 breadth 'extent' (*OED* 3).

30.1 *Exeunt Petitioners* Q gives no SD for the ***Petitioners*** to leave. They have been instructed to do so by Marcus Clodius at 28, and Dilke therefore provides them an exit at 28, presumably to make clear that the 'Be gone' at 31 is directed at Marcus Clodius and the Lictors. This double exit is likely to be more dramatically effective if the **Lictors** entering *afore* Appius assist, as part of their duties, in shepherding out the Petitioners, and are taking up their regular stations in attendance when, unexpectedly, they are dismissed.

31 only spar'd for us 'reserved for us alone' (OED spare *v*.^{1} 8b).

35 pray your courtesie i.e. 'please leave off your respectful obeisance' (see *OED* courtesy 8, 9). Presumably Icilius has maintained a bow, or been kneeling, either since Appius's entry, or accompanying his preliminary 'My Lord' at 34 (which is perhaps as Appius sets himself in the 'Judgement seate' [14]). Lucas glosses as 'put on your hat'; removing the hat would be Jacobean etiquette when bowing in what is in effect a presence chamber, but is not in itself normally referred to as a curtsy.

38 second Chaire A **Chaire** is a more elaborate piece of furniture than a stool, and what is brought on may equate to Appius's 'Judgement seate' (14), which is called a 'Chair' at 92.

47 Revenues Accented on second syllable.

52 consist in The context seems clearly to require 'depend on' (*OED* consist 4b), though *OED* limits **consist in** to less germane meanings such as 'be vested in'.

61 contract 'enter into an agreement' (*OED* 2), but with a sense of 'matrimonial contract' (*OED* 3). Accented on second syllable.

62 bases 'foundations' (*OED* 2a); cf. 'basis' (12).

63 mauger 'defy' (*OED* maugre).

71 interpose me i.e. 'obstruct [*OED* 6a] the payment to me'. Cf. Heywood, *Gynaikeion*, V.258: 'robbers that interposed him in his way to Athens'. For this use of **me** (dative) see Abbott, Sect. 220.

79 mispriz'd 'scorned' (*OED* 1a). Cf. Heywood, *The Royal King and the Loyal Subject*, II.ii (D3^r): 'It sorrows me that you misprize my love.'

80 Lustful Lord At some point Icilius must rise from his chair, and hereabouts (or perhaps at 86) seems dramatically most likely, as punctuating his move to direct accusation.

81 trace Probably (though the first citation is 1642) 'search out, ascertain by investigation' (*OED* 8a), rather than 'track' (*OED* 5a), since Icilius has been observing Appius's cunning, and establishing its direction, rather than pursuing him.

82–3 You would . . . to cheat On the insertion of 'to' before the second of two infinitives, see Abbott, Sect. 350.

82 Appian Trull the lowest class of Roman prostitute, who operated among the tombs lining the Via Appia (Violaine Vanoyeke, *La Prostitution en Grèce et à Rome* [Paris, 1990], p. 102); cf. Juvenal, *Satires*, VI.O16: 'flava ruinosi lupa sepulchri' ('yellow-haired whore in a crumbling graveyard'; tr. Niall Rudd [Oxford, 1992], VI.O15).

87 Thy Letters Lucas supplies an SD '*Shows letters*', presumably based on III.i.88, where Icilius recalls he 'Shewd him his hand as witnesse 'gainst himself'. This is unlikely, however, since (1) Icilius says in III.i he did this after, not before, threatening Appius with his poniard (see 91–2 and n), and in this scene there is no evidence he does so at all; (2) the **Letters** are linked with **guifts** that he **perus'd** (see n), which would encumber him somewhat if he brought them too; (3) the rhetorical and gestural point of this speech is to enumerate the senses which confirm the accusation: his 'hand' (86), his 'ears' (88), and his 'eyes' (89), a catalogue that would be weakened by the use of props; and (4) he is just about to draw his poniard, and will need his hands free.

87 perus'd . . . guifts Given 'hand' (86), the sense of **perus'd** here is 'handle, examine one by one' (*OED* 2), not 'read' (*OED* 5), which would need to go with 'eyes' (89). Dyce's emendation of Q's 'guefts' to 'gifts' is confirmed by the association with **Letters** (see n); but the Q form strongly suggests that the original read **guifts**, a spelling very common in Heywood and found four times in *DM* (I.i.366, IV.ii.212, V.i.36, V.ii.41).

89 subscrib'd 'signed, written at the bottom' (*OED* 1).

91–2 Sit . . . Chair The actions accompanying Icilius's threat to **nail** Appius **to the Chair**, and prevent him rising or crying out for help, are fully described (possibly with some exaggeration) by Appius at 151–5 and Icilius at III.i.78–83. The essential is that Icilius with his 'Poinyard . . . threatned death' (III.i.78–80).

93 Our Secretary! Appius calls out to Marcus Clodius. The office of **Secretary** was one of some importance; cf. *WD* II.1.301n.

94 Tempt not . . . fury Action is called for: 'when he would have clamor'd, [I] threat-ned death' (III.i.79).

95 insculpt 'carved, engraved' (*OED* insculp 1).

96 But withal revengeless i.e. 'nevertheless without revenge (yet)'. The implication seems to be that Appius remains dangerous, and that Icilius will therefore continue to hold him at knife point.

103 shalt . . . will Here, and at 102 and 107, the use by both men of the determinative 'Thou shalt . . . I will' form (rather than regular 'thou wilt . . . I shall') suggests both Appius's fear and an attempt to placate the furious Icilius (cf. 94, 115).

104–5 Judges place . . . souls i.e. above Minos, Rhadamanthus (cf. IV.i.10), and Aeacus, the underworld judges of the dead, with perhaps therefore a suggestion of the Christian god (cf. *H8* III.i.99–100: 'Heaven is above all yet; there sits a judge, | That no king can corrupt').

118–19 forfeiture . . . life i.e. 'liable to the death penalty'.

121 graft i.e. 'graffed' = 'grafted' (*OED* graff 4).

123 misprision 'mistake' (*OED* 3). Cf. *DM* V.iv.80.

124 wee Appius is again using the royal plural; cf. I.iii.58n.

129 in his own behoof 'to his own advantage' (see *OED* behoof 1).

130 our hand Appius is probably now standing to indicate his release from Icilius's threat, unless he remains seated to indicate the power of his office. If the latter, one would expect him to be on his feet as soon as Icilius leaves (cf. 147n).

131 remit 'pardon' (*OED* 1).

133 Repair 'return' (*OED* 2a).

136–7 Morrow . . . no more Lucas glosses as '"It is indeed not yet noon" (after which "good morrow" or "good morning" would be out of place)'. H. D. Gray cites a parallel from Heywood's *The Royal King and the Loyal Subject*, II.ii (D3ᵛ): 'Morrow Gentlemen.—The morning's past, 'tis mid-day at the least.'

142 cast 'condemned' (*OED* 17a). Sykes compares *The Thracian Wonder*, V.ii.101–2: 'if a jury of women go upon me, I'm sure to be cast' (ed. Michael Nolan [Salzburg, 1997]).

147 tempest Appius's anger may well be signalled by angry movement. Cf. Ferdinand in *DM* (II.v.2n); and cf. 130n.

148 Panthean i.e. 'constituting the pantheon' (= all the **Gods**). *OED* does not record this sense.

151 brave 'challenge, defy' (*OED* 1). Cf. Heywood, 'A Panegerick to the worthy Mr. Robert Dover', in *Annalia Dubrensia* (1636): 'Ossa and Pelion? That so brave the sky'; also *WD* IV.ii.50.

152 Play . . . beard Icilius presumably seized Appius by the beard, an insult in both Roman and Renaissance contexts: cf. Livy, *Romane Historie*, p. 206: 'M. Papirius . . . when a Gaule began to stroke his beard . . . gave him a rap on the pate'; and *Lr.* III.vii.35–6: 'By the kind gods, 'tis most ignobly done | To pluck me by the beard'.

154 me unarm'd i.e. 'unarmed as I am'.

156 toyes 'trifles' (*OED* 5). Cf. *Mac.* II.iii.92–4: 'from this instant | There's nothing serious in mortality: | All is but toys'.

157 front 'demeanour, outward appearance' (*OED* 3b).

159 Bandetto 'bandit'.

166 taxt 'taxed, accused'.

170–1 bit . . . lure As Lucas points out, the metaphor is from falconry. A young hawk is first allowed to **play** with a **bit** (a 'morsel' of food [*OED n.*² 2]), prior to being **train'd** to come to the **lure** (feathers swung on a cord to resemble a prey; see *WD* IV.i.132 and n).

172 strike Appius now applies the language of falconry to himself (**strike** = 'dart at and seize its prey' [*OED* 39]).

180 probable 'demonstrable, provable' (*OED* 1, citing Hall, *Chron. of Hen. VII* [1548], 33: 'It is probable by an invincible reason and an argument infallible').

183 infallid 'infallible' (*OED*). Clark compares Heywood, *The Hierarchie of the blessed Angells* (1635), V.308: 'infallid testimonies'.

187 dispose 'deal with, dispose of' (*OED* 1c).

187 spurne 'kick *against*; manifest opposition' (*OED v.*¹ 3).

188 Clap him up close i.e. 'imprison him in strict confinement' (*OED* close 3).

189 redound to you i.e. 'reflect (negatively) upon you'.

192–3 Warrants . . . answer The syntax is elliptical, but Clodius evidently seeks **Warrants** authorizing the **Arrest** of Virginia so that she will be forced to appear in a court **To answer** the charges. The use of **by** is odd, however, both syntactically and legally. *LION: Drama* records no sixteenth- or seventeenth-century instances of warrants by, of, or for arrest, so it cannot be readily explained as a misreading of either of the other two prepositions; nor does the immediate context afford another 'by' that might have provoked a compositor or scribe into accidentally using the word here. Conceivably **by Arrest** is intended as an independent clause subordinate to **To answer**.

193 Judgment bar i.e. the **bar** in a court of law, akin here to the frequent 'Judgement seat'.

201 manage 'management' (*OED* 5); Clark compares Heywood, *1 The Fair Maid of the West* IV.i (H1ᵛ): 'the manage of the fight | We leaue to you'.

ACT III, Scene i

0.1 *Nurse* An 'old woman' who has been with Virginia since her birth (see IV.i.151–2, and p. 641).

4–7 come upon ... come on Corbulo puns upon **come** in various idiomatic uses, some sexual and others military, first asking the Nurse why she has 'swept down' (**come upon**: see *OED* come 51) upon him **in such haste**, suggesting that it may be because she is keen that he **come over** her (i.e. 'mount her sexually' [Partridge 1955, p. 90]). When she, suspecting a sexual innuendo, objects to **come over**, Corbulo responds with an offer that, if she will **come off** (i.e. 'retire' [as from a field of combat: see *OED* come 65] but also with a theatrical joke), he will **come on** (i.e. 'advance' [*OED* come 66a]).

9 when 'exclamation of impatience' (*OED* 1b); cf. *DM* II.i.106. Corbulo may be dawdling in interplay with the audience.

10 bed ... board Playing upon 'bed and board'; **board** = 'table' (9).

11 light 'wanton' (a common quibble; see *DM* IV.i.41 and n).

14.1 HORATIO There is little to identify this character other than his presence at this family conference and the trial scene (IV.i), and his subsequent association with the forces led by Icilius. He is perhaps young like Valerius, with whom in Act V he shares a command subordinate to Icilius. He may also be a senator (see pp. 477–8).

17 None interrupt Spoken to Corbulo and Attendants.

18 whose This spelling of modern 'who's' is also found in *WD* (IV.iii.23) and *DM* (II.iii.10).

18 masters (Lucas) Q's 'most—' presumably registers a scribe's or compositor's inability to decipher what followed in his copy or his recognition that something had accidentally been left out. Straightforward identification of Virginia by the Nurse as her **master's child** is more suited to the dramatic context than a gushily proprietorial 'My most dear child' (Dyce) or a neutrally proprietorial 'My foster child' (Hazlitt), the latter also having little to recommend it graphically. Confusion of 'o' and 'a' is very common, and as Lucas notes, '-er is not infrequently omitted by mistake, being sometimes contracted to a flourish above the line'.

20 forbear us 'leave us alone' (*OED* 4c).

25 under . . . tempest Cf. *DM* III.i.21–2.

27 cozen Having referred to his niece as 'cozen' (20), Numitorius here extends the courtesy title to her fiancé.

30 Censurer 'judge' (*OED* 2). Cf. Heywood, *Gynaikeion*, IX (p. 454): 'How can I bee a just and equall censurer of such diuine Beauties?'

34 wage eminence and state i.e. 'contend against rank and power' (*OED* wage *v.* 10c, eminence 4, state 16b). Some obscurity results from the unusual absence of 'against' after **wage** (an omission for which *OED* cites no example). As Lucas notes, however, 'contend against' is supported at 35 by 'Chuse out a weaker opposite' (i.e. 'opponent' [*OED* 3]).

38 scandal 'revile' (*OED v.* 2b). Cf. *WD* III.ii.130 and *JC* I.ii.74–6: 'if you know | That I do fawn on men and hug them hard, | And after scandal them'.

42 smooth crest i.e. his **crest** is not elevated, which would be a symbol of pride (see *OED* crest 1b).

42 palped film i.e. 'a film so dark and thick it can be felt'. Heywood uses **palped** (= 'palpable, tangible' [*OED*]) in this odd sense elsewhere; cf. *Great Britain's Troy* (1609), XV.42 (p. 395): 'Fearlesse, he through the palped darknesse scowres.' The usage perhaps derives from the marginal note in the Geneva Bible to Exod. 10: 21, 'darcknes, even darcknes that may be felt'. Lucas finds the 'whole phrase closely paralleled in Heywood's *Dialogues* (1637), p. 73, "The Man-hater": "over their eies | Casting a shadowie film"'.

43 Juggler 'one who deceives by trickery' (*OED* 3).

47 lend a face i.e. 'support, countenance, provide my reputation as a front for' (see *OED* lend 2e, face 7).

58 stale 'whore' (see *OED* 4).

73 Colossus . . . bestrides 'a clear reminiscence of *JC* I.ii.135–6: "he doth bestride the narrow world | Like a Colossus"' (Lucas).

77 Lobby 'a waiting-place or ante-room' (*OED* 2a).

84 Keep fast the door Numitorius's need both to ensure the door is locked, and to speak low in his own house, emphasizes the sinister power Appius is felt to wield.

88 Shewd him his hand II.iii contains no reference to such action (see II.iii.87n), but subsequent elaboration of what an audience is understood to have seen is not uncommon.

96 regreets Though *OED* does not record this sense, the meaning here is clearly 'renewed greetings' (so Lucas, who notes the same signification in *Jn.* III.i.241).

112 Statist 'powerful politician' (see *OED* 1); cf. I.iii.110 and n.

116 conduct . . . lodging This exit emphasizes Virginia's independence of movement, upon which her arrest in III.ii depends, as well as reinforcing Icilius's care and concern for her. Strict logic seems not to be observed: Numitorius has already countermanded Icilius's suggestion that Virginia 'lodg in secret' (101), and at I.ii.32 Numitorius instructed her to 'take your chamber' (presumably in his house).

ACT III, Scene ii

0.1 *foure Lictors* As the dialogue from here to 26 makes clear, the role of the **Lictors** is indistinguishable from that of sheriff's officers in plays set in London; cf. I.i.o.1n and, e.g., *WHo* III.ii, where Tenterhooke is assisted by Ambush and Clutch. Since the Lictors are armed, and this is not a ceremonial occasion, they presumably do not carry fasces. The 'weapons' (III.iii.98–9) they carry are not specified, but some form of halberd seems most likely. See p. 479, and Fig. 7.

1 **close shops** Perhaps 'secluded shops', but the sense of **close** = 'concealed' suggests 'shops in which you can hide' (see *OED* 4a).

5 Sempsters 'tailors''.

7 action 'legal suit' (*OED* 8).

8 carefull Here, presumably, 'painstaking, watchful' (*OED* 4).

9–10 strange . . . strange Lucas notes a similar repetition in *DM* I.i.376–8.

12 Calender . . . dog dayes The **dog dayes** were regarded as the hottest and most oppressive time of the year (cf. *WD* III.ii.202 and n, and *WD* III.iii.63). Lucas compares Overbury, *Characters* (N3ᵛ), 'A Prisoner': 'He is an Almanacke out of date: none of his dayes speakes of faire weather.' The **Calender**, in its additional sense, 'list of canonized saints' (*OED* calendar 4b), is used by 1 Lictor as a preparation for moving on to the 'book of common-prayer' at 14.

13 dog unthrifts 'pursue (quibbling on 'dog dayes' [12]) spendthrifts, prodigals' (see *OED* unthrift 3).

14 book of common-prayer Since 1 Lictor, taking up 'Calendar' (see 12n) and 'common' (13), puns on **common-prayer** as 'usual entreaty', and '*Book of Common Prayer*' (i.e. the liturgy of the Church of England), the playwrights clearly conceive the Lictors as London sheriff's officers; cf. 0.1n.

16 banquerouts i.e. 'bankrupts'.

17–19 back . . . hourely 1 Lictor is presumably playing on **back** as 'support with physical force' (*OED* v. 4a), as **valiant** men would do, and the fact of the support actually being to prevent those arrested from fleeing (which would also, in the common jest, prove the valour of those from whom they fled). Lucas, however, reads **back** as 'subdue', as an extension of *OED* 10a: 'to break [a horse] in to the saddle'. Either way, 2 Lictor continues with **we have them by the back** = 'we seize them by the shoulder' (from behind, in arresting them). Sykes notes a similar quibble in *WHo* (III.ii.55–7). See 0.1n and 14n.

19 French flye *Cantharis vesicatoria*, usually called 'Spanish fly', a poisonous beetle, source of cantharides, a drug used for raising blisters. Cf. Topsell, *Historie of Serpents* (1608), p. 97: 'Their vertue and quality is to rayse blisters', and p. 808: 'He scarified the place and drawed it with cupping glasses'.

20 French Rheume 'venereal disease, the pox'. Although *OED* (French 6) does not specifically record this term, it is a common rendering of *morbus gallicus*; see Johannes Fabricius, *Syphilis in Shakespeare's England* (London, 1994).

21 drawer 2 Lictor puns on the medical sense of 'draw' (see 19n) and, here, on 'draw' =

'pull' (*OED* 1a), whence **drawer** = 'one who seizes' (by 'the nape of the neck' [20])
(see 17–19n).

22 **little timbred** 'slightly built' (see *OED* timbered 2b). The choice of metaphor
allows the pun on 'logerhead' at 23.

23 **logerhead** 'blockhead', punning woodenly on 'little timbred' (22), and with a suggestion of much greater size.

23 **kennell** 'gutter'. Lucas compares Marston, *The Malcontent*, IV.iii.81–2: '*Shoulder not a
huge fellow, unless you may be sure to lay him in the kennel.*'

23–5 **shoulder . . . counter** 1 Lictor plays on the verbal structure of 22–3, with **shoulder** the equivalent of 'justle' (22), the **Knight** by implication a 'logerhead' (23), **sure**
now meaning 'safe from escape' (see *OED* 3), **kennell** ('gutter' at 23) now a verb
meaning 'confine' (see *OED* v. 2b), and the gutter replaced by the **counter** ('debtors'
prison'; see *OED* n.[3] 7, with a possible pun on 'encounter', for which cf. *WHo*
III.ii.76–7 and *NHo* I.iii.55). There is probably a further pun on **shoulder** = 'seize by
the shoulder' (see 17–19n), although this usage is not recorded by *OED*.

24 **Knights fellow** Presumably 'of the same sort of standing as a knight', as Lucas sur-
mises, rather than a 'knight's servant'.

ACT III, Scene iii

III.iii A new scene starts here, since the stage has been cleared; but cf. 2–9n.

1 **amorous** i.e. 'enamoured, in love' (*OED* 2a).

2–9 **looke back . . . regardant** Corbulo enters ahead of both women, since his looking
back is taken by Virginia to be to observe the Nurse, who is evidently with Virginia
('we are your clogs then' [8]). This teasing sets up the extended sexual banter that
follows. Presumably, however, Corbulo is actually looking back at the Lictors who are
to be imagined as following them. This may be best suggested on stage by the Lictors
exiting at III.ii.26 sufficiently slowly (perhaps observing Virginia enter) that Corbulo
sees them leave, and continues to watch behind for 'what . . . followes him' (6–7).

3 **Frenchman . . . buttock** The reference may be to 'French saddles', which Gervase
Markham describes as offering little stability for the rider: 'the generall and greatest
fault which our Sadlers heere in England doe commit in making these French pads is,
that they make the seates thereof too broad, so that when a man comes to bestride
them, they doe make him open his thighes so wide, that he can neither sit fast nor at
his ease, but after a little trauell put him to such paine, as if they would splyt or deuide
him' (*Cavelarice* [1607], p. 51). The point seems to be that Corbulo's constant looking
backwards makes him resemble a rider who cannot 'sit fast'. Given 'amorous' (1) and
Frenchman, there is no doubt a sexual joke intended as well. The relative density of
derogatory references to the French in this scene (cf. also 3, 4, 13) may relate to the
unpopularity of the French in negotiating a separate peace with Spain in February
1626, or perhaps to the expulsion of the French household of Queen Henrietta
Maria, threatened in July 1626, and carried out in August. See p. 444, and Lockyer, p.
300.

5–6 **Monky . . . clog** Lucas compares John Selden, *Table Talk* (1689), 'Wife': 'You shall see a Monkey sometime, that has been playing up and down the Garden, at length leap up to the top of the Wall, but his Clog [a heavy block attached to prevent escape] hangs a great way below on this side' (Arber repr. [London, 1869], p. 117).

9 crest . . . regardant Heraldic hyperbole for 'your head [OED crest 5a] is looking backwards' (OED **regardant** 2), punning on 'observant, watchful' (OED 3a) and, with reference to the Nurse, 'full of regard, consideration' (OED 3b, not cited until 1647).

14–15 matchlesse . . . matches A common jest; cf. WD IV.ii.129–30.

17 powder'd 'salted' (OED 2a).

18–27 widowes teares . . . husband A comic elaboration of stock attacks on widows considered indecently keen to remarry; cf. Chapman, *The Widow's Tears*, II.iv.23–5: 'her open and often detestations of that incestuous life (as shee term'd it) of widdowes marriages; as being but a kinde of lawfull adulterie; like vsurie, permitted by the law, not approv'd', and *DM* I.i.285n.

20 fresh Lucas notes the quibble on **fresh** as (1) 'not stale' (OED 7a) and (2) 'not salted' (OED 4a; see 'powder'd' [17]). Cf. CC II.iii.17.

23 old rule . . . belly Cf. Tilley E261: 'His eyes are bigger than his belly.'

24–7 fingers . . . husband 'Corbulo, I suppose, having taken down two middle fingers for "debts and legacies", "makes horns" with the remaining two' (Lucas).

26 reversion that portion of the dead husband's estate which was granted to him only for life, and now reverts to the original owner or another grantee (probably, as Lucas suggests, the dead husband's next of kin). Cf. *DM* III.i.14, IV.ii.189.

28 Tribe i.e. of widows (see OED 4).

29–31 fish . . . pleasure 'The combination of natural history and "as the learned divulge" recalls Euphuism and its earlier parodies'; so Lucas, who compares *1H4* II.iv.412–13: 'This pitch (as ancient writers do report) doth defile'. This attitude of mock learning allows Corbulo to develop a series of sexual innuendos directed at the Nurse, where for the most part the **sharke**, although described as 'he', is to be understood as a lascivious female: **feede** = (1) 'eat', (2) 'satisfy sexual appetite'; **lies upon his back** = (1) 'swims with mouth upward', (2) 'adopts the female posture for sexual intercourse' (see Partridge 1955, p. 143); **takes it** = (1) 'feeds', (2) 'accepts sexual penetration', (3) 'possesses, penetrates sexually' (of a man; see Partridge 1955, p. 200); **at pleasure** = (1) 'whenever wished', (2) 'enjoying sexual gratification'. Corbulo may be recalling Pliny (*Nat. Historie*, IX.xxiv.248) on sharks: 'all the sort of them that devour flesh are such: and their manner is to feed lying backward'.

34 clarks of the kitchin Cf. 'caters' (40 and n), and Shirley, *The Lady of Pleasure*, V.ii.104–7: 'My clerk o' th' kitchen's here, a witty epicure, a spirit that to please me with what's rare can fly a hundred mile a day to market and make me lord of fish and fowl' (ed. Ronald Huebert [Manchester, 1986]); also Beaumont and Fletcher, *The Captain*, II.i.71–7: 'Thou art young and handsome yet, and well enough | To please a widow [who will] make ye Clarke a'th kitchen.'

35–6 Woodcocks . . . spoke with The Clown's point is that because 'there's a great feast towards' (i.e. in preparation) **Woodcocks** (meaning both game birds and fools) will be hard to come across. Given the sexual innuendo of 'cod' (38), and with 'calves head' (40) having a similar sense to woodcock as a potential foolish husband, there may also be a pun on **cock** = 'penis'.

38 fresh cod ... threefold Since the Clown puns on **cod** as (1) 'fish', and (2) 'penis' (see Partridge 1955, p. 88), **taken down** = (1) 'lowered' (from its place of sale), (2) 'swallowed' (*OED* take 82b[a]), and (3) 'reduced in sexual turgidity' (by completion of sexual intercourse; Partridge 1955, p. 200). Proverbial (Tilley T100), **thick and threefold** may also refer to 'the proverbial three, the male genitals, penis and testicles' (Rubinstein, p. 274). The point throughout is the sexual appetite of women.

38–9 women ... ears for't i.e. 'women who are not pregnant fight for it' (see *OED* go 94a, ear *n.*[1] I 1d).

40 caters 'in large households the officer who made the necessary purchases of provisions; caterers' (*OED* 1a).

40 calves head Inexpensive meat; but given double entendres on 'cod' and 'mutton', there is probably a play on 'stupid fellow' (*OED* calf 3), and perhaps a further sexual innuendo with **head** = 'the head of the penis' (Henke 1975, II, 174).

41–4 Muttons ... common The Clown's (ostensible) point is that a shortage of other cheap meat means that **mutton** is in demand, hence the literal meaning of the word, practically obliterated by its slang use (= 'whore') by **the sinners i'th' Suburbs** (see II.ii.75n), is now restored.

44 sweet 'agreeable' (*OED* 5).

45 Terme ... muttonmonger i.e. 'the presence of lawyers and their clients during the law term results in great consumption of (1) mutton, (2) whores' (*OED* muttonmonger 2, 1). This common perception may be historically inaccurate; see Paul Griffiths, 'The Structure of Prostitution in Elizabethan London', *Continuity and Change* VIII, 1 (1993), p. 55.

47 sallets 'another word with improper associations, salads being highly seasoned': so Lucas, who compares *Ham.* II.ii.441–2: 'no sallets in the lines to make the matter savory'.

48–9 revellers ... heeles At least three levels of meaning seem intended: (1) that young lawyers spend money on condiments for their meat until, as a result of deceit (**shuffling** = 'using shifty pretences' [see *OED* shuffle 7]) they are impoverished (**out at heeles**); (2) that Inns of Court students dance (**capers** = 'leaps in dancing' [see *OED* n.*[2] 1]; **cutting** = 'springing from the ground, and, while in the air, twiddling the feet one in front of the other alternately with great rapidity' [see *OED* cut 30]) at their revels until they have worn out their hose; and (3), continuing the previous sexual references, that merry-making lawyers frolic (caper) with their whores (**mutton**) until their sexual activities (**shuffling** = 'mixing or jumbling together' [see *OED* 3 and, for 'jumble', *CC* IV.i.8n], and **cutting** = 'copulating' [Henke 1975, II, 128]) leave them impoverished. For the common initial double entendre on capers and mutton, cf. *TN* I.iii.121–2: '*Sir And.* Faith, I can cut a caper. *Sir To.* And I can cut the mutton to't'.

48–9 so long till 'until'.

50 bountifull ... purse Corbulo may be seeking a tip (so Wellington 1999).

53 cuckoes 'with a play on "cuckolds", whence the point of 57' (Lucas).

60 not know me In fact Virginia was serenaded by Marcus Clodius in II.i, and she appears to remember him at 89. He may be preparing to deny any previous encounter.

63 followers 'officers of justice after you' (Lucas).

64–5 Gentlemen . . . geldings Corbulo presumably intends this as an insult to the Lictors.

69 *Seizes her* Given 'Unhand me villaine' (71) and Marcus Clodius's reply it seems that he lays hold of Virginia himself. It is possible in performance for the Lictors to act for him (cf. 'pulling and haling' [85]).

76 King or Consull Since the **Consull** was 'the supreme civil and military magistrate of Rome under the Republic' (*OCD*), he may be considered the equivalent of both the **King** whom the Republic replaced, and a Jacobean monarch.

80 presse 'force to serve in the army' (*OED* press 2a).

81 in ure 'in use, practice' (*OED* ure 1a).

82–3 any eares With, as Lucas notes, 'insulting allusion to the cropping of criminals' ears'. Cf. II.iii.18n.

83 take a Castle i.e. 'take refuge in a castle' (as a proverbial place of security). Lucas compares Drayton, *Nimphidia*, 367–8: 'And lying downe they soundly slept and safe as in a Castle' (*Works*, III.136), and *AQL* (Lucas) V.i.454.

85 pulling and haling Marcus Clodius may still have hold of Virginia, or by now the Lictors may be holding her; cf. 69n.

87–8 whip Shall cease i.e. 'the whip which shall seize'. Lucas emends to 'sease', of which there are three other instances nearby (III.ii.7, 75, 95) and one at *DM* II.v.8. But, as Lucas notes, **cease** is a seventeenth-century spelling of 'seize' recognized by *OED*, and, although W never uses it in this sense elsewhere, reserving it for the verb meaning 'to stop', *LION: Drama* shows it appearing in Heywood's *The Hierarchie of the blessed Angells* (1635) and *An Emblematical Dialogue* (1637): 'stoopes downe to cease her prey'. III.ii seems to be a predominantly Websterian scene, but we have retained the rare spelling as possibly Heywood's and as more likely to be authentic than due to a scribal or compositorial slip.

90 approve 'prove, demonstrate' (*OED* 1a).

98–9 What's . . . weapons on us i.e. 'what has Virginia done (that) you aim [*OED* bend *v.* 17b] your halberds [cf. III.ii.0.1n] at us?' Evidently the Lictors form a defensive screen to keep Icilius away from Virginia, and this presumably remains the stage arrangement until the entry of Appius.

99–100 Sir . . . rescue Apparently a warning to Icilius not to advance, but possibly a warning to Clodius behind them.

102 Your incredulity This accusation of Icilius is counter to the fact of his believing Appius to be a threat to Virginia, and to his attempt to persuade Numitorius to hide her (III.i.100–3). Lucas explains away Rupert Brooke's concern by saying that 'Virginia in her dismay very naturally complains that if her warnings had been taken more seriously and she had been hidden out of Appius' reach, all this trouble would never have happened. It is true that Icilius himself had urged this course; but he allowed himself to be overruled. Virginia's outcry is thus very human without being quite fair; and, if we wish, we may suppose "Your" [102] to be plural and referring to the family council as a whole.' At Wellington 1999 Virginia's anger was at Icilius's willingness to believe in and accede to Numitorius's counsel of caution in III.i. Alternatively, since Numitorius replies to Virginia's speech, plot and character consistency could be maintained by 'O my *Icilius!*' being a separate preliminary acknowledgement of his presence and her plight before she turns to blame her uncle for **incredulity**.

105 publish't for 'proclaimed to be' (see *OED* publish 1).

112.1 *Secretary* Previously Marcus Clodius (II.iii.93, 139), but another *Secretary* is needed at 283.

113 in presence The usual sense of 'ceremonial attendance upon a person of superior rank' (*OED* 2b) emphasizes the power of Appius.

116 reach i.e. 'give me' (see *OED v.*[1] 2a). Marcus Clodius does have papers with him, although he does not give them to Appius until 163.

120–1 The Fox ... yet 'these words must be addressed to Numitorius, not to Appius, who is himself the fox that has not yet been exposed to the light of day. Numitorius is similarly called "My Lord" in 114 above' (Lucas). **winde** = 'perceive by some subtle indication; get wind of' (*OED v.*[2] 1c).

122 Stooles ... sit Either **Stooles** for Appius, Numitorius, and Icilius transform this street scene into an impromptu court (with, presumably, Marcus Clodius and Virginia on one side, and Icilius and Numitorius on the other; cf. *DLC* IV.ii.0.1n); or, if the scene is imagined to have changed to a place of formal hearing, Appius will ascend his 'Judgment seat' (I.iii.108).

138 Imposture 'fraudulent deception' (*OED* 1).

144 overflow 'overwhelm' (*OED* 2a).

147 wage Law 'go to law' (*OED* wage 4b[b]). Cf. Jonson, *The Staple of News*, V.i.117: 'I am not able to wage *Law* with him.'

151 High ... or'eflow Cf. *DM* III.v.140 and *DLC* IV.ii.647–8.

154 acrue 'incur' (see *OED* accrue 4a).

155 double 'act deceitfully' (*OED* 11).

162 tripping 'making a mistake or false step' (*OED* trip 9).

165 Nurse The Nurse's prattle, and her despatch by Icilius on an errand, allow time for Appius to pretend to read the 'proofes' (163).

165 had a sore hand with her 'had hard work with her' (Lucas).

167 green sicknesse 'An anaemic disease which mostly affects young women about the age of puberty, and gives a pale or greenish tinge to the complexion' (*OED*). Cf. *CC* I.i.122n.

170 view it my Lord Probably passing the paper to Icilius, who takes it aside to read it (at 174 he is at a distance); but this could be directed to Numitorius, especially if he is sitting next to Appius. For the wording, cf. *WD* III.ii.195.

173 this black forgerie Probably Icilius is reading it, but it is just possible he is observing from a distance as Numitorius reads; cf. 170n.

174 come near By calling both Icilius and Virginia to him, Appius appears to be releasing Virginia from the 'hold' (144) of Marcus Clodius and the armed Lictors. Presumably she stays with Icilius for the rest of the scene, with the result that Marcus Clodius will appear more isolated.

175 Compound i.e. 'come to terms with' (and pay a sum in settlement) (*OED* 13a), given 'Disburse some trifle' (176).

178 handfull of a bribe i.e. 'even a very small bribe' (see *OED* handful 2).

179 take your course i.e. 'do what you intend'.

180–1 I onely . . . for't Cf. *WHo* V.iv.83, *WD* I.ii.81, and *DLC* I.ii.261–2.

183–99 character . . . undone men On 'the device of judicious bankruptcy' Lucas compares Dekker, *Seven Deadly Sins of London* (1606), 'Politick Bankruptisme'. Cf. also Monticelso's 'character' of a whore (*WD* III.ii.79–80 and n), though Appius's 'character' of a 'pettie Notary' is closer in its detailing to the prose characters of Overbury and W than to the metaphoric catalogue of Monticelso.

184 pettie 'subordinate'.

188–9 Couching . . . course Appius compares the **cunningly** planned bankruptcy to successful participation in a tournament. As Lucas notes, a **tilting staffe** provides an apt simile, since it was 'meant to break *easily*, and made accordingly'. Thus **Couching** = 'lowering (like a lance) to the position of attack' (see *OED* couch 7), **brake** carries a pun on 'breaking' in bankruptcy, and **course** = 'passage at arms' (as in a tournament) (*OED* 5), but with a pun on 'circulation of money' (*OED* 10).

192–3 compounded . . . moity i.e. 'settled by payment [*OED* compound 8a] of a third of what he owed' (see *OED* moiety 2a, and *1H4* III.i.95–6: 'my moi'ty . . . equals not one of yours').

193–4 buyes . . . place i.e. 'buys a position [*OED* office 4a] in my service' (see *OED* place 14a).

194 depends on In the sense both of 'relies upon, is sustained by' (see *OED* depend 4) and 'is a subordinate of' (see *OED* 3).

200–3 plague . . . rise Cf. *Tim.* IV.iii.109–11: 'Be as a planetary plague when Jove | Will o'er some high-vic'd city hang his poison | In the sick air'. Although the **bright Sun** might disperse clouds of contagion, one of the causes of **plague** was, paradoxically, thought to be **infection** being drawn up into the air by the sun. Cf. Dekker, *The Wonderfull Yeare* (1603), C1ʳ⁻ᵛ, 'vp rises a comfortable Sun out of the North, whose glorious beames (like a fan) dispersed all thick and contagious clowdes'; and *Newes from Graves-end* (1604), B2ʳ, Epistle Dedicatory: 'mustie bodies putrifying, the inavoydable stench of their strong breath be smelt out by the Sun, and then there's new worke for Clarkes and Sextons'. In times of increased plague-deaths (such as the 'great plague' of 1625; see F. P. Wilson, *The Plague in Shakespeare's London* [Oxford, 1963], pp. 129–73) both passing **bells** and the handbells accompanying corpses to their **graves** would be constantly heard. Cf. Jonson, *Volpone*, III.v.4–6: 'My Madam, with the euerlasting voyce: | The bells, in time of pestilence, ne're made | Like noise, or were in that perpetuall motion.'

206 riotous 'wanton, dissolute' (*OED* 3).

215–16 subscribed Unto 'written at the bottom of, signed' (*OED* subscribe 1). Cf. II.iii.89.

224 *Enter* SERTORIUS Q's '*Valerius*' does not match the summoning of Sertorius at 168, nor the repetition of his name, and provision of a speech prefix, at 301–4. Given confusion about Valerius elsewhere (see II.ii.94n), and the fact that this is a strangely inappropriate moment for a subordinate character to enter, we may suspect some uncertainty in the allocation of minor roles, or some corruption in the text.

224 colour 'pretext'.

233–4 referring . . . censure i.e. 'deferring and reserving consideration of the injury to me to separate judgement' (see *OED* refer 7b, c, censure 2).

238 slights i.e. 'sleights'. *OED* recognizes Q's spelling, which is common in Renaissance drama.

239–40 Camelion . . . colour Cf. Pliny, *Nat. Historie*, VIII.xxiii.215, *Chameleon*: 'his colour naturally is very straunge and wonderfull, for ever and anon he chaungeth it, as well in his eye, as taile and whole bodie besides: and looke what colour he toucheth next, the same alwaies he resembleth'. Cf. also Tilley C221: 'As changeable as a chameleon'.

240 presently 'forthwith, immediately' (*OED* 3).

247 travel There is the usual pun on 'travail'.

252 thicket . . . plain Cf. Isa. 10: 34 (Authorized Version): 'he shall cut down the thickets of the forest with iron' and 40: 4: 'Every valley shall be exalted, and every mountain and hill shall be made low: and the crooked shall be made straight, and the rough places plain.'

259–61 To-morrow . . . you This sounds like a dismissal, and is probably accompanied by Appius rising to leave, thus providing an opportunity for Marcus Clodius to feign more anxiety, and eventually to be taken into custody.

266 motion 'proposal' (*OED* 7a).

276 use her . . . as my wife Cf. *DLC* I.ii.192: 'you may use me at your pleasure.'

280–1 lye . . . forth coming This appears to mean 'be held by a man in safe custody ready to be produced in court', though this meaning is given by *OED* only for the adjectival sense of 'forthcoming', not the substantive. In Livy, *Romane Historie* (p. 118), Appius rules that Marcus Clodius 'might lead away the wench, promising and assuring to have her forthcomming, and to present her in court'. Lucas suggests that W misread 'forthcomming' as a noun; i.e. 'to have her forthcomming' = 'to have the reponsibility for her forthcoming'.

283 Our Secretary Cf. 112.1n.

284 Take bonds Presumably the Secretary will do the necessary paperwork with Icilius and Numitorius during the next few lines.

285–6 you that were . . . casheire you Lucas notes the similar mock dismissal of Antonio by the Duchess (*DM* III.ii.178–208).

286 shrowde 'conceal' (*OED* 4); cf. *WD* I.ii.33.

288 hangmans hook Here **hangman** = 'executioner' (*OED* 1), and the **hook** refers, as Lucas notes, to Roman execution at 'the Gemonian steps . . . on which bodies were thrown to dishonour them, sometimes dragged by the hangman's hook' (Jonson, note to *Sejanus*, IV.309; several uses in the play). Cf. Massinger, *The Roman Actor*, IV.ii.295: 'haue thy limbes | Rent peece meale by the hangmans hook'.

290–1 I am . . . service Cf. *DLC* IV.ii. 478–9 and n.

291 Harke you The theatricality of their charade will be served by Marcus Clodius starting to leave before being brought up short by Appius.

294 commit him The Lictors now guard Marcus Clodius in place of Virginia.

295 starting 'escaping' (*OED* start 6).

297–8 Judges heart . . . hand Cf. I.i.109–11.

299–300 O were . . . Rome! Sykes compares Jonson, *Sejanus* (1605), I.ii.400–2: 'If this man | Had but a minde allied vnto his words, | How blest a fate were it to vs, and *Rome?*'

301 Post 'ride with haste' (*OED* 2).

302 effect 'result, consequence' (*OED* 1a).

305–11 O my Lord . . . miscarries 'Virginia's speech is so full of rhyme that it is a little hard to follow its reasoning. She seems, however, to be warning her lover against either trusting or defying the hypocrisy of Appius' (Lucas).

306 flattering '(delusively) encouraging hope' (*OED ppl. a.*).

308–9 men o're born . . . friends i.e. 'men oppressed by the powerful (should) continue to regard as dreadful, and to be feared [*OED* dread *ppl. a.*], false and apparent (not genuine) friends'.

311 He that . . . miscarries Cf. 306–7.

313 to Dyce's insertion of this word, which could easily have been omitted from Q accidentally, improves metre and syntax (**both to . . . And to**).

313–14 confounding . . . in a mist Cf. *WD* V.vi.254–5, *DM* V.v.93. **confounding** = 'confusing, perplexing' (*OED*).

315 have fell i.e. 'have fallen', perhaps, given 316–19, with something of the sense of a tree being felled.

316–19 The bending Willow . . . foote A variant of Tilley O3: 'Oaks may fall when reeds stand the storm.' For the willow–oak comparison, cf. J. W., *The Valiant Scot*, III.i.317–8: ''Tis not so sinfull, nor so base a stroke | To spoile a Willow as an old reverend Oke.'

ACT III, Scene iv

0.1 Servant He may well be wearing boots, spurs, and a cloak, ready for immediate departure; cf. I.iii.63.1n.

7 policy (1) 'political cunning' (*OED* 3), and (2) 'stratagem' (*OED* 4b).

8 poison'd . . . sweet meats Cf. *WD* III.ii.81 and n.

12 suspect 'suspicion' (*OED* 1).

15 committing 'being taken into custody' (*OED* commit 3b).

17 *Mercury* Here associated with cunning; cf. *Tro.* II.iii.11–12: 'Mercury, lose all the serpentine craft of thy caduceus.'

19 One ill . . . another Cf. *WD* II.i.314n.

20–1 *Aconitum* . . . Serpents stings Wolfbane and monkshood are both plants of the genus ***Aconitum***, from which poisons of great potency are derived; cf. *2H4* IV.iv.47–8. For its use as an antidote, Lucas compares Jonson, *Sejanus*, III.651–4: 'I haue heard, that *aconite* | Being timely taken, hath a healing might | Against the scorpions stroke; the proofe wee'll giue: | That, while two poysons wrastle, we may liue', and Pliny, *Nat. Historie* (XXXVII.ii.270). Cf. also *WD* III.iii.56–7.

21 present 'immediate' (*OED* 9b).

23 necessity . . . wise Cf. Tilley N60: 'Necessity is the best schoolmistress', and N61: 'Necessity is the mother of invention.'

26 I'l break . . . broken i.e. Appius will break the wheel on which he is tortured. Cf. *WD* III.iii.87, where Flamineo explicitly invokes the wheel of Fortune.

ACT III, Scene v

0.1–.2 *one door* . . . *melancholy* The SD requiring entry at opposite doors indicates that the ***Serving men*** will have time to observe Corbulo's ***melancholy***, which may include weeping (see 33). Cf. I.iii.0.1 and n.

3–4 Times . . . halter i.e. 'our situations change, and (however well-off we may have been in the past) fate has determined that some men become judges and others are sentenced by them to be hanged'.

10 Wide of the bow hand 'wide of the mark'; literally, 'wide to the left', since the left is the **bow hand** that holds the bow in archery (see *OED* bow-hand 1, and Tilley B567). Cf. *LLL* IV.i.133: 'Wide a' the bow-hand! I' faith, your hand is out', and Dekker, *Satiromastix*, III.i.1, 'a the bow hand wide'.

14 treble . . . base Corbulo puns on **base** and 'bass' (cf. **treble**).

19 you serving Creatures Although this clearly includes the two Serving-men, it may also be addressed to any servants in the audience.

19–20 this is . . . *Virginia* Cf. Antonio's (mock) complaint (*DM* III.ii.207–8): 'You may see (Gentlemen) what 'tis to serve | A prince with body, and soule.'

23–6 borrowed . . . bondwoman Corbulo embarks on a series of puns around **bond** and **bonds**, thus: though Virginia has not borrowed money (for which she would have to sign a 'bond' guaranteeing repayment), she is in **bonds** (i.e. 'fetters, custody' [*OED* 1]); and though she may be thought not **sufficient** (i.e. 'of adequate means': see *OED* 4, and cf. *MV* I.iii.17), her **bond** (which would only be accepted from someone who had the means to pay) is likely to be accepted, and she, the **bond woman** (i.e. the woman who signed the 'bond') is **challenged** ('laid claim to': *OED* challenge 5b) as a **bondwoman** (female slave).

27 Woodcock 'proverbially foolish'; cf. *CC* IV.i.56n and *DM* IV.ii.87.

28 Hodmondod 'snail' (*OED* hodmandod 1).

28　amongst flies 'Hazlitt is much worried by the snail being classed among flies; but surely they can be classed together in the mouth of a clown. And the quickness of the fly contrasts effectively with the slowness of the miserable snail' (Lucas).

28　trindle tale 'dog with a curly tail; low-bred dog' (*OED* trundle-tail 1a). Cf. *Lr.* III.vi.70: 'Or bobtail tike or trundle-tail'; also Jonson, *Bartholomew Fair*, II.v.123: 'you dogs-head, you Trendle tayle!', where, as here, the term is applied to a person (*OED* 1b).

29　poor Jhon 'hake salted and dried for food; a type of poor fare' (*OED* Poor John 1a); cf. *DLC* IV.ii.141–4n. Defending his excellent emendation of Q's meaningless 'poor Iper', Lucas suggests that 'Iper' was a misreading of manuscript 'Ihon', noting that 'confusions of *h* and *p*, *o* and *e*, *n* and *r* are of the commonest'. We have therefore emended to the seventeenth-century spelling of the name John that is most likely to have given rise to the Q error (while normalizing 'I' to 'J' in accordance with our invariable practice).

30　Yeoman Fewterer 'keeper of greyhounds' (*OED*). Sykes compares Massinger, *The Maid of Honour*, II.ii.29–31: 'You sirrha Sheepes-head . . . You yeoman phewterer'.

33　*weeping* His performance of '*melancholy*' (0.2) may have included *weeping* since he entered.

35–6　but . . . taken i.e. 'although she was **taken** (into custody), my offer (of bail) was not accepted (**taken**)'.

37　free . . . own man i.e. 'until I am freed from (1) servitude, and (2) grief, I cannot (1) take employment with myself as my own servant, (2) be my own master, or (3) be myself'. Lucas compares Heywood, *A Maidenhead Well Lost*, I.i (C3ᵛ), and *AQL* (Lucas) V.i.62.

38　Ward 'custody, imprisonment' (*OED* 3).

39–40　Knight side . . . Hole 'In the London Counters or prisons there were four divisions, wards, or "sides" in descending order of comfort and of cost—(1) the master's ward; (2) the knight's; (3) the twopenny; (4) the hole (which may perhaps have had a lower depth "the hell")'; so Lucas, citing *The Miseries of Enforced Marriage*: 'from the feather bed in the Maisters side, or the Flock-bed in the Knights warde, to the straw-bed in the hole' (MSR, 1178–9). Cf. *WHo* III.ii.78–9, and Chapman, Jonson, and Marston, *Eastward Ho!*, V.ii.41–51. Lucas's emendation to **Twopenny** of Q's nonsensical 'Troping' assumes the misreading of 'w' as 'r', 'e' as 'i', 'y' as 'g' and perhaps the mistaking of the number of minims in 'nn', though the manuscript may have read 'Twopeny'.

39–41　will . . . taken up Using the sexual implications of **Hole** (= 'vagina'), Corbulo puns successively on **have his will with** ('have intercourse with'), on **Warrant** (here = 'penis', given **hath been out for her**, rather than, as Rubinstein glosses [p. 300], 'alluding coarsely to fornication'), on **case** ('vagina'; cf. *DLC* IV.ii.236n, and *CC* III.ii.94–8n), on **stands** ('has an erection': Partridge 1955, p. 194), and on **taken up** (cf. *CC* II.iii.67 and n).

49　Ænigmaes 'enigmas'.

50　apprehensions 'comprehension'. Cf. Heywood, *Loves Mistress*: '*It was above my apprehension to conceive*' (To the Reader [A2ᵛ]).

53 my hand 'my pledge' (in token that).

54–5 timber . . . Posts Corbulo puns on **Posts** (as both 'courier' [*OED n.*² 2a] and 'support, prop' [*OED n.*¹ 1a]) in relation to the **timber of his house**. Cf. III.ii.204.

56 spur cut i.e. 'ride hard', using spurs and whip (not in *OED*); cf. *NHo* IV.i.254: 'spur cut and away'.

61–2 Tears . . . sorrow Corbulo's elaborate word play pivots on a multiple pun on **Role** as (1) 'fresh bread roll', which will be his **sops** ('bread or the like dipped or steeped in water, wine, etc., before being eaten' [*OED n.*¹ 1]) for breakfast, (2) his new 'role' or situation as serving-man to a slave, and, possibly, (3) for him as company Clown, a new theatrical 'role' in place of Corbulo as the Orator (see p. 489). Drinking a quart of salt **Tears** with his bread is both a bathetic sign of grief and a recollection of 2 Chr. 18: 26: 'Put this man in the prison house, & fede him with bread of affliction and with water of affliction'; cf. Massinger, *The Bondman*, IV.iii.20–1: 'Wee haue so long fed on the bread of sorrow, | Drinking the bitter water of afflictions.' This strengthens the proverbial force of **sops of sorrow** (Tilley S661); cf. Lyly, *Mother Bombie*, I.iii.193–4: 'And you, pretie minx, that must be fed with loue vpon sops, | Ile take an order to cram you with sorrows.' (Lucas canvasses further possible punning on 'sorrow' and the bitter 'sorrel', sometimes served as a medicinal sop, and on 'sop' and 'sob'.)

62 *Exeunt* Presumably Corbulo leaves by a different door from the Serving-men.

ACT IV, SCENE i

0.1, .2 *like a slave* i.e. wearing the 'habit' of slaves (see 12 and n, and 55), and, in Virginia's case, without her 'Jewels' (203). Virginius is presumably without his sword, since only a '*knife*' is mentioned at IV.ii.74.1.

0.2 *Orator* Q has no entry direction, but he must enter now rather than at 48.1 (as Lucas) in order to be pointed at by Virginius at 29 ('yon Lawyers Gown'). He evidently keeps his distance. Perhaps he cannot enter with his client, Marcus Clodius, because Clodius has been in custody; or perhaps he is needed to supervise setting up the court, possibly including a 'pleading bar' (V.ii.48), or even two (cf. *DLC* IV.ii.46.2n). He is also identifiable by his English lawyer's coif (cf. 111n), and may well have a buckram bag and a comically excessive number of papers like the lawyer in *DLC* IV.ii.

0.2 JULIA, CALPHURNIA Although Julia and Calphurnia are ghost characters, with no lines or identified function, possibly the intention here is to depict female as well as male support for the family (Livy, *Romane Historie* [p. 119], cites 'the traine of women, with their still & silent weeping'), and to utilize available boy actors to swell a public scene. Virginia sent Corbulo with a message to Calphurnia at II.i.1.

3 ranges 'is inconstant' (*OED* 8); cf. *Shr.* III.i.91–2: 'If once I find thee ranging, | Hortensio will be quit with thee by changing.'

4 dance . . . changes Cf. Ford, *The Broken Heart*, V.iii.90: '*Time alone doth change and last.*' Alan Brissenden defines 'change' as a 'finite passage of a dance, apparently equivalent to a strain in music in the sense of "a musical idea or passage, more or less complete in itself"' (*Shakespeare and the Dance* [Atlantic Highlands, N.J., 1981], p. 113), a more accurate description than *OED*'s '? A round in dancing' (1c), citing only *LLL* V.ii.209: 'in our measure do but vouchsafe one change'. Lucas cites *The Broken Heart*, V.ii.12

SD: *'They dance the first change'*, and 'To the other change'. Cf. *H8* IV.ii.82.4–.6: *'They . . . dance; and, at certain changes, the first two hold a spare garland over her head.'*

7 to our merit 'according to our merit'; see Abbott, Sect. 187.

8 memory to vertue i.e. 'memory of virtue'.

9 carousing *Lethe* Cf. 'I have drunke Lethe' (*WD* IV.ii.125); the waters of this river of the classical underworld induced forgetfulness.

11 *Rhadamant* Rhadamanthus was one of the three judges of the dead in Hades.

12 Then . . . yonder i.e. 'than the unfortunate accused appears before Appius's "Judgment seat" over there', presumably with, as Dilke suggests, an accompanying gesture.

13 habit Cf. Livy, *Romane Historie*, p. 119: 'he himselfe being in soiled and simple array, brought his daughter in her old worn clothes'. It was conventional for those in mourning or under accusation in Rome to appear 'in soiled and simple array' (Latin *sordidatus*), but here both Numitorius and Appius are surprised, and Virginius clearly stresses the irony of their 'form and shew' (16) of slavery to face a trumped-up charge of slavery. Cf. 0.1n and 56–62n.

20–1 Tryer . . . fire Cf. Georgius Agricola, *De Re Metallica* (1556), trans. Herbert Clark Hoover and Lou Henry Hoover (New York, 1950), p. 253: 'the touchstone with which gold and silver are tested . . . although the assay made by fire is more certain'. A **Tryer** is an 'assayer' (see *OED* trier 8); assaying the purity of gold or silver may first be done by rubbing it on a touchstone and comparing its colour against known samples, but fire was at the time the only fully reliable method. Minting of debased coinage was initiated in 1626, but Charles I halted it by proclamation on 4 September (see Gardiner, VI, 138).

28–9 fear'd . . . Gown Stoll (*Periods*, p. 140) compares Chapman, *Byron's Tragedy*, V.ii.39–42 (a passage based on Grimeston's *History of France*): 'These Scarlet robes, that come to sit and fight | Against my life; dismay my valure more, | Than all the bloudy Cassocks *Spaine* hath brought | To field against it.' For the possibility that the **Lawyers Gown** may be scarlet, cf. *DLC* II.iii.21–2n, and *WD* III.ii.69–72n. Virginius is evidently indicating the Orator, who is at a distance, and by implication not of their party (cf. 0.2n).

32 forfeit '"penalty for loss of that freedom"; Blackstone defines "forfeiture" as a punishment annexed by law to some illegal act or negligence, on the part of the owner of lands, tenements, or hereditaments, whereby he loses all interest therein. Virginia is of course guiltless of any negligence; none the less she is, I feel, thinking of this legal sense and of death as the forfeiture and atonement due for loss of her liberty and honour' (Lucas).

32–4 take the life . . . Lust By emphasizing that her **life** was given her by Virginius, and by urging him to kill her as a **sacrifice . . . to the gods** rather than let her be prey to **a villains Lust**, Virginia ensures that her death at her father's hand will not be seen as murder.

36 lustful projects bent upon 'lustful schemes [*OED* project 5a] directed [*OED* bend 17a] against'.

40 their . . . doom i.e. 'the evil and predetermined legal judgement [*OED* doom 2] which they will impose'.

44 second deluge i.e. a second Noah's Flood (or possibly that of Deucalion, the Greek Noah).

45 *Tenerife*'s high head The central peak of Tenerife (in the Canary Islands) soars from sea level to 3,718 m. Lucas compares Donne (*The First Anniversarie*, 287–8): 'Doth not a Tenarif, or higher Hill | Rise so high like a Rocke, that one might thinke | The floating Moone would shipwracke there, and sink.'

46–8 snow ... winter The traditional comparison of white hair and **snow** is here given particularity by the reference to the peak of Tenerife.

48 SD APPIUS will no doubt mount to his 'Judgment-seat'. The *six Senators* are more likely to be the 'reverend Lords' (198) to whom Appius appeals for confirmation of his justice (as Monticelso's does to the Ambassadors in *WD* III.ii) than to be, as Lucas thinks, the 'six . . . Knights' (195–6) who have deposed against Virginia. Probably no more than two actors are left to provide *Lictors* to precede Appius in this ceremonial entry (see pp. 489–90).

48–9 Is he come . . . General Appius, realizing Virginius is present, swears to be revenged (see *OED* quit 11) on Minutius for not preventing him; cf. III.iv.10–12.

50–1 reverence ... complement As Numitorius urges Virginius to make his **reverence** ('bow or obeisance' [see *OED* 2]), Virginius responds ironically with the word **complement**, which can mean the same thing, but often carries the sense of 'mere courtesy' (*OED* 9). Whether Virginius bows to Appius immediately after delivering his sententia to Numitorius (52–3), and has to remain thus until Appius speaks to him at 54, or delays his bow until 'I am here' (54), is unclear.

52–3 Blest ... any i.e. 'Fortunate are those of low station who dread and reverence (see *OED* fear *n.*[1] 3d) many, and cursed are those of high rank because they reverence no-one.'

55 Here 'We should expect Virginius himself to answer the question: "Where is your daughter?" But perhaps he hesitates and the conciliatory Numitorius hastens to answer for him' (Lucas). Or perhaps Virginius has stepped forward to a prominent stage position at 54, and Virginia is now brought forward from her previous discreet place in the background.

56–62 Your habit . . . many The stage picture now has the meanly attired father and daughter facing the 'spruce Orator' (146). There may be a quibble on **habit** and **sutes**. Numitorius's comment on Virginia's *sordidatus* creates a parallel with his earlier comment on Virginius's attire (cf. 13n), and also provides another private interchange, like that at 50–4, in which attention is on the defendants rather than Appius. Lucas, following Dyce, assumed an error here, and allocated 56 to Appius, on the grounds that Numitorius 'has already remarked on her father's similar clothing (13). To repeat the same criticism of the daughter would be a little too tedious even for Numitorius. Besides, Appius is clearly firing off a whole train of remarks, which is interrupted if we give this one to N.' Character analysis as a basis for emendation apart, one would logically expect Lucas's argument to extend to allocation to Virginia of 59–63, for which the Q speech prefix is the ambiguous '*Virg.*', especially as that speech is in some respects at odds with speeches undoubtedly by Virginius at 65–70 and 72–6 (see 65–70n). But although an Appius–Virginia exchange, begun at 56 and continued by

Virginia with an idealistic statement that 'Truth needs no Advocate', would present an
impressively independent and courageous Virginia, the evidence points in a different
direction. The scribe or compositor seems to have recognized the danger of ambiguity
in the speech prefixes, and to have been careful to spell out '*Virginia*' when necessary (as
at 56). Hence confusion at either 56 or 58 is unlikely. Further, for her to speak out for
herself directly to Appius at this early stage of the trial would seem counter to the
decorum she has displayed up till now as an unmarried woman allowing her male pro-
tectors to speak for her. Finally, for Virginia to say at 58–62 that she has decided against
having a lawyer would be to arrogate to herself agency which neither the playwrights
nor legal custom allow her; as is made clear at 82–4, Virginia is a chattel under dispute,
not a principal in the case (see p. 487).

59 Truth . . . Advocate Cf. Tilley T575: 'Truth has no need of rhetoric.'

60 travel i.e. 'travail'.

63 Lordships Appius, Oppius, and the six Senators; cf. 48 SDn.

63 What are you Since his 'Lawyers Gown' (see 28–9n) will make clear the Orator's
function, Appius's question is probably a satirically contemptuous introduction of the
comic lawyer. Cf. *WD* III.ii.11 and (for the identical query, but concerning a virtuous
lawyer) *DLC* IV.ii.75.

65–70 My Lord . . . against me Virginius's idealistic contempt for mercenary lawyers
at 58–62 is not reversed here; but he acknowledges that he may be at a legal disadvantage because of his decision not to employ one. Cf. 56–62n.

68 travell'd 'learned' (see *OED* travail 2c: 'to study'). Cf. 60.

70 wrested 'twisted' (*OED* 2b).

73–4 place . . . Court Perhaps with reference to Buckingham's accumulation of
high titles and offices. The first three articles of his impeachment dealt with 'the
excessive number of high positions which the favourite held' (Lockyer, p. 321); cf.
I.i.30–1n.

76 stand . . . have at you As at *WD* III.ii.23–5, the accused is ready to 'withstand'
(*OED* stand 52a) the attack of the Lawyer.

77–86 May it . . . circumstance Cf. the Lawyer's address (*WD* III.ii.26–32) and particularly Contilupo's (*DLC* IV.ii.99–102).

81 My practice more i.e. 'my experience in practising law even greater' (see *OED*
practice 5).

82 pursenet 'a bag-shaped net' (*OED* 1), and hence, figuratively, a snare. Cf. *DLC*
IV.i.32: 'new stratagems, new pursnets'.

82–3 Here . . . Heres another The Orator seems to have taken centre stage between
Virginius and Marcus Clodius.

86 two words only Cf. Contilupo in *DLC*, whose 'I'll conclude in a word' (IV.ii.178),
is likewise a prologue to a long-winded speech.

87 Fall to 'begin, proceed to' (*OED* fall 66d).

87–90 papers . . . prating This charade, similar to Appius's feigned irritation in III.ii,
casts Marcus Clodius in a role similar to that played by Sanitonella in *DLC* IV.ii.

91–110 That honourable . . . lying in Cf. Contilupo's slandering of Leonora (*DLC* IV.ii.179 ff.).

95–7 *Numitorius* . . . your side If *Numitorius*, at the first suggestion that he is implicated, has turned to Virginius or others in their party, then **I pray Sir** is probably directed to him, to be followed by a further demand for his attention at 96–7. As Lucas notes, 'This attempt to appeal to the self-interest of Numitorius and divide the house of Virginius against itself, is not unskilful.'

99 observe it The Orator directs his pleading throughout to Appius and the Senators. Cf. *WD* III.ii.57 and n.

101–4 She . . . stuff Cf. *DLC* III.iii.179–81.

104 imposterous 'of the nature of an imposture; false' (*OED* 1). Lucas notes its use 'some half dozen times in Heywood', but that 'it occurs embedded in a passage of the most obvious W'.

106 a Dyce supplied the word, which is not in Q. There is such a plethora of indefinite articles hereabouts that Q's accidental omission of this one is not unlikely, and its presence not only regularizes the metre but slightly improves the rhetorical balance of the line.

107 Bumbasted 'padded out' (*OED* bombast *v.* 2). Cf. *DLC* III.iii.184–5: 'Make to your petticoat a quilted preface, | To advance your belly.'

109 it skils not 'it matters not' (*OED* skill *v.*[1] 2b).

111 fellow i'th' night cap i.e. the Orator, wearing the coif or skullcap of an English serjeant at law. Cf. *DLC* II.i.42 and *DM* II.i.4n and 19n.

116 A thousand Drachmas Somewhat under £50; see I.iii.166n.

119–20 deposition . . . other testimony The Orator, like Contilupo in *DLC* and the Lawyers in *CC* (see, e.g., *DLC* IV.i.11–17 and *CC* IV.i.22.1), has a vast quantity of paper; even in tragedy W employs this trademark (cf. *WD* III.ii.46).

125 your claim The case has been brought by Marcus Clodius. It would be possible for this question to be addressed to the Orator, but both logic and characterization are better served by his interrupting with the answer.

126 discontinued 'abandoned' (legal usage; *OED* 3a).

127 fourteen years This is the only indication of Virginia's age.

128–9 I vow . . . off Cf. *DM* I.i.315–16, *FMI* IV.ii.230.

130 this Gentleman i.e. Marcus Clodius.

131 accident 'incident' (*OED* 1a).

132–3 mother . . . bond-woman The mother is the dead 'bond-woman' referred to at 114 and 117, and, as stage gesture will make clear, **this fair bond-woman** refers to Virginia.

138 put case i.e. 'suppose that' (see *OED* put 22).

143–4 Cast . . . dunghil Appius and the **Judges** are characterized as the sun shining on a **dunghil**, the Orator; the image is proverbial (see Tilley S982, *Wiv.* I.iii.61–3, and, indirectly, *Ham.* II.ii.181–2).

146 spruce 'brisk' (*OED* 1), probably with the accompanying sense of 'dapper; smart in appearance' (*OED* 2a). Cf. *DLC* IV.i.79: '*Enter Contilupo, a spruce lawyer.*'

149 glosses 'explanations, interpretations', with a connotation of 'sophistical or disingenuous' (*OED n.*¹ 1). Lucas suggests that 'deceptive appearances' (*OED n.*² 1b) may also be intended.

153 Soft you For the first time Appius turns the court's full attention to Virginius.

158 belike 'perhaps; in all likelihood' (*OED*).

165 Command . . . Lictors Either the **Lictors** take the Nurse off (in which case they must re-enter so as to be available by 245.1) or they merely threaten her. She is heard from no more.

168 This is a trick Probably indicating the depositions which constitute the case against Virginia.

173 his soul or thine Gesture will clarify that **his** refers to Marcus Clodius (or just possibly the Orator; cf. 125n). If Virginius pauses before **or thine**, it will be a deliberate, perhaps coded, challenge to Appius's integrity. Even without such emphasis, this speech is the first time Virginius's anger results in him addressing Appius as 'thou' (169).

174–6 thy love . . . loathing Appius puns on **natural** and **nature**: his hypocritical point being regret that Virginius has become accustomed (*OED* custom 1a) to a normal (*OED* natural 3c) love for Virginia where he should, in the **nature** of things, feel **absolute loathing**.

176–9 Sparrow . . . nest Cf. *1H4* V.i.59–65:

> And being fed by us you us'd us so
> As that ungentle gull, the cuckoo's bird,
> Useth the sparrow; did oppress our nest,
> Grew by our feeding to so great a bulk
> That even our love durst not come near your sight
> For fear of swallowing; but with nimble wing
> We were enforc'd for safety sake to fly.

180 have it drest With, it seems, the senses both of 'set in order' (*OED* dress 2a) and 'made ready' (*OED* 5a). Lucas compares *Shr.* III.i.83: 'to dress your sister's chamber up'.

183–4 souldiers . . . Pleaders i.e. lawyers are as vulnerable as soldiers to being cuckolded while they are away from home. Cf. Henry Fitzjeffrey's satiric observation of lawyers 'That from their Wiues must all the *Terme-time* tarry. | O Sir! If *Termely absence* breeds the *Feare*, | How many *Frights* each *Lawyer*, in a yeare?' (*Satyres: and Satyricall Epigram's* [1617], D5ʳ, epigram 40; cited by Wilfrid R. Prest, *The Rise of the Barristers* [Oxford, 1986], p. 123).

187–8 Janus . . . several wayes Because the god *Janus* is depicted with two heads facing opposite ways, his name can indicate, as here, 'two-faced, hypocritical'.

189 go to th' point Cf. *DLC* IV.ii.150 and 177; also *WD* III.ii.136.

190 At points end As if with a sword or pike, punning on 'point' at 189.

195–6 six ... Knights Since these **Knights** are not present (see 48 SDn), Appius may have their written depositions to hand. The assertion that their oaths are 'currant' (197 and n) ironically raises the likelihood of fraud, and may also be satire against English knights, given the disrepute into which knighthood had fallen since King James's commercializing of the honour.

197 currant 'genuine, authentic' (*OED* current 5).

199 *Virginius*. Addressing Appius, Virginius insists on the validity of the outraged scepticism he has been expressing since the start of the scene. Q's speech prefix is '*Virg.*'; although almost certainly, as in most instances, indicating Virginius, it is just possible that Virginia is intended, addressing either Appius or Icilius.

200 Policy 'craftiness, cunning' (*OED* 4a), or perhaps the 'crafty device, stratagem' (*OED* 4b) which they have introduced today.

201 Confounds 'confutes' (*OED* 3b).

204 More ... Tribe Lucas notes 'a clear echo' of *Oth.* V.ii.346–8: 'one whose hand, | Like the base Indian, threw a pearl away | Richer than all his tribe'. **Tribe** may be simply general (= 'a class of persons' [*OED* 4], as at III.ii.59), but here it may invoke the specifically Roman divisions of society; cf. *Cor.* III.iii.11: 'Have you collected them by tribes?'

207 proper 'suitable, befitting' (*OED* 10).

208 by th' hand Probably 'by the bargain'; see *DLC* IV.ii.141n.

209–10 *Appius ... Appius* Probably these three outraged responses are in effect simultaneous.

210 juggling 'trickery, deception' (*OED* 1b).

213 brought up 'elevated, brought into a higher position' (*OED* bring 27a), rather than 'reared from childhood' (*OED* 27b).

214 probable 'likely' (*OED* 3a).

215–17 our wife ... ours The use of the plural here may be Roman *gravitas*, or possibly carry familial implications.

222 writ in snow Cf. *DM* V.v.114–16: 'his print in snow; | As soone as the sun shines, it ever melts, | Both forme, and matter', and *MonC* (Lucas), 110.

224 hot livers 'unbridled lust'; cf. *DLC* IV.ii.517–18n.

225–9 Remember ... divels Virginia's only significant speech to Appius, brief though it is, will be the more effective from its contrast, in content, stage position, and vocal quality, to what has gone before. Use of **thee** and **thy** is the more striking from a deferential young woman.

227 Aspick i.e. 'asp, serpent'. Cf. Massinger, *A Very Woman*, V.iv.163–6: 'If *Portia's* burning coals, | The Knife of *Lucrece*, *Cleopatra's* Aspicks, | Famine, deep waters have the power to free me | From a loath'd life, I'll not an hour outlive him.'

233–4 That place ... sanctuary 'the high seat which holds you as judge is really the sanctuary that shields your felony' (Lucas).

234 Lye? Q's punctuation may be correct, or may indicate an exclamation (so Lucas). Either way, Icilius is picking up Appius's 'lye' at 232.

235 My Lords Appius appeals to the 'reverend Audience' (233) of Senators; cf. *WD* III.ii.129–30: 'See my Lords, | Shee scandals our proceedings.' The theatre audience may possibly be included in the appeal.

235 shifts 'stratagems, fraudulent devices' (*OED* 4a).

240–1 Office . . . another Cf. *DM* IV.ii.293–4.

243 no man view The refusal of the Senators, under the eye of Appius and the advancing Lictors (see 245 SD and n), to **view these papers** (see 231–5), which Icilius tries to present to them, may constitute an eloquent dumb show.

245, 250 SDs The precise manner in which the *Lictors* undertake the command at 242 to 'take charge of him' will be determined in performance, but it seems unlikely that they seize Icilius until after he has unsuccessfully sought help of the Senators, and knelt to Appius. At Wellington 1999 he was forced to his knees by a Lictor.

246–8 The Ass . . . reverence Lucas identifies this fable as no. 324 in the Teubner Aesop (ed. Halm). Sykes quotes Joseph Hall, *Meditations and Vowes Divine and Morall* (1606), p. 116 (III.63): 'The rich man hath many friends; although in truth riches haue them, and not the man: As the Asse, that carried the Egyptian Goddesse, had many bowed knees, yet not to the beast, but to the burden.'

251 in hold 'in custody' (*OED* hold 4).

253 lye with thee Nothing in the text indicates that Virginius is actually taken into custody. 'The apparent quibble with *truth* in the previous line may be merely due to unconscious association in W's mind as he wrote' (Lucas).

254–6 injuries . . . revenged i.e. 'we shall pardon the injuries you have done us, but it is at least justice that those wrongs which we forgive are the ones the gods have a duty to revenge'. Cf. Rom. 12: 19: 'Vengeance is mine: I wil repaye, saith the Lord.'

257 *Plebeian* See I.i.10n.

288–9 Ancestors . . . years The eleventh article of impeachment against Buckingham stated: 'the noble barons of England, so well deserving in themselves and in their ancestors, have been much prejudiced, and the crown disabled to reward extraordinary virtues in future times' (Lockyer, p. 322).

263 thy opinion old *Pythagoras* i.e. teachings of the Greek philosopher about metempsychosis, the transmigration of souls.

266 weeping Crocodile Cf. Topsell, *The Historie of Serpents* (1608), p. 135: 'The common prouerbe also, *Crocodili lachrimae*, the crocodiles teares, iustifieth the treacherous nature of this beast, for there are not many bruite beasts that can weepe, but such is the nature of the Crocodile, that to get a man within his danger, he will sob, sigh & weepe, as though he were in extremitie, but suddenly he destroyeth him.'

268–9 lov'st . . . swallow me Cf. Donne, 'A Nocturnall upon S. Lucies day, being the shortest day', 5–6: 'The world's whole sap is sunke: | The generall balme th'hydroptique earth hath drunk'; and Shakespeare, *Son.* 75, 1–2: 'So are you to my thoughts as food to life, | Or as sweet-season'd showers are to the ground.'

272 just defence i.e. the power of speech and his right to 'speak freely' (270). Cf. *WD* III.ii.126.

273–4 wink . . . sink (1) 'sleep during the storm, and so foolishly drown', (2) '"shut their eyes", are complaisant, about something wrong, and so foolishly perish' (see *OED* wink *v.*[1] 3, 5a, and *OED* fondly 1).

276 farwel let me borrow There is no indication in the text that either Virginius or Virginia is under guard (cf. 253n), so this may simply preface a move by them both to a central stage position.

281 fruit . . . blessed hope i.e. grandchildren.

285 Target 'a light round shield' (*OED n.*[1] 1).

286 burganet . . . neck Since Virginius's **burganet** (i.e. 'burgonet, helmet', usually with hinged cheekpieces) is very unlikely to have **hung** from his **neck**, Q's punctuation requires the assumption that the playwrights confused 'burganet' with 'gorget', a standard military costume accessory on the stage (see MacIntyre, p. 301), to which the helmet was sometimes attached (see *OED* b), and which would provide a reflective 'bright mettall' (287) surface **hung** from his **neck**. The alternative, that Virginia **hung 'bout his armed neck,** could be achieved by repunctuation (as **steel;**), but is unlikely given the succession of tenses from 'Would kiss' (286) to 'smile' (288).

290 go 'walk' (*OED* 1a).

293 bring . . . asleep i.e. 'lull my girl to sleep' (*OED* asleep 2).

294–5 When . . . growes 'When we were born our sorrows began, and they continue to increase, just as all life still grows even as it approaches death.' Cf. *WD* V.vi.267–8.

297 attend her Sentence Cf. *DLC* V.vi.65 and *WD* III.ii.263.

303 *Kills her* With a '*knife*'; cf. IV.ii.74.1.

306 Bury her in thy bowels 'a last faint echo of the literal Thyestean banquets of human flesh affected by Senecan revenge-tragedies' (Lucas). Stoll compares *Alphonsus Emperor of Germany* (1654), pp. 55–6 (IV): 'There murderer take his head, and breathless lymbs, | Ther's flesh enough, bury it in thy bowels.'

311 hang-men i.e. the Lictors trying to seize him (cf. I.i.0.1n).

312–13 Some . . . Others This seems to imply at least four Lictors or other attendants. Cf. 0.2n.

ACT IV, Scene ii

3–8 how many . . . Cattel i.e. fleas or lice (see 8n), as low-comedy stage business may emphasize.

6 Comrague Specifically 'a fellow rogue' (see *OED* comrogue), but often, as here, taken as a variant of 'comrade'; cf. Jonson, *The Masque of Augurs*, 56–7: 'you and the rest of your Comrogues shall sit disguis'd in the stocks'.

7 *Acteons* death Actaeon was torn to death by his own hounds (after being transformed into a stag by Diana, whom he had seen naked, bathing).

8 Cattel (1) 'animals held as property' (here, Actaeon's hounds), (2) 'vermin, insects' (here, fleas or lice) (*OED* cattle 4a and 7a). Cf. Dekker, *The Welsh Ambassador*, V.ii.63–4: '*Edmond.* Dow knowst our cuntry [Ireland] too has noe virmine in't. | *Clowne.* Oh noe, yett more cattell by far then *Wales*', and Davenant, *The Just Italian* (1630), IV.i (G1ʳ): 'I feele a heard | Of small cattell graze on my left shoulder.'

9 **My stomack has struck twelve** Sykes compares Heywood, *The English Traveller* (1633), I.i (B3ʳ): 'my stomacke hath strucke twelue', and *The Lancashire Witches* (1634), I.i (B2ᵛ): 'my stomacke is now much upon 12'.

10 **provant** 'provender, allowance of food' (*OED* 1).

13 **taste like date stones** i.e. the crust 'feels' (see *OED* taste 3) as hard as date stones (because it is stale and tough).

15 **struck in years** i.e. 'advanced (or stricken) in years'.

17 **frighted** 'as though the cheese had been congealed by terror' (Lucas).

22 **Gentles** 'maggots'.

23 **by profession Gentlemen** Ironic; but cf. *H5* IV.iii.61–3: 'For he to-day that sheds his blood with me | Shall be my brother; be he ne'er so vile | This day shall gentle his condition.'

25 **strong water** 1 Soldier puns bitterly on (1) 'spirits' (*OED* 2), and (2) water that is 'strong smelling', 'rank' (*OED* strong 15a, b).

26 **green ditch** Cf. *Lr.* III.iv.133–4: 'drinks the green mantle of the standing pool'.

29–30 **Cat . . . flead** More usually a horse would be flayed, hence incongruity is being played on, as well as desperation.

31 **Dutch . . . souldiers** The hardships of service in the Low Countries were notorious. During the withdrawal of Mansfeld's troops after the fall of Breda in May 1625, for instance, 'four days passed after their arrival at the frontier before even a piece of bread was served out to the famished soldiers' (Gardiner, V, 335); see pp. 443–4. The point of the heavy irony is that although when they 'dine' (30) on no food at all they will starve, at least when they 'sup' they will starve 'Bravely' (32) on dead cat.

32 **Bravely** 'excellently' (*OED* 3).

32 **Leaguerers** 'troopers' (*OED*), usually, as here, associated with the Dutch; cf. Henry Glapthorne, *The Hollander* (1640), D1ᵛ (II.i): 'My naturall Dutch too is a Clownish speech, and only fit to court a leagurer in'. The **Roman** camp garrison is, however, referred to as 'the leaguer' at V.ii.4; cf. *DM* I.i.208.

32.1 **SD** Probably *his Souldiers* are four of the '*six Souldiers*' of II.ii.0.1 (two more are already on stage; cf. 35n); they will carry pikes as before (cf. 'partisan' [77]). The **Letter** was despatched by Appius in III.iii, but has arrived too late for Minutius to prevent Virginius reaching the trial.

33 **give him place** i.e. 'get out of his way' (see *OED* place 23).

34 **dainties** 'delicacies'.

35 **SD** Clearly 1 Soldier must exit here, since he re-enters at 58.1, but there is no need for 2 Soldier to do so, since he also speaks later in the scene. Possibly 1 Soldier's stated intention to leave to get a drink (24–7), and his instruction to 2 Soldier to prepare supper (29–30), are more than mere jokes.

42–4 **fly . . . escape** Presumably this refers to Virginius making a hasty departure immediately prior to Minutius receiving this letter (which seems to be confirmed by 97–8), although it is just possible that Virginius did literally **escape**.

46 **hand** 'part, share' (*OED* 3b).

46 of faction i.e. 'in (my) conduct; manner of behaving' (*OED* faction 1a).

48 Tribuneship Military tribunes were senior officers in the Roman republican army, six to a legion, although historically more often administrative than tactical leaders.

51 Colours 'A flag, ensign, or standard of a regiment' (*OED* 7); cf. *Cor.* I.iv.0.1–.2: '*Enter MARTIUS, TITUS LARTIUS, with Drum and Colors*'. Roman standards, however, were historically, and at least sometimes on stage, metal eagles rather than fabric banners; cf. Jonson's *Catiline*, III.563–4: 'Behold this siluer eagle, | 'Twas MARIVS standard, in the *Cimbrian* warre'. It is just possible that Virginius is thought of as having personal family **Colours** (*OED* 6) like an English knight, since evidently the Souldiers will have to learn to 'Know [the Roman's] Colours' (55); cf. 112n.

55 worthy Roman The Lieutenant would be the most appropriate candidate for promotion, but casting constraints mean it was probably one of the Soldiers (see pp. 489–90).

60 shape 'appearance, guise'; cf. 'forme' (I.ii.34).

62 growths 'sizes attained by growing' (*OED n.*¹ 2).

63 frighted Presumably 'affected with fright, scared' (*OED*, not first cited until 1647). Although Virginius never appears frightened on stage, 1 Soldier describes the crowd as pursuing him either with hostile intent or in anticipation of violence (see also 104–5).

64 Room's This spelling of 'Rome's' reflects a common pronunciation; cf. *JC* I.ii.156: 'Now is it Rome indeed and room enough.'

66 uncouth 'unfamiliar; strange' (*OED* 3), perhaps also with a sense of 'unpleasant, unseemly' (*OED* 4). Lucas compares *The Lamentable Tragedy of Locrine*, II.ii.61–2: 'what uncouth novelties | Bringst thou unto our royal majesty?' (ed. Jane Lytton Gooch [New York, 1981]).

68 Martial i.e. 'marshal'. Cf. 'order' at II.ii.94, similarly in a situation in which a 'ring of steele' (69) is part of the stage picture (see II.ii.86n).

68 novel 'novelty' (*OED* 1). Cf. Heywood, *The Brazen Age*, II.ii (E3ʳ): 'To see this Prince lye dead? why that's no nouell, | All men must dye.'

74.1–.2 SD For a similar image of arms and weapons *all bloudy* as a symbol of Roman liberty, cf. *JC* III.i.105–10. On the costume implications of *stript up to the elbowes*, see p. 481. As he *makes a stand* (i.e. halts as if facing an enemy [see *OED* stand *n.*¹ 4]) he will be encircled by the 'ring of steele' (69).

77 thrill Given **partisan** (see next note), the sense here must, as Lucas notes, be 'thrust' (see *OED* 1a), not the frequent 'hurl' (*OED* 3a, which cites Heywood, *Great Britain's Troy*, canto 13, verse 70 [p. 347]: 'He thrild a Iauelin at the *Dardans* brest').

77 partisan 'A long-handled spear, the blade having one or more lateral cutting projections' (*OED*). References to 'pikes' at II.ii.112n may in fact be to partisans. According to *Shakespeare's England* (I, 137–8), the **partisan** was often referred to as a pike; at about nine feet (just under 3 m), it would have been a handier size for stage use than a full twelve- to eighteen-foot-long (3.7 to 5.5 m) infantry pike. It may be that shorter stage versions were made of both weapons.

79 prison The body as the prison of the soul is a commonplace. Cf. Donne, *The Second Anniversarie*, 'Of the Progres of the Soule', 169–74:

Thinke that no stubborne sullen Anchorit,
Which fixt to'a Pillar, or a Grave doth sit
Bedded and Bath'd in all his Ordures, dwels
So fowly'as our soules, i'their first-built Cels.
Thinke in how poore a prison thou didst lie
After, enabled but to sucke, and crie.

Also *DM* IV.ii.120–3.

80 christal pallace i.e. 'heaven', as a gesture will probably make clear. Cf. Heywood, *The Silver Age*, II.i (C3^r): 'let *Iuno* skold, | And with her clamours fill the eares of heauen . . . And through our christall pallace breath exclaimes'. There may be an additional association with the ideal of absolute chastity that Virginia represents: cf. Middleton, *The Revenger's Tragedy*, IV.iv.152: 'A virgin honour is a crystal tower.'

81 inthronis'd 'enthroned'.

90 obdure 'obdurate' (*OED* 1); a word, as Lucas notes, regularly used by Heywood, though otherwise rare. Cf. Heywood and Rowley, *Fortune by Land and Sea*, I.406: 'The boy's inflexible, and I obdure.'

97 stay 'confine' (*OED* 20d).

102 face of blood i.e. 'bloody visible state' (see *OED* face 9). Though Virginius's arms and clothes are still stained with his daughter's blood, it seems unlikely that **face of blood** is to be taken literally. See 114n.

106 Parricide 'one who murders either parent or other near relative'; also often associated with treason (*OED n.*^{1}). For **Parricide** as an archetypally Roman crime, see Ronan, pp. 140–50.

110 advice 'deliberation' (*OED* 4).

112 colours Virginia's **crimson** blood on his clothing is imagined as the insignia which Virginius wears in service; cf. 51n.

114 I lov'd her life An odd phrase, and slightly bathetic in its weakening of the plainer declaration of love which we might expect, unless we take **life** to mean 'live, alive'. *OED* provides no exact equivalent.

115 speaking Organ 'tongue'.

118 How agrees this? i.e. 'How can this discrepancy [love her, and murder her?] be resolved?' (see *OED* agree 4).

121 agree them well Virginius picks up Minutius's use of 'agrees' (118) in explaining that he will 'explain the apparent contradiction'.

122–36 Alas . . . fathers hand From Livy, *Romane Historie*, p. 121 (see p. 641).

124 Lay in her bosom i.e. 'would have lain in her bosom'; presumably Virginius means he would have given his life for hers.

124–6 pull'd . . . drag'd Apparently rhetorical, since there is no evidence of Virginia having been in custody between III.ii and IV.i, nor during the trial (cf. III.ii.284n and 294n). Nevertheless, the audience has seen the Lictors 'pulling and haling' her (III.iii.85).

126 Sessions house 'court of justice' (Lucas); see *OED* session 7.

127 fore Spousals i.e. 'betrothal' (Lucas). *OED* lists the word (fore- *prefix* 2), citing only this instance, under the misleading heading 'beforehand, previously, in advance', which would imply (wrongly) that Virginia and Icilius were already married.

130 Peramour (Q 'Permour') *OED* cites a 'per' spelling of 'paramour' as late as 1652, where the form is 'peramore'. Q's omission of the medial vowel must be accidental: 'Permour' is not an authenticated variant, and the metre requires the extra syllable.

131 twinings 'embracings, writhings' (*OED*). Cf. Marston, *The Malcontent*, II.v.53: 'And in your lustful twines the Duke to you?'

137 O villain . . . Virginius! Lucas compares the exclamations of the crowd in *JC* III.ii.199–201: 'O noble Caesar!'—'O woeful day!'—'O traitors, villains!'

138 Sentencers 'those who pass sentence' (see *OED* sentence *v.* 8b). Cf. Heywood, *2 The Fair Maid of the West*, V.i (L4ʳ): 'The thief is found . . . I beg | That I may be his sentencer.'

140 Fact 'action', whether noble or criminal (*OED* 1).

144 fry 'crowd of insignificant people' (*OED* 4b).

153 Roman Presumably the *Roman* earlier appointed to take Virginius's place (see 55 and n).

157 take my Charge Possibly Minutius signals the change of responsibility by transferring to Virginius a token of command, such as a truncheon (cf. *MM* II.ii.61: 'The marshal's truncheon').

170 proscribe The publication of names of those outlawed (with a price on their heads) was not introduced until 82 B.C., but lies behind the more general English sense 'condemn'.

171–9 Thou oughtest . . . have time From Livy, *Romane Historie*, p. 121 (see p. 641).

175 Elysian Vestals i.e. 'Vestal Virgins in the Elysian Fields, dwelling place of the blessed after death'.

176 none 'no-one' (*OED* 1a).

ACT V, Scene i

0.1 Orator 'a professional advocate' (*OED* 1). Cf. Rowley, *All's Lost by Lust* (perf. 1619–20, publ. 1633), I.i (B2ʳ): 'Indeed in rightfull causes, weake Lawyers will | Serve turne, but the wrong had need have | The best Orators.' Despite Q's SD '*Advocate*' and various abbreviations of it for the speech prefixes, the dialogue makes clear that he is the Orator from IV.i. The audience will therefore see the same man.

4 I wonder . . . imprisonment Cf. *WD* I.i.38–9: 'So, but I wonder then some great men scape | This banishment.'

5 Hedghog . . . tempest Cf. Montaigne, *Essayes*, II.xii.270: 'he had learn't the qualitie of the hedge-hogge, whose propertie is to build his hole or denne, open diverse wayes, and toward several windes, and fore-seeing rising storms, he presently stoppeth the holes that way', and Topsell, *Historie*, p. 278: 'the wild ones have two holes in their cave, the one north, thother south, observing to stop the mouth against the wind'. Lucas further notes Bartholomaeus, *Batman*, XVIII.lxii.369, and Browne, *Pseudodoxia*, III.x (*Works* II, 187).

7–8 Bear-whelp . . . clawes Sykes quotes Pliny, *Nat. Historie*, VIII.xxxvi.216: 'beares be as weake and tender [in the head]: and therefore when they be chased hard by hunters and put to a plunge, ready to cast themselves headlong from a rocke, they cover and arme their heads with their fore-feet and pawes, as it were with hands, and so jumpe downe'.

10–11 sand . . . shelf Cf. Heywood, *2 The Iron Age*, IV.i (G2ʳ): 'the Seas | With tempests, stormes, rocks, shipwracks, shelues and sands | More dammag'd them then all the Troian siege'. Here **sand = shelf** ('sandbank' [*OED* 1]), and implies drowning; see *CC* II.iii.87n. Cf. also *H5* IV.i.97–8, 114–15.

12 Hee's . . . himself Cf. Tilley F684 'Be a friend to thyself and others will be so too.'

18 Court of Guard In context, 'defence' is the meaning required. A **Court of Guard** is 'the small body of soldiers stationed on guard or as sentinels', or their 'guardhouse' (*OED* corps de garde 1, 2). Cf. Massinger, *The Unnatural Combat*, V.ii.253–4: 'Our outworkes are surpriz'd, the centinell slaine, | The corps du garde defeated too.'

19 uncoupled 'set free for the chase', as hounds are (*OED* 1). Lucas glosses the **dogs** as Virginius and Icilius, hunting down the Orator, but the danger the Senator warns of is probably more general in its application, since Virginius and Icilius are currently set to confront each other.

21 distaste 'render distasteful' (*OED* 5).

23–4 Lord . . . Benefactor Presumably Appius, ironically intensifying the reference at 20–2. Cf. also 27–8. Reference to Marcus Clodius, as the Orator's ostensible client in IV.i, is possible, but unlikely.

26 By the way 'in passing'.

30–1 Art . . . Rhetorick Although reference to the **Art Of flattery** is common, the Orator seems to be playing not only on **Rhetorick** as **flattery**, but also on the seven liberal arts, which include both rhetoric and 'Arithmatick' (36).

36–8 Arithmatick . . . twenty i.e. 'in order to continue fraudulently to collect the pay of soldiers who have died [see *OED* dead pay 2], their arithmetic is good enough to make twelve live soldiers appear on a false muster-roll [*OED* muster 3, 5] as if they were twenty'. Cf. *Char.* (Lucas), 'A vaine-glorious Coward in Command', 2–3: 'he loves a life dead paies, yet wishes they may rather happen in his Company by the scurvy, then by a battel.'

40–1 commend . . . observation i.e. 'recommend [*OED* commend 2a] that you take note [see *OED* observation 5a] of this (the couplet which follows)'.

41 shake-rags 'tatterdemalions, beggarly fellows' (see *OED*).

42 Helmet . . . spider 'an ancient image. Thus the spider's web upon the spear appears in a famous fragment of Euripides's *Erechtheus* which helped to make Athens conclude peace with Sparta, according to Plutarch, *Nicias*, 9.' So Lucas, who notes that here 'the spider symbolizes the change, not from the use of war to the dusty neglect of arms in peace, but, less aptly, from neglected hardships and squalor to revelry and ease'. If the couplet is, as Lucas feels, 'almost like a garbled recollection of the classical phrase', the garbling is presumably intended to make the Orator look ridiculous.

43 Sack and Sider Possibly referring to the perennial sharp practice of adulterating wine with cider; see *CC* IV.i.21n.

44 *Proteus* A minor Greek god who could change his shape at will. Cf. Tilley S285 'As many shapes as Proteus'.

46 Bastinado 'cudgel' (*OED* 4). The jingling rhyme with 'bravado' (45) suggests that Oppius is mockingly parodying the Orator here.

48 foulded i.e. 'furled'.

48 *Exeunt* The Orator could exit at any point after 44, and by a different door.

ACT V, Scene ii

0.1–.3 SD Since ICILIUS is now evidently Rome's 'General' (2), he may be in military costume (see pp. 476–7). VIRGINIUS probably still has hands and arms '*all bloudy*' as at IV.ii.74.1–.2 (cf. 96); he is shaking with a 'burning Feaver' (see 10–12 and n). The *others* are Soldiers. Q has the succinct direction *Wine* justified against an inner right-hand margin created by quads, after Virginius's 'Make a stand' at 1. This anticipates Virginius's call for wine at 11–12 and may have been added by the book-keeper as he prepared the authors' manuscript for stage use. Among similar 'anticipatory' directions is one in *The Spanish Curate*, where at IV.v.6, in the Beaumont and Fletcher Folio of 1647, '*Diego ready in Bed, wine, cup*' anticipates '*Enter* Diego (*in a Bed*)' at line 41 and 'Give me a cup of wine' at line 61 (W. W. Greg, *The Shakespeare First Folio* [Oxford, 1955], p. 140; see also Dessen and Thomson, 'wine').

1 Make a stand 'halt' (*OED* 2a).

1 parly i.e. 'parley'.

2 'twixt the Armies The entry of the two **Armies** was by opposite doors at 0.1–.3, and their stage position has evidently remained confrontational, with space between them for the 'parly' (1).

4 leaguer 'a military camp; an investing force' (*OED n.*[1] 1); both senses are appropriate here.

5.1 SD The two hostages *meet, embrace* centre stage before each continuing to the opposite army, there to *salute* the opposing general. In Q the SD is opposite 5, where space was available.

9 despaire A response to Virginius's 'I am forsaken of the gods' (7), Numitorius's comment carries implications Christian rather than classical Roman. Cf. IV.i.254–6; also *DM* IV.i.73–4n.

10–12 Feaver ...Wine Virginius **shakes** with a **burning Feaver**, which he likens to **a divel**, presumably because of Numitorius's comment (8–9) warning him against 'despaire' (see *WD* V.iv.136n). His repeated **Wilt a** (**Give me some Wine**) may be a verbal equivalent of his physical weakness. There is no basis for Lucas's supposition of a convulsive fit. A marginal note in Q at 1, just after the entry, specifies '*Wine*', so it is presumably visible now, held in readiness by an attendant or Soldier.

12 hurtful Cf. William Turner, *A Book of the Natures and Properties of all Wines* (1568), D8ʳ: 'Wine is ill also for them that are of a hote burning complexion, and haue any inflammation within them in their bodies, or haue any burning agues.' For 'degrees' cf. *CC* II.ii.5–6 and n.

17–21 When . . . Here Virginius's impatience to get the cup of wine, even assuring them his estate will pay for it, emphasizes the loss of his 'wonted temper' (32), just as his inability to guide the cup to his lips (having to be assisted by Numitorius) suggests age and grief.

22 guide it to you i.e. 'assist you to bring the wine cup to your lips'.

23 palsie i.e. 'shaking palsy'; see *DM* II.v.55n.

24 this i.e. his trembling hand, holding the wine cup.

25 So, I thank you Having drunk, he returns the cup.

28 serve my belly i.e. by drinking; cf. 25 and n.

28 *to Icilius* Just as Numitorius crossed to Virginius's army as a hostage and spoke to him, now the other hostage, Minutius, addresses Icilius prior to the two generals meeting.

32 wonted temper 'habitual disposition' (see *OED* temper 9).

33 powred i.e. 'poured'.

34 You . . . Lord The two generals will now have centre stage ''twixt the Armies' (2) for what is something of a rhetorical set piece.

40–3 Lions . . . Scorpions Cf. the similar list in *Jn.* III.i.258–61: 'France, thou mayst hold a serpent by the tongue, | A cased lion by the mortal paw, | A fasting tiger safer by the tooth, | Than keep in peace that hand which thou dost hold.' For **Dragons taile** cf. Pliny, *Nat. Historie*, VIII.ix.198, probably referring to pythons in India: 'dragons, that are . . . evermore fighting, and those of such greatnesse, that they can easily claspe and wind round about the Elephants, and withall tye them fast with a knot'. Pliny also describes **Bulls** (*Nat. Historie*, VIII.xlv.225): 'their hornes so standing, as if they were ever disposed and readie to fight'. For **Cormorants beak** cf. *Tro.* II.ii.6: 'hot digestion of this cormorant war'. **Scorpions** were reputed by Pliny to have **teeth**: 'It is said moreover, that the Scorpions have the like tooth in their taile, and most of them three together' (*Nat. Historie*, XI.xxxvii.337).

47 peach 'accuse formally, indict, impeach' (*OED* 1a). Emendation of Q's 'teach' is required for Virginius to say he *indicts* himself no less severely than does Icilius *accuse* him, but to assert that, were he minded to do so, he could speak in his own defence. Virginius's use of **peach** fits well with the implication that he is on trial. Q's 'teach' would have to mean 'instruct, school' (*OED* 7), with perhaps also a sense of threat (see *OED* 6d), but 'teach me for this act' is not really idiomatic; besides, Virginius could hardly be said to *teach* himself for his killing of his daughter, as he claims to do. Dyce's 'tax' provides good sense, but could scarcely have provoked Q's 'teach'; 'touch', in the sense of 'reprove' or 'convict', is a possible alternative, but would be clumsy in view of the use of the verb at 61 in a different sense, namely 'affect'. See MacD. P. Jackson, '*Appius and Virginia*, 5.1.20: to Explicate or Emend', *ANQ: A Quarterly Journal of Short Articles, Notes, and Reviews* (forthcoming).

48 approve 'prove, demonstrate' (*OED* 1a).

49–50 posterity . . . praise Virginius's confidence that **posterity** will **praise** him for his actions is thematically central to the tragedy.

52 Here's a fury i.e. his feverish trembling.

54 oath . . . Knighthood A conflation of the Roman equestrian order ('equites' = knights) with Jacobean **Knighthood** which did include an **oath**.

55 parcel 'part' (*OED* 1a).

56–7 honour . . . servitude Cf. Tilley H576 'It is better to die with honor than to live with shame.'

66 unthrifts 'unworthy (unthriving) shiftless persons' (see *OED* 3 and unthriving 1).

67 Hearten 'encourage' (*OED* 1).

70 common Wealth (1) 'general good', (2) 'whole body of people constituting a state', and (3) 'republic' (*OED* 1, 2, 3).

72–8 tame . . . watching The language of taming wild animals or hawks is used by both men. Icilius, referring to himself as a **Lion** (to be feared and respected), says that harsh means will not work. (A whip that is **wierd** is 'strengthened or stiffened with wire' [*OED* wired 1]. Cf. *Ant.* II.v.65: 'Thou shalt be whipt with wire.') Rather, the tamer should be gentle and **fearful** ('timid, frightened' [*OED* 3a]), and **ply** ('continue to supply with food' [*OED v.*² 4]) its **wanton** ('unmanageable' [*OED* 1b]) hunger. **Want of sleep**, as Virginius retorts, is the standard most efficacious technique (cf. *DM* II.iv.31–2n), and he sarcastically warns Icilius of the dangers to a tamer himself **watching** (staying awake) in order to prevent the animal sleeping.

77 wake for others ruine i.e. 'remain awake in order to achieve **others ruine**'.

83–4 disgrace . . . place Cf. Beaumont and Fletcher, *Love's Cure*, IV.iii.128–9: 'However corrupt officers may disgrace | Themselves, 'tis not in them to wrong their place.'

87 Piteous 'lamentable, deplorable' (*OED* 3).

88 chance 'happen, occur' (*OED* 1a).

88–9 Towrs of stone . . . Flax shops Cf. *DLC* IV.ii.207–12 and 218–20.

90 to Virginius Minutius is apparently seconding Icilius's attempt to calm Virginius's 'rage' (71) and 'passion' (91); so Wellington 1999. The alternative, that Icilius's anger is now matching that of Virginius, and needs calming by Minutius, seems less likely.

92 good Dyce filled Q's metrical gap with this adjective, and the collocation **good deed** does seem more natural than the unqualified noun. A scribe or compositor could have been thrown by the presence of 'good' in the previous line.

94–6 reconcilement . . . bloody hand The refusal by Icilius to **seale** his **friendship** with Virginius by shaking his hand will be most emblematically forceful if Virginius has offered his literally and figuratively **bloody hand** first (so Wellington 1999).

97–8 No . . . borrowed President Lucas compares *DM* V.iv.81–2: 'I will not imitate things glorious, | No more then base: I'll be mine owne example.'

102–3 those . . . perfumes 'Cf. *Char.* (Lucas), "A Divellish Usurer" 22–3: "like the

Jakesfarmer that swouned with going into Bucklersbury" (where spices were sold)'
(Lucas).

104–7 no more . . . wakes i.e. 'Tell no more of this unhappy story (we can call our own
grief a tell-tale, which repeats the story when sleepless, envious that others are asleep').

112 *Exeunt* Whereas the two armies entered by opposite doors, their new joint purpose
will be emphasized by their departure as a single force, and by one door.

ACT V, SCENE iii

0.1 *Enter . . . gyved* Their shackled legs (*fettered and gyved*; both words normally mean
the same thing) signal that they are *in prison* (see Dessen, pp. 98–9); cf. Heywood, *The
Silver Age* (B1ᵛ): 'Gyue his legges in Irons, | Till we determine further of his death.'
There is therefore no need to suppose discovery here (as Lucas does). Having their legs
chained together would not prevent them walking, so even if they are discovered, they
may advance somewhat onto the stage (see Dessen and Thomson, 'prison').

2 Hydra headed multitude i.e. the Roman mob. Cf. Alexander, *Alex. Trag.* V.i (M1ʳ):
'the multitude more rash than wise, | A *Hydra*-headed beast whilst nought it binds, |
Doth passionately praise, or else despise', and *Cor.* III.i.92–3.

3 gape for innovation i.e. 'long for [*OED* gape 4] the introduction of novelties [*OED*
innovation 1]'; cf. *1H4* V.i.76–8: 'fickle changelings and poor discontents, | Which
gape and rub the elbow at the news | Of hurly-burly innovation'.

5 one rear'd . . . suffrage i.e. an individual 'raised, exalted' (*OED* rear *v.*¹ 11) by the
'collective vote' (*OED* suffrage 7) of the people.

6 station 'metaphorical standing-place' (*OED* 15); cf. Isa. 22: 19 (Authorized Version):
'I will drive thee from thy station, and from thy state shall pull thee down.'

6 Avees i.e. 'shouts of "Ave!"' (Latin, 'Hail!'). Cf. Heywood, *The Golden Age*, I.i (B2ᵛ):
'all the people, with lowd suffrages, | Have shrild their Auees high aboue the clouds',
and *MM* I.i.70.

7 airy (1) 'lofty' (*OED* 3), (2) 'unsubstantial, flimsy' (*OED* 7), and possibly with a glance
at 'Avees' (6) as shouted air or at 'base' = bass musical pitch.

7 Bases (1) 'pedestals' (*OED* 4), (2) 'supports, foundations' (see *OED* 1, 2).

9 consciate 'deliver an oration' (*OED* concionate).

10 Oratorize 'deliver an oration' (*OED*). Lucas notes Heywood's *The English Traveller*,
IV.i (H1ᵛ): 'This your absence . . . Orators | In your behalfe'. Q's 'Orarorize' is not rec-
ognized by *OED*.

10 rung shril Plaudits Although **Plaudits** requires 'hands' (8) to be clapping, both
rung and **shril** suggest voices or bells, and perhaps therefore suggest a religious sense
of 'grace' (11), as well as the primary one of 'favour'.

12 place of darkness A reinforcement of the prison location signalled by their fetters
(cf. 0.1n), with perhaps implications of hell, in opposition to 'grace' (11).

17 impart 'share' (*OED* 4). Cf. Heywood and Rowley, *Fortune by Land and Sea*,
III.1176: 'I am likely to impart his losse.'

19 climb'd (Dilke; 'climb' Q) The syntax requires the past tense. Lucas followed Dyce 2 in reading 'clomb', but it is unknown in English drama of the period, whereas there are a few instances of 'climbd' and many of **climb'd**.

21 trac'd 'followed the footprints or traces of' (*OED v.*[1] 5).

21–2 golden path . . . promotion i.e. advancement would have brought financial reward.

23 right 'exactly, to the full' (*OED* right *adv.* 5); cf. *DLC* III.iii.144.

33.1–.2 SD One or more of the Soldiers or other attendants may possibly carry torches to further emphasize the 'darkness' (12) of the 'loathsome dungeon' (28).

39 convince 'convict' (*OED* 4).

39 *Exeunt Souldiers* Most of the Soldiers will exit as directed, but probably at least two remain as a guard, and available to haul Marcus Clodius away at 167.

39 See This cry would support a staging in which Appius and Marcus Clodius are in or near a central discovery space, almost emblematically on display. Cf. 0.1n.

40 fronts 'faces' (*OED* 2).

43 damned Q has 'damn'd', but Dilke's emendation improves the metre, and Q is untrustworthy in its printing of such endings.

43 purge 'purify' (*OED* 2).

47 Chair i.e. his 'Ivory Chair' (64); cf. I.i.91n.

53 indifference 'impartiality' (*OED* 1).

57–8 yesterday . . . *Rome* Stoll (*Periods*, p. 196) compares *JC* III.ii.118–19: 'But yesterday the word of Caesar might | Have stood against the world.'

58 torved i.e. 'torvid, stern' (*OED* torve *a.*). Lucas notes Heywood's use of 'torvity' in *Londini Speculum* (B2^v).

64 Ivory Chair Cf. 47 and I.i.91n. Here, ironically juxtaposed with 'black deed' (63).

67 Common Weal (1) 'common well-being' (*OED* 1), (2) 'body politic, commonwealth' (*OED* 2); cf. V.ii.70n.

68–9 Nay . . . sin Although possibly spoken to Virginius, this may well be direct address to the audience prior to Icilius's exit.

70 remiss to punish i.e. 'slack in punishing' (see *OED* remiss 2).

76 Make good 'hold, secure' (*OED* good 22d).

80 place and Office An intensifying repetition, given that **place** = 'office' (*OED* 14a).

90 bleeding . . . presence Cf. *R3* I.ii.55–8: 'see, see, dead Henry's wounds . . . bleed afresh! . . . 'tis thy presence that exhales this blood'. On the wider significance of stage blood on her costume, see p. 481.

92 stench 'stanch, cease flowing' (*OED* stanch 2c). Understandably, Lucas alters to 'stanch', but **stench** is among seventeenth-century spellings recorded by *OED*.

93–4 soul . . . in the blood Lucas notes Heywood's *The Hierarchie of the blessed Angells* (1635), IX.1–2, 21–2 (p. 586): 'Some grant a Soule, but curiously desire | To have th'essence thereof deriv'd from Fire . . . Empedocles would have it understood | The Sole place she *resides in* is the Bloud.' Sykes suggests a source for the idea in Montaigne,

Essayes, II.xii (p. 315): '*Empedocles*, in the bloud: as also *Moises*, which was the cause he forbad the eating of beastes bloud, vnto which their soule is commixed'.

98 operant powers 'faculties' (Lucas; see *OED* operant *adj.* 1a). Cf. *Ham.* III.ii.174: 'My operant powers their functions leave to do.'

100–1 daughters . . . wounds It seems likely that Icilius will have laid her down in a central position on stage by now; Virginius evidently weeps over her, perhaps embracing her body.

104 Give . . . swords It does not matter who gives him the **two swords**, but Valerius and Horatio seem the most likely.

105 hang-men 'executioners' (*OED* 1).

111 lust-burnt 'again Heywoodian': so Lucas, who compares, e.g., *The Silver Age*, III.i (H3ᵛ): 'lust-burn'd and wine-heated monsters'.

111 confine 'banish' (*OED* 3); cf. *MonC* (Lucas), 254–5: 'be shee confin'd as farre | From his sweete reliques as is heaven from hell!' Lucas notes also its frequent use by Heywood: e.g. *Gynaikeion*, IV.207: 'Alcippus intended to abrogate their lawes, for which he was confind from Sparta.'

113–14 Had I . . . ballance i.e. 'If I had directed (*OED* level *v.*[1] 7d) my irregular (dishonest) path in accordance with (*OED* by 23) yours, I would not have weighed down (*OED* sway 5) one side of the scales of justice (see *OED* balance 8a).'

117 strage 'slaughter' (*OED*). Used frequently by Heywood: cf. *The Hierarchie of the blessed Angells*, VIII (p. 549): 'He did as much dammage, and made as great slaughter on his Enemies, as he had received strage or execution from them.'

123 constancy A crucial Roman Stoic virtue (Latin *constantia*); see Geoffrey Miles, *Shakespeare and the Constant Romans* (Oxford, 1996). Cf. *JC* V.i.90–1: 'For I am fresh of spirit, and resolv'd | To meet all perils very constantly.'

124 mulct 'fine, penalty'.

125–6 family . . . nobler Appius was a plebeian (I.i.10), but seems to be thought of as having been ennobled by his elevation to the decemvirs; cf. Virginius's taunt at IV.i.256. The claim that he and his family are 'of noble blood' (147) serves the dramaturgical contrast with Marcus Clodius better than strict genealogy. See pp. 461–2.

127–9 Learn . . . dy Cf. *WD* V.vi.72–3.

128 studiest The past tense would be more 'correct' here, so that Lucas emends to 'studiedst'. It was perhaps to avoid just such a tongue-twister that the playwright (probably Heywood in this scene) used **studiest**, thinking of it as 'continuous': **what thou never studiest yet** means 'what you have never studied until now'. There is a comparable usage in *1 Edward IV* (1599), ascribed to Heywood: 'Opprobrious villaine . . . That neuer dreamst of other manhood yet', where, strictly speaking, 'dreamst' is in the present tense.

129–30 Judges . . . Gods on earth Cf. Hall, *Characters*, p. 62: 'He is the guard of good lawes, the refuge of innocencie, the Comet of the guiltie, the pay-maister of good deserts, the champian of iustice; the patron of peace, the tutor of the Church, the father of his Countrey, and as it were another God vpon earth.'

131 Read me 'study the lesson of my fate' (Lucas). See *OED* read 5c.

133 *Kils himself* On the importance of suicide in the Renaissance view of Rome, and its association with 'constancy' (cf. 123n), see Ronan, pp. 87–107.

139 not being Stoll (*Periods*, p. 82) compares *DM* IV.ii.288, while Lucas suggests that 'the general contrast between the courage of the noble and the cowardice of the base may recall the similar difference between the deaths of the Duchess and Cariola'.

142 *Elizium* The dwelling place of the blessed in the classical underworld; hence, in opposition to **Hel**, 'paradise'.

145 mercy The contrast between Appius and Clodius is likely to be further emphasized by the latter falling on his knees at this point (so Wellington 1999).

147 noble blood See 125–6n.

156 And note Icilius, having removed Appius's sword (155), now turns from him to address either Virginius and the others on stage, or, instead or as well, the audience.

160 both wayes knowing Presumably, as Lucas suggests, 'knowing how to behave nobly as well as basely'. Lucas, crediting Brooke, compares Heywood and Rowley, *Fortune by Land and Sea*, II.756: 'Come I am both waies armed against thy steel.' Cf. *DLC* V.iv.116: 'You know not how to live, nor how to dye.'

161 sensible 'conscious; aware' (*OED* 11a).

162 apprehensive 'having an apprehension or notion' (see *OED* 5). Cf. *DLC* V.iv.94: 'Can you feed, and apprehend death?'

163–5 base Malefactor . . . Hangman The determining of punishment by social rank was familiar to Stuart England, but it is also authentically Roman. 'Capital punishment for the [upper class in Rome] was often in the form of exile, but even when he was put to death he was spared the horror of being crucified, burnt alive or thrown to the beasts in the arena, all of which awaited his more humble counterpart' (Richard A. Bauman, *Crime and Punishment in Ancient Rome* [London, 1996], p. 7).

167–8 *Decemviri . . .* **free** Cf. Livy, *Romane Historie*, p. 124, beside the marginal note '*Decemvirs resign up their government*': 'Then was an Act made by the Senat, that the Decemvirs out of hand should surrender their place: & that *Q. Furius* the Archbishop or Highpriest, should create Tribunes of the Commons . . . These Actes being passed, and the Counsell risen, the Decemvirs came abroad into the open place of assamblies, and there to the exceeding joy of all men, they resigned up all their power and author-itie.'

170 Consuls It is clear in Livy that Virginius and Icilius and others were actually created tribunes; but **Consuls** dramatically links the play's resolution back to the Lucrece story, and to *Junius Brutus* as the father of Roman liberty; cf. 170–8n.

170–8 *Junius Brutus . . . Virginia* According to Roman legend, **Lucretia** was raped by Sextus, son of Tarquinius Superbus; having told her husband, she took her own life. This incident led to *Tarquins* **fall**, for *Junius Brutus* led a popular uprising against the Tarquins, expelling the kings from Rome and establishing the republic. Comparison between **Lucretia and Virginia**, and the tyranny of the Tarquins and Appius, is common. Cf. Livy, *Romane Historie* (pp. 116–17): 'Now followeth the other heinous deede committed within the cittie: which began of wanton lust, and had as foule and shamefull an end, as that, which upon the carnall abusing and bloudie death of *Lucretia*, cast the *Tarquines* out of the cittie, and deprived them of their regall dignitie: that both

638

KK. [i.e. Kings] and Decemvirs, might have not only the like successe and issue, but also one and the selfesame cause, of loosing their rule & dominion.'

174 martial i.e. 'marshal'.

175 these golden bayes Possibly metaphorical, of being **Consuls**, but perhaps Minutius has crowned them with wreaths at 171–3; cf. Heywood's *The Rape of Lucrece* (1614), V.vi (K1ʳ), 'you *Collatine* | Shall succeed *Brutus*, in the consuls place, | Whom with this Lawrel wreath we here create', followed by the SD '*Crowne him with a Lawrel.*'

176 Ladies fair . . . infortunate Lucas emends, comparing Heywood, *Love's Mistress*, I.i (B3ʳ): 'shee alone | Of three most faire is most infortunate'. This creates a much more orthodox word order and assumes the kind of transposition that can easily occur when a compositor or scribe carries a phrase or sentence in his head.

180 Rome pronounced, as it was often spelt, 'Room'; see IV.ii.64 and n.

181 Corse *OED* lists Q's 'Course' as a sixteenth-century spelling of **Corse** ('corpse'), but since in over two hundred instances of 'course' in the works of W and Heywood it never means corpse, we have regarded it as accidental here, rather than as a late survival of a rare spelling.

181 SD Q's *Flourish* indicates a trumpet fanfare to accompany the formal *Exeunt* bearing Virginia's body in state.

Sources

The tragic tale of Appius and Virginia is told by Livy in Book III of *Ab Urbe condita* and, far more fully, by Dionysius of Halicarnassus in his *Roman Antiquities*. Of the latter an edition in the original Greek with Latin translation had been published by Sylburg in 1586, while Livy's history appeared (as *The Romane Historie*) in an English translation by Philemon Holland in 1600. The story is told elsewhere, as in Painter's paraphrase of Livy in *The Palace of Pleasure* (1566), source of *The Duchess of Malfi*. But it is clearly from Livy (in English) and Dionysius (in Greek or Latin) that Webster and Heywood drew the bulk of the material used in *Appius and Virginia*.

Lucas summarizes the dramatists' reliance on Dionysius thus:

> Here alone, for instance, is the feigned reluctance of Appius to accept office: whereas Livy describes him as soliciting with abject eagerness to be elected. Here, again, not in Livy, we find two of the chief objections which are raised in the trial-scene against the story of Marcus Clodius—'If the wife of Virginius palmed off a child on her husband, why did she not choose a boy rather than a girl?'—and 'Why did not Marcus bring the case before?'[1]

Lucas also notes that 'the bond-woman is actually mentioned only by Dionysius', and finds compelling evidence for the use of this version of the story in the reference at I.i.123 to 'The army that doth winter 'fore Algidon' (i.e. Mt. Algidus, in Latium). As Lucas notes, Q reads 'Agidon', for which 'Algidon' is 'clearly meant', and this false rendering of the Latin name occurs (along with several correct renderings) in Sylburg's Greek text.[2]

Webster and Heywood's use of Dionysius is particularly clear in IV.i, the tribunal scene, where his lengthy account of proceedings, and of the arguments of Appius, Clodius, and Virginius, is in marked contrast to the brevity of Livy, who has Appius interrupt Clodius's opening statement and, without allowing Virginius the right of reply, proceeds to judgement. Livy comments (in Holland's translation):

> What preamble it was that he made before his decree, peradventure some auntient writers have for truth recorded. But for as much as I cannot any where find, in so shamefull a decree, that which carrieth but a shew and soundeth like a truth: therefore, that only which is of all agreed upon, I thought best to set downe, even the sentence barely without any preface at al: namely, *That he iudged her in the behalfe of the Plaintife to be his bond-servant.*[3]

Telling much the same story, though almost everywhere more briefly than Dionysius, Livy is nonetheless a significant source, as Lucas notes:

> He alone mentions Virginius' refusal of office on the plea of being broken-hearted by his daughter's death (cf. his words in IV.ii.162ff and in Holland p. 122) and his final relenting, not indeed towards Appius, but towards Marcus Claudius, who was by his intercession let off with banishment.[4]

Lucas also points out the resemblance between Virginius's address to the soldiers at IV.ii.170–9 and part of the speech he makes in Livy.

Reliance on Livy, however, is more extensive than Lucas realized, and includes the use of other parts of the same 'complaint and mone of Virginius in the campe', as the marginal gloss terms it, in Virginius's earlier speech of justification (IV.ii.122–36). Holland's translation of the relevant sections runs thus:

> Then lifting up his hands to heaven, and calling to all his companions and fellow souldiers, hee besought them not to impute that foule act unto him, whereof in truth Appius Claudius was the authour and cause: not to detest and abhorre him as a parricide and murderer of his owne children: saying, that his daughters life was more deare unto him than his owne, if she might have lived free and honestly. But when he saw her once haled by force, as a bondmaid to be ravished and made a strumpet, he thought it better to be bereft of his children by death, than by contumlie and reproch: and so upon meere pittifulnesse incurred the shew and apparence of crueltie . . . I know well (saith he) that you also have daughters, sisters, and wives of your owne: And it is not the death of my child that hath killed and mortified the lust of Appius, but rather the longer it escapeth unpunished, the more outrageous and unbridled would it be. So that by the calamitie of another man, yee are well taught and warned to beware of the like injurie. As for me, I have buried my wife before, who died on gods hands: and now my daughter, for that she might not finish the course of her daies, with the safetie of her maidenhead and chastitie, hath died, I confesse, a pitifull and lamentable, but yet an honest kind of death. As to Appius (quoth he) now can he not fulfill his lust in this my house: and for any other violence of his whatsoever, I carrie the same mind and heart still, to defend mine owne bodie, wherewith I have already saved my daughters. Now let other men looke to themselves and their children, as well as they can.[5]

Unnoticed also by Lucas is the derivation of Virginia's Nurse from Livy's mention that she was accompanied by her nurse when seized by Clodius. In Dionysius, by contrast, Virginia is accompanied by governesses. Equally, the presence of Horatio and Valerius at Numitorius's house (III.i) is developed out of the mention in Livy that Valerius and Horatius were 'the chiefe captaines and ringleaders of the multitude'[6] who led the opposition to Appius following the death of Virginia.

One further point about the relationship between Livy's *Romane Historie* and *Appius and Virginia* remains to be noted, one first made by Brooke. This is what Lucas calls 'the curious legal use' of 'forthcoming' at III.ii.282–3 and in Holland (p.118). In Holland, Appius rules that Claudius 'might lead away the wench, promising and assuming to have her forthcomming, and to present her in court'. As Lucas points out, Webster (or Heywood) misreads Holland (as indeed did Brooke), taking the participial 'forthcomming' for a noun.[7]

Dionysius and Livy are the primary sources, then, of *Appius and Virginia*. But there are also significant additions to the story which seem to be Webster and Heywood's own. The characters of the Orator (closely related to Contilupo in *The Devil's Law-Case*) and the clown Corbulo (likewise related to several Heywood clowns, and particularly one in *The Rape of Lucrece*) are added, while the Nurse is built up from the single mention in Livy. Deviations from the narrative, too, are clearly the dramatists' own: in particular the plight of the army, including the famine scenes at the camp, and Virginius's mission to the

Senate seeking relief for the army. For possible reasons for their inclusion see pp. 443–4.

There remains only to be considered a possible indebtedness to Shakespeare, and in particular to *Julius Caesar* and *Coriolanus*. Stoll, noting that these two plays became available in print for the first time in the 1623 Folio, argues an 'indebtedness—in language, technique, and inspiring spirit— . . . so various and minute as to indicate the use of the printed page'.[8] His case is overstated, particularly in relation to *Coriolanus*, where many of what Stoll claims as significant situational parallels are simply the product of the sources, while his claim that the handling of the soldiery in *Appius and Virginia* and the citizens in *Coriolanus* is identical in attitude is unsustainable (see pp. 449–51). With *Julius Caesar*, however, the evidence seems more substantial. For Webster and Heywood not only appropriate the name of the ghost character, Calphurnia, but also borrow verbally at several points (see, e.g., I.iii.5–8n, II.ii.103n, III.i.73n, and V.iii.57–8n). Yet even if to these may be added Lucas's suggestion that the quarrel of Virginius and Icilius (V.ii) may echo that of Brutus and Cassius, and Icilius's entry with the bleeding body of Virginia to stiffen Virginius's resolve (V.iii) may be reminiscent of Antony's speech over the dead Caesar,[9] *Julius Caesar* must be considered less a source for *Appius and Virginia* than an influence.

1. Lucas, III, 131.
2. Ibid.
3. Livy, *Romane Historie*, p. 119.
4. Lucas, III, 132.
5. Livy, *Romane Historie*, p. 121.
6. Ibid., p. 120.
7. Lucas, III, 239–40.
8. Stoll, *Periods*, p. 197.
9. Lucas, III, 133.

Corrigenda Volume one:
music (*Webster*, I, 710–12)

These corrigenda to the music printed in Volume one of *The Works of John Webster* for 'O Let Us Howle' in *The Duchess of Malfi* follow the conventions described by Peter Walls in his Note on the music (*Webster*, I, 709).

GB–Lbl Add. MS. 29481

2   The slur is not editorial (hence should not have a stroke through it). The comma preceding the line of continuation after 'howle' should follow the line of continuation.
5   The comma preceding the line of continuation after 'howle' should follow the line of continuation.
21   The *b'-flat* should be approached by a slide (or *coulé*) *g'-a'* written as small semiquavers leading on to a minim. (Compare bars 3 and 10.)
33   The comma preceding the line of continuation after 'blest' should follow the line of continuation in bar 34.
37   A comma should follow the line of continuation.

US–Nyp MS. Drexel 4175

IncipitV Incipit should include the time signature C.
2V   The slur is not editorial (hence should not have a stroke through it). The comma preceding the line of continuation after 'howle' should follow the line of continuation.
3V   The comma preceding the line of continuation after 'note' should follow the line of continuation in bar 4.
5V   The comma preceding the line of continuation after 'howle' should follow the line of continuation.
27T   The notes before the double bar should be written as dotted minims. There should be a crotchet rest in the upper stave (above the quavers in the bass line) after the double bar.
31V   The slur is not editorial (hence should not have a stroke through it).

33V The comma preceding the line of continuation after 'blest' should follow the line of continuation in bar 34.

35V A bar line should separate bar 35 from bar 36.

36V The comma preceding the line of continuation after 'Swans' should follow the line of continuation in bar 37.